HAVES AND HAVE-NOTS

HAVES AND HAVE-NOTS

An International Reader
on Social Inequality

Edited by

James Curtis
University of Waterloo

and

Lorne Tepperman
University of Toronto

With the assistance of Alan Wain

Prentice Hall, Englewood Cliffs, NJ 07632

Library of Congress Cataloging-in-Publication Data

Haves and have-nots : an international reader on social inequality /
   edited by James Curtis and Lorne Tepperman with the assistance of
   Alan Wain.
      p. cm.
   Includes bibliographical references.
   ISBN 0-13-011669-6
   1. Equality. 2. Poverty. 3. Power (Social sciences) 4. Social
status. I. Curtis, James E. II. Tepperman, Lorne. III. Wain,
Alan.
HM136.H328 1994
305—dc20   93-13442
                                                         CIP

Acquisitions editor: Nancy Roberts
Editorial assistant: Pat Naturale
Editorial/production supervision and
   interior design: Joan Powers
Cover design: Maureen Eide
Production coordinator: Mary Ann Gloriande

© 1994 by Prentice-Hall, Inc.
A Paramount Communications Company
Englewood Cliffs, New Jersey 07632

Printed in the United States of America
10 9 8 7 6 5 4 3 2 1

ISBN 0-13-011669-6

Prentice-Hall International (UK) Limited, *London*
Prentice-Hall of Australia Pty. Limited, *Sydney*
Prentice-Hall Canada Inc., *Toronto*
Prentice-Hall Hispanoamericana, S.A., *Mexico*
Prentice-Hall of India Private Limited, *New Delhi*
Prentice-Hall of Japan, Inc., *Tokyo*
Simon & Schuster Asia Pte. Ltd., *Singapore*
Editora Prentice-Hall do Brasil, Ltda., *Rio de Janeiro*

CONTENTS

PREFACE

Today's college students realize that events in other parts of the world influence their own lives. Political unification in Europe, economic prosperity in the Pacific basin, environmental destruction in South America, military conflict in the Middle East, and famine and epidemic in Central Africa affect them in one way or another. What's more, the worldwide forces of industrialization and democratization have affected different parts of the world differently. A generation ago, sociologists expected the opposite, that is, a convergence of social patterns across modern and modernizing countries. This did not come to pass; thus, today no one is quite certain what to expect next.

Amid this general awareness of unpredictable change in a shrinking world, more and more people are aware of changes in social inequality—the complex web of class, gender, race, and other relations of unequal access to rewards. Recent theoretical and practical concerns have led researchers to focus their attention on the possible future of inequality. They have begun to look for clues about the future of inequality in other societies, where societal life is different from our own. They have also looked to history for clues to the trends and forces that will shape inequality in North America.

A rapidly changing world calls for new kinds of textbooks. Instructors in sociology need textbooks that talk about societal life in ways that undergraduate students can relate to this fluid, changeable world. Students need books that teach them about the world and its variety while introducing the topics and traditions of sociology.

With this in mind, we have examined other textbooks on inequality, reviewed our own experiences in teaching undergraduates, spoken to other sociology instructors, and finally, remembered our own first years in sociology. The book we have put together reflects our sense of what instructors can tell undergraduate students of inequality that is true, important, clear, and interesting.

Specifically, we show students some of the varied *forms* of inequality, including inequalities of wealth, power, and prestige, as well as resulting differences in work experience, lifestyle, and belief. We show how class, gender, and race (or ethnicity) are major *influences* on the unequal distribution of rewards. We also show how these inequalities give rise to resistance, protest, group mobility, and legislation. This book examines the way these phenomena show up on the local, national, and global scale. In addition, it examines the varied ways sociologists analyze different forms of social inequality throughout the world.

Our book fills the gap in the range of existing readers by providing a cosmopolitan selection of up-to-date excerpts. It offers a worldwide variety of materials on all the topics typically covered in a lower level sociology course on inequality. Learning aids make the materials as accessible as they need to be for lower level students.

We have designed *Haves and Have-nots* to support a mainstream textbook on social inequality, by supplementing the historical and cross-cultural materials in such a textbook, strengthening the future orientation of the book, and augmenting the textbook's more conventional approaches with other, competing approaches. The effect is to give students a richer, more lively exposure to thinking about inequality around the world. Overall, *Haves and Have-nots* shows how the major forms of inequality fit together in different societal contexts.

FEATURES OF THIS TEXT

International outlook. The only way for students to learn about the various influences on inequality, the many forms of inequality that exist in a modern world, and the kinds of institutional arrangements that support these inequalities is by studying inequality from an international perspective, which is what this book provides. Some of the excerpts are cross-nationally comparative, comparing structures and processes according to uniform standards; others are "idiographic," based on the country's own frame of reference.

We are concerned both with global inequality, the stratification and struggle of nations, and with varying inequalities *within* nations of the world, that is, how inequalities are different in Lesotho and Luxembourg, Brazil and Bangladesh. All sections of this book contain articles from a wide variety of countries and perspectives; many contain explicitly comparative articles.

Historical perspective. Some of the factors affecting inequality today have been developing for decades, if not centuries. They include the spread of capitalistic values and of modern technology throughout the world. Other factors, like the internationalization of capital and collapse of world communism, are much more recent. And some other factors, like movements of equality for women and racial minorities, have varied in form as well as in content over the course of time.

To understand inequality today and to make informed guesses about inequality in the future, students must know about these historic forces and trends. For this reason, all sections of the book include historical materials.

Useful introductions. The opening section of the book introduces students to the sociology of inequality. It organizes the discussion around those features of social research that we consider essential for a comprehensive understanding of inequality, including cross-cultural variation, historical perspective, and future orientation. The introduction also makes clear the relevance of the articles we have chosen for this book. It discusses some implications of the findings both for the future of the sociology of inequality and for patterns of inequality.

Professional social scientists have written all of the articles in this volume. Since professional writing is often telegraphic and sometimes obscure, each *article* is introduced by a paragraph or two that describes the purpose and sets the context for the piece. As well, each of the three parts of the book is introduced by a brief essay that foreshadows and integrates the excerpts that follow.

Learning aids. Because of the great diversity of materials and approaches examined, learning aids play a critical role in making this book successful. Fully one third of the book is made up of learning aids.

Each section ends with a brief set of discussion questions and exercises that help the student understand and review the pieces. These questions will stimulate classroom discussion by suggesting unresolved issues and calling attention back to earlier readings. Also each of the three parts contains a list of suggested readings that describes books of lasting importance concerned with the topic at hand, as well as some recent publications. A glossary at the end of the book defines the key concepts.

Again, the purpose of this elaborate pedagogical armament is to help students unpack the case studies they are reading and find links among them. In this way we guide the student to seeing meaningful patterns in what is, admittedly, a world's worth of material.

To conclude, we think this book makes teaching and learning about social inequality much more interesting—even more fun. We hope you enjoy using it. Let us know what you think.

ACKNOWLEDGMENTS

Putting together a book of readings like this one is a lot of fun but plenty of work too. Many people helped with the work and we want to thank them all.

First, we want to thank the people at Prentice-Hall for their help. Nancy Roberts, the Acquisitions Editor, has greatly supported this project since we proposed it about two years ago. Joan Powers, the Project Editor, has helped by getting permissions and otherwise moving the book through production from start to finish. Durrae Johanek, the copy editor, has helped us make sure the manuscript was readable and without too many loose ends.

Then, we want to thank the reviewers, including Norval Glenn at the University of Texas at Austin. We appreciate the effort they put into reviewing our proposal and suggesting ways to improve the book.

A great many people at our end have helped us create this book. First, a grant from the University of Toronto Provost's Fund for Broadening Ethno-Cultural Initiatives helped us pay the costs of collecting and assessing a wide array of materials, only a small fraction of which are presented here. Then, a large number of assistants were actually involved in collecting and assessing these articles. They included Amy Ma, Dorceta Taylor, Victoria Tehmasabi, and Janaki Weerasinghe. Another student assistant, Tom Bellman, both reviewed articles for us and summarized many of them; we have drawn on his written materials freely throughout this book. Thanks, Tom.

Mighty big thanks go to our article editor, Alan Wain. Alan brought the interesting but often long articles down to manageable size without sacrificing the main arguments. Al's rare skill for this task was demonstrated here and in earlier projects we have done together. You will more readily appreciate what he has accomplished by comparing Al's edited excerpts with the generally much longer original articles.

Finally, our main thanks go to the authors whose articles we have excerpted and who have allowed us to reprint them in a shortened, sometimes modified form. This book could not have existed without their insights and efforts.

As you will discover, this book is mainly about the "have-nots" of the world. We dedicate this book to efforts to improve their lives.

Introduction

WHY SOCIAL INEQUALITY OCCURS

Jean-Jacques Rousseau (1712–1778) begins his famous book *The Social Contract* with the paradox "Everywhere men [sic] are born free and everywhere they are in chains." This sets the stage for a long argument that claims equality is natural and inequality, unnatural.

In the course of this book, we will disagree with that famous conclusion. But before we go very far, let's define our terms. When we, and Rousseau, discuss "social inequality," we have in mind all those differences in the ways people treat other people that are (1) important, (2) predictable, and (3) common.

In particular, we are focusing on what Weber called "life chances": the *important* ways people's living conditions (and opportunities for improving these conditions) are affected by other people's behavior. Some people enjoy better life chances than others. Everything that affects how well a person can meet the basic requirements of life (food, shelter, good health), how much control a person can exercise over where and how to live, work, marry, spend leisure time; even, how much dignity and respect a person is permitted in everyday life are all aspects of one's "life chances." All of these aspects are, certainly, very important. And as we shall see, life chances vary from one person, group, and society to another.

Second, these differences in experience are *predictable* in several respects. For one thing, they persist over time. Typically, people's life chances change very slowly—over years, not days. For many people, they never change. So we are able to predict how people are going to be living months and years from today, particularly if their life chances are especially good or bad.

For another thing, we can predict people's life chances as a whole because they tend to be interrelated. Typically, people who suffer from poor economic conditions *also* suffer from a lack of power and dignity (or respect). To say someone has poor life chances is to say he/she suffers from inequality in a great many areas of life. So even though we have organized the materials in this book into separate sections on economic, power, and status inequalities, these different types of inequality are connected. People are likely to score high, low, or medium on all three types.

It is precisely this consistency in types of inequality that allows us to lump people together into "social classes," or "status groups," about which we will say more later.

As well, social inequality is predictable in the sense that certain situations, or characteristics of individuals, are more likely to provoke differences in behavior than others. For example, we will see repeatedly in this book that men are treated differently from women, whites differently from nonwhites, rich and powerful people differently from poor and powerless people. We will also see that conditions of strife, uncertainty, and poverty also increase differences in behavior. Times like these are particularly dangerous for the poor, for women, and racial minorities.

Finally, social inequalities are differences in treatment that are *common*. As we have seen, they apply to very basic issues of everyday life, and they are problems for huge numbers of people (women, the poor, minority groups, and the like). In fact, most people on earth, at some time or another, are victims of social inequality.

Beyond that, we are talking about differences in treatment that are so common we are likely to ignore them. We are not often going to talk about rare or dramatic events: a political coup in some distant country, a royal marriage, or a war between two countries—events that get discussed in the news. Most inequality *never* gets discussed in the news because it is *not* new and it is not unusual. It is the content of everyday life, influencing the ways people live, work, marry, die, and so on.

In the end, this book is about the reasons some people get a better—safer, healthier, happier—life than other people do. But as individuals, we are rarely aware of the patterns in our lives and their similarities with other people's lives.

Given such a broad subject matter, what can there be to argue about? Well, the question is, *why* do people treat one another unequally, often with terrible consequences; and *what* if anything can be done about it?

For his part, Rousseau felt a great deal could be done about it. In particular, he believed most social ills are caused by social life and the ways we are educated, not a flawed human nature. Many have followed Rousseau's line of thinking. For example, his beliefs about the "state of nature" and the naturalness of equality have influenced many important streams of intellectual thought: anarchist, socialist, and even liberal.

The most important thinkers he influenced are communists, starting with Marx and Engels. Like Rousseau, Friedrich Engels (1820–1895) argued that primitive societies had been egalitarian. Class and gender inequality arose for the first time with the development of settled agriculture and private property. Engels believed this process could be reversed. Along similar lines Karl Marx (1818–1883), with Engels, proposed a social movement—communism—that would restore the natural social equality of primitive societies in a new, more complex but still classless society.

The "fall of communism" in Eastern Europe in the past few years has provoked many explanations. On the one hand, the Eastern Bloc may not have exemplified communism in its truest form. There never was a "withering away of the state," as Marx had expected. In fact, much economic, power, and status inequality remained throughout the so-called communist period. Perhaps communism had too little opportunity to develop: it died before it could flower. But equally likely, the *underlying* premise of Marxist communism—that equality is natural—may simply be wrong. Let's consider the reasons why.

All humans are naturally equal (meaning "identical") in only one respect: they all die. And even in this respect, people differ: it takes some humans much less time to die than others. Typically, women live longer than men, for biological as well as social reasons.

In fact, it may be far more fruitful to start from the assumption that inequality is natural and equality is *un*natural—a social construct, invention, aspiration, or goal. Because it's unnatural, equality is rare and hard to achieve. And there are good statistical reasons to think that inequality is natural and inevitable.

To see this for yourself, try an experiment: get together with a friend and start flipping coins. Each head is worth 1 point and each tail is worth nothing. Keep track of how many total points you have won after 5 flips, 10 flips, 15, and so on, compared with how many points your friend has won. If you do this, say, 100 times, you will find that most of the time one of you is ahead of the other. You will almost never have an equal number of points (on this, see Feller, 1964).

As you play this game even more times, with more people, you will produce ever less equal outcomes. The range of points will diverge more and more widely. Pure chance yields a wide variety of results, few of them equal.

If you now impose certain preferential rules on this game—for example, people with blond hair get 2 points for every head they toss, while everyone else gets only 1 point per head; or men start out with 10 points while women start out with 0; or the value of a head doubles once you have scored 50 points—the outcomes will be even more varied and unequal. Under rules like these, it is virtually certain that "favored" players (in this case, blonds, males, and people getting past 50) will stay in the lead, and even pull ahead, in a majority of contests.

What does this have to do with real life? First, all lives begin with a genetic coin toss. People are programmed, by chance, to have certain characteristics that are available in their parents' gene pool. So, strictly by chance (that is, without conscious intervention), some people will be short or tall, dark or fair, male or female, heavy or light, handsome (or beautiful) or plain, and so on. For similar reasons, some will be more or less aggressive, sociable, artistic, and so on.

But imposed on this set of random processes—this biological coin toss—is a set of social meanings. These meanings define, often very arbitrarily, which of the outcomes should be seen as "better" than others: for example, whether it is better to be tall or short, ugly or beautiful, fat or thin, male or female, dark or light skinned. Where some of these outcomes are concerned, there is a lot of agreement across cultures; for others, there is less agreement. But within any given culture, these social meanings change a randomly determined biological difference into a socially meaningful inequality.

All social life is made up of rules that confer advantages on one type of person or another. These advantages may be minute or enormous, obvious or hidden, intended or unintended, changing slowly or rapidly. One thing is certain: even rules that seem mild and fair in themselves may, cumulatively, yield results that are extreme and unfair.

This is what causes the conflict between political liberals and political radicals. Liberals seek adherence to the rule of law and a "free" market economy even though they may produce unfair outcomes (for example, large differences in wealth and life chances). For their part, political radicals seek fair outcomes—for example, small differences in wealth and life chances—even if this requires coercive measures, such as the abolition of private property, to achieve them.

As noted, different societies make different rules and attach different meanings to particular traits; but all societies do make rules. They also rank people and people's activities, and reward them differently. This ensures there will be inequality in every society, a fact that has led sociologists to ask, "Why do people rank others at all?" and "What purpose, if any, could be served by this translation of differences into inequalities?"

Historically, sociologists have answered this question in several ways. One group has argued that people in power attach social meanings in ways that justify, or legitimate, their own power and wealth. This is the so-called **conflict approach**, which splits into two main branches over the question of what might be done to remedy the problem.

Those following Roberto Michels (1876–1936) argue that if we removed one elite group, we would simply open the door for another one to take over. Elites perform leadership and management roles in society and we cannot eliminate these roles. We are stuck with leadership if we are to coordinate and manage our social activities. By this reasoning, there can be no end to the rise of elites and their exercise of oligarchic power. So, in complex societies, if Michels is right we must always have the inequality that grows out of leadership.

On the other hand, those following Rousseau, Marx, and Engels argue that by overthrowing the system of classes and private property which supports these leaders we could "return to equality" once and for all. But there is a lack of evidence that complex societies can exist without leaders, classes, private property, and inequality of at least some kind.

The other way of explaining inequality stresses differences in values. It holds that social inequalities arise because we generally view some kinds of people as more useful than others. So, for example, in a society where people must hunt animals for their food, there will be a role of "master hunter" or "leading hunter," which commands general respect. Only people who are good hunters will stand much chance of entering that role.

Other societies will make other roles more important, according to the needs of the group. "Functional" value will determine how a role is rewarded and what skills are required of people seeking the role.

This way of thinking about inequality has been called the **functional theory of stratification**, and it is attributed to Davis and Moore (1945) and Parsons (1952). This theory argues that inequality is natural and inevitable. It also explains why: people (and societies) give the most rewards to those who perform social functions they consider most valuable, whatever those functions might be, whether hunting, military, religious, managerial, scientific, and so on. Unequally high rewards motivate people with rare skills to come forward and use them, whatever the risk or cost to themselves.

Sociologists have criticized this functional approach by demonstrating that in many societies (1) there is little agreement on what qualities and activities are valuable; (2) rewards are often out of proportion to what most people value—either the "wrong" people are rewarded, or some people are rewarded too much or too little; (3) people who get the most are often more or less "parasites" with no "objective" social value—for example, criminals, pop singers, baseball players, heirs to large fortunes; and (4) it is possible to extort rewards—both money and deference—from others, if you have enough power whether you have a social value or not (see, for example, Tumin 1953).

So a debate continues on the question of *why* we find social inequality in nearly every society, why some social roles carry more rewards than others, and why some kinds of people have more access to the social rewards of better economic circumstances, power, and prestige than other people do. These debates run under the surface of many excerpts in this book, in the context of a variety of countries.

As we shall see, some people have more rewards than others, and some people are given better opportunities to achieve highly rewarded roles than others. These are two different forms of inequality, of course, and we should be clear on the distinction.

Inequality in the distribution of wealth, power, and prestige among members of society is called **Inequality of condition**. Equality of condition would mean that all have roughly the same wealth, power, and prestige. Inequality of access to these things is called **inequality of opportunity**. Equal opportunity means that all positions in society are equally open to everyone, regardless of background such as race, gender, and social class. Recruitment, then, is done according to merit or on the basis of personal talent.

As we have said, in our society as in every other, there is unequal distribution of rewards. Inequalities of condition for wealth, power, and prestige also often translate directly into differences of physical and material well-being: food, shelter, physical security, good health. Indirectly, they translate into differences of mental health and happiness. Inequalities of opportunity are differences in the chance that people (or their children) will get to enjoy an improved social condition.

Inequalities of condition and opportunity are not scattered randomly among members of a society. Rather they vary from one social class to another, from one race or ethnic group to another, and across the genders. People in the same social class have similar conditions and similar chances for changing those conditions. People in higher classes have both better conditions and better chances for further improving those conditions. What is more, their children also have better chances than the children born into lower classes.

Better conditions and better opportunities for improving those conditions go together. People cannot have an equal opportunity to get what they want if they start out with vastly unequal wealth, power, and respect. Thus a society cannot equalize opportunity without greatly reducing the range of unequal starting points. If everyone were born with the same wealth, power, and social respect, a great many people would have much more chance of getting what they want out of life than they do today.

MECHANISMS OF INEQUALITY

Social inequality affects people's lives by affecting the conditions they live in and opportunities for changing these conditions. Four mechanisms of inequality seem to limit people's opportunity to get what they want out of life. We shall call them exclusion, disability, decoupling, and scarcity. We briefly discuss each of these below.

Exclusion is one mechanism controlling access to rewards and opportunities. It keeps people from entering contests they might win, and rewards people unequally for equal performances. Organizations practice exclusion against other organizations, ethnic groups practice it against other ethnic groups, classes practice it against other classes, and individual people practice it against other people. So exclusion is a very widespread way of limiting opportunities.

If power is nothing else, it is certainly the ability to make rules about who will get the biggest share of "goodies"—wealth, authority, and prestige—in our society (Murphy, 1982). Research on American society by Mills (1956) and Domhoff (1967) and on Canadian society by Porter (1965) and Clement (1975) suggests that power is exercised by people in **elite** positions—the dominant group in any society.

Societies vary in the extent to which their various elites (political, intellectual, economic, etc.) form a cohesive ruling group. In Canada and the United States, the dominant elite is the corporate elite: a group of top executives of the largest businesses. Through their executive positions, these people hold more economic power than anyone else. Their decisions affect economic conditions (like the availability of jobs) and, in this way, affect all of our lives.

We also find exclusion exercised by nonelite persons in the job market. Increasingly, access to high-paying jobs has required a credential, often in the form of an educational degree, that proves the possessor has qualified for selection. Degrees from medical schools are particularly valuable in this way, since almost no doctors are unemployed or poorly paid. Who decides how these scarce degrees will be handed out? Who will get them, and in return for what investments?

To practice medicine, a person needs a medical degree. In the end, this requirement protects doctors. We see exclusion at work in the continuing battles over health care—debates about who shall pay and who is entitled to receive how much; and the exclusion of such competitors as chiropractors, homeopaths, and midwives from public recognition and coverage under public health plans. The medical monopoly on activities that generate high incomes prevents competent nurses, paramedics, and other health professionals from enjoying similar rewards.

Professional associations protect the interests of these groups. In many respects, these associations are little different from trade unions. Both aim to protect and promote the economic interests of their members.

The example of medicine shows clearly that successful professionalization means the power to exclude others and to control public and private spending on specialized (health) services. Further, this kind of power arises under certain kinds of historical, political, and economic conditions: it is far from inevitable. Especially in North America, professionalization advances the private interests of particular occupational groups by capitalizing on our fear of harm, belief in education, and inability to evaluate and control the people who serve us. It is a form of social mobility for the groups involved, and it perpetuates inequality.

Another kind of exclusion is based on ethnic or racial origin, not educational credentials. Many workplaces recruit people with similar ethnic backgrounds, with the result that people of the same ethnic origin come to control particular organizations and even entire industries. When an ethnic group becomes able to monopolize an economic activity and allow entry into that activity on ethnic grounds, it is practicing exclusion. All "the wrong" ethnic types are excluded.

All ethnic groups practice exclusion to some degree, but they vary widely in this respect, for ethnic communities differ as much from one another as they do from the dominant Anglo-Saxon community. But for all, ethnic community organization is what makes this kind of exclusion possible.

An ethnic community that is highly organized has created enough social, cultural, and economic organizations to insulate group members from the rest of society. These include schools, camps, churches, business associations, social clubs, and credit unions. They all provide a context within which community members can meet and do business with other community members. Such organizations make people more conscious of their common ethnic origins. And like professional associations and unions, these organizations press for group interests.

Certain groups face serious discrimination on their arrival in North America. Living in a highly organized community can protect immigrants from a hostile social environment. The Jews and Chinese, both victims of serious discrimination, have historically practiced this strategy of protecting themselves. However, a community's ethnic organization often persists long after the discrimination that created it has died down (Reitz, 1980). Institutions formed within an ethnic community create a demand for the services they provide. Thus the mere survival of an ethnic community does not prove discrimination has continued.

Disability is a second mechanism controlling access to rewards and opportunities. By this method, certain categories of people are discouraged from competing for the rewards everyone desires. Some people simply don't think of themselves as able to compete. Women, the poor, the old, the physically disabled, and younger people have all been taught that certain kinds of behavior are inappropriate—unladylike, undignified, hopeless. That is why these socially disabled people "choose" not to compete for what they want out of life.

As adults and children, we learn to live effectively in the real world. Socialization teaches us how and why to conform to cultural values and social norms. Socialization also teaches us how *not* to function in the real world. For many of us, "disability" means learning ways of thinking about ourselves that make us less than what we might otherwise be. It is any kind of socialization that teaches us low self-esteem, a low sense of mastery and control, alienation, and distrust.

Generally, disability makes people believe that they cannot and should not try to do what they want to do. Such training leads to lower aspirations, a lack of assertiveness, and even withdrawal from competition.

The dominant ideology teaches all of us, including people who are victimized by the class structure, to blame ourselves (Ryan, 1976). In a sense, everyone knows about things like exclusion, decoupling, and scarcity. But people rarely confront their personal knowledge consciously and take the appropriate action. Our thinking is largely "ideological," based on beliefs we keep insulated from reality and everyday experience.

Moreover, many of our ideological beliefs are very old. Some have called these beliefs the principles of "laissez-faire capitalism," "liberal democracy," and the "liberal ideology." Whatever we call it, this package of beliefs emphasizes the rights of individuals against government interference, and protects people's rights to carry out economic exchange any way that is legal.

Liberal democracy rests on (supposedly) free choice, free competition and a free market in labor, goods, and ideas (Macpherson, 1965). As Anatole France said, we guarantee everyone the freedom to sleep under bridges. We usually find freedom of this kind—freedom from interference—in societies with a capitalist economy, universal suffrage, and two or more political parties. But given social inequality—unequal starting points—freedom *from* interference is not the same as freedom *to* live a full and equal life.

Our own experiences tell us these ideological beliefs are false (cf., Marchak, 1987). People we know are often not rewarded for hard work and merit. At the same time, upper-class children inherit enormous wealth, generation after generation. These facts tell us that hard work and merit have little to do with rewards. As well, corporate crime, government patronage, and tax laws that favor the rich over the poor all prove that the cards are stacked against ordinary people, however hardworking.

What keeps our society together in the face of this systematic inequality and demonstrated untruth? Surveying studies of public opinion from several capitalist countries, Mann (1970) concludes there is little evidence that people generally agree with the central tenets of liberal democracy. To a large degree, it is people's ambivalence that keeps the system working. "Cohesion in liberal democracy depends on the lack of consistent commitment to general values of any sort and on the 'pragmatic acceptance' by subordinate classes of their limited roles in society" (Mann, 1970, p. 423).

Mann also finds evidence that "false consciousness" helps to maintain order and social cohesion. False consciousness is a view of society that incorrectly describes the world to disadvantaged people. For example, it holds disadvantaged people responsible for circumstances beyond their control; in that way, false consciousness disables them.

This is why a person who is unable to find work is likely to blame himself—not the high unemployment rate, discrimination, business mismanagement, and bad government handling of the economy. It is also the reason why a two-income family that is struggling unsuccessfully to meet all its obligations may turn its aggression inward—spouse against spouse, parent against child, child against parent. In this way family members end up destroying their family, rather than blame exploitive employers, inadequate legislation, and uncontrolled prices.

Mann argues that false consciousness disables voters. The main political parties lead voters to believe in vague political philosophies that contradict their everyday experience and support the status quo. Conservative politicians appeal to patriotism, tradition, harmony, and national unity, while neglecting and mismanaging the economy. In this way, voters are disabled by their own optimism and gullibility.

Along with these types of false consciousness—a willingness to blame oneself, a readiness to reinvest in the status quo, a tendency to see public issues as personal problems—we find a more general set of beliefs about social inequality. In our society, people have been taught to believe that social inequality—even extreme inequality—is necessary and useful. Further, they have been taught that people at the top of the heap deserve to be there.

People who are not rich, not powerful, and not famous have a hard time living with themselves because our culture tells them they are not trying hard enough. Rather than working for social change, they pour their energy into making themselves feel better.

One way is by humiliating other people who are even less powerful: poor whites against poor blacks; poor men against their wives and children; and children against other children or pets, for example. This is where bullies and fascists come from (Adorno, Frenkel-Brunswik, Levinson, and Sanford, 1969).

Another way to cope is by using "dreams and defenses" to soothe hidden injuries (Sennett and Cobb, 1973). If people feel worthless, they dream of becoming "worthwhile" through promotions, winning a lottery, and other strokes of good fortune. Women's romance books and magazines dwell on this dream. They are full of Cinderellas who, as nurses and secretaries, capture a Prince Charming with a mixture of good luck, virtue, and wile.

A third way of coping is through the use of humor. Simon (1990) reports that humor doesn't increase life satisfaction, but it does help people keep their spirits up in the face of adversity. Finally, Marx characterized religion as a fourth way of coping—an "opiate" of the people that deadened them to the pain of inequality and injustice.

Decoupling is a third mechanism controlling people's access to rewards and opportunities. It disconnects certain groups from rewards by keeping them uninformed about good opportunities and ways of taking advantage of them. It also keeps people from firsthand acquaintanceship with others who could help them gain rewards. People who are decoupled simply do not "know the ropes" and "have the contacts."

The word *decoupling* makes us think of a disconnected railway car that has been shunted onto a side track. Like train cars, people are connected to one another and often pull one another forward and back. The dominant ideology holds each of us personally responsible for our own fate; but much of what happens in life is due to others, many unknown and distantly connected to us.

Take an unlikely example—the careers of church ministers—as sociologist Harrison White did. The job vacancy created by a minister's death or retirement may set off a chain reaction and lead to the upward movement of dozens of other ministers (White, 1970). For this reason, social mobility is as much the result of "vacancy chains" as it is the accomplishment of individuals.

Depending on economic conditions, an initial change (e.g., retirement or death) may produce longer or shorter chains of reaction. In some cases, the chain reaction may lead to dozens of promotions, but retirement and death do not always lead to such long chains of movement. Sometimes the organization eliminates the departed person's job, makes it into a part-time job, or fills the job with a newcomer brought in from outside. Then, no one inside the organization benefits. These kinds of reactions are probably most common in organizations "downsizing" in the face of economic difficulty.

Your contacts with other people affect your opportunities whether or not a vacancy chain fails to operate. We see this clearly in studies of the upper class in North America (for example, Baltzell, 1958; Clement, 1975; Newman, 1979). Upper-class people are tied to one another by a variety of activities and experiences: marriage; kinship; attendance at the same private schools, summer camps, and universities; membership in the same social clubs; and service on the same boards of directors. In these ways, upper-class people get to be much better acquainted with others in their class than middle-class and working-class people are.

But social contacts are important in every social class. A survey of managers showed that people typically find the best white-collar jobs through personal contacts (Granovetter, 1974). That's because hiring through networks of personal contact is the simplest, most trustworthy way of hiring.

When an employer has a job to fill, many people have suitable qualifications. If the employer advertises the job opening, many applicants will have to be screened and interviewed. Investigating every applicant to find the best would be very expensive, so employers often ask their personal contacts—people they know and trust—to recommend someone good enough for the job. In this way, the employer can find someone with the right qualifications at relatively little cost. That person will be good enough to do the job, and that's just fine with employers. They want a satisfactory candidate for the job, not an ideal one.

This method of hiring also gives the employer information that is unlikely to surface in a candidate's résumé. For example, it can often provide some information about the candidate's personal habits and attitudes (and "attitude problems"). The candidate who is recommended by a trusted acquaintance probably has the right attitude as well as credentials.

This strategy is not limited to employers, and people find jobs in the same way as employers find candidates for jobs. For their part, job seekers want to know if the job is a good one, the boss a good boss, the prospects for advancement good, and so on. (They may want to know if the boss has an "attitude problem," too!) They are bound to find out more by talking to an acquaintance with firsthand knowledge of the organization, the job, and the boss than in any other way. Other sources of information—for example, organizational brochures and formal interviews—are less likely to tell the candidate as much.

So on both sides of the job market—among people who are hiring and people who want to be hired—"networks of personal contact" provide the best information about jobs and candidates. As a result, many jobs find people, and people find jobs, through networks of personal contact. In fact, the best-paying jobs are filled in this way.

Granovetter found that the most valuable job information is passed on by acquaintances. Acquaintances are people you call by their first name, though they are not close friends. We have a great many more acquaintances than close friends, so we are more likely to get useful information from an acquaintance. Also, close friends tend to have the same information about jobs. They are likely to know one another and know the same things. By contrast, acquaintances are less likely to know one another and likely to know many other people and therefore, more things. Acquaintance networks can become very large indeed, numbering hundreds and even thousands of people.

In theory, job referral chains could be enormously long; in practice, they are not. People do not trust information that comes from a person at some distance from them, people they do not know personally. It is like getting information from a stranger. After all, we live in a "small world," as psychologist Stanley Milgram showed in his studies of social networks (Travers and Milgram, 1969). People are likely to have thousands, even tens of thousands, of "acquaintances of acquaintances of acquaintances." (If we follow this logic far enough, every pair of people in the country probably has *someone* in common.)

So, in practice, only acquaintances and acquaintances of acquaintances are likely to pass on valuable job information. Each acquaintance provides information and connections that other acquaintances are unlikely to duplicate. That's what makes them so valuable in getting a job. Your chances of hearing about a job or having an employer hear about you are best if you have many acquaintances.

With this in mind, there is one strategy that is likely to increase opportunities. Granovetter found that people who have changed organizations often have many acquaintances. In fact, a person changing jobs three or four times over 15 years might end up knowing people in 30 or 40 different companies. (Remember, his or her acquaintances have also been changing companies.) People who stay in a job for three to five years seem to do best, according to this research.

What's more, people who begin moving between organizations early in their careers seem to benefit most. This process snowballs career opportunities: like a snowball rolling downhill, they increase with the passage of time. By contrast, people who stay with the same organization for much of their working life have a lot of trouble finding a new job when they have to.

Some classes and ethnic groups benefit more than others from these processes. The value of acquaintanceships for finding good jobs within ethnic communities will vary according to the kinds of jobs the ethnic community controls. For example, acquaintanceship will be much more likely to uncover a good job in prosperous and economically diverse Jewish or Italian communities than in more limited Portuguese or West Indian communities.

The process Granovetter describes may also favor middle- and upper-class people. Higher-status people usually have much larger and more varied networks of contact than lower-status people. They also have more time and money to travel, meet people and interact socially; this helps upper-class people form acquaintanceships.

Second, because they have a higher status and more access to scarce resources, higher-status people are likely to receive more attention from other people. Lower-status people seek *them* out for advice, encouragement, and help. This also gives the higher-status people a great many contacts, even without making an effort. Finally, as we noted earlier, elite and upper-class institutions bring higher-status people together on a regular basis.

The networking process works against groups (like women and blacks) who are underrepresented in the better jobs and socially decoupled from the dominant group. The reason is simple: whites usually make the acquaintance of other whites, and men, the acquaintance of other men. When asked to recommend people for jobs, white men will recommend their acquaintances—other white men. Without people intending to discriminate, the process has a discriminatory outcome and the workplace remains racially and/or sexually unbalanced.

Scarcity is a fourth mechanism controlling access to rewards and opportunities. A shortage, or scarcity, affects how many opportunities are shared out in total; and true scarcity can be reduced if we produce more of the desired rewards. Most often, we become aware of scarcity when we get a poor return on an investment we have made. One example is the "underemployment" of recent postsecondary graduates. They have invested a great deal of time and effort in their education, but have not always gained the result they desire.

Now, scarcity varies with the ratio of competitors to desired rewards; so it can be reduced by eliminating competitors (through exclusion disability, and decoupling) or by increasing the supply of rewards. This helps to explain why people in our society practice exclusion, disability, and decoupling and also strive to increase the gross national product.

Yet scarcity remains; we see it all around us. The poor are its greatest victims, but most of us suffer from scarcity some of the time. Increasingly, even the middle class falls prey to scarcity, as witnessed by the falling opportunity of young adults to own homes as their parents had done (Berljawsky, 1986). In fact, a gap is widening between the rich and everyone else. As the rich get even richer, the rest get poorer and the traditional middle ground declines.

Beyond this material deprivation, we find "social limits to growth" (Hirsch, 1978) and reasons for a growing *sense* of scarcity. Increasingly, people value scarce items—the unique vacation, the unusual home, designer clothing, and so on—*because* they are scarce. People want something that is all their own because we live in a society of growing uniformity. The sheer growth in our numbers makes this goal more and more attractive and also ever harder to attain.

Often we adapt by giving up something that we have long valued and even loved. It is becoming ever more difficult to enjoy such truly scarce things as quiet, good craftsmanship, and privacy. We cannot bring the old things back, and only if we have a lot of money can we replace them. So people tend to seek satisfactory, though imperfect, solutions. This often means looking at choices in a new way and giving value to things they had not valued before.

Consider the problem in scarcity demographers have called the "marriage squeeze." Between 1945 and 1957, more babies were born each year than in the year before. Of these, roughly half were male and half were female. Now remember that women tend to marry men who are a few years older. A woman about 30 years old in 1987 would find a shortage, or scarcity, of men between 33 and 35 years old. Men of this age would have been born between 1952 and 1954, and fewer men were born in each of these years than were born in each of the years 1955 through 1957, when the woman in question was born. This is the "marriage squeeze" from the standpoint of a single woman about 30 years old in 1987.

Eventually, the situation reverses. A woman about 30 years old in 1992 would find no shortage of men several years older, since more males were still being born in each of the years 1959 through 1961 than females in 1962 through 1964. On the other hand, there is a shortage of brides, a marriage squeeze, for single *men* under 25 years old in 1992.

People use creative strategies to deal with scarcity. For example, in response to these marriage squeezes, many traditional constraints on mate selection are disappearing. First, people are marrying mates who, in the past, might have been considered too old or too young. Others are marrying outside their own racial and ethnic groups. More often than before, people are marrying previously married people and people from other social classes.

Some others opt for unmarried motherhood or sequential cohabitation. Others still adjust to a single life by putting their energies into work, leisure, and friendship. (After all, people do not stigmatize singles today the way they did in the past.)

Adjustments to the marriage squeeze are both personal and cultural; they include new conceptions of adult life, family, and marriage. Making adjustments always helps when people are faced by scarcity, and scarcity is a normal state of affairs. But scarcity is not inevitable. Often, it is due to exclusion—the monopolization of desired goods by people powerful enough to control their access. The powerful can always get far more than their share of what everyone wants: money, good housing, respect, and so on.

In fact, Marx and Engels (Meek, 1954) argued that capitalism itself tends to produce scarcity. Employers want a large "reserve army of the unemployed" to keep down wages, and shortages to keep up prices. Moreover, under capitalism, jobs tend to disappear. The investment in technology rises continually and the capital invested in workers' wages falls. That is why, according to this theory, capitalism creates too few, indeed ever fewer, jobs; prices rise; and inequality increases steadily.

Marx and Engels believed a political revolution was needed to break the monopolies on production and prices. Yet, most North Americans reject this solution. While some people see revolution as a creative solution to the problem of scarcity, most see higher productivity as the better solution. Typically, high rates of economic growth give most people more of what they want without breaking the existing monopolies. Such growth makes inequality less visible and less painful.

RECURRENT PATTERNS OF SOCIAL INEQUALITY

This book collects, in 54 excerpts, information on patterns of social inequality from many societies. As we will see there is much that is different, in the specifics of social inequality, across societies. However, at the same time, there are also certain frequently recurrent phenomena. Our excerpts will clearly show the following recurrent patterns.

First, the four mechanisms of social inequality that we just described—exclusion, decoupling, disabling, and scarcity—occur everywhere. For one type of social inequality after another, and whatever the specifics of that inequality in the particular country, we find evidence of one or more of the four forms of social obstacles. These are very common social strategies employed by haves to maintain their advantage over have-nots.

Second, three types of social inequality are widespread—inequality by gender, social class, and ethnic/racial group. We will later describe these as "risk factors" for social disadvantage. Everywhere the **genders** differ in economic circumstance, power, and prestige, and the advantage always goes to males over females. Likewise, there are very frequently differences in rewards by *social class* backgrounds (by the wealth and income of people's families). Those from advantaged backgrounds have more opportunity to attain wealth, power, and prestige than those who do not have such backgrounds. And frequently some *ethnic/racial groups* prosper over others in economic resources, power, and prestige. The only real exception to this seems to be ethnically/racially homogeneous societies (of which there are very few), where there is no sizable racial/ethnic out-group to be opposed by a majority in-group.

Third, there have been, and are now, numerous episodes of *bloody conflict* between racial/ethnic groups. Conflict around ethnic/racial inequality extends to violent encounters and even warfare. Sometimes, too, there is out-and-out fighting between classes. This occasionally culminates in a class revolution, where a once less powerful group wins out over the elite, and the representatives of the former take power. There is much less organized, violent conflict between genders. It is true there is physical violence against women by men in most societies, but it is not as organized as is much ethnic and class conflict—namely, as warfare. Also, it is comparatively seldom that women reciprocate in individual violence, much less organized violence against men.

Fourth, status consciousness and status group activity are comparatively low for women, and for the lower class, and comparatively high for ethnic/racial groups. This may partly explain the differences in the occurrence of bloody conflicts just described.

Fifth, whenever the workworld is at all complex and bureaucratized, managers have control over workers. Never do the workers share control equally with managers, although there are marked differences across societies in the specifics of how workplace power and authority are arranged. There seems to be an "iron law of oligarchy" in bureaucratized work; some must lead, and some must follow.

Sixth, in all reasonably complex societies, there is elite domination. While particular governing elites come and go—through elections, revolutions, and such—there are always governing elites.

Seventh, governments and the courts everywhere are squarely involved in legitimizing social inequalities, though sometimes they attempt to change inequalities and to legitimize the changes. The maintenance and shaping of patterns of inequality is clearly one of the major "tasks" of governments and the courts in all societies.

Eighth, inequality is legitimized through supporting ideology everywhere.

As we have suggested, this is promoted most strongly by governments and the courts. Also, family socialization, schools, churches, and the media are part of the process. At the same time, everywhere there is some resistance to inequality and development of counterideology among have-nots—among organizations of some women, some in the disadvantaged racial ethnic groups, some of the lower classes. The counterideologies justify other ways of arranging inequality, with a better lot for the have-nots.

Ninth, "external" power has affected relations of ethnic/racial groups and classes in many societies. For example, most nations have had some experience with being colonized in the past; and always it has affected inequality in the colonies in some way. Colonizing societies have imposed upon other societies their views on how economic rewards, power, and prestige should be arranged. And, sometimes long after the colonial power has withdrawn, its effects remain in the structure of inequality of the colonized society.

HOW INEQUALITY VARIES

As we shall see from the excerpts in this book, inequality varies from one society to another. For example, there is a lot of evidence that inequality increases with population size, economic surplus, and social complexity. This should not surprise us, given what we learn from the coin-toss game. There, inequality increases as we increase the game's complexity (i.e., number of preferential rules) and number of players. For similar reasons, it is bound to happen in a real society with a market economy, vested interests, and "elites."

Equality, as a social idea, construct, or invention, is of fairly recent vintage, not an ancient practice. There have been few groups or societies in history that even aspired to equality, much less made progress toward achieving it. In that sense, we are far closer to equality today than at any time in history.

Of course, equality is nearly inevitable when people lead simple, poor lives and when there is little property to possess (or, often, even food to eat). The trick is not to achieve equality through a lack of resources; it is to achieve equality despite a surplus. But as property and surplus increases, so does inequality (Lenski, 1966; Turner, 1984). As a chosen state of affairs in the midst of surplus, equality is a new idea, a new human goal. Societies have only started to attempt to achieve it in the past few centuries.

We have argued that an increase in size and surplus increases differentiation: a wider variety of outcomes in the competition for rewards. So equality is even less inevitable or "natural" in large societies than in small ones. But more differentiation also permits a wider range of social responses to inequality. It is in the largest, most prosperous, and complex societies— where the widest range of inequality is possible—that we find some of the most dramatic efforts to create equality. Here we find policies and legislation designed to minimize the social effects of biological chance—the social costs of being born disabled, for example. Here we also find efforts to limit the range of inequality that results from a free play of "the market."

One thing cannot be doubted: some societies make stronger, more conscious efforts to limit inequality than others do. In this sense, equality is an accomplishment—a successful limit placed on the operation of natural inequality. Creating full equality—and no society has done this yet—would require a very high degree of cultural, economic, and political functioning. As we will see, modern societies like Japan, the United States and Sweden all deal with inequality in different ways, because they have different cultural, political, and economic agendas.

To repeat, *inequality is natural* and that's why we find it everywhere. What is fascinating about social life is not how unequal it is, but how people strive to overcome inequality: to bridge the gap between haves and have-nots. That is why this book focuses on how, when, where, why, and to what degree people actually accomplish equality at different times and places.

One main problem facing those who would like to bring about equality is that it is not clear precisely what equal conditions would look like. Treating different people the same way does not always result in fairness or justice. For example, Christopher Jencks (1988) asks, "Whom must we treat equally for educational opportunity to be equal?" He asks us to imagine a certain Ms. Higgins, a third grade reading teacher who must decide how to allocate her time and attention among students in order to "equalize" their treatment. Jencks examines five different versions of equal educational opportunity.

1. Democratic equality requires Ms. Higgins to treat everyone equally regardless of ability, effort, past treatment, or chances of benefiting;
2. Moralistic justice requires her to reward those who make the most effort;
3. Weak humane justice requires her to compensate those who have gotten less than their share in the past;
4. Strong humane justice requires her to help her worst readers, regardless of why they read badly; and
5. Utilitarianism requires her to help those who will benefit most from her attention.

So exactly what is "equal treatment"? If Ms. Higgins gives everyone equal time, then those who are most talented won't get the nurturing they need to develop excellence. But if she concentrates on those students she considers the most talented, she will be helping the already advantaged, and increasing the disadvantages of the less able. And by what measurement are we to even decide who is most talented? Jencks suggests that Ms. Higgins should have to give convincing reasons for treating her pupils unequally. However, since no rationale for *unequal* treatment enjoys general agreement, Ms. Higgins may well feel obliged to simply give everyone equal time.

This problem of fair or equal treatment is not restricted to the allocation of teaching time: sometimes it can be a matter of life and death, as in the allocation of medical services. An eminent law professor, Guido Calabresi, shows in his book *Tragic Choices* (1979) that people disagree whenever scarce resources are being shared out.

Take the distribution of kidney dialysis machines, which are in short supply. We want to save people's lives by giving them access to scarce kidney dialyzers, without which they will die—their body will poison them. Should we put these machines on the market, and charge for the use of these machines, so that rich people survive and poor people die? Or should we charge everyone according to his or her ability to pay? Or should we give younger people more chance at these machines than older people, since young people have longer lives at stake, hence more to lose. Should we give more intelligent, or more productive, members of society more chance at these scarce machines? Or, should we simply use a lottery method and let pure chance decide who gets access to a dialyzer?

This discussion, of course, begs an important question: namely, why are kidney dialysis machines in such short supply? More generally, who gets to decide how much money is allocated to hospital equipment and staffing, and how much is used for other purposes, such as "national defense"? And on what basis do they make these decisions? Is it on the basis of a real concern for the safety, well-being, health, and prosperity of the nation, or are such decisions based on political motives and business interests?

Everyone wants a bigger piece of the pie and can give you good reasons for having it. So, how do we go about giving people fairer chances, when it means taking something valuable away from someone else? The fact is, we don't know what "equal treatment" means in practice. Deciding the issue is a political matter, not a philosophical one. In the final analysis, inequality changes through political action, not speculation or scientific research.

Consider access to jobs on the police force. Historically, working for the police has required meeting a certain size requirement and wearing a certain uniform (among other things). Women and certain racial or ethnic minorities have often had great difficulty meeting the size requirement. Should they be excluded from the police force, or should the rule be changed? What is the best decision in this case? There are arguments on both sides, and, ultimately the question is a political one and has to be resolved in the political arena. As a result, in some countries and in some cities of the United States the rules have been changed: smaller people can be police officers now.

Likewise, members of certain ethnic groups may be forbidden, by the rules of their religion, from wearing precisely the uniform the police typically wear. For example, Sikhs may be obliged to wear their ceremonial dagger at all times. Should Sikhs be prevented from joining the police force unless they give up their religion? Again, this is a political question, and increasingly the rules have been changed under pressure from people demanding more justice.

These are all very difficult, interesting questions, and ultimately they are all political questions. We cannot deduce a right and wrong answer until we make certain important assumptions about the social values we want to maximize. Even so, the outcome will typically be determined in the political arena by politicians or voters, or both. These issues of allocation and opportunity will all reveal public opinion about who deserves what, and why.

Nowhere is this issue more evident than in discussions of "comparable worth," which Gleason and Moser (1985) have called "the civil rights issue of the 1980s" and perhaps the 1990s. Comparable worth "is based on the notion that women in traditional female occupations such as nursing earn, on the average, 20% less than men in traditionally male occupations, such as truck drivers, despite the fact that both jobs are of equal value to the employer."

According to Gleason and Moser, "the question is whether employers are willing to implement comparable worth [payments] or female employees will bear the cost of this differentiation. . . . Comparable worth [payments] would help the women who work full time, but are still below poverty; while it would cost employers, taxpayers would realize a savings of $186 million, unless the employer is a public agency, in which case the taxpayer burden remains constant."

Women are bearing the direct cost of wage discrimination. Indirectly, taxpayers are bearing part of the cost, by having to subsidize impoverished women victimized by discrimination. If women were paid what their work merited, taxpayers would save money; employers would have to pay their workers more, and would probably pass the higher cost on to consumers. So, in the end, we all would still end up paying, but at least the wages would be nondiscriminatory.

That is one aspect of comparable worth, but when you get down to determining what the term really means, it proves elusive. In fact, women and men do different kinds of work, which are hard to compare. Even when they do the same work, they sometimes do it in different ways.

In our society, women have historically been socialized to provide emotional leadership and support. This is important work they are doing, whether they do it at home or on the job, and perhaps it has comparable worth to more technical, "male" approaches to the task. But emotional or symbolic labor has been associated with the female sex, so it has traditionally been treated as unimportant. This serves to justify a gender inequality in wages that favors men over women. This is very convenient for males, and for employers, who pass along the consequences such as female poverty to the taxpaying public. It is not so convenient for females, nor is it arguably just.

On the other hand, it is difficult to devise a way of measuring comparable worth so that we can give things like emotional labor the rewards they deserve. So part of the reason some people get ahead and others do not is due to this difficulty in figuring out how to reward comparable worth. At present, many governments and organizations are trying to fix this problem. On the other hand, most of the difficulty is political, not a problem of measuring comparable worth. There is still plenty of discrimination against women, blacks, gays, and old people—these groups still have more limited opportunities to get ahead—because some people stand to benefit by keeping these others behind.

Who gets ahead is a function of political bargaining; how many people get ahead, and whether the rules will be made more inclusive or "fair," is also a function of economic growth. If we want less discrimination against women, racial minorities, and the poor, we will get more changes in that direction in a period of growth than in a period of stagnation or decline. Better conditions, and better opportunities for improving those conditions, go together.

HOW THIS BOOK IS ORGANIZED

Today's college students realize that events in other parts of the world influence their own lives. Political unification in Europe, economic prosperity in the Pacific basin, environmental destruction in South America, military conflict in the Middle East, and famine and epidemic in Central Africa will all affect them in one way or another. What's more, the worldwide forces of industrialization and democratization have affected different parts of the world differently. A generation ago, sociologists expected the opposite: namely, a convergence of social patterns across modern and modernizing countries. This did not come to pass, so today no one is quite certain what to expect next.

Amid this general awareness of unpredicted change in a shrinking world, more and more people are aware of changes in social inequality—the complex web of class, gender, race, and other relations of unequal access to rewards. Recent theoretical and practical concerns have led researchers to focus their attention on the possible future(s) of inequality. They have begun to look for clues about the future of inequality in other societies, where social life is different from our own. They have also looked into history for clues to the trends and forces that will shape inequality in North America.

A rapidly changing world calls for new kinds of textbooks. Our own textbook aims at showing students some of the varied forms of inequality, among them, inequalities of wealth, power, prestige; and resulting differences in work experience, lifestyle, and belief. It also shows how class, gender, and race (or ethnicity) are major influences on the unequal distribution of rewards.

Articles included in this text show how these inequalities also give rise to resistance, protest, group mobility, and remedial legislation. They examine the way these phenomena show up on the local, national, and global scale. And, finally, they demonstrate the varied ways sociologists go about analyzing different forms of social inequality throughout the world.

Haves and Have-nots shows how different kinds of inequalities—class, race, and gender, among others—interact and change in response to different social and economic conditions.

All of the articles included in *Haves and Have-nots* were published in the past ten years or so and describe dozens of developing (as well as developed) societies, providing the student with a cosmopolitan selection of up-to-date excerpts. They include a worldwide variety of materials on all the topics typically covered in a first sociology course on inequality

The book is divided into three major sections: economic inequality, power inequality, and status inequality. Each of these is divided into three smaller sections: patterns of inequality, causes of inequality, and consequences of inequality.

Each of the nine subsections contains excerpts on how a particular type of inequality is affected by the three most important factors—class, race (or ethnicity), and gender. Indeed, many articles discuss more than one of these influences at a time. It could be argued that other factors—for example, Western values, modern technology, the internationalization of capital, the collapse of world communism, and movements of equality for women and racial minorities—are important, too, but no one could argue that class, race, and gender are *less* important. Rather than try to cover a wide variety of factors superficially, we have chosen to focus on these.

The book also includes a variety of research approaches. Some of the excerpts are cross-nationally comparative and "nomothetic"—comparing structures and processes according to uniform standards—while others are "idiographic" based on the country's own frame of reference. A secondary goal of this text is to show that both approaches to sociology—nomothetic and idiographic—are widespread and accepted parts of the sociological tradition.

Because we are concerned with showing how inequalities are different in China and Haiti, Germany and Bangladesh, all sections of this book contain articles from a wide variety of countries and perspectives. Many contain explicitly comparative articles.

Naturally, the historical dimension is important. Some of the factors affecting inequality today have been developing for decades, if not centuries. They include the spread of capitalistic values and modern technology throughout the world. Other factors, like the internationalization of capital and collapse of world communism, are much more recent. And still other factors, like movements of equality for women and racial minorities, have varied in form as well as content over the course of time.

To understand inequality today, and make informed guesses about inequality in the future, students must know about these historic forces and trends. For this reason, most sections of the book include historical material.

To make things easier, the book also provides useful introductory materials. As well as this opening section of the book, which introduces students to the sociology of inequality, there are three section introductions and brief introductions to each of the 54 excerpts. Professional social scientists have written all of the articles in this volume. Since professional writing is often telegraphic and sometimes obscure, each article is introduced by a paragraph describing the purpose and setting the context of the piece.

Other learning aids are provided, too. Because of the great diversity of materials and approaches examined, learning aids play a critical role in making this book successful. Fully one third of the book is made up of learning aids. For example, each section ends with a set of discussion questions and exercises that will help the student understand and review the pieces. The questions can stimulate classroom discussion by suggesting unresolved issues and calling attention to related issues in other readings.

A glossary at the end of the book defines the key concepts. At the end of each section, a list of suggested readings describes books of lasting importance concerned with the topic at hand, as well as some recent publications.

The purpose of this elaborate pedagogical armament is to help students unpack the case studies they are reading and find links among them. In this way we guide the student to seeing inequality is a complex, constantly evolving product of many social forces. Meaningful patterns will be pursued in what is, admittedly, a world's worth of material.

CONCLUDING REMARKS

This book documents the many varieties of *inequality* one can find in different parts of the world today. It also describes some of the struggle for equality that is central to modern politics and modern lives. This struggle for equality has been a struggle to establish new kinds of societies and new ways of living, not to return to an earlier state of equality. In particular, it has been a struggle to win rights and benefits for three traditionally disadvantaged groups: the poor, women, and racial minorities—groups that had an even worse time of it in the past than they do today.

The creation of equality will mean raising questions about and indeed fighting against prejudice, whether directed at poor people, women, or racial minorities. It will also mean limiting the range of inequality that we allow to result from competition, and preventing people from falling below a floor, or minimum level, of existence.

Clearly, people cannot have an equal opportunity to get what they want if they start out with vastly unequal wealth, power, and respect. Thus a society cannot equalize opportunity without greatly reducing the range of unequal starting points. The goal of ensuring equal opportunities within a system of unequal rewards is impossible. But there is some chance of reducing the range of inequality nonetheless.

Creating equality means making a cultural commitment to achieving something that has never existed; maintaining a political system that is responsive and powerful enough to enact laws that would increase equality; and enjoying an economic system that is healthy and buoyant enough to provide improved benefits for the disadvantaged.

Efforts to create equality mean raising questions about the attribution of values to simple differences (call this an "antiprejudice revolution"); setting limits to the range of inequality that can result from chance and competition (call this a "redistributive revolution"); and establishing a floor below which people will not be permitted to fall (call this a "citizenship [or human rights] revolution").

The point of this book is not that people should give up struggling for equality, any more than they should give up struggling for truth, justice, love or beauty. The point is, simply, that equality won't come easily. We must give up searching for a mythical state of natural equality to which we can all return, for that state of nature never existed. We can no more pin our hopes on returning to a natural state of equality than we can plan on returning to natural goodness in the Garden of Eden.

In our own society, professional associations, workers' unions, ethnic groups, and other groupings all use monopolization to their own advantage. In the long run this strategy cannot succeed. If every collectivity in the world mobilizes to gain a greater advantage, inequality will take more aggressive forms. Compare the situation to a parade people have gathered to watch. First a few people stand on their toes to see the parade better, then a few more, and so on. When everyone is standing on tiptoe, each person's ability to see the parade is as unequal as it was before, and everyone has sore toes.

Long-run solutions to the problem of unequal opportunity must be worldwide and cooperative. Anything less will result in economic, political, and military warfare. What the human race has working against it is greed, extreme and widening inequality, and rapid population growth. Working in its favor is a proven ability to use knowledge and science creatively, adapt to new circumstances, and occasionally to cooperate for mutual benefit.

This book will cover a wide variety of themes related to social inequality, focusing primarily on the influences of class, race, and gender. The difficulty in finding a single best way of organizing these articles is compounded by the fact that many types of inequality are interlinked. There are connections between class and gender inequality, gender and race inequality, and so on. What's more, the consequences of one kind of inequality may be causes of another kind of inequality.

There are any number of ways this material might have been organized:

by topic, region of the world, cause of inequality, consequence of inequality, and so on. We cannot claim to have found the single best pattern of organization. In fact, we encourage readers to dip into these articles in any way they find most useful. So in closing, we urge you to think of this collection as a kaleidoscope of thinking about inequality around the world. Its diversity and complexity may help you spin off new ideas of your own about relationships between types of inequality in North America and around the world.

REFERENCES

Adorno, T.W., E. Frenkel-Brunswik, D.J. Levinson, and R.N. Sanford (1969). *The Authorization Personality*. New York: W.W. Norton.

Baltzell, E.D. (1958). *Philadelphia Gentlemen: The Making of a National Upper Class*. New York: Free Press.

Berljawsky, A. (1986). "Mortgage rates and the housing market." *Canadian Social Trends*, Winter, 30–33.

Calabresi, G. (1976). *Tragic Choices*. New York: W.W. Norton.

Clement, W. (1975). *The Canadian Corporate Elite*. Toronto: McClelland and Stewart.

Davis, K. and W.E. Moore (1945). "Some principles of stratification." *American Sociological Review*, 10 (2), 242–249.

Domhoff, G.W. (1967). *Who Rules America?* Englewood Cliffs, NJ: Prentice-Hall.

Engels, F. (1962). *The Origin of the Family, Private Property and the State*. Reprinted in Volume II of *Selected Works in Two Volumes*. Moscow: Foreign Language Publishing House.

Feller, W. (1964). *Introduction to Probability Theory and Its Applications*, Vol. I, 3rd ed. New York: Wiley, 1968.

Gleason, S.E. and C. Moser (1985). "Some neglected policy implications of comparable worth." *Policy Studies Review*, 4 (4), 595–600.

Granovetter, M. (1974). *Getting a Job: A Study of Contacts and Careers*. Cambridge, Mass.: Harvard University Press.

Hirsch, F. (1978). *The Social Limits to Growth*. Cambridge, Mass.: Harvard University Press.

Jencks, C. (1988). Whom must we treat equally for educational opportunity to be equal?" *Ethics*, 98 (3), April, 518–533.

Lenski, G. (1966). *Power and Privilege: A Theory of Social Stratification*. New York: McGraw-Hill.

Macpherson, C.B. (1965). *The Real World of Democracy*. The Massey Lectures (4th Series). Toronto: Canadian Broadcasting Corporation.

Mann, M. (1970). "The social cohesion of liberal democracy." *American Sociological Review*, 35 (3), 423–439.

Marchak, P. (1987). *Ideological Perspectives on Canada*, 3rd ed. Toronto: McGraw-Hill Ryerson.

Meek, R.L. (ed.) (1954). *Marx and Engels on Malthus*. Translated by D.L. Meek and R.L. Meek. New York: International Publishers.

Michels, R. (1962). *Political Parties*. New York: Free Press.

Mills, C.W. (1956). *The Power Elite*. New York: Oxford University Press.

Murphy, R. (1982). "The structure of closure: A critique and development of the theories of Weber, Collins and Parkin." *British Journal of Sociology*, 35 (4), 547–567.

Newman, P. (1979). *The Canadian Establishment*, Vol. I. Toronto: McClelland and Stewart.

Parsons, T. (1964). "A revised analytical approach to the theory of social stratification." pp. 386–439 in *Essays in Sociological Theory*, rev. ed. New York: Free Press.

Porter, J. (1965). *The Vertical Mosaic*. Toronto: University of Toronto Press.

Reitz, J.G. (1980). *The Survival of Ethnic Groups*. Toronto: McGraw-Hill Ryerson.

Rousseau J.J. (1950 [1762]). *The Social Contract and Discourses*. Trans. and edited by G.D.H. Cole. New York: E.P. Dutton.

Ryan, W. (1976). *Blaming the Victim*. rev. ed. New York: Vintage.

Sennett, R. and J. Cobb (1973). *The Hidden Injuries of Social Class*. New York: Vintage.

Travers, J. and S. Milgram (1969). "An experimental study of the small world problem," *Sociometry*, 32, 425–443.

Tumin, M. (1953). "Some principles of stratification: A critical analysis." *American Sociological Review*, 18, August, 387–393.

Turner, J.H. (1984). *Societal Stratification: A Theoretical Analysis*. New York: Columbia University Press.

White, H. (1970). *Chains of Opportunity: System Models of Mobility in Organizations*. Cambridge, Mass.: Harvard University Press.

Part I

INTRODUCTION TO ECONOMIC INEQUALITY

Why are some people very rich and other people very poor? And what are the results of this inequality in wealth, or economic *inequality?* This section contains excerpts from a variety of countries that examine the causes and consequences of economic inequality, particularly poverty. We find poverty all over the world, and there are many factors that lead people into poverty, but certain typical patterns repeat themselves over and over again. Excerpts in this section try to explain why by looking at economic inequality in a variety of social contexts.

But before we begin, what do sociologists mean by *poverty?* Well, they usually distinguish between different kinds of poor people by distinguishing between "relative" and "absolute" poverty. People suffer from *absolute poverty* when they do not have enough of the basic necessities—food, shelter, and medicine, for example—for physical survival. They suffer from *relative poverty* when they can survive but are far from reaching the general living standards of the society or social group in which they live. As a result, what people consider "poor" varies from one society to another and, within a given society, from one group to another. In North America, we would consider people with much less than the average income to be poor.

Western governments usually measure poverty relatively, in relation to "low income cut-off points," which vary with family size and the size of the community in which a family lives. For example, large families who live in large communities generally need more money to live at a given level than they would if they lived in smaller communities. And, of course, large families require more than small families, regardless of the size of community they live in.

Typically, the incidence of such poverty is highest in families with three or more children and in those headed by mothers (mostly single parents). In the United States and Canada, for example, half of all lone-parent families headed by women are poor, and this percentage has increased since 1981. Indeed, families headed by lone female parents make up about one third of all poor families (Methot, 1987: 2). Among unattached individuals, the incidence of poverty is highest among the young (under age 25), the old (65 and over), and women. This is largely because these groups are least likely to be in the paid labor force or to hold a well-paying job.

Many unemployed people simply cannot find a job. In some regions and for some groups, the unemployment rate has been very high indeed, especially during the recession of the past several years. In addition, certain groups such as female lone parents of small children cannot afford to pay the daycare costs that would allow them to take a job that is offered them. Others still, like the physically disabled, cannot find a job suitable to their ability (or disability).

One result is the impoverishment of children. By 1990, over one child in six was living in a poor family. That percentage had increased since the early 1980s, while the proportion of elderly with low incomes was decreasing. Of all age groups, children are the most numerous and blameless victims of poverty. It is clear the poverty of children is due to forces beyond their control, especially the inability of parents to find work and the inadequacy of social supports (like inexpensive daycare), which would permit them to do the job.

CAUSES OF ECONOMIC INEQUALITY

Throughout North America, single mothers and chronically unemployed people receive less-than-generous welfare assistance, since many people consider them the "undeserving poor." Welfare payments to this group often fail to meet actual living expenses, especially for people living in large cities where rents are high. Why are welfare payments so low? The answer is that many believe that if welfare payments were higher, unemployed people would be reluctant to get off welfare and take a job.

Of course, North Americans hold varied beliefs about the causes of poverty. Consider a study by Smith and Stone (1987) that asked 200 adults, randomly chosen from a metropolitan area in southeast Texas, to answer this very question. They found people's thoughts about wealth and poverty reveal three general approaches or "meta-theories." The researchers call these meta-theories *individualism, structuralism,* and *fatalism;* of these, individualism and structuralism prove to be the most popular.

A person with individualistic views about poverty thinks the poor lack drive and perseverance, have loose morals and abuse drugs and alcohol, are not thrifty, and are lazy or unmotivated, perhaps because they can get welfare. Likewise, a person with individualistic views about wealth, usually the same person, thinks that people get wealthy because they possess drive and perseverance, are willing to take risks, are hardworking, and are thrifty.

These are individualistic views because they attribute success and failure to the personal characteristics of the individual. Only the individual is to blame for failure or due praise for success.

By contrast, a person with structuralist view focuses not on the individuals, but on the situation in which an individual finds himself or herself. So, a structuralist explains poverty by saying that poor people lack contacts or pull, suffer from discrimination in hiring, promotions, and wages, are taken advantage of by the rich, have to attend bad schools, and get little attention from an insensitive government.

On the other side, the structuralist explains that people become wealthy when they have a lot of pull or contacts, can attend good schools, inherit lots of money, are favored in hiring, wages, and promotions, get special treatment from the government, and take advantage of the poor. The most common meta-theory in the Texas community was individualism, especially in explaining poverty.

However, the excerpts in this section tend to support a much more structuralist view. Namely, they support the view that poverty is usually the result of factors well beyond the control of individuals.

In general, we shall find that three factors—class, gender, and race (or ethnicity)—all play a central part in determining whether a person will be rich or poor. Throughout the world, women are more likely to be poor than men; racial (and ethnic) minorities are more likely to be poor than racial (and ethnic) majorities; and working-class people are far more likely to be poor than people who own the lands, factories, and controlling shares in the largest companies.

Race, class, and gender are not causes of economic inequality and poverty per se, but they are factors that increase the risk of falling into, and remaining in, poverty. In the excerpts that follow we shall see how jointly and individually they have this effect.

PATTERNS OF ECONOMIC INEQUALITY

The first section contains six excerpts that describe patterns of economic inequality in different parts of the world. It includes excerpts on absolute and relative poverty, stateless people, immigrant minorities, visible minorities, and what we might call "ideological minorities."

This section begins with an excerpt on absolute poverty. To see what absolute poverty looks like, consider Sadeque's description of the lives of poor people in Bangladesh. Poor people's lives are filled with uncertainty. Some seek out whatever work they can find each day, with no guarantee of finding any. Bad weather, drought, or poor crops all spell disaster for farm workers, and there is a constant threat of employers hiring outside workers for cheaper wages. It is common for people to work at many different jobs in a day or week.

At the best of times, a family's income is scarcely enough to meet its basic needs, and food is the family's number one priority. In fact, many families spend their entire income on food. When income is diverted to other essential needs, such as shelter or health, it is often at the expense of an already insufficient diet. In extreme cases people will starve themselves to meet a need other than food.

When getting enough food to survive takes one's full energy, all other aspects of life suffer. Many village people live in dilapidated, unsafe huts surrounded by filth. Rather than take advantage of modern medical facilities when illness sets in, they resort to home remedies, faith healing, and the services of quacks. Few villagers even know how to prevent illness.

The second excerpt, by Wilson, helps us to understand relative poverty: a lifestyle that is deprived but not by any means as harsh as life in Bangladesh. As an example, we consider poor urban blacks in America.

According to this excerpt, racial discrimination is not the main problem facing poor black Americans. There are other, more important reasons blacks make up such a large percentage of the urban poor in the United States. Wilson notes that affirmative action has benefitted educated blacks, but has done little to help the poor blacks. This is because affirmative action tried to eliminate discrimination. Discrimination may have helped to create a black underclass, but other groups in American society have overcome discrimination in the past. Why haven't black Americans done the same?

Wilson argues the answer has more to do with factors that promote poverty in general, than with the unique history of African-Americans. In particular, the presence of large numbers of unsupervised youth has harmed the black community. A high concentration of youth in any population is accompanied by the worst characteristics of ghetto life—low income levels and high unemployment and crime rates, among others. And the sheer size of the black population makes it more threatening, to the white majority, than many other minority and immigrant groups. This has provoked a backlash from some portions of the white community.

American blacks have been particularly hard hit by the economic shift from manufacturing (the traditional area of black employment) to services. The consistent inability of black males to get jobs and support families has also eroded their self-esteem and sense of family responsibility. (In the introduction to this book we called this process **disability**.) That is why black family life is so unstable.

As fertility in the black population declines and the average age rises, crime and unemployment rates will fall, Wilson argues. However, meaningful change may also require the U.S. government to enact better social programs, particularly in the areas of education and employment.

We see a somewhat different combination of factors at work in the case of Palestinian women. In an excerpt by Rockwell, we consider how a stateless people, the Palestinians, and particularly the women among them, experience economic inequality.

The economic position of Palestinian women has worsened since the occupation, of the Gaza Strip by Israel. These women can no longer work on the family farm as they have done in the past. At the same time, inflation has forced Palestinian women to work for pay in order to supplement the family income. However, Israel's occupation of Palestinian lands has limited the types of jobs they can perform. Most women remain unskilled. The jobs open to them are in sewing, tinning, and packaging factories in Israel.

Rockwell points out that among Palestinians and other Arabs women avoid working for pay, due to their heavy domestic responsibilities. Social stigma also limits their participation in the work force. The patriarchal family structure makes men responsible for protecting the family and isolates its women. This system holds men to be the primary breadwinners, and wives are expected not to work for pay.

Women who *do* work for pay are likely to be single, widowed, or divorced. As unskilled workers, they receive only a fraction of what Arab men make, even when performing the very same task. Many Palestinian families try to hide the fact that a female family member works for pay, because this proves the family is poor. Likewise, male family members offer these women little support. For example, when the women are ill-treated, the menfolk are unwilling to help them get their due. The women themselves often fail to protest their treatment.

According to Rockwell, Palestinian women are not mainly concerned with their own emancipation. Rather they feel that they must first free Palestine from the oppression of occupation. Some might consider this an example of what Marx called "false consciousness"—a way of thinking that keeps power in the hands of men at the expense of women, as has been the case for millennia. As such, it is another type of disability.

Women accustomed to thinking of themselves as family property may be slow to demand the rights and respect to which people in our society think they are entitled. Whatever the reason, unskilled unmarried women are the losers.

Another type of disability is the alienation that is caused by a process sociologist call "commodification," which turns people and human activities into "things for sale." Typically, people who are poor are most vulnerable to commodification, since they are most in need of money at virtually any cost. In the world as a whole, the commodification of human life and experience is most common in Third World countries.

One piece in this part of the book, Excerpt 2.5, talks about the ways tour operators and travel literature sell tourists on "authentic" Third World experiences. To qualify as worth seeing, a country and its people must provide "authentic" experiences. But these experiences only appear to be *real*: in fact, they hide as much as they reveal about the country. As you might imagine, such as charade does not contribute much to the self-image of the people who live in this society.

Among the most decoupled people in any society are its immigrant minorities. That is because immigrants are often cut off from information and social contacts that would allow them to prosper in a competitive job market. This effect may even be reinforced by the actions of the immigrant community itself and the "sending" nation from which they have come.

When immigrants are "temporary workers" in a very different cultural and economic milieu—as, for example, Turkish workers in Germany—little effort may be made to integrate these immigrants into the receiving society. In fact, a continued strong contact with the home state may keep immigrant workers isolated from the receiving society. Extensive social bonds with their countries of origin, and plans to return there as soon as possible, may produce what are in effect political barriers between the immigrant communities and the host country. For their part, the sending countries may show as much interest in having their migrant workers return as the host countries do.

Under these circumstances, there is little likelihood the temporary workers will, with the passage of time, gain a greater foothold in the society they are visiting. They will remain decoupled from the best opportunities in the host society.

Another economically vulnerable group is visible minorities, such as the black Britons described in an excerpt by Howitt and Owusu-Bempah. Often laws are powerless to prevent the harmful effects of discrimination against such groups.

For example, Britain's laws forbid discrimination on the basis of race. Yet racism often achieves its goal in hidden ways. In the past whites expressed their disdain for blacks openly to help to maintain their advantage. Today, even positive (but weak) valuations of blacks by whites serve the purpose of racism equally well.

A final excerpt in the first section discusses another kind of minority group: people who are ideologically suspect. In this case, these people are China's new entrepreneurs. An excerpt by Shuqi and Liping discusses the effects of economic change of China's class structure. The authors show that a market-oriented economy increases social differentiation in the countryside. Peasants either combine other work with part-time agriculture or leave the farm altogether, taking nonagricultural work. Their new jobs include factory work, privately operated transport, handicrafts, and work in service businesses.

Today, farming peasants still make up the bulk of China's rural population, but there is a rapidly growing, increasingly prosperous working class. In the industrial sector of society, private enterprise is permitted, even encouraged. For their part, entrepreneurs are still far from loved in China, but they are seen as necessary for the country's modernization. The main problem facing China is how to incorporate this emerging capitalist class into the economy without giving up on socialism as an ideal. Seen another way, the problem is finding a way to accept a group—private entrepreneurs—who have always been ideologically suspect under communism but are now needed for economic growth.

CAUSES OF ECONOMIC INEQUALITY

In the second section, we consider six important causes of economic inequality: economic modernization, the de-skilling of work, the state's redistribution of wealth, sexism in economic policies, constraints on women's earning power, and the effect of labor markets on wealth distribution.

In Bangladesh, economic modernization, combined with discrimination against divorced women, often leads to poverty, according to an excerpt by Alam. Divorce used to be very rare in Bangladesh, but that is no longer the case. Often, divorced and abandoned women are blamed for the failure of their marriages. The community and even their relatives shun them. So these women are in the difficult position of having to provide for themselves and their children in a society that does not help its women to be economically independent.

Yet Bangladeshi women get divorced and deserted for a number of reasons beyond their control. For example, some men leave the community to seek employment elsewhere. Others return to a previous spouse. The women themselves tend to blame changes in the attitudes of men. The practice of paying dowries, which has replaced the traditional bride price, has made men more greedy, they say. Men consider marriage a business and when a marriage is no longer profitable, they leave. Whatever the reason, with increased rates of divorce and desertion the situation is getting worse for women in Bangladesh and elsewhere. In North America, it has contributed to what researchers call a **feminization of poverty**.

De-skilling is another cause of poverty, and we see it at work in an excerpt by Reiter. Typically the worst paying jobs are also the worst jobs to work at. Consider North America's fast-food industry as an example. Fast-food organizations place little value on the skills of their employees, so they treat them like machines and pay them poorly.

Reiter finds fast-food organizations treat workers as interchangeable units. Technology has reduced restaurant work to the monitoring of machines—a job anyone can do. In fact, management often treats its machines better than its employees.

Machines greatly reduce the amount of skill needed to work in a fast-food restaurant. Cash registers that calculate how much change to give a customer eliminate the need for cashiers to know arithmetic, for example. Fryers and ovens let workers know when the food is ready. Drink dispensers pour precise amounts of soft drink into cups. These labor-saving devices are very efficient but they leave little to the worker's discretion. Management limits what little freedom remains in these jobs by explicitly outlining how a task should be performed. It isn't surprising to find out that three in every four workers is a teenager.

Throughout the modern world, industry relies on poorly paid, socially vulnerable labor. Consequences of such work include poor pay, low productivity, and a sense of alienation from one's own life.

A third cause of economic inequality is the state's role as a redistributor of national wealth. For its part, Britain is kinder to its poor than many less-developed societies like Bangladesh. But even in Britain, welfare provides the poor with barely enough to survive. As an excerpt by Townsend shows, British social programs fail to provide people with enough to get by.

In Britain, as in other countries, the poor often have to neglect other needs in order to get enough food. They leave bills unpaid, put off buying needed new clothing, and withdraw from social life. By providing poor people with too little money to obtain the necessities of life, welfare keeps people in poverty. And according to Townsend, "poverty" means more than not having enough to eat. It means not having enough to participate fully in society. To be poor is to be socially, as well as physically, deprived.

Townsend argues that unemployment—due to a scarcity of jobs—is the most important cause of poverty in Britain. In this respect, multinational corporations worsen the problem. They wield more power than some governments and are not responsible to any single government. They can often escape efforts to limit their wealth by moving to another country, leaving massive unemployment in their wake. Solving the problems of poverty in a modern society may mean ensuring full employment despite the free movement of multinationals, says Townsend.

This effect of unemployment on economic inequality illustrates something we argued in the introduction to this book: the role of *scarcity* as a factor in shaping people's life chances. When there are not enough jobs to go around, some people will end up unemployed. And where people's economic well-being rests primarily on their ability to get and keep a job, some people will necessarily suffer economically from this job scarcity. Payments of welfare and unemployment insurance benefits provide only a slight, often temporary relief. The inescapable fact is that without work most people will be poor.

A fourth cause of economic inequality is sexism in a nation's economic policies. For Third World women, a lack of control over what they earn has profound consequences for the economy. When people are poorly paid for their work they reduce their output, and women are no exception. As an excerpt by Blumberg points out, women in developing countries do most of the work, yet they control very little of the income they generate. Assistance programs generally pay money exclusively to men, who then pay their wives much less than their work merits. Such projects fail because they ignore the needs of women to have control of their own income.

When women do control their own income, they exercise more power in household decisions. One result is that they have fewer children. Since development strategists universally recognize overpopulation as the Third World's biggest problem, a reduction in childbearing is a very good reason to increase women's control over family income.

Family well-being and child nutrition also improve when women have more control over incomes. The breakdown of traditional male-controlled family life has led some people to suggest increases in male income: this would remove the need for men to migrate to find work and allow families to remain intact.

However, there is no guarantee that increased male incomes would improve the condition of women and children. An excerpt by Jiggins suggests that placing income under female control will contribute even more to family welfare. A fifth cause of economic inequality is the existence of constraints on women's earning power.

Women suffer from a subordinate position to males in most societies, so they have a harder time establishing businesses. This causes particular problems in some African countries, Jiggins emphasizes. After all, how can a female entrepreneur run a successful business if she cannot discipline a male employee? And what recourse does she have if her husband suddenly appropriates all her money?

In sub-Saharan African rural poverty is increasing, and one effect of this is a change in the composition of households, according to Jiggins. More and more men are leaving their families in search of work. Yet female heads of household do not enjoy the same rights as their male counterparts (for example, land titles are seldom awarded to females). As a result, they have less access than men to many services and loans; as we noted earlier, they exercise little control over their income.

Change must occur from the top down, with governments guaranteeing women more rights in law. Jiggins argues that to change the situation more countries will have to follow the lead of Zimbabwe, where agricultural banks give loans directly to women. In general, governments will have to recognize the essential role women play by supporting and encouraging female income-earning activities.

The risk factors affecting economic well-being do not always work independently. Often, two or three factors combine to influence economic inequality. So, for example, in many societies female agricultural workers or factory workers suffer the greatest economic hardship. In other cases, impoverished racial minorities form a hard core of the chronically unemployed or underpaid classes. In these instances, we have a hard time separating out the effects of class, gender, and race on economic inequality.

That is the problem illustrated in an excerpt by Kelley, which asks whether the problems faced by Bolivian Indians are due to race or class. In particular, this excerpt examines the ways labor markets influence the distribution of wealth and, in that way, economic inequality within a society. But seen another way, this article is about the difficulty we have disentangling the effects of race and class on economic well-being.

RESPONSES TO ECONOMIC INEQUALITY

In the third section, we consider six important consequences of, or responses to, economic inequality: envy, state policy, the working woman's dual burden, illegal livelihoods, the commercialization of relationships, and changes in family structuring.

The first excerpt, by Keyfitz, is about economic development as a response to national poverty, and envy as a response to economic development. The supposed goal of development projects is to raise the living standards of poor people, thus reducing inequality. However, critics note that development projects typically encourage the growth of wealth differences and social inequality in peasant communities.

If adequate food and clothing, basic medical services, and literacy were truly the main objectives, development would go on in a very different way than it does now. For example, Keyfitz notes that Brazil, with its per capita income of $1,400, could easily provide these amenities to its millions of inhabitants. Yet a majority of Brazilians lack them altogether, while a minority have much more than the bare necessities.

Keyfitz believes development programs pursue a less noble goal than we usually acknowledge: the spread of the culture of consumerism. This way of life is exported from America and Europe to the rest of the world. It teaches people to want a centrally heated and cooled home, a television and refrigerator, food purchased at self-service supermarkets, and a car.

We usually find this lifestyle in cities with paved streets to accommodate the automobile. A network of paved roads and air transport between the city and surrounding rural areas ensures a continuous supply of goods. Unfortunately, this level of prosperity exceeds the capacity of many national economies. Thus, only a minority can benefit from development programs that aim to provide people with the things listed above. Some will become middle class (by our standards); the majority will not.

In the end, a rapidly expanding middle class creates more inequality and relative poverty. Keyfitz estimates that each year about 20 million people join the middle class, yet two or three times as many join the ranks of the poor. To claim that development aims at wiping out poverty in the Third World is hypocritical. Poverty might be reduced if the middle-class standard were acheived gradually by all members of a society. However, people in poor countries who obtained some part of the middle-class lifestyle want the new lifestyle quickly. They are not prepared to wait the time that making their fellow citizens middle class would require.

In trying to explain this pattern of unequal development, Keyfitz notes that the middle class controls the levers of power in nearly every society. They determine the policies that make cities grow while rural areas shrink. He sees a relentless, one-way, global trend from countryside to city. Even current efforts to modernize the countryside support this trend. Mechanization will put even more peasants out of work, forcing more people to head for the city.

An excerpt by Zimbalist is about a second response to economic inequality: namely, a national strategy to fight poverty. It shows that some countries succeed in the fight against poverty much better than the United States and Canada do.

An excerpt by Xuewen et al. is about a third response to economic inequality: the double burden working women have to take on in order to make ends meet. In a great many societies, women's involvement in the paid labor market is a result of too little household income. Wives need to help the family earn *more*. But in every society, women take on paid work in addition to the domestic work they have always been responsible for doing. That means that, when women take paid work, they take on a dual burden.

The point of the research by Xuewen et al.—a comparative study of women's work in three societies—is that this burden is heavier in some societies than in others. Some societies, like China, are less willing to simply assume that women will bear the domestic burden single-handedly, as we seem to assume in North America. The question, of course, is *why* societies differ in this way, or, to put the question in a more theoretical form, why, in some societies, economic inequalities intensify gender inequalities more than they do in other societies.

A fourth response to economic inequality is recourse to crime and, more generally, illegal livelihoods. These kinds of activities have a long history in North America, as elsewhere.

In what is now considered a classic article on the effects of poverty and discrimination in the United States, Bell (1962) wrote about the "queer ladder of social mobility." Historically, Bell notes, urban minorities have had to use three "queer" career ladders—especially in sports, entertainment, and crime—to gain success in a hostile environment. No wonder, then, that the history of American organized crime recalls the successive passage of minority groups— the Irish, then Germans, Jews, Italians, blacks, Hispanics, and most lately, Asians—from poverty and rejection to wealth and acceptance.

We see this same pattern at work in an excerpt by Bourgois that details the operation of an underground "crack economy" in Spanish Harlem (New York). There, unemployment and a general concern about the ability to provide one's family with the bare necessities of life translates itself into crime, drug abuse, and violence. For these people, it may not be easy or even rational to "just say no" to the use and sale of drugs.

In this community, drug use and sale is more than a self-destructive response to poverty and discrimination: for many, it is a way of carving out a career. As Bourgois notes, at least the drug economy is an "equal opportunity employer" for inner-city young people victimized by high rates of unemployment and lousy job opportunities. In terms of pay and working conditions, work in crime may appear more attractive than the few low-paying jobs that are open to poorly educated young people.

True, violence is occasionally necessary in this line of work, to maintain credibility and prevent rip-offs by customers and competitors. But this, too, is part of the logic of the drug business, not a random pathology. For many, the ends—high profits—may justify the means, including a high risk of personal harm. And in a society like our own that hates losers and typically holds that, in business, the ends justify the means, the crack economy may be little more than a caricature of law-abiding, everyday life.

A fifth response to economic inequality is seen in the commercialization of interpersonal relations. It takes its clearest form in traditional practices of what people have called the sexual *double standard*, especially the requirement that women be virgins when they marry, even if men are not. An excerpt by Schlegel reports on a study of a sample of preindustrial societies from around the world that finds that a cultural preference for, or prescription of, female virginity at marriage is part of a general conception of women as property. At marriage, this human property is traded by the bride's family to the husband (and his family) for certain economic considerations.

This double standard is slow to die. Even when the practice of treating women like property dies out, the cultural beliefs that support it hang on for a long time. For example, recent research by Bo and Wenxiu (1991) shows that urban Chinese people are more opposed to premarital sex than Americans are—in fact, about 50 percent more likely to be opposed. The reason is, in large part, because the Chinese still place a high value on virginity in their women. Bo and Wenxiu report that 73 percent of men and 78 percent of women say virginity is a girl's most valuable possession. Women are still preferred if they are virgins at marriage, while men are not.

Lest we feel too smug about this evidence of a cultural lag in China, we should note that changes to American attitudes on this matter are fairly recent. Darling et al. (1984) report that until the late 1940s or early 1950s there was a similar double standard in the United States: nonmarital sex was permitted for males and prohibited for females. From about 1950 to 1970, there was a period of "permissiveness with affection," during which premarital intercourse was acceptable so long as it was in a love relationship that was expected to lead to marriage.

It is only since about 1970 that we have seen a general acceptance—especially among young people—that sexual intercourse is a natural and expected part of a relationship for both males and females, whether or not the relationship is expected to lead to marriage.

So today, Americans place less value on virginity at marriage than they did in earlier decades. Women are not as likely to be considered sexual property—at least, not in any blatant sense. However, past battles are still being fought on this issue. For example, it is still unclear in many jurisdictions whether wives can legally accuse their husbands of rape or must consider themselves sexual property after marriage.

On the other hand, even in China some conflict remains between what we would call ideal culture and real culture. Virginity at marriage is part of China's ideal culture. In reality, a large proportion of men and women are having premarital sex, especially sex with a person one expects to marry. So it would seem that the urban Chinese are endorsing ideal norms like those that held in the United States before 1950, but (in practice) are following the norms that held between 1950 and 1970.

A sixth response to economic inequality is change in family relations, often for the worse. Poverty can have disastrous effects on family life. In Bangladesh, for example, family tensions are high and divorce and desertion are common. Where starvation is always just around the corner, education cannot be an important value for villagers because they see no hope of their children's lives being any better than their own. As a result, few achieve even the most minimal education and there is a high dropout rate among those who do attend school. Illiteracy, in turn, worsens the problem of poverty by limiting opportunities for employment outside farming.

Poorer families work much harder, yet earn less for their work and barely survive; this is bound to have an effect on childrearing and the lives of children. Consider the lives of Colombian street children described in an excerpt by Aptekar. In Colombia, one finds two kinds of family (and childhood). The wealthier Spanish classes tend to live in traditional families led by a strong father figure. Here, women learn to serve and depend on men. Adolescence is prolonged and supervised by the parents, especially the father.

In contrast, the poorer classes include a large number of female-led families of indigenous or African origin. Here, the mother is the dominant figure. Women function independently of their mates, and men are valued to the extent that they can contribute economically to the household. The children of these families are encouraged to be independent at a young age. It is from these poorer female-led families that Colombia's notorious "street children" are drawn.

The ruling classes, who control the government and press, criticize the street children as misfits, criminals, and drug addicts. They blame the methods of childrearing in poorer families for the increasing numbers of street children. However, Aptekar claims these children manage quite well, under the circumstances. Like their parents and fellow poor in other parts of the world, they are simply devising their own strategies for survival in a difficult, unequal terrain.

CONCLUDING REMARKS

The poverty problem is not going to get better without decisive actions. They will include the creation of new jobs for people to fill, job retraining for people whose job skills are inappropriate, and social supports, such as free, good-quality daycare, for women who need to go out and earn an income. In the long run, unemployment and discrimination against women, racial minorities, and working-class people will have to abate before we see a serious reduction in poverty around the world.

The excerpts in this section shows us that, throughout the world, gender, race, and class all serve to define the nature of economic inequality. And throughout the world, in different ways, the processes creating inequality are exclusion, disability, decoupling, and scarcity. There will be no significant reduction in economic inequality until the harmful influences of race, gender, and class are dealt with.

REFERENCES

Bell, D. (1960). "Crime as an American way of life," Reprinted in *The End of Ideology*. New York: Free Press.

Bo, Z. and G. Wenxiu (1992). "Sexuality in urban China," *Australian Journal of Chinese Affairs*, 28, July, 1–20.

Darling, C.A., D.J. Kallen and J.E. VanDusen (1984). "Sex in transition, 1900–1980." *Journal of Youth and Adolescence*, 13, (5), 385–399.

Keith, V.M. and C. Herring (1991). "Skin tone and stratification in the Black community." *American Journal of Sociology*, 97, (3), 760–778.

Methot, S. (1987). "Low income in Canada," *Canadian Social Trends*, Spring, 2–7.

Smith, K.B. and L.H. Stone (1989). "Rags, riches and bootstraps: Beliefs about the causes of wealth and poverty," *Sociological Quarterly*, 30, (1), 103–107.

SUGGESTED READINGS FOR PART I

Baltzell, E. Digby (1964). The *Protestant Establishment: Aristocracy and Caste in America*. New York: Vintage. *This beautifully written book describes the upward mobility of immigrants in America and the attempts the upper classes made—in the long run, without success—to keep ethnic minorities out. It spells out how and why minorities must be accepted, for the good of society and the upper class itself.*

Bridenthal, Renate, Claudia Koonz and Susan Studard, eds. (1987). *Becoming Visible: Women in European History.* Second edition. Boston: Houghton Mifflin Company. *This somewhat mistitled book hops around the world, and around human history, to show how women's economic condition has been tied up with family life, politics, and cultural ideas about sexuality, among other things. The result is exciting and provocative—a kind of history you may not have learned in high school.*

Coleman, James et al. (1966). *Equality of Educational Opportunity.* U.S. Department of Health, Education and Welfare. Washington, D.C.: U.S. Government Printing Office. *Commissioned as a report to the U.S. government, this monumental study had an enormous impact on the ways Americans think about education and economic inequality. The analysis showed that* separate but equal *cannot possibly work as a model for race relations.*

Hochschild, Arlie (1989). *The Second Shift.* New York: Avon Books. *Packed with everyday examples, this study shows the connection between women's economic inequality and inequality in the home. By the end of the book, we see that it is impossible to solve either problem without solving both problems.*

Ianni, Francis (1974). *Black Mafia: Ethnic Succession in Organized Crime.* New York: Simon and Schuster. *As in his earlier study of the Italian-American Mafia, anthropologist Ianni writes clearly about the day-to-day organization of urban crime. This book illustrates how the crime business passes through the hands of one disadvantaged group after another, providing the poor with means of gaining wealth.*

Myrdal, Gunner (1973). *Asian Drama.* New York: Harper and Row. *This multi-volume overview of Asian societies, by the author of a classic work on American race relations,* An American Dilemma, *outlines the reasons for economic inequality between and within Third World countries and the consequences of poverty in that part of the world.*

Orwell, George (1933). *Down and Out in Paris and London.* London: Heinemann. *This amusing autobiographical work tells about the experiences Orwell had as a tramp in England and an underpaid worker in a posh Parisian restaurant. A first-hand experience of how inequality and poverty feel to a middle-class Englishman; poverty hasn't changed much since then.*

Porter, John (1965). *The Vertical Mosaic.* Toronto: University of Toronto Press. *A classic of Canadian sociology, this book shows how the economic inequality of different ethnic groups is related to a society's history of development and the exercise of power by its elites. In the end, the book is a snapshot of an entire society working unequally.*

Stinchecombe, Arthur (1961–62). "Agricultural enterprise and rural class relations," *American Journal of Sociology,* 67, 165–176. *A tiny, jewel-like discussion of the variation in class relations on manors, plantations, ranches, family farms and other rural lands. This gives us a starting point for understanding the varieties of economic inequality throughout the rural Third World.*

Turner, Jonathan (1984). *Societal Stratification: A Theoretical Analysis.* New York: Columbia University Press. *This book is an adventurous attempt to tie together theories about social change with theories about economic inequality, status inequality, and power inequality. It's a small book with a big view of human history.*

Vicinus, Martha (1985). *Independent Women: Work and Community for Single Women, 1850–1920*. Chicago: University of Chicago Press. *This book is about the beginnings of feminism and women's struggle against economic inequality. It shows that the struggle will not only mean changes in domestic organization—it will also demand new social roles, new identities, and new communities to support these efforts at gender equality.*

SECTION 1
Patterns of Economic Inequality

1.1. How the Poor Survive in a Bangladesh Village

Mohammed Sadeque

The first excerpt is about absolute poverty—about people who are "down and out." George Orwell had it right in his classic work of autobiography, *Down and Out in Paris and London*: being poor is hard work. It means spending a lot of time on things you would rather not think about at all, like how to pay for your next meal, how to fill your time (if not employed), or how to put up with a hard, unpleasant, often repetitive job (if you are employed).

Things haven't changed for the poor since Orwell wrote down his views over sixty years ago. Poverty is still hard work, as we learn from the next excerpt on village life in Bangladesh. There, the working lives of poor people are filled with uncertainty. Some spend every day looking for whatever work they can find, without any guarantee of finding work at all. Bad weather, drought, and poor crops can spell disaster for agricultural laborers, and there is a constant threat of employers hiring outside workers for cheaper wages.

At the best of times, a family's income is scarcely enough to meet its basic needs. Food is the number one priority of families, and many spend their entire income on food. When income is diverted to other essential needs, such as shelter or health, it is often at the expense of an already poor diet. In extreme cases people will starve themselves to meet another need. Not surprisingly, the residents of Meherchandi live in dilapidated, unsafe huts in filthy surroundings—many in poor health. Education seems unimportant to these villagers because they see no hope of their children's lives being any better than their own. As a result, few complete even a minimal education and there is a high dropout rate among those who begin school. Poverty has also had a disastrous effect on family life. In these families, tension is high, divorce and desertion common.

According to the author, education is the best hope for the poor masses of Bangladesh. Illiteracy worsens the problem of unemployment by limiting job opportunities. People will never have stable employment and a stable income until they improve their education. But they will never improve their education until they have stable employment and a stable income. So the vicious circle of poverty continues.

Excerpted from Sadeque, Mohammed (1986), "The survival characteristics of the poor: A case study of a village in Bangladesh," *Social Development Issues*, 10(1), Spring, 11–27.

CONCEPTUAL FRAMEWORK

... In Bangladesh, poverty has been one of the major concerns in social studies in recent years. The present study adopted a multidimensional stance to analyze the interrelationship between economic and non-economic features of deprivation and their impact on the survival of the poor. The study is expected to help develop appropriate social policies for Bangladesh where methods for mobilizing the poor do not exist. . . .

Village Meherchandi

The study village was located on the northern border of the University of Rajshi. . . .

Two criteria—land ownership and income—were adopted to single out the poor households which constituted about 86% of the 632 households in the study village. *The Second Five Year Plan of Bangladesh* estimates the number of poor and extremely poor at 83% and 53%, respectively (Bangladesh Planning Commission, 1980).

Location, cost consideration, and familiarity with the community prompted the selection of the study village. Data were collected in three stages: preliminary survey of all households in the village; an intensive interview of selected households; and twelve case studies.

TABLE 1   Land Ownership in Meherchandi

Land Holding	Percentage of Total Households	Percentage of Total Land
Landless	39.24	—
Less than 1 acre	21.84	6.28
1.00–2.50 acres	23.58	26.93
2.50–5.00 acres	8.70	21.08
5.00–7.50 acres	3.80	16.68
7.50–12.50 acres	1.58	11.33
Over 12.50 acres	1.26	17.70
Total	100.00	100.00

PRESENTATION OF THE FINDINGS

Income-Earning Activities

. . . The daily wage earners had to undertake whatever they could manage on a day-to-day basis for eking out a bare subsistence. The day laborers were faced with uncertain employment opportunities due to the seasonal nature of agricultural and non-agricultural income-earning activities, unfavorable natural conditions, and the pressure of outside laborers. Others who had relatively stable sources of income could not count on any single activity throughout the year, and had to engage in additional activities to supplement their income.

On the basis of the major income-earning activities, we broadly categorized the households into eight specific groups: day laborers, small farmers, petty service holders, rickshaw pullers, petty traders, artisans, and beggars. The day laborers were the largest group. They constituted 40% of the households at the preliminary survey stage.

The monthly average household income of the classified categories based on data collected at the interview phase indicates very low income levels. The average monthly income of all the categories was about Tk.377, or roughly U.S.$13 (1 taka = $0.035). An average household size of 5.48 persons put the per capita monthly income at slightly more than two dollars, which is about one-fourth of the presumed national per capita income in Bangladesh.

The abysmally low income of the day laborers, service holders, and beggars was confirmed by the case [studies].

Meeting Basic Needs

The poor spent all or most of their income for consumption purposes only. Analysis of a month's expenditures shows that more than 90% of the total expenses were for daily food requirements (Table 2).

The various household categories show a similar expenditure pattern. Four house-

TABLE 2 Expenditure Pattern of Poor
Households in a Particular Month

Expenditure Item	Percentage of Total Expenses
Rice	47.11
Wheat	15.73
Pulses	3.16
Vegetables	5.06
Other Foodstuffs	20.08
Cloth	6.15
Medicine and Medical Expenses	1.53
Recreation	0.82
Social responsibility	0.36
Total	100.00

holds (Cases II, III, XI, and XII) spent their entire yearly income on food. Four others (Cases I, IV, VI, and VIII) allocated nearly 90% for food. The remaining four cases had to divert . . . part of their incomes for meeting extraordinary expenses such as payment of marriage gift, purchase of medicine, etc. In other words, they . . . decreased food intake to meet other unavoidable expenses.

The poor adopted varied means to survive a decrease in income: credit-buying from village grocers, informal loans, institutional credit, disinvestment of assets (if any) or, in extreme circumstances, starvation.

Since they purchased foodstuffs daily, they were subject to recurring price fluctuations. Certain essential items of daily living for the years 1981–1983 demonstrated wide variations in [local] prices.

Because their earnings were uncertain and irregular, so was their food-intake pattern. It was clearly linked to income and the manner in which it was earned. Thus, they had little control over what and when they ate. Food-intake information for a particular 24-hour day and for a particular month strongly suggests the poor recorded a much lower intake of carbohydrates (their dominant form of food) than the desirable minimum of 450 grams of rice/wheat per capita per day.

Food-intake information from the twelve case studies collected for two consecutive months on a weekly basis shows an equally depressing picture. None of these households could afford a minimum carbohydrate diet.

The vast majority of households cooked rice and/or wheat only once in the evening and ate the evening's leftover, if available, the next morning. The curry consisted of leafy vegetables or *marichbata*, a peculiar combination of onions, chilies, and mustard oil. None of the households purchased any fish or meat from the market.

This near-starvation diet had a deleterious impact on health. About one-fourth of all members in the households studied and one-half of the labor force reportedly were suffering from diseases.

The incidence of chronic and severe gastrointestinal diseases on a wide scale was clearly indicated. Deficiency diseases related to malnourishment seemed to be highly concentrated among the poorest households.

Health problems were exacerbated by at least two conditions: first, their huts (78% had a one-room dwelling of about 127 sq. ft.) were made of rustic material, were substandard, dilapidated, and unsafe, and they lacked the minimum facilities of rest, sleeping, and healthful living; second, their living environment was filthy, as only 15% used service latrines, whereas the vast majority evacuated their bowels in the fields and banks of rivers, polluting soil and water. Moreover, 50–80% of the households utilized home remedies, faith healing, and herbal medicines, and went to locally available quack alopaths and homeopaths when disease conditions deteriorated. Most people had no awareness of prevention.

Education of children was not conceived of as relevant to the realities of living. They could not imagine that the lifestyle of their children could differ from theirs. Only about 25% of the children were attending primary schools. The dropout phenomenon was also colossal. Most school-aged boys and girls had to help their parents with household tasks, collected firewood, or earn an income.

In summary, food was the overriding need. Families were so engrossed in meeting this requirement that the rest of their basic needs were grossly neglected—consciously or unconsciously.

Impact on Family and Kinship Relationships

Economic insecurity and hardship and the consequent interpersonal complications appeared to pave the way for the division of joint families into nuclear ones. About 85% of the poor households could be classified as nuclear. . . . This division took place upon any pretext. At times, far-sighted parents took the initiative in setting up separate households for married sons in the interest of amity or to make them independent. All the cases except one were nuclear in the present study.

[Many] of the nuclear families were wracked by internal conflicts and mutual distrust. Familial peace and harmony seemed to be disturbed constantly by two particular conditions: first, grown girls were a perpetual source of anxiety for parents because the burden of a dowry or marriage gift was beyond their means. Second, the poor households recorded about a 25% rate of divorce/desertions. Unfortunately, neither the traditional local leadership was of any help in checking indiscriminate divorce/ desertions, nor was there any effective legislation passed to protect the victimized married women.

Interestingly, most of the divorced/ deserted women earned their own food. We also found instances where rich and powerful employers were having illicit sexual relationships with such working women.

Sons-in-law, on the other hand, enjoyed a somewhat privileged position. Sometimes their fathers-in-law lent or gave them money to do petty business. They also were presented with gifts from their fathers-in-law on special occasions. The primary concern of the girls' parents was to ensure that the marriages of their daughters survived. The weaker social position of women was clearly indicated. It is likely that the daily preoccupation with ceaseless efforts to find work and food changed the traditional mode of kinship relationships. Such relationships (both patrilineal and matrilineal) were limited to the exchange of visits at the most, and proximity was an important determinant. Relatives living in distant villages did not maintain connections with one another.

Status in the Community

Relationships with neighbors could be termed diffused. The pressure of outside laborers and the preference of some local employers to engage outside laborers at cheaper rates might have led to the ejection of a few of the working poor from the local employment market. But the majority were dependent on co-workers and poor neighbors for mutual support during emergencies or on rich and powerful neighbors for employment and other exigencies. There was a patron-client relationship between the rich and the poor, and the poor neighbors re-ciprocated by offering free services or supporting patrons in local elections (Khan, 1978). This dependence might have lowered their social position.

Their political awareness and participation seemed to be at the lowest ebb. Most adults voted in a ritualistic manner. The desire to achieve economic gains (e.g., relief goods) and the opinion and influence of the patrons acted as motivating factors. Local politics virtually became the monopoly of the local power elites.

Alternative opportunities for participation could be provided by voluntary social agencies and other programs that sprang up in the study community in recent years. Two voluntary organizations established to cater to the recreational needs of the local people had a very brief existence. At the time of research, two other organizations were working as cooperative saving societies.

Attitude

Almost everybody felt God had ordained their sufferings. The old, physically weak, and chronically sick were the most frustrated. Their sense of insecurity was obvious. Their ability to work and earn was their most valued possession and when that was threatened, their physical survival was endangered. Households with very young dependents or grown-up/divorced/deserted young girls were found to sulk in their pent-up frustrations.

Despite the fact that most of the poor were fatalistic, the majority were not content with their living conditions. They were unhappy because they failed to meet even the minimum food needs, let alone other basic necessities. The majority, however, did not give up and continued working hard for their basic survival. We agree with Gans (1970) in asserting that their reaction to present living conditions might be called fatalistic, "not because they were unable to conceive of alternative conditions but because they have been frustrated in the realization of alternatives."

Our observations did not support the prevalence of a so-called culture of poverty among our respondents.

IMPLICATIONS FOR SOCIAL POLICY

The study found survival by all the categories of the rural poor to be precarious. The problems of unemployment and lack of purchasing power appeared to have spread widely. The main problem is employment. It is, therefore, urgent that the nation adopt appropriate strategies of planned mobilization of our vast landless manpower through agro-based employment schemes, promotion of rural non-farm activities, and labor-intensive rural industrialization schemes. The traditional rural artisans should be incorporated into these schemes.

The productivity of small, marginal farmers should receive equal attention. Previous studies indicate that they were more productive than larger farms, provided they are given access to a regular flow of necessary credit, extension facilities and inputs at the proper time (Hossain, 1974). The existing Integrated Rural Development Programme (IRDP) has failed to meet their needs because the cooperatives are dominated by the rural rich (Jones, 1979).

The deteriorating socioeconomic status of disadvantaged women is largely linked to the failure to make them economically independent. Those without any productive role in their families must be provided with one to supplement family income. Others should be taught alternative ways of performing household chores; the time saved may be used in undertaking additional income-producing activities. Moreover, the legislation enacted to protect their rights needs to be enforced.

To enable rootless people to derive the full worth of their work, their asset base has to be steadily created by suitable land and other asset reforms and by funnelling a substantial portion of the annual development funds to them. We found an unprecedented increase in the vulnerability of the old, infirm, and the young dependents who were previously supported by the joint family system. Society must introduce social security measures for them.

Health services were in disarray. The existing *union* level health care centers can be revitalized with essential medicines and equipment, and locally recruited paramedics may be trained to provide elementary health information as well as curative and preventive services. These centers could also serve as a nucleus for providing additional family welfare services.

In conclusion, we may emphasize two things. First, mass illiteracy reinforces the unemployment problem. The nation has to mobilize resources to introduce compulsory education in order to arrest illiteracy and raise the skill level of children and young adults. Second, organizations for the poor need to be turned into viable action groups by a gradual process of education, and consciousness-raising. Existing poverty-focused programs and voluntary social agencies may be utilized as institutional bases for reaching and organizing them.

REFERENCES

Bangladesh Planning Commission. (1980). *The second five year plan 1980–85.* Dacca: Bangladesh Government Press.

Gans, H.J. (1970). Poverty and culture—Some basic questions about methods of studying life style of the poor. In P. Townsend (Ed.), *The*

concept of poverty (pp. 146–164). London: Heinemann.

Hossain, M. (1974). Farm size and productivity in Bangladesh agriculture: A case study of Phulpur farms. *The Bangladesh Economic Review,* 2(1), 469–500.

Jones, S. (1979). An evaluation of rural development programme in Bangladesh. *The Journal of Social Studies,* 6, 51–92.

Khan, F.R. (1978). Problems and model of the study of elites in a district town in Bangladesh. *The Journal of the Institute of Bangladesh Studies,* 3, 149–172.

1.2. The Black Underclass in America

William Julius Wilson

This excerpt is about relative poverty, a condition people face when they are not completely "down and out," like those we read about in the first excerpt, but very poor by national standards. The Los Angeles riots of 1992 rudely reminded us that America's urban poor live in such a state of relative poverty. The people who looted and set fires did so because they had nothing to lose. Comparatively speaking, their lives could not get any worse.

Black Americans make up a large share of the urban poor. Why is this so? In this excerpt, the author examines traditional views about the persistence of poverty among urban American blacks. Wilson finds that attacks on **discrimination** have had little effect. Affirmative action may have helped educated blacks, but has done little to help the poor. Wilson argues that this is because affirmative action aimed at reducing discrimination. This is a problem, to be sure, but not what prevents most urban blacks from improving their economic situation.

The author believes there is much more to the problem of black poverty than discrimination. These factors promote poverty in general, for whites and African-Americans alike. In particular, he argues that large numbers of unsupervised youth have a devastating effect on the community. In any population, a high concentration of youth predicts low incomes and high rates of unemployment and crime. (We will say more about poverty and crime in a later excerpt on the crack economy of Spanish Harlem.)

Blacks have been particularly hard hit by the shift in the economy to services from manufacturing, the traditional sector of black employment. Discrimination may have helped to create a black underclass, but it cannot account for the poverty of most urban blacks. If discrimination were to blame, how could we explain the prosperity of Chinese and Japanese-Americans? They, too, were subjected to equally brutal forms of discrimination earlier in this century, yet escaped poverty.

Much of the research on black poverty has focused on the family. But recent research suggests that, even under slavery, black families were actually quite strong and stable. The high percentage of single-parent families we see today first appeared in the middle of the twentieth century, not during times of slavery.

Ironically, this change for the worse coincides with the passage of civil rights laws designed to improve the situation of black Americans. It also coincides with a drop in employment opportunities. Limited opportunities make it hard for black men to support their families. In this way, a bad economy erodes their self-esteem and sense of family responsibility. Meaningful change will occur only when the education and employment chances of urban black men improve.

It is no secret that the social problems of urban life in the United States are, in great measure, associated with race.

While rising rates of crime, drug addiction, out-of-wedlock births, female-headed families, and welfare dependency have afflicted American society generally in recent years, the increases have been most dramatic among what has become a large and seemingly permanent black underclass inhabiting the cores of the nation's major cities.

And yet, liberal journalists, social scientists, policy-makers, and civil-rights leaders have for almost two decades been reluctant to face this fact. Often, analysts of such issues as violent crime or teenage pregnancy deliberately make no reference to race at all, unless perhaps to emphasize the

Excerpted from Wilson, William Julius (1984), "The black underclass," *Wilson Quarterly*, Spring, 88–99. From the *Wilson Quarterly*, Spring 1984. Copyright 1984 by the Woodrow Wilson International Center for Scholars.

deleterious consequences of racial discrimination or the institutionalized inequality of American society.

Some scholars, in an effort to avoid the appearance of "blaming the victim," or to protect their work from charges of racism, simply ignore patterns of behavior that might be construed as stigmatizing to particular racial minorities.

Such neglect is a relatively recent phenomenon. During the mid-1960s, social scientists such as Kenneth B. Clark (*Dark Ghetto*, 1965), Daniel Patrick Moynihan (*The Negro Family*, 1965), and Lee Rainwater (*Behind Ghetto Walls*, 1970) forthrightly examined the cumulative effects on inner-city blacks of racial isolation and class subordination. All of these studies attempted to show the connection between the economic and social environment into which many blacks are born and the creation of patterns of behavior that, in Clark's words, frequently amounted to a "self-perpetuating pathology."

Why have scholars lately shied away from this line of research? One reason has to do with the vitriolic attacks by many black leaders against Moynihan upon publication of his report in 1965—denunciations that generally focused on the author's unflattering depiction of the black family in the urban ghetto. The harsh reception accorded to *The Negro Family* undoubtedly dissuaded many social scientists from following in Moynihan's footsteps.

The "black solidarity" movement was also emerging during the mid-1960s. A new emphasis by young black scholars and intellectuals on the positive aspects of the black experience tended to crowd out older concerns. Indeed, certain forms of ghetto behavior labeled pathological in the studies of Clark et al. were redefined by some during the early 1970s as "functional" because, it was argued, blacks were displaying the ability to survive and in some cases flourish in an economically depressed environment.

In the end, the promising efforts of the early 1960s—to distinguish the socioeconomic characteristics of different groups within the black community, and to identify the structural problems of the U.S. economy that affected minorities—were cut short by calls for "reparations" or for "black control of institutions serving the black community." In his 1977 book, *Ethnic Chauvinism*, sociologist Orlando Patterson lamented that black ethnicity had become "a form of mystification, diverting attention from the correct kinds of solutions to the terrible economic condition of the group."

Meanwhile, throughout the 1970s, ghetto life across the nation continued to deteriorate. The situation is best seen against the backdrop of the family.

In 1965, when Moynihan pointed with alarm to the relative instability of the black family, one-quarter of all such families were headed by women; 15 years later, the figure was a staggering 42 percent. (By contrast, only 12 percent of white families and 22 percent of Hispanic families in 1980 were maintained by women.) Not surprisingly, the proportion of black children living with both their father and their mother declined from nearly two-thirds in 1970 to fewer than half in 1978.

In the inner city, the trend is more pronounced. For example, of the 27,178 families with children living in Chicago Housing Authority projects in 1980, only 2,982, or 11 percent, were husband-and-wife families.

TEENAGE MOTHERS

These figures are important because even if a woman is employed full-time, she almost always is paid less than a man. If she is not employed, or employed only part-time, and has children to support, the household's situation may be desperate. In 1980, the median income of families headed by black women ($7,425) was only 40 percent of that of black families with both parents present ($18,593). Today, roughly five out of 10 black children under the age of 18 live below the poverty level; the vast majority of these kids have only a mother to come home to.

The rise in the number of female-headed black families reflects, among other things, the increasing incidence of illegitimate births. Only 15 percent of all births to black women in 1959 were out of wedlock; the proportion today is well over one-half. In the cities, the figure is invariably higher: 67 percent in Chicago in 1978, for example. Black women today bear children out of wedlock at a rate nine times that for whites. Almost half of all illegitimate children born to blacks today will have a teenager for a mother.

The effect on the welfare rolls is not hard to imagine. A 1976 study by Kristin Moore and Steven B. Cardwell of Washington's Urban Institute estimated that, nationwide, about 60 percent of the children who are born outside of marriage and are not adopted receive welfare; furthermore, "more than half of all AFDC [Aid to Families with Dependent Children] assistance in 1975 was paid to women who were or had been teenage mothers." A 1979 study by the Department of City Planning in New York found that 75 percent of all children born out of wedlock in that city during the previous 18 years were recipients of AFDC.

WHY NO PROGRESS?

I have concentrated on young, female-headed families and out-of-wedlock births among blacks because these indices have become inextricably connected with poverty and welfare dependency, as well as with other forms of social dislocation (including joblessness and crime).

As James Q. Wilson observed in *Thinking About Crime* (1975), these problems are also associated with a "critical mass" of young people, often poorly supervised. When that mass is reached, or is increased suddenly and substantially, "a self-sustaining chain reaction is set off that creates an explosive increase in the amount of crime, addiction, and welfare dependency." The effect is magnified in densely populated ghetto neighborhoods, and further magnified in the massive public housing projects.

Consider Robert Taylor Homes, the largest project in Chicago. In 1980, almost 20,000 people, all black, were officially registered there, but according to one report "there are an additional 5,000 to 7,000 who are not registered with the Housing Authority." Minors made up 72 percent of the population and the mother alone was present in 90 percent of the families with children. The unemployment rate was estimated at 47 percent in 1980, and some 70 percent of the project's 4,200 official households received AFDC. Although less than one-half of one percent of Chicago's population lived in Robert Taylor Homes, 11 percent of all the city's murders, 9 percent of its rapes, and 10 percent of its aggravated assaults were committed in the project in 1980.

Why have the social conditions of the black underclass deteriorated so rapidly?

Racial discrimination is the most frequently invoked explanation, and it is undeniable that discrimination continues to aggravate the social and economic problems of poor blacks. But is discrimination really greater today than it was in 1948, when black unemployment was less than half of what it is now, and when the gap between black and white jobless rates was narrower?

As for the black family, it apparently began to fall apart not before but after the mid-20th century. Until publication in 1976 of Herbert Gutman's *The Black Family in Slavery and Freedom*, most scholars had believed otherwise. "Stimulated by the bitter public and academic controversy over the Moynihan report," Gutman produced data demonstrating that the black family was not significantly disrupted during slavery or even during the early years of the first migration to the urban North, beginning after the turn of the century. The problems of the modern black family, he implied, were a product of modern forces.

Those who cite racial discrimination as the root cause of poverty often fail to make a distinction between the effects of *historic* discrimination (that is, discrimination prior to the mid-20th century) and the effects of *contemporary* discrimination. That is why they find it so hard to explain why the economic position of the black underclass started to worsen soon after Congress enacted, and the White House began to enforce, the most sweeping civil-rights legislation since Reconstruction.

MAKING COMPARISONS

My own view is that historic discrimination is far more important than contemporary discrimination in understanding the plight of the urban underclass; that, in any event, there is more to the story than discrimination (of whichever kind).

Historic discrimination certainly helped to create an impoverished urban black community in the first place. In *A Piece of the Pie: Black and White Immigrants since 1880* (1980), Stanley Lieberson shows how, in many areas of life, including the labor market, black newcomers from the rural South were far more severely discriminated against in Northern cities than were the new white immigrants from southern, central, and eastern Europe. Skin color was part of the problem, but it was not all of it.

The disadvantage of skin color—the fact that the dominant whites preferred whites over nonwhites—is one that blacks shared with Japanese, Chinese, and others. Yet the experience of the Asians, whose treatment by whites "was of the same violent and savage character in areas where they were concentrated," but who went on to prosper in their adopted land, suggests that skin color per se was not an "insurmountable obstacle." Indeed, Lieberson argues that the greater success enjoyed by Asians may well be explained largely by the different context of their contact with whites. Because changes in immigration policy cut off Asian migration to America in the late 19th century, the Japanese and Chinese populations did not reach large numbers and therefore did not pose as great a threat as did blacks.

Furthermore, the discontinuation of large-scale immigration from Japan and China enabled Chinese and Japanese to solidify networks of ethnic contacts and to occupy particular occupational niches in small, relatively stable communities. For blacks, the situation was different. The 1970 census recorded 22,580,000 blacks in the United States but only 435,000 Chinese and 591,000 Japanese. "Imagine," Lieberson exclaims, "22 million Japanese Americans trying to carve out initial niches through truck farming."

THE YOUTH EXPLOSION

Different population sizes also helped determine the dissimilar rates of progress of urban blacks and the new *European* arrivals. European immigration was curtailed during the 1920s, but black migration to the urban North continued through the 1960s. With each passing decade, Lieberson writes, there were many more blacks who were recent migrants to the North, whereas the immi-grant component of the new Europeans dropped off over time. Eventually, other whites muffled their dislike of the

Poles and Italians and Jews and saved their antagonism for blacks. As Lieberson notes, "The presence of blacks made it harder to discriminate against the new Europeans because the alternative was viewed less favorably."

The black migration to Northern cities—the continual replenishment of black populations there by poor newcomers—predictably skewed the age profile of the urban black community and kept it relatively young. The number of central-city black youths aged 16–19 increased by almost 75 percent from 1960 to 1969. Young black adults (ages 20–24) increased in number by two-thirds during the same period, three times the increase for young white adults. In the nation's inner cities in 1977, the median age for whites was 30.3, for blacks 23.9. The importance of this jump in the number of young minorities in the ghetto, many of them lacking one or more parent, cannot be overemphasized.

Age correlates with many things. For example, the higher the median age of a group, the higher its income; the lower the median age, the higher the unemployment rate and the higher the crime rate. (More than half of those arrested in 1980 for violent and property crimes in American cities were under 21.) The younger a woman is, the more likely she is to bear a child out of wedlock, head up a new household, and depend on welfare. In short, much of what has gone awry in the ghetto is due in part to the sheer increase in the number of black youths. As James Q. Wilson has argued, an abrupt rise in the proportion of young people in *any* community will have an "exponential effect on the rate of certain social problems."

The population explosion among minority youths occurred at a time when changes in the economy were beginning to pose serious problems for unskilled workers. Urban minorities have been particularly vulnerable to the structural economic changes of the past two decades: the shift from goods-producing to service-providing industries, the increasing polarization of the labor market into low-wage and high-wage sectors, technological innovations, and the relocation of manufacturing industries out of the central cities. . . .

BEYOND RACE

Roughly 60 percent of the unemployed blacks in the United States reside within the central cities. Their situation continues to worsen. Not only are there more blacks without jobs every year; many, especially young males, are dropping out of the labor force entirely. The percentage of blacks who were in the labor force fell from 45.6 in 1960 to 30.8 in 1977 for those aged 16–17 and from 90.4 to 78.2 for those aged 20–24. (During the same period, the proportion of white teenagers in the labor force actually *increased*.)

More and more black youths, including many who are no longer in school, are obtaining no job experience at all. The proportion of black teenage males who have *never* held a job increased from 32.7 to 52.8 percent between 1966 and 1977; for black males under 24, the percentage grew from 9.9 to 23.3. Research shows, not surprisingly, that joblessness during youth has a harmful impact on one's future success in the job market.

There have been recent signs, though not many, that some of the inner city's ills may have begun to abate. For one, black migration to urban areas has been minimal in recent years; many cities have experienced net migration of blacks *to* the suburbs. For the first time in the 20th century, a heavy influx from the countryside no longer swells the ranks of blacks in the cities. Increases in the urban black population during the 1970s, as demographer Philip Hauser has pointed out, were mainly due to births. This means that one of the major obstacles to black advancement in the cities

has been removed. Just as the Asian and European immigrants benefitted from a cessation of migration, so too should urban blacks.

Even more significant is the slowing growth in the number of *young* blacks inhabiting the central cities. In metropolitan areas generally, there were six percent fewer blacks aged 13 or under in 1977 than there were in 1970; in the inner city, the figure was 13 percent. As the average age of the urban black community begins to rise, lawlessness, illegitimacy, and unemployment should begin to decline.

Even so, the problems of the urban black underclass will remain crippling for years to come. And I suspect that any significant reduction of joblessness, crime, welfare dependency, single-parent homes, and out-of-wedlock pregnancies would require far more comprehensive social and economic change than Americans have generally deemed appropriate or desirable.

The existence of a black underclass, as I have suggested, is due far more to historic discrimination and to broad demographic and economic trends than it is to racial discrimination in the present day. For that reason, the underclass has not benefitted significantly from "race specific" antidiscrimination policies, such as affirmative action, that have aided so many trained and educated blacks. If inner-city blacks are to be helped, they will be helped not by policies addressed primarily to inner-city minorities but by policies designed to benefit all of the nation's poor.

I am reminded in this connection of Bayard Rustin's plea during the early 1960s that blacks recognize the importance of *fundamental* economic reform (including a system of national economic planning along with new education, manpower, and public works programs to help achieve full employment) and the need for a broad-based coalition to achieve it. Politicians and civil-rights leaders should, of course, continue to fight for an end to racial discrimination. But they must also recognize that poor minorities are profoundly affected by problems that affect other people in America as well, and that go beyond racial considerations. Unless those problems are addressed, the underclass will remain a reality of urban life.

1.3. Palestinian Women Workers in the Gaza Strip

Susan Rockwell

This excerpt is about stateless people and the effects of statelessness on economic well-being. Israel has occupied the Gaza Strip—site of the next excerpt—since the 1967 Six Day war. Most of the inhabitants of the Strip are refugees who had fled what was then Palestine during the 1948 War of Independence. They had hoped to return to their homes after the Arab defeat of the new Jewish state, an event that never occurred.

Today, many continue to live in refugee camps. Some are unable to move to more permanent housing in towns and cities. Many, however, refuse to become integrated into the social structure of the Strip. To do so would be to accept the Israeli occupation and give up the possibility of returning to their homes.

This is the backdrop for the subordination of Palestinian women. Their condition reflects a combination of disabilities, among them class and occupation by what they consider a foreign power. And sex discrimination is important, too. Middle Eastern culture discourages women from entering the work force. This reluctance to have women working outside the home is the result of a patriarchal family structure, in which men are held responsible for protecting the family even if that means isolating its women.

Because they violate the traditional norms, women who work outside the home tend to be stigmatized. As a result, only women who have to work for pay do so; they tend to be single, widowed, or divorced and without a male breadwinner. Most of them are also unskilled.

Since the Israeli occupation of the Gaza Strip, women can no longer work on the family farm as they had in the past. Inflation has forced Palestinian women to work in order to supplement the family income. Yet the Israeli occupation has limited the types of jobs women can perform. The jobs open to most women are local subcontracting, conversion industries, and sewing, tinning, and packaging factories in Israel.

Arab factory owners take advantage of the prevailing poverty and the shortage of jobs to pay women less. In fact, women receive only a fraction of what men make performing the same task. For their part, families often try to hide the fact that a female member works, because that proves the family is poor—a source of shame.

So Palestinian women find themselves in a terrible position, subordinated by their bosses, their families, and the occupying Israeli government. No wonder they have trouble knowing who to seek out as allies and which struggle—class, gender, or political—to fight first.

PALESTINIAN WOMEN: A RESERVE ARMY OF LABOR

. . . Palestinian women have been affected by the erosion of the subsistence economy, due to the sudden loss of land in 1948, and the rapid, post-1967 absorption of Palestinian workers into the Israeli economy.[1] The loss of land terminated women's work on family farms, a role which still characterizes much of female labor in the Middle East where women are heavily represented as "unpaid family workers," especially in the rural areas. In the Gaza Strip, forty-eight percent of the population lives in refugee camps, whose urban character limits woman's role to domestic work in the home.

The makeshift conditions of the refugee camps and the lack of basic services require female provision of subsistence through work at home. Even today, although concrete shelters have replaced the refugee's tents, the primitive housing and the lack of state services increase women's workload.

In independent nations, capital profits from women's "invisible" labor at the subsistence level, since it can pay semi-proletarian male workers less than the subsistence familial wage. Women's roles as marginal workers, whether as unpaid family labor, casual laborers or seasonal laborers, "serve a function, structurally conditioned by the dynamic of capital accumulation, that depresses wages in the formal sector thus yielding to the capitalist a higher rate of surplus value extraction through this reduction in the cost of labor."[2] For Palestinians, the Israeli occupation additionally exploits the sexual division of labor, as Israeli capital profits from Palestinian women's subsistence production. In the West Bank, approximately forty-nine percent of the total active labor force is employed in Israel, the hourly wages of West Bank construction workers are 50–60 percent of the hourly wages of Jewish "permanent" workers with the same labor specifications.[3] Although a similar empirical comparison is not available for the Gaza Strip, the pattern appears identical; indeed, Gazans are worse off since no subsistence agricultural production supplements wages.

In factories, the majority of workers are single, and the turnover rate, due to early marriage, is high. Divorced and widowed women also work, but their number is few in comparison to single women. Married women rarely work: out of a sample of 156 Palestinian women, only one was married. Palestinian women said they worked because their families depended on their wages, and some earned the only income for the family. While some Palestinian women enjoyed getting out of the house, factory work remains an undesirable interlude before marriage.

In the Gaza Strip, women constituted 9.9 percent of the mining and manufacturing workforce in 1980, concentrated in small, sub-contracted sewing factories, conversion industries, and seasonal food industries like citrus and ice-cream packaging.[4]

As unskilled workers, women usually engage in one "step" of a production process, and are prevented from accumulating skills

Excerpted from Rockwell, Susan (1985), "Palestinian women workers in the Israeli-occupied Gaza Strip," *Journal of Palestine Studies*, 14(2), 114–136. © 1985 by Institute for Palestine Studies.

and wage increases. Raises in salaries depend foremost on women's duration on the job, when the risk of marriage has declined. The monthly wages of a sample of women working in small factories ranged from $15 to $150. Men receive higher wages for performing identical jobs in both the Gaza Strip and Jordan. Palestinian factory owners paid men twice what they paid women, rationalizing that men head the household, and need higher wages.

Women in the Gaza Strip constitute the majority of workers in local sewing and conversion industries. Factory owners said they preferred hiring women since they had to pay men higher wages as an incentive not to work in Israel, where wages are five to six times higher. In the Gaza Strip many consider the pool of cheap female labor to be all that is keeping the outdated factories from going under in the face of Israeli competition. One sewing factory owner readily admitted that the workers were actually paying him, since their daily wage of 500 shekels ($10) was covered by the first three hours of work, giving him five hours of free labor. Arab factory owners profit from societal stigmas that consider men to be the traditional breadwinners and that discourage women from working in Israel.

Woman's status as second sex, already exploited by Arab factory owners, is also exploited by Israel. Subcontracting, described as "small-scale operations loosely tied to an integrated industry on the other side of the Green Line," involves little financial investment.[5] The system is based entirely on cheap female labor. As Brian Van Arkadie points out in his study of the economies of the occupied territories in 1975, the growth of the sub-contracting system would require an increasing mobilization of female labor.[6] Israeli managers foresaw the need for Palestinian female labor and also realized that Arab tradition barred women from commuting to factories within the Green Line. They therefore sub-contracted instead of integrating

Palestinians from the occupied territories into their plants.[7]

Palestinians' rapid and obligatory transformation to a capitalist system suddenly pushed women into wage labor. Moreover, like Arab women elsewhere, they have also been affected by the internationalization of labor which both male unemployment and the rapid growth of the oil-based economies of the Gulf States have accelerated within the region. Migration has had varied effects on family structure and the sexual division of labor. While remittances from laborers abroad have relieved some women of the necessity to work, the absence of family members has compelled others to assume greater workloads within the household or as wage earners.[8]

While male migration to jobs in the capitalist sector has, in the Gaza Strip, affected the marital and fertility characteristics of the population, in the Gaza Strip, a surplus of women exists due to Israeli policies. Several people there suggested that more women worked after 1967 because their husbands or fathers, working abroad at the time of the 1967 war, were not included in the census which determined residence status. Consequently, they are without Israeli identity papers and are unable to return except for short visits. The male/female ratio was also affected by severe Israeli repression in Gaza in the late 1960s and early seventies, when many of the refugees participated in PLO resistance activities. The death, imprisonment or deportation of Palestinian men reinforced women's role in the reproduction of the community.

The fertility rate in the Gaza Strip is high, with a crude birth rate of fifty per thousand, or more than 20,000 newborns per year.[9] Marital and fertility characteristics today are affected by UNRWA health facilities, and by sex-differentiated emigration. In 1981, 5,400, or 11.8 per thousand, emigrated from Gaza.[10] The predominantly male outmigration sustains the surplus of women, and Dr. Eitan

Sabatello suggests its implication for the marriage market:

(i) The women surplus (which however is declining) has not favored, *prima facie*, any modernization of the family formation in the Areas since 1967; on the contrary, it may have continued to give advantage to men's choices, and preference for very young wives: evidence exists that even in urban or semi-urban localities, or among relatively developed sections of the Territories' population, the average age at marriage of the women is low and the age difference between the spouses is high.
(ii) Therefore, assuming as actual such implication of the marriage market structure on the family formation patterns, it may fit the high fertility levels still prevailing in the Territories, despite other signs of modernization.[11]

Families tend to hide or deny the fact that female members work, since a house in which women work is poor. Reluctance to have women working outside the home stems from the patriarchal family structure, where men have traditionally been responsible for all their female dependents, and where male prestige rests on the ability to protect family honor through the isolation of women. For Palestinians, the issue of female employment becomes particularly sensitive, since the community perceives wage labor as an affront to a tradition already threatened by Israeli society.

Women in the Gaza Strip tend to find work passively through relatives and neighbors, and contact sometimes seems almost clandestine; one woman was with her father in the back of a taxi when the driver convinced the father to allow her to work in his brother's sewing factory.

Gazan society's negative opinion of female employment is reflected in the circumstances surrounding women who do work. As women work solely out of economic necessity, the work force consists primarily of three types of women: single women between the ages of sixteen and twenty-two who work because their families

depend on their incomes; divorced women, who are frequently childless; and widows. As in Egypt, divorced women exceed widows in the Gaza work force, implying that it is the divorcee—the outcast—who first loses family support. As Raymonda Tawil put it, "In the Arab world, there is no one so despised as a divorced woman."[12]

The fact that Palestinians tend to be more tolerant of divorced women working implies wage labor is equated with low moral standards, since it is better for one already "dishonored" to be employed. As one journalist for *Al-Fajr* noted, while families are increasingly recognizing the necessity of women's labor outside the home, "many women who work, especially in factories in Israel, are looked down on as immoral because of the absence of family supervision there."[13] When asked if they would like to work in Israel, girls in UNRWA sewing training centers nodded their heads, but quickly added that "their families would kill them."

Seen as "women's work," sewing is the most acceptable occupation for wage laborers. Conversion industries cannot find sufficient female workers, despite the fact they offer higher wages than sewing factories and may involve the same traveling time. Women interviewed at a toilet paper packaging factory outside Gaza City mostly came from the poorer, southern camps of Rafah and Khan Yunis. Women who worked in Israeli factories just within the Gaza Strip's northern border also came from the south; most would be considered too old to marry, and had stayed on the job for five or six years.

Although in most factories men and women worked side by side, some of the smaller factories encouraged women to work by segregating male and female employees. Owners also frequently provide workers with machines inside their homes in order to avoid employee registration with the Israeli labor office. While such an action may economically benefit both worker and owner, it also accommodates society's desire to keep women's work in the home, and thus invisible.

POLITICAL EFFECTS OF THE ISRAELI OCCUPATION

. . . For Palestinians two specific repercussions of the Israeli occupation—a lack of labor unions and passports—condition the terms of employment. In the Gaza district, there is one registered trade union—the Federation of Workers in Gaza. Due to Israeli restrictions, its outreach is minimal, so much so that most people in Gaza say that unions don't exist.

No sort of minimum wage or basic standards exist for workers. The lack of official regulation is evident in the range of monthly salaries for female workers in sewing factories—from $15 to $150. Those with higher salaries usually had worked for a fair time in a large factory, or were employed by owners associated with Gaza's Communist Party and who considered themselves sympathetic to the workers.

Palestinian workers, especially professional ones, are affected by the lack of passports. Lily Saba Artin estimated that as many as seventy percent of female university graduates had to find employment abroad. But Palestinian women, like their male counterparts, encounter barriers resulting from the Israeli-Palestinian conflict. Stateless, Palestinians are without passports and foreign governments do not generally recognize Palestinian travel documents as official; Palestinians from the Gaza Strip travel on an Israeli *laissez-passer* to non-Arab states, and on an Egyptian *laissez-passer* to Arab countries.

For those Palestinians, jobs with private firms reportedly depend on an employer who will guarantee to the government that he will be responsible for the employee, and that he will produce him whenever the government requests. Understandably, employers in the Gulf states prefer to hire Palestinians from the West Bank, who have Jordanian passports and whom, "the Gulf countries are obligated in a sense to accept since there are agreements between them and Jordan."[14]

Other political repercussions of the Israeli-Palestinian conflict affect employment for professional women. For internal security reasons, Arab countries do not want a large Palestinian work population. Most countries have also responded to the PLO's request that they limit job opportunities in order to avoid a mass exodus from the occupied territories.

For professional women, political repercussions affect access to education. After 1967, Egypt began closing its universities to Palestinians from Gaza in acknowledgment of the end of its claim to rule over the territory and in recognition of the Arab stand against contact with the Israeli state. Unofficially, Egypt does not want any problems with a large Palestinian population. The last year that Gazans could study teaching and engineering in Egypt was 1983, and now only one hundred students from Gaza are accepted annually for a degree in the humanities.

The closing of Egyptian universities my also push more women into wage labor. Families that can still afford to educate children will send sons abroad, as they are expected to look after the parents when they grow old. In any case, many see educating girls as an indulgent gamble, since they will probably marry and leave the household. In order to pay for the more expensive education—often taking place outside the Arab world—more women enter the work force, and girls are often pulled out of school to help out. Several people interviewed in the Gaza Strip believed the number of girls attending secondary school had declined in the last four years.

People in Gaza said a major effect of the lack of opportunity for professionals was that the younger generations questioned education's merit, and tended to quit school early. As many pointed out, what child will value a secondary school education or a university degree if he or she sees a family member trained as a lawyer or a doctor working at a construction site in Israel? . . .

The influence of politics in motivating female employment is also evident in the case of professional women who chose their careers in reaction to political events. . . .

One lawyer interviewed lost her brother in the 1948 war, and said a concern with human rights led her into law.

Among Palestinians, the question of women's place in society falls behind nationalism to such a degree that Rosemary Sayigh writes of "the need to decide where there is a problem of women independent of the collective national problem."[15] Palestinian women themselves place nationalism as the first priority, as shown by the statement of Mouna, a Palestinian woman from South Lebanon who was interviewed by Ingela Bendt. "We are stateless!" she exclaimed. "Compared to that, other problems seem to shrink. The women, women's struggle, has a long way to go when the whole people is oppressed. Not even the men are free."[16]

Bendt's book, which consists primarily of conversations with Palestinian refugee women in southern Lebanon, raises an interesting point. While Israeli control over the Gaza Strip forbids any form of a national movement, the relative freedom enjoyed by the Palestinians until recently in Lebanon produced some government structure, which gave opportunities for women's employment in the service sector.

. . . in addition to the PLO, all the main Resistance groups supported educational, health and productive projects that were largely staffed by women. And, as well as employment, the PLO and Resistance groups provided women with multiple types of technical and professional training, through scholarships, subsidized courses, and on-the-job training. There was not only an increase in the size of the female work-forces up to 1982, but there was a strong development of work-skills, and an evolution in attitudes towards women's employment.[17]

In the Gaza Strip, women do not occupy significant enough positions to cultivate admiration; in fact, women who work in factories often discourage female family members from joining them. Without a

government, women are unable to occupy some of the most acceptable and visible positions.

Under the Israeli occupation, charitable organizations have become, in a sense, the social service branch of an absent government, and see themselves as the only structure capable of providing basic services for the unmet needs of the population. The organizations adopted literacy programs, vocational training programs, educational programs, and created committees for the preservation of heritage and culture.[18]

One goal of the societies is to stop the erosion of the Palestinian social infrastructure, which many feel Israel tries to sabotage in order to have "the land without the people." Israeli restrictions on private Palestinian organizations include the registering of any funds received from abroad, if they are indeed even allowed to come through. . . .

As well as outlawing the Palestinian flag, Israel forbids any combination of the Palestinian national colors—red, black and green; in defiance, some Palestinian women embroider the traditional black dresses with red and green thread. . . .

Palestinians try to resist Israeli domination. For Palestinians in the Gaza Strip, resistance takes form in part through isolation from Israeli society, which is aided by Gaza's geographical isolation. The reaction against the Israeli occupation has resulted in a growing conservatism.

(Gaza's conservatism results in part from the population's reaction against dependency on the foreign culture of Israel.)

In the face of Israeli hegemony, an idealization of the past arose among Palestinians in Gaza. . . .

The home is the place where men, deprived of power or influence in their work, can still exert their control. Women spoke of an acceleration of so-called "honor" crimes in the Gaza Strip, whereby a woman is killed to preserve the family's reputation. In her visit to the Gaza Strip in 1980, Rosemary Sayigh heard similar stories, and attributed them to the influence of Israeli hegemony: "The fear of loss of control over the female sector, of sexual revolution, of emancipation on the Israeli model (with mini-skirts and pre-marital sexuality falsely equated with 'emancipation'), have added new dimensions to the 'woman problem'."[19]

CONCLUSION

The Israeli occupation exacerbates the Palestinian woman's traditional role as low-paid labor by curtailing job opportunity and by causing both sex role and class distinctions to assume negative political connotations.

For female workers in Gaza, two future trends are possible. Ever-spiraling Israeli inflation may cause more women to enter the work force. Or Israel's economic recession may force men to take jobs in factories within the territories where they would replace women. For those who are able to emigrate, their female family members will be more than ever put in the role of preserving the heritage of a stateless people. . . .

Palestinian women perceive their problem as less a problem of oppression within their own society, more a problem of the oppression of the Israeli occupation. Israeli military attempts to destroy Palestinian society and culture make the priority of national issues both justified and nec-essary. . . . What remains to be seen is whether women's admirable levels of political organization and awareness under occupation will continue after a Palestinian state is established, or whether, once nationhood is achieved, women will lose the incentive to organize.

NOTES

1. Information on female workers in Gaza comes from research undertaken in the Gaza Strip in the summer of 1983, and from secondary literature. Original research was based on interviews and, for factory workers, on a questionnaire. Seventy secondary interviews were conducted out of an original sample of 156 primary interviews of women employed in factories. Information on professional women came mostly from interviews and from statistics provided by local charitable societies and private organizations.
2. *Ibid.*, p. 6.
3. Benvenisti, *op. cit.*, p. 6.
4. An employee from the Department of the Interior said that there were 243 factories in the Gaza Strip with 1,112 female employees officially, but added that there was probably two to three times that number.
5. Frisch, *op. cit.*, p. 54.
6. Brian Van Arkadie, *Benefits and Burdens: A Report on the West Bank and Gaza Strip Economies since 1967* (Washington, D.C.: Carnegie Endowment for International Peace, 1977), p. 124.
7. Frisch, *op. cit.*, p. 55.
8. Hammam, "Labor Migration," p. 10.
9. Eitan Sabatello, "The Populations of the Administered Territories: Some Demographic Trends and Implications," *The West Bank Data Base Project* (July 1983), p. 18.
10. *Ibid.*, p. 41.
11. *Ibid.*, p. 55.
12. Raymonda Tawil, *My Home, My Prison* (New York: Holt, Rinehart and Winston, 1979), p. 24.
13. Taylor, *op. cit.*, p. 8.
14. Interview with Ahmed Majdalawi of the UNRWA Social Welfare Office, Gaza Strip, June 21, 1983.
15. Rosemary Sayigh, "Encounters with Palestinian Women Under Occupation," *Journal of Palestine Studies* 10, 4 (Summer 1981), p. 3.
16. Ingela Bendt and James Downing. *We Shall Return: Women of Palestine* (London: Zed Press Ltd., 1982), p. 18.
17. "Three Cases of Human Rights Violations; Case 1—Palestinian Women in Lebanon," *Palestine Human Rights Bulletin* 37 (Fall 1983), p. 3.
18. Giacaman, "Palestinian Women," p. 9.
19. Sayigh, "Encounter," p. 26.

1.4. Marketing Authenticity in Third World Countries

Ira Silver

In a market economy, just about everything is for sale. In principle, human lives are *not* for sale—for example, slavery is not permitted. Nor, in principle, is human dignity for sale. But when we look at world tourism, we find reasons to doubt that even these assumptions about market economies are valid.

For example, in many parts of the world slavery *does* exist. The most common form of slavery is prostitution in such Third World countries as Thailand, where poor parents often sell their sons and daughters into prostitution in order to meet their own expenses. In turn, these countries become tourist havens for wealthy travellers from Japan, Europe, and North America who crave varied sexual experiences with cheap, compliant young partners.

The problem of child prostitution is only the most extreme example of a more general problem: namely, the commodification of Third World people. Because they are poor, these people need tourist dollars. But to earn tourist dollars they must sell something: not merely hotel rooms and beach space, but an "image" or illusion of themselves that *seems* friendly, understandable, and real.

In fact, tourists do not want to experience the real life of ordinary Third World people: in a great many cases that would be too depressing, grimy, boring, and possibly dangerous. What tourists want is a cleaned-up fantasy version of Third World Life that *seems* authentic.

As the next excerpt shows, the art of selling Westerners on travel to Third World countries is the art of glamorizing or hiding poverty. Selling travel also requires hiding social variation, change and conflict: freezing people and their lives in a simple, once-upon-a-time version of pre-industrial culture.

INTRODUCTION

Tour operators play a pivotal role in shaping motivations for travel because tourists usually lack access to information that can provide them with insight about the places they seek to visit. Thus, most people turn to

Excerpted from Silver, Ira (1993). "Marketing authenticity in Third World countries," *Annals of Tourism Research*, 20, 302–318. Reprinted with permission from Pergamon Press.

advertisements and brochures in order to help them plan vacations (Adams 1984:472). Like most marketing strategies, the images that the tourism industry promotes are geared toward selling the product that is being advertised. Tour operators are chiefly concerned with marketing images of authentic culture, and they tend to be motivated more by profit than by any genuine sensitivity toward representing indigenous peoples in a fair and accurate manner (de Kadt 1979:56).

The tourism industry did not create the many images of the authentic non-Western Other that are so prevalent in travel literature. Indeed, *orientalism* (the ideological discourse that makes distinctions between "West" and "Other") has been a part of Western consciousness at least since the first contacts were made between European and Arab peoples (Said 1979:1–2). Examining the development of orientalism provides an historical context in which touristic images of the Other can be properly understood. Such images appear in many media besides tourist advertisements and brochures. These include films, documentaries, and magazines like *National Geographic* and *Smithsonian*. Indeed, images of the Other are so prevalent that they are virtually ubiquitous, and can be found blatantly within the surface of most forms of Western discourse (Bruner 1991:248). Because most tourists rely upon travel literature for information about the Third World, their understandings about indigenous peoples seems to derive most immediately and explicitly from images marketed in travel magazines, advertisements, and brochures.

Tourists are not alone in overlooking the many changes that have occurred within indigenous societies. Others, including even anthropologists, have viewed native peoples as static and unchanging. Asad (1973) and Fabian (1983) have each documented how anthropology emerged during the 19th century in conjunction with, and as an implicit legitimation of, colonialism. Perhaps, then, inventing tradition and orientalizing the Other are characteristic of Western industrial societies. In his definitive analysis of touristic motivations, MacCannell (1976) construed the tourist's quest for authenticity within such a post-modernist perspective (see also Clifford and Marcus 1986; Clifford 1988; and Cohen 1988).

Yet, touristic representations of indigenous peoples do not merely reinforce cultural stereotypes. They also often portray the notion that natives exist primarily for the consumption of Western tourists. Indeed, this is precisely what gives advertisements and brochures their enormous power and influence upon potential tourists. Consider a recent article in a travel magazine that implies (and thus seems to assume) that tourists have a right to photograph native peoples. The author does not consider why natives might prefer not to be photographed, nor the overall implications that photography might have within the larger touristic process. Instead, he offers strategies for, in essence, subduing Others in order to photograph them (Houser 1990:48). Indeed, very little travel literature informs tourists that many natives do not want to be photographed, or that they at least expect to be paid for it. Thus, tourists are often left unaware that natives might view the context in which photography takes place differently than Westerners do. This can cause tourists to disrespect local restrictions about appropriate camera use, and to assume that all natives are "open game" for photographing (Chalfen 1979:440–441).

Therefore, successful marketing seems to be based on a few simple ideas being effectively manipulated in order to sell something that people want. Various examples indicate that travel literature does not portray indigenous people as they might represent themselves, but rather according to Western markers of authenticity. However, these markers differ according to the type of tourist who is consuming a particular marketed image. The implications of selling culture in these ways cannot adequately be assessed without specifically focusing on how tourism is marketed to particular types of tourists. It is clear, though, that developing such a typology has political importance given that marketed images tend to encapsulate, if not also distort, how tourists come to view the societies they visit (Britton 1979:320). Marketing trends to insulate tourists from the historical processes that have made tourism possible, as well as many of the social realities present within tourism destinations (Kirschenblatt-Gimblett nd:64).

MASS TOURISM

Mass tourists desire to see the authentic primitive, but they also believe that what they are experiencing will be greatly changed during the coming years (Errington and Gewertz 1989:43). While mass tourists acknowledge the inevitability of social change within the Third World, they overlook the degree to which it has already occurred. Their belief that Third World countries should develop is consistent with the typically middle class context from which these tourists have come, and in which they have succeeded economically (Gewertz and Errington 1991:68–69). Thus, advertisements for expensive package tours tend to depict tourism as a modernizing force in the Third World, but one that does not threaten the primitiveness of indigenous peoples. This image caters to these tourists' ambition to see a changing, but as yet unchanged, primitive (Britton 1979:322).

The term "primitive" is used rather loosely by this author even though social theorists have made various comments about the different ways in which Westerners evaluate this concept. In reference to tourism, the term is used here to emphasize that tourists often make fundamental distinctions between their lives in the modern world, and what they tend to view as the timeless and unchanging—thus primitive—lives of many native peoples.

In travel literature, what is necessary in fusing images of the modern and the primitive is to show the potential mass tourist that resort destinations are neither too remote (with too few amenities), nor too touristy (lacking all authenticity). Therefore, travel literature seeks to draw a fine line between these extremes. It claims, for example, that "Barbuda is not really out of the way, just overlooked" (Rattner 1990:82); that Tana Toraja is "remote yet easily accessible" (Adams 1984:473). However, even these representations may not sufficiently cater to the tourist who seeks both an authentic experience and the luxury of Western amenities. Therefore, advertisements not only portray

places as accessible, they also minimize the foreignness of host countries by claiming, for instance, that English is spoken, or that top hotel personnel are European (Britton 1979:322).

This fusion of modern and primitive indicates that images directed at mass tourists represent the Other as an unchanged primitive living within a society that has undergone Westernization. Generally, the only forms of development that advertisements and brochures acknowledge are those that enable mass tourists to enjoy all of the amenities that they have at home. Consider, for example, that many brochures for luxury hotels in the Caribbean juxtapose images of natives in the background (often as menial laborers) with captions suggesting that the finest attributes of tourism derive from the hotel's Western amenities. Such images seem to convey to the mass tourist that natives only matter insofar that they fulfill a Western desire to experience authenticity.

Another implication of mass tourism marketing that needs to be considered is that tours are often sold as standardized packages. Brochures for these tours tend to ignore the particular cultural identities of the indigenous peoples among whom the tourists will descend, and instead they focus on the similar climates or Western amenities that most mass tourism destinations have. Because advertisements for package tours tend to market the four s's—sun, sea, sand, and sex—it seems to matter little to mass tourists whether they are in Hawaii or the Bahamas. The tourism industry places many geographically and ethnically distinct places in what has been termed the "pleasure periphery," which includes sunspot resorts that are as dissimilar as the Caribbean and Pacific islands (Matthews 1978:81–83). In many advertisements, references to indigenous peoples are entirely omitted, and instead, images of the purely Western attributes (golf, fine cuisine) are depicted (Dilley 1986:60). Examining travel magazines, such as *Caribbean Travel and Life*, illustrates how culturally distinct islands are marketed as undifferentiated products. The overall sense one seems to derive from the advertisements in this magazine is that all of the islands of the Caribbean are very similar. Although an advertisement may highlight the unique qualities of a particular island, the mass tourism products for all of the islands are virtually indistinguishable. They are all, it seems, identically unique.

The Case in Point

An analysis of particular advertisements and brochures substantiates many of the earlier general comments about the marketing of mass tourism. It seems implicit to suggest that brochures and advertisements are effective when they market a product concomitant with tourist motivations. Even though it is difficult to measure the precise relationship between tourism marketing and motivations for travel, advertisements and brochures do lend some insight into the nature of this dialectic. For example, one brochure begins by stating that "our well-executed tours show you the Africa and Middle-East of your dreams" (Olson-Travelworld brochure 1990:2). It suggests that these places are enticing to Westerners for particular reasons, and that tours to Africa and the Middle East will confirm one's expectations of those places.

Consider an advertisement for the island of Bonaire. It conveys a clear image of how the tourism industry attempts to market a cure for what social theorists have called *post-modern alienation*. MacCannell (1976) argued that tourism can be viewed as a post-modern phenomenon; it is an attempt by post-modern subjects to neutralize the alienation produced in contemporary societies, by holding on to disappearing elements of pre-modernity. Because individuals in Western industrialized societies tend to differentiate work from leisure, tourism enables them to escape the alienation of their working lives by descending upon the authentic world of indigenous peoples (MacCannell 1976:8-9).

Many social theorists have argued that the routinization and bureaucratization of living in an industrialized society have literally caused people to lose a sense of what is real or authentic in their lives. As tourists, people want to encounter cultures that appear radically different from their own, in order that they may gain some sense of purpose in a world that often seems to be lacking one (van den Berghe and Keyes 1984:345). Thus, the notion that an authentic reality exists may indeed derive from and be rooted in the experience of living in the modern industrialized world. Moreover, many Westerners seem to believe, at least implicitly, that they can only find authenticity beyond the scope of the inauthenticity of their own lives; that is, among other means, through tourism. Western tourists also tend to believe that they must find this authenticity in the non-Western Other because modern life has undermined the connections between them, by fragmenting social relations, often solely in economic terms (Cohen 1988:373). Through the contrary images of crowded masses on the beach and the carefree woman floating alone in the clear, blue Caribbean Sea, Bonaire is portrayed as an alternative to the alienation of modern life, "the last unspoiled island in the Dutch Caribbean and surely the most unique."

These notions of the authentic and unspoiled conjure up images that are central to all types of tourism marketing. Other advertisements depict authenticity by marketing the discovery of "previously untouched worlds." This image that tourists can, in a sense, experience first contact with an authentic Other is portrayed in various ways. One brochure characterizes Irian Jaya, a territory belonging to Indonesia, as a "stone-age society," and it describes Tana Toraja as a place where tribes "still adhere to their animistic beliefs and are best known for their elaborate funeral festivals." An advertisement for swimwear presents an archetype of the "exotic" pan-Caribbean native. Similarly, a brochure about tropical paradises contains a photograph of a woman who is described in the caption as "a traditional hula dancer."

While tourists (like other consumers) are not passive recipients of these marketed images, their views toward host populations tend to be shaped by advertisements and brochures. Indeed, even though tourists are usually fully aware that natives perform many of their traditions explicitly for them, their experiences tend to mirror their own imaginary projections about the Other (Bruner 1991:243-244). Moreover, because many tourists are motivated by a desire to escape their own alienation, they may behave insensitively toward natives in order to satiate their touristic expectations. While probably very few tourists deliberately intend to devalue or disrespect native traditions, tourism marketing allows, indeed often encourages, them to view host populations insensitively. Many seem to believe that it is the natives' job to adapt to them, rather than their responsibility to adjust to the particular conditions of the host society (Nash 1989:41). Moreover, tourists may overlook the fact that many natives live amidst wretched poverty, both because tourism marketing tends to de-emphasize such "inauthentic" images, and also because tourists may feel that the amount of money they are spending to travel entitles them to leave their problems at home (Nettekoven 1979:137).

Tourism marketing, thus, ought to be viewed as just one facet of a larger touristic process which, as briefly outlined earlier in reference to orientalism, is itself only a small part of a complex asymmetrical relationship between the West and the Other. The implications of selling indigenous culture must be assessed within this historical asymmetry. Indeed, it seems that tourists and indigenous people are incommensurately different within the touristic process, and indigenous peoples can only continue to be attractive to tourists so long as they remain undeveloped, and, hence, in some

sense primitive. To the extent that natives attempt to become what they see as more equal (more developed), they will inevitably begin to lose their appeal, and more importantly their value, to Western tourists (Gewertz and Errington 1991:87).

While natives are hardly passive in accepting marketed images about them, their ability to subvert touristic discourse is often constrained. Natives usually have no choice but to present themselves according to romanticized imagery, because Western travel agents control the terms of the touristic encounter (Bruner 1991:241; Hitchcock and Brandenburgh 1990:22). However, resistance to tourism can take many forms. A few Native American tribes have devised jokes about tourists to counteract feelings of objectification and subordination (Evans-Pritchard 1989:93-94). The Balinese have also been able to enhance some of their traditions and profit from performing them for tourists (McKean, 1989:123-124; Noronha 1979: 201-202).

Yet, while natives do stand to gain economically from certain touristic encounters, they can only do so by performing a set of traditions derived largely from the Western imagination. Even those natives who take pride in such traditions and ostensibly see themselves in opposition to the West, such as the Balinese and Masai of East Africa, must construct a sense of self and identity that mirrors Western discourse (Bruner 1991:247).

Thus, viewed within the context of this asymmetry, advertisements and brochures do not merely represent the Other; they also present a particular view of indigenous tradition that in many cases seems to cause mass tourists to devalue native peoples. For example, when mass tourists look at photographs of native Papua New Guineans, their impressions of these people are shaped not just by such images, but also by notions that they already hold about the Other. This is not to imply that every marketed image fits within a defined category, but rather that because such categorizations already exist and are reinforced by touristic discourse, it is often difficult for tourists to ignore them. Thus, both of these images might suggest to tourists that these natives are savages whose traditions are important only insofar that they are performed for Western tourists; perhaps because many of their traditions *are* performed only for Western tourists.

It is also important to consider what is omitted from the images depicted in travel literature. Because mass tourists depend upon advertisements and brochures to gain a knowledge of the Third World destinations they aspire to visit, they never learn many of the ethnographic "facts" that might challenge the stereotypes they hold about the Other. In this light, then, it matters profoundly that a description of a tour to the South Pacific neglects to inform its readers of the historical reasons—pertaining to colonialism and years of profound social changes—why the Fiji Islands were "a feared cannibal country a hundred years ago, but are now called the 'friendly islands'" (Travcoa brochure 1991:8).

CONCLUSIONS

Chic travel has recently become popular because the tourism industry has successfully constructed and marketed a new niche of authenticity. This type of tourism development is growing, even in places like Papua New Guinea that used to receive only a small number of alternative travelers annually. As it grows, so does the West's power to determine where and how development occurs. In Papua New Guinea, chic travel is marketed as a better and less disruptive alternative to mass tourism development. Yet, such marketing, designed as it is in order to sell a product, also suggests the inevitability of large-scale development in the future, should it prove profitable. Thus, the crucial distinction between chic travel and the other two types of travel is that the former reflects the newest version of how the industry packages indigenous peoples as marketable products. Chic tourist

marketing is particularly effective because it depicts new images of authenticity and suggests to sophisticated (and usually highly-educated) people how they may travel in morally responsible and politically correct ways.

Moreover, the emergence of this new category of travel seems to illustrate that even though most tourists share a similar desire to experience authenticity, how they specifically wish to fulfill that desire varies among different types of tourists. However, these categories are not rigidly defined, and most of the distinctions among tourist types outlined in this paper are constructed by travel agents and affirmed in the minds of tourists, rather than through their experiences. Indeed, such constructions are central to how tour operators sell the authentic Other. Because the touristic encounter is asymmetrical and natives must cater to the wishes of the tourist's imagination, most natives are positionally unable to affect how images of authenticity are constructed and marketed. Natives can usually distinguish "mass tourists" from "alternative travelers," but they generally lack the power to influence the discourse that has created these different categories of tourists (Bruner 1991:247).

Travel literature continues to present multifaceted images of authenticity through new marketable tourism products or practices developed or popularized by tour operators. Consequently, it is operators and their agents who continuously redefine and reconstruct notions of "authentic" culture. It is them who contribute to how ideas of the Other are imagined and conceptualized within Western consciousness.

REFERENCES

Adams, Kathleen M.
   1984 Come to Tana Toraja, "Land of the Heavenly Kings": Travel Agents as Brokers in Ethnicity. Annals of Tourism Research 11:469-85.

Asad, Talal
   1973 Anthropology and the Colonial
      Encounter. New York: Humanities Press.
Britton, Robert A.
   1979 The Image of the Third World in
      Tourism Marketing. Annals of Tourism
      Research 6:318–329.
Bruner, Edward M.
   1989 Of Cannibals, Tourists, and
      Ethnographers. Cultural Anthropology
      4:339–349.
   1991 The Transformation of Self in Tourism.
      Annals of Tourism Research 18:238–250.
Chalfen, Richard M.
   1979 Photography's Role in Tourism: Some
      Unexplored Relationships. Annals of
      Tourism Research 6:439–447.
Clifford, James
   1988 The Predicament of Culture. Cambridge:
      Harvard University Press.
Clifford, James, and George E. Marcus
   1986 Writing Culture. Berkeley: University of
      California Press.
Cohen, Erik
   1988 Authenticity and Commoditization in
      Tourism. Annals of Tourism Research
      15:371–386.
   1989 "Primitive and Remote": Hill Tribe
      Trekking in Thailand. Annals of Tourism
      Research 16:30–61.
de Kadt, Emmanuel
   1979 The Encounter: Changing Values and
      Attitudes. In Tourism: Passport to
      Development? Emanuel de Kadt ed., pp.
      50–67. New York: Oxford University Press.
Dilley, Robert S.
   1986 Tourist Brochures and Tourist Images.
      Canadian Geographer 30:59–65.
Errington, Frederick, and Deborah Gewertz
   1989 Tourism and Anthropology in a Post-
      Modern World. Oceania 60:37–54.
Evans-Pritchard, Deidre
   1989 How "They" See "Us": Native American
      Images of Tourists. Annals of Tourism
      Research 16:89–105.
Fabian, Johannes
   1983 Time and the Other: How Anthropology
      Makes its Object. New York: Columbia
      University Press.
Gewertz, Deborah, and Frederick Errington
   1991 Altered Contexts: Representing the
      Chambri in a World System. New York:
      Cambridge University Press.
Houser Dave G.
   1990 Gone to Market: How to Capture the
      Vibrancy and Emotion of the Marketplace.

Caribbean Travel and Life
   (November/December):48–49.
Kirschenblatt-Gimblett, Barbara
   nd Authenticity and Authority in the
      Representation of Culture: The Poetics and
      Politics of Tourist Production. Unpublished
      Manuscript.
MacCannell, Dean
   1976 The Tourist: A New Theory of the
      Leisure Class. New York: Schocken Books.
Matthews, Harry G.
   1978 International Tourism: A Political and
      Social Analysis. Cambridge MA:
      Schenkman.
McKean, Philip Fricke
   1989 Toward a Theoretical Analysis of
      Tourism: Economic Dualism and Cultural
      Involution in Bali. In Hosts and Guests:
      The Anthropology of Tourism. Valene L.
      Smith, ed., pp. 119–138. Philadelphia: The
      University of Pennsylvania Press.
Nash, Dennison
   1989 Tourism as a Form of Imperialism. In
      Hosts and Guests: The Anthropology of
      Tourism. Valene L. Smith, ed., pp. 37–52.
      Philadelphia: The University of
      Pennsylvania Press.
Nettekoven, Lothar
   1979 Mechanisms of Intercultural Interaction.
      In Tourism: Passport to Development?
      Emanuel de Kadt, ed., pp. 135–145. New
      York: Oxford University Press.
Noronha, Raymond
   1979 Paradise Reviewed: Tourism in Bali. In
      Tourism: Passport to Development?
      Emanuel de Kadt, ed., pp. 117–204. New
      York: Oxford University Press.
Northwest Airlines
   1992 Northwest World Vacations: Hawaii.
      Minneapolis MN: Northwest.
Olson-Travelworld
   1990 Olson's Africa and Middle East. New
      York: Olson-Travelworld.
Rattner, Robert
   1990 Call of the Wild: Barbuda. Caribbean
      Travel and Life (November/December):
      82–85.
Said, Edward
   1979 Orientalism. New York: Vintage Books.
Travel Corporation of America
   1991 Travoa's South Pacific, with New
      Guinea. Travel Corporation of America.
van den Berghe, Pierre L., and Charles F. Keyes
   1984 Tourism and Re-created Ethnicity.
      Annals of Tourism Research 11:340–351.

1.5. Racism Needs No Words in England

Dennis Howitt and J. Owusu-Bempah

This excerpt is about visible minorities and their struggle to achieve economic equality in the face of "polite" racism.

When we think of racism, we usually think of something loud, rude, and violent: the Nazi death camps, lynchings of black Americans, or the forced segregation of South African "kaffirs." But racism doesn't always work that way. Some people believe a *new* kind of racism has emerged in polite societies like England. The authors of this excerpt believe racism against blacks has merely changed its public face and lost none of its traditional effectiveness.

What form does racism assume in a society that prohibits it? Not long ago, Britons tolerated blatant racism. Today, this kind of racism is socially and legally unacceptable in many Western societies. The authors argue that racism changes to suit the social climate of the moment in order to achieve its goal. After all, racism is not just personal animosity toward a group of people, it is a societal attitude that preserves the status quo.

In Britain, antiblack racism has always maintained the material and social advantage of whites over blacks. With laws that forbid discrimination on the basis of race, racism achieves its goal in hidden, simple ways.

To study the new racism, researchers sent identical letters to 162 voluntary organizations. The imaginary letter-writers offered to volunteer their time to the organization, free of charge. Half of the letters were signed with a traditional English name—Irene Croft. The other half were signed with a typically African name—Arima Kumari. Then impartial raters, unaware of the race of each "applicant," evaluated the level of encouragement expressed in letters of reply.

Researchers found the response rate was the same across the board, whether the imaginary applicants were English or African (i.e., white or black). But there was a significant difference in the amount of encouragement white and black applicants received. In fact, black applicants were four times as likely to be refused outright. When white applicants were refused, they were 50 percent more likely to receive encouragement than black refusees.

This illustrates that, in a subtle way, white Britons are more willing to encourage white initiative than black initiative. In the letters of reply we find no racist language or lack of politeness. It is impossible to accuse any respondents of open racism. Yet, as this simple experiment shows, racist attitudes reveal themselves in the differential treatment of blacks and whites. This treatment demonstrates and maintains racial inequality just as well as the old-fashioned methods.

Excerpted from Howitt, Dennis and J. Owusu-Bempah (1990), "The pragmatics of Institutional racism: Beyond words," *Human Relations*, 43(9), 885–899. With permission of Plenum Publishing Corp.

The present study concentrates on the joining practices in the voluntary social services. The joining process is of interest as it has been previously demonstrated that Black people are treated differently from

White people in this respect by industrial employers (Brown, 1984a,b; Commission for Racial Equality, 1980, 1987a,b; Thomas, 1984; Smith, 1974) in that virtually identical enquiries from Black people produce less positive responses than ones from White people. The joining process is more complex than simply writing letters of enquiry and involves stages like publicity and presenting an ethos welcoming of Black people. However, this previous research demonstrates that simple racism explains significant facts in the relatively disadvantaged employment position of Black people which are not reduceable to qualifications and experience. It also demonstrates the ease with which racist acts can be perpetrated in an anti-racist political-legal climate in a way which is only readily detectable using experimental and statistical methods.

The theoretical problem has the following elements: (1) How are discriminatory acts perpetrated in a macro climate antagonistic to racial discrimination? (2) How does the perpetrator of the discriminatory act effect this discrimination? and (3) How does the perpetrator of the discriminatory act present the discrimination? These questions relate to the difficult question of the relationship between action, attitude, and the macro-ideological context.

METHOD

. . . Drawing on a simple but effective measure which had been used to identify racism (Howitt et al., 1977), a method was devised to both identify a racially discriminatory act and to provide some insight into how this act is managed without provoking embarrassing "gaffs" (Semin & Manstead, 1983) such as complaints of racism being made. It was found that letters "wrongly" addressed to a White household were less frequently returned to the sender if the addressee was Black rather than White. This method was adapted by sending identically worded letters to a variety of organizations requesting voluntary work but randomly signing them with a name which was identifiably White or identifiably Black.

The contents of the replies would provide information about the degree of helpfulness or rejection and the means by which any racism was disguised.

The names and addresses of voluntary organizations in Leicester and Leicestershire, a county in the East Midlands of England, were obtained from a directory of voluntary organizations. Organizations unlikely to recruit females as volunteers were excluded. One hundred and sixty-two organizations were sent the following letter signed either by Mrs. Irene Croft, the White name, or by Mrs. Arima Kumari, the Black name:

Dear Sirs:
  Would you please let me know if you have any need for voluntary workers. A prepaid envelope is enclosed.
                    Yours faithfully,

The letters were all handwritten. Eighty-one of each type were sent.

Coding Procedures

The coding procedure was developed once the replies had been examined by the researcher. This inspection of the replies suggested a coding scheme which consisted of four categories:

Category 1. A positive response saying "yes they did have a need for voluntary workers" or suggesting further letters or telephone calls. A positive response means that basically work was being offered.

Category 2. An apparently positive response but the reply contains some excuses for the volunteer not to take up the offer implied, e.g., it is a long way to travel or some implication that the volunteer would not be able to keep up the commitment.

Category 3. The reply refuses the volunteer work for some reason.

Category 4. The reply passes the volunteer over to another organization or suggests another organization.

There was an additional category, which was non-classifiable contents.

Further to this coding procedure, overall ratings of the encouragement or reaction of the volunteer were obtained from raters. They were asked to: "Please give each letter a rating according to how much it appears to be encouraging or rejecting of the volunteer: (1) very encouraging, (2) encouraging, (3) slightly encouraging, (4) neutral, (5) slightly discouraging, (6) discouraging, and (7) very discouraging." Coders were ignorant of the race of the volunteer and the name of the addressee was obliterated before the categorizations and ratings were made. Two independent raters were used but were asked to meet to agree on categories where there was disagreement between them. They were not asked to agree over ratings of encouragement. A third rater acted independently as a precautionary final check at a later stage and yielded similar results. The raters were White, one male and one female. The use of White raters was justified in this case as their task was to evaluate the underlying intent of the writers of the replies.

RESULTS

The overall rate of response was 65% replies to the 162 letters sent out. White enquiries had a reply rate of 65% and Black enquiries one of 64%.

Preliminary investigations suggest a high level of inter-rater correlation on the ratings of overall tone of the letters, . . . reflecting substantial agreement about the implications of the replies for the recipients. Correlations between the first two raters were of the order of 0.74 for the White letters, and 0.81 for the Black letters, these being significant at better than the 0.1% level.

There was a consistent trend for the White applicants to average more encouragement than the Black applicants. While overall the replies tended to be encouraging, there was greater encouragement given to White applicants. . . .

Fewer Black applicants proportionately

were offered work though this does not reach statistical significance using chi-square. Table I shows that a major difference in the treatment of Black and White applicants was that Black volunteers were four times more likely to be simply refused work than White ones. When Whites were not made an offer of work, there was a tendency to suggest alternative organizations which might be suitable or make similar helpful comments. For every White volunteer refused work, three were refused work but alternative suggestions made, whereas for Black volunteers for every person refused work only 0.5 were made suggestions of alternative avenues!

DISCUSSION AND CONCLUSIONS

The significant feature of this is the radically different experiences Black and White people have in this . . . "labor" market. Black applicants are much more likely than White

TABLE I.   Classification of the Letters into Content Categories

	White letters	Black letters
Category 1: positive response need for workers	36[b]	30[b]
Category 2: apparently positive but excuse given	3	3
Category 3: work refused	3[a]	12[a]
Category 4: no work but alternative suggestions	9[b]	6[b]
Not classified	1	2

[a] The difference between the return rates for White and Black letters in this category is significant at 5% level using chi-square.

[b] Combining Category 1 and Category 4 as they both reflect encouragement, produces a significant difference (at the 5% level using chi-square) between the Black and White letters.

applicants to receive replies which simply offer no work and no encouragement. There are two possible explanations for this. One is that there is a paternalistic assumption that in order to protect Black applicants from further disappointment, knowing there is prejudice against Black people in voluntary organizations, no encouragement to contact other organizations is made. While this is not a racist act from a social psychological point of view in that it involves no personal negative valuation of Black people, from the sociological point of view it is the sort of collusion with racism which leads to the maintenance of racism.

Maintenance of racist social systems may be variously motivated and "well meaningness" in protecting Black people from the distress of racism is one method which traditional social psychological approaches do not properly accommodate because they adopt the "individual racial animosity" approach to racism. The second explanation of this aspect of the data is in terms of the idea that racist ideology is built on the "assumption of the superiority of White people over Black people." From this viewpoint, the social psychological dynamic involved is clear. "Peace offerings" might be expected to be less common in differential power and status relationships emanating from the "superior" than in the reverse situation or in exchanges between equals. "Defusing" the situation by offering something other than had originally been requested in these circumstances prevents the disruption of status relationships. This suggestion is much closer to social psychological conceptions of racism since superiority issues imply valuations including those which social psychologists include as racism.

Superficially there seems to be a difference between the outcome of the present research and that of Howitt, Craven, Iveson, Kremer, McCabe, and Rolph (1977) insofar as in the present data more replies were sent to Black people than White people while in the previous research more letters were returned when the addressee was White. However, they are substantially the same outcomes if one considers "helpfulness." In the present study, Black people were not "helped" as much as White ones, and in the 1977 study the same was true.

It is doubtful whether the organizations realized in the present study that they were perpetrating a racist act. Indeed they do show signs of being keen to deal with Black people on a "fair" basis. Black applicants were actually no less likely than White ones to receive a reply to their letter. So, at the level of common courtesy, the organizations were putting on a good face (Owusu-Bempah, 1989). There is no suggestion that Black applicants were being ignored or overlooked. Nothing in the content of the replies reflected White racist attitudes, stereotypes, or ideology as such. It would be pointless to try and find the hidden "new" racism in them.

An important issue is the relationship between the gently-expressed discriminatory acts of the so-called "new racism" such as those found in the present research and the concept of institutional racism. Institutional racism includes the policies, practices, and procedures of organizations which lead to the disadvantage of Black people. New racism and institutional racism are mutually entwined. It was obviously impossible to determine in the present study whether those who replied to the applicants acted in a racist manner because of their personal views or because of features of their organization's procedures, policies, or practices. Our concern was with the interaction between the Black individual and the organization, not the causes of the discrimination. In most respects, the issues are identical whether broader institutional or individual factors are the most important. Indeed, if institutional policies, practices, and procedures do not prevent the expression of individual racism, then it might be argued that this failure is an example of institutional racism.

Whatever the complete social psychological explanation of the actions of the letter writers in this study, the social consequences of the process are to encourage White initiative and to discourage it in Black people. This is yet another example of the wearing down process of racism which destroys individual motivation.

Theoretically, for social psychologists, the outcome of this study is intriguing. In terms of the idea of a new racism or "aversive racism" the genteel nature of the social acts found in the study fits the description well. There was nothing in the individual letters which could be identified as racial hostility. At the same time, the study demonstrates the sort of discriminatory acts which are key components of the crudest forms of racism. As such, it becomes problematic to under-stand how any value-based explanations of discriminatory behavior remain tenable. Attitudes as an explanation of racist acts are problematic because of the ease with which the social context of the racist act may change the behavior, the attitude, or both. However, to move from attitudes to ideology as an explanation of racist acts seems to invoke similar difficulties. The idea of a new racism which has an element of more circumspect thinking does not easily explain why a new ideology can go hand-in-glove with long-familiar types of acts. Perhaps even more difficult is the fact that the present study revealed that rather than embarrassment-saving work being done when Black applicants were refused voluntary employment, it was when the White volunteers were being refused that this occurred. One might assume . . . the risk of social embarrassment would be greater with a new ideology which is broadly anti-racism if Black people were refused.

. . . The present research has shown it is easy to detect racist effects and that the rhetorical and other language correlates of this are not what might have been expected since the effort went more toward placating and encouraging White applicants than discouraging Black ones. While White applicants received broadly encouraging replies even if they were not significantly more likely to be offered work, Black ones tended not to receive the same encouragement. Why there seems to be a need to tone down the reply to White applicants as if to reduce "injury" perhaps tells us something of the mundane nature of racism.

REFERENCES

Brown, C. Patterns of employment among Black and White people in Britain. *Employment Gazette*, July 1984. (a)

Brown, C. *Black and White Britain: The third Policy Studies Institute survey*. London: Heinemann, 1984. (b)

Brown, K. Turning a blind eye: Racial oppression and the unintended consequence of White "non-racism." *Sociological Review*, 1985, 33(4), 670–690.

Commission for Racial Equality. *Half a chance: A Report on job discrimination against young blacks in Nottingham*. London: Commission for Racial Equality, 1980.

Commission for Racial Equality. *Employment of graduates from ethnic minorities: A research report*. London: Commission for Racial Equality, 1987. (a)

Commission for Racial Equality. *Living in terror: A report on racial violence and harassment in housing*. London: Commission for Racial Equality, 1987. (b)

Howitt, D., Craven, G., Iveson, C., Kremer, J., McCabe, J., & Rolph, T. The misdirected letter. *British Journal of Social and Clinical Psychology*, 1977, 16, 285–286.

Owusu-Bempah, J. The new institutional racism. *Community Care*, September 14, 1989, 23–25.

Semin, G. R., & Manstead, A. S. R. *The accountability of conduct*. London: Academic Press, 1983.

Smith, D. J. (1974). *Racial disadvantage in Britain*. London: PEP, 1974.

Thomas, D. The job bias against Blacks. *New Society*, November 1, 1984.

1.6. How Social Classes are Changing in China

Pang Shuqi and Qiu Liping

This excerpt is about ideologically based inequality, and particularly, about such ideologically "suspect" groups as the entrepreneurs in modern China. Since its founding in 1949, the People's Republic of China has been committed to *both* economic growth and economic equality. What is not clear is whether these two founding goals are compatible. And if they are not, how will the Chinese resolve this problem?

The most recent signs suggest that China prefers continued economic growth even at the expense of equality. Debates about the future focus on the ability of socialism to adapt private ownership to China's needs, given a socialist ideology that opposes private ownership. Entrepreneurs are far from loved in China, but they are now seen as necessary for modernization.

Already, a more complex market-oriented economy has developed in the rural areas. Peasants, who have traditionally farmed, are either combining part-time agriculture with other work or leaving farmwork altogether. Today, the peasantry is more differentiated and less equal than before.

Industrial work is also becoming more market oriented and specialized. These changes in agriculture and industry are producing new social strata. Farming peasants still make up the bulk of the rural population, but there is a rapidly growing, increasingly prosperous working class and more private businesses than before.

One result is uneven growth: for example, a less-developed area resembling Japan in the 1950s and a more-developed area resembling Japan in the 1980s. Another is the growth of economic inequality. The main problem facing China's rulers is how to incorporate such changes into Chinese society without giving up socialism.

The authors suggest allowing the capitalists to function under the watchful eye of the state. In their view, free enterprise does not have to mean unlimited wealth and power. It is not clear how the rulers will achieve this control.

Nor is it clear how planners and other intellectuals will be treated. Chinese peasants have always viewed intellectuals with suspicion, if not contempt. President Mao Tse-tung used these feelings for his own political advantage. During China's cultural revolution (1967–1977), university professors were publicly humiliated and removed from their jobs. But China's current rulers know that economic growth will require more respect for knowledge and intellect as well as entrepreneurship.

Excerpted from Shuqi, Pang and Qiu Liping (1989–90). "Preliminary study of the current structure of social classes and strata in China," *Chinese Sociology and Anthropology: A Journal of Translations* 21(2), Winter, 5–20.

A THEORETICAL INVESTIGATION INTO THE CURRENT STRATIFICATION

. . . Chinese society is in transition from a society of ascription to a society of achievement, and thus appears to be a structure in which caste, classes, and strata are all mixed up with each other. Further, Chinese society is moving toward a modernized society. In a modern society, each individual plays multiple social roles and therefore fits into many classes or strata. Thus, the criterion for social stratification should also be multiple rather than singular. . . . As we see it, the criteria for social stratification can be divided into two levels. Social strata determined according to the criteria of interests, educational background, lifestyle, income, and political affiliation comprise the surface level, or outer layer, of society while those determined according to the criteria of the ownership and distribution of wealth (including the ownership of means of production) and the division of labor comprise the inner layer, or inner structure of society.

Marx and Engels placed special emphasis on the ownership of the means of production for the purpose of pointing out the antithesis between the proletariat and the bourgeoisie in a Capitalist society. According to their view, classes would become extinct once society took over ownership of the means of production. What Marx was implying in the term "class" was really the antithesis between classes. . . . Therefore, we should discard the method of determining classes according to the ownership of the means of production once the socialist revolution is brought to a successful end. Instead, social classes (that is, nonantagonistic classes) should be divided according to the criteria of the division of labor, income, educational background, and lifestyle. . . .

Second, the criterion to be used in stratification is also contingent on the researcher's understanding of changes in the whole society. Generally, social change is highlighted in two areas: steady growth and social crisis. When . . . researchers are of the opinion that a society is in the stage of steady growth, they would generally analyze the outer-layer structure of social classes in light of such criteria as earnings, educational background, and lifestyle. Only when society is

experiencing a crisis would ownership and distribution of wealth be used as the criteria for an inner-layer structure analysis to explore the profound contradiction within the social crisis. . . . Right now our society is in a stage of steady growth. Multicriteria based on occupation are instrumental in studying the different strata in society. . . .

Changes in rural areas

Modernization is, to begin with, a process in which the farming population is transformed into a nonfarming population and an agricultural society into an industrial society. . . .

A 1987 survey of Jiading County in the suburbs of Shanghai indicates that pure peasants (those engaged basically in farming) account for 9.54 percent [of the total population], peasants engaged mainly in farming but who work at other jobs on the side account for 5.25 percent, peasants engaged mainly in nonfarming production with farming as their sideline (those engaged more than half the time in other production undertakings) account for 9.38 percent, and purely nonfarming peasants (those who do no farming at all) account for 75.83 percent. . . .

If we use occupation as the criterion for social stratification, we find five major social strata in the countryside.

The peasant stratum refers to those who are mostly engaged in planting and breeding; those of the household nonfarming economy operators stratum are engaged in privately operated transport, handicraft, and industrial and service businesses; the worker stratum refers to production workers in village- and town-run enterprises; the administrator stratum refers to party and government cadres and managers of village- and town-run enterprises, and functionaries of state organs; those of the specialized and technical personnel stratum are teachers and agricultural technicians. Judging from statistics, the strata of peasants and of workers have become the major components of society. In terms of economic growth, the workers have gained the most ground in relationship to the other social strata. They have become the most important stratum in the suburbs of Shanghai.

The traditional farming population, under a commodity economy, is becoming a nonfarming population. Furthermore, with the expansion of the agricultural economy, the peasants are also undergoing a qualitative change, becoming either ranchers or farm workers. Moreover, social differentiation in the countryside basically results from the pluralization of the rural production structure. As long as this trend continues, the social differentiation and stratification of rural areas is inevitable.

Finally, the cities exert a strong impact on the social differentiation and stratification of rural areas. Our surveys show that the areas where there is the most differentiation are those adjacent to large and medium-sized cities. . . . Chinese peasants still suffer from ignorance and backwardness and are mostly traditional farmers. Only by matriculating in "the school of the commodity economy" can they overcome the shortcomings inherent in traditional peasantry and become a new social stratum.

Social stratification in the cities

Based on our 1987 survey of more than one thousand people in the urban district of Shanghai, Table 1 presents the makeup of the social strata in the cities.

The worker stratum refers to manual laborers in industrial production. They comprise both technical and nontechnical

TABLE 1. Make-up of Social Strata [In Urban Shanghai]

Social Strata	%
Workers	49.38
Service people	7.00
Managers and administrators	13.23
Specialized and technical personnel	14.28
Private economy operators	0.86
Retirees	15.15
Total	100.00

workers, with the former accounting for 31.26 percent and the latter 68.74 percent. Service workers work in trade and hotel businesses. The retiree stratum refers to people who have retired from their work. Obviously, the working class still constitutes the main body of urban society.

Labor-intensive industries still command the dominant position in an urban economy. If this situation continues—and the possibility does exist, especially if the foreign-trade oriented economy focuses on developing labor-intensive industries—nontechnical or unskilled workers will continue to comprise the major portion of the working class, and the transformation of nontechnical workers into technical workers will take a protracted course. As diverse economic sectors continue to coexist, it is possible for hired laborers to be split off from the worker stratum. And this will lead to a disparity in interests between hired laborers and laborers who . . . are assigned to their jobs by the state. Following the reform of the labor employment system, a portion of the worker stratum will become unemployed and . . . form an "industrial reserve force." A gap will emerge in the living standards of workers who hold jobs and those who are unemployed. And, finally, with the expanded autonomy of the enterprises and changes in the way they operate, the workers' own interests will be tied directly to the interests of their enterprises. The workers' identification with their class will possibly be replaced by an identification with their enterprise or department. Increasingly, the workers' destiny will hinge upon the destiny of their factory or enterprise. Furthermore, as the gap in earnings widens among different enterprises and departments, the social mobility of workers will increase. On the other hand, they will gradually form their own overall interests in contrast to other classes, strata, or interest groups, thus shaping up as a true working class.

The second characteristic marking the social stratification in the cities is the expansion and growth of the stratum of service workers. . . . As the market economy matures, it will further expand the social stratum of service workers.

The third characteristic of social stratification is the growing stratum of retirees. Members of this stratum, when compared with their peers in the West, are still extremely able to exert influence in Chinese society. Within the retiree stratum are three main forces that continue to hold sway in society. First are the cadres who have retired by taking leaves of absence with full pay. Under the "hierarchy" system, they still hold great power. Their continued existence not only accentuates the problem of aging as a social issue but also remains a strong force to reckon with in the nation's economic and political life. The second category consists of intellectuals such as professors, senior engineers, and technical personnel who continue to play an important role in society and in the arena of science and technology. The third group of retirees are skilled in certain technological fields and still play an important role in economic construction. The abrupt growth of village- and town-run enterprises over the last decade is directly related to this group of retired technical workers. Without them it would have been impossible for the village and town industries to have grown to such a large extent within such a short time.

Based on our preliminary analysis of the urban and rural social strata, we can epitomize the structure of social strata as follows: First, there is the peasant stratum. A portion of these peasants are evolving into modern farmers. Second is the stratum of workers, made up of three segments, namely, skilled workers, nonskilled workers in the cities, and workers in village and town enterprises in the rural areas. Third is the stratum of administrators, ranging from leaders of the state all the way down to functionaries of the grass-roots organizations. They all hold power, more or less, and thus can be called the power stratum. Fourth is the stratum of specialized and technical personnel. These individuals are

still [few] and their position in society is not high. But they are the vanguards in construction and modernization, and therefore the most promising stratum in society. Fifth is the stratum of service-related personnel. Under a market economy, this stratum will play an increasingly important role. This stratum can be extended to include the strata of administrators and specialized technical personnel, or at least the majority of them, making it the principal stratum in society. Sixth is the stratum of private economy operators. This stratum includes self-employed trade people and owners of private enterprises. Seventh is the stratum of retirees. Many members of this stratum have not faded from the scene after stepping down from their work posts. They continue to influence China's political and economic life.

Intellectuals and the Middle Class

. . . In China, intellectuals have not yet become a defined concept in social stratification, and it is better to regard them as a social group with no definite parameters rather than a social stratum. China has not long regarded its intellectuals as "a part of the working class." In the past, our intellectuals were regarded as a part of the petit bourgeoisie or the bourgeoisie. However, this is an ideological classification, that expresses how members of society were politically classified at that time. It is both reasonable and possible for intellectuals, especially those at the middle and higher levels, to become an independent social stratum unaffiliated with any other social class on the strength of their own occupational characteristics, value, work style, and life-style. Society should acknowledge the progressive role of intellectuals, both historically and in the course of modernization, and allow them a leading roll in society. A look at modernization trends around the world will show the intelligentsia holds high the banner of modernization, earnestly practices what it advocates, and plays the dominant role [in the modernization endeavor]. Regrettably, intellectuals in China have never been able to attain the position to which they are entitled. That is partly because their numbers are negligible and they can never become an independent social force; they can only demonstrate their strength by affiliating with another class. Moreover, China's traditional culture has also been self-contradictory toward them. On the one hand, "scholars are ranked the highest of the four types of people [namely, scholars, farmers, workers, and merchants]"; on the other hand, "a scholar should die for one who has trust in him." With such a cultural upbringing, the intelligentsia can hardly develop its own personality and function as a separate entity.

It is possible today for intellectuals to become the main body of the middle class. Originally, the middle class was designated according to the amount of property owned. Now it refers to those whose income is at the middle level. Technically, there is always a stratum of middle-income property in either developed or underdeveloped countries. Obviously, such a definition is inadequate. In Western societies, the middle class can be divided into the new and the old. The old middle class refers to small owners, small businessmen, land-holding peasants, and usurers. The new middle class refers to managers, teachers, engineers, doctors, lawyers, officials in the middle and lower echelons, and office workers. The old middle class is in the process of disintegration. Therefore, the middle class in a modern society is basically the new middle class. In Western countries, the middle class performs the functions of managing society, disseminating knowledge, creating technology, and keeping society in operation. The middle class also promotes and maintains . . . modernization and has high prestige. Because the middle class is composed mainly of intellectuals, intellectuals are the principal force of the middle class.

. . . The middle class is once again taking shape in China. It is inevitable that a middle class will form because such a class is needed in the modernization endeavor. The middle class being formed should comprise the social stratum of management personnel, entrepreneurs, technical personnel, self-employed businessmen, owners of medium and small-sized private enterprises, and those workers who have a higher educational background. Among them are many who are the "elite" of society. It is only by relying on their leadership that the modernization program can be fulfilled through the concerted efforts of the whole society.

About the bourgeoisie

According to recent statistics, there are 115,000 privately owned enterprises with eight employees or more with a total payroll of 1,847,000. There are 50,000 nominally collectively owned enterprises that are actually private enterprises and 60,000 nominally cooperatively operated ventures that are private businesses. In sum, China now has 225,000 privately owned businesses with a total payroll of 3.67 million. If we include the 14.13 million individually operated business ventures as privately owned enterprises, we have 25.91 million people engaged in privately operated economic activities.[1] Obviously, China's private economy is growing rapidly. This is by no means a repetition of class relations in the early 1950s. It represents a new recognition and understanding of socialism. The emergence of this social stratum not only makes it possible for society to be differentiated into haves and have-nots but also makes the differentiation a reality. This is because the majority of this sector belongs to the category of people who "get rich first." The question is whether it is possible for them to form an independent new class that can push China onto the road of modernization without going against the socialist direction. We do not equate the current group of private owners to the bourgeoisie because they fall short of that capitalist class, in terms of both quality and size. In the long term, however, it is possible for them to evolve into a capitalist class. As long as we acknowledge that socialism in its initial stage is a society in which diverse economic sectors coexist and both socialist and capitalist elements are found side by side, then the presence of a capitalist class is logical. . . .

In fact, acknowledging that the capitalist class is still a motivating force for the development of productivity does not mean we should follow a capitalist road. Why should it be impossible to recognize the legitimacy of the bourgeoisie and guide them into a direction that is conducive to the growth of socialism? If an unrestrained power is a corrupted power, then we may ask: Where does this unrestrained power come from? It comes from an unrestrained stratum or class. The existing "two classes (the working class and the peasantry) and one stratum (the leadership stratum)" have lost their opposites. . . . Thus, it is possible different social groups—the working class, the peasantry, the middle class, and a restricted bourgeoisie—will complement each other as well as provide each other with checks and balances.

NOTES

1. Quoted from *Wen hui bao*, November 23, 1988.

Section Review

Discussion Questions

1. How are poor *women* particularly disadvantaged in Bangladesh? Should special social policies be aimed at improving the conditions of women; if so, what should they be?
2. What will determine whether Bangladesh adopts Chinese policies of rural change? In the long run, will the rural areas of Bangladesh begin to prosper whether they follow Chinese policies or not?
3. In what ways (if any) are poor people better off without tourists around? Can you think of any conditions under which tourism is likely to make things *much worse* for the poor? And are men and women affected equally by the growth of tourism?
4. Is there an underclass of Palestinian women, in the same sense as there is an underclass of American blacks? What are the main differences in the experience and organization of these two groups?
5. Given what Wilson has to say about racism in the United States, would you likely get the same results if you carried out an American study like the one Howitt and Owusu-Bempah carried out in Britain?
6. Rockwell focuses on the poverty of rural women while Shuqi and Liping ignore it. Are there reasons to think we would find the same conditions among Chinese peasant women as we do among Palestinian peasant women?

Data Collection Exercises

1. Examine some ethnographic evidence about the black underclass in an American city of your choice, to find out whether poor blacks live in conditions that are better or worse than those facing poor Bangladesh peasants.
2. Collect some data on the places where American tourists travelling abroad are most likely to go. What fraction of tourist dollars is spent each year on "authentic" experiences in Third World countries?
3. Collect some evidence from a society in Africa or South America to determine whether peasant women *usually* suffer from the economic inequalities we find among Palestinian women.
4. Like Britain and America, China contains a great many ethnic and racial minorities. Collect some data on the extent of economic inequality between these groups and the dominant (majority) Chinese group. Is there a racial underclass?

Writing Exercises

1. Write a brief (500-word) essay on the day-to-day personal experience of poverty, as though you were a Bangladeshi man.
2. Imagine you are William Julius Wilson, about to send a brief (500-word) letter to the leader of a Palestinian women's organization. What has American history taught you about poverty that Palestinian women need to know?
3. Write a brief (500-word) travel brochure that glamorizes a Third World country (your choice) that is actually suffering from widespread poverty, civil violence, and environmental destruction.
4. "Palestinian women suffer economically because they are Palestinian, and only secondarily because they are women." Write a brief (500-word) response to this statement as though you are Howitt and Owusu-Bempah.

SECTION 2
Causes of Economic Inequality

2.1. Women and Poverty in Bangladesh

Sultana Alam

The first excerpt in this section is about one of the causes of economic inequality: economic modernization.

In the short run at least, economic modernization may not have entirely beneficial results. An excerpt in the previous section showed that poor people in Bangladesh are caught in a seemingly endless cycle of poverty. This affects their incomes, health, and education. It even harms their family lives, as widowhood, divorce, and desertion all become more common. As the number of households led by women rises, the position of women and their children gets worse and worse.

At the time of writing, 65 percent of women age 55 and over are widows. They are unlikely to remarry, because men prefer to marry younger women—ideally, ten years their junior. Because they are younger, these women are less experienced. They are also less likely to gain power in the household. The same preference for younger wives makes it likely that divorced and abandoned women will also remain single.

Divorce used to be very rare but that is no longer the case. What's more, divorced women are treated worse than any other women. Often, people blame them for the failure of their marriages. The community shuns them, and relatives rarely take them in as they do women who have been abandoned. It puts them in the difficult position of having to provide for themselves and their children. Yet this is a society that assumes men will be the breadwinners.

Even those who receive help are in desperate straits. Women invited to live with relatives are often given the poorest accommodation and fewest privileges in the use of common facilities. They rarely eat with the extended family and must wait until others are finished before using the stove or bathroom.

Perhaps blame doesn't really matter, but these women are not to blame in any case. There are several reasons why women are divorced and deserted. Chiefly, men have to go elsewhere to seek employment and leave their families behind. Others return to an earlier marriage. Women themselves see the emergence of female-headed households as a bad thing. They blame both their loss of a spouse and the poor treatment they receive from their families on the economy. Poverty is worse in Bangladesh than it was 20 years ago. That's what forces husbands to leave homes, and families to withhold *support from some of their own members—especially single women who have lost their husbands.*

In general, women and children are worse off than ever in Bangladesh and conditions will not improve until the economy improves.

. . . The present study is a qualitative exploration of the situation of women heads-of-households as reported by rural women in Bangladesh. . . . The study attempts to understand how poor women view the emergence of the woman head-of-household, the causes to which they attribute the new formation, the resources commonly used by women heads-of-households and the adjustments made by the community to accommodate women who find themselves on their own.

The sample is based on landless and poor women living in Shagatha Thana, in Rangpur district in northeastern Bangladesh. The area was chosen because it is economically depressed and contains a large proportion of widowed, divorced, and deserted women. . . .

METHODOLOGY

The data for this report are based on several sources:

A. A demographic survey of four women's groups with a total membership of 182. The purpose was to provide clues as to the living arrangements of single women; and about the age, number of children, kind of support received by women heads-of-households who are otherwise unable to find reabsorption with relatives.

B. Five group interviews during which 25–40 women participated. The interviews were

Excerpted from Alam, Sultana (1985), "Women and poverty in Bangladesh," *Women's Studies International Forum*, 8(4), 361–371. With permission from Pergamon Press Ltd. Oxford, England.

discussions of the problems of widows, divorced and deserted women.

C. Individual interviews with selected women who are single, heads-of-households, or related to such women.

D. Individual interviews with the organizing staff of the NGO which operates in Shagatha. . . .

THE RESULTS OF THE SURVEY

Out of 182 women in the survey, 70 (38 per cent) are single and divide into 54 widowed, 12 divorced and four deserted women. A majority of the single women live as heads-of-households. Forty (57 per cent) of all single women are the primary adult managing their households. Twenty-two of the 30 single women who live as members of households headed by relatives live with adult sons. Only five women live with parents, and three with brothers.

Women who . . . find relatives willing to provide shelter and social protection are older . . . with grown sons or . . . are able to invoke social shame mechanisms. The latter includes very young women whom society defines as being . . . in need of protection; and women who have been abandoned . . . without . . . a divorce and are legally unmarriageable.

. . . The mean age of women living with sons is 46.1 yr; that of women who live with parents and brothers is 25.7. The mean age of women who head their households is 41.1. . . .

As already indicated, deserted women are the most effective among single women in mobilizing family support for reabsorption. Widows are the next most effective group. Least fortunate . . . are divorced women. . . .

Only 25 per cent of divorced women are living as members of households headed by relatives (see Table 1). . . .

Slightly over a quarter of the women—49 (27 per cent)—have been married more than once. Of these, 40 have been married twice; seven have had three marriages and two, four marriages. The younger age groups are more prone to multiple marriages. The mean number of marriages in the oldest age group (45 + yr) is 1.19 while the mean number for the 25–34-yr age group is 1.51. Even among the group under 24 yr of age, the mean number of marriages is higher than for the higher age ranges.

Although women heads-of-households are not reabsorbed in other households they are still eligible for support: ranging from the gift of a coarse sari (costing Taka 80); to help in paying for a doctor, or medicine; to periodic contributions of rice or wheat. The survey sought information about such contributions over the previous year. Only nine (23%) of the 40 who head households receive regular support; 22 (55 per cent) receive support sporadically, and the remaining nine receive no support at all. . . .

THE INTERVIEWS AND FIELD OBSERVATION

The living arrangements of women heads-of-households

Few women heads-of-households own their own homesteads. Most depend on kin to provide them with housing. The women share the courtyard with their relatives but

TABLE 1.   Marital status by living arrangement

	Head of household	Lives with others	Total
Deserted	0	4 (100%)	4 (100%)
Widowed	31 (57%)	23 (43%)	54 (100%)
Divorced	9 (75%)	3 (25%)	12 (100%)
Total	40	30	70

cook and eat separately. A few do not have kin who are able to help and squat on land belonging to others. Uniformly, the households under women are small, and consist mainly of children or adolescents who are not able to bring in full wages.

A few examples reported by the women show the variations in arrangements.

Lives with parents but eats separately. Sharifa, 32, was deserted by her husband because her parents could not meet his demand for Taka 1000 with which he wanted to start a grain business. She lives in the homestead of parents, occupying the kitchen-cum-bedroom hut but eats separately. The parents are too poor to feed her. Sharifa supports herself by working like her mother, in other homes sweeping and clay-plastering yards and floors; fetching water; grinding spices, and helping with rice husking. . . .

Lives with mother and assumes primary responsibility for household. Alta, a widow of 28 yr of age, no children, lives in her mother's homestead. Her mother is old, has no land, but occasionally gets wheat from government relief programs. Alta supports her mother with food and other necessaries. She works in other homes and occasionally takes orders for thin quilts.

Lives next to parents in house provided by other relatives. Mallicka, a widow of 36, lives next door to her elderly parents and two brothers who are between the ages of 18–22. Space for her small hut was provided by an uncle who owns the adjoining homestead. The expenses for building her hut were pooled through the help of her savings, and contributions from her parents and brothers. . . .

Mallicka, like the other women, works in other homes. She owns a cow which her father cares for. She has three sons who have been farmed out to other people because she cannot support them. . . .

Lives with brothers but eats separately. Bele, 38, was divorced by her husband nine years ago after a history of conflict with her mother-in-law. She was married nine years. She lives in a house built by her three brothers. The brothers are all married and have families of their own. They all live in the same courtyard, occupy separate huts and eat separately. Bele's brothers are . . . landless and work as agricultural day laborers. She raises chickens and works in peoples' homes. She also sews quilts on order.

Bele has eight children, all of whom were taken back by their mother-in-law. Her oldest son visits occasionally and gives her Taka 15–20 for personal expenses.

Owns own home. Shopiron, age unknown, mother of three sons, owns her own house and lives with her youngest son who is twelve. . . . Her eldest son is married and lives in another village. Her second son, also married, lives with his wife and daughter in a separate hut in the same courtyard but cannot feed his mother. He has no land and works occasionally as an agricultural wage worker. Shopiron occasionally gets relief, works in other homes. Her youngest son does weeding and grazing.

Women in de-centralized living structures. Many women whom the community identifies as 'living with relatives' rather than 'living on her own' because they eat jointly in fact occupy highly decentralized structures in which the women take equal economic responsibilities, and in which the level of poverty is such that all attention is consumed by the need to secure food on a day-to-day basis. Two such examples include:

Bachani, 28, separated a year ago from her husband who left her to return to his first wife. Bachani has no children and moved back to her parents' homestead. Her parents are deceased and she lives with two minor brothers between the ages of 14 to 16. All three work. Bachani works in the homes of neighbors, her brothers do light work such as weeding, and grazing.

Shona, 38 yr of age, is widowed. She poaches on someone's land on which she has built a shack and lives there with her eldest

son who is crippled, and a younger son of around 10 yr of age. Her daughter is married and lives with her husband.

Shona begs for a living as does her eldest son.

The social status of women heads-of-households

. . . When women heads-of-households are provided housing, they are given the least desirable, least durable, and least central hut in the courtyard. They take second place in the use of common facilities, waiting for others to finish using the stove, never claiming a fallen branch for fuel but using leaves and stalk, declaring an occasional fruit-tree in the homestead off limits for their own children.

Families having once invested in the marriage of a daughter or sister deeply resent the obligation to support her in difficult times. The resentment is most acutely felt by women who are young and considered of 'marriageable' age.

There is constant pressure from relatives for their re-marriage. If their parents fail to find a match, they are taunted and ridiculed by cousins and aunts. Soon parents join in pushing the women to take whatever work they can find. The women feel that every mouthful of food they consume is begrudged. They survive by 'making ourselves small', i.e. by attempting to strike an impossible balance between being both non-existent and helpful around the household.

Women heads-of-households by assuming responsibility for earning their food avoid the overt expressions of resentment directed at women dependents. But they do not fully escape the fate of the single woman. The presence of these women and their children in the same courtyard provokes guilt over their helplessness and generates anger. Women heads-of-households indirectly affect the quality of life possible to other occupants in the homestead. Sons and brothers are forced to put on a show of greater poverty than they really experience. They are forced to eat less well than they would otherwise do, to conceal the sari they have bought for their wives or daughters. To do otherwise would undermine their plea of inability to support relatives.

EMPLOYMENT AND THE WOMAN HEAD-OF-HOUSEHOLD

. . . . Traditionally the most important form of employment for landless women is the tedious, time consuming process of parboiling, drying, and husking rice. Husking usually requires two to three women.

Because rice is better preserved from mould and insects with the husk on, families prefer to store the rice as is after harvesting, taking out small quantities two or three times a week for husking. This results in a steady flow of work for landless women. However, rice mills have sharply cut into this form of employment. . . .

While rice mills have been introduced no steps have been taken to create alternative employment for women.

Food-for-work programs provide some work for women. These programs centered around the construction of rural roads, embankments, and irrigation canals pay in kind (wheat or rice). They are eagerly sought by women because they pay up to three seers per day as opposed to the local rate of a seer of rice.

In practice, though, food-for-work programs do not provide work regularly even on a seasonal basis. In Shagatha, the women report having worked on only two food-for-work programs in three winters and some found only three days during each project. In addition, the women have had to fight bitterly to receive their full payment.
. . . The women understand that economic hardship is forcing families to withdraw support from widows and divorced or deserted women. In their view, women would receive a warmer welcome were they self-sufficient, but:

'At the same time there is even less work for us. There is a lot we can do to earn money. But where is the opportunity?'

The homes of the well-to-do landowners [employ] only a handful of women. . . .

The mainstay of single women, particularly women who head households, are their relatives who form part of that thin stratum of subsistence cultivator families owning 3–6 bishas (1–2 acres) of land. This group provides the little employment that women heads-of-households are able to find in rice husking and heavy housework (clay plastering, fetching water, repairing clay stoves etc.).

In most cases when relatives do the hiring, the work is 'created' for the less fortunate women, i.e. the work would normally be undertaken by the householders themselves with the help of neighbors on an exchange basis. In token of the artificial nature of the services received, the women are paid half the normal wages.

Women in the landless groups contribute towards community solution by observing a system of triage among themselves. In an unspoken arrangement, the women who are less in need remain behind so that women who are on their own can have first choice of the available jobs. This ensures that women heads-of-households get four to five days of work a week at half pay, while other single women may average one to three. Among the former, again, those who own goats or a cow or chickens take second place to their counterparts who are solely dependent on wage work.

One response from policy-makers to the plight of women heads-of-household has been to institute relief programs directed at older widows and mothers with young children. These programs suffer from the usual corruption through which a large portion of the supplies are misappropriated by local politicians who administer the programs. . . .

How women view the emergence of a new formation

The women in Shagatha universally view the emergence of the woman head-of-household with alarm and ascribe it to two factors.

(A) Women ascribe the loss of support from parents, brothers and sons to economic pressures. There is no doubt in the women's minds that living conditions have deteriorated significantly in the last 20 years, making it impossible for families to welcome single women when they lose their husbands. A large segment of families that are now landless owned land one or two generations ago. Compounding the problems of rural families cut off from land, is the lack of employment. And with the disappearance of work, there is the loss of what the women term their 'value' in the eyes of society.

'Today there is no food, no clothes. If a daughter is sent back to her family by her husband now, she catches hell. Because of the lack of things women have lost their value. We have no worth left.'

. . . Younger women whose parents are alive see the impossibility of fathers and mothers to feed another mouth. Women who are in their late twenties and whose parents are either deceased or too old, are more sensitive to the in-built conflicts of interest between their brothers and themselves.

'Brothers do not want to feed us any more. So long as our mothers are alive, brothers take care of us. After that they want to steal from us. No matter how much fathers leave, daughters get nothing. . . .'

Women who are older and have grown up sons also perceive growing insecurity:

'Now there is no caring. Now sons say "I cannot even take care of my wife. What can I do for my mother?"'

Older women see themselves as vulnerable once their daughters-in-law become assertive. They do not deny that relationships between mothers- and daughters-in-law have always been tense. The difference is that nowadays sons are more apt to welcome a reduction in the number of mouths they must feed.

(B) However, when the women talk about husbands, they talk about qualitative changes in the attitudes of men.

In the view of the women, men today have become acquisitive and greedy. They are moved by the new vogue for dowries to marry and leave wives. As a result the risk that a woman will be sent back to her family has greatly increased. Shagatha, like other rural areas of Bangladesh, is beginning to experience modernization. As a result, the system of dowry has begun to spread. Prior to the 1970s the system that prevailed was the system of 'Pon' or a bride-price. In all probability Pon only meant that the women's parents did not have to pay dowry. . . .

All the group interviews rapidly developed into discussions over the new trend for dowries and its negative effects on marital stability.

'There was not so much breaking of marriages before. Now greed is pushing a lot of men to leave their wives and make demands from new wives.'

Another woman dwells on the inhuman burden dowries place on families, and the way it leads to the devaluation of daughters:

'It is better not to have daughters. Mothers have to work hard and beg to meet demands (for dowries). Men today have gone mad. They want watches, bicycles, Taka 1000, plus clothes. Even then they are not content and think nothing of leaving their wives when they please.'

The women speculate about the sources of the new marital instability and blame the men.

'There are so many marriages today (i.e. multiple marriages for one person). And it is not the women who leave. Women look for security, calm. It is the men who leave.'

They find the plea that men leave their wives because of poverty unconvincing and point out that every man who has left a woman in Shagatha has gone on to remarry or to return to a former wife.

According to the women, men have also become more pleasure-seeking, more self-centered, and more oriented towards using women as objects.

'Now the eyes of men have become bad (corrupt). They roam from woman to woman. At first they marry within their villages. Then they go away where nobody knows them and do what they please.'

The women feel helpless. They complain about their loss of authority over sons and nephews who do not listen when their elders rebuke them for leaving their wives. . . .

2.2   Life in a Canadian Fast-Food Factory

Ester Reiter

The next excerpt is about a second cause of economic inequality: the deskilling of work. It is specifically about the organization of work in a fast-food restaurant, but the implications extend far beyond this particular restaurant, and even beyond the food industry. In the end, this excerpt is about the deskilling, underpayment, and undermotivation of workers in a highly industrialized country—in this case, Canada. Increasingly, deskilling is a cause of economic inequality.

According to what sociologists call the theory of postindustrial society, work is becoming more creative, more dependent on information and technology, and more demanding of skills. Accordingly, people with the most skills at work-sites making the most use of information and technology will be the best rewarded. By these standards, flipping burgers at a Burger King is unlikely to be rewarding on many counts. Yet many such jobs exist, and their numbers are increasing. As their numbers increase, so will the numbers of working poor increase. The gap between well-paid creative workers and poorly paid service workers will widen, increasing economic inequality.

This relatively new development is related to the growth of food-store franchising. The small, independently owned restaurant places a lot of importance on its employees and their skills. A restaurant's success depends on consistently high quality and service, so owners try hard to hold on to a good cook or a competent waiter. But not so in the fast-food industry!

Here, machines standardize food preparation, so the focus of management's concern is equipment. Organizations such as Burger King and McDonald's have reduced the human jobs to a minimum of skill and interest. Cash registers that calculate how much change to give eliminate the need for cashiers to know arithmetic. Fryers and ovens inform workers when food is ready. Drink dispensers pour precise amounts of soft drink into cups.

These labor-saving devices are very cost efficient and leave little to the worker's discretion. As a result, fast-food restaurant work strongly resembles work on a factory assembly line. The tasks take little time to learn, are boring and repetitive. Technology has reduced restaurant work to the monitoring of machines—work anyone can do.

In particular, teenagers and young women fit the requirements of the job perfectly. The work demands speed and endurance. Training is simple and teenagers, eager to work, are in plentiful supply. Is the Burger King work experience, and its economic consequence, the wave of the future; or can we expect work to more creative and better paying in the future?

. . . This paper focuses on the technology and the labour process in the fast-food industry. Using Marx's description of the transitions from craft to manufacture to large-scale industry it considers the changes in the restaurant industry, brought about by the development of fast-food chains. The description of life in a fast-food factory is based on my experience working in a Burger King outlet in 1980/1. . . .

Founded in 1954 by James McLamore and David Edgerton, Burger King became a wholly owned subsidiary of Pillsbury in 1967. The company grew from 257 restaurants at the time of the merger to 3,022 by May 1981. About 130,000 people are employed in Burger Kings all over the world. By November 1982, there were 87 Burger King stores in Canada, 40 of them company owned.[1]

TRANSFORMING THE OPERATIONS OF A KITCHEN

Until approximately twenty-five years ago, all restaurant work involved an extensive division of labour: a complex hierarchy within the kitchen required workers with varying

Excerpted from Reiter, Ester (1986), "Life in a fast-food factory," pp. 309–326. In Craig Heron and Robert Storey (eds.), *On the Job: Confronting the Labour Process in Canada*, Kingston and Montreal: McGill-Queens University Press.

levels of skill and training. For a restaurant to be successful, all workers had to co-ordinate their efforts. A supervisor's function was not only to ensure that the work was done, but to see that the various parts of the operation were synchronized. . . .

This production arrangement resembles what Marx called "manufacture." The skill of the worker remains central to the production process. The commodity created (the meal served to the customer) is the social product of many workers' efforts. Human beings, using tools to assist them in their work, remain the organs of the productive mechanism.

In the fast-food industry, the machines, or the instruments of labour, assume a central place. Instead of assisting workers . . . the machines are dominant. . . . Marx described this as the transition from "manufacture" to "large-scale industry."[2] Since the motion of the factory proceeds from the machinery and not from the worker, working personnel can continually be replaced. Frequent change in workers will not disrupt the labour process—a shift in organization applauded by *Harvard Business Review* contributor, Theodore Levitt.[3] According to Levitt, this new model is intended to replace the "humanistic concept of service" with the kind of technocratic thinking that in other fields has replaced "the high cost and erratic elegance of the artisan with the low-cost munificence of the manufacturer." . . .

The labour process admired by Levitt has been adopted by many of the large fast-food companies [including] Burger King. . . .

MANAGING A STORE

The brain centre of all Burger King outlets lies in Burger King headquarters in Miami, Florida. There the Burger King bible, the *Manual of Operating Data*, is prepared. The procedures laid down in the manual must be followed to the letter by all Burger King stores. To ensure that procedures are followed, each outlet is investigated and graded twice yearly by a team from regional headquarters. . . .

In order to maximize volume and minimize labour costs, there is tremendous emphasis on what Burger King management calls speed of service. Demand is at its peak during the lunch hour, which accounts for about 20 per cent of sales for the day; the more people served during the hour twelve to one, the higher the sales volume in the store. . . .

Ideally, service time should never exceed three minutes.[4] Labour costs are also kept down by minimizing the use of full-time workers and by hiring minimum-wage part-time workers. Workers fill out an availability sheet when they are hired, indicating the hours they can work. Particularly when students are involved, management pressures them to make themselves as available as possible, though no guarantees are provided for how many hours a week work they will be given, or on which days they will be asked to work.

Scheduling is done each week for the coming week and workers are expected to check the schedule each week to see when they are supposed to show up. The *Manual of Operating Data* recommends that as many short shifts as possible be assigned, so that few breaks will be required.

Food and paper costs make up about 40 per cent of the cost of sales in Burger King outlets. These costs are essentially fixed, owing to company requirements that all Burger King outlets buy their stock from approved distributors. In effect, individual stores have control over food costs in only two areas—"waste" of food and meals provided to employees. Both together make up less than 4 per cent of the cost of sales. . .

Store operations are designed from head office in Miami. . . . By late 1981, it was possible to provide store managers not only with a staffing chart for hourly sales—indicating how many people should be on the floor given the predicted volume of business for that hour—but also where they should be positioned, based on the type of kitchen design. Thus, what discretion managers formerly had in assigning and utilizing workers has been eliminated.

Having determined precisely what workers are supposed to be doing and how quickly they should be doing it, the only remaining issue is getting them to perform to specifications. "Burger King University," located at headquarters in Miami, was set up to achieve this goal. Burger King trains its staff to do things "not well, but right," the Burger King way.[5] Tight control over Burger King restaurants throughout the world rests on standardizing operations—doing things the "right" way—so that outcomes are predictable. . . .

WORKING AT BURGER KING

I did fieldwork . . . at a Burger King outlet in suburban Toronto in 1980/1. The Burger King at which I worked was opened in 1979, and by 1981 was the highest volume store in Canada with annual sales of over one million dollars. . . .

Workers use the back entrance at Burger King when reporting for work. Once inside, they go to a small room (about seven by twelve feet), which is almost completely occupied by an oblong table where crew members have their meals. Built-in benches stretch along both sides of the wall, with hooks above for coats. Homemade signs, put up by management, decorate the walls. . . .

The crew room is usually a lively place. An AM/FM radio is tuned to a rock station while the teenage workers coming off or on shift talk about school and weekend activities or flirt with each other. Children and weddings are favourite topics of conversation for the older workers. . . . Each worker must punch a time card at the start of a shift. A positioning chart, posted near the time clock, lists the crew members who are to work each meal, and indicates where in the kitchen they are to be stationed.

There are no pots and pans in the Burger King kitchen. As almost all foods enter the store ready for the final cooking process, pots and pans are not necessary. The major kitchen equipment consists of the broiler/toaster, the fry vats, the milkshake and Coke machines, and the microwave ovens. In the near future, new drink machines will be installed in all Burger King outlets that will automatically portion the drinks. At Burger King, hamburgers are cooked as they pass through the broiler on a conveyor belt at a rate of 835 patties per hour. Furnished with a pair of tongs, the worker picks up the burgers as they drop off the belt, puts each on a toasted bun, and places the hamburgers and buns in a steamer.

The more interesting part of the procedure lies in applying condiments and microwaving the hamburgers. The popularity of this task among employees rests on the fact that it is unmechanized and allows some discretion to the worker. However, management is aware of this area of worker freedom and makes efforts to eliminate it by outlining exactly how this job is to be performed. . . .

Despite such directives, the "Burger and Whopper Board" positions continue to hold their attraction for the workers, for this station requires two people to work side by side, and thus allows the opportunity for conversation. During busy times, as well, employees at this station also derive some work satisfaction from their ability to "keep up." At peak times the challenge is to not leave the cashiers waiting for their orders.

As with the production of hamburgers, the cooking of french fries involves virtually no worker discretion. The worker, following directions laid out in the *Manual of Operating Data*, empties the frozen, pre-cut, bagged fries into fry baskets about two hours before they will be needed. When cooked fries are needed, the worker takes a fry basket from the rack and places it on a raised arm above the hot oil, and presses the "on" button. The arm holding the fry basket descends into the oil, and emerges two minutes and twenty seconds later; a buzzer goes off and the worker dumps the fries into the fry station tray where they are kept warm by an overhead light. To ensure that the proper portions are placed into bags, a specially designed tool is used to scoop the fries up from the warming table. . . .

Even at this station, though, management is concerned about limiting worker discretion. Despite the use of a specially designed scoop to control the portions each customer is given, a sign placed in the crew room for a few weeks admonished crew about being too generous with fry portions.

At the cash register, the "counter hostess" takes the order and rings it up on the computerized register. The "documentor" contains eighty-eight colour coded items, ensuring that all variations of an order are automatically priced. As a menu item is punched in at the counter, it will appear on printers in the appropriate location in the kitchen. In this manner, the worker at sandwiches, for example, can look up at the printer and check what kind of sandwich is required. When the customer hands over the money, the cashier rings in "amount tendered" and the correct amount of change to be returned to the customer is rung up. Thus, cashiers need only remember to smile and ask customers to come again.

The computerized cash register not only simplifies ordering and payment, but is used to monitor sales and thus assist in staffing. If sales are running lower than expected, some workers will be asked to leave early. Output at each station is also monitored through the cash register. Finally, the computer at all company stores is linked through a modem to the head office in Miami. Top management has access to information on the performance of each store on a daily basis, and this information is routed back to the Canadian division headquarters in Mississauga.

Skill levels required in a Burger King have been reduced to a common denominator. The goal is to reduce all skills to a common, easily learned level and to provide for cross-training. At the completion of the ten-hour training program, each worker is able to work at a few stations. Skills for any of the stations can be learned in a matter of hours; the simplest jobs, such as filling cups with drinks, or placing the hamburgers and buns on the conveyor belt, can be learned in minutes. As a result, although labour turn-over cuts into the pace of making hamburgers, adequate functioning of the restaurant is never threatened by people leaving. However, if workers are to be as replaceable as possible, they must be taught not only to perform their jobs in the same way, but also to resemble each other in attitudes, disposition, and appearance. Thus, workers are also drilled on personal hygiene, dress (shoes should be brown leather or vinyl, not suede), coiffure (hair tied up for girls and not too long for boys), and personality. Rule 17 of the handout to new employees underlines the importance of smiling: "Smile at all times, your smile is the key to our success."

While management seeks to make workers into interchangeable tools, workers themselves are expected to make a strong commitment to the store. If they wish to keep jobs at Burger King, they must abide by the labour schedule.

Workers, especially teenagers, are, then, expected to adjust their activities to the requirements of Burger King. . . .

THE WORKERS

One of the results of the transformation of the labour process from one of "manufacture" to that of "large-scale industry" is the emerging market importance of the young worker. While artisans require long training to achieve their skills, a machine-tender's primary characteristics are swiftness and endurance. Thus, young workers become ideal commodities: they are cheap, energetic, and plentiful. As well, they can be used as a marketing tool for the industry: the mass produced, smiling teenager, serving up symbols of the good life in North America—hamburgers, Cokes and fries.

Making up about 75 per cent of the Burger King work force, the youngsters who worked after school, on weekends, and on holidays were called "part-timers." The teenager workers (about half of them boys, half girls) seemed to vary considerably in background. Some were college-bound youngsters who discussed their latest physics exam while piling on the pickles. Others were marking time until they reached age 16 and could leave school. . . .

The daytime workers—the remaining 25 per cent of the workforce—were primarily married women of mixed economic backgrounds. Consistent with a recent study of part-time workers in Canada, most of these women contributed their wages to the family budget.[6] Although they were all working primarily because their families needed the money, a few expressed their relief at getting out of the house, even to come to Burger King. One woman said: "At least when I come here, I'm appreciated. If I do a good job, a manager will say something to me. Here, I feel like a person. I'm sociable and I like being amongst people. At home, I'm always cleaning up after everybody and nobody ever notices!"[7]

Common to both the teenagers and the housewives was the view that working at Burger King was peripheral to their major commitments and responsibilities; the part-time nature of the work contributed to this attitude. Workers saw the alternative available to them as putting up with the demands of Burger King or leaving; in fact, leaving seemed to be the dominant form of protest. During my period in the store, on average, eleven people out of ninety-four hourly employees quit at each two-week pay period. While a few workers had stayed at Burger King for a few years, many did not last through the first two weeks. The need for workers is constant. . . .

Burger King's ability to cope with high staff turnover means that virtually no concessions are offered to workers to entice them to remain at Burger King. In fact, more attention is paid to the maintenance of the machinery than to "maintaining" the workers; time is regularly scheduled for cleaning and servicing the equipment, but workers may not leave the kitchen to take a drink or use the bathroom during the lunch and dinner rushes.

The dominant form—in the circumstances, the only easily accessible form—of opposition to the Burger King labour process is, then, the act of quitting. Management attempts to head off any other form of protest by insisting on an appropriate "attitude" on the part of the workers. Crew members must constantly demonstrate their satisfaction with working at Burger King by smiling at all times. However, as one worker remarked, "Why should I smile? There's nothing funny around here. I do my job and that should be good enough for them." It was not, however, and this worker soon quit. Another woman who had worked in the store for over a year also left. A crew member informed me that she had been fired for having a "poor attitude." . . .

Management control and lack of worker opposition is further explained by the fact that other jobs open to teenagers are no better, and in some cases are worse, than the jobs at Burger King. The workers all agreed that any job that paid the full rather than the student minimum wage would be preferable to a job at Burger King; but they also recognized that their real alternatives would often be worse. Work at a donut shop, for example, also paid student minimum wage under conditions of greater social isolation; baby sitting was paid poorly; and the hours for a paper route were terrible. Work at Burger King was a first job for many of the teenagers, and they enjoyed their first experience of earning their own money. And at Burger King these young men and women were in the position of meeting the public, even if the forms of contact were limited by a vocabulary developed in Burger King

headquarters: "Hello, Welcome to Burger King. May I take your order?" Interaction with customers had some intrinsic interest.

In sum, workers at Burger King are confronted with a labour process that puts management in complete control. Furnished with state-of-the-art restaurant technology, Burger King outlets employ vast numbers of teenagers and married women—a population with few skills and little commitment to working at Burger King. In part, this lack of commitment is understood through reference to a labour process that offers little room for work satisfaction. Most jobs can be learned in a very short time (a matter of minutes for some) and workers are required to learn every job, a fact that underlines the interchangeable nature of the jobs and the workers who do them. The work is most interesting when the store is busy. Paradoxically, work intensity, Burger King's main form of assault on labour costs, remains the only aspect of the job that can provide any challenge for the worker. Workers would remark with pride how they "didn't fall behind at all," despite a busy lunch or dinner hour. . . .

It would be reassuring to dismiss the fast-food industry as an anomaly in the workplace; teenagers will eventually finish school and become "real workers," while housewives with families are actually domestic workers, also not to be compared with adult males in more skilled jobs. Unfortunately, there are indications that the teenagers and women who work in this type of job represent an increasingly typical kind of worker, in the one area of the economy that continues to grow—the service sector. The fast-food industry represents a model for other industries in which the introduction of technology will permit the employment of low-skilled, cheap, and plentiful workers. In this sense, it is easy to be pessimistic and agree with Andre Gorz's depressing formulation of the idea of work:

The terms "work" and "job" have become interchangeable: work is no longer something that one *does* but something that one *has*.

Workers no loger "produce" society through

the mediation of the relations of production; instead the machinery of social production as a whole produces "work" and imposes it in a random way upon random, interchangeable individuals.[8]

The Burger King system represents a major triumph for capital. However, the reduction of the worker to a simple component of capital requires more than the introduction of a technology; workers' autonomous culture must be eliminated as well, including the relationships among workers, their skills, and their loyalties to one another. The smiling, willing, homogeneous worker must be produced and placed on the Burger King assembly line.

While working at Burger King, I saw the extent to which Burger King has succeeded in reducing its work force to a set of interchangeable pieces. However, I also saw how insistently the liveliness and decency of the workers emerged in the informal interaction that occurred. Open resistance is made virtually impossible by the difficulty of identifying who is responsible for the rules that govern the workplace: the workers know that managers follow orders from higher up. The very high turnover of employees indicates workers understand that their interests and Burger King's are not the same.

As young people and women realize that their jobs in the fast-food industry are not waystations en route to more fulfilling work, they will perhaps blow the whistle on the Burger King "team." The mould for the creation of the homogeneous worker assembling the standardized meal for the homogeneous consumer is not quite perfected.

NOTES

1. Promotional material from Burger King Canada head office in Mississauga, Ontario.
2. Karl Marx, *Capital*, vol. 1 ([1867]; New York 1977), ch. xv.
3. Theodore Levitt, "Production Line Approach to Service," *Harvard Business Review* 50, no. 1 (Sept.–Oct. 1972): 51–2.
4. A "Shape Up" campaign instituted at the beginning of 1982 attempted to set a new goal of a 2 1/2-minute service time.
5. Personal communication, Burger King "professor," 4 January 1982.
6. Labour Canada, *Commission of Inquiry into Part-Time Work* (Ottawa 1983) [Wallace commission].
7. Personal communication, Burger King worker, 8 August 1981.
8. Andre Gorz, *Farewell to the Working Class* (Boston 1982), 71.

2.3. Why Are So Many People Poor?

Peter Townsend

The next excerpt is about a third cause of economic inequality: the state's role in redistributing wealth (and poverty). Sometimes redistribution is so ill-planned or inadequate as to have no beneficial effect on economic inequality. For example, during the 1980s, poverty in Great Britain increased. According to the author of this excerpt, the rise in economic inequality was a direct result of government policies aimed at creating two Britains—a rich one and a poor one.

Rather than attempting to reduce, or at least maintain the level of inequality, Margaret Thatcher's government cut social programs and increased the incomes of the rich by lowering their taxes. Thatcher's successor, John Major, comes from a working-class family, and this may make him more sympathetic to the needs of the poor. But there is little reason to hope for miracles. Conservatives are unlikely to pay any more than lip service to antipoverty measures in the 1990s, because of their party's traditional view of poverty.

The conservative right would have one believe that poor people are to blame for their own situation because they are unwilling to work. But Townsend, the author of this excerpt, argues otherwise, citing the fact that there are 20 unemployed people for every job vacancy in Britain. Unemployment may not be the sole cause of poverty. However, Townsend sees it (along with government policy) as the most important factor causing recent increases in inequality.

For their part, multinational corporations worsen the problem. These companies wield more power than many governments do, yet they are not responsible to any single country. They can always avoid attempts to limit their wealth by moving elsewhere, leaving massive unemployment in their wake.

Given this globalization of the economy, what steps should governments take to deal with poverty, whatever its causes? The traditional antipoverty approach accepts high rates of unemployment, and taxes wealth to fund social programs for the poor. But this way of reducing inequality has failed: the rich resist paying high taxes. In fact, most people oppose paying higher benefits to welfare recipients, even though the existing benefits are too low for people to survive on. (For more about this resistance to social programs, see an excerpt by Swaan in a later section.)

Townsend believes we need to reassess basic strategies for dealing with poverty. Government must place reasonable limits on people's income, wealth, and power and guarantee everyone a minimum income. Underlying this approach is a need to believe that full employment is possible and mass unemployment is *not* inevitable. Defensive strategies cannot reduce poverty, he argues.

The [British] government estimated there were, in 1981, 15 million people with very low incomes, including those with lower incomes than the state poverty line, those with incomes on that line, and those with incomes only marginally above. . . .

Excerpted from Townsend, Peter (1986), "Why are the many poor?" *International Journal of Health Services* 16(1), 1–32. With permission of Baywood Publishing Co., Inc.

The numbers in the categories I have described have doubled, from seven and three-quarters of a million to 15 million in 20 years under successive governments but have accelerated in the last five years. Between 1979 and 1981, the total increased from just over 11 million to 15 million—or by nearly 4 million—and there is no discernible halt to that trend. Since 1981 long-term unemployment has increased substantially. Instead of 15 million poor the total could now be 18 million.

[WHO IS POOR?]

. . . The recent increase in poverty in Britain is partly due to an increase in unemployment. In the early 1960s only about 250,000 people were in families with very low incomes because of unemployment which had lasted three months or longer. By the late 1970s the figure was in excess of one million. Between 1979 and 1981 the figure leapt to 2.6 million. . . .

But other categories of poor have also increased. Between 1971 and 1981 the number of one-parent families increased by 71 percent and now stands at nearly one million families. This is approximately one family in every seven with children. The long-standing inequality between the sexes in access to resources and the institutional bias in favor of conventionally married couples contribute to the poverty which lone parents and their children experience.

There have been fluctuations in the percentage of old people drawing supplementary benefit. During the last 25 years there has been a slight increase in the total proportion living on low incomes from around 60 percent to 68 percent. The actual number living *below* the state's standard has increased. Much of the poverty of the elderly has been "created" by the modern institutions of retirement and inadequate employer and state pensions. The total number of younger disabled people living on low incomes has stayed around the three-quarter million mark in the last ten years, but within that total the number below the poverty line has increased. Again, employment opportunities, and access to social associations, continues to be denied to many people with disabilities.

The number of low paid in poverty or on its margins has also increased. The tenth of wage earners with lowest earnings have a wage which has fallen to 64.1 percent of the median in the case of men and 66.4 percent in the case of women (1983). Further evidence of the multiplication in number of low earners is to be found in the doubling in recent years of the numbers drawing Family Income Supplement. . . .

The Life Cycle [And Poverty]

Another method of getting closer to the structural causes of poverty is to examine changes in the distribution of incomes by age. . . . A disproportionately large number of children and of old people, especially over 75, have incomes below or on the margins of the government's poverty line.[1] In middle life, between the ages of 45 and 60, disposable incomes tend on average to be nearly twice or more than twice the incomes available to the households in which young children and old people live.

The reasons for the growing inequality by age in the distribution of resources are several. Young people have been marrying younger and having their children younger than preceding generations. This means many couples in middle age do not have dependent children to support. More married women of this age are now taking paid employment and this means that for many households in middle life there are two wage earners rather than one at a time when there are no dependent children. More of the employed population are in nonmanual employment and therefore eligible for age increments in pay. "Seniority" payments among manual workers have also become more common. People who reach the most powerful managerial, professional, administrative and political positions are generally in this age group. Finally, the spread of owner-occupation means that more people have high costs when raising a family and low housing costs when they have no dependent children.

[What Causes Poverty?]

. . . A theory of poverty depends on a two-fold analysis. One strand shows how different institutions of economic and social management operate to distribute resources unequally. The other shows how the terms of social membership are continually revised by new laws, new housing, new transport systems, new environments and modes of living. This explains what individual members of society *need* to do at any time and what resources they require to minimally fulfil their obligations as citizens.

Control of poverty therefore lies not just in controlling the allocation of resources but controlling the construction and reproduction of those institutions which govern social behavior.

[INSTITUTIONAL CAUSES OF POVERTY]

1. Jobs and Wages

The problem arises first and foremost in the institutions of employment and the wage structure. The growth in influence and power of the large corporation has been succeeded by the crucial phenomenon of the multinational corporation. Because of their flexibility to enter and leave international markets, multinational companies are overcoming the restraints imposed on them by some national governments. Threats of nationalization, for example, can be met by shifting production to other countries or by separating production into stages, so denying any single country access to control of all the stages of production.

For workers and representative trade unions this means a weakening of bargaining powers. It is felt that concessions have to be made to management in order to preserve jobs. For management, there is a less widely discussed problem. Loyalties to family concerns, work groups and local communities are replaced by the uncertain disciplines of international camaraderie within big organizations. There is bound to be loss of national as well as local affiliation, and certainly among some a growth of social cynicism which knows few geographical roots and depends more and more upon the advancement of self-interest.

It is disinvestment and the relocation of employment overseas, and not just world recession, which has brought about mass unemployment in the 1980s. An example is Scotland. The authors of one study describe the disinvestments of Singer, Chrysler-Peugot, Hoover, NCR, Honeywell and Goodyear, and the resulting loss of 45,000 jobs between 1976 and 1981.[2] . . . To the

problem in Britain of disinvestment and relocation of industry overseas have to be added the increasing use by management of the threats of robotics, computerization and privatization to suborn and reduce labor forces. The politics of wage control is being replaced by the politics of redundancy.

. . . The internationalization of finance is a parallel trend. Those in charge of insurance companies, unit trusts, pension funds and other institutions have been transferring money overseas. This means that the health of the British economy is of lesser importance than it used to be to those in leading positions in the city of London. The financial viability and profits of concerns and individuals is more and more dependent on developments overseas rather than at home. . . .

The growth of corporations and multinational companies as well as international agencies has also had its effect on augmenting pay at the top, introducing more grades of pay and lowering the pay of subordinate groups like temporary staff and wholly or partly dependent subsidiaries. On June 3, 1984 the *Sunday Times* listed the salaries, as far as they are known, of the leading 100 public company directors. . . .

"Many a highly paid director's salary is of course dwarfed by the earnings of his super salesmen or vital executives. At Grand Met, for example, the chairman, Stanley Grinstead, earns £111,000—but two of his top casino executives, Max Kingsley and Philip Isaacs, earn nearly £400,000 apiece. . . . But then, for many a chairman or highly paid director, his salary is simply the loose change in his pocket. Tiny Rowland earned over £4m in the final Lonrho dividend in his £56m stake in the Company, compared to a mere £265,000 salary in 1983."[3]

[The Unfair Tax System]

The gains to the rich since 1979 have been in profitability to companies, as partly engineered and encouraged by the government. Some salaries include bonuses for additional profits. But they have also come from deliberate redistribution. Of a total of £4.17 billion cuts in income taxes since 1979 the richest 1 percent receive 44 percent and the poorest only 3 percent. The average reduction in income tax for those earning over £50,000 is £11,700, but for those earning under £5,000 is £20.[4]

Fringe benefits have not figured prominently in the debates about tax allowances and tax rates. During the 1960s and 1970s inequality was therefore made out by different interest groups to be diminishing when in fact it was increasing. . . .

Tax allowances have made a mockery of the personal income tax system. Because of their existence the tax base is narrow.[5] Tax is now collected on less than half gross declared income and perhaps only a third of total real income. Chartered accountants working on behalf of the rich can save their clients huge sums of money. "For the rich," concluded one recent review, "Britain has become a fiscal paradise."[6] Wealth taxes in Britain (Capital Gains, Estate Duty, and Capital Transfer Taxes) have never been very consequential but have declined in value and percentage of total taxes since 1975. They accounted for 7.5 percent of total Inland Revenue taxes in the early 1970s but only for 2.5 percent by 1983–84, and had declined, expressed as a percentage of GNP, from 1.2 to 0.5 percent. The tax structure has become far less progressive. Higher tax rates on higher incomes were reduced and the thresholds raised. In 1984 it was estimated that only 3 percent of tax units are paying tax above the standard rate of 30 percent. At 650,000 their numbers are half what they were in the late 1970s.

The government . . . analysis of income distribution[7] shows a shrinkage since 1975–76 and especially since 1978–79 in the share of disposable income of the poorest 20 percent and a substantial increase in the share of the top 20 percent of taxable units. The figures are summarized in Table 1. . . .

Engineer[ed] Dependency

Just as the tax structure became less egalitarian, the dependent population increased—in largest measure "artificially" through unemployment and premature retirement, and some postponement of the completion of education. Between 1973 and 1983 the number of men aged 55 to 59 who

TABLE 1.   Shares of Income After Tax[a]

	1975–76	1978–79	1981–82
Top 10 percent	23.1	23.4	25.6
Top 20 percent	39.0	39.7	42.0
21–40 percent	24.8	24.8	24.0
41–60 percent	17.3	17.0	16.1
61–80 percent	11.6	11.5	11.5
Bottom 20 percent	7.3	7.0	6.4

Estimated Average Real Income at 1981–82 Prices[a]

	1975–76	1978–79	1981–82	Gain or loss 1978–79 1981–82
Top 10 percent	£10,638	£11,295	£12,851	+£1,557
Top 20 percent	£8,980	£9,572	£10,542	+£970
Bottom 20 percent	£1,681	£1,688	£1,606	–£82

[a] Source: Central Statistical Office, *Economic Trends*, July 1984. . . .

are economically active fell from 94 percent to 85 percent and, at ages 60 to 64, from 85 to 63 percent. There were corresponding reductions among divorced and other single women in these two age groups from 69 percent to 53 percent, and 34 percent to 17 percent. This increase in dependency at such youthful ages is nationally self-destructive. The need to finance this increase in dependency has brought the tax threshold down and caused taxes to be increased on the goods purchased by the mass of the population.

[Cuts In Government Benefits]

The Thatcher Government is seeking change by drastically reducing public expenditure and ensuring that more of it is paid for by the poor. Taxation has been introduced for unemployment benefit. Changes in regulations have stopped some groups of unemployed getting any supplementary benefit at all and have stopped others from getting as much as their former entitlement. Earnings related supplement has been abolished. The activities of the Special Claims Control Teams to identify fraud have been stepped up. As a percentage both of earnings and of the benefits received by long-term claimants, other than the unemployed, the unemployed person's weekly benefit has declined. Unemployment benefit is at its lowest level relative to earnings since the early 1960s. Housing benefit is now payable by local authorities. The transfer of its administration, like the reorganization of supplementary benefit beforehand, has involved reductions in weekly income for hundreds of thousands of recipients, as conceded by Government Ministers.

[SUMMARY: THATCHERISM AS CLASS WARFARE]

. . . The government is following a policy of "get tough with the poor." This is its major raison d'être and far more important in fact than its well-advertised neo-monetarism. It is a covert form of class warfare. . . . The Government is aiming to lower prices first by lowering already low levels of pay (we can cite decisions in public sector industries, on wages councils and the history of the Youth Training Scheme); second, by refusing to set principled limits on the extent or growth of unemployment; and third, as we have seen, by lowering benefits in order to make lower pay acceptable. It is a downward spiral whereby the government fails to recognize the ultimate destination—the establishment of Third World wages and Third World social conditions in an otherwise rich country for more than a third of its people.

For the first time since the war a majority of the British Cabinet seem prepared to allow conditions of life for a large minority of the people to deteriorate in the mistaken belief that conditions for the rest of the population will thereby be improved. That is a departure from the consensus politics of post-war Britain. But there is a worse implication still. For the first time Government Ministers seem prepared to depart even from the most tenuous principles of one nation and consider seriously that certain sections of the British population are beyond redemption, have to be taught some rough lessons and are expendable. . . .

REFERENCES

1. Townsend, P. Fewer Children, More Poverty: An Incomes Plan. University of Bristol, England, 1984.
2. Hood, N., and Young, S. Multi-nationals in Retreat, the Scottish Experience. Edinburgh University Press, Scotland, 1982.
3. Beresford, P. Boom at the top. Sunday Times (London), June 3, 1984.
4. Hansard, April 4, 1984.
5. Report by the Board of Inland Revenue, Table 1–5, London, 1983.
6. Bellini, J. The tax avoidance boom. The Listener, April 5, 1984.
7. Economic Trends, July, 1984.

2.4. Income Under Women's Control in the Third World

Rae Lesser Blumberg

The next excerpt is about a fourth cause of economic inequality: the role of sexism in economic policies.

The author of this excerpt believes women need more control over their own lives and incomes. They will benefit from a reduction in economic inequality, and so will their respective societies. Today, most development strategies are flawed because they place income under the exclusive control of men.

In developing countries women do most of the work yet they control very little of the wealth they produce. Assistance programs generally pay money out to men, who then pay their wives much less than their work merits. But when people are poorly paid for their work they reduce their output, and women are no exception. One result is a limitation on food production, with food crises occurring in much of the Third World.

On the other hand, when women *do* have control of their own incomes, they have more say in household decision making. For example, they bear fewer children. Since development experts all view overpopulation as the Third World's biggest problem, a reduction in childbearing is perhaps the best single reason to give women more control over their income.

Family well-being and child nutrition also improve when women have more control over income. In cultures where women help to provide income for the family, women contribute virtually all their earnings to basic needs, especially food. By contrast, men tend to withhold a significant portion of their income for personal use (e.g., drinking and socializing). So even though women earn less than men, their incomes contribute more to family health than men's incomes do.

In most cultures, women are expected to be selfless caregivers, while men are permitted to behave irresponsibly. But this cannot continue, says the author. What goes on within the family matters greatly, and development planners cannot afford to ignore this fact. Improving the economic well-being of Third World people will have to mean dealing with gender inequality at the same time.

This excerpt illustrates several important facts about economic inequality. First, there is a direct connection between inequalities of income and inequalities of power. Second, there is a direct connection between inequalities in the home and inequalities outside the home. Third, gender inequality is not only unjust but also can harm every member of society by hindering economic growth.

Excerpted from Blumberg, Rae Lesser (1988), "Income under female versus male control. Hypotheses from a theory of gender stratification and data from the Third World," *Journal of Family Issues*, 9 (1) March, 51–84. Reprinted with permission of Sage Publications.

The relationships among control of income, marital power, and gender stratification in the capitalist societies of the "First World" raise questions that provide food for academic thought. In contrast, in much of the Third World, especially sub-

Saharan Africa, the consequences of their interconnections involving food are not metaphorical but *literal*. Relative male/female control of income and marital power, I propose, affects outcomes that run the gamut from how much food is available to the children in a family to how much food is grown in a country. In much of Africa, in fact, the implications of husbands' versus wives' control of resources may extend all the way to the region's recent food crises. . . .

HOW LACK OF RETURNS TO LABOR FOR WOMEN FARMERS CAN AFFECT THE AFRICAN FOOD CRISIS

. . . In the macro context of Africa, development experts rarely consider women as autonomous economic actors who generally *require* income under their control to fulfill responsibilities toward family provisioning and kin. When development planners—especially in Africa—ignore the "internal economy" of the household at the micro level, women's possibilities and incentives for food production may be reduced. That's serious; women tend to be the primary cultivators of food crops in most of sub-Saharan Africa. Indeed, the Economic Commission for Africa credits women farmers with from 60% to 80% of all labor in agriculture (United Nations, 1978, p. 5). Nevertheless, women are rarely *seen* as farmers by development officials. They are still overwhelmingly shut out of agricultural extension, training, credit, fertilizer, and other assistance. . . . This neglect of female farmers (and their incentives) may contribute to outcomes ranging from failed development projects to famine.

Female Farmers, Income Incentives, and the African Food Crisis

The argument can be summarized in . . . six points:

1. Women in much of Africa raise the bulk of locally produced/marketed food crops but rarely obtain direct benefits from agricultural development projects.
2. In Africa, especially, men and women not only tend to have some separate income, but also separate obligations for spending it. Women's duties often include providing much of the family food. Accordingly, the sexes tend to maintain "separate purses" for at least part of their resources—especially where polygyny and/or marital instability are high (see Staudt, 1987 for a fine overview).
3. Women's control of income has direct implications for family welfare: . . . Where women have resources under their independent control, they tend, more than men, to devote them to feeding the family and to children's well-being.
4. Given so many African women's needs for resources to provision their family, they will tend to allocate their labor *toward* activities that put income and/or food under their direct control and—to the extent culturally possible—*away* from activities that don't. This seems to hold true even if the latter activities are substantially more profitable (see Jones, 1983, below).
5. Therefore, if development projects fail to provide (sufficient) economic returns, especially income incentives, for the women's labor, both the project's and the women's goals are likely to suffer (see below). In other words, the impact of new macro-level "structural adjustment" policies that try to "get the prices right" to provide incentives for agricultural producers (see World Bank, 1981) will be reduced if *women* producers don't get enough of the resulting income to provide incentive.
6. In effect, then, the combination of a gender-differentiated "internal economy" of the household, female predominance in food crops grown for local consumption or market, and insufficient incentives for women producers may be an important but unheralded factor in Africa's recent food crises.

When Development Projects Need Female Labor But Decrease Their Income

Space constraints limit this section to four projects from Africa. But the annals of the "gender and development" (also known as "women in development") literature document this phenomenon around the world. Since Boserup (1970) first noted the "double whammy" whereby both planned and unplanned development were likely to increase poor Third World women's workload while undermining their economic autonomy, researchers have provided considerable empirical documentation of just such negative effects on *women*. Recently, however, attempts are being made to compile empirical documentation of the negative effects on the *projects* themselves when women are bypassed and undercut (see, e.g., Carloni, 1987). The rationale, of course, is that this is a tack more likely to result in policy changes that will "make them stop doing it."

Cameroon: Women's return to labor affects how much rice they grow. In the Cameroon SEMRY I irrigated rice project, Jones' (1983) sophisticated econometric analysis provides the best documented case of a development project suffering because women were not given sufficient compensation for their labor. Jones' data stem from a random sample of 102 Massa women from three villages. They provide support for the following: (1) The project's long-term prospects are doubtful since it has not been able to get farmers to grow enough rice; (2) There is a clear relationship between women's incentives and their rice output; and (3) Women who grew rice on their own account—*or* were especially well compensated by their husbands—cultivated approximately twice as much rice acreage as women whose husbands provided lower compensation.

1. SEMRY's problem with uncultivated fields: The SEMRY 1 project in Cameroon involves about 5,400 hectares of pump-irrigated rice fields. Although yields and prices have both been good,

every year many fields go uncultivated for lack of farmer interest. . . . In the 1981 rainy season . . . only 3,228 hectares were cultivated, despite [a 45%] increase in the producer price in 1980 (Jones, 1983, p. 30).

Unless SEMRY can get farmers to cultivate those unused fields, its prospects are grim: At present hectarage, its "revenues

are not sufficient to cover both operating costs and amortization" (Jones, 1983, p. 31). To understand why SEMRY can't find takers for its idle irrigated fields, we must see who works versus who benefits.

2. Women with more incentive raise more rice: Irrigated rice cultivation on SEMRY fields is a *joint conjugal activity*. But *the husband gets all the income*—and then compensates his wife as he sees fit. "In return for [her] sweat,

a woman receives about 7,700 CFA in cash and about 9,200 CFA worth of paddy from her husband after the harvest, or about 16,900 CFA in total. This is less than a quarter of the net returns from rice production—about 70,000 CFA. Valued at the market wage rates . . . a woman's labor contribution is worth about 31,200 CFA, so her husband makes a profit of about 14,300 CFA from her labor (Jones, 1983, p. 51).

And "husbands are quite aware that their wives' continued participation depends on their own generosity [i.e., their wages]" (p.51); wives' rice labor—especially transplanting—is done "at the expense of [women's] sorghum production and other income-generating activities" (p. 4). Specifically, sorghum, which is the mainstay of the diet (100% of households surveyed cultivated it), is grown on an *individual* basis by both men and women. In other words, even though a married woman uses her sorghum primarily for subsistence, it is her *own* sorghum. Not surprisingly, then, Jones' first regression analysis establishes a very strong "relationship between the amount of compensation women receive from their husbands and the number of days they worked on their husbands' rice fields" (p. 52).

Moreover, Jones establishes empirically that the average 16,900 CFA that husbands gave to wives as "wages" is about one-third more than the "opportunity costs" of women's labor—that is, what they could have earned if they had engaged in their own income-generating activities. But even this one-third "premium" was insufficient to induce the average wife to raise more rice: She devoted some labor to growing rice for her husband, but spent the rest of her time on less profitable activities under her *own* control.

. . . Jones' regressions show that women must make a literally one-to-one tradeoff between the number of days they work on rice versus sorghum cultivation during the peak transplanting season. Yet rice gives the better return. So, not surprisingly, independent women (mostly widows) who grew rice on their *own* account spent 24.7 days transplanting it. This is half again as many days as married women transplanting their husband's rice (they transplanted for only 16.4 days; the difference is significant). As a result, the married women transplanted only .31 hectare per adult worker versus the .47 hectare transplanted by independent women's households.

Furthermore, since both independent and married women obtained yields of about 4,300 kilos/hectare, it was *quantity* of rice land planted, not quality of cultivation, that differentiated the two groups.

3. Specifically, women with more incentives cultivate as much rice land: One subgroup of married women *did* cultivate as much land as independent women—and these were wives who received a significantly *higher rate of compensation* from their husbands. In one village, Jones compared independent women with two groups of married women: those whose households grew more than .75 "piquet" (1 piquet = .5 hectare) per household worker and those whose households grew less. The independent women averaged .94 piquet per household worker. And the 13 households in the .75 + piquet category averaged an almost identical .95. This was *twice as much* rice land as that cultivated in the 18 households below .75 piquet, which averaged only .47 piquet per household worker. The secret? Married "women who cultivated .75 piquet or more per household worker were compensated at the mean rate of 363 CFA/day, while the group of women who cultivated less than .75 piquet per household worker received only 302 CFA/day from their husbands."

In sum, although wives were compensated above opportunity costs, lack

of sufficient incentive explains why so few "take on the cultivation of an additional rice field" (p. 83). And this surely is a major reason why SEMRY can't get farmers to cultivate its unused fields.

The next three African examples tell the same story.

Kenya. In an area where Kenyan women traditionally grew pyrethrum (used in insecticide), sold the dried flowers, and kept the income, a project organized a co-op to exploit this crop. But it enrolled (and paid) men almost exclusively. The discouraged women reduced their output (Apthorpe, 1971).

The Gambia. An irrigated rice project was developed by male Taiwanese technicians. Men were targeted, despite the fact that women traditionally not only cultivated swamp rice but also controlled its disposition and cash returns. But men needed women's labor. So they blocked women from owning or cultivating irrigated rice land on their own account. The results? Rice production decreased under the project as women held back their labor (Dey, 1981, 1982).

The Turkana of Kenya. Traditionally, Turkana males were herders; Turkana females were cultivators, and produce from their rain-fed sorghum plots long had been under female control. An irrigation project was launched. It paid all cash earnings to the (male) head of household, but counted on women providing unpaid family labor for their husband's irrigated crops. Instead, women neglected the irrigated project crops in favor of their own rain-fed sorghum plots located away from the project area. Those few women who had their own irrigated plots, however, allocated relatively less time to off-project cultivation. Output on the project's one-acre irrigated plots proved so far below projections that women had to work on off-project activities for their family to survive. (Two other consequences also bear mentioning. First, a nutrition study found that children in project tenant households had the worst nutrition of all groups studied, including people in famine relief camps receiving food rations. Second, to fill their provider role, women sold surplus sorghum, did petty trading, and brewed beer from their sorghum. Accordingly, another outcome of concentrating all project income in male hands has been an increase in beer drinking [Broch-Due, 1983].)

Women: The Missing Variable in Analysis of the African Food Crisis

The list of variables found in analyses of African food crisis and famine reads almost like the biblical 10 plagues: War. Drought. Ecological degradation. Unfavorable insertion into the capitalist world economy. Bad government macroeconomic policies (including (1) inefficient "parastatals" and government marketing boards that don't pay farmers enough to stimulate output; (2) distorted, urban-biased factor prices that may make it cheaper to import wheat from the United States than get farmers to grow local food staples; (3) misguided exchange rate policies; and (4) a long list of other "macroeconomic mortal sins"). Lack of breakthrough research on African food crops. Inadequate extension. Insufficient use of agricultural inputs (fertilizer, chemicals, etc.). Inadequate management of development projects. Corruption. Insufficient funding from the international donor agencies. Indeed, this list could be doubled without depleting the factors found in the growing literature on the African food crisis.

But with few exceptions, when the *African farmer* is discussed, the personal pronoun used is *he.* That women are the main producers of African food crops—and *especially* their need for incentives—are almost never mentioned (see Staudt, 1987, for a first-rate discussion of this blindness).

As background on Africa's food situation, here is Hyden's summary:

According to a recent African survey (ECA, cited in Hyden, 1986, pp.8–9) for the whole of [the 1970s], when Africa's population was expanding at an average annual rate of around 2.8%, total food production in Africa was rising by no more than 1.5%. Food self-sufficiency ratios dropped from 98% in the 1960s to approximately 86% in 1980. This means that, on average, each African had about 12% less homegrown food in 1980 than 20 years earlier. With food production stagnating and demand, particularly for cereals, keeping pace with population growth, the volume of food imports between 1970 and 1980 increased by an average annual rate of 8.4%. In 1980, imports of food grains alone reached 20.4 million tons, costing African countries over $5 billion (not including heavy ocean freight costs). Food aid to Africa in 1980 was 1.5 million tons (ECA, cited in Hyden, 1986, p. 11).

All this was before the drought that brought Africa's second major famine since the early 1970s to the world's television screens in 1984–1985. Now, dire reports mention a third famine beginning in Ethiopia in 1987. Yet most of even the newest "mainstream" analyses largely ignore women (e.g., Mellor, Delgado, and Blackie, 1987).

The consequences of this omission are indeed serious at both micro and macro levels.

REFERENCES

Apthorpe, Raymond, 1971. "Some Evaluation Problems for Cooperative Studies, with Special Reference to Primary Cooperatives in Highland Kenya." In *Two Blades of Grass: Rural Cooperatives in Agricultural Modernization,* edited by Peter Worsely. Manchester: Manchester University Press.

Boserup, Ester. 1970. *Woman's Role in Economic Development.* New York: St. Martin's.

Broch-Due, Vigdis. 1983. "Women at the Backstage of Development: The Negative Impact on Project Realization by Neglecting the Crucial Roles of Turkana Women as Producers and Providers." Rome: Food and Agricultural Organization.

Carloni, Alice Stewart. 1987. *Women in Development: A.I.D.'s Experience, 1973–1985, Vol. 1. Synthesis Paper.* Washington, DC: Agency for International Development.

Dey, Jennie. 1981. "Gambian Women: Unequal

Partners in Rice Development Projects?" In *African Women in the Development Process*, edited by Nicci Nelson. London: Frank Cass.

—,1982. "Development Planning in the Gambia: The Gap Between Planners' and Farmers' Perceptions, Expectations and Objectives." *World Development* 10(5): 377–396.

Economic Commission for Africa. 1983. *ECA and Africa's Development 1983–2008: A Preliminary Perspective Study*. Addis Ababa: Economic Commission for Africa (April).

Hyden, Goren. 1986. "The Invisible Economy of Smallholder Agriculture in Africa." In *Understanding Africa's Rural Households and Farming Systems*, edited by Joyce Lewinger Moock. Boulder: Westview.

Jones, Christine. 1983. "The Impact of the SEMRY I Irrigated Rice Production Project on the Organization of Production and Consumption at the Intrahousehold Level." Washington, DC: Report prepared for the Agency for International Development, Bureau for Program and Policy Coordination.

Mellor, John W., Christopher L. Delgado, and Malcolm J. Blackie, eds. 1987. *Accelerating Food Production in Sub-Saharan Africa*. Baltimore: Johns Hopkins.

Staudt, Kathleen. 1987. "Uncaptured or Unmotivated? Women and the Food Crisis in Africa." *Rural Sociology* 52(1):37–55.

United Nations. 1978. *Effective Mobilization of Women in Development*. Report of the Secretary General. UN A/33/238. New York: United Nations.

World Bank. 1981. *Accelerated Development in Sub-Saharan Africa: An Agenda for Action*. Washington, DC: World Bank.

2.5. How Poor Women Earn Income in Sub-Saharan Africa

Janice Jiggins

This excerpt is about a fifth cause of economic inequality: the constraints on women's earning power in much of the world.

Rural poverty is increasing around the world, especially in sub-Saharan Africa. One effect of this is a change in the composition of households: more and more men are forced to leave their families in search of work. As a result, women now head 30 percent of the region's households, and economic inequality has risen.

This is because female household heads do not enjoy the same rights as their male counterparts. In families, and in society as a whole, women stand in a subordinate position to men. Land titles are seldom awarded to females, for example. As a result, women have little access to many services and loans they need. More generally, women exercise little control over their incomes.

They also have little control over their time. In order to meet the needs of their families, more women are turning to self-employment or wage work. But they remain responsible for all the household duties. This means that for women who must support their family without the help of a spouse, the workday is getting longer. Women already do most of the work and produce most of the food, and now they must work even harder. The stress on women has become so bad that death during childbirth is more common than anywhere in the developing world. Infant mortality rates are double the Third World average.

The deterioration of the traditionally male-led family has led some to suggest increasing men's incomes. This would remove the need for men to migrate to find work and allow families to remain intact. However, there is no guarantee that increasing men's incomes would improve the condition of women and children. On the contrary, there is strong evidence that placing income under women's control contributes more to family welfare. So the solution would seem to be increasing women's incomes.

Women's rights need to increase, too. How, for example, can a female entrepreneur run a successful business if she cannot discipline a male employee? What can she do if her husband suddenly runs off with all her money? Change must occur from the top down, by governments guaranteeing women's rights in law. A female head of household should enjoy the same rights a man does. More countries should follow the lead of Zimbabwe. There, agricultural banks know that many men are absent and lend money directly to women.

To fight economic inequality, governments will have to recognize the essential role women play in the health of the region. This will mean supporting and encouraging women's income-earning activities.

RURAL POVERTY

. . . Rural poverty in sub-Saharan Africa seems to be increasing. For analytic purposes, six types of poverty can be distinguished in terms of their consequences for women. . . .

Poverty of Cash

Poverty of cash is typical of areas of low population density, where a strong local market economy has not developed, market infrastructure remains weak, and diversified opportunities for savings and investment are lacking. The main sources of cash are government wages and salaries, but this stimulus is limited by the weakness of government investment. . . .

Excerpted from Jiggins, Janice (1989), "How poor women earn income in sub-Saharan Africa and what works against them," *World Development*, 17, 953–963. Reprinted with permission of Pergamon Press Ltd. Oxford, England.

Poverty of Resources

Poverty of resources takes at least three forms. The first is found in areas of high population density, where the trend toward permanent cropping on smaller and smaller plots is accompanied by inadequate soil management and replenishment of fertility. Natural resources in the medium to long tern decrease in productivity. Women tend to be particularly affected by declines in the availability of fuelwood, and by the marginalization of their access to land.

The second form of poverty of resources is in areas of low population density, where soils are poor or infertile and vulnerable to decertification. In these areas, people themselves are the chief resource. Men migrate in the worst dry years in search of wage income, leaving women to struggle alone.

Third, the number of areas . . . in which the demand for fuelwood and charcoal is outstripping supply is growing. Poor women switch to less fuel-demanding foodstuffs or reduce the number of times they cook; better-off women divert scarce cash to purchasing fuel.[1]

Poverty of the Range

Poverty of the range is a special case of "poverty of resources," where rangeland [is degraded] through overgrazing of common property resources by larger herd owners.[2] Women are affected by having little access to land and water for their own small stock, the migration of small herders or stockless men in search of alternative livelihoods, and the impact of overgrazing on the supply of fuelwood.

Poverty of Labor Supply

In areas of high male outmigration, the remaining households find it harder to make a sustained response to the market, provide balanced diets year-round, or maintain environmentally sound farming practices by hiring the labor of those unable to maintain self-provisioning.

Poverty of Labor Demand

In areas where farm productivity, opportunities for market sales or diversified sources of nonfarm income are inadequate to absorb the increasing population, rural stagnation is likely to drive out increasing numbers of young men, leading to a scarcity of labor. . . . Recently, women and children who do not have means to support themselves are beginning to move out in large numbers; they often become vulnerable casual laborers or live without secure livelihoods on the fringes of rural towns.

Poverty of Health

There are still large areas of severe endemic disease such as river blindness, and of disability related to dietary deficiencies such as cassava-related cretinism. . . .

From Survival to Security

. . . Case histories suggest that considerable numbers of women move over time from survival to higher-yield entrepreneurial activity. . . . However, four factors make it difficult for rural women in poverty areas to maintain or consolidate their entrepreneurial activity:

—fluctuating supply and demand in line with seasonal climatic variations;
—frequent product market failures, which encourage women to retain basic food production capacity;
—poor opportunities for diversification;
—women's multiple roles which limit their freedom to exploit assets solely as commercial assets.

LABOR PROCESSES AND FAMILY COMPOSITION

Changing Position of Women in the Labor Process

Structural changes are forcing changes in women's position in the labor process and in the composition of the family. There appear to be two constants however, irrespective of culture, community, or location: (1) gender remains a fundamental principle for organizing the division of labor within the family and the wider socio-economy; and (2) the specialization of women in food farming, processing, and trading remains predicated on a particular definition of household production which is embedded in the cultural expectations of African patriarchal society.

Given these two constants, structural change in agrarian economies has put women at a greater disadvantage in the labor process. The new arrangements do not support the underlying constants in the social organization of production.

Modern land law, for example, tends to collapse complex patterns of land use rights into ownership of land as the property of a single title holder.[3] Titles to occupy, cultivate, and own land usually have been awarded to men, as presumed heads of households. Modern land law does not reflect the actual organization of production which allows, for example, a man in Ibadan,

Nigeria, to cultivate yams and his wife tomatoes on the same piece of land at the same time, i.e., two cash intercrops on one land unit, managed by two people maintaining separate budgets and who have individual and not joint rights to the use of that unit.

Women continue to cultivate land privatized under male title, or on irrigation and settlement schemes, irrespective of the rules governing land use, cropping patterns, labor allocation, and tenancy. They do so, however, in a kind of legal limbo, with impaired access to services and inputs, weak control over income, little stake in the maintenance of infrastructure, and with no diminution in their multiple roles and tasks....

Family Composition

. . . Marriage is no longer the only way in which rural households are formed, and there is no longer a necessary connection between adulthood, fecundity, and marriage. The synonymity of residential unit, biosocial unit, and economic unit is weakening. These trends may have divergent consequences for rural women. On the one hand, their traditional social support group and their access to resources through their lineage can be weakened or destroyed, thus increasing their responsibilities for family support. On the other hand, the changes can open up new horizons beyond the restrictions of traditional gender expectations....

. . . Given the women's increasing responsibility for the daily support of themselves and their children, the immediate objective must be to provide women with the means to provide that support.

Three emergent household formations tend to increase the need for women to augment their independent income: ...

Rural-based Wives and Children with Migrant Husbands

. . . Given low and uncertain urban and industrial incomes for most male wage seekers, remittances can be only intermittent sources of support. They are often accompanied by expenditure instructions which further compromise women's management flexibility. Insofar as women's access to the support and resources of their lineage depends on the presence of their spouse, male migration also weakens women's social base....

Residentially Separated Spouses and Fractured Marriages

Women who remain separated spouses are especially vulnerable, but a divorced woman's status is also often problematic because she has less access to production resources, credit, and social support. Additionally, the law and practice often do not recognize women as legal persons able to sign contracts and enter into commercial transactions without a male guarantor.

Many countries tie access to inputs (including bank and cooperative credit), services, and formal market crop sales to *de jure* marital status, the holding of land title, and the presence of a male household head or guarantor....

Networks of Female-headed Households

Women's networks are emerging in areas in which male outmigration has been particularly severe, and the percentage of households headed by women is as high as 60 or 70 percent'....

These households, taken as corporate production units, are not necessarily poor. Individually, each appears to be marginalized, but together, they can spread costs, pool savings, and diversify enterprises without the risks and uncertainties of dependence on menfolk.

THE INFORMAL ECONOMY

The informal economy in African usage denotes all those activities not protected, financed, licensed, or run by ministries of state and their parastatal or quasi-autonomous agencies. Informal sector activities range from self-employment and petty enterprise to wholesaling, export trading, and sizeable financial operations. Many of these activities are illegal or untaxed, operate wholly or in part outside the money economy through barter and exchange, and make unsanctioned use of public or licensed private sector resources. . . .

Most of these activities go unrecorded. Yet, female entrepreneurship is concentrated in these areas.

. . . The many difficulties women entrepreneurs experience are: . . .

[Male] Interference, [Competing] Domestic Expenditures, and Fragmentation [of Profits]

These three problems are closely linked to women's multiple roles as women. Because women as wives and daughters stand in a subordinate position to men, it can be hard for them to prevent their menfolk from appropriating cash or taking management decisions as a condition of acting as a loan guarantor, or to discipline male employees, or to refuse to submit to sexual harassment. Many women thus choose group organization and management of an enterprise as a protection against male interference and manipulation.

Domestic expenditures are more often under women's individual control but because of women's feelings of responsibility toward the family and the domestic environment, it can be hard for them to keep separate the money required to operate an enterprise and domestic finance.

Lack of Infrastructure

The lack of infrastructure along entire production and marketing chains is a particular handicap to women who are trying to develop small agroindustries. . . .

Competition with State Enterprises

Many of the enterprises run or licensed by the state are competitive with women's enterprises in the parallel economy. In many countries, governments have . . . large vested interests in industrial beer brewing. The natural evolution of women's local brewing into a larger-scale, higher-profit industry has been preempted.

Credit and Financial Services

By far the largest part of women's economic activity is financed by informal savings, banking, and credit services. . . . However, such services hardly exist in some areas and in others have limited development potential. Several factors work as constraints: a slow buildup of investment capital and poor mobilization of working capital; the need to keep funds relatively liquid to recycle among members; and the limited range of profitable investment opportunities. At the same time, formal services in banking and farm credit have shown little interest in making their services accessible and attractive to women.[5]

Competition with Other Women

The concentration of women within particular sectors, and their weak access to male-dominated sources of inputs and services, forces women to rely on each other and, at the same time, to compete with each other. On the one hand, older wives, sisters, grandmothers are typical sources of start-up capital, skills training, information, and contacts. Women's savings groups, banking and credit organizations, trade associations, and producer groups provide the social and corporate strength to enter and maintain business activity. On the other hand, market conditions encourage competition between women in the same activity. . . .

BREAKING THE BARRIERS

. . . [Ways of] helping women strengthen their position in the labor process, within households, and as independent wage and income earners are:

[Improving the Infrastructure]

Expanding women's access to land, credit, and services in areas of poverty seems to do little to improve women's capacity to earn income unless additional measures are taken to augment the productivity of the resource base. Particularly useful [are] improving land quality, energy use, and water availability; developing alternative social support structures; and strengthening transport and construction capacities.[6] . . .

Expanding Income From Food Production Through Land Redistribution and Provision of Services

. . . Expanding income opportunity through land redistribution and provision of services is based on the assumption that existing gender divisions of labor and responsibility will continue with women maintaining a primary role in food production and income earning. . . . Changes in women's legal status would help women gain access to the factors of production.

Strengthening Women's Negotiating Power in the Labor Market

Given continued male control of women's labor through household relations, support to strengthen women's negotiating power at policy levels and within alternative rural labor markets might be a more powerful strategy for improving women's position within emergent labor processes. One way to do this is to expand their income-earning opportunities through the organization of group-to-group production and sales.[7] The concomitant strengthening of leadership, social skills, and access to information are additional gains. However, the costs of organizational membership may prove too high for the poorest rural women.[8] Another strategy is to develop advocacy skills among women and to encourage women's participation in [advocacy] groups.

Enhancing Women's Labor Productivity

Three areas seem to have a high payoff. One is to increase the opportunities for girls' schooling and professional training of women in agriculture and enterprise management.[9] Another is to develop

drudgery-reducing machinery such as cassava peelers and grain mills.[10] . . . The third way is to provide services and facilities that support women's management of pregnancy and child care.

Linking Women's Enterprises to the Formal Sector

. . . An increasing number of successful strategies widen rural women's access to formal sector resources and services. Women's World Banking, for instance, is helping to develop affiliate institutions in 13 sub-Saharan African countries, which provide loan guarantee funding for women's credit within commercial and development banks.

Concentrating on Informal Sector Activities

Considerable scope exists for expanding enterprises in the informal sector. One disadvantage is that the most successful businesses will tend either to run into competition with state or licensed enterprises or to stimulate duplicate economic structures which might prove wasteful. Another difficulty is that the most worthwhile interventions are often hard to identify from a donor office. A larger debate [concerns] the extent to which informal activity is robust enough to withstand recession in the public and formal sectors.

CONCLUSION

Support for rural women's income-earning activities and capacities is essential to check further deterioration in the welfare, economic viability, and food security of rural households and to build market demand in rural areas. Any such support will require sensitivity to complex environmental and legal issues, a sustained capacity and willingness to assist and to respond to local initiative, and a sharp eye for what is strategically opportune and practically possible.

NOTES

1. Huss-Ashmore in Jiggins (1982), pp. 147–160.
2. Ghai and Smith in Mellor, Delgado and Blackie (1987), pp. 278–289.
3. Armstrong and Ncube (1987) and Davison (1987).
4. Kerven (1979) and Izzard (1979).
5. AFRACO/FAO (1983).
6. Carr (1984). Dankelman and Davidson (1988), Chavangi and Ngugi (1987), and Traore and Kouakou (1985).
7. Ikpi *et al.* (1986) give a detailed example for women and cassava in Nigeria. Agatha Nji, Chief of Service, Ministry of Agriculture, Yaonde, reports a growth in the organized linkage between women producer groups and urban women's marketing groups (personal communication, October 21, 1988).
8. Muzale with Leonard (1985).
9. FAO (1984d) notes that overall resource constraints are likely to restrain the achievement of targeted expansion in the majority of countries.
10. Ikpi *et al.* (1986) and Nweke *et al.* (1987).

2.6. Why Indians in Rural Bolivia Do So Badly

Jonathan Kelley

This excerpt is about a sixth cause of economic inequality: namely, the way class origins and labor markets affect wealth distribution. The author sets out to determine whether, in rural Bolivia, it makes any difference if people are of Indian or Spanish descent. In many respects, this is a lot like studies of "status attainment" carried out in the industrial world. Unlike these studies, however, it assesses the importance of achieved and ascribed statuses in a pre-industrial milieu.

It is no simple matter to distinguish among the effects on income of such closely related factors as ethnicity, class, education, and occupation; yet this is precisely what this study achieves. And, perhaps surprisingly, the study finds that Indian descent is really no disadvantage. To the extent that Indians fail in rural Bolivia, it is *not* because of their racial origin but because of their educational attainment. Indians get much *less* education because of their fathers' class background.

In this respect, the result is what we routinely find in North American studies, and this result can be stated in a number of different ways. One is that education, as a form of "human capital," makes an extremely important contribution to people's social status and income. Another is that a market economy prevents irrelevant factors, like race or ethnicity, from assuming great economic importance. Or, as the author hypothesizes, "A free labor market prevents exploitation" and erodes discrimination.

The author concludes with some speculations about the potential for exploitation. Particularly, he examines the ways in which local and national elites can control the labor market to exploit indigenous peoples or, alternately, tax prosperous independent peasants. So what begins as a conventional statistical study ends up an exercise in speculative theory-making.

Discrimination on the basis of race, religion, or ethnicity exists in many nations under diverse political systems. . . .

That subordinate ethnic groups have worse jobs and lower incomes is incontrovertible. That these differences are created by discrimination rather than the natural working of economic forces is not. . . .

The weight of evidence begins to suggest that economic differences between nationality, language, and religious groups—but probably not racial groups—are mainly due to differences in family background, education, place of residence, and language rather than discrimination. In modern societies, free markets and relatively universalistic standards of education and government seem to have eroded most discrimination.

But there is little evidence from the less-developed, mainly rural societies where most of the world's population still lives.

This paper addresses these questions with data from a society where ethnic differences loom as large as anywhere in the contemporary world: rural Bolivia. . . . The data are from a large, representative sample of male heads of household collected in 1966 as part of the Bolivia Project of the Research Institute for the Study of Man. . . .

Excerpted from Kelley, Jonathan (1988), "Class conflict or ethnic oppression? The cost of being Indian in rural Bolivia," *Rural Sociology*, 53(4), 399–420.

DATA AND METHODS

Data

The survey involved detailed ethnographic surveys of [six towns] based on anthropological field studies, each lasting seven to eleven months. The questionnaire was designed after the anthropological fieldwork was well under way. Interviewers were recruited primarily from the ethnographic field teams, and they interviewed in both Aymara and Spanish. . . .

The sample, selected from a complete house-to-house census, is confined to adult male heads of household; the completion rate was 83 percent. It is representative of the towns from which it was drawn. . . .

Measurement

Social Race. In Bolivia a clear, universally recognized distinction exists between the monolingual peasants of Indian origin who speak Amerindian languages (derogatively called *indios* before the revolution, *campesinos* now) and Spanish-speaking, Western-oriented groups. Marked differences exist in culture, dress, and diet, as well as language (McEwen 1975). An intermediate group, the *cholos*, is in transition from an Indian past to a Spanish future. These people were born Amerindian but have acquired some Spanish, along with some of the cultural, dress, and dietary characteristics of the Spanish elite.

Cholos are properly treated as being of Indian origin, since they were born to Indian parents, grew up in Indian homes, and faced the disadvantages common to Indian children. But, unlike most of their peers, they learned Spanish, succeeded in school, and entered the labor force with those advantages. Since we are concerned with the economic effects of being born Spanish or born Indian, *cholos* are properly considered Indian; treating them as a separate group would bias the results for Indians by excluding many of the most successful.

By this definition, 62 percent of the population are of Indian origin, and the rest are Spanish. Only 3 percent could not be classified.

Education. Education is measured in years of schooling.

Occupation. . . . While half of the respondents had secondary occupations, the primary occupation analyzed here is clearly central: on the average, the respondents worked 7.7 hours a day, 5.9 days a week, and 11.0 months a year at that occupation.

I developed a scheme for classifying the respondents into broad status. The 14 categories (and their status scores) are:

100: Elite white collar (doctor, clergy, school principal, etc.)
75: Large-farm operator
72: Cattle rancher
71: Higher white-collar worker (school teacher, contractor, middle-rank administrator, etc.)
66: Skilled modern blue-collar worker (mechanic, truck driver, and the like)
62: Clerical and sales
57: Small business
33: Specialized farmer (coffee or fruit planter, etc.)
31: Skilled traditional blue-collar worker (carpenter, mason, leather worker, baker, blacksmith, tinker, etc.)
31: Unskilled nonfarm (day laborer, muleteer, etc.)
12: Tenant farmer
9: Farm laborer (peon)
4: Small-farm operator
0: Small livestock owner (landless farmer, llama herder, etc.)

I measured the occupational status of each of these groups by the average standard of living of its incumbents (Kelley and Klein 1982: 62–63).

Standard of Living. . . . Using factor analytic procedures, I constructed a composite measure including characteristics of housing, servants, food consumption, and the like (Kelley and Klein 1982: 58–59). I rescored it as a cumulative percent. Thus, the poorest person gets a zero (no one is lower), someone in the middle gets 50 (half the population lives worse and half better), and the richest person gets 100 (everyone else is worse off).

Family background. The class aspects of family background are measured by the father's occupational status and the father's education. . . .

Methods

. . . The key technical problem is distinguishing differences that arise out of class background (i.e., father's education and father's occupation) from differences that arise from ethnicity. This can be done by extending the Blau-Duncan model by applying it separately to Spaniards and to Indians, using the Indian regression equations to estimate what would have happened to an Indian son born into a family with the same class background as the average Spanish son has; and comparing that (hypothetical) Indian to the actual average for Spanish sons (e.g., Duncan 1968). . . .

Class, Ethnicity, and Education

(1) Having a father with an additional year of education is worth about half a year of education for those born into Aymara-speaking homes, but fractionally less for those born to Spanish homes. For example, an Indian father with six years of primary schooling could expect his son to get about four years more education than the son of an unschooled Indian (6 X .634 = 3.8 years), whereas a Spanish father with six years of schooling could expect his son to get three years more than the son of an uneducated

Spaniard (6 X .483 = 2.9). The difference between Spaniard and Indian is not, however, statistically significant, so we have no good grounds for saying that the advantage is larger for one than the other. (2) An elite white-collar Spanish father, at the top of the occupational hierarchy with 100 status points, would give his son an advantage worth about four years of education, whereas an Indian parent at the top would give his son an advantage worth about three years. This difference is small and not statistically significant. (3) Finally, the constants in the regression education—estimating the education of a son whose father has no education and the lowest occupation (small livestock owner)—do not differ greatly either.

Although both the educational and occupational advantages of the father are thus passed on to the son in much the same way, Indian fathers have less to pass on, and this explains why their sons get less education than Spanish sons. The regression equations express this more precisely. Although the differences are small here, the procedure is worth detailing since it is used later to analyze the large differences in occupation and standard of living. Begin with sons born into Indian families: on the average they get 1.2 years of education. We use the regression equation to break that up into three components—one part due to the father's education, one part due to the father's occupational status, and a constant. These three components are calculated as follows: an Indian son gets .634 years of education for each year of his father's education, so a son whose father has average education for an Indian father, 0.4 years, will get .634 X 0.4 = 0.2 years of education from that. In addition, an Indian son gets .029 years of education for each point of his father's occupational status, so a son whose father has the average status of all Indian fathers, 13 points, will get .029 X 13 = 0.4 years of education from that. Finally, every son gets the constant, 0.61, which gives in all:

$$.634 \times 0.4 + .029 \times 13 + 0.61 = 1.2 \text{ years of education (Eq. 1)}$$

What would happen to an Indian son if his father had the same class background as the average Spanish father; that is, to what extent does class background account for differences between Indian and Spanish? We estimate this by putting the mean levels of *Spanish* fathers' occupations and educations into the Indian equation—in effect constructing a hypothetical Indian whose father had Spanish levels of education and status, but who was still subject to the Indian stratification system:

$$.634 \times 4.2 + .029 \times 43 + 0.61 = 4.5 \text{ years of education (Eq. 2)}$$

This shows that an Indian son, had he the class background typical of Spanish sons, would get 4.5 years of education. That is much more than the 1.2 years of education Indians actually get and, indeed, is exactly the same as the average for Spanish sons. Thus, differences in class background explain *all* of the difference between Aymara and Spanish levels of education.

Class, Ethnicity, and Occupation

There are important differences in how Indian and Spanish sons get their jobs. Among Indians, the father's occupational status is crucial: having a father at the top of the status hierarchy is worth 54 points, enough to get the son halfway up the hierarchy himself. In sharp contrast, having a father at the top is worth only 17 status points to Spanish sons. For them, education is crucial; each year of school is worth three status points, so a son who finished secondary school gets a job 33 points higher than an uneducated Spaniard. In stark contrast, schooling is worth only half as much for Indians.

Father's education has no appreciable direct effect for either Spaniards or Indians. This is not because it is irrelevant, but because it influences occupational status only indirectly, through the son's education. If this indirect effect is included, it is quite important for Spaniards: each year gives two status points, twice what an Indian father's education is worth. Indeed, in standardized terms, the father's education is more important than the father's occupation for Spanish sons, whereas the reverse is true for Indian sons. So in this way too, education is crucial for Spaniards but not for Indians.

In all, occupational success comes in very different ways for Indians, for whom the father's occupation is crucial, than for Spaniards, for whom education is crucial. What causes this divergence? One possibility is a dual labor market (e.g., Boeke 1942; Doeringer and Piore 1971): Spaniards enter a modern job market, in which linguistic and educational skills (i.e., human capital) dominate, whereas Indians go into business, traditional crafts, and farming, in which financial resources and land (i.e., physical capital) are crucial. Such a dual labor market can endure because the Spanish have a comparative advantage in one and the Indians in the other.

The regression analysis again provides an estimate of what would have happened *if* Indian sons had started out with the same education and family background as Spanish sons. Indian sons' occupational status would then average 38 points, far above their actual 16 points and barely 3 points lower than Spanish sons' status. Thus, differences in family background explain almost all of the wide gap between the jobs Indians and Spaniards have.

Class, Ethnicity and Standard of Living

Influences on standard of living again suggest a dual labor market. Occupation is dominant, and education virtually irrelevant in the Indian sector, while education is vital in the Spanish sector. For Indians, a man's own occupation is crucial, and his father's occupation is also important, but neither his own education nor his father's matters. For Spanish sons, occupation is also vital, though not as important as for Indians, but education is almost as important. Neither the father's occupation nor the father's education have any direct effect.

The effects of family background are mainly indirect. Men born into a well-educated, high-status family are not paid more because of that per se, but because it helps them indirectly by getting them more education and better jobs. When we count these indirect effects, the dual labor market is again evident. Consistent with the emphasis on education in the Spanish labor market, a Spanish father's education has a larger effect than his occupation. And consistent with the emphasis on occupation in the Indian system, an Indian father's occupation dominates.

Although these labor markets are different, standard of living is nonetheless

TABLE 1.   Indian/Spanish differences

	Education	Occupation	Income
Gap to be explained (percent)[a] Indian versus Spanish in Bolivia	73	60	40
Percent of gap explained by class differences[b] Indian versus Spanish in Bolivia	101	88	88

Source: Head of Household Survey for Bolivia; N = 675 for Indians and 421 for Spanish.

[a] Difference between Indian and Spanish means, expressed as a percentage of the Spanish.

[b] Difference between Indian mean and actual Spanish mean, as a percentage of line 1.

determined by class, not by ethnicity. If Indians had the same family background, education, and occupation as the Spanish, the regression estimates suggest they would have a standard of living less than 3 percentiles lower than Spanish sons actually have. Thus ethnicity and other factors play a minor role, if any.

CONCLUSIONS

. . . By the 1960s, class accounted almost entirely for the vast gap between the Indians and Spanish. Most Indian sons were born into families with no education and miserable jobs; as a result, they themselves got little education, poor jobs, and lived in poverty. Most Spanish sons' families had a bit of education and modest jobs; so the sons got some education, middling jobs, and lived in modest comfort. Indian and Spanish lived in separate economic worlds, in a dual economy. For Indians, property and occupation were crucial, but education mattered little; for the Spanish, education and literacy were crucial, and property and occupation less important. But these different economic worlds were equally rewarding. The (few) Indian sons born into families with the education and occupation typical of Spanish families did just as well as Spanish sons; they got just as much education, just as good jobs, and lived just as well. This is my key result: inequality in Bolivia is basically a matter of class, not ethnicity. . . .

. . . Despite their manifest power, the Spanish elite failed to preserve their ethnic advantage because the free market erodes discrimination. Unlike a slavery or bonded labor system, peasants could seek a living elsewhere; even *hacienda* peasants could run away. The threat was that other *Spanish* employers would hire the Indians away. For example, if the traditional elite was extracting, say, 10 percent of the Indians' production, a "rebel" Spanish employer could offer to take only 5 percent. Indians then would abandon their first master for the new one, and the rebel Spaniard would get rich from his 5 percent. But then there is a clear incentive for yet another rebel to

offer to take only 2 percent. And so the logic of the market goes, until in the end Indians are keeping almost all their output. . . .

Hypothesis 1. A free labor market prevents exploitation.

Because competitive markets undermine the exploitative elite, they must prevent competition from other potential exploiters. In Bolivia, the Spanish elite had to control other Spaniards; with a third of the population Spanish, there was no shortage of poor Spaniards desperate for riches. The elite also had to keep foreign competition out and keep successful Indians from competing:

Hypothesis 2. To effectively exploit the peasantry, an elite must use a political power to prevent competition from other elites.

Strong and effective government control is required to prevent competition because potential employers have strong incentives to compete. A strong local elite can prevent competition. . . .

Hypothesis 3. Exploitation is more likely under strong, efficient governments having wide-ranging economic powers than under weak, inefficient governments having modest economic powers.

Lemma: Political modernization—the emergence of large, efficient, centralized governments—makes exploitation by local elites less likely (by undermining their power), but exploitation by national elites more likely (by increasing theirs).

By providing more attractive opportunities, economic development undermines the old elite's interest in exploiting peasants. In poor countries, jobs in business, the government bureaucracy, and even teaching pay handsomely. . . . Working at jobs like those compares . . . well with exploiting peasants. . . . So once opportunities open up outside agriculture, most elites would do better there:

Hypothesis 4. Increases in industrial productivity and the expansion of employment outside agriculture reduce the incentive for elites to exploit peasants.

In Bolivia, one of the Spanish elite's fundamental difficulties was that the Indians were subsistence farmers who produced so little that there was hardly anything to be taken from them. So the easiest way to exploit them—taxing them—was not especially profitable. Instead the Spanish, like feudal European nobles before them, had to raise productivity by setting up commercial farms that used corvée labor. By contrast, exploiting prosperous peasants by taxing them is easy. And the prosperous will not resist taxes as desperately as the impoverished since a loss of luxuries is easier to bear than a loss of necessities:

Hypothesis 5. Gains in agricultural productivity increase the incentive to exploit peasants and so make such exploitation more likely, all else equal.

Thus economic development is a two-edged sword: the usual and dominant effect is to increase productivity outside agriculture and expand the reach of the free market, both of which undermine exploitation. But development also boosts agricultural productivity and provides profitable new markets for agricultural goods. Both make exploitation more likely. . . .

Lemma: Economic development generally reduces exploitation (by increasing productivity outside agriculture and expanding the free market), but may also increase it (by making prosperous peasants a more tempting target).

REFERENCES

Blau, Peter M., and Otis Dudley Duncan
  1967 The American Occupational Structure. New York: John Wiley.
Boeke, J. H.
  1942 The Structure of Netherlands Indian Economy. New York: Institute of Pacific Relations.
Doeringer, Peter B., and Michael J. Piore
  1971 International Labor Markets and Manpower Analysis. Lexington, Mass.: Heath.
Duncan, Otis Dudley
  1968 "Inheritance of poverty or inheritance of race?" Pp. 85–110 in Daniel P. Moynihan (ed.), On Understanding Poverty. New York: Basic Books.
Kelley, Jonathan, and Herbert S. Klein
  1982 Revolution and the Rebirth of Inequality: A Theory Applied to the National Revolution in Bolivia. Berkeley, Calif.: University of California Press.
McEwen, James M.
  1975 Changing Rural Society: A Study of Communities in Bolivia. London, England: Oxford University Press.

Section Review

Discussion Questions

1. Does Jiggins have anything to say about the causes of poverty among African women that does not apply equally well to British women? To British men?
2. Are the British poor disconnected from the mainstream of British society in the same ways as Bolivian peasants are disconnected from the mainstream of their society?

3. Has economic modernization had the same effects on economic inequality in Bolivia as it has in Bangladesh? For example, has development affected Bolivian Indians the way it has affected Bangladeshi peasant women?
4. Is an increase in jobs of the kind one finds at Burger King likely to increase income inequality between men and women in the way that Blumberg describes in the Third World?
5. Given what you know about gender differences in income (from the excerpt by Blumberg), what guesses can you make about the experiences of (Indian) peasant women in Bolivia? In Bangladesh?
6. What connection can you see, if any, between the withdrawal of the state from responsibility for public welfare (described by Townsend) and the deskilling of workers by multinational employers (described by Reiter)?

Data Collections Exercises

1. What is the connection between overall income inequality in a given country (e.g., Britain) and income inequality between men and women in the same country? Or, said another way, do men and women become more equal economically as poverty becomes less common for everyone? Collect data from at least four countries that will help to answer that question.
2. Collect some evidence to show that, in Britain, prejudice has no more effect on people's economic well-being than it does in Bolivia (or another South American country).
3. Collect some evidence on the effects of automation on workers, to find out whether women (or other vulnerable groups—e.g., young people, poorly educated people, or minority people) are most likely of all workers to be replaced or "deskilled" by mechanical innovations.
4. Collect some data on the experiences of women factory workers in Third World or industrializing societies. Are these experiences (e.g., pay levels, job discrimination, sexual harassment) different from what we find in industrial countries?

Writing Exercises

1. Write a brief (500-word) essay outlining the ways in which Reiter's excerpt proves Townsend's analysis of poverty is incomplete.
2. A fictitious organization, the African Development Corporation, is thinking about encouraging Western interests like Burger King to open businesses throughout sub-Saharan Africa. Write a brief (500-word) letter to the president of that organization discussing the likely impact on women's well-being.
3. How do changes in the organization of work affect economic inequality? Answer this question in a brief (500-word) essay that draws upon the insights provided in excerpts by Blumberg and Alam.
4. One finds an increasing number of immigrants, racial minorities, and middle-aged women working in fast-food restaurants. Write a brief (500-word) essay explaining the causes and economic consequences of this increase.

SECTION 3
Responses to Economic Inequality

3.1. Development and the Elimination of Poverty

Nathan Keyfitz

This excerpt is about responses to economic inequality and, particularly, about the growth of envy during the course of economic development.

Many believe that economic development will *reduce* economic inequality, both within countries and between countries of the world. However, paradoxically, the next excerpt suggests that economic inequality shapes the direction of economic development and may end up creating even more inequality. In large part, the problem is envy.

For example, Brazil, with its high per capita income, could easily provide adequate food and clothing, basic medical care, and literacy to its inhabitants. Yet a majority of Brazilians lack these amenities altogether, while a minority have them, and much more.

Perhaps this is because development programs tend to spread a culture of consumerism, not economic equality. Consumerism is a way of life exported from America and Europe to the rest of the world. It generates a desire for centrally heated and cooled homes, televisions and refrigerators, food purchased at self-service supermarkets, and cars among other things: in short, a desire for middle-class city living

People aspire to a level of consumption they read about in magazines and newspapers, see on TV and in movies. But this level exceeds the capacity of their national economy. Only a minority can benefit from development programs that aim to provide these things. Since the budget is limited, money spent on the urban middle class is money *not* spent on the rural poor. It follows that an expanding middle class will necessarily create more poverty.

It might be possible to reduce the number of poor by approaching the middle-class standard gradually, bringing along all members of a society. However, people in poor countries who obtain some part of the middle-class lifestyle want the rest quickly. They are not prepared to wait until all of their fellow citizens catch up.

The result is an unequal pattern of development. Remember that middle-class people control the levers of power in nearly every society. They are the people who shape the policies that make cities grow and rural areas dwindle. More money spent on subways to transport city people means less money spent on irrigation schemes to improve agriculture, employ the rural poor, and feed everyone.

So villagers stream out of the countryside. They crowd into densely packed shantytowns, often worse off than they were before. Nearby, in plain view, the middle-class lifestyle flourishes. For most migrants, it will remain beyond their grasp.

. . . The influence of the middle class in determining the course of development is strong even in those countries in which there is full democracy and in which the peasants are by far the largest part of the electorate. The middle class has access to education and can understand the issues, is aware of its interests and able to act politically to further them. Schooling and influence enable it to pass its status to its young, and so it tends to be hereditary. It results from the peasantry through urbanization, in highly selective fashion. Its initial task is to break the rural landholding class; once that is accomplished its influence is decisive, for the dispersed, uneducated peasantry are no match for it. . . .

DIFFUSION OF THE MODERN CULTURE

Development may be seen as the diffusion of a certain culture and the dominance of a new class that carries that culture. This article attempts to place the economics of development in a social and cultural framework.

THE MODERN WAY OF LIFE

The middle-class style has been taught to the Third World by the United States and Europe. It consists of centrally heated and cool homes equipped with television sets and refrigerators, transport by automobile,

Excerpted from Keyfitz, Nathan (1982), "Development and the elimination of poverty," *Economic Development and Cultural Change*, 30(3), 649–670. Reprinted with permission of the University of Chicago.

and procurement of foodstuffs and other supplies in self-service supermarkets. It is found typically in cities with paved streets, the countryside between those cities being laced with a network of paved roads and another network of air transport. Literacy is essential to it, and the daily press and monthly magazines are conspicuous, along with television. The content of its media has remarkable similarity worldwide: local, national, and world politics; urban crime; and the cost of living. . . .

. . . Economists have written on one aspect of this modern conception of how to live and work, calling it the demonstration effect. People learn from films and other media to want a level of consumption that is for the moment beyond the capacity of their national productive apparatus to support. Such wishes cause premature spending and impede the saving and investment that would bring such benefits within the scope of national production and trade. But in fact the demonstration effect has not had a large impact on economics. It should be taken seriously, both in its negative aspects and positively as the motor of development.

MEASURING THE POOR AND THE MIDDLE CLASS

. . . In the United States it is easier to measure poverty and take the middle class as a residual; in other countries it is on the whole easier to measure the middle class, the minority, and take the poor as the residual.

The U.S. Department of Agriculture designed a 1961 Economy Food Plan that forms the basis for the calculation of . . . poverty income thresholds, recognizing family size, sex, and age of the family head;

number of children under 18; and farm-nonfarm residence. Annual adjustments are made on the basis of the Consumer Price Index, but the consumption levels continue to be those for the base year 1963.[1] The number of families below the poverty line in the United States was just under 40 million in the late 1950s, and had dropped to 25 million by 1977.[2] . . .

The figures, extrapolated to 1980, show 24 million poor, 196 million middle class, for a total population of 220 million. Our task is to find how this can be extended to the world.

. . . The middle class can be traced broadly through statistics of ownership of certain artifacts. An automobile is one indicator, and we have statistics of automobile ownership for 75 countries. Counting two persons per automobile, the American standard, is a first approximation.

The *United Nations Statistical Yearbook* gives 271,620,000 passenger vehicles in the world in 1976, of which 109,003,000 were in the United States. Using this ratio to bring the U.S. middle class of 196 million to a world total gives us 196 X 271,620/109,003 = 488 million. But because automobiles are less used elsewhere by people who could afford them than they are in the United States, this is a low figure. It is also low insofar as families elsewhere are larger than in the United States. A figure of 2.5 or 3 middle-class persons per vehicle would bring us closer.

Energy consumed is one indicator. The total in million tons of coal equivalent for the world in 1976 was 8,318, and for the United States it was 2,485.[3] This ratio would bring us to 656 million middle-class people in the world. Better than automobiles, but still probably too low; the American burns more energy than middle-class people elsewhere.

The problem is distribution is not the same in all countries and is difficult to measure. We note the total for the market economies of the world in 1976 at 5,426 billion, and the United States in that year at 1,695 billion.[4] The ratio used crudely gives us 627 million people above the poverty line. To it would have to be added the middle

class in nonmarket economies on the order of 150 million. (The United Nations calculates for the centrally planned a weight of 0.196 in the world economy.)[5]

On the basis of such evidence, the number of middle class in the world in 1980 might be 700–800 million. . . .

. . . A similar calculation gives 200 million for the middle class of 1950. The entry of Europe and Japan, plus some progress in the Third World, brought the total to 800 million by 1980. . . .

PRODUCTION

Being middle class is not a matter of consumption alone; certain kinds of work are middle class and other kinds are not. Office work at a salary that permits owning a car and an adequately equipped house is the ideal; if the salary does not permit buying a car, then obtaining one as a perquisite of office will do. The boundary of the middle class does not coincide with that of nonmanual workers. Wages converge so that all can aspire to middle-class style.

Middle-class workers seek to avoid the hazards of entrepreneurship. Much better is the job of senior administrator, working according to fixed rules within a framework of law, with no personal capital at stake. Next in desirability to a job in government, and paying better, is being hired by a multinational corporation.

The multinationals have access nearly everywhere partly because their kind of operation is understandable and gratifying.

The entry of such cultural preferences into the work world creates a difficulty. The kind of work people like to do, and which they get jobs doing, diverges from the kind of work that produces the goods on which collectively they want to spend their salaries. The government employee may be engaged in the collection of taxes, or the organization of cooperatives, or the country's foreign policy. These activities make little contribution to producing the groceries he seeks to buy at the supermarket or the plumbing fixtures for his new house. . . .

RELIEF OF POVERTY VERSUS
A NEW CULTURE

. . . Growth in the form of an expanding middle class is consistent with an increasing number of poor. Of course the middle-class way by itself is relief of poverty for some. Yet this relief of poverty seems incidental. For if adequate food and clothing, basic medical services, and literacy were the main objectives of development it would go on in a very different way from that now pursued. Brazil's national income per capita of $1,400 could provide these amenities for every one of its inhabitants. Yet in fact the majority of its inhabitants lack these altogether, while others have them and much more. After 30 years of formal development effort in 75 countries we can infer the objective of the process from actual observation. As much as anything it is the diffusion of the artifacts that support a certain way of life, and in a poor country only a minority can benefit.

While the particular culture of the middle class belongs to the second half of the twentieth century, the idea of an urban industrial group with incomes far higher than their rural contemporaries goes back much farther. Adam Smith saw development as taking place in the measure in which material capital accumulated in cities. With each increment of city capital some jobs would be created. A new factory or mill could offer wages high enough to attract people from the countryside. Until the call to city employment came, the peasant would remain in his ancestral village. . . .

INCENTIVES TO RURAL-URBAN
MIGRATION

. . . Whatever expands city facilities, or lowers the price of foodstuffs, increases the size of the city. We can even suggest a positive feedback that results from legislation and administrative action. The price of rice is, in many countries, fixed well below the world market, and a law requires peasants to deliver part of their crop at this price. Officials go into the countryside to execute the procurement. The unpleasantness and actual loss contribute to causing some . . . peasants to leave and go to the city. That increases the need for foodstuffs in the city, so the procurement activity is intensified.

One might think there would be an equilibrium point in migration. When enough have left, the living should be equal to what migrants could get by going to the city, and at that point migration should stop. One reason it does not, as Alfred Marshall pointed out (quoted by Lipton), is that there is selection on who comes to the city; on the whole those who come are better educated, and have more initiative.[6] Thus their departure does not make things better but worse.

. . . We can imagine policies that would discourage internal migration. For one, taxes to provide urban services could be levied on urban real estate rather than coming out of the national budget. Inputs to agriculture could be subsidized. . . . An effect similar to subsidies would be obtained by better prices for farm outputs. . . .

. . . The elite cannot make the city better for themselves without making it better for the newcomers, and so encouraging further newcomers. They could forcibly prevent migration, or expel existing migrants, and this has been tried in Moscow, Jakarta, and elsewhere, but by and large has not been successful.

The masses in the capital city are physically close enough to the government to communicate their wishes, as those of Cairo did 2 years ago when they forced the government to cancel its increase of food prices. Such an increase would have helped the peasant and discouraged migration, but the political forces did not permit it. In the same way . . . Governments cannot always resist the reasonable demands of the protected segment of the labor force for decent places to live. Government often builds houses with funds that could have gone to rural investment.

Local transport within the city is often government run. The costs of the buses it imports, and the fares it charges, are public matters, and very much the business of administrators and legislators. They do not always set the fares high enough for even their low-cost imported buses, and when the bus operations make a loss it is covered from general revenues, which means in some part from the rural sector.

Other public utilities run by government at a loss even more clearly favor the middle class. Electricity is largely used by them. The view has been that industry needs protection more than agriculture, that manufactured exports are better than farm exports, that agriculture's decreasing returns justify removing resources to help industries giving increasing returns.

The need for food supplies to permit the town people to engage in manufacturing was accepted by all the classics: thus Smith says, ". . . it is the surplus produce of the country only, or what is over and above the maintenance of the cultivators, that constitutes the subsistence of the town, which can therefore increase only with the increase of the surplus produce."[7]

Holding the price of grain down is not the way to increase the supply. Investment in agriculture is called for. Szcaepanik shows that the gross marginal capital/output ratios for 1960–65 are much higher for nonagricultural than for agricultural investment.

On the whole the capital required to produce a given amount of income is more than double in industry what it is in agriculture.

Some of these points are now being recognized, and efforts are being made on behalf of agricultural output. The Mexican government is investing in modernization and stressing the use of machinery. The man with the bullock is to be replaced by a tractor operator, with backing by soil chemists, agronomists, irrigation specialists, and bankers ready to advance rural credit. All this will indeed provide employment, but for specialists and not for the masses in the countryside. Indeed, it could accelerate the move to the city.

Here much depends on the patterns of consumption and residence of the new classes in the rural areas. If the tractor operator and the soil chemist live in the city and commute to the rural area, or if they live in the village but use their new incomes on city goods, then unemployment in the countryside will be greater than ever, and cityward migration will continue and even accelerate. . . .

In few fields does the middle-class urban bias reveal itself as clearly as in education. Most schools above the primary level are in cities, and the ordinary peasant's children stand little chance of attending. The disparity in numbers of secondary schools between rural and urban areas is matched by some disparity in the quality of instruction. Moreover, the primary schools that are now attended at least long enough for most peasant children to learn to read and write, have little to do with peasant life. Rather than being planned to make better farmers, they serve as a selection device, by which ability is discovered and sent to secondary school, usually in the city. . . .

EXPLANATION RATHER THAN POLICY GUIDANCE

. . . The present paper stands back from development and refrains from offering policy advice, at the same time that it tries to look at it from [the] point of view of the citizen undergoing the process. The citizen of poor countries sees development as the advent of goods that make possible a modern style of life. The goods are above all symbols that one has attained a certain status.

This wish for middle-class status is an engine of development—it can induce acceptance of the hard work and abstinence that development requires. Yet it is not a readily manipulated policy variable, like a tariff or the rate of interest. The object of this paper is not to reveal some easy way by which development can be brought about but to make it look as difficult on paper as it is in reality. I have tried to show why excellent policy advice is disregarded. Thus, reaching for middle-class status is an explanatory rather than a policy variable. It tells us why government has grown, why cities have expanded, why poor countries aim to produce automobiles rather than bicycles, why the import of consumption goods is everywhere so large an element in the balance of payments. . . .

Within each of the poor countries is an expanding middle-class enclave. We need to observe more closely the social mechanisms that cause the spread of the middle class to take precedence over the alleviation of poverty.

NOTES

1. U.S. Bureau of the Census, *Statistical Abstract* (Washington, D.C.: Government Printing Office, 1978), p. 438.
2. Ibid., p. 465.
3. United Nations, *United Nations Statistical Handbook* (New York: United Nations Department of International Economic and Social Affairs, 1978), p. 389.
4. Ibid., p. 748.
5. Ibid., p. 10.
6. Michael Lipton, *Why Poor People Stay Poor: Urban Bias in World Development* (Cambridge, Mass.: Harvard University Press, 1977), p. 376.
7. Lipton, p. 94.

3.2. Winning Sweden's War on Poverty

Sydney Zimbalist

This excerpt is about a second response to economic inequality: progressive policy-making. In particular, this excerpt is about the Swedish strategy for fighting poverty.

This excerpt holds that the Swedes have succeeded in dealing with basic human needs where American society has failed. Unlike the United States, Sweden has a minimal number of poor, no large urban slums, low unemployment, relatively high and equitable survival chances for all levels of the population, and so on.

Sounds too good to be true? Well, there are some costs, to be sure. First and most obvious, the taxation level in Sweden is about twice what it is in the United States. This should come as no surprise: you can't help the poor without taking something away from people who are not poor. Taxation redistributes national wealth: the less you tax, the less you can do for the poor.

Another cost, much in the spotlight today, is the creation of a deficit. The social programs of Sweden certainly contributed to the creation of a deficit. On the other hand, today the United States has an even more impressive deficit than Sweden's *without* having helped the poor nearly as much. Thus, if deficits are inevitable, even if only in the short run, at least they should be helping someone.

Perhaps worst of all, Sweden has been helping the poor in a relatively quiet and undogmatic way. In the United States, the poor are helped less but *probably hated more. Political rhetoric dramatizes poverty without helping us understand it or reduce it. As hatred and fear of the poor increases, the middle-class becomes ever less likely to give in (willingly) to demands for higher taxes and more generous programs.*

With much fanfare, President Johnson committed the United States to the eradication of poverty in the mid-1960s. By the 1980s, the war on poverty had deteriorated into President Reagan's "war on the poor." In 1984, there were a half million more Americans below the official poverty line than in 1965, despite a slight improvement over the previous year.[1] The reasons for this failure are too familiar to require restatement. Suffice it to say that despite all its wealth and power, the United States has been unable—or unwilling—to make lasting headway toward this historic challenge.

During the same period, Sweden, another Western democracy, has been making continuing progress in its conquest of poverty, probably reducing it to the minimum that has been achieved anywhere else in the world. In effect, Sweden has largely accomplished what was proclaimed in the United States to be its highest social priority two decades ago.

How did these opposite results come about? What does Sweden "know" about fighting and overcoming indigency—and, as we shall see, unemployment, slums, infant deaths, and so on—that we don't? At what costs are such social gains made? A recent sabbatical stay in Stockholm provided the author with clues and materials bearing upon these vital questions for American observers. That it is possible for a society to lift itself above many of the social problems that afflict this country gives some ground

Excerpted from Zimbalist, Sydney E. (1988). "Winning the war on poverty: The Swedish strategy," *Social Work*, January-February, 46–49. Copyright 1988, National Association of Social Workers, Inc.

for hope, a commodity that is hard to come by in face of the persisting material needs of millions of Americans.

THE SWEDISH SUCCESS

Poverty

Social progress in Sweden in recent decades is impressive. In 1976, an authoritative comparative analysis that employed a standardized relative measure of poverty yielded an estimate of 13.0 percent of the United States population below the poverty level (as compared with 11.9 percent, according to the "official" United States poverty line). For Sweden, the same measure yielded a poverty rate of 3.5 percent.[2] Only one of the eight Western nations in the comparative analysis came out with a poverty proportion similar to Sweden's, namely, West Germany with 3.0 percent. According to the relative measure used, the poverty yardstick for a three-person family was set equal to the average per capita income for the given country. In other words, if a three-person family received a household income below the mean income per inhabitant of that nation, the household was considered as "poor." Poverty levels for other sizes of households were adjusted upward or downward according to the number of household members. Based on this approach, 3 percent was the minimum in the mid-1970s among the eight industrialized Western countries. By way of contrast, only one of the nations was measured to have a higher poverty level than the United States: France, with 16 percent.

More recently, a study with a somewhat different definition of relative poverty and an overlapping, but not identical, group of countries, pegged the United States at 16.0 percent in poverty in 1980. The measure was the highest proportion among the seven nations included in the study. Sweden again was in the lowest bracket with 5.0 percent. This time Norway was slightly lower, with 4.8 percent.[3] In both studies, the Swedish poverty percentage was less than one-third that of the percentage in the United States, and in the bottom group of countries studied. Because Sweden was the only country in both comparisons that was in the lowest pair of countries, it may be argued that overall it came out below the rest. The United States, in contrast, was the highest in one study and second highest in the other. Clearly, a much better performance record than ours is feasible for a modern affluent society.

What of homelessness and hunger? Unofficial estimates in Stockholm place the total number of homeless at around 100, out of a total metropolitan area population of some 1 1/2 million. The homeless are for the most part alcoholics, drug addicts, and mentally ill who are not accessible to rehabilitation despite the extensive service resources of the Swedish welfare state. A few alcoholics may be seen at times in the vicinity of the main subway stations, presumably attracted by the underground shelter available there. An occasional beggar–musician will be encountered in the downtown area playing for coins. One or two homeless women frequent the center of the city looking for scraps or handouts. And there is some prostitution, related at least in part to drug addiction. In sum, these people apparently form the hardcore casualties of urbanization, whom even the efficient Swedish social services have been unable to salvage, though the numbers are small.

Slums and Housing

It is difficult to make objective comparisons of housing conditions on a cross-national basis; therefore, my observations are necessarily brief and impressionistic but hopefully

of some value nonetheless. One of my self-assigned projects was to locate the worst slums of Stockholm, Sweden's largest city and its capital. Repeated inquiries were made, both of officials and of private residents, and many excursions were taken, both on foot and by public transportation, to the lowest income neighborhoods and older parts of the metropolitan area. By consensus of our various informants, the Alby and Tensta neighborhoods were identified as the location of the poorest families with a high proportion of recent immigrants to the country and a high rate of dependency on Social Assistance—the Swedish counterpart of our public assistance programs. The two districts are the site of large-scale, multiple-unit apartment complexes, one of them inside the city limits and one outside. They correspond roughly to what would be considered in this country as public housing projects. A persistent search through the housing developments, and through older neighborhoods in other parts of Stockholm, failed to turn up much deteriorated housing anywhere. There was an occasional dilapidated structure or town to be seen, but none of the American urban phenomenon of blocks and blocks of razed, abandoned, or ramshackle housing. The infrequent spots of physical blight apparently were not permitted to spread and take over entire streets and neighborhoods. There was nowhere to be found the bleak expanses of extended wastelands such as in the slums of urban America.

Health Conditions

Life expectancy and infant mortality are common indicators of the general health of a population. Here, too, Sweden is in the forefront of international standing. Average length of life is 76 years, as compared with 74 years in the United States. In 1983, infant deaths were at an international record low of 7.0 per 1,000 live births versus 11.2 per 1,000 in the United States.[4] Equally significant is the fact that wide variations in infant mortality in the United States between different income groups and between racial and ethnic groups have been largely eliminated in Sweden. Moreover, for many years now the preexisting linkage between out-of-wedlock births and high infant death rate has been broken, contrary to their persistent close association in the United States.[5] Thus, life expectancy has been largely equalized at a high level by Western standards.

Unemployment and the Labor Force

An unemployment rate appreciably above 2 percent historically has been considered too high in Sweden, and a great public investment—amounting to as much as 3 percent of Gross Domestic Product—is made in programs to make jobs available for all who wish to work.[6] Job training, job placement, job subsidies, job security, and job creation through public and private channels are national priorities, particularly in periods of economic slack. As a result, Sweden has maintained an unusually low level of unemployment in recent decades, averaging considerably less than half the rate in the United States.[7] And Sweden does not resort to the foreign "guest workers" utilized by some other West European nations to cushion their economic cycles. In the recession in 1983, unemployment was up to 9.5 percent in the United States, compared with 3.5 percent in Sweden. By 1984, the postrecession level had fallen to 7.4 percent and 3.1 percent, respectively.

An aggressive labor-force policy, supported by strong and politically active unions in Sweden, has made it possible for exceptionally high proportions of the working-age population to find employment. In 1982, comparison of the Swedish and U.S. male labor forces was 86 versus 84 percent and 76 versus 61 percent for the female labor force. The greater edge in female employment follows through for married women, for mothers of small children, and for female heads-of-households.[8] In the later case, the implications for self-support of a

major risk population in terms of welfare dependency are obvious.

An additional outcome, perhaps not unrelated, is the surprisingly high ranking of Sweden in standard-of-living as measured by gross per capita income. Over the past few years for which data are given in the 1985 U.S. Statistical Abstract (from 1975 through 1982) Sweden has ranked second of 61 countries reported, behind Switzerland but just ahead of the third-ranked United States.[9] So much for the alleged deleterious effect of a relatively generous and comprehensive welfare state on work motivation and economic productivity.

THE WINNING STRATEGY

Sweden is by no means a perfect or near-perfect society. But, as we have seen, on a number of indices this late-comer among the industrialized nations has reduced to a virtual minimum many historical social plagues that still beset the United States and other Western countries. And Sweden has been successful with the help of an advanced welfare state that apparently has not impaired labor force activity, economic productivity, or per-capita income. In fact, these measures have attained near-record levels.

What is their "secret weapon" that we have yet failed to discover? How did they manage practically to wipe out poverty, while we remain mired in the mud-trench conditions of the 1960s? There is to be sure no single answer to these questions. Many distinctive features of American and Swedish circumstances and history are obviously involved. Separate treatises might well be devoted to such differences—cultural, demographic, economic, geographic, and political—and indeed have been. At any rate, of the contributing features may be found in the contrasting social policy strategies adopted in the post-World War II period in Sweden and the United States. In Sweden, public social benefits were made available on an increasingly universal—that is, not means-tested—basis, whereas in the United States more and more emphasis was placed on rigorous means-testing of welfare programs. For example, Social Assistance in Sweden accounted for 16 percent of public social expenditures in 1945; by the 1970s this proportion had dwindled to between 1 and 2 percent.[10] In the United States, public aid—a broad means-tested classification that includes public assistance, food stamps, Medicaid, and closely related services—rose from 7 percent of public social spending in 1960 to 21 percent in 1981, a threefold proportionate increase in two decades.[11]

The significance of these dramatically opposed trends for our discussion here may lie in the fact that a large and growing proportion of social benefits in Sweden has been allocated to the poor as well as to the nonpoor, whereas in the United States, a declining proportion has been so distributed in an attempt to "economize" by selective targeting of the most needy. As a plausible political consequence, however, Swedish public support for broad social programs has been strong, while the dwindling American constituency for social benefits aimed at the destitute paved the way for the "welfare backlash" with which we are well familiar.[12] One key, therefore, to the contrasting experiences in the two countries may well lie in a divergence in social policies two decades ago. In Sweden, social policies turned more universal; in the United States, more means-tested. This parting of the ways seems to have contributed to the sharply different attitudes toward welfare-state programs. For example, basic pensions for the elderly, general child allowances for all children, "advance payment" of child-support for mothers by the government, housing allowances for many families with children, sickness benefits for all workers, free education through college, almost-free medical care and part-free dental services are some of the social utilities that appear to have helped "sell" the Swedes on their welfare state. The foregoing benefits, it should be noted, are either not available at all in the United States, or only to a fraction of the popula-

tion. Thus, the scales of public support for benefits may have been tipped in opposite directions in Sweden compared with the United States.

COSTS

What is it worth to a society to have a minimal number of poor, no large urban slums, low unemployment, relatively high and equitable survival chances for all levels of the population, and so on? There is no calculus for such values other than the political process. The Swedes have for the past several decades opted to "pay the bill." They consistently have supported and elected governments that have maintained and strengthened their welfare state. Even the two terms of conservative coalition government from 1976–82 witnessed no slowdown in growth of social programs—indeed, quite the reverse. All political parties in Sweden have apparently found it to their advantage to support these popular priorities. In the last election (September 1985) the late Olaf Palme led the Social Democrats to another term in office, with a campaign pledge to boost the position of pensioners and children.

But such values come dearly. To support them, Swedes pay overall tax revenues, both direct and indirect, that are almost twice the burden borne by Americans—in 1982 a total of 60 percent of Gross Domestic Product as compared with 32 percent here. Personal income tax rates reach a high of 80 percent in the upper income brackets, rather than the new 38.5-percent ceiling in the United States for 1987. And a value-added tax amounting to an indirect national sales tax comes to 23.6 percent on top of the price of most goods. Such sacrificial tax burdens are widely resented, deplored, and evaded where possible (as are the much lower American taxes here), but obviously the Swedes have been willing to put up with this albatross for the advantages received.

Another means by which Sweden has been making ends meet is not so heroic. The national budget had been balanced until 1978, when the combination of international economic slowdown, stagflation, and governmental obligations led to a growing deficit, which peaked at 13 percent of the Gross Domestic Products in 1982–83. Since then the budget shortfall was reduced to 10 percent in 1983–84 and is projected at 7 percent for 1985–86.[13] This recent reduction in national deficit is being achieved through a combination of an improving economy, adjustment of exchange rates, limitation of demands by unions, and so on. Clearly, however, there are fiscal hazards as well as dividends associated with large governmental commitments. The United States, too, as we well know, has been running substantial deficits (approaching 6 percent of Gross National Product) despite its considerably smaller public sector overall.

Another liability that should be mentioned is the fact that inflation has been higher in Sweden in the past few years, about twice the rate in the United States. In 1984, for example, the increase in consumer prices in Sweden was 8.0 percent, and 4.3 percent here. Urgent efforts are underway to lower inflation through wage and price restraints, devaluation of the Swedish kronor, and other measures.[14]

Steadily and quietly, without much flourish or self-congratulation, Sweden has been overcoming poverty as well as other (but by no means all) social ills. Despite near-record total government spending, public social expenditures, and correspondingly high tax burdens, there does not seem to have been any diminution of the Swedish standard of living, economic productivity, or work ethnic.

In contrast, the United States found itself with more officially poor in 1984 than in 1965. Some of the resulting differences in quality of life, and some of the means by which Sweden has been able to succeed where America has failed have been discussed. Notably, the social policy strategy of providing a wide array of generally universal social benefits, available to broad segments of the population, might have

assisted in gaining majority public support for maintaining welfare-state programs. The opposite strategy in the United States has been accompanied by increasing political resistance to social spending. In particular, the growing emphasis here on rigorous means-tested benefits targeted on the "truly needy" may have in effect set up the poor for political isolation and backlash.

Of course, this is not the only possible factor influencing the contrasting welfare attitudes and outcomes in the two nations. Nor is the implication intended that Sweden is a trouble-free society, either socially or economically, as we have noted. But the message is clear from the Swedish experience, namely, that there are democratic alternatives to the dismal record of the United States in dealing with basic human needs.

NOTES

1. U.S. Department of Commerce, Bureau of the Census, *Current Population Reports*, Series P-60, No. 149 (Washington, D.C.: U.S. Government Printing Office, 1985), table 15, p. 21.
2. Organisation for Economic Co-operation and Development, *Public Expenditure on Income Maintenance Programs* (Paris: Organisation for Economic Co-operation and Development, 1976).
3. P. Hedstrom and S. Ringen, "Age and Income in Contemporary Society: A Seven Nation Study" (Stockholm: Swedish Institute for Social Research, 1985), table 9, p. 25. (Mimeographed draft report for the Luxembourg Income Study.)
4. Nordic Council, *Level of Living and Inequality in the Nordic Countries* (Stockholm, Sweden: The Nordic Council, 1984), p. 31.
5. W. Korpi, "Poverty, Social Assistance, and Social Policy in Post-War Sweden," *Acta Sociologica*, 18 (1975), p. 135.
6. R. Taylor, "The Best of a Bad Job Situation," *Sweden Now*, 19 (February 1985), p. 23.
7. U.S. Department of Commerce, Bureau of the Census, *Statistical Abstract of the United States: 1985* (Washington, D.C.: U.S.

Government Printing Office, 1984), table
1494, p. 852.

8. A. J. Kahn and S. B. Kamerman, *Income
Transfers for Families with Children: An Eight
Country Study* (Philadelphia: Temple
University Press, 1983), table 21, p. 59.

9. U.S. Department of Commerce, Bureau of
the Census, *Statistical Abstract of the United
States: 1985*, table 1481, p. 846.

10. Korpi, "Poverty, Social Assistance, and Social
Policy in Post-War Sweden," p. 121.

11. U.S. Department of Commerce, Bureau of
the Census, *Statistical Abstract of the United
States: 1985*, table 589, p. 354.

12. W. Korpi, "Approaches to the Study of
Poverty in the United States: Critical Notes

from a European Perspective," in V. T.
Covello, ed., *Poverty Research and Public
Policy* (Boston: G. K. Hall and Co., 1980), pp.
301–305.

13. Organisation for Economic Co-operation and
Development, *Sweden* (Paris: Organisation
for Economic Co-operation and Development, 1985). Economic Surveys 1984/1985,
p. 37.

14. *For an elaboration of the economic aspects of
Swedish welfare trends compared with those in
the United States, see* S. Zimbalist, "A Welfare
State Against the Economic Current: Sweden
and the United States as Contrasting Cases,"
International Social Work, 30 (January 1987),
pp. 15–30.

3.3. Women's Working Lives in China, Japan, and Great Britain

Sheng Xuewen, Norman Stockman, and Norman Bonney

This excerpt is about a third response to economic inequality: a doubled burden on working women in three societies.

Virtually every culture still views housework as primarily the woman's responsibility and as we have seen, this seriously limits women's opportunities outside the home. But the lives of working women in different societies can vary quite a lot. This is evident in this excerpt by Xuewen, Stockman, and Bonney, which compares data from surveys in Japan, Great Britain, and urban China. They examine the degree to which housework is shared between spouses and the attitudes of women to their position in the work force and the home. All of their respondents were employed married mothers with young children.

The results show sharp differences between the three countries in disabling attitudes for women and burdens on time from housework. As Kato shows in excerpt 4.5, Japanese women have low status in their society. Kato contends they are not without power at home, but the Japanese portion of this comparative study seems to reject that view. It shows Japanese women are socially isolated and largely restricted to doing housework. Upon marriage, they are expected to quit their jobs and assume the role of housewife. Gender roles in the household are very clearly defined. With few exceptions, husbands do little or no housework.

Compared to Japan, China is a paragon of gender equality. Women's wages are identical to men's or very close. Families in which only the husband works are the exception rather than the rule. To some extent, this reflects the economic need for two fulltime incomes. It is also a partial fulfillment of the promised equality of the sexes under communism.

To achieve this equality, the state provides extensive social support in the form of daycare services. As well, Chinese women are under no pressure from the prevailing ideology to quit their jobs when they become pregnant, and maternity leave is extremely fair. Work for women is legitimized. In general, women interrupt their work lives only briefly to have children. Three quarters return to work within six months after the birth of a child.

The results from a comparable British survey resemble the Japanese findings more than they do the Chinese. That is to say, British women accept the role of housewife almost as readily as their Japanese counterparts. Unlike Japanese wives, however, they handle the dual responsibilities of housewife and income earner by taking on parttime work. They also lower their expectations when they reenter the work force after childbearing, and recognize they are likely to have a job, not a career.

. . . Modern societies are confronted with structural dilemmas as to how to allocate labour between the conflicting priorities of production in manufacturing and service industries in the public sphere and production and reproduction in the private domestic sphere. Political processes at the level of the state influence the institutional solutions which are evolved to determine the allocation of labour between these spheres. At the micro-level individuals, couples, families, communities and individual enterprises are confronted with similar dilemmas. In particular, and related to the interests of this paper, parents of young children are faced with how to allocate their time and labour between parental, domestic and employment responsibilities. . . . This paper [examines] three societies which have adopted different responses to these dilemmas.

Excerpted from Xuewen, Sheng, Norman Stockman, and Norman Bonney (1992), "The dual burden: East and west (women's working lives in China, Japan, and Great Britain), *International Sociology*, 7, 2, 209–223.

METHODOLOGY

The findings reported below draw from data collected by sample surveys in China, Japan and Great Britain. The respondents in the three samples were all employed married mothers of pre-school and school-age children. The Chinese and Japanese surveys used a common methodology, involving the administration of a self-completed questionnaire to mothers of children attending workplace nurseries, kindergartens and child-care centres, in Beijing, Shanghai and Xian in China and a sample of urban areas in Japan in 1987. There were 2,072 respondents in China and 1,865 in Japan.

. . . The British data are taken from interviews with 1,000 respondents in each of six medium-sized British urban labour markets in 1986 and 1987. The data reported in this paper derive from a sub-sample of respondents who were female, married, employed and who had children of school or pre-school age. The data derive from 466 such women interviewed in 1986 and the 246 re-interviewed in 1987.

CHINA: THE DUAL BURDEN

In urban China a 48-hour six-day working week is the norm for both mothers and fathers of young children. Eighty-two per cent of the respondents and 83 per cent of their husbands have such working hours. Women's working careers exhibit only brief interruptions following childbirth. Eighty-four per cent of the sample had held jobs continuously since they left school and almost three-quarters had returned to paid work within six months of the birth of the child. When asked for their reasons for working, Chinese women were most likely to mention financial necessity.

Chinese women's employment patterns are much closer to men's than they are in the other samples. There is, for instance, no gender difference in the time of travel to and from work in China. Almost all of the female Chinese sample has regular worker status rather than being temporary workers or engaged in family enterprise. Their average income is much closer to their spouses' than is the case in Britain or Japan. Educational differences are also far less marked.

Chinese women in the urban labour force are not under pressure when married or pregnant to sever their employment. Indeed the situation is the reverse. Enterprises are currently extending the statutory 56-day maternity leave by up to six months, during which time the female worker qualifies for full pay. Further leave can be obtained for up to two years, but with 75 per cent of the pay in the first year and 50 per cent in the second. Mothers retain their employment position throughout this period, but may lose seniority rights. There are extensive child-care facilities for pre-school children. A further factor minimising the effects of maternity on employment is the one-child policy which has been very effective in urban areas.

Chinese women exhibit slightly more dissatisfaction with their working life than do their Japanese peers, and are much more likely to consider there to be unreasonable differences between women and men in their employment. 50.5 per cent of Chinese respondents, compared to 15.7 per cent of Japanese respondents indicated affirmative responses to the question: 'Are there any unreasonable differences between men and women at your workplace?' The most frequently cited 'unreasonable difference' amongst the Chinese sample was 'few opportunities to receive training' (29.7 per cent compared to 9.9 per cent among the Japanese sample). The Chinese sample was also twice as likely (15.3 per cent compared to 8.8 per cent) to cite lack of promotion possibilities as a source of dissatisfaction. This greater dissatisfaction among Chinese women with gender inequalities at work may seem paradoxical, given their greater objective equality with men. The paradox may be resolved by emphasising the greater expectations for gender equality aroused among Chinese women by the official ideology. Chinese women expect a dismantling of gender divisions, and are therefore more disillusioned by those remaining gender differences at work.

With respect to domestic labour, the data indicate a greater sharing of tasks between marital partners in China than in either Japan or Great Britain. Table 1 indicates the gendered division of domestic labour in the three samples for a range of tasks. In each society exclusive female responsibility for washing-up, cooking, cleaning the house and washing clothes is considerably more common than is exclusive male responsibility. In China, however, there is a much more marked incidence of partners sharing these tasks.

The differing domestic division of labour in China and Japan was also demonstrated in an item which requested respondents to describe the husband's role in household work. While 75.3 per cent in China said the husband did most of it, shared it with his wife or did it together with his wife, only 4.1 per cent reported this to be the case in

TABLE 1   The Division of Domestic Labour Tasks in the Three Countries (Percentages)

Task	Female, entirely or mainly			Both			Male, entirely or mainly			Other		
	C	J	B	C	J	B	C	J	B	C	J	B
Washing-up	36	91	53	36	3	36	20	1	5	8	5	6
Cleaning the house	47	89	77	39	6	17	10	2	3	4	3	3
Washing clothes	43	92	94	44	4	5	9	2	1	4	2	0
Cooking	35	94	77	37	2	19	13	1	4	15	3	0

C = China; J = Japan; B = Britain

Japan, and whereas—according to the respondents—over half of Japanese men (54.7 per cent) do almost no housework, the comparable figure for China was 7.3 per cent.

The greater sharing of domestic roles in China can be attributed to the logistics of managing a household when both partners are undertaking demanding extra-familial employment. There is evidence from the Japanese and British data that where the female partner is in full-time paid work, there is a less extreme gendered division of domestic labour compared to cases where the respondent is in paid work for fewer hours. In general, dual full-time labour market partnerships lead towards less inequality in the domestic divisions of labour. In China the prevalence of dual full-time working partnerships is a factor contributing towards a less extreme domestic gender role segregation. Where both partners face demanding extra-familial employment responsibilities, the male is under pressure to contribute more to household labour. While much needs to be done to achieve full gender equality in China, the evidence presented above is an indication of the considerable changes on this front in urban areas since pre-revolutionary times.

Such advances have not, however, been made without a price. Because of their extensive employment and domestic commitments, Chinese women were much more likely than their Japanese counterparts to say they found housework a heavy or very heavy burden (62.5 per cent compared to 38.2 per cent), that their work was too tiring (31.9 per cent compared to 12.7 per cent) and that their hours of work were too long (39.7 per cent compared to 15.7 per cent). They were also more likely to report they did not get enough sleep (35.8 per cent compared to 29 per cent). Despite these negative aspects of their circumstances, the Chinese women were more likely to express satisfaction with their family life (93.1 per cent compared to 82.7 per cent); they were far less likely to be dissatisfied with their husbands' contribution to domestic tasks (25.8 per cent compared to 48 per cent) and they expressed more satisfaction with their relations with their husbands (96.2 per cent compared to 81.9 per cent) than did the comparative group in Japan.

JAPAN: WORKING HOUSEWIVES

The pattern in Japan contrasts markedly with that of China. Home and paid work are spheres which are much more differentiated by gender in Japan. Typically in Japan women leave the labour force upon marriage or the birth of a child, and when they return to paid work they return to subordinate and marginal employment (Eccleston 1989 : Ch. 6; Smith 1987). This is borne out in the data which demonstrate labour market interruptions occasioned by childbirth and child care being much more common in Japan than China. Over half the sample was not in paid employment for two to five years for such reasons. Only 39 per cent had worked continuously since leaving school, compared to 84 per cent in China. Forty-one per cent were employed in temporary work and 22 per cent in private or family enterprises. Fifty-eight per cent worked less than an 8-hour day compared to 8 per cent of their husbands. Their income averaged just under 1 million yen per annum compared to 3.3 million yen for their husbands.

The data are consistent with the view that female self-identity in China is more anchored in working life, while in Japan it is more rooted in the home. Thus, despite their lower involvement in—and rewards from—paid employment, the Japanese respondents were slightly more satisfied with their working life than their Chinese peers. 70.4 per cent of the Japanese sample expressed satisfaction with their working life, compared to 66.2 per cent of the Chinese respondents. The Japanese women also expressed significantly less dissatisfaction than the Chinese on such aspects of work as: the work being too tiring, the hours being too long, the work not being suitable, and a lack of promotion possibilities. The major exception concerned income. About a quarter of respondents in both China and Japan mentioned dissatisfaction over income. For the Japanese, this represented by far the most frequently mentioned source of dissatisfaction, whereas for the Chinese it was only the third most frequently mentioned item. . . .

Japanese respondents were considerably more likely to agree that the husband should go out to work and the wife should be a housewife. 38.1 per cent of the Japanese respondents and 19.2 per cent of the Chinese expressed degrees of agreement

with this view. Japanese respondents and their husbands, according to the wives' reports, were much more likely to endorse the view that housework and child-care were the responsibility of the wife even if she was in paid work, than were their Chinese equivalents. Twenty-nine per cent of respondents and husbands endorsed this view in Japan, and 1.8 per cent and 9.8 per cent respectively of these categories supported it in China. The Japanese respondents were also more likely to feel that a married woman in paid work would neglect housework (23.7 per cent compared to 0.3 per cent) and that the increase in married women working might result in family problems (40.1 per cent compared to 13.8 per cent). Japanese respondents also displayed less enthusiasm for married women engaging in paid work, in that only 63.7 per cent of them endorsed the view that 'the increase in married women working will promote social equality and progress,' compared to 83.5 per cent of the Chinese sample.

Because of their lesser involvement in paid work the Japanese respondents were less likely than the Chinese to report experiencing too heavy a burden of housework and child-care deriving from their work commitments (31.4 per cent compared to 37.5 per cent). Only 38.2 per cent of the Japanese respondents, compared to 62.5 per cent of the Chinese felt housework was a heavy or very heavy burden. Amongst the Japanese there was, however, a difference in this respect between those in part-time and those in full-time paid employment. The latter found housework more burdensome than did the former (44.6 per cent compared to 29.7 per cent respectively). In both countries, then, being in full-time paid work contributed to a feeling that housework was burdensome.

Seventy-eight per cent of the Japanese respondents, compared to 51 per cent of the Chinese, believe men are advantaged over women in family life, politics, law, and social ideas and customs. Few of them, unlike their Chinese counterparts, believe paid work can produce equality between husband and wife (2.3 per cent compared to 19.8 per cent in a fixed choice item which allowed other responses on the virtues of married women working). Reflecting their relative social isolation in the household, Japanese respondents were also more likely to recognise the value of paid work in providing a link with society than were the Chinese (16.7 per cent cf. 3.4 per cent). Thus, while the housewife role finds considerable endorsement among Japanese mothers, it is not without a recognition of the penalties that it results in for them.

GREAT BRITAIN: PART-TIME WORKERS

Data for the British sample are closer to that of the Japanese than the Chinese model, although gender role segregation in domestic labour tasks does not appear to be as extreme. The British respondents worked fewer hours than the Japanese. Seventy-six per cent of the Britons worked part-time—fewer than 30 hours per week, compared to 45 per cent of the Japanese. The median number of hours of paid work per week was 18 in Great Britain compared to 37 in Japan and 48 in China. The net wages of respondents in Britain were 35 per cent of their husbands' net average wage. In Japan the comparable figure was 41 per cent and in China it was close to 100 per cent. Part-time work in Great Britain is generally of low status and poorly rewarded. Seventy-five per cent of female employment is in routine non-manual sales and service occupations and semi- and unskilled manual work. Such occupations are often resorted to by mothers of young children since they provide part-time work at hours consistent with their domestic child-care responsibilities. As in Japan, maternity results in women, if they return to paid work, occupying low-status and marginal types of employment.

In China, both wife and husband average 43 minutes daily travel times to and from work. In both Britain (data relate to Aberdeen only) and in Japan, the median travel time for women is 20 minutes, while the median times for their husbands are 44 minutes in Britain and 33 minutes in Japan. These differences could be due to a number of factors. In China, work allocation procedures give workers much less choice as to where they work and women may not have the opportunity to choose to work closer to home. In Britain and Japan, in contrast, women are more able to choose work which fits in with their domestic responsibilities, and their shorter travel to work times may reflect their greater symbolic attachment to the home compared with their husbands. In Britain, an additional factor is that female respondents were much more likely than their partners to travel to work by bus or on foot. Male partners were more likely to travel in their car.

Working Japanese and Chinese parents are much more able to take advantage of kindergartens and child-care centres than are their British equivalents. The latter depend upon relatives, friends and neighbours for such assistance. The marital partners are the major providers of care in this respect, juggling their work schedules to take turns looking after the children. The male partner's role is particularly important when children are below school age. In 21 out of 33 such cases in Aberdeen, male partners were the source of child care. Only two were cared for in day nurseries. When children are of school age, mothers fit their working hours around the school-day. The constraints of providing care for children in the absence of formal institutional provision is one reason British women's hours in paid work are relatively so low.

Only 9.5 per cent of the British respondents are dissatisfied with their hours of work, compared to 39.7 per cent of the Chinese and 15.7 per cent of the Japanese. Twenty-two per cent of the Britons are dissatisfied with their level of pay, compared to slightly higher proportions of the other two samples who indicate that their income is too low or unstable. Twenty per cent of the Britons were dissatisfied with their promotion prospects, compared to 15.3 per cent of the Chinese and 8.8 per cent of the Japanese. Twenty-two per cent of the British sample expressed overall dissatisfaction with their job, compared to 34 per cent of the Chinese and 30 per cent of the Japanese. The British were also most likely to express satisfaction with their leisure. The figures were 49 per cent for Britain, 42 per cent for China and 41 per cent for Japan. For British women, part-time work resolves the competing pressures of domestic obligations and paid employment and generates higher levels of satisfaction with employment and leisure.

Like the Japanese respondents, traditional gender role attitudes were espoused by substantial proportions of the British sample. Fifty-two per cent expressed degrees of agreement with the statement 'I'm not against women working, but men should still be the main breadwinner in the family' and 18 per cent agreed 'In times of high unemployment married women should stay at home.' Evidence of a commitment to the domestic sphere was also expressed by the minority of respondents who had never engaged in paid work while their last child was of pre-school age. Only 19 per cent reported they would have preferred to work. Of those who had worked while their child was small, 40 per cent reported they would have preferred to stay at home. . . .

Fifty-nine per cent stated the female partner *should* be ultimately responsible for ensuring the housework is properly done; 43 per cent believed the male partner *should* be ultimately responsible for ensuring the family gets an adequate income and 26 per cent believed the female partner *should* be ultimately responsible for looking after the children. An item similar to these attitudes, i.e., 'the husband should go out to work, the wife should look after the home' was endorsed by 38 per cent of the Japanese but only 19 per cent of the Chinese. Similarly, 29 per cent of Japanese respondents, but only 1.8 per cent of the Chinese, supported the

view (in a forced choice item with three other possible responses) that 'even if the wife is working, housework and child-care should mainly be done by the wife.'

Overall, the Chinese respondents were least committed attitudinally to gender role differentiation. Surprisingly, given the emphasis of the literature on the strength of the 'housewife' role in Japan, it is difficult with the data available to detect any difference between Japan and Great Britain in the prevalence of attitudes supportive of this role set. . . .

CONCLUSION

Each of the societies examined has found distinctive institutional solutions to the problems of allocating the labour and time of parents of young children between the competing demands of employment and family life. Certain common features can be discerned, particularly the greater dual burden falling upon employed mothers in each society. In each society they combine primary responsibility for domestic work with their paid employment. There are, however, important variations in this pattern, with women in urban China having a greater total load of obligations, a relatively advantaged position in the sphere of employment and greater help in the home from their husbands. In Britain and Japan the pressures generated by the dual burden are resolved more by mothers of young children lowering their activity and status in paid employment. This process is most marked in Great Britain. . . .

NOTES

Eccleston B. 1989. *State and Society in Post-War Japan.* Cambridge: Polity Press.

Smith, R.J. 1987. 'Gender Inequality in Contemporary Japan'. *Journal of Japanese Studies* 13 (1): 1–25.

3.4. Crack in Spanish Harlem

Philippe Bourgois

This excerpt is about a fourth response to economic inequality: the development of illegal livelihoods.

One of the primary goals in North American society is success in obtaining money and living the "good" life. Almost everyone has been socialized to value material success. Yet in real life, many people do not have a good chance to gain success honestly. Because of this gap between their goals and means, people are often pushed to seek other, not-so-legitimate means of achieving success.

One adaptation to this gap between goals and means is what Merton (1957) has called *innovation*. Innovation means developing unconventional—even criminal—methods of achieving success. A criminal adaptation is most likely among poor people who have been socialized to want success but have the least chance of gaining it through legitimate channels.

According to Daniel Bell (1962), crime is as American as apple pie— America's own "queer ladder of success." It is a tried and true method of upward mobility in a society where everyone's hopes are high but people's opportunities are unequal. For over a century, crime has made enormous fortunes for many thousands of people: people who started out poor, had few marketable skills, and had to "innovate" in order to get ahead.

Professional criminals tend to be quite skillful and resourceful. They have to be, or they end up dead or in jail. In particular, criminals who operate drug businesses, large-scale prostitution, illegal gambling, and loan-sharking rings are the most successful of all.

Bell notes that professional crime, like sports and entertainment, has traditionally been staffed by the urban poor. And as the poor of North America's cities have changed, so has the ethnic makeup of crime. In the 19th century, the Irish were very active in crime; then came the Germans; then, the Jews; then, the Italians and Al Capone's remarkable innovations; then came the blacks; and most recently, the Asians and Hispanics.

The next excerpt is about a new version of criminal entrepreneurship in America's inner cities—the sale of crack cocaine in Spanish Harlem. Like much profitable crime, drug selling panders to people's weaknesses. Poverty is a breeding ground for people who need to escape reality—hence the demand for crack. And poverty and discrimination are excellent reasons to enter the underground crack economy: The work pays well, racial and ethnic origins are no liability, and you don't need a high school diploma. The downside is danger, violence, and a chance of prison or death at an early age.

So long as wealthy societies hold out the lure of easy living, then make easy living hard to get for a huge number of urban poor, there will be drug users and drug dealers in America's cities.

Excerpted from Bourgois, Philippe (1989) "Crack in Spanish Harlem," *Anthropology Today*, 5(4), August, 6–11. With permission of the Royal Anthropological Institute of Great Britain and Ireland.

A MUGGING IN SPANISH HARLEM

The undercover policeman pushed me across the ice-cream counter, spreading my legs and poking me around the groin. As he came dangerously close to the bulge in my right pocket I hissed in his ear 'It's a tape recorder.' He snapped backwards, releasing my neck and whispering 'Sorry.' Apparently, he thought he had intercepted an undercover from another department because before I could get a close look at his face he had left the *bodega* grocery-store cum numbers-joint. Meanwhile, the marijuana sellers stationed in front of the *bodega*, observing that the undercover had been rough with me, suddenly felt safe and relieved—finally confident I was a white drug addict rather than an undercover.

As we hurried to leave we were blocked by Bennie, an emaciated teenager high on angel dust who was barging through the door along with two friends to mug us. I ran to the back of the *bodega* but Gato had to stand firmly because this was the corner he worked, and those were his former partners. They dragged him onto the sidewalk surrounding him, shouting about the money he still owed, and began kicking and hitting him with a baseball bat. Gato owed them for his share of the marijuana confiscated in a drug bust. . . . After we finished telling the story at the crack/*botanica*[1] house where I had been spending most of my evening hours this summer, Chino jumped up excitedly calling out 'what street was that on? Come on, let's go, we can still catch them—How many were they?' I quickly stopped this mobilization for revenge, explaining it was not worth my time. Chino looked at me disgustedly, sitting back down and turned his face away from me, shrugging his shoulders. Julio jumped up in front of me raising his voice to berate me for being 'pussy.' He also sat back down shortly afterwards feigning exasperated incredulity with the comment 'Man you still think like a *blanquito*.'

CULTURE AND MATERIAL REALITY

The above extract from sanitized fieldwork notes is a glimpse of the day-to-day struggle for survival *and for meaning* by the people who stand behind the extraordinary statistics on inner city violent crime in the United States.[2] . . .

The inner city residents described above are the pariahs of urban US society. They seek their income and subsequently their identity and the meaning in their life through what they perceive to be high-powered careers 'on the street.' They partake of ideologies and values and share symbols which form the basis of an 'inner city street culture' . . . excluded from the mainstream economy and society but ultimately derived from it. Most . . . have a few direct contacts with non-inner city residents, usually with people in a position of domination: teachers, bosses, police officers, and later parole or probation officers.

How can one understand inner city poverty without falling into a hopelessly idealistic culture of poverty and blame-the-victim interpretation? Structural, political economy reinterpretations of the inner city dynamic emphasize historical processes of labour migration in the context of institutionalized ethnic discrimination. They dissect the structural transformations in the international economy which are destroying the manufacturing sector in the United States and swelling the low wage, low prestige service sector. These analyses address the structural confines of the inner city dynamic but fall prey to a passive interpretation of human action and subscribe to a weakly dialectic interpretation of the relationship between ideological processes and material reality, or between culture and class.

Street-level inner city residents are more than passive victims of historical economic transformations or of the institutionalized discrimination of a perverse political and economic system. They do not passively accept their fourth-class citizen fate. They are struggling determinedly to earn money, demand dignity and lead meaningful lives.

In the day-to-day experience of the street-bound inner city resident, unemployment and personal anxiety over the inability to provide one's family with a minimal standard of living translates into intra-community crime, intra-community drug abuse, intra-community violence. The objective, structural desperation of a population without a viable economy, and facing systematic barriers of ethnic discrimination and ideological marginalization, becomes charged at the community level into self-destructive channels.

Most importantly, the 'personal failure' of those who survive on the street is articulated in the idiom of race. The racism imposed by the larger society becomes internalized on a personal level. . . .

CULTURAL REPRODUCTION THEORY

. . . Cultural reproduction theory has great potential for shedding light on the interaction between structurally induced cultural resistance and self-reinforced marginalization at the street-level in the inner city experience. The violence, crime and substance abuse plaguing the inner city can be understood as . . . manifestations of a 'culture of resistance' to mainstream, white racist, and economically exclusive society. This 'culture of resistance,' however, results in greater oppression and self-destruction. More concretely, refusing to accept the outside society's racist role playing and refusing to accept low wage, entry-level jobs, translates into high crime rates, high addiction rates and high intra-community violence.

Most of the individuals in the above ethnographic description are proud that they are not being exploited by 'the White Man,' but they feel 'like fucking assholes' for being poor. All of them have held numerous jobs in the legal economy. Most hit the street in their early teens working odd jobs as delivery boys and baggers in supermarkets and *bodegas*. Most held jobs recognized as among the least desirable in US society. Virtually all of these street participants have had deeply negative . . . experiences in the minimum-wage labour market, owing to abusive, exploitative and often racist bosses or

supervisors. They see the illegal, underground economy as not only offering superior wages, but also a more dignified work place. For example, Gato had formerly worked for the ASPCA, cleaning out the gas chambers where stray dogs and cats are killed. Bennie had been a night shift security guard on the violent ward for the criminally insane on Wards Island; Chino had been fired a year ago from a job installing high altitude storm windows on skyscrapers following an accident which temporarily blinded him in the right eye. . . . Julio's last legal job before selling crack was as an off-the-books messenger for a magazine catering to New York yuppies. He had become addicted to crack, began selling possessions from his home and finally was thrown out by his wife. Julio had quit his messenger job in favour of stealing car radios for a couple of hours at night in the same neighbourhood where he had been delivering messages for ten hour days at just above minimum wage. Nevertheless, after a close encounter with the police Julio begged his cousin for a job selling in his crack house. Significantly, the sense of responsibility, success and prestige that selling crack gave him enabled him to kick his crack habit and replace it by a less expensive and destructive powder cocaine and alcohol habit.

The underground economy, consequently, is the ultimate 'equal opportunity employer' for inner city youth (cf. Kornblum and Williams 1985). As Davis (1987: 75) has noted for Los Angeles, the structural economic incentive to participate in the drug economy is overwhelming:

With 78,000 unemployed youth in the Watts-Willowbrook area, it is not surprising that there are now 145 branches of the rival Crips and Bloods gangs in South L.A., or that the jobless resort to the opportunities of the burgeoning 'Crack' economy.

The individuals 'successfully' pursuing careers in the underground economy are no longer 'exploitable' by legal society. They speak with anger at their former low wages and bad treatment. They make fun of friends and acquaintances who are still employed in factories, in service jobs, or in what they (and most other people) would call 'shitwork.' Of course, many others are less self-conscious about the reasons for their rejection of entry-level, mainstream employment. Instead, they think of themselves as lazy and irresponsible. They claim they quit their jobs to have a good time on the street. Many still pay lip service to the value of a steady, legal job. Still others cycle in and out of legal employment supplementing their bouts at entry-level jobs through part-time crack sales.

THE CULTURE OF TERROR IN THE UNDERGROUND ECONOMY

. . . Regular displays of violence are necessary for success in the underground economy—at the street-level drug dealing world. Violence is essential for maintaining credibility and for preventing rip-off by colleagues, customers and hold-up artists. Behaviour that appears irrationally violent and self-destructive to the outside observer can be reinterpreted according to the logic of the underground economy, as a judicious case of public relations, advertising, rapport building and long-term investment in one's 'human capital development.'

The importance of one's reputation is illustrated in the fieldwork fragment at the beginning of this paper. Gato and I were mugged because Gato had a reputation for being 'soft' or 'pussy' and because I was publicly unmasked as *not being* an undercover cop: hence safe to attack. Gato tried to minimize the damage to his future ability to sell on that corner by not turning and running. He had pranced sideways down the street, though being beaten with a baseball bat and kicked to the ground twice. Gato was not going to be upwardly mobile in the underground economy because of his 'pussy' reputation.

Employers in the underground economy look for people who can demonstrate their capacity for effective violence and terror.

For example, in the eyes of Papito, the owner of the crack franchises I am researching, the ability of his employees to hold up under gunpoint is crucial as stick-ups of dealing dens are not infrequent. Since my fieldwork began in 1986, the *botanica* has been held up twice. . . .

On several occasions in the midst of conversations with active criminals I asked them how they were able to trust their partners in crime. In each case, in slightly different language I was told somewhat aggressively: 'What do you mean how do I trust him? You should ask "How does he trust me?"' Their ruthlessness is their security: 'My support network is me, myself and I.' They made these assertions with such vehemence as to appear threatened by the concept that their security might depend upon the trustworthiness of their partner or employer. They were claiming they were not dependent upon trust: because they were tough enough to enforce all contracts they entered into. . . .

PURSUING THE AMERICAN DREAM

The underground economy and the violence emerging out of it are not propelled by an irrational cultural logic distinct from that of mainstream USA. On the contrary, street participants are frantically pursuing the 'American dream.' The assertions of the culture of poverty theorists that the poor have been badly socialized and do not share mainstream values is wrong. On the contrary, ambitious, energetic, inner city youths are attracted into the underground economy to try to get their piece of the pie as fast as possible. They often even follow the traditional US model for upward mobility to the letter by becoming aggressive private entrepreneurs. They are the ultimate rugged individualists braving as unpredictable frontier where fortune, fame and destruction are all just around the corner. . . .

Entry-level jobs are not seen as viable channels to upward mobility by high school dropouts. Drug selling or other illegal activity appear as the most effective and realistic options for getting rich within one's lifetime. Many street dealers claim to be strictly utilitarian in their involvement with crack and snob their clients despite the fact they usually have considerable alcohol and cocaine habits themselves. Chino used to chant at his regular customers 'Come on, keep on killing yourself; bring me that money; smoke yourself to death; make me rich.'

Even though street sellers have to maintain regular hours, meet sales quotas and be subject to being fired, they have a great deal of autonomy and power in their daily routine. The boss only comes once or twice a shift to drop off drugs and pick up money. Frequently, a young messenger is sent instead. Sellers are often surrounded by a bevy of hanger-oners—frequently young teenage women in the case of male sellers—willing to run errands, pay attention to conversation, lend support in arguments and fights and provide sexual favours. In fact, even youths who do not use drugs will attempt to befriend respectfully the dealer just to be privy to the excitement of people coming and going, copping and hanging.

Besides wanting to earn 'crazy money,' people choose 'hoodlum' status in order to assert their dignity at refusing to 'sling a mop for the white man' (cf. Anderson 1976: 68). Opulent survival without a 'visible means of support' is the ultimate expression of success and it is a viable option. There is plenty of visible proof of this to everyone on the street as they watch teenage crack dealers drive by in convertible Suzuki Samurai jeeps with the stereo blaring, 'beem' by in impeccable BMWs, or—in the case of the middle-aged dealers—speed around in well waxed Lincoln Continentals. The impact of the sense of dignity and worth that can accompany selling crack is illustrated by Julio's ability to overcome his addiction to crack only after getting a job selling it: 'I couldn't be messin' up the money. I couldn't be fucking up no more! Besides, I had to get respect.'

In New York City the insult of working for entry-level wages amidst extraordinary opulence is especially painfully perceived by Spanish Harlem youths who have grown in abject poverty only a few blocks from all-white neighbourhoods commanding some of the highest real estate values in the world. As messengers, security guards or Xerox machine operators in the headquarters of FORTUNE 500 companies, they are brusquely ordered about by young white executives who sometimes make monthly salaries superior to their yearly wages.

This humiliating confrontation with New York's ethnic/occupational hierarchy drives the street-bound inner city youths deeper into the confines of their segregated neighbourhood and the underground economy. They prefer to seek meaning and upward mobility in a context that does not constantly oblige them to come into contact with people of a different, hostile ethnicity wielding arbitrary power over them.

In this context the crack high and the ritual and struggles around using the drug are comparable to the millenarian religions that sweep colonized peoples attempting to resist oppression in the context of accelerated social trauma. Substance abuse in general, and crack in particular, offer the equivalent of a millenarian metamorphosis. Instantaneously users are transformed from being unemployed, depressed high school dropouts, despised by the world—and secretly convinced their failure is due to their inherent stupidity, 'racial laziness' and disorganization—into being a mass of heart-palpitating pleasure, followed minutes later by a jaw-gnashing crash and wideawake alertness that provides their life with concrete purpose: get more crack—fast!

One illustration within the crack economy of how resistance to exploitation can lead contradictorily to greater oppression and ideological domination is the conspicuous presence of women in the growing cohort of crack addicts. In ten random surveys undertaken at Papito's crack franchises, women and girls represented just under 50% of the customers. This contrasts dramatically to estimates of female participation in heroin addiction in the late 1970s.

The spectacle of young, emaciated women milling in agitated angst around crack copping owners and selling their bodies for five dollars, or even merely for a puff on a crack stem, reflects the growing emancipation of women in all aspects of inner city life. Women are no longer as obliged to stay at home and maintain the family. They no longer readily sacrifice public life or forgo independent opportunities to generate personally disposable income.

Similarly, national statistics document increased female participation in the legal labour market—especially in the working class Puerto Rican community. By the same token, more women are also resisting exploitation in the entry-level job market and are pursuing careers in the underground economy.

Although women are using the drug and participating intensively in street culture, traditional gender relations still largely govern income-generating strategies in the underground economy. Women are forced disproportionately to rely on prostitution to finance their habits. The relegation of women to prostitution has led to a flooding of the market for sex, leading to a drop in the price of women's bodies and to an epidemic rise in venereal disease among women and newborn babies.

Contradictorily, therefore, the emancipation which has enabled women to demand equal participation in street culture and in the underground economy has led to a greater depreciation of women as ridiculed sex objects. Addicted women will tolerate a tremendous amount of verbal and physical abuse in their pursuit of crack, allowing lecherous men to humiliate and ridicule them in public. . . .

NOTES

1. A *botanica* is an herbal pharmacy and *santeria* utility store.
2. Pseudonyms have been used in order to disguise identities of persons referred to.

Anderson, Elijah. 1976. A *Place on the Corner*. Chicago: U. of Chicago.
Davis, Mike. 1987. *Chinatown*, Part Two? The 'Internationalization' of Downtown Los Angeles. *New Left Review'*. 164: 65–86.
Kornblum, William and Terry Williams. 1985. *Growing Up Poor*. Lexington, MA.: Lexington Books.

3.5. Status, Property, and the Value on Virginity

Alice Schlegel

This excerpt is about a fifth response to economic inequality: the commercialization of personal relationships and, particularly, the placing of an economic value on female virginity.

In the past, sex was largely confined to marriage, and marriage was a transaction between families—a kind of business connection. People gained their social status from the family into which they were born or into which they married, and this was particularly true for women.

For their part, women could provide their husbands with labor power, kinship connections, property in the form of a dowry, and children. No less important, they could bring their virginity to the marriage. The author of the next excerpt finds that virginity is valued most in societies where families exchange gifts upon marriage. Virginity is part of the marriage bargain—proof that the family has controlled a girl's sexuality and kept her from intimate relations with lower-status, ineligible men. The more exclusive her sexuality, the more valuable is her gift of it in marriage.

The higher the status of the families whose children are marrying, the more important virginity becomes. As a result, we find more concern with female chastity among rich and middle-class people than we do among the poor, since the poor have no property or status to lose.

This excerpt illustrates the operation of a "double standard," which applies different sexual rules to men and women. It also reminds us that economic relations can intrude into even the most intimate parts of people's lives. Third and most important, the excerpt shows that economic inequality can have different consequences for societies as a whole, and for different parts of society.

Presumably, the least equal societies (economically) will place the highest value on virginity. To protect their honor, families will take up much of their time protecting and secluding wives and daughters. This will set serious limits on the ability of women to participate in activities outside the home. In this way, a value placed on virginity ensures the economic inequality and dependence of women in a society.

Today, this practice largely has disappeared in North America and, increasingly, the rest of the world. This is because of the declining importance of family as a source of property and status and the declining importance of children to a family's well-being. Today, both sons and daughters are expected to win a social position on their own, through achievements at school and work. As the economic equality of men and women increases, the value of female virginity becomes a relic of the past.

. . . There may be some connection between marriage transactions and the value on virginity, but it is not readily apparent what that connection is.

To illuminate this question, it is necessary to understand the varying effects marriage transactions—the movement of goods (most usually) or services at the time of a marriage—have on the transmission or

Excerpted from Schlegel, Alice (1991), "Status, property, and the value on virginity," *American Ethnologist*, 18(4), November, 719–734. Reproduced by permission of the American Anthropological Association. Not for further reproduction.

retention of property and on the social debts incurred thereby. This question was addressed in Schlegel and Eloul (1987, 1988) and will be summarized here. Following that, marriage transactions and attitudes toward virginity will be analyzed. It will be argued that the virginity of daughters protects the interests of brides' families when they use marital alliances to maintain or enhance their social status.

MARRIAGE TRANSACTIONS

The form of marriage transaction that has received the most attention in the literature is bridewealth, goods given by the groom, usually with the assistance of his kin, to the family of the bride. Bridewealth generally does not remain with the family that receives it: it is used to obtain wives for brothers of the bride or an additional wife for her father. Thus, goods and women circulate and countercirculate.

Women exchange is also a form of replacement, the exchange being direct rather than mediated by a transfer of property. Women exchange and bridewealth are most frequently found where women have economic value through their large contribution to subsistence (cf. Schlegel and Barry 1986). In each case the result is a kind of a social homeostasis.

Brideservice is often considered analogous to bridewealth, with payment in labor rather than goods. They differ in that the benefit of brideservice goes directly to the bride's household and is not circulated, as are bridewealth goods. Thus, families with many daughters receive much free labor, while families with few get little.

While gift exchange, in which relatively equal amounts are exchanged between the families of the bride and groom, can occur at all levels of social complexity, it is often found in societies with important status differences in rank or wealth. Since residence is predominantly patrilocal in gift-exchanging societies, the bride-receiving household is socially in debt to the bride-giving one. The exchange of equivalent goods is a way of ensuring intermarrying families are of the same social status, as indicated by the wealth they own or can call up from among their kin and dependents.

Status is a major consideration in dowry-giving societies. The bride's dowry is sometimes matched against the groom's settlement, thus ensuring equivalence, a usual practice among European land-owning peasants or elites. Dowry can also be used to "buy" a high-status son-in-law, a common practice in South Asia and one also known in Europe.

The final form of marriage transaction examined here is indirect dowry, which contains some features of both bridewealth,

in that goods are given by the groom's family, and dowry, in that the goods end up with the new conjugal couple. Sometimes the groom's kin give goods directly to the bride, but more often they give goods to her father, who then gives goods to the new couple. Indirect dowry appears to be a way of establishing the property rights of the conjugal couples that make up larger households, in anticipation of eventual fission. In addition, it allows for status negotiation without either family being put in the other's debt (cf. Schlegel and Eloul 1988).

There are variations within these major types, and additional features that are secondary and limited in distribution. In complex societies, the form of transaction may vary according to region or class. When the forms differ by status, the preferred form, practiced by the elite, is the one considered here.[1]

MARRIAGE TRANSACTIONS AND THE VALUE ON VIRGINITY

Information on the value placed on virginity comes from two sources. The primary one is the code "Attitude Toward Premarital Sex (Female)" in Broude and Greene (1980). Using the Standard Sample of 186 pre-industrial societies, Broude and Greene found information on this subject for 141 societies. Their code is divided into six levels of value: (1) premarital sex expected; (2) premarital sex tolerated; (3) premarital sex mildly disapproved of but not punished; (4) premarital sex moderately disapproved of and slightly punished; (5) premarital sex disallowed except with bridegroom; and (6) premarital sex strongly disapproved of. For the present study, the first three categories were collapsed into "virginity not valued" and the second three into "virginity valued." I have made four alterations to the code based on my reading of the ethnographic literature.

The second source is data collected by Herbert Barry and me on adolescent socialization in Standard Sample for societies not coded by Broude and Greene. The data were collected on adolescent behavior, not cultural attitude; coders were asked to assess whether premarital sex was tolerated. Because the code is less detailed than Broude and Greene's and because it measures behavior rather than attitude, I offer information only on societies in which premarital sex is not tolerated and thus, by definition, virginity is valued.

The value on virginity is not randomly distributed among societies with all types of marriage transaction. Table 1 shows the distribution, which is statistically significant: $p < .0001$. Even when those societies without marriage transactions are eliminated, the distribution is still statistically significant: $p < .001$.

Others have also found associations between premarital sexual permissiveness and structural or cultural features (see Broude's [1981] summary). Sexual permissiveness is shown to be associated with the simpler subsistence technologies, absence of stratification, smaller communities, matrilineal descent, matrilocal residence, absence of belief in high gods, absence of bridewealth (but bear in mind that in earlier studies, bridewealth has been conflated with indirect dowry), high female economic contribution, little or no property exchange at marriage, and ascribed rather than achieved status. These features are all highly intercorrelated, and some correlate

with types of marriage transactions (Schlegel and Eloul 1988).

. . . Goody (1973, 1976) has shown virginity is prescribed in societies in which dowry or inheritance by women is customary, and this article pursues that line of thinking. The advantage of an explanation grounded in type of marriage transaction is that it does not simply assign premarital permissiveness to the less complex societies and restrictiveness to the more complex; it suggests motives for parental control of adolescent girls' sexuality.

WHY VALUE VIRGINITY?

. . . I argue virginity is valued in societies in which young men may seek to better their chances in life by allying themselves through marriage to a wealthy or powerful family. In preserving a daughter's virginity, a family is protecting her from seduction, impregnation, and paternity claims on her child. This is most critical when certain kinds of property transactions are involved. In societies in which dowry is given (or daughters inherit), it would be attractive to seduce a dowered daughter (or heiress), demanding her as wife along with her property. Her parents would be reluctant to refuse, since the well-being of their grandchildren would depend upon their inheritance from both of their parents, and another man would be unlikely to marry the

TABLE 1   A Test of the Value on Virginity According to the Type of Marriage Transaction.

| Virginity valued | Marriage transaction* | | | | | |
	None	Bride-wealth[+]	Bride-service	Gift exchange	Dowry and indirect dowry	Total
Yes	3	16	6	9	18	52
No	26	27	10	3	7	73

$N = 125$; Chi-square $= 27.13$; $p < .0001$.

* Women exchange is omitted because of the small number of cases.

[+] Includes token bridewealth.

mother if it meant he had not only to support her children but to make them his heirs.

To illustrate that upward mobility through marriage with a dowered daughter or heiress is not foreign to dowry-giving societies, consider a common theme of European fairy tales. A poor but honest young man goes through trials to win the hand of the princess, who inherits her father's kingdom. Or, he wins her heart, and through the good offices of a fairy godmother or other spirit helper, they evade her wrathful father and are eventually reconciled with him. This more or less legitimate means to upward mobility is not so different from the illegitimate one, by which he wins the girl through seduction.

This line of reasoning was familiar to the 17th- and 18th-century English. As Trumbach tells it:

Stealing a son . . . was not the great crime. It was, rather, the theft of a daughter that was the real nightmare. For a woman's property became her husband's and she took his social standing. . . . To steal an heiress was therefore the quickest way to make a man's fortune—this was the common doctrine of the stage before 1710—and it had a special appeal to younger sons. [1978:101–102]

All of the dowry-giving societies in the sample value virginity except the Haitians. Nevertheless, as Herskovits, writing about Haiti, points out: "Even though pre-marital relations are commonplace, . . . the pregnancy of an unmarried girl is regarded as both reprehensible and unfortunate, and she is severely beaten for it by her family" (1971:111).

The majority of societies that exchange gifts and give indirect dowry also expect brides to be virgins. This is particularly true in the case of gift exchange, in which a bride's family gives property along with her, receiving a more or less equivalent amount from the family of the groom. As noted earlier, gift exchange is a way of ensuring . . . the two families are of equal wealth or of equal social power. Impregnating a girl would give a boy and his family a claim on

that girl and an alliance with her family, even though they would have to come up with something themselves for the exchange. As in dowry-giving societies, an emphasis on virginity discourages a man who is tempted to jump the status barrier by claiming fatherhood of a woman's child. The sample does, however, include three exceptions to the general requirement of virginity in gift-exchanging societies, and it is instructive to examine these deviant cases.

Malinowski (1932) has discussed the sexual freedom of Trobriand Island girls at length. However, Trobriand Islanders do not, at least ideologically, associate sexual intercourse with pregnancy. Weiner (1976: 122) relates two cases in which pregnancy was attributed to magic, and her informants maintained women could conceive without male assistance. No boy, then, can make a claim on a girl simply because he has been sleeping with her and she has become pregnant.

Among the Omaha, virginity was not considered important for most girls (as coded in Broude and Greene [1980]), but according to Fletcher and La Flesche (1911), virgins were held in greater esteem than those who had lost their virginity. It was a privilege to marry a girl who had been tattooed with the "mark of honor," which was given to a virgin of a prominent family. Only the marriages in prominent families involved significant gift exchange. In ordinary marriages, the young husband was expected to work a year or two for his father-in-law, making brideservice more common than gift exchange. Thus, it was in the important marriages, accompanied by the exchange of goods of much value, that the bride was expected to be a virgin. Omaha elite families faced the danger that a daughter might be seduced by a youth who would persuade her to elope. As long as his family recognized the marriage and brought some gifts to the bride's father, the marriage was legitimate in the eyes of the community. Maintaining the virginity of high-status girls protected their families from unwanted alliances.

In Samoa, similarly, girls from untitled

families had sexual freedom (as coded in Broude and Greene [1980]) but the daughters of titled chiefs did not. Children could be affiliated to the mother's group rather than the father's, Samoa having an ambilateral descent system. If the mother's rank was higher than the father's, the children's status would be elevated above their father's. High-status families would wish to guard their daughters against potential social climbers, who might be tempted to improve their children's position in life by seducing and marrying socially superior girls. It appears that only the arranged marriages, generally of high-status people, involved much gift exchange. Most marriages were of the "elopement" type and were much less expensive than the arranged ones (Shore 1981).

When no property accompanies the marriage, virginity is of little interest. If the groom gives goods or labor, the picture is mixed, but fewer societies are restrictive than permissive. In societies in which the bride's side gives considerable property, as with gift exchange, dowry, and, in many cases, indirect dowry, virginity is most likely to be valued. Thus, there is an association between the giving of property, particularly from the bride's side, and control of the girl's sexuality. I have interpreted this as a means by which the families of girls prevent their being seduced by ineligible boys, resulting in alliances that could be an embarrassment. . . .

DISCUSSION

. . . The question of the value on virginity revolves around whether premarital sexual intercourse leads to pregnancy, and whether biological fatherhood alone gives a man a claim on a child and its mother. . . .

Virginity is not such an issue if abortion is freely available, as in Southeast Asia. Even there, however, the elite have secluded their daughters, possibly in imitation of the Hindu, Buddhist, or Moslem aristocrats whom they have emulated in other ways (cf. Reid 1988:163).

Although abortive techniques are widely known and practiced, even where proscribed (Devereux 1976), abortion is a last-ditch measure for preventing unwanted births and must take a distant second place to the maintenance of virginity.

Impregnating a girl does not automatically give a boy or man a claim to her child or to her. In the Trobriand Islands, as we have seen, biological fatherhood alone is simply not recognized. In other places, it may be recognized without giving the impregnator a paternity claim. Such a claim may have to be paid for through bridewealth and marriage to the mother; if it is not, the child is absorbed into the mother's kin group. This practice appears to be more common in Africa than in other regions. I suggest the acceptance of illegitimate children is greater when children are a distinct economic asset. . . .

If children are not an unqualified asset to the mother's family, the rules of social life are likely to include the prescription that fathers take responsibility for their children, thus bringing biological and social fatherhood closer together. The responsibility for one's child can be restated as the right to that child, and biological fatherhood becomes a claim on social fatherhood. When the status of the mother is equal to or lower than that of the impregnator, it is to her advantage to press for marriage or at least support, so long as the impregnator is willing (or is unable to escape). When the mother is of greater wealth or higher status, particularly when her status or property will be inherited by her child, it is to the advantage of the impregnator to press *his* claim on the child and its mother. It is in such situations, I propose, that virginity is valued, as it is the surest way of preventing such claims.

This is not to deny virginity may acquire secondary meanings. . . . The idealization of virginity is most common in Eurasia, and it is found in some other areas, such as Polynesia or native North America, where certain categories of girls are expected to be virginal. It is noteworthy that belief in the purity or spiritual power of virginity, chastity, and celibacy developed in those regions where dowry or gift-exchange was the established form or the form practiced by the elite and aspired to by those who would imitate them. Ideology does not arise *de novo* but is grounded in existential concerns and issues. I suggest the ideology of virginity has its source in pragmatic concerns about status maintenance and improvement. . . .

NOTES

1. Coding on marriage transactions can be found in Schlegel and Eloul (1987). The Pawnee form has been recoded from absence to gift exchange, based on Grinnell (1891). The Somali, Teda, and Toda forms have been recoded from bridewealth to indirect dowry, based on Lewis (1961), Chapelle (1957), and Walker (1986), respectively.

REFERENCES CITED

Barry, Herbert, III, and Alice Schlegel
    1986 Cultural Customs That Influence Sexual Freedom in Adolescence. Ethnology 25:151–162.
Broude, Gwen J.
    1981 The Cultural Management of Sexuality. *In* Handbook of Cross-Cultural Human Development. Ruth H. Munroe, Robert L. Munroe, and Beatrice B. Whiting, eds. pp. 633–673. New York: Garland.
Broude, Gwen J., and Sarah J. Greene
    1980 Cross-Cultural Codes on Twenty Sexual Attitudes and Practices. *In* Cross-Cultural Samples and Codes. Herbert Barry III and Alice Schlegel, eds. pp. 313–334. Pittsburgh: University of Pittsburgh Press.
Chapelle, Jean
    1957 Nomades noirs du Sahara. Paris: Librairie Plon.
Devereux, George
    1976 A Study of Abortion in Primitive Societies. Rev. ed. New York: International Universities Press.
Fletcher, Alice, and Francis LaFlesche
    1911 The Omaha Tribe. Annual Reports of the Bureau of American Ethnology 27:17–672.
Goody, Jack
    1973 Bridewealth and Dowry in Africa and Eurasia. *In* Bridewealth and Dowry. Jack Goody and S. J. Tambiah, eds. pp. 1–58. Cambridge Papers in Social Anthropology no. 7. Cambridge: Cambridge University Press.
    1976 Production and Reproduction. Cambridge: Cambridge University Press.
Grinnell, George B.
    1891 Marriage among the Pawnee. American Anthropologist 4:275–281.
Herskovits, Melville J.
    1971[1937] Life in a Haitian Valley. Garden City NY: Doubleday and Company.
Lewis, I. M.
    1961 A Pastoral Democracy: A Study of Pastoralism and Politics among the Northern Somali of the Horn of Africa. London: Oxford University Press.
Malinowski, Bronislaw
    1932 The Sexual Life of Savages in Northwestern Melanesia. London: Routledge and Kegan Paul.
Reid, Anthony
    1988 The Lands Below the Winds. Southeast Asia in the Age of Commerce 1450–1680, Vol. 1. New Haven, CT: Yale University Press.
Schlegel, Alice, and Herbert Barry III
    1986 The Cultural Consequences of Female Contribution to Subsistence. American Anthropologist 88:142–150.
    1991 Adolescence: An Anthropological Inquiry. New York: Free Press.
Schlegel, Alice, and Rohn Eloul
    1987 Marriage Transactions: A Cross-Cultural Code. Behavior Science Research 21:118–140.
    1988 Marriage Transactions: Labor, Property, and Status. American Anthropologist 90:291–309.
Shore, Bradd
    1981 Sexuality and Gender in Samoa: Conceptions and Missed Conceptions. *In* Sexual Meanings. Shery B. Ortner and Harriet Whitehead, eds. pp. 192–215. Cambridge: Cambridge University Press.
Trumbach, Randolph
    1978 The Rise of the Egalitarian Family. New York: Academic Press.
Walker, Anthony R.
    1986 The Todas of South India: A New Look. Delhi: Hindustan Publishing.
Weiner, Annette B.
    1976 Women of Value, Men of Renown. Austin: University of Texas Press.

3.6. The Family Lives of Colombian Street Children

Lewis Aptekar

This excerpt is about a sixth response to inequality: changes in family structure and control over children.

As time goes on, the household consisting of father, mother, and children is becoming just one of an increasing number of alternatives. As the next excerpt shows, economic inequality produces different kinds of families and childhoods. The traditional definition of "family" makes several assumptions about family composition that no longer represent the norm in many societies.

For example, it assumes the presence of two adults, a legal marriage between the two adults, and the presence of children. Supporters argue the traditional family provides the best environment for raising children. Children require the stability of a conventional structure, with its unconfused sex roles and clearly defined sexual division of labor. But advocates of a new definition of family disagree. At the least, they believe that family life will evolve and must evolve with changes in the society as a whole.

In terms of family structure, Colombia is split into two categories. The dominant Spanish classes tend to live in traditional families led by a strong father figure. In these households, women are subservient to and dependent on men. Adolescence is prolonged and highly supervised by the parents, especially the father. By contrast, the poorer classes include a large number of female-led families of indigenous or African origin. In these families, the mother is the dominant figure. Women function independently of their reproductive partners. Men are valued to the extent that they can contribute economically to the household.

Adolescence comes earlier to the children of poor, female-led families. These children are encouraged to be independent at a young age. Early on, many are out on the streets, living their own lives, making ends meet as best they can. Is this a social problem for Colombia? The ruling classes, who control the government and press, think so. They blame the methods of childrearing in the poorer families for the increasing numbers of street children.

However, this excerpt presents data that contradict these claims. The author argues these children manage quite well, under the circumstances. They are about as well-off as their parents, or the Bangladesh poor we examined in the first section of this book. Drastically different interpretations of the street life reflect the economic division of family life in Colombian society. Colombia's street children are not envied, but should we blame their parents?

Excerpted from Aptekar, Lewis (1990), "Family structure and adolescence: The case of the Colombian street children," *Journal of Adolescent Research*, 5(1), January, 67–81. With permission of Sage Publications, Inc.

. . . This article explains how Colombia has responded to the growing number of children on the streets. It will be shown that the response has been guided by (a) the historic tension between different family structures, (b) problems of epistemology, and (c) the changing fabric of Colombian society. . . .

This study was a part of a larger (Aptekar, 1988a) that outlined the characteristics of the street children. The present study focuses on the dynamics between the children and the society in which they live.

METHOD

Data Compilation

Ethnographic data were collected in Cali, Colombia, with the help of Colombian research assistants from the Universidad del Valle. The information was obtained from four different locations: a private store front program, the streets, a state diagnostic center, and the press. . . .

Family Structure and Street Children

Research has not corroborated the assumption that street children were abandoned and living without family connections. In a study of 56 street children, Aptekar (1988b) found only 16% had no known family, 9% were under the care of a grandparent or other relative, and the remaining 75% had at least one parent who could be contacted, usually the mother, Felsman (1981) reported in his study of a similar Colombian group that nearly three-quarters of the children did not have their biological father in the home, but 84% had their biological mother in the home. From a study by Tellez (1976), the data (also from Colombia) illustrated a similar family situation. In all three studies, as well as the information from the diagnostic center in this study, the family constellation was comparable. The children, as a rule, were in contact with at least one parent. In addition, when they lived at home, it was usually with their mothers, who were almost always separated from their biological fathers.

Other studies (Aptekar, 1988a; Felsman 1981), as well as this present work, reveal entry into street life was slow and measured. The children tested their adaptability to street life by leaving home for short periods and returning home frequently until they felt comfortable on their own. During this period, the children maintained contact with their mothers, and even when fully involved with street life returned periodically to visit their homes.

RESULTS

Matrifocal Families

The families of the street children in this study were a mixture of indigenous and African descent, and of a matrifocal structure. Their marriages began with informal ceremonies without church sanctions. As time progressed, the women had several male partners so their families could be characterized as having "male kin marginality" (Siegal, 1969), which meant adult men were marginal to their homes. When present and appropriate (neither abusive or too expensive to keep), the men were valued, and the economic products of their labor were used. When the women determined the men were not valuable, the men were asked to leave. The children were raised with a subjective, if not conscious, understanding of this. For these children, the mother was the source of wisdom, to whom they turned when there were issues to be clarified, or when they needed protection from dangerous situations.

A female child was expected to leave her mother only after the mother, usually in her forties, was ready for a more permanent union with a man. At this time, the daughter was well past puberty. Sometimes a girl chose to leave if she became pregnant and wanted her own home. Should her conjugal relationship end, it was not uncommon for her to return home. Other girls, when they became pregnant, chose to remain with their mothers. In some cases, there were three generations of women in the same home, with no men.

In the matrifocal family, male children were urged to leave home and be independent of their mothers. At a very early age they often explored areas of the city beyond their mothers' immediate view. The liberty to move around was considered by their mothers to be the proper way to raise them, since the boys would learn the skills needed to survive in an urban economy where there were no steady employment opportunities. After reaching puberty, their welcome at home depended on their ability to bring in money. Their experiences and expectations were such that they did not assume they would have an enduring conjugal relationship with one woman. . . .

Patrifocal Families

In the middle and upper social classes, the dominant family tradition was Spanish and patrifocal. Families began with formal church marriages. Adult men were central to the home, and they put the conjugal relationship at its core, which was used to publicly define the family. This was done to place the family within a strata of the civic order, hence the value middle and upper class Colombians gave to the father's family name.

Family life revolved around the father. The children turned to him to obtain resources and to receive preparation for entry into appropriate adult social roles. Their futures were planned by him and he kept strict control over his children. Both boys and girls were expected to stay at home years after puberty. Even then they did not leave without the father's blessing. Not only before leaving home, but often afterwards, children's fathers supervised them strictly.

Girls were taught the acceptable behaviors of their class by their mothers. It was through the supervision of their fathers, however, that their mothers disciplined them. The girls also turned toward their fathers for clarifying information. Their

mothers were consulted about relationships between the sexes. As children, girls rarely left their homes without their mothers. When girls began to date they were supervised (ultimately by their fathers) not only about whom they could go out with, but also about the extent of their involvement. Only with the father's permission were they able to leave their homes as adult women, and nothing would be more disgraceful to their fathers than for them to become pregnant out of wedlock. Girls were thus raised to define themselves within, and dependent on, their relationships with men.

Boys learned how to be "men" in sanctioned social groups or clubs. In these clubs they learned there were two kinds of girls, those to be respected, and those with whom sexual relations were allowed. Friendships with other boys were made at the social clubs, also arranged by their fathers. By the time the boys reached puberty they had few experiences away from home not sanctioned by their fathers. The boys were raised to value marriage as a means to further the family name and place in society.

Adolescence in patrifocal families was prolonged, with adulthood beginning only after being placed into an appropriate social standing. Patrifocal families viewed matrifocal children as wild and uncontrolled, and matrifocal families saw patrifocal children as sheltered and helpless in the real world. Within their homes, the children were also raised differently with respect to how they would relate to their future spouses. In the matrifocal family, boys and girls learned they would be independent of their future spouses. In patrifocal families, girls grew up to be dependent on their future partners, while boys learned to have women dependent on them. Children in the two family structures were also raised with different expectations of the conjugal relationship—it had little value in matrifocal families and was very important in patrifocal families.

Problems of Epistemology

There was a great discrepancy between the governmental information about the children and several research studies. For example, in a study funded by Colombia's national welfare agency (Piñeda, de Muñoz, Piñeda, Echeverry, & Arias, 1978), the structure of poor families and women's place in them was described in terms that reinforced commonly held beliefs about the origins of street children and their families. The authors claimed

the mother is the stable progenitor figure, placed in front of the family group as the result of the fruit of successive unions with men. The biological father almost always abandons his descendent and many times another man replaces him as father. In her status of covering the roles rejected by the man, the woman's job is very difficult and rarely successfully accomplished. The ambiance of the home is one of conflict between the stepfather and his stepchildren. This conflict also involves the mother. The pressing economic needs of the family, only semiprotected by the stepfather, threaten the family with dissension. When the domestic tranquility is threatened, the mother has to choose between working to protect and provide for her children or accepting the stepfather who can help her out of this economic difficulty. Very often she chooses the stepfather. (Piñeda et al., 1978, p. 12)

As a result of her lack of security the mother abandons her children in favor of a life with the stepfather.

If this scenario was as likely, it would have resulted in more psychopathology in the children than has been found. Several studies have shown that many of the children were performing adequately emotionally, intellectually, and neurologically. In the only study (Lopez & Lopez, 1964) that compared street children with their siblings who remained at home, the evidence indicated the street children weighed more and had fewer health problems than their homebound siblings. Felsman (1981) suggested the strongest children in the family were choosing to go to the streets.

Although it was commonplace to assume the Latin American woman would not leave her male partner because she was unable to live without his income, there was considerable evidence to discount this. "For many women in La Laja [a poor barrio in Caracas], having a man in the house is no firm solution to the economic problem, either because the man is likely to be unskilled, to be employed intermittently, or to be expensive to keep in food and beer when out of work" (Peatrie, 1968, p. 46).

In spite of the fact that poor women in Latin America [are] generally perceived to be victims, studies of Latin American women in poor families have not always borne this out. According to Burkett (1978, p. 117),

in recent years, anthropologists and sociologists have discussed the character of the *chola* [a woman of Spanish and Indian blood] in Andean towns and cities. She is depicted as a strong, willful woman, either Indian or *mestiza* [a woman of Spanish and Indian blood], aggressive economically and socially. She stands in sharp contrast to her *cholo* [a man of Spanish and Indian blood] brother who is seen as drunk, bumbling, meek and not very bright. . . .

The differences were exactly the opposite of what was described in the official social welfare document (Piñeda et al., 1978).

There was also a problem in the archival data of ascertaining the characteristics of the street children, with respect to their [number]. For example, Piñeda et al. (1978) claimed that in Bogotá there were about 130,000 *gamines* (the name refers to all street children). In 1973, Diaz published an article in *Educacion Hoy*, a national periodical, giving a figure of 3,000 street children in Bogotá (Diaz, 1973). A September 1976 article published in *El Tiempo* ("El censo de gamines"), one of two leading Bogotá daily newspapers, indicated there were about 60,000 street children in the city. Gutierrez (1972), claimed there were about 5,000.

In addition to the disparate numbers given for the size of the street children population, there were problems for understanding these children's alleged use of drugs. The inflated estimates of both the number of children and the extent of drug abuse were frequently used to adopt certain policies.

Basuko is the Colombian name given to the unrefined residue of coca leaves left over after the purer cocaine is distilled. Popular and governmental opinion held basuko was widely used by street children.

How common was the use of basuko? Another article in *El Tiempo* indicated 60% of the youth under 15 years of age in one town "have followed in the path of drug addiction" (Patino, 1983, p. 11A). The article went on to say that in many cities the statistics were even more alarming. In one city "of one thousand youths, six hundred are drug addicts in the extreme. On September 28, 1983, *El Espectador*, another of Bogotá's leading newspapers, claimed "in Colombia thirty-eight percent of the children below fourteen years of age have problems with drugs" ("Mas de 25 millones," p. 5A). The article continued by saying "the problem is made worse because each of these children contaminates ten other children."

The speculation in their articles attempted to show the use of basuko was as widespread as it was debilitating. If this were true, the children would have been severely affected by it. Another study (Aptekar, 1988b), which gave similar street children three psychological tests, indicated the children's emotional and neurological functioning were adequate. A similar study by Felsman (1981) showed through psychological testing and participant observation that the children had no overt signs of severe psychopathology. Other studies (Jaramillo, 1976; Lopez & Lopez, 1964; Villota, 1979) on similar populations of children illustrated the children were faring adequately.

State Involvement

Why [were] there so many conflicting pieces of information about the children? The confusion was in part the result of the two family structures with their different methods of child-rearing and expectations

about family life. However, the discrepancies were also related to Colombia's concern for civic order. In fact, street children found themselves in the middle of a civic struggle that began April 9, 1948, when Colombian society erupted, beginning *La Violencia* (the violent civil war). On that day, a dictatorial government was overthrown, and the popular leader, Jorge Eliecer Gaitan, was assassinated. After the populace heard of his assassination, Bogotá erupted in violence. In La Violencia, which lasted nearly a decade, 200,000 people were killed (Alape, 1984). As a result of this disruption, many social customs were changed. These changes brought a great deal of tension between social classes.

Before La Violencia, civic life was dictated by family connections, and political parties were synonymous with families' names. Thus political parties were nearly feudal family empires. Likewise, participation in social groups depended on the family empires. La Violencia brought about the breaking down of family as the determiner of citizenry, and life became more equalitarian and meritocratic. The civic changes included an opportunity for the nonSpanish racial groups with their matrifocal family tradition to become participants in the civic politic.

Although there were children on the streets in Colombia before La Violencia, they were not viewed as a social problem. After La Violencia, they were labeled as "abandoned" and were referred to as "street children". The emotive nature of these terms implied street children's families were remiss, irresponsible, and in need of restructuring to help them improve.

CONCLUSION

Colombia's response to the growing number of children on the streets has been guided by the continuing tensions between various structures, most notably differences between the middle- and upper-class patrifocal families and the lower socioeconomic families of primarily matrifocal orientation.

Problems in epistemology have also affected how Colombians have responded to the children. Research revealed most street children were functioning adequately, particularly given their low socioeconomic status. Yet press and governmental documents claimed the majority were not faring well, indicating the children were in need of emotional help or incarceration.

As the opening up of Colombian society after La Violencia allowed for a larger number of the working class to gain entry into the middle class, the matrifocal method of child-rearing, exemplified by the supposedly abandoned children in the streets, was met by the privileged class with pejorative comments. This segment of the populace directed the governmental reports and wrote the journalistic accounts of the children.

The children and their families were judged by ethnocentric standards. Moral values were applied to support the claims of those making the accusations. In great part, this was a way to avoid the expansion of society to include different social and racial groups. In addition, new rules changed the nature of participation in civic life from one based on family identity to one associated with personal merit.

The street children also gained support from those in society who had prospered without having to rely on family connections, because they viewed the street children as having similar struggles. These adults were often small entrepreneurs—restaurant owners who gave them food, street vendors who shared their space, or laundry owners who allowed them to sleep in a warm place. Ironically, being able to gather support added to their burden. If they were seen as healthy or even as managing, they would have further reduced the power of the dominant social class to define "family" from the patriarchal point of view.

The children themselves contributed to heightening the drama of their plight. In their conspicuously dirty appearance, their flirtation with danger and their cunning thievery, all of which took place in full public view, they contributed to their being viewed as defiant of adult authority. It possibly was not hunger or family disintegration that caused the children to be so public in their displays, but a rebellion against the inevitability of inheriting the lowest social status.

As adolescence was the time when young adults were on the verge of citizenship and the psychological issue of independence was paramount, it was at this time that the demands of the state for control and the needs of the individual for freedom were most in conflict. Thus independence from authority or respect for it became poignant areas of tension. . . .

NOTES

Alape, A. (1984). *El Bogotazo: Memorias del olvido* [The Bogotano: Forgotten memories]. Bogotá: Editorial Pluma.

Aptekar, L. (1988a). *Street children of Cali.* Durham, NC: Duke University Press.

Aptekar, L. (1988b). Street children of Colombia. *Journal of Early Adolescence, 8,* 225–241.

Burkett, E. C. (1978). Indian women and white society: The case for sixteenth-century Peru. In A. Lavrin (Ed.), *Latin American women: Historical perspectives* (pp. 111–144). Westport, CT: Greenwood.

El censo de gamines [The census of the gamines]. (1976, September). *El Tiempo,* p. 22.

de Mantilla, N. (1980). El gamin: Problema social de la cultura urbana [The gamine: A social problem of the urban culture]. *Revista Javeriana, 94,* 457–464.

Diaz, B. G. (1973). Un esayo de autoeducacion de niños marginados: Los gamines [An essay on the self-education of the marginal children: The gamines]. *Educacion Hoy,* (November-December), 33–58.

Felsman, K. (1981, April). Street urchins of Colombia. *Natural Histories,* pp. 41–48.

Gutierrez, J. (1972). *Gamin: Un ser olvidado* [The gamine: The forgotten person]. Mexico City: McGraw-Hill.

Jaramillo, O. (1976). El sub-mundo de los Gamines [The sub world of the gamines]. *Nueve Frotera, 73,* 5–16.

Lopez, A., & Lopez, E. (1964). *Estudio medico-*

social de la vagancia infantil de Bogotá [A social and medical study of child vagrants in Bogotá]. *Revista Colombiana de Psiquiatria, 1* (1), 37–44.

Mas de 25 millones consumen drogas en los Estados Unidos [More than 25 million consume drugs in the United States]. (1983, September 28). *El Espectador*, p. 5A.

Patino, N. O. (1983, July 11). 600 de mil niños consumen "basuko" [600 out of a thousand children consume "basuko"]. *El Tiempo*, p. 11A.

Peatrie, L. R. (1968). *The view from the barrio.* Ann Arbor: University of Michigan Press.

Piñeda, V. G., de Muñoz, E. I., Piñeda, P. V.,

Echeverry, Y., & Arias, J. (1978). *El gamin su alberque social y su familia,* Vol. 1 [The gamin's social home and family]. Bogotá: Instituto Colombiano de Bienestar Familiar.

Siegal, J. (1969). *The rope of God.* Berkeley: University of California Press.

Tellez, G. M. (1976). *Gamines.* Bogotá: Editorial Temis.

Villota, R. (1979). Problematica de la niñez de la calle [The problema of the children of the streets]. *Revista Javeriana, 91,* 473–477.

Section Review

Discussion Questions

1. Are Bourgois and Aptekar just talking about the same kinds of people—street people—at two different points in time?
2. Is the rise of crack dealing an inevitable result of too-fast and faulty economic development, such as Keyfitz describes? If so, will drug use and drug dealing increase in all industrial societies with pockets of urban poor?
3. Why don't working women rebel against the dual burden they are forced to carry? Or have they already done so in *some* countries, with the result that have had a lighter load to carry in those countries?
4. How and why is Sweden's strategy for fighting poverty different from, say, Brazil's or the United States'? Why do they even have a "strategy"? Wouldn't increased economic growth do the job?
5. Would you expect to find that, in countries where virginity is valued most highly, women are *least* likely to carry a dual burden? Or *most* likely to do so? Explain your answer.
6. "Everyone wants to be middle-class, but no one wants to help the poor do the same thing." Do you agree? Would Keyfitz agree? How about Zimbalist?

Data Collection Exercises

1. Collect data from urban slums on two continents to find out whether there is a high incidence of criminal behavior (e.g., drug dealing), deviant behavior (e.g., drug use), and early initiation into sex (e.g., early loss of virginity) in both. What is the connection among these behaviors, if any?

2. Use a time-budget questionnaire (see Xuewen's et al. excerpt) to collect two days' worth of data (one Saturday and one Wednesday) from each of six married women and six single women of (roughly) the same age. How much difference among these time budgets could be attributed to the marital status of the women?
3. Collect evidence from ethnographies, history books, diaries, or even novels about dating practices in a society where virginity is idealized. How are these dating practices different from our own?
4. Collect some anecdotal, biographic, or quantitative data from Sweden (or another European society) to determine whether the problems urban poor people face are likely a result of their rural, or agricultural, origins.

Writing Exercises

1. Pretend you are a middle-class person writing a long (500-word) letter to the editor of a national newspaper. It is on the topic of "Drugs in America: Why there is a problem and what to do about it."
2. You are a 12-year-old street child in Colombia. Keep an imaginary diary for two days, documenting what you are doing, with whom, and how you feel about it. What are your relations with your family?
3. Write a brief (500-word) essay on whether the social value of virginity is likely to increase or decrease with industrialization, taking into account what Keyfitz has to say about people's aspirations.
4. "Groups with more money usually have more status, and they take actions to ensure they get more of both." Comment on this statement in a brief (500-word) essay that takes into account the findings of Zimbalist and Keyfitz.

Part II

INTRODUCTION TO POWER INEQUALITY

POWER INEQUALITY AND ITS SOURCES

The struggle for equality not only means setting limits to inequalities in wealth and poverty but also setting limits to the range of inequality in power.

But what is power? Who holds power over whom, and why? How do people get power, and how do they lose it? These are some of the questions sociologists ask when they study domination and submission. **Domination**, or the exercise of power, has four aspects: (1) differentiation, (2) inequality, (3) legitimation, and (4) symbolization. When people dominate others, they start out by demonstrating a difference between "us" and "them," then convert that difference into an inequality that the majority are willing to accept as legitimate—sensible, moral, just. Once this pattern of inequality is established, those who are powerful tend to develop symbols by which people can be reminded of the relationship of domination, can recognize who is most powerful, and who should submit.

Max Weber was one of the first sociologists to study domination, which he defined as "the probability that a command with a specific content will be obeyed by a given group of persons" (Weber, 1968: 53). The flip side of domination is **submission**, the act of yielding to the control of another, or doing what others tell us to do. To understand domination and submission means understanding inequality and social differentiation, for there is no domination without inequality, and inequality without differentiation.

Differentiation is the making of social distinctions. The characteristics we use to differentiate ourselves are socially significant because they are considered "natural" differences and "rightful" bases of inequality. Take skin color. This only becomes a socially significant characteristic when people attach meanings to it. They may attribute moral superiority to light skin over dark skin, for example.

These meanings are **socially constructed**; they are established by people through social interaction. They have no basis in biology. For this reason, different societies are able to attach different meanings to the same characteristics. So, female gender, dark skin, and old age have less effect upon social inequality (are less disabling and less characterized by exclusion, decoupling, and scarcity) in some societies than they are in others.

The social distinctions we make may be based on ascribed *or* achieved characteristics, or statuses. Ascribed statuses include gender, race, and age. Achieved statuses include education and demonstrated merit. An **achieved status** is based on characteristics over which a person exercises some control—for example, educational attainment, type of job held, or marital status. Becoming pope or a university graduate would be examples of achieved statuses. By contrast, an ascribed status is based on the position into which an individual is born, or on characteristics over which the individual has *no* control—for example, sex, ethnicity, or the caste or social class of one's parents.

Among children born into very rich or very poor families in North America (say, the top 10 percent and bottom 10 percent), most will remain in precisely the same social stratum when they are an adult. For them, their social class is largely ascribed at birth. However, among children born into the middle 80 percent of the population, few will remain in *precisely* the same social class as their parents. Most will end up slightly higher or somewhat lower than their parents. In that sense, their social class is achieved, not ascribed.

As we have said, in many societies race and/or ethnicity is given social meaning, making for social differentiation, and social inequality. In even more societies the same occurs for gender. For these two forms of ascribed statuses at birth there is even less likelihood of change or achievement of a different status than for class.

People tend to behave differently toward those of one sex compared with the other, toward members of different racial and ethnic groups. The differentiation of people by sex, in particular, leads to (gender) inequalities everywhere.

Age is another ascribed characteristic that differentiates people, and it often provides a basis for inequality. Some people—especially parents—believe that older people are wiser, more experienced, more reasonable, and are therefore more suited to positions of authority than younger people. Of course, after a certain age, this belief seems to change. Then, middle-aged people consider old people and young people to be less competent to hold power than themselves.

People dominate other people who they believe are different from themselves: There is no domination without differentiation. In a society that did not distinguish culturally between men and women, white and nonwhite, rich and poor, old and young, there would be no domination along these lines. And, there is no known society without some kind of differentiation.

However, the differentiation—hence, domination—that takes place in societies is far from random. Every known society differentiates people by sex and age. In small tribal societies, there is little differentiation beyond this, so we do not find class or racial inequalities in such societies. Differentiation by race, ethnicity, and class are typical of larger, more advanced societies. Once people settle down to an agricultural way of life and the population starts to grow, social differentiation increases rapidly; so does domination.

As societies get larger, they become more differentiated still, so they have a greater potential for domination than smaller societies. However, for domination to take place, a social *difference* must be turned into a social *inequality*.

Not every social difference is converted into a social inequality. We can imagine many kinds of difference. For example, Mr. X can run faster and farther than Mr. Y, but for most people in our society this has little social importance (unless they happen to be Carl Lewis or Florence Joyner). In a hunting society, though, speed may mean the difference between success and failure in getting food. In this instance, people with speed are likely to be given more wealth, power, and respect than others. So, speed may be the basis of social differentiation and inequality in some societies, and not others.

And, even if speed becomes a basis for differentiation and inequality, it may not become part of what we call a **system of stratification**—a stable pattern of inequality that persists over generations. Unless the running gene is passed from parent to child, it may not produce family dynasties, such as exist in our own society. So, we can have differentiation without inequality, and inequality without stratification.

Stratification results when parents are able to hand their power, wealth, or status over to their children. In a highly stratified society, people are likely to stay in approximately the same social position they were born into—they pass that position along to their children. Also, their power is tied up with a particular income, lifestyle, and set of opportunities. Stratification means there are fairly stable groups of people with similar amounts of wealth, status, and power.

How do people exercise power? Of course, they can always try to dominate others through naked force. But coercion is a poor basis for ongoing social relations. Something more than sheer physical force is needed if one person is going to consistently, and without question, get another to do what he or she wants. That something more is **legitimacy**. Gaining legitimacy means converting domination based on force, or the threat of force—a highly unstable relationship—into domination based on **authority**, a much more stable relationship. Thus, legitimation is very important in some people establishing domination over others.

Authority, or legitimate domination, exists when people accept that the person taking charge has the right to do so. In other words, "authority" is power that has become legitimate in the eyes of people who are subject to that power. Elements of authority underlie all four mechanisms of inequality—exclusion, disabling, decoupling, and scarcity—in the sense that advantaged people provide legitimizing "explanations" for the occurrence of these processes and others often accept these explanations.

Max Weber (1968) identified three types of authority—traditional, charismatic, and rational-legal—according to the source of its legitimacy. People are obeying **traditional authority** when they obey a rule simply because that is the way things have always been done.

For example, the authority of elders in a small, preindustrial village is traditional. So is the authority of males over females in our society. Until recently in North America, the courts took for granted that women were subject to the authority of their fathers; or if married, of their husbands; or if widowed or divorced, of some other male guardian. Supposedly, this was for their own good, as women were "naturally" inferior in their capacity to reason and make sound decisions. These practices are still common in many societies.

By contrast, people obey **charismatic authority** because they believe the person in authority has abilities that are out of the ordinary. Examples of charismatic leaders include Mahatma Gandhi, Martin Luther King, Jr., and Adolf Hitler. In various ways, each challenged the status quo and persuaded millions to commit themselves to movements for change. Charismatic authority is hard to explain and almost impossible to fake. We know when leaders have it, because we can see large numbers of people responding to the charisma. The followers are willing to make extreme, unusual sacrifices for their leader. They are likely to grant their charismatic leaders greater powers, more second chances, and more trust in uncertain situations.

Weber's third form of authority—**rational-legal authority**—is the most important kind in modern industrial societies. It is based on a "belief in the legality of enacted rules and the right of those elevated to authority under such rules to issue commands." In this case, people obey an order because they see the order as coming from a legitimate office or position.

Rational-legal authority resides in the role or office, not the individual. Under a system of rational-legal authority, it is the legality of the rules—not tradition or charisma—that brings compliance. Traditional authority commands little respect in most areas of life and charismatic authority is rare and volatile. For these and other reasons, in our society rational-legal authority is by far the most important form of authority.

To summarize, effective domination depends on people believing in the naturalness of socially constructed differences, the rightness of social inequalities, and the legitimacy of a dominant leader or group. From this standpoint, politics is the art of making people think they should submit to the authority of one leader, or group, rather than another.

Each of the three forms of authority results in particular "elite" individuals dominating. An elite is a small group that has power or influence over others and that people regard as being legitimate leaders. The top few percent of power holders in government and the economy, for example, are members of the society's elite.

In his study of elite domination in American society, for example, C. Wright Mills (1956) argued that what he called the **power elite** dominates American society. Typically the elite make decisions that affect the larger society and set the trends the society follows. Mills suggested that the elite does not form a "ruling class" because they are not a class—they come from different sectors of society, especially the military and political elites, if not the economic elite.

The exercise of power in modern society, Mills argued, is not based on the use of force but by the elite reserving for itself the ability to make or influence the crucial political, economic, and military decisions that affect society. They are able to do this not only because of their own positions, but because by and large the public is unaware that these decisions are even being made. Moreover, those who do know are convinced that those at the top are best suited to be making these decisions. In effect, the elite dominates as a consequence of the ignorance and indifference of the public. Elites are more unified and less confused about their interests than other groups in the society.

When we study political power, whether in public institutions like Congress or the Houses of Parliament, or interpersonal relationships like marriage, we should not only focus on open disputes but also examine the control of information and the ways people acquire the values that lead them to accept authority. Domination always means controlling other people's knowledge and attitudes and, thereby, helping to disable, decouple, or exclude them and create scarcity for them. In this respect, the creation of symbols of inequality is also very important. (We will discuss the latter further in the introduction to Part III on status inequality.)

Note, though, that an analysis of gender inequality does not seem to fit neatly into the traditional sociological approaches to power inequality. It does not fit well the Marxist scheme because gender inequalities in power are not about class inequality or relations to the means of production. It does not fit the Weberian scheme because gender has not, historically, been a basis on which people have formed status groups and have mobilized to compete for power. (Gender inequality has had a strong basis in the legitimation provided by Weber's traditional and national legal forms of authority.) So new theories of gender inequality are needed.

Feminist scholars have made a significant contribution to our understanding of power and gender in the past few decades. Compared with traditional sociological approaches radical feminism is a relatively recent political theory and is still developing. What distinguishes radical feminism from earlier theories is the claim that the oppression of women is fundamental. By this feminists mean some or all of the following depending on the theorist's approach (see, for example, Jaggar and Rothenberg, 1984:87):

1. Women were, historically, the first oppressed group.
2. Women's oppression is the most widespread, existing in virtually every known society.
3. Women's oppression is deeper than any other, in that it is the hardest form of oppression to eradicate and cannot be removed by other social changes such as the abolition of class society.
4. Women's oppression causes the most suffering to its victims, although this suffering may often go unrecognized.
5. Women's oppression provides a conceptual model for understanding all other forms of oppression.

Despite their differences, radical feminists all hold the view that *the personal is political*. What this means is that politics does not just go on in the public sphere—it is also a feature of the day-to-day, night-to-night lives of women everywhere. This insight is very similar to C. Wright Mills's (1959) idea that "public issues" are the flip side of "personal troubles."

To label a certain area of human life as merely personal (as opposed to public and political) is to trivialize and conceal the problem: in this case, the domination of women in everyday life. Further, it denies the legitimacy of women's struggle against personal forms of domination. The radical feminist argues that male domination infects every area of life and must be fought against in every sphere, including the home.

For this reason, sexuality is an issue of central political concern. Many radical feminists argue that the roots of male dominance lie in the male control of women's bodies. Men have traditionally defined women as primarily sexual beings and have identified heterosexual intercourse as the norm for sexual activity. Thus, redefining "normal" sexuality and giving women control over their own bodies are both essential actions in radical feminist thinking.

A society has to reconceive of the relationship between public power and personal life—as the feminists have done—if it is to achieve equality. It has to ensure that no group or individual is allowed to fall below a certain level of economic well-being and respect, and this can only be done by redistributing power within the society.

Many of the points radical feminists make about the domination of women by men also can be applied to an analysis of racial inequality and the domination of nonwhites by whites. Thus, radical feminism is not only a new way of viewing relations between the sexes; it is a new way of viewing power inequality in general.

If the *risk factors* for inequality—of gender, race, and class—occur for power inequality so, too, do the four *mechanisms* of inequality we identified at the beginning of this volume. The readings in Part II will show again and again how social exclusion, decoupling, disability, and scarcity—all rooted in some form of accepted legitimation—support inequalities in power. Let us briefly refer to one excerpt included in Part II, to illustrate.

The paper by Fabricant (excerpt 6.3) shows that when it comes to power, the homeless of America are at the bottom of North America's social ladder. Many homeless people are former mental patients. Others are jobless or working people who could not find affordable housing. Together they form an underclass of utterly destitute, powerless people—the untouchables of America. And, homelessness is increasing in North American cities at an alarming rate.

Homelessness is partly rooted in *scarcity*, of income and employment and affordable accommodations. But, there is more to it than that, as Fabricant shows. There is also a problem of political inaction. The latter occurs in large part because of the widely shared belief that homeless people are to blame for their condition. Often the homeless people come to believe this, too; certainly they feel powerless to improve their lives. Both sets of beliefs "legitimize" their situation. These beliefs are, of course, *disabling*.

Social service agencies tend to reinforce these attitudes. Many treat the homeless with cold, rational detachment as "clients." But advocates of the empowerment approach believe in creating warmer, more equal relationships with their clients. They want to remove unnecessary bureaucratic obstacles to getting help. And they try to create an environment in which the homeless person will feel welcome. In short, they try to enable the homeless and to work against their state of extreme *decoupling* and *exclusion*.

Central to the empowerment approach is the development of group consciousness. By discussing their predicament with others, homeless people come to realize that their problems are not unique. They begin to recognize the things that have affected their lives and made them homeless. As they shift the blame from themselves to outside factors, they gain the motivation to do something about their situations.

Much of the problem of the homeless, then, is a matter of the absence of political will to change mechanisms of the inequality. However, some of the change needed to bring about more equality will come through the efforts of the disadvantaged themselves. The homeless, and poor people generally, have fewer community resources than rich people do. Involvement in community organizations is important, but it takes time and energy—scarce resources to the poor person struggling to just get by.

In addition, the poor tend to be fatalistic about their situation and skeptical that they can do anything to improve it. These views, and the decoupling, need to be changed if attempts to lessen inequality are to be very successful.

This is just one illustration from among many provided in Part II of the effects of processes of exclusion, disability, decoupling, and scarcity in making for inequalities in power across the genders, races, and classes. There is much sobering evidence in this part for the cross-cultural generality of these mechanisms of inequality and the three forms of inequality. There are also several examples of social arrangements that are helping people move in the direction of some greater inequality, if ever so slowly.

CONSEQUENCES OF INEQUALITIES IN POWER

As we saw in Part I, there are many serious consequences of economic inequality. The same is true, as might be expected, of inequalities in power. The consequences for individuals of economic and power inequality are of three broad types: (a) effects upon life chances, (b) effects upon lifestyles, and (c) effects upon political behavior and beliefs.

In section 1, we emphasized many of the consequences for life chances ranging from differential access to basic needs—food, shelter, and health care—to problems of working conditions, harmful effects on the family, and violence and drug abuse. Lifestyles, it will be remembered, refer to patterns of behavior, patterns of social interaction across status.

Part III will present several excerpts that emphasize these consequences. In this part we focus more on consequences for political behavior and beliefs of inequality in power, although evidence of life chance consequences of inequality also continues to mount here.

Differences in economic and power advantage involve differences in interests, so we can expect that sometimes an awareness of these interests will develop, and the haves and have-nots will vie with each other over their interests. If the pursuit of interests becomes at all pronounced, it can be expected to lead to differences between haves and the have-nots in political beliefs and values and behavior.

For the same reason, barriers of social exclusion between the haves and the have-nots will be developed, largely by the haves who have more resources and the greater need for exclusion. These, in turn, may lead to still other differences in beliefs and behavior. In other words, *subcultures of different ways of thinking and acting politically* can easily develop out of the interests that surround social classes, the genders, and races and ethnic groups.

There is no easy way of predicting the full details of these subcultures, no way of saying precisely how people will come to differ in beliefs and behavior. For an understanding of the character and prevalence of inequality-based subcultures, a large-scale research effort across societies is required. The selections in this section will suggest what a very large task this is, and will give examples of appropriate research techniques.

Karl Marx made a now-famous observation that it is not the consciousness of people that determines their being, but rather their social being, primarily their relation to the mode of production, and class, that determines their consciousness. We can ask to what extent this view is correct for different societies: Does social class determine beliefs and outlook? Are the different social classes aware of their differences? Do individuals in similar economic positions see themselves as having similar interests? Do people try to safeguard or pursue their interests?

Going further, we can ask whether the different classes develop still other differences in beliefs and behaviors. Likewise, we can ask the same questions about differences between races and ethnic groups, differences between the genders. Various excerpts in Parts II and III pursue these questions.

Consciousness of common class interests has developed in many places and has led, at times, to organized class struggles that changed the whole structure of societies. But class consciousness does not follow automatically from class differences. People having a particular class position may not be aware of their position and the consequences flowing from it. Thinking and conduct are not determined merely by position in the economic order or power structure but depend in part upon the way in which people come to perceive and interpret their social circumstances.

Socialization—through the educational system, the media, and churches—has effects upon people's thinking about their class, race, or gender position and its meaning. Some observers say that much of what is taught in the educational system, media, and churches either obscures social inequality or is supportive of and justifies it.

So, for example, people are taught that everyone has an equal opportunity to get whatever they want in income, power, and status. Or, they are taught that some inequality is a necessary outcome of the workings of the economy, but that this should be tolerated because it is for the common good. Such disabling beliefs work against the development of group consciousness among the disadvantaged and help contain conflict.

Moreover, people "carry with them" *various* achieved and ascribed statuses, and related sets of experiences, at any given point in their lives. For example, a person has, simultaneously, the experiences of a class position, an ethnic status and race, a gender, and an age group. These statuses often compete for people's attention and action.

It is therefore difficult to know which of these sets of experiences will influence most of the person's perceptions of social inequality. We cannot assume the presence of common group consciousness, but must, in each circumstance, investigate how people evaluate and respond to the inequality they experience.

NOTES

Jaggar, Alison M. and Paula S. Rothenberg (1984). *Feminist Frameworks: Alternative Theoretical Accounts of the Relations between Women and Men.* Second edition. New York: McGraw-Hill.

Mills, C. Wright (1956). *The Power Elite.* New York: Oxford University Press.

Mills, C. Wright (1959). *The Sociological Imagination.* New York: Oxford University Press.

Weber, Max (1968). *Economy and Society.* New York: Bedminster Press.

SUGGESTED READINGS FOR PART II

Abercrombie, Nicholas, Stephen Hill, and Bryan S. Turner (1980). *The Dominant Ideology Thesis.* London: Allen and Unwin.

Crompton, Rosemary and Michael Mann, eds. (1986). *Gender and Stratification.* Cambridge: Polity Press.

Howard, Robert (1985). *Brave New Workplace.* New York: Viking.

Kanter, Rosabeth Moss (1977). *Men and Women of the Corporation.* New York: Basic Books.

Lerner, Gerda (1986). *The Creation of Patriarchy.* New York: Oxford University Press.

Michels, Robert (1962). *Political Parties.* New York: Harcourt Brace.

Rossi, Peter H. (1989). *Down and Out in America: The Origins of Homelessness.* Chicago: University of Chicago Press.

Skocpol, Theda (1979). *States and Social Revolutions.* Cambridge, MA: Harvard University Press.

Walby, Sylvia (1991). *Theorizing Patriarchy.* Oxford: Basil Blackwell.

Weber, Max (1946 [1922]). *From Max Weber: Essays in Sociology* (H. Gerth and C. W. Mills, eds. and trans.). New York: Oxford University Press and his (1947 [1922]) *The Theory of Social and Economic Organization* (T. Parsons, ed. and trans.). New York: The Free Press.

SECTION FOUR
Patterns of Power Relations

4.1 Workplace Relations in Advanced Capitalist Societies

Stephen Frenkel

This article is about one particular pattern of power relations: the conflict between employers and employees.

How is power distributed in the workplace in industrialized societies? The answer, it turns out, is that there is not a single pattern. Somewhat different patterns occur in different societies, depending on the history of labor-management relations and cultural values.

In this excerpt, comparisons are drawn among workers in Japan, Great Britain, and France. They have one main thing in common: Management always has the greater power, and workers are controlled. Beyond this, though, there are significant national differences in how workplace control is exercised.

For example, the Japanese system generally has reasonably secure employment (often for the working lifetime), a seniority-plus-merit wage system, enterprise-based unions, enterprise-based training, and a high level of positive feeling for the enterprise among workers. This stands in marked contrast to the British system, with its considerable interfirm mobility of employment, a market-based wage and salary system, publicly provided training, industry-wide unions, and greater class consciousness and worker-management conflict.

The author argues that the reason for differences between these two countries is that Japan's industrialization took place later. The British system, including its national unions, was established before the emergence of large corporations, when working conditions were harsh and work organizations were less effective at "managing" their workers. In Japan, on the other hand, corporations developed rapidly with more effective management and without strong countervailing unions. National differences in state planning and control of the economy also helped to create workplace differences.

Differences in cultural values may have been important, too, in that Japan is a more collectivity-oriented society. Management that placed a high value on the collectivity was perhaps more sensitive to the needs of the worker. Likewise, workers sharing this value might have more positive feelings for the enterprise.

Excerpted from Frenkel, Stephen (1986) "Industrial, sociology, and workplace relations in advanced capitalist societies," *International Journal of Comparative Sociology*, 27(1–2), January-April, 69–86. With permission of E. J. Brill, Leiden.

This paper begins with a critical review of three studies which reveal connections between the wider society and workplace relations. I shall show how insights from these studies can be used as a basis for theory construction and application. For the sake of illustration the interpretive schema developed in the paper will be applied to the workplace in Australia.

WORKPLACE RELATIONS: (1) THE JAPANESE-BRITISH CONTRAST

Dore's (1973) classic study of four electrical engineering workplaces—two in Japan and under common Japanese ownership, the other two in Britain and owned by a British company—permits him to claim the existence of two different employment systems. The Japanese system involves 'lifetime employment, a seniority-plus-merit wage system, an intra-enterprise career system, enterprise training, enterprise unions and a high level of enterprise consciousness . . .' (Dore 1973: 264). This enterprise-based employment system stands in contrast to the British market-based arrangement with its 'considerable [inter-firm] mobility of employment, a market-based wage and salary system, self-designed, mobile rather than regulated careers, publicly provided training, industrial or craft unions, more state welfare and a greater strength of professional, craft, regional or class consciousness . . .' (Dore 1973: 264).

Dore argues that while cultural values foster and maintain certain aspects of workplace relations, the Japanese employment system bears the imprint of two trends which affect all advanced industrial societies. These are: (1) the emergence of the large corporation and (2) the extension of democratic ideals to the workplace.

Dore contends that employment relations in most advanced industrialized societies that developed late resemble the Japanese system. In time, Dore believes, British workplace relations will come to resemble the Japanese system. This convergence—which will never be complete owing to cultural differences between societies—is not simply one-way. Dore maintains that growing state intervention is characteristic of all advanced capitalist economies, a trend which will shape employment and welfare systems in a similar way.

Dore's analysis has three major strengths: it integrates workplace analysis with a theory of social change; second, this is accomplished by means of detailed comparative empirical research; and third, his study pays close attention to the impact of history.

Notwithstanding the importance of this study, there are several weaknesses worth noting. First, as Dore recognises (1973: 302), the employment systems of large Japanese firms are not typical of Japanese industry. A second criticism concerns Dore's assertion that late and rapid industrialisation necessarily implies a significant role for large corporations in the shaping of industrial relations. This is refuted by the Swedish and Australian cases, which indicate the importance of labour movements in structuring labour relations.

A third related weakness of Dore's analysis lies in his assumption that because capital intensive technology is costly, large firms will necessarily establish internal labour markets, extensive welfare measures and, where possible, enterprise unionism in an effort to ensure employee loyalty. Not only are alternative industrial relations strategies available to large corporations—witness the history of employer attempts to avoid all forms of unionism in the United States—but the strategies adopted depend crucially on the political economic environment. Thus, Koshiro (1983) takes Dore to task for over-emphasising the role of management, arguing that workers played an important part in perpetuating the dominant features of the Japanese employment system.

The final and most serious shortcoming of Dore's study is his failure to examine the way changes in the distribution of class power influence industrial relations institutions and employee behaviour. . . .

WORKPLACE RELATIONS: (2) THE FRENCH-BRITISH CONTRAST

Gallie looks mainly to the politics of the labour movement in explaining the more radical attitudes of French workers and their lower commitment to the procedural and substantive norms of the industrial enterprise compared to their British counterparts. He mainly draws upon empirical data relating to the structure and content of managerial control practices, trade unionism and industrial relations in four workplaces in the oil industry, two in France and two in Britain.

The distinguishing features highlighted by Gallie are claimed to represent general patterns in French and British industrial relations (Gallie 1978: 315; 1983: 96). These can be briefly summarised. First, French paternalist management, with its emphasis on unilateral control and concern for the individual employee, differs from the British approach which is characterised by limited acceptance by management of unions as negotiating partners. Second, French employees reporting less control over work than their British counterparts. Third, French workers are less strongly integrated into the enterprise than their British colleagues. . . .

According to Gallie, French employees' experience of inequality at work is sharpened by radical union policies but the unions are weak at the point of production. They are divided along ideological lines and remain pre-occupied with wider political issues. This enables management to retain unilateral control in the workplace. Gallie argues that the left-wing parties in France, in particular the Communist Party, furnish a vocabulary which enables workers to understand and articulate their sentiments. These parties also act as a medium for resolving work-related problems at a national level. . . .

Gallie's analysis has the merit of directing attention to the policies and role of the labour movement in workplace relations. Moreover, state politics, particularly the role of governments at critical historical junctures, is also shown to be important. A further advantage of Gallie's study is his reference to the way industrial relations arrangements, or what I have elsewhere referred to as accommodation structures (Frenkel, 1980: 15–16; Frankel and Coolican, 1984: Ch. 9) have served to bolster management domination in France. Being centralised and offering the unions little

opportunity for bargaining, these structures have reinforced the union's preoccupation with state policies. This contrasts with Britain where decentralised collective bargaining has encouraged greater co-operation between management and employees.

There are several problems with Gallie's analysis. Gallie provides no detailed discussion of management ideology and strategy during industrialisation. Nor is it clear why Right wing parties have tended to dominate the French polity, an observation which draws attention to the most serious weakness of Gallie's analysis: his failure to systematically explore the role of the state in industrial relations. . . .

WORKPLACE RELATIONS (3): PRODUCTION POLITICS AND THE ROLE OF THE STATE

Burawoy's (1983) study takes the state as its central theme arguing that the state plays a crucial role in shaping, what he terms, factory regimes. A distinction is made between *despotic* and *hegemonic* regimes, the former being characterised by workers being highly dependent on employers. The workers are unable to resist arbitrary coercion while employers are forced to intensify their control over labour in response to competitive pressures. Hegemonic regimes, on the other hand, are characterised by a less unequal distribution of power between management and workers, where 'consent prevails, although never to the exclusion of coercion' (Burawoy, 1983: 590). The transformation from despotic to hegemonic regimes depends on reducing worker dependence on wage labour and limiting managerial discretion in labour matters. According to Burawoy, this is accomplished most decisively through state intervention: by providing social insurance for the unemployed and through labour legislation regulating management control. This implies factory regimes will vary from one country to another depending mainly on the extent and effectiveness of state intervention.

This proposition is illustrated by reference to factory regimes in Sweden, Japan, the U.S. and England. I shall concentrate on England and Japan as these countries have been discussed earlier in connection with Dore's analysis.

In England, industrialisation occurred early against a background of labour dependence on factory wages. According to Burawoy, this fostered the development of unions. Thus, early craft unionism laid the groundwork for a continuing emphasis on sectional workplace bargaining. State intervention in the workplace was viewed with suspicion. This attitude was also held by employers, who, during the long wave of imperialist expansion and consolidation, had little incentive to seek state assistance in industrial relations. The unions, and the Labour Party in particular, nevertheless pressed for government intervention in the labour market, resulting in the establishment of a relatively high social wage compared to other advanced capitalist societies.

Japan's corporate paternalism is explained historically by the presence of a labour surplus coupled with the dominance of large enterprises in a late and rapid industrialisation. By comparison with England, the balance of class power was more inclined towards employers who were able to shape trade unionism and workplace relations more decisively than in England. They did so in part, by ensuring that state intervention in the labour market and in the workplace was minimal.

Burawoy argues that a new crisis of profitability is currently underway. With the balance of power having shifted more in favour of employers, a new form of factory regime has emerged. Burawoy terms this form of regime *hegemonic despotism*. It represents the granting of concessions by labour to capital based on the threat of capital mobility and consequent unemployment. In sum, the shifting balance of class forces in production, both historically and currently, represents the key to understanding employers, unions, and the state.

Burawoy's analysis has the merit of developing a number of key concepts. These include the notion of factory regime and the state's role in the economy. Burawoy's analysis is also more comprehensive than those of Dore and Gallie in that it covers four societies rather than two, and so pays greater attention to the role of the three key actors— employers, unions, and the state—rather than focusing mainly on employer (Dore) and the labour movement (Gallie) as explanatory factors.

There are several deficiencies in this study . . . . The concept of factory regime is too restricted to encompass the varieties of accommodation structures that mediate class power and workplace behaviour. Thus, in countries like Australia, Sweden and, to a lesser extent, West Germany, where the main structures of accommodation involve multi-employer groupings and multi-union organisations, many of the major features of workplace relations are fashioned beyond the factory gates.

Another problem with Burawoy's analysis is [that he] ignores the role of ideology or consciousness. . . .

When we turn to Burawoy's explanation of variations in workplace relations, four shortcomings are noteworthy. First, although his typology of state intervention is useful in explaining differences in the four selected countries, its more general applicability is open to question. Variations in the *extent* of state intervention in most advanced capitalist societies does not differ markedly although the *form* of intervention in workplace relations varies a good deal. This suggests the nature and role of the state require further clarification.

A second weakness stems from the contradictory position assumed by the state in Burawoy's theory. On the one hand, differences in state intervention are assigned a primary explanatory role, while on the other, the state's role reflects the balance of class power.

This brings me to the third problem: Burawoy's failure to explicitly incorporate state politics into his conception of class power. I am referring here to the capacity of employer and worker collectivities to galvanise public opinion and secure the support of party organisations in order to influence legislative and judicial decision-making.

The fourth problem concerns the connection between changes in the distribution of class power and changes in the role of the state. From Burawoy's analysis it seems that a change in the balance of class forces is a necessary, but not sufficient, condition for a change in the level of state intervention. Nevertheless, appreciable changes in the level of state intervention occur irregularly and infrequently, for example, in the aftermath of war.

IMPLICATIONS FOR A THEORY OF WORKPLACE RELATIONS

Emerging from the above review are several propositions that merit further empirical application. These propositions go some way towards a theory of workplace relations, and can be stated briefly: (1) Contemporary workplace relations are reproduced and changed in the context of a set of constraining factors which only very rarely permit these relations to be created *de novo*. (2) Three principal factors tend to shape the dominant patterns of workplace relations in any advanced capitalist society. These are (a) large enterprises; (b) the labour movement and (c) the state. (3) In most advanced capitalist societies the basic pattern of workplace relations is inscribed at critical historical junctures. Such crises have a significant impact on the distribution of power between capital, labour, and the state. (4) Arising from such crises is a process of institutional change in the regulation of industrial conflict. (5) There will be differences in the way the major collectivities institutionalise conflict and regulate workplace relations. Factors promoting convergence in workplace relations include the rise of the large corporations, state intervention in national economies and the tendency towards greater integration of the world economic system. . . .

APPLYING THE CONCEPTUAL FRAMEWORK: WORKPLACE RELATIONS IN AUSTRALIA

The framework developed above can explain the typical features of Australian workplace relations. These include comparatively high union density (50 per cent or more) with employees being immediately represented by lay, part-time union representatives. These shop stewards are accorded a marginal negotiating role by management. Australian workplace representatives have therefore had little incentive and often insufficient power to create durable shop steward organisations.

The second feature is the relatively high level of organised industrial conflict. Short duration strikes and other pressure tactics are frequently deployed by strategically placed work groups (Frenkel, 1980: Ch. 6). Third, the adjustment of workplace rules is mainly through unilateral imposition by management or the product of a compromise arising from protest by work groups. Fourth, the reward system is characterised by two major principles: (a) wages and conditions are established and changed mainly by employers, unions, and statutorily regulated tribunals according to market *and* social criteria. And (b), wage rates are set by reference to occupational categories (job titles) rather than on the basis of performance, additional acquired skills, or seniority.

To explain the Australian pattern it is necessary to go back to 1860–1890 [when] permanent unions developed. They inherited their forms, customs, and ideology largely from the British immigrants who comprised the great majority of the population at that time. These unions were structured mainly along occupational lines; their leaders favoured control of the labour supply, collective bargaining, and where necessary, the use of political influence. Ideologically the unions favoured economic prosperity and better wages and conditions for their members.

The growing power of the unions—who by 1890 comprised one fifth of wage and salary earners (Macintyre, 1983: 99) mostly in strategic industries—was resented by employers. An opportunity to reassert control occurred in the last decade of the century when economic recession reduced the economic power of the unions. A series of massive strikes occurred essentially over the recruitment of non-union labour. The unions were defeated and with little economic leverage they sought to redress the new balance of class power through political means. This entailed greater emphasis on parliamentary representation through the labour parties in the various States. Substantively, the unions sought the establishment of conciliation and arbitration arrangements. The distribution of class power moved towards labour in the first decade of the 20th Century as trade improved and the labour parties consolidated their position. The upshot of this was the creation of conciliation and arbitration arrangements in most of the States. In the federal sphere a new class compromise was concluded under the banner of 'New Protection'. Tariff protection—'fair compensation'—went hand in hand with 'fair wages'. Thus, in 1904, legislation was introduced enabling a new court to make and enforce awards determining fair and reasonable wages. This Court, like its State counterparts, encouraged the growth of registered organisations of employers and employees.

By 1910, the Australian accommodation structure had been forged. It embodied two salient features of the British system: support for independent trade unions based on the expression of widespread sectional working class interests and limited direct government intervention (Fox, 1985). But unlike British voluntarism, the Australian accommodation system encouraged the development of statutory conciliation and arbitration tribunals which continue to occupy a central place in regulating capital-labour relations to this day.

By the time secondary industry expanded rapidly in the 1920s, large corporations lacked the power to reconstruct the system of industrial relations. Nor was there much incentive to do so. According to Connell and Irving (1980: 279), there was a substantial reserve of unemployed labour until the 1940s and thereafter mass immigration from non-English-speaking countries ensured a relatively compliant workforce. In any case, the continuation of tariff protection meant that the pressure to reduce unit labour costs was not as strong as in some other industrialised countries. Last but not least, the accommodation system proved flexible enough to forestall any threat to its existence. Thus, in 1931, the Federal tribunal was able to enforce a 10 per cent wage reduction (Committee of Review, Vol. 2, 1985: 38).

To sum up: it is to the labour movement that we must look to understand workplace relations in Australia. These were forged at a time of crisis and have not changed fundamentally since the early years of this century. The state has remained a dominant and stabilising actor in the drama.

The marginal role played by shop stewards and the absence of formal consultative or negotiating structures at workplace level derive partly from the small scale of workplaces in Australia, but more particularly from the fact that awards, determined outside the plant, are viewed by employers as authoritative and comprehensive. Union leaders too have been reticent to promote workplace consultation or bargaining except as an adjunct to award determination.

It is not surprising that Australian workplace relations are characterised by a high level of organised conflict for this is closely associated with attempts by management to impose their policies on the workforce. The scope for doing so is wide. Awards, though detailed, do not cover many issues relating to work organisation and work performance, nor are the award clauses specific enough to cater for the special conditions in different workplaces. The net result is tension and irregular skirmishes as management and labour continue to extend and defend their positions along the frontier of control. . . .

BIBLIOGRAPHY

Burawoy, M. 1983. 'Between the Labor Process and the State: The Changing Face of Factory Regimes under Advanced Capitalism', *American Sociological Review*, 48, 5.

Committee of Review 1985. Report of the Committee of Review on Australian Industrial Relations Law and Systems, Vol.2, A.G.P.S., Canberra.

Connell, R. W. and Irving, T. H. 1980. Class Structure in Australian History, Documents, Narrative and Argument, Longman Cheshire, Melbourne.

Dore, R. P. 1973. British Factory—Japanese Factory, George Allen and Unwin, London. *The Economist*, December 7, 1985.

Fox, A. 1974. Beyond Contract: Work, Power and Trust Relations, Faber, London.

Fox, A. 1985. History and Heritage: The Social Origins of the British Industrial Relations System, George Allen & Unwin, London.

Frenkel, S.J. (ed.) 1980. Industrial Action, Patterns of Labour Conflict, George Allen and Unwin, Sydney.

Frenkel, S.J. and Coolican, A. 1984. Unions Against Capitalism? A Sociological Comparison of the Australian Building and Metalworkers' Unions, George Allen and Unwin, Sydney.

Gallie, D. 1978. In Search of the New Working Class, Automation and Social Integration within the Capitalist Enterprise, Cambridge University Press, Cambridge.

Gallie, D. 1983. Social Inequality of Class Radicalism in France and Britain, Cambridge University Press, Cambridge.

Macintyre, S.F. 1983. "Labour, Capital and Arbitration, 1890-1920', in Head, B. (ed.), State and Economy in Australia, Oxford University Press, Melbourne.

4.2 Racial Conflict in Post-Industrial America

Joseph Antoine

The next excerpt is about affirmative action for a disadvantaged minority. It concerns the dynamics of class, gender, and race in North America's labor market.

The piece deals with power struggles around **affirmative action** policies, and questions about the legitimacy of these policies by those whose interests are being adversely affected.

These state-supported affirmative action policies are directed at improving the lots of women and racial minorities in employment. But they are creating a "backlash" among middle-class (largely male) workers, it is argued. The latter, especially young males just starting their careers, tend to see the policies as lessening their chances for attractive employment, compared to a situation without such policies. The resulting economic anxieties fuel racial antagonism and gender conflict in the middle class.

The anxieties of the white middle-class men will also result in political action.

The author emphasizes that this group already has a comparatively high involvement in politics, particularly in conservative politics. The economic and status anxieties raised by affirmative action programs will push more middle-class male voters in the direction of conservative politicians who oppose affirmative action.

It remains to be seen whether this kind of backlash will affect politics, or policies, in any important way.

. . . This essay will examine changes occurring in postindustrial America. I argue that recent controversy over affirmative action symbolizes a resurgence of racial antagonisms (as well as a possible intensification of conflict along gender lines). Although the immediate sphere of engagement is in employment, the effects are probably most clearcut in political competition, a not infrequent result when competition over scarce resources leads to a political contest between racial and ethnic groups. The potency of affirmative action as an issue is due to its interweaving questions of the fairness of the economic structure of American society with competing claims for economic gain and political power.

The following premises underlie this hypothesis: social conflict in post industrial America cannot avoid the distributive consequence of material insecurity. Its particular resonance in the United States is a consequence of the public sector's minimal role in mitigating economic insecurity by comparison to other capitalist democracies. Given the relative parsimony of the American welfare state, the possession of a good job is critical for the acquisition and maintenance of middle and upper middle class life styles. However, the contemporary service economy produces fewer good jobs

Excerpted from Joseph, Antoine (1991), "The resurgence of racial conflict in post-industrial America," *International Journal of Politics, Culture, and Society,* 5(1), 81–93. With permission of Human Sciences Press.

than its industrial predecessor did in its heyday.

Yet, even if the number of jobs providing access to middle class standards of living were not declining in absolute terms, there is still a basis for the perception of a relative decline in their availability. Competition among potential candidates for good jobs has increased due to the higher rates of college attendance among the general population and the entry of women and minorities into occupations to which their access was once restricted. Their wider access to good jobs translates into a perception of relative deprivation for younger white males who face a deterioration of their life chances in contrast to their formerly privileged access to secure well paying employment. Such competition provides a catalyst for a resurgence of racial (and sexual) conflict in the political economy. . . . The competition for scarce resources in education and housing as well as increasing racial competition in employment suggest there may be a resurgence of racialism and an accompanying backlash.

Affirmative action provides an attractive target because of the entry of blacks and women into positions which were once a nearly exclusive preserve of white males. For occupations in which whites and blacks compete, the presumption that blacks are unfairly aided by quotas, special programs, etc. contributes to a rise in racial antipathy.[1] That the improvement in the occupational standing of blacks is partly at the expense of whites is supported by a number of investigators (Burstein, 1985; Featherman and Hauser, 1977; Lieberson, 1980). Burstein finds that in terms of group income shares the gap between white men and other groups narrowed between 1953–1978 (Burstein, 1985:138).

But affirmative action's symbolic significance is magnified well beyond its actual impact since only about half the private sector non-education workforce is covered by statutes (Smith and Welch, 1986). What makes affirmative action so potent politically is that it provides a microfoundation for conflict in the workplace while simultaneously channeling increasing anxieties about future economic security. Concerns about economic insecurity are creatively translated into a preoccupation with gains made by minorities. Peretz has used the term "demand transference" to describe situations in which "people whose financial situation is getting worse for reasons unrelated to inflation, come to blame their misfortune on inflation rather than on its real cause" (1983:93). I argue that "racial transference" similarly heightens racial tensions by providing a scapegoat for anxieties stemming from economic insecurity. . . .

. . . Although the transition to a postindustrial economy has affected the livelihood of all groups in the population, white males with a high school education or less face the greatest relative decline. That economic insecurity is overladen with status anxiety and impressions of relative deprivation is evident in the indications that women's political attitudes and behaviour are less volatile than men's notwithstanding their greater economic insecurity. While young less educated male workers of all races face a squeeze due to deindustrialization, the greater deterioration in the life chances of young blacks does not lend itself to such status anxiety, given their already impoverished circumstances.[2]

THE DYNAMICS OF RACE IN A ZERO SUM POLITICAL ECONOMY

The major contributors to this resurgence in race consciousness as an axis of political and economic competition are: dein-

dustrialization and the emergence of zero-sum economic competition; the dealignment of the party system; and the disintegration of the Keynesian Welfare State in conjunction with the end of the American century.

It is hardly coincidental that less educated white males are the group whose political stance has moved most to the right. Compositional factors weigh heavily in explaining their increasing conservatism. The movement from unionized manufacturing employment to nonunionized service employment has had a conservative influence. Even though American unions are conservative by crossnational standards, industrial unions have consistently supported equalization and social justice since the New Deal. Freeman and Medoff (1984) have shown that on balance industrial unions' wage and employment policies promote greater economic equalization. The role of unions in political coalitions that support progressive causes is also well established.

By shifting employment from union organized mass production to less organized and unorganized occupations, deindustrialization has undermined a major bulwark of social reform. The decline of mass production industries especially diminishes the supply of good jobs available to non-college graduates. Although service industries are not uniformly hostile to unionization, the net effect of the absence of strong unions in many service occupations is the diminution of union benefits. As the benefits of unions are restricted to an ever smaller proportion of workers, the base of support for such benefits shrinks even more. Thus support for strong unions has become an electoral loser in ever more areas of the country.

The onset of an economic squeeze in 1973 ended the at best moderate tolerance of affirmative action policies. The economic downturn, stagflation, and the emergence of a postindustrial economy have collectively meant economic competition has turned increasingly zero-sum (Thurow, 1980). In this climate the acceptance of affirmative action has ceased....

Furthermore, political conflict over the distribution of good jobs is both shaped by and strengthens the dealignment of the party system. Difficult economic conditions alone often shift political competition rightward. But an additional conservative influence is the departure of middle and working class whites from the Democratic party, a departure closely attuned to an increasing discomfort with heightened intra-party competition with recently organized constituencies and what is taken to be an embrace of civil rights by the national Democratic party. For middle and working class white males this multiplicity of resentment coalesces around a presumption that minorities are unfairly advantaged, that contemporary welfare state programs offer few benefits to the majority, and that higher taxes to pay for such benefits, primarily for those unlike oneself are unacceptable.

The major changes in urban politics, specifically the increased competitiveness of minorities in the politics of urban America contribute to this perception that minorities garner unearned advantages. Increasing rates of political participation, changes in legal statutes, and suburbanization have combined to make minorities a plurality if not an outright majority in many large cities.[3] Such changes reduce the possibility of maintaining the nonreciprocal political linkages that once typified interracial political relations.

The dissolution of the Keynesian welfare state (KWS) strengthens the conservative counterthrust because it reflected not merely an economic strategy but served as a political and social mechanism of integration.

In the United States, Keynesian society was an exercise in coalition building—the political integration of previously marginal social groups and the harmonization of diverse constituencies—in the singular American sense, set against the backdrop of a very shallow welfare state" (Krieger, 1986:118). Accordingly, the "Reagan Revolution" has economically disadvantaged and marginalized two central constituencies which had been partly integrated into the affairs of state by the KWS programs and the New Deal/Kennedy coalition politics of the "War on Poverty" (Krieger, 1986:198).

The Reagan-led coalition's repudiation of Keynesianism transcends its economic functions by repudiating this assimilative dimension. Furthermore, by idealizing an economy without a society, the retrograde Social Darwinist vision embodied in Reaganism reinforces everpresent negative stereotypes of minority groups.

Essential in sustaining the contemporary conservative movement is this relative deterioration in the life chances of white males who have historically formed the most privileged race by gender stratum, a deterioration exacerbated by the declining imperial status of the United States.

The backlash against affirmative action thereby synthesizes the uncertain prospects and increasing insecurity which affects those who until recently enjoyed a privileged access to the pool of good jobs while offering a convenient scapegoat....

Fears which surface as resentment to affirmative action incorporate anxieties stemming from several sources: the dynamic effects of labor markets, the current economic transformation, and social policy. Affirmative action serves as a useful foil in translating anxieties attributable to economic insecurity, interracial political competition and apprehensions about minorities into a potent source of conservative political mobilization.

THE DILEMMAS OF AFFIRMATIVE ACTION

... Affirmative action policies are a consequence of both the failure as well as the limits of broader policies to provide equity and equality. For example, earlier support for equal employment opportunity legislation reflected a changing political universe due to the consolidation of the New Deal coalition. But notwithstanding the breadth of this support, that it took until the 1970's for legislation to be enacted outlines the arduous path to be traveled for social reforms which benefit mostly minorities even within an economic context of sustained growth (Burstein, 1985).

Affirmative action policies are attuned to a political, social, and legal environment that possibly no longer exists, given the decline of the New Deal coalition and the tendency for issues of political economy to be framed within a zero-sum context. But saying this does not mean I agree with the conservative critique of affirmative action which assumes key decision makers and institutional structures are now capable of an objectively dispassionate neutrality (Glazer, 1978). The presumption made here is both unduly optimistic and questionable in light of the legacy of discrimination. Conservative critics typically overstate the progress which has been made, and curiously find some criteria of discrimination acceptable whereas others remain unacceptable in a highly arbitrary manner. None for example object to regional balancing as a criteria for admission to prestigious colleges and universities. Yet the effective packaging of the conservative critique, in terms of reverse discrimination, is a sign both of the changing political culture and of the difficulties of reallocating group shares in a period of stagnation (Gamson and Modigliani, 1987).

Reverse discrimination is an effective device because it identifies "innocent victims"—whites who have not discriminated themselves—but who are now being disproportionately assessed with the costs of programs for minorities. . . .

This controversy reflects the problems faced by affirmative action programs. . . . The negative effects of affirmative action policies include: 1) an orientation towards relatively narrowly defined special interests; 2) a dependency on legalistic definitions that diminish if not avoid the need for popular assent while maintaining the drawbacks inherent in such approach—fragmentation and demobilization of directly affected constituencies; and 3) the paradox that diminishing individual inequities between individuals with similar credentials may well increase overall inequality and lessen the incentive to search for alternatives to meritocracy.

Meritocracy, for all its pretenses to the contrary, tends to reward individuals for qualities that are heavily influenced by the success of their parents. White males who presently occupy positions in the professions, for example, are themselves in large measure the beneficiaries of the advantages derived from their parents and grandparents (Livingston, 1979:120).

Affirmative action is a blunt instrument. Quotas and statutes are divisive, and generate undesirable consequences. They disproportionately tax the generation of white males currently entering the employment and educational hierarchies, while primarily benefiting the current cohort of educated minorities. This encourages young white males in particular to redirect the target of their disaffection from the changing economic environment to the relatively paltry preferences reserved for minorities, a misdirection strongly encouraged by politicians seeking electoral support.[4]

CONCLUSION

. . . Political opposition to affirmative action taps into a backlash which concentrates anxieties from disparate sources. With individual credentials increasingly the primary means of access to the middle class, the allocation and distribution of good jobs has become more important. That the possession of a good job is the strongest protection against economic insecurity for the non-wealthy has negative connotations for any future provision of social goods which depends on strong collective organizations. But it is the parsimony of the American welfare state which is the most important underlying problem. The most effective way out of the dilemmas presented by affirmative action is to directly address the meritocratic principles which underly it. By comparison to the current emphasis on equality of opportunity, a shift to greater equality in results would diminish the risks and consequences of private actions.

Limited power necessitates participation in political coalitions. But coalitions require a submergence of differences to some common denominator. This can only happen within a new political coalition very different from the coalitions which formed the backbone of Keynesian welfare states during periods of economic plenty.

The dilemmas of affirmative action run up against the obstacles of race and class. The continued growth of the low wage sector of the economy illustrates the need for a class based political movement, yet race consciousness can thwart class-based appeals. Thus even as the potential of a more universalistic political movement is tantilizing, it remains illusory. But if class based politics is often a mirage, there may be no alternative for lasting gains in spite of the glacial pace at which such changes often occur. . . .

NOTES

1. Kanter (1977:154) argues that within corporate hierarchies, affirmative action is most resented by those most vulnerable to competition from women and minorities. Verba and Orren (1985) find affirmative action to be unpopular with elites even among those who favor income redistribution.

2. "The falling earnings of young men with no more than a high school education account for most of the shrinkage in the middle of the earnings distribution and for most of the expansion at the bottom. In 1973 64% of high-school-only men aged between 25 and 39 earned more than 20,000 (in 1987 dollars). By 1986, the ratio had dropped to 40%." (The Economist, November 12, 1988).

3. According to John Kasarda in an interview discussing data from the Current Population Survey for March 1985 "These data reveal huge losses of Non-Hispanic whites in central cities of the Northeast and Midwest and their partial replacement through minority increases" (The New York Times 10-22-86 pp. A1).

4. Burstein's (1985) careful analysis finds little evidence of widespread reverse discrimination.

REFERENCES

Burstein, Paul. 1985 Discrimination, Jobs, and Politics Chicago: Univ. of Chicago.

Featherman, David and Robert Hauser. 1977 "Changes in the Socioeconomic Stratification of the Races, 1962–1973," AJS 82 (3):621–651.

Freeman, Richard and James Medoff. 1984 What Do Unions Do? New York: Basic Books.

Gamson, William and Andre Modigliani. 1987 "The Changing Culture of Affirmative Action" Research in Political Sociology 3 pp. 137–177.

Glazer, Nathan. 1978 Affirmative Discrimination: Ethnic Inequality and Public Policy New York: Basic Books.

Kanter, Rosabeth M. 1977 Men and Women of the Corporation. New York: Basic Books.

Krieger, Joel. 1986 Reagan, Thatcher and the Politics of Decline. New York: Oxford Univ.

Livingston, John. 1979 *Fair Game? Inequality and Affirmative Action* San Francisco: Freeman.

Lieberson, Stanley. 1980 *A Piece of the Pie* Berkeley: Univ. of California.

Peretz, Paul. 1983 *The Political Economy of Inflation in the United States* Chicago: University of Chicago Press.

Smith, James and Finis Welch. 1986 *Closing the Gap: Forty Years of Economic Progress for Blacks* Santa Monica, Calif.: The Rand Corp.

Thurow, Lester. 1980 *Zero-Sum Society* New York: Basic Books.

Verba, Sidney and Gary R. Orren. 1985 *Equality in America*. Cambridge: Harvard Univ.

4.3 Social Inequality and the Wars in Lebanon

Boutros Labaki

The last excerpt, on affirmative action policies, dealt with a situation of modest, slow change. We often think of the relative power of social groups (classes, genders, and racial and ethnic groups) as changing very slowly, and generally, this is what happens. Powerful groups tend to try to maintain and increase their power, to protect their interests. The previous excerpt showed how very grudgingly groups give up their power.

Yet, if we look at things over a broad sweep of time, there is a lot of change in power distribution in most societies, particularly for classes and ethnic groups. The next selection by Labaki provides a good example of such change in power among religious groups in Lebanon.

This excerpt is about religious and ethnic rivalry in a political arena. Labaki begins by reminding us what the Ottoman society of the 18th century to the beginning of the 20th century looked like. During this period, according to the author, the Muslim community—especially the Druze and the Sunni—had better socioeconomic status and greater power than the Christians or the Shiite communities.

This situation began changing with the European expansion during the first half of the 19th century, which in many ways benefited the Christian communities. Commercial and financial expansion, and European political and military intervention in the region, allowed for a shifting of power and privileges to the Christian group. Over recent decades the Lebanese government has taken steps to narrow the gap in the standard of living between Christians and Muslims and to encourage a greater amount of sharing of state power between the two communities.

The author believes that the improvements in standards of living and increased participation in power for Muslims awakened them to the remaining marked inequality in Lebanon. This factor, he believes, has caused a growing number of Muslims to back groups such as the PLO. At the same time, the Christians have responded by arming themselves and by developing their militia.

Thus, as we said earlier, governments attempt to change inequalities and provide legitimacy, which shores them up. And, the inequalities and legitimization is often questioned by the disadvantaged.

... This article attempts to shed some light on the relationship between Lebanon's horizontal societal cleavages of a socio-economic nature and vertical social cleavages of a communal nature. It attempts to clarify the internal causes of the wars which have broken out in Lebanon since 1975.

WHAT IS A "CONFESSIONAL COMMUNITY" IN LEBANON?

Confessional communities in Lebanon are social groups linked by their origins to a unity of beliefs and religious rites. Historically, these communities have their own distinctive religious networks. These networks control the judiciary system of the community. They often control the community schools and universities network. They also partly control the many community social work and charity associations, sanitary systems, cultural associations, clubs and youth movements, specifically religious associations, etc. ...

EUROPEAN EXPANSION AND THE RISE OF THE CHRISTIAN COMMUNITIES

At the end of the 18th century in the Ottoman regions which made up the Lebanon the Muslim communities—the Druze and the Sunni in particular—had a better social status and participation in power than those of the Christian [mostly Maronite] and Shi'ite communities.

However, during the first half of the nineteenth century ... European expansion profoundly modified the balance-of-power between the different social strata and between the communities, especially in Mount Lebanon [because]:

Excerpted from Labaki, Boutros (1988), "Confessional communities, and social stratification and wars in Lebanon," *Social Compass*, 35(4), 533–561.

- The sanitary improvement measures of European inspiration affected principally the Christian population and provoked a sharp demographic rise in this population.
- The European commercial expansion [based in Beirut] brought about a rapid weakening of the rural and urban craft industries, and a development of export oriented primary productions (especially silk), for the European market.
- The centralizing measures [initiated by the Ottomans in an attempt to counter the European threat with modernization, helped] curb the power of the notables (iktai'yins) of all the communities and increased fiscal pressure on the population.

These modifications brought about a crisis in the rural sector resulting in peasant revolts (between 1820 and 1858) and a weakening and impoverishment of the notables. As these were majority Druze in Mount Lebanon, this associated with the demographic, cultural and economic expansion of the Christian population, resulted in a clear modification in the balance-of-power between these two communities. ...

Frictions continued up to 1858 when the most important of the peasant revolts against the local Maronite notables took place in the Maronite district of the Kesrwan. The revolt rapidly spreading towards the Metn and the mixed (Maronite-Druze) districts, alarmed the Druze notables who succeeded in rallying Druze peasants under their direction. The whole lot degenerated in a civil war in 1860, with European political and French military intervention.

The Protocols of 1860 and 1864 confirmed the abolition of the privileges enjoyed by the notables (iktai'is), and established a representative regime based on proportional communal representation. The status of the clergy and the A'ama (literally the common run of mankind) was reinforced. Within this A'ama emerged new strata of rich peasants, merchants, money lenders, silk manufacturers, liberal professionals, intellectuals and also impoverished peasants, craftsmen and a nucleus of industrial workers of the silk industry.

The political balance-of-power between the Druze and Christian communities became aligned with the demographic, economic and educational balance-of-power. A few advantages were maintained in favour of the Druze notables, who kept the position of Caimacam (equivalent to district governor) of the Shuf, despite the minority of their community in that region.

Between 1860 and 1914, the same factors remained: the expansion of Western educational systems, the extension of commercial relations, the flow of European investments in finance, transport, industries for the processing of raw materials (especially silk), insurance and urban public services. To these factors may be added massive [mainly Christian] emigration towards Egypt and America. This emigration while weakening demographically the Christian communities, strengthened them culturally and economically.

Finally, Mount Lebanon which was predominantly Christian enjoyed some privileges: The population was exempted from military service, and from paying tithe on agricultural production. The population paid only 7.4% of its total income in taxes. In districts which did not belong to this province, the population paid about 10% of its total income in taxes. The majority of this population belonged to Muslim communities. The structure of public expenditure in Mount Lebanon was also less unproductive than in the other districts. And the transfer of income to the central Ottoman treasury in Istanbul was more important in these peripheral districts.

. . . This public financial structure contributed to deepening the economic and social disparities between Mount Lebanon (mainly Christian) and the other regions (mainly Muslim) between 1861 and 1914. . . .

THE BEGINNINGS OF READJUSTMENT IN MANDATORY LEBANON [1918–1941]

The Development of Public Schools Under the Mandatory Authorities

The Mandatory authorities undertook to develop the public educational system, particularly in regions where private schools were lacking. Their number of students rapidly increased from 8,611 in 1925 to 13,632 in 1930.[2] This benefited principally pupils from Muslim communities. At the same time the development of schools by the foreign missions came to a relative stop. In the private educational system, proportions were reversed. Out of 55,358 boys, there were 46,408 Christians (83.8%).

[But] disparities [in literacy rates] persisted. At the end of the Mandate in 1941, the percentage of educated Christians was 71.3% while that of the educated Muslims was a mere 27.2%.[3]

Disparities in secondary education were not negligible either: in 1921, the proportion of Christians in secondary education was 82%.

The Consequences of the World Economic Crisis

The world economic crisis occurring during a large part of the French Mandate period affected the Christian communities' standard of living [in that]:

a) The raw silk export industry was affected by the economic crisis in France, its main importer.
b) Emigration diminished because the economic depression was also occurring in North and Latin America and in Egypt; main host countries of Lebanese Christian emigrants.

The slowdown of the Christian communities' economic progress resulted in a narrower gap between the Muslim communities' standard of living and theirs.

The Role of France
in Promoting Agriculture

. . . . The Mandatory authorities undertook the development of agriculture in several fields (credit, irrigation, land survey, technical support, fiscal incentives). And in 1936, the tithe on agricultural production was suppressed in the peripheral Lebanese areas belonging previously to the Ottoman Wilayas of Beirut and Damascus. The world economic crisis stimulated the orientation of agricultural products towards the local market. This, along with the French policies, benefited the agricultural regions of Lebanon and especially the peripheral areas of the Bekaa, North and South Lebanon. These areas had a slight Muslim majority.

The Political Rise of
the Muslim Communities

Finally, in 1936, Lebanese Muslims achieved two important objectives in the field of power-sharing with the Christian Communities[4]:

a) The principle of a "fair distribution" of the public service positions among the communities was introduced in an addendum to the French-Lebanese friendship and alliance treaty of 1936.
b) The responsibility of Prime Minister was assumed for the first time by a Muslim Sunni leader and this became a tradition in Lebanese political life up to the present day.

INDEPENDENT LEBANON: THE
ACCELERATION OF READJUSTMENT
[1943–1970]

Independence

The accession of the Lebanese state to independence in 1943 required a consensus between the communities on the sharing of power and a redistribution of wealth between regions.

This consensus was realised by equal sharing of public functions between the Christian nd the Muslim Communities and a proportional sharing within each of these communities. Also, from 1950 on, the State progressively applied an active public equipment policy (roads, electricity, telephone, water works, schools and public health).

A progressive policy was also applied in public schooling. From 1943–1953, the percentage of students attending public schools (primary and complementary) rose from 16% to 48% of the total number of students.

As for secondary education, the percentage of the public sector rose from 22% in 1962–63 to 29% in 1970–71. The same applied to higher-level education.

All these developments contributed to narrowing the gap in the standard of living between the regions and the communities. Statistical data on the Lebanese University during the period 1960–66 shows the large proportion of Muslim students [at] the University. The growing proportion of Christian students in this University, reflects its role in bringing together people from various communities.

The Increase of Private Institutions

The various Lebanese communities and, in particular, the Muslim communities, developed their own institutions in the fields of education, health and social and cultural services. These institutions received large donations from the oil-producing Arab countries.

The Muslim communities [also] established a series of universities. . . .

The Economic Boom [in Lebanon and
the Arab Oil Countries]

The rapid economic growth that occurred in Lebanon [after] 1945 brought deep changes in Lebanese income levels. This is due to the growth of production and export of industrial and agricultural goods, and services towards the Arab countries.

The massive emigration of Lebanese to the Arab oil countries generated a flow of remittances resulting [also] in a higher standard of living for the emigrants' families in Lebanon. These remittances were partially used for private investments [especially within the Sunni community].

Demographic Increase of the Shi'ite Community

This economic growth had been preceded and accompanied by an increase in the demographic growth particularly of the Shi'ite community, whose sanitary conditions had undergone large improvements.

This growth strongly contributed to improving the bargaining power of this community in the Lebanese political system.

The same demographic growth also provoked huge internal migration of the Shi'ites from the South and the Baalbek region towards Beirut and the city suburbs, which contributed also to reinforcing their bargaining power [there].

Decreasing Socio-economic Disparities in Independent Lebanon

The quantitative indicators for the period from 1943 to the present converge on the fact that social and economic disparities between the Lebanese tend to decrease regardless of their groups (income, regional and confessional):

a) *Evolution in the distribution of Lebanese according to income.*

The first estimate available on the distribution of Lebanese according to categories of income was carried out by Prof. Elias Ghannage [in 1953]. The IRFED Mission carried out a second estimate of the same distribution in 1960.

Finally, the last available estimate on the social distribution of revenues in Lebanon comes from an investigation carried out by Yves Schmeil, with the help of the students of the Lebanese University and of St. Joseph's University and concerns 1973–74.

The following phenomena become apparent. First, a growth pattern in the volume of the middle categories of income beween 1960, 1973 and 1974 and second, a growth pattern in the volume of higher categories of income between 1960 and 1973 with a contraction of the volume of these categories between 1973 and 1974.

b) *Changes of the standards of living in the various (Lebanese provinces) between 1960 and 1970.*

In 1960, the IRFED Mission carried out an investigation of rural standards of living. The investigation was repeated ten years later, on the request of the Ministry for Planning. The results [showed] that the peripheral regions of Lebanon (which are majority Muslim) enjoy the larger increase. South Lebanon, in particular, (70% Muslim) underwent a rise in standard-of-living of approximately 44% between 1960 and 1970; North Lebanon (40% Muslim) progressed by 40% and the Bekaa (more than 60% Muslim), progressed by 36%. Central Lebanon (70% Christian), only progressed by 15.6%. Therefore, despite the major differences in the standards of living which reached 22% between the various rural areas in Lebanon in 1970, it should be noted that these differences had reached 35% in 1960. The whole of the rural areas in Lebanon had a rise in standards-of-living of 32% between 1960 and 1970.

This type of evolution seems to result from several factors, i.e. migrations, remittances, investment of emigrants in rural areas, and finally the Lebanese Government's [investments] in the rural regions.

c) *Evolution in the confessional composition of some professions*

Professions requiring a high level of education (lawyers, doctors, engineers, etc. . .) are those in which the gap in participation of the various communities is being rapidly bridged over the last decades.

The same phenomena for professions requiring a certain capital investment before being set up, was slow before 1975. After 1975, the narrowing of this gap accelerated mainly in banking, and insurance due to the "oil boom" and consequent important financial resources made available for countries like Lebanon.

FROM POWER SHARING TO CIVIL WAR

The Lebanese Government adopted policies [to] reduce socio-economic disparities between the Lebanese, particularly under Fouad Chehab (1958–1964). These policies had been partly followed up until 1970 under Charles Helou. However, the elites of various communities, united to overthrow the Chehabist candidate and to have a leader of a traditional Maronite, North Lebanon family, Suleiman Franjieh—elected President of the Republic. They were supported by [the] PLO and what become known as the "National Movement."

The efforts of Fouad Chehab to build a strong modern state acting as a social and confessional regulator were gradually eroded. From 1970, inflation accelerated, the exodus from Southern Lebanon towards the capital increased (provoked by the Palestinian Israeli-guerilla warfare on the Lebanese-Israeli border). The PLO, thrown out of Jordan in 1970–1971 moved into Lebanon. The Lebanese Government, unable to deal with this new situation, wavered between repression and acceptance.

The rising Moslem economic and cultural elites found a fertile ground for transforming their new status—the political level: with each conflict between the Lebanese army and the PLO, the Sunni Muslims' claims for a greater share of political power became more pressing. The Christian elites, frightened by a change in the balance of power symbolised by the alliance of PLO, National Movement and Islamic elites, reacted defensively. They were in no mood for flexible negotiation.

. . . [Reacting to] the arming and training of the PLO and their Lebanese sympathisers and the groups linked with the Syrian regime, the Christians responded by arming themselves and by massive training of militia, parties and groups.

For the PLO, Syria and Israel, this country divided along confessional lines, [appeared ideal] for external intervention. The ground had been prepared for all that has happened since: the expression of three different types of conflict on Lebanese ground; local, regional (inter-Arab, Arab-Iranian and Arab-Israeli) and international conflicts.

REFERENCES

1. Boutros Labaki, "An introduction to the economic history of Lebanon and its environment 1840–1914." Publications of Lebanese University, p. 5–30.
2. Theodor Hanf, "Erziehungswesen in Gesellschaft und Politik des Libanon," Bertelsman Universitas-verlag, 1969, p. 101–137.
3. Jean Charro, "The policy of Education in Lebanon," Beirut, July 1979, p. 180.
4. Muhib Himadeh, op. cit., p. 305 and 320.

4.4 The Legacy of Anti-Democratic Traditions in Haiti

Yolaine Armand

The next excerpt is about the unhappy history of violence in Haiti, and how that history reflects a struggle between democrats and authoritarians. As we have said, skin color plays a part in legitimating domination throughout the world. The following excerpt also provides examples of this from the history of Haiti.

When the French ruled Haiti, whites held absolute power over black slaves. After the French left the country, a ruling class of lighter-skinned, racially mixed people—the mulattoes—took over, and exclusion from the elite on the basis of race persisted. To this day, the mulatto elite considers itself French, not Haitian. In contrast, the black majority speaks Creole. Their customs and values reflect their African origins. The mulattoes scorn black Haitian culture, which they consider primitive.

Under mulatto rule, many black Haitians became poorer. However, there eventually rose a black middle class. Its climb to political power in the 1940s brought hope that things might improve for the masses of Haitian poor. This hope culminated in the election of black president Francois Duvalier in 1957. But Duvalier became a ruthless dictator. His son Jean-Claude, who succeeded him, was equally corrupt. Things continued to get worse for the poor.

Black leaders did not make life easier for poor black followers. Duvalier was ousted in 1986, renewing hope of improvement in Haiti. But experiments with democracy and more equitable power sharing have all been short-lived. The black middle class oppresses the poor as much as the upper-class mulattoes did, and the poor have too few resources in terms of power, organizational support, and enabling beliefs to do anything about it.

... This paper examines Haiti's enduring political instability in terms of cultural and socio-historical variables. [It] examines the legacy of Haiti's political and economic past and an assortment of other obstructions that seriously impede the establishment of democracy in Haiti.

POLITICAL OBSTACLES

A Tradition of Political Autocracy

Political power in Haiti is highly centralized in a chief of state with lesser power delegated to a handful of friends. The latter in turn, control all other legal or political apparatus, including the Executive Branch, the Legislative, the Judiciary, the Armed Forces, all of which are rubber stamping

Excerpted from Armand, Yolaine (1989), "Democracy in Haiti: The legacy of anti-democratic political and social traditions," *International Journal of Politics, Culture and Society*, 2(4), Summer, 537–56.

institutions expressing the will of the supreme ruler. Once political power has been taken, most often by force or fraud, it becomes legitimized by its mere existence. The way it is usually challenged is again by violence.

For the Haitian people, it is so much easier to follow a familiar, undemocratic process. Attempts at changes are met with resistance, denials, skepticism, and a great deal of reticence. For example, when General Namphy regained political control last June 20 by ousting President Manigat, it was reported that people met the event with indifference. They went about their daily activities as if nothing significant had happened. The old pattern of favoritism and paternalism was so familiar that people seemed ready to fall back into it matter-of-factly. By the same token, General Avril's successful coup three months later seemed no less expected. A number of Haitians polled in New York reported only two general concerns: that the new ruler be "a good guy" and that he satisfy the demands set forth by the people after Duvalier's departure.

The Direct Legacy of 29 Years of Dictatorship

The long-awaited departure of former President Jean-Claude Duvalier [in 1986] was greeted with elation among Haitians both in Haiti and abroad. The first few weeks after the overthrow saw a tremendous surge of relief and hope for a brighter future. People visiting the country reported seeing Haitians sweeping the sidewalks, disposing of long-accumulated garbage that defaced city streets and painting tree trunks with bright colors. Neighborhood community councils were spontaneously created to channel the ideas, needs, and suggestions of the people. All Haitians seemed willing to work together to defend their newly won freedom and to participate in the creation of a truly democratic system.

This euphoria was short-lived, however, for it soon became evident that twenty-nine years of absolute power had left the country with a burdensome political legacy that would impede the establishment of a democratic system.

The Particular Remnants of an Anti-Democratic Political Structure

The Duvaliers created some peculiar institutions whose influences ran strongly counter to the democratic process:

A unique party system akin to a "political mafia." For many years, the only recognized (i.e., openly functioning) political party was the one represented by the ruling dictatorship. It is perhaps a misnomer to even call it a political party since it possessed neither a political platform open to discussion, nor any other democratic mechanisms responsive to the public. Adherents held membership cards identifying them as "Volunteers for National Security" (VSN),

the official designation of the dreaded "Tontons Macoutes."[1]

An army dominated by Duvalier sympathizers. High army echelons and most officers were compelled by fear of reprisal to display loyalty to the system or at least to not demonstrate open opposition against it. Officers who were. . . critical of the regime would be "retired" or went into exile. The rank and file expressed a similar loyalty for fear of denunciation by other soldiers or by the "tontons macoutes."

A cadre of undisciplined para-militaries (the "macoutes"). Some estimates place the number of "macoutes" as high as 100,000 at the time of Duvalier's departure. Since their purpose was to guarantee the security of the regime, the "macoutes" were left in disarray, with no recognized leadership. Many were armed, but afraid of popular vengeance.[2] Moreover, the upper to middle echelons were divided between the "old guard" attached to Francois Duvalier's rigid doctrine and the more liberal followers of Jean-Claude Duvalier.

An Inadequate Political Process

Although classifying itself as a "republic," Haiti has never had a tradition of institutions that could ensure the democratic process. The recent years of dictatorship have simply eliminated whatever embryo of democracy may have once exited in the country. Following are three major political obstacles left by the former regime.

Non-existence of key political institutions. No political institutions are sufficiently established to channel the demands and articulate the needs of the people. The Congress which traditionally rubber stamped presidential wishes had been abolished by Francois Duvalier. The press was heavily censored and local news of any significance was unilaterally broadcast by the biased government owned media. The Constitution itself had no real weight since it had been routinely amended to reflect the many whims of ruling regimes.

Lack of alternatives in political leadership. Because it stifled all dissenting voices, the dictatorship left no real political leadership. Of those few opponents who managed to remain in the country, the most outspoken were in hiding most of the time and the remainder voiced only occasional timid protests. Except for the amorphous leadership of the Church, no effective political opposition existed. Shortly after Duvalier's departure, however, a flock of presidential candidates and political activists surged to the fore, several from abroad. As many as 20 odd political parties were created or came to action many with undefined programs of government. The sudden surge of politicians caused people to divide their allegiance.

The controversial role of the Church in political leadership. When all dissenting voices were silenced, the Church-owned radio stations became the public voice, serving as the link both among the people and between the people and the government. Individuals and groups went to "Radio Soleil"[3] and "Radio Lumiere"[4] to report police brutality, riots, illegal arrests, murders, missing persons, and so forth. They used the Church sponsored radio stations to report hardships and to complain about poor public services. . . .

ECONOMIC OBSTACLES

Widespread Poverty Hampering the Political Process

Haiti is among the poorest nations of the hemisphere, with a net per capita income currently at around $360 per year. The steady deterioration of rural farms due to years of unchecked land erosion, frequent hurricanes, the absence of governmental agricultural policy, the land workers' ignorance and lack of resources, and the dispos-

session of the farmers due to the corrupt political system all contributed to the steady impoverishment of the peasants and their exodus to urban areas.

This situation had worsened considerably during the Duvalier dictatorship. The last thirty years witnessed the neglect of the secondary towns, called "provinces." Under Duvalier, military—and therefore political—control was more easily maintained when all significant economic activities were centralized in the "Republic of Port-au-Prince." As a result, an estimated 20% of the total Haitian population (of about six million) is concentrated in the capital city of Port-au-Prince. As is usually the case in under-developed countries, there is a wide socio-economic gap between the few haves and the vast majority of have-nots.

The Political Elites

Political power has usually been seen as one means for gaining access to everything that can lead to the good life such as education, employment, and the countless lucrative forms of favoritism. Throughout Haitian history, each new political regime was expected to fire as many public employees as possible in order to replace them by a new hungry crowd. People pledged allegiance not to a political philosophy but solely to individuals who assured them of political favor, most often in the form of a salaried government position or other lucrative benefits.

Public political fund raising is not generally practiced. As a tradition, the financially well-to-do are able to "buy" potential voters by spending lavishly on food, money gifts, advertising, and anything else that will impress the public. By the same token, poor candidates are easily bought by private interest groups or wealthy industrialists who will finance their campaign in return for personal favors when elected. As a result, successful candidates for political power are often members of a privileged class bound by their own class interests, or have their hands tied by a powerful group whose interests they have pledged to support.

The Electorate

Haitians' widespread poverty is reinforced by a 75% rate of illiteracy. Illiteracy is another impediment to democracy. Ignorance of the political process and misconceptions about political issues, goals, and objectives make it easier for demagogy, intimidation, and sheer violence to take hold. . . .

SOCIO-CULTURAL OBSTACLES

Political implications of Class and Status in Haiti:. . . The last three decades have brought significant changes in the social structure of Haiti. The previous two-class society in which income, education, occupation, skin color and status were positively correlated has been modified. Research done by the author between 1981 and 1986 (Armand: 1988) found two patterns of social organization in Haitian cities: a system of *class* inequalities determined by the distribution of income, education and occupation, and one of *status* inequalities based on such subjective factors as prestige, honor, and social recognition of worth. . . .

A person's class, in turn, determines ownership of goods, patterns of consumption, areas and types of residence and general lifestyle.

Honor and prestige, which is more characteristic of *families* than of *individuals*, are based on such inherited attributes as family name, skin color, and wealth and occupation passed on by the family, as well as by such acquired distinctions as money, education, refined manners and tastes, and a mastery of the French language. The inherited or achieved sources of status further subdivides Haitian society into six status layers. These layers can be represented in descending order as follows:

- *White foreigners* who work with foreign or international agencies in Haiti.
- *The Higher Positive Status Group,* designated as "Elite," "Haute Bourgeoisie," or "Bourgeoisie Traditionnelle." Consisting of upper class elites

and a few black families, this group has some of the characteristics of a caste since membership is assigned at birth. Moreover, members retain their high prestige even if they lose (or fail to acquire) one or several of its identifying characteristics, such as education or occupation.
- *The Lower Positive Status Group,* known as "Bourgeoisie Noire," "Nouvelle Bourgeoisie," or "Nouveaux Riches."
- *The Neutral Status Group,* referred to as "Gens de Bien," "Honnetes Gens," "Bons Mounes" (Creole for "Good Folks").
- *Negative Status Group,* identified as "La Masse," "Gens du Peuple," "Pitit So Yette," "Vagabonds," "Mounes Mone," "Gros Zoteye" (Creole for "Mountains Folks, Peasants").
- *The Lowest Negative Status Group,* considered as "Vauriens," or "Sans Zave" ("Good for Nothings, Trash").

Class, Status and Politics in Haiti

The dual pattern of class and status differentiation affects Haitian politics. Throughout the history of the country, the upper and middle classes have taken turns as the dominant political groups and have used politics as a means to strengthen their class positions, obtain new socio-economic gains, and acquire status. In the ongoing class and status competition, politics has become another battlefield.

. . . For well over a century after independence, the economic upper class of mainly lighter skinned people entered politics as a way of sustaining or enhancing their status rather than to gain material privileges. The few well-educated dark-skinned persons of lesser economic rank also saw in politics a way to acquire status. The exercise of politics seemed to reflect the status conferred upon it by the upperclass, high-status group.

With President Magloire[5] and, to a greater extent with the two Duvalier presidents, politics became the best avenue to intra-generational class mobility. Under the Duvalier regime, well-paid positions and all sorts of financial advantages could be obtained by allying oneself with the government. . . .One entered politics not to espouse an ideology but to obtain power and material advantages.

This helped to organize political practices and define political culture in a way that is antithetical to the principles of democracy.

As the traditional high status group was pushed out of politics by the black majority, they used their economic advantages to gain control of the business and industrial sector. The exercise of political power ceased to be a status symbol since it now belonged to those of lower status, but it remained the surest avenue of intra-generational class mobility. While the dark-skinned middle and lower classes used politics as a way of making status distinctions among themselves, the upper class now denied all such claims, regarding it as more prestigious to acquire wealth outside the arena of "dirty" and "shifty" politics.

Status and Political Leadership

The prevalence of status distinctions led to a tradition of political autocracy in Haiti. The authority of the president has been similar to that of a Patriarch. His authority was as undisputed as that of the old-fashioned husband and father over his family. The president expected to receive and was generally given respect and obedience, if not love and admiration. He centralized and epitomized the exercise of final authority, and was accepted as a legitimate ruler by a majority of people.

This authoritarian, paternalistic pattern has made the delegation of authority difficult in the country, imposed a heavy burden on higher-level administrators, and aroused temptations to abuse authority. Its consequence has been twofold: autocracy by those who hold power and dependency by those who do not. . . .

Preeminence of Status as an Impediment to Democracy

Because of the predominance of status inequalities in Haitian society, the concept of equality that is inherent in democracy will be difficult to implement. The acceptance of inequality seems an integral part of Haitian culture and it conditions relationships among all groups and individuals. It is evident in the way people refer to and treat each other.

It is therefore not surprising that Haitians at different status levels attach different meanings to the idea of democracy. Both the upper class and the middle class welcome guarantees of human rights and freedom of expression, but are fearful of misinterpretations which could lead to "encroachment" and "invasion" by the lower class masses. With widespread illiteracy among the poor, it is assumed. . . the latter will see democracy as unrestrained freedom to do so and say what they please, with no self-restraint or respect for others. . . At the bottom levels of the society, even illiterate Haitians in Port-au-Prince understand democracy to mean the absence of arbitrary physical abuse and the freedom to vote without coercion or intimidation.

CONCLUSION

This paper has attempted to place Haiti's effort at democratization in its proper sociocultural context. The Haitian case challenges the notion that in third-world countries with unstable political regimes, democracy needs only to be given a chance (i.e., to remove a dictator or a corrupt ruler) in order to be on its way. In their desperate efforts to survive and initiate socio-economic development, the less developed countries must often overcome age-old traditions and overwhelming internal constraints when political options are presented to them. As a case in point, Haiti's struggle for democracy is hampered by several serious obstacles whose origins lie deep in the country's history. Besides widespread poverty and illiteracy, the country faces a tradition of autocracy and a pervasive acceptance of social inequalities which run counter to the basic egalitarian principles of democracy. Class and status inequalities which permeate Haiti's social and political cultures and institutions may prove to be one of the most serious roadblocks to the institutionalization of Haitian democracy. . . .

NOTES

1. The term "Tontons Macoutes" refers to members of a civilian force appointed by Francois Duvalier to maintain his dictatorship. They often fulfilled their mission by threatening, intimidating, beating, jailing, torturing and physically eliminating known opponents or people suspected to be nonsympathizers of the regime.

2. There were widely publicized documented reports of a handful of incidents where angry mobs lynched or burned to death former Duvalier tortionaires in Port-au-Prince and in the countryside.
3. "Radio Soleil," a regular broadcasting station sponsored by the Catholic clergy.
4. "Radio Lumiere," the regular broadcasting station of the Protestant faith.
5. Dumarsais Estime, a black politician, was elected President by a two-house Congress in 1946, and overthrown four years later, before the end of his six-year term, by Army General Paul Magloire who then became President from 1950 to his overthrow in 1956.

4.5 Japanese Women: Subordination or Domination?

Ryoko Kato

The last excerpt was about power relations between people in general. This next excerpt is about relations between husbands and wives in particular.

As we noted earlier, women suffer domination by men. By feminist criteria, Japanese women have little control over their lives because few of them work for pay. They are in this sense decoupled and excluded. But are we being ethnocentric in judging that Japanese women are powerless? An excerpt by Ryoko Kato suggests we are, and rejects the stereotype of the helpless, exploited Japanese woman.

Women may be inferior in the work force, but they play a dominant role in the home, according to this author. Japanese children are much more physically and psychologically dependent on their mothers than North American or European children. The parental contribution of the father, who is absent much of the time, is insignificant. Because of their influence in the home, women exert a strong influence on Japanese society as a whole. They are in this way powerful, according to Kato.

Japanese people consider the mother's role crucial to the formation of a child's character. Japanese childrearing encourages interdependency and sensitivity to other people's expectations. Researchers often point to these personality traits as the reason for Japan's great productivity. If so, then the Japanese woman's influence on enabling beliefs in her society is considerable indeed.

Yet, in Japanese society public displays of power and control by women are unacceptable. Women must use covert means to control their families and achieve their goals; the manipulation of guilt is a common method, for example. This kind of control is effective and, at present, it is one of the few kinds of power women in Japan have at their disposal.

> We should be cautious about Kato's arguments on the power of Japanese women because they portray the domestic enslavement of women in a positive light. The analysis shows that there *are* many subtleties to power and authority, and that have-nots may have some access to power. However, the haves in this case, the men, experience nothing like the same barriers of decoupling, exclusion (e.g., from jobs), and disabilities as women.

. . . The literature on Japanese women continues to point out the low status of women in Japan compared to their counterparts in other leading industrialized countries. It is considered a paradox, an exception to the general principle that industrialization will bring about the dissolution of traditional values concerning the family and women.

Another paradox concerning Japanese women has not been as stressed. Alongside the continuous flow of work that points to the low status of women in Japan, people have consistently referred to the crucial role of the Japanese woman in the formation of Japanese character and society. As Hayao Kawai puts it, Japan is seen as dominated by the "maternal principle" (1976).

How can the Japanese woman's status be so low and yet women be so influential at the same time? In this paper, I examine this paradox.

THE MATERNAL ROLE

Although in most contemporary societies, child-rearing is still primarily a woman's job, Japan is considered extreme in its reliance on the "mother."

The role of the mother is considered so crucial to the development of Japanese character, that for example, Keigo Okonogi came up with an ajase-complex in contrast to the Oedipus-complex of the "West" where one's target is not to overcome the "father" but the

Excerpted from Kato, Ryoko (1989), "Japanese women: Subordination or domination?" *International Journal of Sociology of the Family*, 19(1), Spring, 49–57.

"mother" (1977). This "mother" fixation (Lebra, 1976:154) is quite conspicuous in the literature on Japanese child-rearing practices.

The Japanese father—the typical image being the middle class businessman (salarii mann)—is perceived as absent in the child rearing scene. He is never at home—coming back late at night, leaving early in the morning, often absent even on weekends. This may be a short-coming of the literature—one may socialize by one's presence as well as by one's absence.

Another problematic aspect of the literature is its relative indifference to factors other than the "mother", such as the school, mass media, and peer relations which influence the development of the Japanese character. The literature tends to jump from early childhood experiences to adulthood seeing personality characteristics developed in those early child-rearing states as definitive. The role of the mother thus may be exaggerated.

. . . The relationship of the mother and child in Japan encourages characteristics such as other (group) orientation, sensitivity to other's expectations (empathy), and interdependency—characteristics seen as important aspects of Japanese national character. In general, Japanese child-rearing practices encourage physical and psychological dependence on the mother (or the maternal figure).

Comparing Japanese and American mothers, William Caudill and H. Weinstein (1974) discovered that Japanese mothers tend to stay around their infants more. She lulls, carries, and rocks the baby and keeps on caretaking after the baby is asleep. This contrasted with the American mothers who left the infants more to themselves.

Japanese infants are said to have long periods of nursing, long periods of co-sleeping (Caudill and Plath, 1974), and passive toilet-training (Vogel, 1963). All such child-rearing practices point to the encouragement of longer periods of dependency on the mother.

Japanese modes of punishment have the characteristic of encouraging sensitivity to others' feelings (empathy) and stressing the close mother-child tie. The Japanese scolding practices are characterized by encouraging sensitivity to what others think such as "people will laugh at you if you do that" and use of threat of abandonment suggesting. . . the child's misbehavior might hurt the close mother-child tie and result in the abandonment of the child.

Comparison with others and the use of ridicule have also been traditional Japanese child-rearing characteristics. The Japanese folklore literature relates such practices to the punishment methods of the tight-knit Japanese villages which used to be scattered throughout Japan. According to Tsuneichi Miyamoto "for a person who lives in a village, to be laughed at was most embarrassing" (1967 : 66). Kunio Yanagida points out that many Japanese proverbs ridicule someone and have the educational effect of making people think they would not do such a silly thing. It also has the effect of making the person being laughed at think he/she will not repeat the act.

It has also been noted that Japanese mothers use guilt as a source of control over the child and even their husbands. Keisuke Okonogi explains this as ruling by sacrifice (Okonogi, 1987). In other words, by acting out the role of the martyr—quietly tolerating and suffering the consequences of the child's (and husband's) selfish deeds—the mother implants in the child (and the husband) the guilt the mother is suffering for his sake and is thus led to spontaneously do as the mother would like him to even when not asked to do so.

George DeVos showed through TAT tests that the Japanese sampled repeatedly chose the stories in which the child does something wrong and the parents suffer. The child sees what he has done and regrets his wrong-doing. DeVos sees this guilt behind the strong achievement drive of Japanese—for the child to lighten his guilt—he must achieve the highest goal expected from him which would also be his parents' success (1974 : 122).

Similar relationships of ruling by guilt, and dependency on the maternal figure, have been observed between wife and husband. Ezra Vogel notes. . . the Japanese wife's way of control is to make the husband spontaneously follow her will (1963). The dependence of the husband on the wife is similar to the dependence of the child on the mother. The husband in the traditional role is completely dependent on the wife for satisfying his daily routines. Takie Sugiyama Lebra notes how the traditional Japanese wife takes care of her husband in every aspect around the house including around-the-body-care (1984 : 133). Lebra calls this the Japanese wife's off-stage dominance compared to the husband's on-stage dominance—a domestic matriarchy where the women control everything in the household including the purse strings (1984 : 134). Indeed, husbands were often referred to by wives as something like their "biggest son".

Psychological dependency (amae) has also been noted to be a general characteristic of Japanese. Takeo Doi, proponent of this term, sees the Japanese mother-child relationship, with the child's dependency on the maternal figure, as the prototype of this tendency (1971). Amae indicates a high level of need to be accepted and cared for.

One problem [with] this concept, amae, is that it carries negative connotations. If the independent individual as in Western "individualism" is considered the ideal, amae would indicate immaturity and lack of self-sufficiency. [But] Eshun Hamaguchi and Shumpei Kumon (1982) question the applicability of the Western paradigm of the individual versus the group to Japanese society. The Western view implies a conflict where the interests of the individual and the group do not coincide and the former has to sacrifice part of his/her individuality to conform to the latter. The Japanese case is different, it is argued, since the individual chooses to pursue his/her interests through group interests, thus the two do not conflict.

However, regardless of the term, people have repeatedly pointed out similar characteristics in Japanese—the sensitivity to others' feelings, the willingness to adjust, the need to be accepted, etc. These characteristics have been seen as encouraged in the child-rearing practices.

It has also been maintained that the basic relationship in Japanese families is the mother and child relationship vs. the father, while in the "West" (specially as in the U.S. case) the basic relationship is the husband and wife vs. the child (Vogel, 1963 : 231; Masuda, 1969). Traditionally, the child is seen as the bond between the spouse in Japan. The importance of the child in a marriage and the fact that child-rearing is exclusively a woman's job are seen as contributing further to the importance of being a mother.

Chie Nakane once said that the Japanese wife is weak but the Japanese mother is strong (Nakane, 1981). However, studies suggest that in a sense, the Japanese wife is also strong when playing a maternal role to her husband, at least in that she can control his behavior through mechanisms such as guilt and is in control of his everyday routine life. Without the assistance of the traditional wife, the traditional husband may have trouble even with his daily routines such as getting something to drink.

Hiroshi Wagatsuma questioned the stereotypical view of the Japanese woman as enslaved, by noting that typically in Japan, the wife holds the purse strings and that Japanese men tend to be emotionally dependent on women (Wagatsuma, 1977 : 189–191).

Feminists may consider Oriental women as "enslaved" and "subjugated". But if Japanese housewives are more economically (and emotionally) autonomous than their Western counterparts and play a more significant role at home, it might be necessary to reexamine the whole notion of the low status of women in Japan (Wagatsuma, 1977 : 191)....

CONCLUSION

... Because of the reexamination of the feminine role which has taken place in the Western countries and the fact that the woman's role in Japan resembles that of the "West" a decade or so ago, Japanese women have often been portrayed as exploited and unenlightened. However, one must be careful in being prejudgemental.

Indeed Japanese women are weak in the occupational sphere. Though there are indications of the heightening of women's occupational status in Japan, in general, Japanese women face both implicit and explicit pressures to assume the traditional roles of a female. Japanese wives may be relatively weak in comparison to other industrialized countries if one judges their strength by such standards as the power to support themselves if deserted. Although more than half of the housewives work, much of the labor is part-time with low pay.

And yet, Japanese women were not the helpless, powerless, enslaved servants of their husbands. Through their maternal roles they exert control on their children, through extending those roles to conjugal situations, they also exert control on their husbands. The influence of the Japanese mother is so strong that it has led many people to regard Japanese society as "maternal" and the mother as the sole key figure in developing Japanese behavior and personality characteristics. This glorification of the maternal role may not reflect the actuality—it may also reflect the mentality of those who have contributed to the literature on the subject. However, studies suggest certain characteristics of Japanese mother-child and wife-husband relationships which would be likely to lead to psychological and physical dependency on the maternal figure. In place of on-stage dominance, the Japanese women in traditional roles have assumed on-stage subordination and off-stage manipulation.

The Japanese child-rearing practices were characterized by a high reliance on the maternal figure. Intimacy and dependency on the mother, both physically and psychologically, to satisfy one's needs were seen as characteristic of Japan in contrast to the "West". This extended into adulthood where the wife then took over the maternal role of the mother. In this situation, the maternal figure is capable of making life extremely miserable for either her children or her husband by no longer assuming her role of the caretaker. Even washing clothes may be a great threat if one has never touched a washing machine. The relative absence of the male figure, and the domestic sphere being almost the sole responsibility of the female (including the household purse strings) reinforces the wife's position inside the house. Thus, in a sense, although economically dependent, the Japanese woman in the traditional maternal role has a strong basis of power in everyday domestic life which is reinforced by emotional aspects of love and dependency.

Such implications from the Japanese case may point to the need to look closer into the mechanisms of power which women in traditional roles have resorted to. Routes of influence available to women may differ across societies. Although superficially helpless, women may develop alternative routes of influence to compensate for their lack of power in other areas.

Lastly however, it is important to note that even in Japan, the traditional roles of women are changing. The predominance of the mother in the child-rearing process, her maternal role as mother and wife, were contingent on the omni-presence [sic] of the mother. With increasing numbers of women in the labor force, more flexibility in occupational conditions, and the impact of Western ideas, this is changing—and with it, may be the Japanese woman's means of influence as well.

REFERENCES

Caudill, W. and H. Weinstein (1974). "Maternal Care and Infant Behavior in Japan and America." in Takie S. Lebra and W.P. Lebra eds. Japanese Culture and Behavior. Honolulu: University of Hawaii Press: 225–276 (reprinted from Psychiatry 32 (1969): 12–43).

Caudill, W. and D. W. Plath (1974). "Who Sleeps by Whom?: Parent-child Involvement in urban Japanese Families." in Takie S. Lebra and W.P. Lebra eds. Japanese Culture and Behavior. Honolulu: University of Hawaii Press: 276–312 (reprinted from Psychiatry 29(1969) 344–66).

DeVos, G.A. (1974). "The Relationship of Guilt Toward Parents to Achievement and Arranged Marriage among the Japanese." In Takie S. Lebra and W.P. Lebra eds. Japanese Culture and Behavior. Honolulu: University of Hawaii Press: 117–141 (reprinted from Psychiatry 23(1960) 287–301).

Doi, T. (1971). 'Amae' no kozo. Tokyo: Kobundo.

Hamaguchi, E. and S. Kumon eds. (1982). Nihonteki shudanshugi—sono shink o tou. Tokyo: Yuhik'aku.

Kawai, H. (1976). Boseishakai Nihon no byori. Takyo: Chou keronsha.

Lebra, T.S. (1976). Japanese Patterns of Behavior. Honolulu: University of Hawaii Press.

———.(1984). Japanese Women: Fulfillment and Constraint, Honolulu: University of Hawaii Press.

Masuda, K. (1969). America no kazoku nihon no kazoku, Tokyo: NHK shuppankai.

Miyamoto, T. (1967). Iemoto no kun: aijo wa kodomo to tomoni, Tokyo: Miraisha.

Nakane, C. (1981). Shakai kozo no hikaku: ajia o chushin to shite,Tokyo; Obunsha.

Okonogi, K. (1982). Nihon jin no ajase complex. Tokyo: Chuokoron.

Vogel, E.V. (1963). Japan's New Middle Class: The Salary Man and his Family in Tokyo Suburbs, Berkeley: University of California Press.

Wagatsuma, H. (1977). "Some Aspects of the Contemporary Japanese Family: Once Confucian, Now Fatherless?" Daedalus 106: 181–200.

4.6 Participation in Four Zimbabwean Co-operatives

Sheila Smith

This next excerpt is about sexism in the structure of economic institutions. It shows that movements to improve the position of a class, racial group, or nation-state may promise equality of the sexes, but they rarely deliver on this. Where women expect to fight side by side with men, they usually end up cleaning uniforms. Where movements promise the enlightenment of the masses, men usually write the manifestos and women run the printing presses. Marx believed that socialism would eventually bring about gender equality, but this has not come to pass, even in socialist countries like Zimbabwe.

The excerpt that follows considers why women are under-represented in the leadership of Zimbabwean cooperatives, which are otherwise quite progressive in their outlook. The author comes up with one main reason: women's double burden. Like women around the world, Zimbabwean women suffer from the double burden of paid employment and domestic work. They do productive work in the cooperatives and all of the domestic and child care work, too. This form of disability, and the scarcity of free time, make it difficult for women to participate in the decision-making of the cooperative as much as men do.

Juggling family duties and political duties is extremely difficult if not impossible. Unfortunately, men do not recognize this problem. For this reason, they make no effort to schedule meetings at times that are convenient for women. As a result, women's attendance at meetings is poorer than men's. Even women who want to participate in decision making find it hard to do so. Smith argues that men and women will have to share domestic work more equally if women are to better participate in running the cooperative.

Also, traditional attitudes and gender roles persist in Zimbabwe. Men are taught highly rewarded skills in construction, mechanics, and livestock care. Women, on the other hand, are usually trained to sew and knit. These skills yield only low-prestige jobs in sideline industries, and further exclude women from involvement in the cooperative. Women are seldom sent on technical or management courses. The familiar processes of disability and exclusion, however unintended, show themselves again.

This paper presents the results of a study on the participation of women and of sexual equality in participation in four producer co-operatives in Zimbabwe. . . .

. . . The progress of co-operatives and the emancipation of women are both major concerns of the Zimbabwean Government. The policy of socialism through co-operative development is seen as the key to the liberation of women. Women are urged to participate in development, to participate in co-operatives and to form new co-operatives. Many women have responded to this call, but it is not yet clear whether they are participating fully in all aspects of co-operative life. . . .

PARTICIPATION

I have used the term 'participation' to refer to both participation in productive labour and participation in the running of the co-operative. Women can only expect to participate in the running of a co-operative, and share the benefits, if they participate in the productive work. Women cannot, however, be considered to be equal to men if their participation is limited to their labour. This study therefore focused on three aspects of women's lives in co-operatives:

1. participation in productive work
2. access to resources
3. participation in decision-making

In each case, the relative position of men and women was examined. . . .

METHODOLOGY

. . . A case study of one co-operative, conducted largely through participant observation, was followed by structured interviews of

Excerpted from Smith, Sheila (1987), "Zimbabwean women in co-operatives: Participation and sexual equality in four producer co-operatives," *Journal of Social Development in Africa*, 2, 29–47.

male and female members of that co-operative and three other co-operatives. The case study co-operative was selected on the basis of a recommendation that it was a well-run co-operative in which the female members participated in all spheres of activity. The other three co-operatives were selected from those in a specific geographical area. They were the largest of the available mixed-sex co-operatives.

Forty-four people (24 men and 20 women) out of a total membership of 102 (60 men and 42 women) were interviewed. In the case study co-operative, equal members of men and women were selected for interview on a random basis. In the other co-operatives, [all] members of the sex which was in the minority were interviewed. A random sample of half the members of the other sex was interviewed. . . .

THE FOUR CO-OPERATIVES

Co-operative A, the case study co-operative, is a mixed farming co-operative. It is not part of the Government resettlement scheme. The co-operative had been registered for three years at the time of the survey. There are 55 members, 28 men and 27 women. Many are ex-combatants and some are former farm workers. The members live communally.

Co-operative B is a mixed farming co-operative, which had been registered for three years at the time of the survey. It is not part of the Government resettlement scheme. There are 19 members, 17 men and 2 women, most of whom are ex-combatants. The members live communally.

Co-operative C is a retail co-operative, which had been registered for three years at the time of the survey. There are 18 members, 14 men and 4 women, and most are ex-combatants. The members do not live communally.

Co-operative D, a dressmaking and tailoring co-operative, had been registered for eighteen months. There are 10 members, 9 women and 1 man. The members do not live communally.

THE ROLE OF WOMEN
IN PRODUCTION

Allocation of Work

Both men and women in the four co-operatives were fully involved in production. None had other productive work, such as farming private plots, outside their co-operative. Members were assigned duties in particular departments, and hours of work were laid down. Although it was not possible to assess the contribution of each interviewee, everyone said men and women worked equally hard.

In the four co-operatives, there was a marked allocation of jobs on the basis of sex, with 54% of men holding managerial jobs or jobs which are traditionally men's, such as driving, mechanics, care of livestock. Fifty per cent of women were found in the jobs which are traditionally women's work, such as sewing, knitting, care of poultry. A few men (13%) and women (10%) did jobs traditionally assigned to the opposite sex. Both men and women worked in agriculture and horticulture. In Co-operative A, the men and women in these departments shared all the duties, with the exception of tractor driving. In all the co-operatives, both men and women worked as typists, book-keepers and sales assistants. (33% of men and 40% of women were in agriculture, office work and sales.)[1] Some men worked full-time as co-operative managers. No women were employed in this capacity.

The members interviewed thought men were best for particular jobs, and women for others. Some thought men and women could do jobs other than those traditionally assigned to them if they were trained for them.

Child Care and Domestic Labour

Female co-operators had a considerable responsibility for young children. Half the women in the sample had children under seven, and a third children under two. These women relied heavily on female relatives for help with child care. Only Co-operative A had a creche, and this was well utilised. The case study, conducted before the creche was established, revealed child care demanded much time and limited [women's] participation in productive work. None of the men interviewed were responsible for the care of young children.

Women in all the co-operatives said child care was a problem. In Co-operative A, they said creche facilities were inadequate because of lack of funds. In Co-operative B, the lack of child care facilities was coupled with a shortage of accommodation. In Co-operatives C and D, women generally had to pay someone to look after their children. Another problem faced by female co-operators was loss of pay through taking time off on account of a sick child or any other domestic difficulties. Few men referred to child care or the lack of creche facilities as problems facing women.

Women had a greater responsibility than men for household work. In Co-operatives C and D women did the cooking in their own homes. Males rarely cooked. In Co-operatives A and B there was a communal kitchen, and cooking was done in working hours, thus reducing the women's workloads. In Co-operative A there was a kitchen working team, usually composed only of women, whereas in B all the members were on a cooking rota.

The women in Co-operatives C and D said they had difficulties finding time for their domestic work, particularly since they spent a considerable time each day travelling to and from work. The women in Co-operatives A and B were more concerned about the lack of adequate accommodation. Few men in the four co-operatives mentioned domestic work as a problem facing women.

Training

In the four co-operatives, there was no significant difference in the proportion of men and women being sent on training courses. The men and women had undergone different types of training, with men predominating in management courses and in courses in traditional 'male' skills, such as building, welding, mechanics and care of livestock. Most women had done courses in sewing and knitting. The case study revealed that men were sent on technical and management courses, and women on courses in crafts and office skills.

The women in the sample utilised their training less frequently than men. This was particularly the case with women who had learnt sewing or knitting.

Men and women in the four co-operatives wanted to go on different types of training courses, with 75% of men opting for management and traditional 'male' skills, and 45% of women for sewing, knitting and cookery. Some women (20%) wanted to study management, driving or mechanics, but very few men (4%) were interested in 'female' skills— 21% of men and 35% of women wanted to follow courses in agriculture, book-keeping and typing.

Some co-operators had said men could do women's jobs, and vice versa, if the appropriate training were offered. Men, however, did not express a desire to learn cookery and dressmaking. Of the co-operators who had done some training, most expressed a wish to do further training in the same subjects. The women who wanted to depart from the norm, and drive tractors or study mechanics, had been inspired by the example of some women at an agricultural centre.

Many women with young children had been on training courses, despite the difficulties involved.

ACCESS TO RESOURCES

All members received equal payment for work. In all the co-operatives those who took leave because of family problems or sickness received no allowances. As noted above, this affected women more than men. In Co-operative A, women going on maternity leave received a loan. Co-operative A also ran a welfare fund to cover bus fares to clinics and hospitals, a scheme which largely benefited the female members. In Co-operatives A and B basic medical care and all food were provided.

THE ROLE OF WOMEN IN DECISION MAKING

Membership Status

All participants in the four co-operatives were full members. However, some men and women were not fully involved in their co-operatives.

Knowledge of Co-operative Affairs

... Women were not as well informed as men in financial matters or on national co-operative development. Many more men knew the purchase price of the co-operative's farm or business (79% of men and 45% of women), full details of the major loans received by the co-operative (67% of men and 30% of women) and at least one of OCCZIM's responsibilities (75% of men and 30% of women). There was no significant difference between men and women in terms of their knowledge of the year of registration of the co-operative, of the number of members, of whether the co-operative had received any loans, and of whether OCCZIM had assisted the co-operative.

Pariticipation in General Meetings

The case study indicated that women's attendance at meetings was not as good as men's. Women, particularly those with young children, often arrived late and left early. Sometimes they left for a period in the middle of the meeting. Men were rarely seen to leave a meeting.

The respondents were not asked directly about participation in meetings, but several raised the issue in response to other questions. Men criticised women for not contributing in meetings and for their lack of self-confidence.

A few suggested ways in which the co-operative could help women develop self-confidence. One suggested women on training courses should hold meetings so that they could practice speaking to a large group.

One woman referred to women's lack of participation in discussion, but offered no explanation. None of the women interviewed mentioned lack of confidence as a particular problem.

Representation on the Management Committee

Women were under-represented on the management committees of their co-operatives. In co-operative A, women had comprised at least 50% of the membership at any time, but had held only 25% of the committee posts since the co-operative started. Co-operative B had had no women on the four committees elected since the co-operative started. Co-operative C had had only one committee comprised solely of men. Both co-operative B and C recently elected a women to the committee—as treasurer and deputy secretary respectively. Co-operative D had had one committee at the time of the survey. The first chairperson had been the one male member, but when he went on a course a woman was elected in his place.

Men predominated in the positions of chairperson, deputy chairperson and secretary (69% of men and 17% of women). These were key posts, involving representing the co-operative, meeting national and international organisations and receiving visiting donor agencies. Women served as deputy secretary, treasurer and committee members (83% of women and 31% of men). Although the post of treasurer involved a great deal of work, it was largely, in all the co-operatives, a job of routine bookkeeping. Similarly, the post of deputy secretary involved very mundane work.

There are many possible reasons for women being under-represented on management committees. Four are considered here:

1. Women's workload prevents them from serving on the committees.

2. Men are better educated than women.
3. Men have more experience in administration.
4. Traditional attitudes prevent women from being elected.

Women's Workload

Women with young children had served on the committees. During working hours most children were cared for by relatives or were in a creche. Only co-operative D, however, confined its meeting to working hours. In the other co-operatives, meetings wre often held in the evenings or at weekends when women were fully committed domestically. This may have discouraged some women from standing for election.

Several men and women said a woman could not serve as chairperson, because the post would necessitate some travel, and women could not leave the co-operative easily.

Formal Education

... Although women were not less educated than men, several men clearly believed they were, and this might have influenced their choice of committee members. Some male co-operators mentioned lack of basic education as a factor hampering women's progress. Others said women needed more basic education in addition to training in specific skills.

Administrative Experience

More men than women in the four co-operatives had previous administrative experience (54% of men and 10% of women). Those elected to the committees were not more experienced than the others. There was, however, a marked difference between the administrative experience of the holders of the key positions, 80% of whom had experience and that of the other committee members, 22% of whom had experience. As more of those in the key positions had had administrative experience, this is one possible explanation for the predominance of men in the key committee posts. ...

Attitudes Towards Women as Committee Members

Most of the co-operators said women were capable of holding any committee post. Some, both men and women, expressed doubts about women's capabilities. A few said women were best suited to particular posts. Several said women could serve on the committee only if they had training and help. Those men and women who thought it would be difficult or impossible for women to sit on the committee, or to hold key posts, gave their reasons as women's lack of confidence, their inability and inexperience.

Many interviewees revealed 'traditional' attitudes about women's roles. When discussing the election of the management committee and the allocation of productive work, they began by stating men and women could all do everything. Later on, it became apparent they did not actually believe this.

Traditional attitudes were not identified as a problem by anyone, nor did anyone say there was a need to change the attitudes held by. . . men or women. . . .

CONCLUSIONS

In the four co-operatives studied, women were working full-time in co-operative production. In two of the co-operatives women's domestic responsibilities had been reduced. In all the co-operatives women and men were paid equally, and on an individual basis. All the women in the four co-operatives were full members, and some had been elected to leadership posts in some of the co-operatives.

Despite this progress, women were not completely equal to men in terms of their participation in productive work and decision-making. Most women still worked a 'double shift', because of their domestic responsibilities. There were clear examples of a division of labour on the basis of sex, and the routine tasks usually fell to women, whilst men predominated in management. The training courses followed by members seemed likely to perpetuate this state of affairs. [Many] women were badly informed on co-operative issues. Women were still under-represented on the management committees, particularly in the key leadership posts.

The women in the four co-operatives seemed to be in a better position than many women in co-operatives in other socialist countries. There are two possible explanations for this. Firstly, the Zimbabwean women were occupied on a full-time basis in their co-operatives, and were not trying to combine this work with private agricultural production. Secondly, three of the four co-operatives were composed largely of ex-combatants, who might be more aware of co-operative principles and of the possibility of sexual equality than many peasant farmers.

The experience of the four co-operatives indicates women's entry into social production does not necessarily lead to sexual equality, and that a socialist mode of production is not a sufficient condition for sexual equality.

The study has identified several factors which may be hindering the further participation of women in their co-operatives. Firstly, there are material constraints on women's participation. Child care and domestic labour not only formed a 'second shift' for female co-operators, but also interfered with their regular work in the co-operatives. Women were restricted in the amount of extra time they could give to co-operative activities.

Another material constraint is women's lack of administrative experience [and] [lack of] administrative training.

Secondly, women's progress is limited by ideological constraints in the form of traditional attitudes. Both men and women held traditional views on the jobs which men and women could do, and on the role of women in leadership. There was little awareness of the existence of such attitudes. . . .

NOTES

1. All percentages given are derived from figures for which the differences between men and women are significant at the .05 level or beyond.

Section Review

Discussion Questions

1. "Opposition to affirmative action creates a backlash, which concentrates anxieties from disparate sources." Explain and discuss this observation.
2. Consider the most common approach to power in the workplace in your country, and compare it with those workplaces in Japan, Britain, and France described by Frenkel. Which of those three workplace patterns is most similar to the pattern in your country? What are the differences?
3. Because it favorably portrays women's household-bound role, some would say that Kato's description of the power of women in Japanese society supports the dominance of women by men. What do you think? Discuss the merits of this view.
4. Compare the access to power of women in Smith's study and in Kato's study. Do differences in culture or political systems, or both, account for the different patterns of power?
5. What influence has racism had on people's access to power throughout Haiti's history, according to Armand?
6. Labaki's study suggests that rising standards of living lead to a growing awareness of inequality. Why might this happen? Do you think this is something we would find happening in many societies? Why, or why not?

Data Collection Exercises

1. Collect some information on how power is organized in a local workplace. Measure how much power workers and managers have in that workplace.
2. Joseph discusses the responses of educated white males to affirmative action policies, but presents us with no data from interviews. To begin to fill this gap, carry out some informal interviews with men who have university training and see whether you get the responses Joseph would have expected.
3. Armand's and Labaki's analyses of power differences between racial and religious groups are historical analyses. Collect some information on the history of power relations between men and women in any country of your choice. Why do you not find evidence of open conflict to the degree described by Armand and Labaki?
4. Collect data from two or more countries to test Labaki's hypothesis that rising standards of living increase people's awareness of inequality. What do your data show?

Writing Exercises

1. Imagine that Smith and Kato read each other's excerpts. What is Smith likely to think about Kato's article, and what is Kato likely to think about Smith's article?

Compose a 250-word letter from Kato to Smith, and a 250-word letter from Smith to Kato, expressing their views.

2 Analyze all the articles on labor-management relations that appear in a major newspaper over a two-week period, then prepare a brief (500-word) report on the patterns of power and legitimizing beliefs you find described there.

3. For one week, keep a journal in which you record all the forms of power and authority you confront, and your responses to them.

4. Write a brief report on power and authority in your family, school, or workplace. Indicate how gender, class, and race/ethnicity are involved.

SECTION FIVE
Explanations of Power Inequality

5.1 Obstacles to Equality Between the Sexes

Patricia Schulz

According to the following excerpt by Schulz, one of the obstacles to equal power is that men, not women, make the laws. Women have been largely excluded from law-making activities of the state elite; indeed, from *all* types of activity in the state elite.

Even in the most progressive nations far less than half the members of parliament, judges, and civil servants are women. Even countries that have had female heads-of-state are far from espousing true gender equality. There is really no nation on earth with an equitable distribution of political power between the sexes.

In this excerpt Schulz shows that, until recently, many Swiss laws put women at a severe legal disadvantage compared to men. Marriage law explicitly defined domestic work and child-rearing as the sole responsibility of a wife. Abortion was illegal and rape by a husband not considered a crime. Violence in the privacy of the home was well tolerated.

However, upon our requesting to reprint her article, Professor Schulz wrote us to explain that "This article [now] has historical, and not a present, value. . . Very important changes that have taken place and/or are considered [include the following:] matrimonial law has become almost egalitarian; rape by a husband can be sued against under certain conditions; women now compose 15% of the federal parliament, and up to 35% of certain cantonal parliaments; the right [to] vote now exists in all cantons; there is an increasing number of women in cantonal and city governments. . . ; a number of projects are under way to increase the number of women in all the state authorities (parliament, government, courts, civil service); a bill is being examined in the federal parliament to improve women's position in the field of employment and to fight gender discrimination." She concludes, "In general, there is a movement towards change, that has been increased by the possible integration of Switzerland in the European community."

So much change in only ten years seems to show that institutional obstacles to gender equality can be cleared away in short order, if there is the political will to do so.

Excerpted from Schulz, Patricia (1988), "Institutional obstacles to equality between the sexes," *Women's Studies International Forum*, 9(1), 5–11. With permission of

Ms. Patricia Schulz, Département de droit constitutionnel, Faculté de droit, Université de Genève, 102 bd. Carl Vogt, 1211 Genève 4, Switzerland.

THE CONTEXT*

Patriarchal law

Today Swiss law remains strongly influenced by nineteenth-century (and earlier) gender role traditions. The naturalist and sexist affirmation of man's superiority to woman, a superiorily expressed countless times in laws, parliamentary debates, government policies, court decisions, and jurisprudence, is equally influential.

Marriage law in particular is organised according to a strict division of labour between women and men, and it influences other fields such as social security and taxes. The basic model is that of the breadwinning husband who is chief of the conjugal community, and the housewife, who is legally responsible for housework and child-raising (articles 160 and 161 Swiss *Civil Code*). Only men are whole legal persons in Swiss law, their status not being dependent on another person.

Many people no longer respect this model. About 30 per cent of women work outside the home in paid employment, as well as working in the home (Commission fédérale pour les questions féminines, 1982: 37, hereafter CFQF). Women alone suffer from the double day, as most husbands consider they are entitled to the domestic work and raising of the children by their wives, who are legally required to undertake these tasks in exchange for being provided for by the husband (CFQF, 1982: 40–44; Kellerhals *et al.*, 1982: 156–172).

As always in Switzerland changes are slow, under the influence of legislative modifications in other European countries, changes in the social and economic conditions in Switzerland, and feminist claims. A modification of marriage law is underway, implying less stereotype roles for men and women without abandoning them altogether (Conseil fédéral, 1979).

*This article describes the situation in Switzerland as of *January 30, 1984.* Since then, the first woman in the Federal Government was elected on October 2, 1984, and the revision of marriage law was accepted on September 22, 1985. The author could not include these modifications in the article itself, due to the complications in publishing this issue.

Constitutional and legislative framework

a. *The Constitution.* Switzerland is a federal state comprising 23 *cantons* (member states, each with its constitution, government, parliament, court system and so on). The present federal constitution dates back to 1874 and has been revised 106 times (as of 30 January 1984), most of the amendments giving new rights and/or guarantees to the people. All amendments must be adopted in a ballot, by a double majority which is formed by the majority of the Swiss citizens participating in the ballot and the majority of the cantons (that is, 12 of the 23 cantons). Amendments can be proposed by the government, parliament, or by 100,000 citizens using the right of 'initiative'. Using this right, women launched an initiative for the equality of rights between men and women in 1975 and in somewhat modified form[1] the proposal was accepted on 14 June 1981, becoming article 4, paragraph 2 of the *Constitution* (Chaponnière-Grandjean, 1983).

b. *The equality rule.* Since 1848, with the first federal *Constitution* (replaced in 1874), Swiss law has contained a basic principle:

'All Swiss are equal before the law. In Switzerland there are no privileges due to regions, birth, persons or family.'

The interpretation of article 4 of the *Constitution* by the courts, in particular by the Federal Court, has been far-reaching. The rule can be invoked against a law or a decision by the courts or administration and is binding for all organs of the state on the federal, cantonal and communal level. It has been the basis of new constitutional rights that the Federal Court inferred despite the silence of the *Constitution*—such as a right to a fair trial, protection against arbitrary state action (Aubert, 1967: 124–125). But it has never been interpreted as a protection for women as women. . . .

It took 133 years for women to gain the constitutional guarantee of equality: in article 4, paragraph 2 of the *Constitution*,

'Men and women have equal rights. Legislation shall provide equality, in particular in the fields of the family, education and work. Men and women have a right to equal pay for work of equal value.'

. . . Contrary to article 4, paragraph 1—which creates direct rights a citizen can claim in court—article 4, paragraph 2 is seen as creating only an obligation for parliament to change discriminatory laws (except in the case of equal pay which can be invoked directly in court (Bérenstein, 1980: 193–200)).

c. *The legislation.* Federal laws are adopted by parliament and must be confirmed in a ballot if requested by 50,000 citizens. Under this threat, a compromise is generally reached by all the interested parties before the proposed law reaches the plenary session of parliament where it is seldom modified on important points.

d. *Importance of the legal institutions for women.* . . Although women gained the right to vote at the federal level in 1971 and have the right on the cantonal level in all but one canton, women are still excluded from the making of the law—in parliament and at the judicial level. Of 246 members of the federal parliament, 25 are women; there is an average of 10 per cent of women in the cantonal parliaments; no woman sits in the federal government; only one woman is in the 23 cantonal governments; about 4 per cent of women in the parliamentary and extra-parliamentary commissions; about 2 per cent of women in the higher levels of the federal administration; and one woman among the 30 judges of the Federal Court (*Domaine public,* 1984; Germann, 1981; 86–87, 198).

Even with article 4, paragraph 2 in the *Constitution,* difficulties remain—first to define the meaning of the principle, secondly to implement equality. Additionally, women are faced with a double bind: as most laws determining the status of women and men are federal, it is necessary to accept new, still discriminatory laws, because they bring some improvements, without touching the fundamental discriminations, or to have them rejected in a referendum in the hope for a future, better law, but with the risk of remaining for decades with the present, very discriminatory, laws.

With legislative modifications underway in marriage law and old age pensions, the relative value men give to the rule of equality when applied to women is evident. Cosmetic improvements are accepted, as long as basic male privileges remain untouched.[2] For example, the modification of the law on old age pensions—ostensibly to implement article 4, paragraph 2—has been deprived of all meaning by the fact it is not supposed to cost anything.[3]

Additionally, there is a deeper problem. That is, the relationship of women to the law as both a means of oppression *and* of liberation. It is necessary for women to look to the state that has oppressed us for an improvement in our situation: it is easier to influence the state than to influence the economy, that cannot be held accountable for women's situation. So women are faced with this contradiction, aggravated by the dichotomy of private and public realms, and all that has been built upon this division of the world.

The evolution of the private and public aspects of patriarchy does not mean freedom for us, even though we have passed gradually from total control by a man (father/husband), to a more diffuse power, defined by the state, and setting limits to the private power of our former owners. As women we still do not have control over our own lives: abortion is illegal in Switzerland; rape by a husband is not considered rape; and private violence against women—especially in the family—is well tolerated (CFQF. 1982: 48–50). Women lose their name, nationality, domicile, individual rights to old age pension, individual status in tax matters, right to work outside the home in paid employment through marriage. In short, women are dependent and are denied autonomy by the state. Therefore freedom and the possibility to participate equally in power is denied (Castoriadis, 1982: 26–32).

CONTROL OF THE CONSTITUTIONALITY OF LAWS

Federal and Cantonal Laws Concerning Men and Women

As mentioned previously the major laws determining the status of men and women are federal. These laws give power to men over women under the guise of 'protection.'[4] They also influence cantonal laws. The economic and social status of women depends on the variations of their civil status (married, divorced, widowed, remarried). Marriage is the central institution because of the consequences federal laws attach to it (CFQF, 1980: 2-31, 1982; Margolis and Margolis, 1981: 291-301). The criterion of sex thus influences our legal situation, and yet only the cantonal laws, having a more reduced importance, can be reviewed and struck down for unconstitutionality.

Lack of Control of the Constitutionality of Federal Laws

Due to a restrictive interpretation of the *Constitution*, the Federal Court has denied itself the right to control the constitutionality of federal laws (Aubert, 1967: 94-95, 173-179; Auer, 1983: 68-70). Article 113, paragraph 3 of the *Constitution* simply states . . . the Federal Court shall 'apply' the laws passed by parliament, not that the Federal Court must *not* apply unconstitutional laws (Auer, 1980). It has been the consistent opinion of the Court that faced with a federal law that violates the *Constitution*, it must simply apply the law; otherwise, the judges would place themselves above the parliament and people. The primary consequence of this interpretation is that parliament can violate the *Constitution* freely, with no remedy for the individual suffering this violation (Auer, 1983: 78-81). On a purely formal level, this means a law (adopted by parliament and the people) is superior to the *Constitution* (adopted by the people and cantons—that is, the most complicated procedure, supposed to guarantee its

formal superiority over all others), and that parliament can violate the *Constitution* that gives it its very existence and power to pass laws.

It is often said that the democratic argument linked to the role of the people in the legislative process has won over the liberal argument of the protection of individual rights against state action (Auer, 1983: 62-68 for a critical review). This reasoning opposes democracy and liberalism, equality and liberty as if one were not the condition of the other and vice versa and it leaves the minorities with no protection against the power of the majority. I do not see how democracy is better respected by accepting violations of the *Constitution* than by giving the Federal Court the power to control federal as well as cantonal laws. . . .

Even with its limits, the control of the constitutionality of cantonal laws has been very important, enabling the Federal Court to define constitutional rights, and to 'create' some new ones. Indeed the fundamental rights of individual freedom, of freedom of opinion and of speech, of free assembly and the guarantee of the mother-tongue have all been created by the Federal Court, even though the written *Constitution* does not mention them. Auer has suggested this is possible thanks to the absence of control of federal laws, because the Federal Court could go ahead without being accused of interfering with the powers of parliament (Auer, 1983: 104-105, 168-169, 220-222). As women we also benefit from these rights, but we must question the system and its logic: the Federal Court 'invented' these rights because it found them necessary for a democracy to exist, in violation of the text of the *Constitution*, and of its rules on modifications; at the same time, the Federal Court refuses to control federal laws to avoid being above parliament, but does not hesitate to place itself above the organ normally competent to revise the *Constitution*, that is, the people and cantons!

So we have a progressive Federal Court which is increasing some constitutional rights but steadfastly refusing to accept that article 4 could also include women among the beneficiaries of the equality rule of 'all Swiss are equal before the law' or of 'all Swiss have the right to vote': in both cases the Federal Court decided the *Constitution* had to be explicitly modified to include women. It may then appear as a contradiction to advocate giving the Court the power to control federal laws in the hope it will protect women against discrimination, but at least it would create a forum and force the system, through court decisions, to make more explicit the unequal treatment to which it subjects women.

The Situation with Article 4, Paragraph 2 of the Constitution

Although most authors agree there are few unconstitutional laws in Switzerland, article 4, paragraph 2 rendered a great number of existing laws unconstitutional: all the laws making differences for 'invalid' reasons between men and women should be changed by parliament. Yet, inequalities against women are watered down by male experts.

The federal government tried to advise the judges to overcome the contradiction of a clear, new constitutional rule of equality, and the impossibility of having it respected (Conseil Fédéral, 1980: 134), but in vain for the system is blocked. The question is therefore to ask if a right without a remedy is really a right? The rule of equality between the sexes, although written in the federal *Constitution*, does not exist on the federal level—for lack of remedy.

Perhaps the best approach would be for women to launch a new constitutional initiative to modify article 113, paragraph 3, so the Federal Court would have to exercise control to ensure federal laws respect the *Constitution*. The absurdity of this situation and the double standard of the rule of equality (for only article 4, paragraph 1 creates direct rights, whereas article 4, paragraph 2 imposes a mandate on parliament to make equal laws—but when?) are generally not seen. This is because the unequal treatment of

women as a group is not acknowledged: though if the group of people with blue eyes were treated as women are, the male establishment might see the discrimination, because it would affect some of its members directly.

CONCLUSION

As a group, even with the constitutional 'guarantee' of equality, women still do not receive like protection as men from the courts, because women cannot challenge the discriminatory laws. This is because the court system is biased against women by its very composition.

There is no escape from the fact that more rights for women will mean fewer privileges for men in certain fields, such as marriage law where men could lose the right to women's unpaid 30–60 hr of weekly domestic work, or the right to impose their name on wives and children. In other fields, more rights for women would mean more rights for all, such as the right for everyone to seek redress of all kinds of violations of the *Constitution*, were article 113, paragraph 3 modified.

More rights for women imply a redefinition of power, equality and liberty, and the acknowledgement that only by taking positive measures in favour of women will we overcome the history of discrimination that has been imposed on us.

REFERENCES

Aubert, Jean-François. 1967. *Traité de droit constitutionnel suisse*, 2 Vols. Ides et Calendes, Neuchâtel.

Aubert, Jean-François. 1982. *Traité de droit constitutionnel suisse*, Supplément 1967–1982. Ides et Calendes, Neuchâtel.

Auer, Andreas. 1980. '. . . le Tribunal fédéral appliquera les lois votées par l'Assemblée fédérale . . .': réflexions sur l'art. 113 al. 3 Cst. *Revue de droit suisse* 1980 (I): 107–140.

Auer, Andreas. 1983. *La juridiction constitutionnelle en Suisse*. Helbing & Lichtenhahn, Basel and Frankfurt.

Bérenstein, Alexandre, 1980. A propos de l'initiative pour l'égalité des droits entre hommes et femmes. Effet vertical ou effect horizontal? *Schweiz. Zentbl. Staatsund Gemeindeverwalung* 81: 193–200.

Castoriadis, Cornelius. 1982. Nature et valeur de l'égalité. In *L'exigence d'égalité*. XXXCIII és Rencontres internationales de Genève. La Baconnière, Neuchâtel.

Chaponnière-Grandjean, Martine. 1983. Histoire d'une initiative. *L'égalité des droits entre hommes et femmes*. Comité d'édition Egalité des droits, Genève-Zurich.

Commission fédérale pour les questions féminines. 1980. *La situation de la femme en Suisse*. Troisième partie: Droit. Berne.

Commission fédérale pour les question féminines. 1982. *La Situation de la femme en Suisse*. Deuzième partie: Bibliographies et rôle. Berne.

Conseil fédéral. 1979. Message concernant la révision du code civil suisse (effets généraux du mariage, régimes matrimoniaux et successions) du 11 juillet 1979. *Feuille fédéralae* II/2, 1179–1405, Berne.

Conseil fédéral. 1980. Message sur l'initiative populaire 'pour l'égalité des droits entre hommes et femmes', du 14 novembre 1979. *Feuille fédérale* I/1, 73–155. Berne.

Domaine public. 1984. *La longue marche des femmes*. No. 713. 12.1.1984.

Germann, Raimund E. 1981. *Ausserparlamentarische Kommissionen: Die Milizverwaltung des Bundes*. Verlag Paul Haupt, Bern and Stuttgart.

Kellerhals, Jean, J.- F. Perrin, G. Steinauer-Cresson, I., Voneche and G. Wirth. 1982. *Mariages au quotidien. Inégalités sociales, tensions culturelles et organisation familiale*. Favre, Lausanne.

Margolis, Clorinda and Joseph. 1981. The separation of marriage and family. In Vetterling-Braggin Mary *et al.*, eds. *Feminism and Philosophy*. Littlefield, Adams & Co., Totowa, New Jersey.

NOTES

1. Parliament can adopt a 'counter proposal' when the people launch an initiative. Both texts are then submitted to the vote (and generally refused), unless the authors of the initiative withdraw their text in favour of the counterproposal that has more chance of being accepted. This is what happened with article 4, paragraph 2.
2. The revision aims at removing the most shocking and visible aspects of legal sexism, such as the definition of men as chief of the family and women as housewives; the power of husbands to prevent their wives from working outside the home in paid employment; the privileges of men in marital property rights, in questions of domicile, or in representation and so on.
3. Only men have an individual right to a pension according to what they have contributed into the system, whereas women's situation will vary according to their civil status: a divorce can thus make them lose the right to what they had previously paid into the system. Also, men's contributions create more rights for their family than the same contributions by women.
4. For instance marital property rights give the husband the near entire control over and property in his wife's property, the justification being that women were not experienced enough to deal with financial questions. . . .

5.2 Towards Sexual Equality in Scandinavia

Birte Siim

This excerpt is also about power relations between men and women. Here the author makes the case that a feminist theoretical perspective is more fruitful than Marxist and liberal perspectives for analyzing the role of women in modern states. This argument is demonstrated through an analysis of the Scandinavian situation.

The author shows that there is good reason for arguing that Scandinavian is more advanced in relation to gender equality than just about all other regions of the world. For example, there is a sort of partnership between women and the state to organize care work with children and human reproduction; and women's economic dependence on husbands has been decreased. However, public policy and laws concerning paid and unpaid work are still guided by male values and interests.

The author sketches out some of the agenda of reform required if there is to be more gender equality. She is not convinced that placing more women in leadership positions in politics and law will lead to the reform. The appropriate changes depend, she argues, upon politicians' acceptance of basic feminist premises about work.

. . . Liberal analyses have often focused on the positive aspects of the Scandinavian welfare states towards women as individuals, while Marxist analyses have focused on the double oppression of women as workers and mothers within the capitalist state. In contrast, I argue the Scandinavian welfare states have had contradictory effects on women's lives: On the one hand the institutionalization of motherhood and care work as a part of social citizenship and women's integration on the labour market, have been favourable to women. On the other hand women have not been able to determine their interests as social and political agents, and the development of the corporate state structure with a high degree of centralization has been detrimental to women's collective interests. . . .

THE NEO-MARXIST UNDERSTANDING OF THE SCANDINAVIAN WELFARE STATES

Neo-Marxist analyses of the Scandinavian welfare states have focused primarily on structural class conflicts. In this perspective the Scandinavian welfare states are built on an alliance between the interests of the capitalist class and the interests of the working class. Gender relations have usually been absent

Excerpted from Siim, Birte (1987), "The Scandinavian welfare states: Towards sexual equality or a new kind of male domination?" *Acta Sociologica*, 30(3-4), 255–270, by permission of Scandinavian University Press.

from the model or subsumed under the category of class and gender conflicts have been understood as a part of the struggle between organized capital and labour. . . .

Women's position in the Scandinavian welfare states

The neo-Marxist understanding of the welfare state has been used to analyse the position of women. Mary Ruggie compared the positions of women in Sweden and Britain in *The State and Working Women* (1984). She contrasts the neo-Marxist understanding of the state with the pluralist understanding where the state is seen as a neutral agent and with the feminist understanding where the state is seen as predominantly oppressive as capitalist or patriarchal or both. She attempts to explain the differences in women's position in Sweden and England by looking at: (a) economic determinants, (b) women-specific factors, and (c) the role of the state. Ruggie acknowledges that each factor plays a part in explaining the differences in women's position, but argues 'the state is critical, for it mediates the effect of the two factors in addition to having an independent impact of its own'. The state is therefore understood as both an independent and an intervening factor.

Ruggie argues further that the key to the changes in Swedish policies for working women is 'the close association between concern for women, the labour market, and economic productivity'. She tries to explain the position of women solely by reference to the position of the working class:

It is my thesis that the differential role of the state vis-á-vis women workers in Britain and Sweden reflects the differential status of labor more generally (Ruggie 1984:298).

There is no doubt women's position is linked to the position of the working class, but she subsumes the situation of women completely under the position of the working class. This thesis raises fundamental problems. One is that historically there does not seem to be any automatic relation between a specific state policy and a specific policy towards women workers. The state often has a general policy which does not apply to women, exactly as a result of 'women-specific factors,' like the ideology and meaning of women and the family in the dominant political culture. Another problem is the tendency to see women primarily as workers, thereby subsuming women's position as mothers, and citizens, under their position as workers.

Ruggie has argued the Swedish state has to a large extent represented women's interests, even though she acknowledges women have allowed other parties speaking on their behalf to pursue their interests (1984:345). Feminist scholars have stressed that women's interests cannot be interpreted and represented adequately by other parties.

Paternalism in the Political Culture of the Scandinavian Welfare States

Niels Ole Finnemann has analysed the political culture of Denmark by focusing on the development of the ideas of the Social Democratic party (1985). He argues there has been continuity in the ideas of the party about the meaning of concepts like the state and nature. The state was understood as the incarnation of reason and nature as a rational universe. In contrast, he finds a radical change in the conception of the private sphere since the Second World War. One thesis in his analysis is there has been both a 'male' and a 'female' perspective on the development of the welfare state, specifically in relation to the family and on democracy.

Finnemann argues that the political culture of paternalism has changed radically since the development of the modern welfare state: On the one hand there has been 'a liberation from the personal-patriarchal aspects of brotherhood where there is no longer given any priority to the male sex with reference to sexual power. On the other hand there has been a subsumption of the subjective female values under the objective male values of rationality' (Finnemann 1985:340–341).

According to Finnemann the female perspective is connected with the 'values of family life and a dream about a democratic harmony between the sexes in the family and in the public sphere and with an ambivalence towards wage work'. The dominant political culture of the Social Democratic party after the Second World War is state reformism. State reformism has strived towards a rational organization of both the public and the private sphere by building new state institutions to take over part of the care of the elderly, the sick, the children and the disabled. The rationality which became the governing principle of state reformism was the male principle of rationality connected to the values of the public sphere. . . .

Finnemann has presented an impressive critique. I find, however, that there is a tendency to idealize the female perspective and to place it outside history. Historically there has been a tension between the values and interests of women in different positions and classes which calls into question the formulation of only one female perspective. It is therefore necessary to analyse in what way and to what extent it would have been possible to develop an alternative female perspective within a given historical period. . . .

THE FEMINIST CRITIQUE OF THE SCANDINAVIAN WELFARE STATES

. . . Feminist scholars have analysed different aspects of the welfare state in relation to women: The immediate objectives and the content of public policies, the values and assumptions behind them and the interests that have guided them, and finally the consequences of different public policies for women. From this perspective the welfare state has through its public policies, political ideologies and organizational principles helped produce and reproduce a sexual division of labour and male domination. . . .

The Critique of the Public–Private Split in Liberal Thinking

Feminist scholars [argue] . . . that the public world of politics can only be understood in connection with the private world of the family, and in this perspective it becomes necessary to rethink fundamental categories of liberalism like the concept of the individual and the concept of citizenship.

Political scientists like Helga Hernes have focused on women's position within the institutional structure of the state and in the formal and informal political system (Hernes 1982, 1983). Although women's representation in the formal political system has been growing in the Scandinavian countries and was by 1985 around 25%, the highest in the western world, this growing representation has not necessarily given women more power in relation to men. Women are still absent from the central arenas of decision-making, i.e. the powerful economic and political elites. Women's representation in the corporate system of interest organizations, state administrators and experts is only around 10%, which is much lower than in the parliamentary system. Hernes' conclusion is that in the Scandinavian welfare states men have mainly been the participators and women the receivers in the political process.

Hernes has argued that in the Scandinavian states women's relations to the state have become critical for women, because they have moved from the private dependency of their individual husbands to the public dependency of the state. [Her] conclusion is that although the modern welfare state has given women important social and economic advantages, women have become

subordinated to a new sexual power hierarchy within the political system.

Other political scientists, like Lise Togeby and Drude Dahlerup, have analysed women's growing participation within political parties, trade unions and new social movements. Although women and men today participate to the same extent in the new social movements, there is a gender profile in the kind of activities women and men engage in and women are still underrepresented in the leadership of the political parties and of the trade union movement. . . .

The feminist critique of liberalism has been the basis for a debate among feminists about the public/private split, the meaning of politics and the perspective of the political struggle. Some have argued to abolish the distinction between the public and the private sphere altogether, while others have argued to maintain a difference. I agree with Pateman, who has argued that the aim of the critical feminist theory of liberalism is to make the political dimension of life part of everyday life and to change the power relations in the private and public world in a way that makes women's participation in political life as social and political agents possible (Pateman 1985a).

The Feminist Critique of the Patriarchal–Capitalist State

Marxist feminists have analysed women's relations to the welfare state by focusing on the structural contradictions between the labour market, the family and the state and between women's different position as workers and mothers. Some have emphasized the oppressive character of the capitalist state vis-á-vis women. Others have emphasized male domination in the public sphere and have tried to rethink the concept of patriarchy and use it in connection with the analysis of the modern welfare state. There have been several attempts to differentiate between a patriarchal family and social patriarchy. In this perspective the emphasis has been on the historical changes in patriarchy and on the transformation of patriarchy from the power of men in the families to the power of men through the state. In this perspective the welfare state can be described as a 'social' or state patriarchy.

In my comparative work, and in the analysis of the Danish welfare state with Anette Borchorst, we have emphasized the contradictory character of women's integration in the public sphere and the interrelation between women's positions as mothers, workers and citizens (Borchorst & Siim 1985; Siim 1987a). In Denmark the welfare state has been based on a new partnership between the state and the family—and to some extent between women and the state. Under the Social Democratic party the state has formulated a policy of socializing care for children, the sick, the elderly and the disabled by building public institutions. On this basis it can be argued motherhood and care work in the Scandinavian countries have become part of social citizenship (Siim 1987a and 1987b).

. . . The partnership between the state and the family can be seen as one precondition for empowering women as workers, mothers and citizens by decreasing women's economic dependency of their husbands (Siim 1987b). This has also influenced women's political activities as citizens, but there is no automatic connection between women's socioeconomic position and the sexual power relations in the public sphere. Women have become integrated into a new sexual power hierarchy within the administrative and political system of the welfare state. In this perspective the development of the modern welfare state can be interpreted as a change from a family to a social patriarchy. The welfare state can be said to be patriarchal to the extent women have been absent from the decision-making process and to the extent public policies have been governed by male assumptions and male values and have predominantly served male interests.

On the one hand the state has helped to decrease women's personal dependency on individual men as mothers and workers. On the other hand the state has subsumed women under a new centralized power hierarchy and disregarded or subsumed women's interests and values under the dominant state rationality. The political culture has also been ambivalent towards women: On the one hand it has stressed equality and solidarity and accepted motherhood and care work as part of social citizenship. On the other hand the conception of motherhood and care work has been governed by male assumptions and has served male interests. The belief in equality has only recently included equality policies between men and women and then only to a limited extent.

The Future Development of the Welfare State

There is no agreement among feminists of what women's interests are or of how to define women's issues and it is still an open question what impact women's political mobilization can have on attempts to restructure the welfare state. Women have disagreed about issues like the right to abortion and the right to voluntary motherhood. On the other hand women have at times expressed common interests and built alliances around goals, as e.g. the right to vote and the right to education and equal pay.

In the Scandinavian countries there is a fundamental difference between the position of the young and well-educated women on the one side and the older and unskilled women on the other. Still an open question is the extent to which, and on what subjects, women will be able to unite and fight for common interests. It has been argued that women have a common interest in politicizing motherhood and care work, but they do not necessarily have the same solutions as to how these issues should be organized. Eisenstein has argued women today have a common interest as working mothers, but women also have different positions on the labour market and therefore different strategies towards the labour market.

Political scientists have traced a gender gap in politics. Women have a tendency to vote to the left compared to men and women to a larger extent than men support the development of the 'social state' and are more positive than men towards a decrease in military spending and towards the peace movement. On the other hand women disagree markedly in some countries around such feminist issues as abortion and equal rights and on moral issues connected with the family.

There have been attempts to link differences in women's sociopolitical profiles to differences in women's socioeconomic and cultural position. It has been argued that the old women's culture, centred around the family, tended to pull women in a Conservative direction. In contrast, the new women's culture defined by women's double identification with the private and the public sphere has tended to pull women towards the Left. From this perspective women could play an important role in the struggle to change the social and political institutions of the welfare state in a more democratic direction.

THEORETICAL CHALLENGES FROM THE SCANDINAVIAN EXPERIENCES

In order to grasp the complexities of the Scandinavian welfare states and the contradictory experiences of women it has become necessary to transcend both the liberal and the Marxist understanding of the welfare state.

The changes in the nature of male domination with the advance of the modern welfare state appear to have shifted the locus of oppression from the private to the public sphere. In this perspective it becomes more important than ever that women strive collectively to be present within public institutions and organizations as one precondition for transforming the values, public policies and priorities and institutional structure of the welfare state. Even though socioeconomic, cultural and political factors both divide and unite women, women have a common interest in being present within the institutions in order to make them more responsive to women's needs and interests.

The Scandinavian welfare states have given women an excellent foundation for collectively changing the social and political institutions and making them more democratic and responsive to women's needs. On the other hand there exist strong structural barriers for any real empowering of women as social and political agents. One of the most important barriers seems to be the high degree of centralization within the administrative and political system of the Scandinavian welfare states and a political culture that has subsumed women's needs and interests under the interests of economic class organizations, and which has only recently begun to recognize women's interests as separate and legitimate vis-à-vis the interests of the working class.

REFERENCES

Andersen, G. J. 1984. *Kvinder og politik* (Women and Politics). Arhus: Politica.

Borchorst, Å. & Siim, B. 1984. *Kvinder og velfaerdsstaten. Mellem moderskab og lønabejde i 100 år* (Women and the Welfare State Between Motherhood and Wagework in 100 Years). Aalborg: Aalborg University Press.

Borchorst, A. & Siim, B. 1985. Women and the Advanced Welfare State—a New Kind of Patriarchal Power? Forthcoming in Showstack-Sassoon (ed.), *From a Women's Point of View: New Perspectives on the Welfare State*. London: Hutchinson.

Finnemann, N. O. 1985. *I Broderskabets Ånd. Den socialdemokratiske arbejderbevaegelses idehistorie 1871–1977* (In the Spirit of Brotherhood). Gyldendal.

Hernes, H. 1982. *Staten—kvinder ingen adgang* (The State—No Admittance for Women). Oslo: Universitetsforlaget.

Hernes, H. 1983. Women and the Advanced Welfare State—the Transition from Private to Public Dependence. Paper presented in Bellagio, Italy and later appeared in H. Holter (ed.), *Patriarchy in a Welfare State*. Oslo: Universitetsforlaget, 1984.

Pateman, C. 1985a. *The Problem of Political Obligation. A Critique of Liberal Theory*. Oxford: Polity Press.

Peterson, A. 1984. 'The Gender-Sex Dimension in Swedish Politics. *Acta Sociologica* 27:1.

Ruggie, M. 1984. *The State and Working Women. A Comparative Study of Britain and Sweden*. Princeton: Princeton University Press.

Siim, B. 1987a. Women and the Welfare State. Comparative Perspective on the Organization of Care Work in Denmark and Britain. Forthcoming in C. Ungerson (ed.), *Women and Community Care. Gender and Caring in the Modern Welfare State*. London: Wheatsheaf.

Siim, B. 1987b. Rethinking of the Welfare State from a Feminist Perspective. Forthcoming in A. Jonasdottir & K. Jones (eds.), *The Political Interests of Gender. Developing Theory and Research with a Feminist Face*. London: Sage Publications.

5.3 Ethnic Antagonism in Yugoslavia

Sergej Flere

As suggested by the excerpts you have just read, struggles between the genders have made their way to the courts and parliaments in many instances. In day-to-day interaction these struggles often lead to out-and-out violence against women, but not to organized warfare. The same cannot be said for struggles among ethnic groups.

The next excerpt is about conflict between ethnic groups in response to regional disparities. One of the many areas seeing a very bloody struggle for power between ethnic groups is the former Yugoslavia. In this excerpt the author asks how adequate are two popular theories of ethnic group antagonism for explaining what has happened in that part of the world.

The two theories are Marxist theory, which says that ethnic group conflict is rooted in class exploitation of one group by another, and **modernization theory**, which sees raised economic expectations and insecurity, due to a breakdown of traditional values and norms, as the basic cause of ethnic group power struggles.

Flere finds both theories wanting; neither explains the Yugoslavian case very well, although the author sees some merit in the modernization theory. The precipitating factor for the current wave of conflict is the breakdown of legitimation around the state's way of regulating conflict between contending ethnic groups. Beyond this, a multifactor theory is required to explain the history of conflict, the author contends. When looked at up close, the reasons for the power struggles are shown to be very complex phenomena.

Yet, the continual pursuit of relative advantage—maximizing perceived group interests—seems to be a constant across struggles like this one. What varies is how interests are perceived, where group barriers are erected, and

Since President Tito's death in 1980, ethnic antagonism has been growing in Yugoslavia. . . We will explore some possible sources of these antagonisms in . . . this paper.

EXPLOITATION AS A SOURCE OF ETHNIC TENSION

The Marxist view holds that behind ethnic tension and antagonism we always find an

Excerpted from Flere, Sergej (1991), "Explaining ethnic antagonism in Yugoslavia," *European Sociological Review*, 7(3), December, 183–193. By permission of Oxford University Press.

infrastructure of exploitation, which takes on ethnic dimensions among others. In the simplest case, this means the exploitative and exploited groups are ethnically distinct. This may be operationalized by emphasizing the use by the dominant class of a reserve labour army composed of one ethnic group in order to combat another, or to keep the first group subjugated or to keep wages in general low.

It may be a paradox that in the field of ethnic tensions, as for socialist, regulated societies, Marxism appears particularly inadequate in offering meaningful explanations. The inadequacy stems from the fact that in Yugoslav society the economy was not an independent subsystem regulated by its own logic and determinisms. Yugoslav socialism was a product of political will. Not only was the political sphere dominant, but other sub-systems were modelled on it, and endowed with political and normative institutional criteria. . . .

. . . The relationship between the political system and the economic system was further burdened by the vast institutional organization of the former, which imposed its model on the latter. In the last decade the rules of this political system had made it almost unchangeable, creating conditions of high integration where dysfunction in one part quickly spreads to the entire system. This made the extra-political spheres continually less adaptable and more inflexible, bringing them into ever greater contrast with the exigencies of the contemporary social system. Therefore, the hypothesis of exploitation must be rejected. . . .

MODERNIZATION AS A SOURCE OF ETHNIC TENSION

The idea of social modernization causing a reaction in the form of ethnic resurgence is initially plausible. Marxism has developed some Hegelian ideas of modernism to the full: that man should be his own master; that he may therefore create a 'transparent' social organization to suit his ends; that no mediation between people in the form of petrified institutions is necessary; that man can use science boldly as an instrument for mastering nature and society, etc. . . .

Nevertheless, we would not be justified in tying modernization in Yugoslavia only to the basic tenets in socialism, as modernization has more to do with empirical social processes as they actually evolve, involving market relations, bureaucracy, civil society, individualism, institutionalization of various segments of society, etc. as bases of sustained growth. Ethnocentrism could appear as a reaction to these processes, according to this line of thought, because of a dislocation experienced by individuals within modern society. This dislocation derives from mobility and the consequent lack of the security that was characteristic of traditional society, where it was based on the extended family, and on local and religious groups. This loss of security may bring about a resurgence of ethnic identity, inter-ethnic tension, and in cases of economic crisis, scapegoating in inter-ethnic relations (see the model discussed by Hannan (1979) and Nielsen (1980)). . . .

Although Yugoslavia has undergone significant modernization . . . it [has been] a partial, incomplete modernization which did not contain components that give rise to ethnic reactions. For example, ethnic mobilization . . . to cope with the merciless market not recognizing individual ethnicities, or a bureaucracy operating solely on impersonal principles, was not relevant. The policy of ethnic parity in the federal administration made it impossible for universalistic criteria . . . to cut across traditional society. Members of different ethnic groups rarely found themselves in a position to compete for the same rewards in a market situation; there was little migration on economic grounds, except into Slovenia.

We must address the . . . following impediments to a full modernization:

1. The lack of bureaucracy in the Weberian sense. The huge bureaucratic edifice was organized on the principle of equal ethnic representation, without producing greater efficiency in the management of affairs. . . .
2. The lack of a market. The market was a taboo for socialism, even in Yugoslavia; it was considered to be linked to the meanest forces of exploitation, oppression, and alienation. On the other hand, an independent market for goods, services and capital would undermine the rule of the political élite. A rudimentary market for commodities did exist, but it was not large enough to leave the individual at the mercy of market forces and force him to seek protection from his ethnic group.
3. The power of the political structure. The . . . system allowed as much modernization as could be absorbed without seriously questioning the legitimacy of the ruling élite. This does open avenues for industrialization, urbanization, and the growth of education and science, but without producing internal moves toward efficiency. . . .

AUTHORITARIANISM

The authoritarian personality syndrome formulated by Adorno and associates (1950) is a theory of a personality structure showing evidence of ethnocentrism and hence relevant to inter-ethnic conflict. . . . In Yugoslavia, authoritarianism has been measured a number of times, following Adorno's methodology, and found to be high. For example, according to a survey in 1987 of adults in Yugoslavia, authoritarianism is high and prevails without great difference between regions (Toš, 1988: supplement).

. . . An analogy may be drawn with Germany in the 1930s. Yugoslavia has experienced similar economic troubles during the last decade: the middle strata were the hardest hit by the economic crisis, and three- and four-digit inflation in the late 1980s has played its part in delegitimizing institutions, bringing about the generalized uncertainty and unreliability of individuals and institutions. Yugoslavia did not lose a war, but ideologically similar phenomena are present: 'scapegoating' for the . . . unfavourable state of one's ethnic group. Though authoritarianism does not offer a full explanation, it may explain the psychological content of ethnic resurgence and antagonism.

ETHNIC STRATIFICATION

. . . This approach holds that ethnic conflicts are the result of the fact that ethnic groups have different positions on the stratification scale [due] to structural barriers to equality of opportunity. It would further mean a particularistic mechanism functions in producing social structures. . . .

In Yugoslavia, social stratification has multiple dimensions but it is evident that political stratification is in question as a cause of ethnic antagonism. It should be remembered that the creators of the Yugoslav political system during the 1960s were aware of the possibility of ethnic conflict arising from such a source. Constitutional provisions as to ethnic parity were built in, making equal representation of ethnic groups compulsory at all levels of political life, and even in the distribution of other positions of power. But nevertheless we shall draw attention to the ethnic populations in the League of Communists—the former ruling political organization. . . .

The incidence of League members was significantly higher among Serbs and particularly among Montenegrins, in contrast with among Croatians and Slovenes. . . . None of these regions is ethnically homogeneous, but in regions where populations of Eastern Orthodox extraction predominate, League membership is more common.

However, to speak of ethnic groups where membership is above average as being on one side of the conflict, and those with below average membership as composing the other would be misleading. Firstly, Yugoslav society in the post-war period was segmented; its component institutions were not strongly tied to each other. Secondly, the roots of the ethnic antagonism date back much further than the present period. Thirdly, the difference in the rate of membership has a cultural explanation, specifically with a higher secularization level in Orthodox regions. Fourthly, the dissatisfaction of the Serbs cannot be regarded as solely manipulative. Serbs question the allegation that they enjoy a favoured position in Yugoslavia. Nevertheless, a small part of the explanation for ethnic conflict may lie in these membership differences.

AN ATTEMPTED EXPLANATION: CULTURE, HISTORY, AND SOCIETY

. . . [To explain] the present conflicts we will have to rely on a multi-factor schema, as follows:

1. Yugoslavia is very heterogeneous in terms of the standard economic, sociological, and demographic indicators.

For now, we shall draw attention only to the first three columns of Table 1, which contain 'hard' data on modernization. . . . One may note the very high birth-rate in Kosovo (predominantly Albanian ethnics)—indicating a population boom—whereas other differentials are not substantial. The per capita income in column two reflects the economic disparities in Yugoslavia, where the variability index is high. The ratio between the extremes of Kosovo and Slovenia is 1:8. The illiteracy figures also point to a high differential in rates. . . . Those disparities were significant. One cannot bypass, however, the presence of Roman Catholicism, of Serbian and Macedonian Orthodoxy, and of Islam on Yugoslav soil as traditional religions, all finding their frontiers in this country, giving the relations between them the flavour and importance of border relations, with numerous attempts at forced conversion in the past. The Catholic lands are generally more economically advanced, and they underwent a Protestant period which may have been a favourable influence for modernization.

Heterogeneity is not a necessarily conflictual factor, though adverse effects are more probable than favourable ones.

2. The Yugoslav policy of ethnic and regional parity in political representation, and the cultural advancement of ethnic groups seemed to function well during President Tito's rule, but problems have arisen since his death.

   (a) Such instruments in the regulation of ethnic relations are not sufficient if they are not part of an overall modernization process. Therefore, the lack of overall modernization, in contrast to processes in Western Europe, instigated ethnic conflicts in the form of 'scapegoating', i.e. in ideological and ethnocentric explanations of the unsatisfactory position of various ethnic groups, compared with other European standards.

   (b) In addition, disputes [arose] concerning the boundaries between federal units. . . . A second part of this framework is the legitimacy of the very existence as autonomous units of Bosnia and Herzegovina, Macedonia, and Montenegro, since all are claimed by other states.

   (c) The nature of the autonomous provinces of Kosovo (Kosova) and Vojvodina, which form part of Serbia but have had direct representation on the federal level of government, [is] also questioned. . . . Such a system presupposes an external, extra-constitutional political arrangement for resolving political dispute. In communism this was found in the principle of 'democratic centralism', but once these extra-constitutional regulative mechanisms ceased

to operate, the long-repressed disputes became overt.

3. A sensitive issue in ethnic relations in Yugoslavia is the question of 'hegemony'. . . . The first Yugoslav state was widely considered one of ethnic hegemony by the Serbs, who played the main role in the formation of that state, who gave it its royal dynasty, and whose church was tied to the dynasty. Serbs were also most numerous in the state repressive apparatuses. Accusations can be heard today that a repetition of such a situation has occurred in the second Yugoslav state.

Reverse accusations as to the subjugation of the Serbs may also be heard. The subjugation of the Serbs in the post-war Yugoslavia is claimed to have been carried out through the imposition of political boundaries within Yugoslavia in such a way that Serbs are dispersed in various republics and provinces. Allegations can be heard that Montenegrins, and to a lesser extent Macedonians, are not true ethnic groups but artificial ones, created by the Communists to decompose the Serbian ethnic unity. Their subjugation is also alleged to be

TABLE 1. Birth-Rate, Per Capita National Income, Illiteracy Rate, and Index of Egalitarianism, by Republics and Provinces

	Birth rate (per 1000; 1987)	Per capita national income (YU) dinars; 1987)	Illiteracy rate[a]	Index of egalitarianism[b]
Yugoslavia	15.3	2 101	13.7	36.5
Bosnia and Herzegovina	16.1	1 478	22.2	38.8
Montenegro	16.9	1 495	13.9	45.8
Croatia	12.7	2 702	8.5	32.9
Macedonia	18.7	1 291	14.8	53.1
Slovenia	13.7	4 828	1.4	28.0
Serbia	12.6	1 871	15.2	31.1
Kosovo	30.4	601	25.7	60.8
Vojvodina	12.3	2 502	8.4	32.2
v =	34%	58%	53%	27%

Source: Statistički godišnjak 1988.
Notes: (a) Percentage aged 15 and more without any schooling, 1981.
(b) Measured by agreement with the statement: 'Income ratios should not be greater than 1:2'. Source: Toš, N. (1988).

found in their lack of representation at the very top of the leadership in the Tito era. . . .

4. The 'numbers game' enters into these relations at the level of the whole country, but also at the republic and province levels. . . .

The chief demographic source of ethnic tension in Yugoslavia is the emigration of Serbs from Kosovo, which is making this area—regarded as the source of Serbian nationhood and statehood—almost empty of Serbs and populated by ethnic Albanians. These demographic changes within Kosovo have divided the Yugoslav polity as to what measures should be taken. . . .

Another demographic change which has had an impact is the emigration of Serbs and Croatians from Bosnia and Herzegovina, mainly into their ethnic homelands.

5. Social-psychological and cultural heterogeneity [has] implications for incompatibility between ethnic groups in Yugoslavia. . . . Two main differences are in question.

(a) Religious affiliations in Yugoslavia have to do not only with differences in doctrine, but they also influence culture, they relate to historical boundaries within Yugoslav territory where there has been a long history of religious warfare and attempts at forced conversions. Most importantly, religious boundaries have much to do with ethnic makeup, in the case of Serbs, Croats, Muslims (in the ethnic sense), and to a certain extent Macedonians.

The greater bearing of historical over doctrinal factors in explaining religious relations comes to the fore in the relationships between Serbs, Croats, and ethnic Muslims (Bošnjaks) in Bosnia and Herzegovina, where the last two are closer socially and politically.

(b) There are traditional differences in culture between mountain herdsmen and lowland agriculturalists, which may develop into incompatibilities, particularly when they take on an ethnic dimension. Mountain herdsmen's ways of thinking and values are embedded in a culture of violence and power-seeking, whereas agriculturalists in the lowlands are more peacefully oriented, more industrious, and readier to accept the imposition of authority. This traditional difference did not disappear after migrations in Yugoslavia but became even more manifest (Tomašić 1950). These differences can be accentuated if we lend credence to the judgement that Eastern Orthodoxy is incongenial to the 'rational and methodical reorganization of the world for capitalistic gain.' (Buss, 1989: 255).

. . . According to some the psychology and culture of the life of mountain-herdsmen was the basis of the egalitarian syndrome. Zupanov (1977) assessed this syndrome as one factor suppressing modernization in Yugoslavia, a cultural factor stemming from traditionalism, and not imposed by communist ideology, though amalgamating well with it. Egalitarianism in this context implies the idea of a limited pool of goods which are to be distributed by a just and authoritarian governor. This presupposes the distributive function of the state, and an obsession with dispossessing private owners and impeding entrepreneurship, professionalism, and innovation.

In Table 1 we see that egalitarianism may function as a restraining factor on modernization in Yugoslavia, as well as that it is unevenly distributed . . .

6. At the level of public opinion and those who influence it, current, contemporary events are interpreted through the prism of historically rooted ethnic grievances and frustrations. The economic crisis, contributed to a growth of frustrations which are then transformed into ethnic grievances and interpreted as a repetition of historic injustices towards one's own ethnic group. . . .

CONCLUSION

. . . Yugoslav socialism was formally a tightly knit system. But Yugoslav society was not substantially integrated. Socially and culturally distinct systems existed in the republics and provinces. This is reflected in the magnitude of economic disparities we have discussed, in the endurance of ethnic traditionalism, and in the fact that loyalty towards Yugoslavia is disappearing when the legitimacy of the political regime and institutional arrangements are withering. Attempts to constitute a Yugoslav identity as an ethnic identity met with little success. Therefore, the only identity which could be found in a time of the general collapse of institutions and their legitimacy remained religion and ethnicity (very much linked to religion), enabling a unique cultural ethno-religious factor to appear in its authoritarian, tradition-invoking form. In a country with such a legacy of ethnic resentment, conflicts between ethnic groups are easily rekindled.

REFERENCES

Adorno T. *et al.* (1950): *The Authoritarian Personality*, New York: Harper.

Buss A. (1989): 'The economic ethnics of Russian Orthodox Christianity: Part I', *International Sociology*, 4: 235–57.

Hannan M T. (1979): 'The dynamics of ethnic boundaries in modern states', in Meyer J W, Hannan, M T (eds): *National Development and the World System*, Chicago: Chicago University Press.

Nielsen N. (1980): 'The Flemish Movement in Belgium after World War II: A Dynamic Analysis', *American Sociological Review*, 45: 76–94.

Statistički godišnjak 1988 (Statistical Yearbook 1988), Beograd: Savezni zavod za statistiku.

Tomašić D. (1950): *Personality and Culture in Eastern European Politics*, New York: George W. Stewart.

Toš N. (1988): 'Klasno bi'ce jugoslovenskog društva: sumarni prikaz z manjkajočimi vrednostmi' ('The class structure of Yugoslav Society: Summary Presentation with Lacking Values'), Ljubljana: Fakulteta za sociologijo, politične vede in novinarstvo.

Županov J. (1977): 'Socijalizam i tradicionalizam' ('Socialism and traditionalism'), *Politička misao*, 1: 129–57.

5.4 Industrial Development and Working-Class Politics in Iran

Val Moghadam

Power struggles sometimes result in the revolutionary overthrow of governments. Indeed, this has been a common occurrence the world around, recently and throughout history. The next excerpt discusses a recent revolution, the 1978–79 revolution in Iran, and the growth of workers' class-consciousness during that revolution.

In this revolution, one form of traditional authority, the Shah's regime, was replaced with another, the Islamic Republic. The author analyzes developments leading up to and following the revolution, with special reference to the role of industrial workers in establishing the legitimacy of the revolution and the new form of government.

Industrial workers were central to the revolution. They did not initiate protests against the Shah's rule; clerics, students, and other workers did. But, once the industrial workers joined in, with strikes, the government was bound to fall because of the importance of the industrial sector to the country's economic stability.

There is some question, though, whether the revolution was a step forward for the power of the working class and the labor movement. Neither workers nor their representatives came to power, a religious elite did. No secular social- ist government followed.

Nonetheless, the author concludes that there were some advances for the working class. These had mostly to do with increases in working-class con- sciousness and some developments in the direction of workers' councils and worker control in the factories.

. . . In Iran, the industrial strikes of Octo- ber 1978 to February 1979 and the rise and fall of workers' councils in the modern indus- trial sector during and immediately after the revolutionary uprising, raised the question of the consciousness and capabilities of Iran's industrial working class. The councils were established in plants where the owners and/or managers had fled or had been expelled during the anti-Shah upheavals and immediately afterwards (Azad 1980; Bayat 1983; Goodey 1980; Moghadam 1984). The councils assigned for themselves the right to manage wholly or in part the production, dis- tribution and financial operations of the workplace. Problems ensued and the councils were undermined by the new Islamic regime, and as a result of contradictions internal to the councils themselves.

. . . This raises three fundamental ques- tions about industrial workers in Iran. First, how to interpret workers' role in the Revolu- tion? Was it reformist, revolutionary, self- interested, progressive? Second, was the Rev- olution a step forward or a setback for the working class and the labour movement? Third, what are the prospects for a revival of the labour movement?

This paper examines the political activities of workers in one major industrial region of Iran, Tabriz and environs. Tabriz was chosen because during the 1978–79 Revolution and afterwards, Tabriz acquired the distinction of being the site of the most radical of the work- ers' councils. Tabriz is located in East Azarbai-

Excerpted from Moghadam, Val (1987), "Indus- trial development, culture and working-class poli- tics," *International Sociology*, 2(2), 151–175.

jan, and is a major Iranian city. . . . I inter- viewed one of the founding members of the Tabriz industrial workers' councils, in 1985 in Paris. Javad, once an activist worker, was now an unemployed member of the Iranian exile community. Javad presented a fascinating pic- ture of work, culture and politics in Tabriz. This paper combines ethnography and struc- tural analysis in seeking to illuminate linkages between industrial development, culture and working-class politics in Iran.

AN INDUSTRIAL WORKER SPEAKS

. . . In 1985, Javad was 28 years old. He had fled Iran two years earlier for political rea- sons. Javad's social class background was industrial working class. His father and grand- fathers had been industrial workers. At age 12 or 13, Javad began employment in work- shops, primarily machine shops. He . . . worked variously as an office sweeper and a tea-boy. He remarked, 'Because of the suffer- ings I experienced in the workshops, I was very receptive to Left ideas'.

I asked him about his family life and the importance of religion. 'My mother and father didn't like clerics; they didn't like beards', he laughed. His parents were, how- ever, believers: 'My mother always prayed'. His father became religious, he said, only as he grew old, because 'he was afraid of what might happen after he died'.

It also emerged that his parents had urged him to attend school.

After obtaining his high school diploma, Javad attended the Institute of Technology, a voca- tional/technical school . . . in Tabriz. . . .

At the Institute, Javad attended book exhibits, read widely, encountered radical students, participated in mountain-climbing expeditions that were really political discussion sessions, and engaged in fights with religious (anti-Left) students. When the anti-Shah movement began, Javad joined other Left students, putting up leaflets, organising protests and other such activities. Javad became drawn to Peykar, one of several Left-wing political groups that emerged during the anti-Shah movement. After the Shah was deposed, he joined Peykar.

After the Revolution, Javad worked in a motor assembly factory, with 100 employees. This plant was among the many medium-sized industrial establishments that sprang up during the 1960s and 1970s. By Iranian standards, this plant is termed 'large', as is any industrial firm employing over 10 workers. In this plant, where Javad was a skilled worker, there were 75 production workers; the balance of the workforce was comprised of drivers (transport workers) and white-collar employees (karmand). Javad became the workers' 'political representative'. At the same time, he became active in the councils movement then spreading throughout the industrial sector in Iran (Azad 1980). In this capacity, he had contact with other factories in and around Tabriz.

INDUSTRIALISATION AND THE STRATIFICATION OF THE TABRIZ WORKING CLASS[1]

Beginning in the early 1960s, the Pahlavi state initiated a capitalist development project based upon import-substitution industrialisation (ISI) and agrarian reform. ISI provided state protection for domestic industry and led to the proliferation of manufacturing that produced commodities primarily for the home market. . . .

Parallel to the rise of a modern industrial sector was the persistence and expansion of 'traditional' industrial activities (Moghadam 1985). . . .

In Iran, large numbers of people are engaged in traditional handicraft industries,

among them silversmiths, coppersmiths, carpet weavers, leather and wood workers. Such industries are mostly carried out in or around the Bazaar, Iran's traditional urban markets. I call this the workshop sector of Iranian industry.

The workshop sector is at once functional and dysfunctional for the large modern industrial sector. It is functional in as much as it carries out operations—such as repair, maintenance and production of goods and services geared toward a certain market—that are not within the purview of the modern sector. More importantly, it is functional because it absorbs the surplus population at no or extremely low cost to the state and to capital. It is dysfunctional in so far as the proliferation of workshops could compete with the modern sector. The intensification of this competition—preferential treatment of larger firms and the government's attempt to regulate the Bazaar's operations—led to opposition.

In the early 1970s, the ILO mission that visited Iran recognised that, given the high rate of population increase and the inability of the formal sector to absorb the entire labour force, the general pattern would be the continued growth of the labour force in the informal sectors of both the countryside and the city (ILO 1973). By the end of the 1970s, much of Iran's 'dynamic' manufacturing was in the informal sector in rural areas.

A notable feature of Iranian industry is the small size of the majority of the establishments. Data for 1972 show over 97 per cent of establishments employed fewer than 10 persons, yet, as there were over 219,000 enterprises in this category, they accounted for nearly 600,000 workers. This constituted two thirds of Iran's total industrial workforce at the time. Thus a typical industrial worker in Iran was either self-employed, engaged in a family business, or employed in a small workshop (Wheeler 1976 : 14). Table 1 illustrates this pattern.

. . . The differentiation of industry, of the labour force and of labour markets, has social, political and ideological implications. These divisions became critical during the Iranian Revolution.

TABLE 1   Employed Population of East Azarbaijan, by Employment Status (1972)

Employment Status	Number ('00s)	Percentage
Total	7972	—
Employer	172	2.1
Self-employed	3468	43.5
Government employee (Karmand)	236	2.9
Government worker (Kargar)	104	1.3
Private sector wage and salary earner	2134	26.7
Unpaid family	1837	23.0
In training	11	0.13
Not adequately described	10	0.12

Source: *Statistical Yearbook*, 1976, Table 12, p. 61.

Javad had his own classification of the Tabriz industrial labour force. In his schema, industrial workers in Tabriz could be separated into three spheres: 1) construction, 2) small-scale manufacturing, 3) modern industrial plants, especially those with over 100 workers. The majority of workers were in construction or in small-scale manufacturing and most were in the latter. Construction workers were often semi-proletarians, still tied to the countryside. As Javad said, 'It took these people a long time to sever their connections to the village'. Most researchers agree that much of the Tabriz working class is in its second or third generation of industrial work. Javad concurred with this.

We shall apply the term *workshop sector* to Javad's second category, small-scale manufacturing. The structure and features of production in the workshop sector are very different from those in the large industrial sector. Javad called it 'anarchy in production'. He meant it was not systematic or regularised. He also explained that most workers in Tabriz began employment at age 12 or 13, and many began at ages eight or nine. These were not 'young adults', as Javad commented, 'They were children; they would cry'.

The mentality of workers in this category was different from that of workers in the large, modern industrial sector. According to Javad, a construction worker, for example, aspired to become a *bana* (independent self-employed builder), while many of those labouring in the workshop sector longed to have their own shops. In neither the construction nor the workshop sector was the question of workers' control considered. 'The objective is petty bourgeois self-employment', Javad said. There is no concern about alienation. There is, instead, social mobility consciousness, as distinct from class consciousness, Javad asserted. Referring to workers for whom the 60-hour work-week is the norm, Javad declared: 'They are incredibly exploited, but all they want is to be *aadam* (human being), or *ostad* (master), or *karfarma* (employer)'.

Workers in the informal sector, for the most part, can identify more easily with traditional religious values than with secular or socialist ideas. Having come from rural areas and facing the complex realities of Iranian urban life, they can expect to be susceptible to recruitment by a religious populist movement. Workers with urban backgrounds are more likely to be interested in secular ideas and modes of life.

It was in the large modern industrial factories that the sporadic strikes, beginning in the early 1970s, took place. In this spate of strikes, many focussing on job classification as well as on wages, Tabriz industrial workers were well represented. It was also in this sector that the industrial strikes which shook the Pahlavi regime took place, from October 1978 to February 1979. Finally, it was in this sector that the workers' councils emerged during and after the Revolution (Moghadam 1984).

I asked Javad if he had noted any tendency for workers in Tabriz to leave the large factories and set up their own small enterprises. . . . Javad did not think this was common in Tabriz. Indeed, it would be a rare worker, he said, who would leave a large modern plant to set up his own workshop. On the other hand, there was some labour transfer from the workshop sector to the modern industrial sector.

Javad said when workers became exposed to the very different conditions within the large plants, the personal relations, long hours, hard work, low income and other features of the workshop sector lost all appeal. And what about workers' own 'control' over labour power and skill? Javad's reply was that, although in the large plants there was external control, supervision and management, he experienced more 'freedom' (*azadi*).

Javad explained that in the industrial sector in Tabriz, many workers are rural-born and have lived in Tabriz for about ten years. Javad asked me to imagine a recent rural migrant coming to a large factory, where he would be given a uniform, shoes, insurance, an 8-hour working day, a 45–46 hour working week. 'This is quite different from the countryside', Javad said, 'where one could work 45 hours in three days'. In the large factories, wages were much better, working conditions easier, and such options as profit-sharing, a luxury. . . .

And what of labour productivity? Javad's response: it was higher in the workshops. The workers in the workshops laboured extraordinarily hard, he emphasised and real skill was developed in the workshops. By contrast, the famous machine-tool factory in Tabriz was always in the red, he said. The factory and the workers worked at low capacity, Javad said. Javad's point about low productivity in the large modern industrial sector was not the first time I had come across it. Sources on Iranian industry all note the low levels of productivity (relative to workers in the same plants in advanced industrial countries). Other comments about industry at the time concerned the higher production costs in Iran and the higher wages accrued to labour. The Iranian labour force was decidedly *not* the cheap and docile labour force found in many other Third World countries.

Neither was management terribly advanced, it appears, in the large modern sector. Johnson (1980), who studied high-level manpower in Iran, makes the point about the less-than-developed techniques of scientific management in the large firms. This, presumably, gave industrial workers some of the leeway

Javad referred to. By contrast, the relations in the workshop between master and apprentice are of a different order: 'The owner is constantly there', as Javad pointed out. There are, clearly, very different relations of domination and subordination in the respective sectors.

Javad was aware of the thesis of a labour aristocracy, of a self-conscious and conservative stratum of the working class which recognises its privileged position. Iranian industrial workers had, by the mid-1970s, become conscious of their important role in the economy and society. This was encouraged by the regime, which, while banning independent labour organisation, exalted industrial workers. In addition, during the 1970s, Iran suffered from a shortage of skilled labour. There was an effort to reduce worker turnover by means of material incentives: higher wages, benefits, profit-sharing, etc. All the talk about the skilled labour shortage and material incentives served to produce a positive self-image on the part of Iranian skilled industrial workers. They were cognisant they were being counted on to realise the Shah's dream of transforming Iran into a major industrial power by the end of the century. . . .

Perhaps due to their privileged position and relative 'youth', . . . the modern industrial workers of Tabriz (and the oil-workers of the southern refineries) were the last to join the Revolution. By contrast, construction workers, students, clerics and others had demonstrated against the regime earlier. However, once the industrial workers joined the Revolution, the Pahlavi state could no longer stand up, due to the importance of the industrial firms.

Javad emphasised the role of the Left in the Tabriz industrial strikes. The slogans and placards were written by Leftist workers, he said. Left groups, such as Peykar and Fedaii, were very active in Tabriz, recruiting workers, encouraging and organising the strikes, and so on. As a result, once the workers decided to turn against the state, they took on a militant stance. In their joint statement of 13 Aban 1357 (4 November 1978), the

Tabriz workers of the tractor-assembly and machine-tool plants raised both political and economic demands. Among other things, they called for the dismantling of existing workers' organisations and yellow unions, the formation of genuine councils and unions 'which defend the rights and social prestige of the workers', and no intervention by outside authorities in the factories' internal affairs (Azad 1980 : 16).

INDUSTRIAL WORKERS AND THE COUNCILS

Most of the workers in Tabriz who created and were active in the councils were Left-inspired, city born and bred workers like Javad, and supporters of Peykar, Fedaii, or Mojahedin. A small number were independent radical workers (that is, not affiliated with political groups). According to Javad, the Left groups would vie with each other in attempts to recruit these workers. Though Javad expressed some criticisms of the Left organisations, after the Revolution he joined the ultra-Left group Peykar. Javad was by no means disdainful of the Left for its activities among workers in Tabriz. Nor was he resentful of the non-working class Leftists, whom he referred to as the 'intellectual kids', who agitated among the workers. He expressed respect and admiration for those among them who were 'martyred'.

In Tabriz, for the most part, the councils' membership was comprised of skilled workers. Almost from the beginning, the councils encountered difficulties. Not least of their problems was the social and ideological heterogeneity of the working class. Javad remarked that, before the Revolution, most skilled workers were not religious. Other workers were observant and believers ('like my mother'), or were what he called 'open-minded religious persons' as opposed to 'reactionary religious persons'. After the Revolution, Javad said: 'We had all kinds of workers: Left, Right, religious, progressive, reactionary'. This was not a homogeneous or united class.

One notable achievement of the industrial workers of East Azarbaijan was the formation, in the winter of 1979-80, of a coordinating council overseeing and uniting eight factory councils. Altogether, the coordinating council represented 5,000 workers (Azad 1980).

According to Javad, most of the radical workers were city-born and bred (i.e. from Tabriz rather than villages). Women workers, a very small minority of the Tabriz industrial workers, also participated in the councils.

Then the Islamic associations were created by the ruling Islamic Republican Party (IRP). These bodies competed with and eventually supplanted the workers' councils. With the purification (paksazi) of 1359 (1980), a large number of workers were affected. Javad emphasised the suppression that took place in the factories at that time. This included the expulsion and disappearance of activist workers followed by a 'tightening of control' in the factories. To recapture factory management and administration from the councils, the regime tried to divide workers on the basis of religion. Another, later, tactic was ironically achieved through a measure widely favoured by workers and the Left—the nationalisation of industries. This allowed the government to undermine activist councils by manipulating inputs. Control was often effected through pure intimidation, and it worked.

WORKING-CLASS POLITICS AND WORKING-CLASS CULTURE

The difficulties encountered by the councils, by radical workers and by the Left were significant. The internal differentiation of the Tabriz working class and the segmentation of the industrial labour force proved an enormous obstacle. Particularly vexing was the Islamic resurgence, the new Islamic populist discourse and many workers' resistance to Left agitation. Javad remarked: 'We easily put up posters in universities, but not in the factories. We found that the workers' consciousness was at odds with our received ideology.

It did not match the formulae we had learned.'¹ Islam is but one factor in the backwardness of workers, Javad believes. It's not determinant. More important, according to Javad, is the backward culture and ideology of workers, their undeveloped working-class consciousness and the absence of a modern, forward-looking and democratic culture.... The Revolution politicised the workers, Javad said, but did not transform them culturally.

His experiences in Tabriz, Javad informed me, reveal 'we cannot begin with Marxist slogans; we must begin with the actual working class itself.' He pressed the point: 'We did not realise at the time that there was such a thing as a reactionary worker. In the council, we'd make allowances for and forgive the pro-Khomeini, anti-Left, or anti-socialist worker'. Why? Because he was a worker, because of 'false consciousness'.

The question of the consciousness of workers is complex. When thinking about industrial labour and working-class politics, we face two paradoxes. The first is that at the same time that the factory is regarded as the crucible of class consciousness and collective resistance, it is presented as an arena of potential embourgeoisement and labour aristocracy. The second paradox pertains more to the advanced industrial economies of the West, where the factory is also presented as an arena of undisputed domination, of fragmentation, degradation and mystification (Braverman 1974). . . .

Javad agreed with my view that Iranian workers today are more advanced than before, because of their experiences in the Revolution (in addition to the dynamics of the labour process). However, a deeper and more continuous process of their cultural development and political maturation is needed. For Javad, the struggle around genuine workers' councils and syndicates is imperative, while seminars should also be organised to provide workers with intellectual understanding of their role in production and society.

I have advanced the proposition that the formation of councils and the movement around workers' control, on the one hand,

and the popular demand for nationalisation of 'the commanding heights of the economy' (industries, banks, insurance companies, foreign trade), on the other, is prefigurative of the democratic-socialist project of autonomy, social ownership and rational planning. For these and other reasons, I regard the Iranian Revolution as essentially progressive—and make a distinction between the Iranian Revolution and the Islamic Republic. Tilly has argued the elements of a repertoire can change with new experiences of collective action—mass demonstrations, strikes, other forms of grievance and protest and revolutions. In as much as the revolutionary experience in Iran added critical elements to the repertoire of the working class, I regard the Revolution as a step forward for the workers' movement. And because industrial development is very much on the agenda of the present Iranian regime, there is no reason to believe the working class has been decentred. When one recalls the major strike in 1985 by steelworkers that derailed the state's plan to break up the huge Isfahan steel complex and render numerous workers redundant, one senses the industrial workers will be heard from again. . . .

REFERENCES

Ashtiani, A. 1986. 'Continuity and Discontinuity in the History of the Iranian Working Class'. Unpublished manuscript.

Azad, S. [Moghadam, V.]. 1980. 'Workers' and Peasants' councils in Iran'. *Monthly Review*, October.

Bayat, A. 1983. 'Workers' Control after the Revolution'. *MERIP Reports*, May.

Braverman, H. 1974. *Labor and Monopoly Capital*. New York: Monthly Review Press.

Goodey, C. 1980. 'Factory Councils in Iran'. *MERIP Reports*, June.

Graham, R. 1979. *Iran: The Illusion of Power*. New York: St. Martin's Press.

Halliday, F. 1979. *Iran: Dictatorship and Development*. Harmondsworth: Penguin.

International Labour Organization. 1973. *Employment and Income Policies for Iran*. Geneva: ILO.

Johnson, G.C. 1980. *High-Level Manpower in Iran*. New York: Praeger.

Moghadam, V. 1984. 'Industrialization Strategy and Labor's Response: The Case of the Workers' Councils in Iran'. Paper presented at the conference on 'Trade Unions and the Changing International Division of Labour', University of Ottawa, Canada, November.

Moghadam, V. 1985. 'Accumulation Strategy and Class Formation: The Making of the Industrial Labor Force in Iran, 1962–1977'. Unpublished dissertation. Washington, D.C.: The American University.

Wheeler, A.C.R. 1976. *The Development of Industrial Employment in Iran before 1353 (1974–75)*. Geneva: Population and Manpower Bureau, UNDP-ILO Planning and Employment Project.

NOTES

1. In an unpublished paper . . . Ali Ashtiani argues that the dislocation of the axis of the communist movement has de-politicised the working class. During the 1920s and 1940s the focus of the radical oppositional movement, and in particular the communist movement, was the factory floor and workplace. After the 1953 coup d'etat against the . . . Mossadeh government and the emergence of the Shah's autocracy, the communist and oppositional movement shifted to schools, universities, mosques and bazaars. For this and other reasons, he argues, the workers' movement during the Revolution showed no important signs of secular or socialist orientation.

5.5 Elites and Ethnic Mobilization in Sri Lanka

Christopher Ellison

It is rare nowadays for a country to be ethnically homogeneous. Most countries consist of more than one large racial or ethnic group, and many smaller ones. Often this has come about because of massive movements of populations to supply labor for colonial powers. This has put groups together in the same country that might otherwise not have come into contact. For example, were it not for the African slave trade, which kidnapped millions of people and shipped them to America, there would be few black people in this area.

The next excerpt is about the divisive legacy of colonialism. In Sri Lanka, the subject of this article, there are two contending groups because of a historic migration of labor. The indigenous Sinhalese, who practice Buddhism, make up the dominant culture of the island state. The Tamils, who come from South India, are primarily Hindu. The Tamil population increased rapidly while Sri Lanka (once called Ceylon) was a British colony.

Under British rule, this group prospered both economically and politically. When the British departed, the Tamils were in an advantageous position with regard to education, employment, and power.

After independence, the majority Sinhalese set out to change the situation. They pursued a policy of political and economic exclusion. During the British period, English had been the language of administration, a fact that favored the English-educated Tamils. After the British left, the Sinhalese made their language, Sinhala, the country's only official language, effectively excluding the

Tamils from political power. Even those who made the effort to learn Sinhala had a hard time finding employment, due to Sinhalese employment quotas.

Also, strict and disproportionate quotas favoring Sinhalese for university places were imposed, in an attempt to counteract the overrepresentation of Tamils in institutions of higher education. The Sinhalese-dominated government also neglected Tamil areas in favor of Sinhalese areas when handing out development and job training assistance.

These changes took place gradually over a period of approximately 40 years. Initially, the Tamils tried to deal with policies favoring the Sinhalese by seeking an equal share of power within the federal system. This approach proved futile, and a new generation of young Tamils shifted its support to separatist parties. Eventually, following the ineffectiveness of political efforts, violent Tamil guerrilla groups emerged. Recently, the country has been in a state of civil war, with brutal interethnic clashes and massacres as common occurrences.

The shift in dominance from Tamil during the British period, to Sinhalese following independence, involved the replacement of one elite by another. But, it had little positive effect on the lives of most Sri Lankans, many of whom have died in the interethnic violence resulting from the shift.

As with several examples in this volume (e.g., the next excerpt by Mah Hui Lim), this one shows how colonial powers created ethnic group rivalry that worsened after colonial control was removed. Many of these rivalries are still characterized by violent conflict today.

. . . The present paper addresses two questions: What factors promote political mobilization to attain ethnic goals in a post-colonial society such as Sri Lanka? Under what conditions do ethnic agendas become more militant? This paper seeks to develop an explanation for (a) geographical and temporal variations in levels of electoral support for Tamil federalism during its heyday (1956–1970); and (b) the swing toward electoral separatism during the early- and mid-1970s. . . .

THEORETICAL ISSUES

. . . Proponents of the ethnic competition framework argue broadly that the mobilization of ethnic groups occurs as group members come to compete for economic, political, and social resources which were previously

Excerpted from Ellison, Christopher (1987), "Elites, competition and ethnic mobilization: Tamil politics in Sri Lanka, 1947–1977", *Journal of Political and Military Sociology*, 15(2), Fall, 213–228.

monopolized by other social groups or were otherwise unavailable. . . .

The "ethnic subnationalism" perspective builds upon the logic of the competition approach, but it takes seriously the roles and interests of ethnic elites in stimulating or supporting ethnic political agendas.

According to Ragin (1986), the dominant strata of an ethnic minority face two actual or potential opponents, the lower strata of its population and the elite strata of the culturally dominant group. Ragin suggests that by encouraging ethnic mobilization, minority elites may defuse class conflict within the minority population, while simultaneously gaining political leverage vis-a-vis the elite strata of the cultural core.

The Argument. The present paper draws on the *ethnic competition* and *ethnic subnationalism* perspectives to explain (a) temporal and spatial variations in support for Tamil federalism between 1956 and 1970, and (b) the increased militancy of Tamil electoral politics after 1970. This analysis focuses on two distinct, sequential mechanisms thought to foster these different forms of political mobilization. First, the initial federalist agenda emerged from *inter*ethnic competition over national identity issues, especially the selection of a national language. However, the resolution of struggles over national language policy—along with regulations allowing the Sinhalese privileged access to educational and occupational opportunities—posed a threat to certain Tamil elites. Thus, these elements were confronted simultaneously with intensified competition from state-backed Sinhalese elements and *intra*ethnic pressures for social reform related to the Tamil caste system. Under these circumstances, a campaign of electoral separatism was an attractive strategy for maximizing both intraethnic solidarity and political bargaining power vis-a-vis the Sinhalese.

NATIONAL IDENTITY ISSUES AND ETHNIC COMPETITION[1]

Ethnic Conflict and "Sinhala Only". Trends toward Sinhalese cultural chauvinism became clear almost immediately after independence. Attempts to dislodge the Tamils from positions of prominence and influence were spearheaded by ascendant social groups with a broad potential constituency. First, traditional religious elites, whose positions were devalued during the colonial era issued their bid for a long-range role in national politics similar to their precolonial status as crucial legitimizers of political leadership.

Second, segments of Sinhalese merchant capital, particularly those not previously linked with the British, demonstrated ideological antagonism toward all Westernized elements—Sinhalese, Tamil, and others—and toward minority ethnic groups, with certain of which they competed. These segments of the Sinhalese bourgeoisie and petty bourgeoisie ardently supported the advance of Sinhalese language and religion.

Third, such key groups drew on a substantial constituency of non-Westernized Sinhalese strata, including traditional (ayurvedic) physicians, schoolteachers, peddlers, agricul-

turists, rural notables, and others who were peripheralized culturally and/or economically during the colonial period. This coalition pressed repeatedly for preferential treatment for the Sinhala language and the Buddhist religion. Although poorly organized for the 1952 elections, the newly-formed Sri Lanka Freedom Party (SLFP) provided an organizational umbrella for the diverse activities of political monks and Sinhalese advocates.

One key plank in the 1956 SLFP platform was the institutionalization of Sinhala as the sole national language, a goal which entailed the reversal of the establishment of dual national languages enacted during the transition to self-rule. The "Sinhala-only" legislation threatened to hinder communication between the national government and non-Sinhala speakers, foreclose long-range prospects for employment in the state sector for non-Sinhala speaking groups, and pose disagreeable questions regarding the structuring and content of state-sponsored education for Tamils and East coast Muslims, most of whom speak Tamil as their home language. . . .

Ethnic tensions degenerated into the first island-wide riots in 1958. By the late-1950s, the SLFP presided over a convergence of diverse and previously antagonistic segments of the Sinhalese population. Further, in the face of SLFP electoral successes, the remaining Sinhalese-dominated parties endorsed "Sinhala-only" and the rhetoric of cultural militancy, furthering the political alienation of the Tamils.

Conflict over language appeared to decline during the mid-1960s. A new government elected in 1965 lacked a working majority in the legislature and was forced to solicit the support of Federal Party leaders. The result was another attempt to enact provisions for reasonable use of Tamil. In addition, the pact allowed for "district" councils with unspecified powers. However, the mobilization of the 'traditionalist' coalition against these language regulations and against any devolution of political power to the Tamils prompted the Sinhalese leadership to abandon the attempt at ethnic conciliation. For many Tamils, this episode demonstrated the bankruptcy of conventional Tamil political strategies in the context of Sinhalese political domination.

The Language Issue and Tamil Politics. The preeminent vehicle of Tamil political expression during the 1950s and 1960s was the Federal Party (hereafter FP). Despite the evident pragmatism of its leaders, and their desire to operate within the national parliamentary system, the FP must be considered more strident than its predecessor, the Tamil Congress. The FP concentrated on promoting solidarity among Tamil-speaking people, including estate workers and lower caste elements of the Northern and Eastern districts. The FP, unlike the Tamil Congress, drew part of its leadership from prominent non-elite castes of the East. Its principal goal was "the establishment of an autonomous Tamil state on the linguistic basis within the framework of a Federal Union of Ceylon" (Kearney, 1973:116)....

SINHALIZATION AND TAMIL ELITE GRIEVANCES

While pre-1970 Tamil politics were dominated by ethnic competition over national identity issues—particularly language—the subsequent turn toward separatism resulted largely from a set of 'elite' grievances which emerged during the 1960s.

State Sector Employment. A number of government employment opportunities were closed to Tamils via the "Sinhala-only" legislation. This resulted in a marked decline in the percentage of Tamils employed in government service by 1970. The losers in the ethnic exclusion have been middle-class urban Tamils, while the winners have been Low Country Sinhalese. Tamil representation in government service has apparently declined further since 1970, due to the unwillingness of Sinhalese officials to recruit Tamils for jobs in such areas as education, police, and defense services (Oberst, 1986:148–49).

Further, the transition from a colonial system to a mixed economy under a democratic socialist state produced an expanded state sector. Thus, the establishment of state industrial and commercial corporations provided additional employment opportunities. Again however, with recruitment at the discretion of Sinhalese officials, the employment of Tamils not educated in Sinhala has been infrequent. One reason for this ... has been the ... expanding use of government jobs as patronage resources by Sinhalese MPs (Tambiah, 1986:84).

Educational Privileges.... Despite evidence of relative and absolute declines in Tamil educational status and opportunities by the mid-1960s, Tamils continued to dominate training programs for high-status, high-reward occupations. The recognition of this pattern led to the adoption of still more stringent policies by the SLFP government after the 1970 elections. A series of university admissions schemes designed to reduce the number of Tamils and to boost the numbers of Sinhalese created immense political controversy.

Between 1969 and 1974, new Tamil admissions dropped sharply in every area associated with professional career paths or the sciences (*see* DeSilva, 1978:494–95). Tamil access improved only with respect to the humanities, an area in which job prospects have long been scarce. More recent figures suggest a continuation of this trend (Tambiah, 1986:153–57).

Regional Development Issues. In addition to these grievances over state sector employment opportunities and access to higher education, Tamil elites have complained of a lack of state support for development projects in Tamil areas. According to Ponnambalam (1983:169–71), the Sinhalese-controlled state shelved proposals by international lending agencies for agro-industrial projects and enhancement of port facilities in predominantly Tamil areas during the 1960s and 1970s. However, the government has financed numerous projects involving state industries in the Southern parts of the island, especially since the insurrection of rural, unemployed Sinhalese youths in 1971....

Resettlement, Caste Dominance and Regional Political Control. Finally, Tamil elites have expressed alarm over the incipient loss of political and social control over largely Tamil areas. The acceleration of state-sponsored colonization programs poses a particular challenge for *Eastern* elites. Although some resettlement projects impact the North as well, most transplant Sinhalese from crowded districts in the South and South-Central rural areas to regions in the North-Central area and along the Eastern coast, ostensibly as part of a national program of agricultural development. These government-sponsored migrations increase interethnic competition for scarce resources in the dry-zone regions, while providing fertile ground for gang violence under the patronage of Sinhalese politicians (Tambiah, 1986:50–53).

Further, these resettlement areas are increasingly viewed by Tamil politicians as attempts by the government to create Sinhalese voting districts within Tamil areas. Moreover, these efforts should be viewed in the context of various Sinhalese attempts to coopt Eastern Tamil leaders, Muslim politicos, and leaders of the Indian Tamil trade union movement with offers of cabinet portfolios. Resettlement thus appears to constitute one arm of a broader Sinhalese strategy of ethnic assimilation, and a comprehensive effort to diminish the social bases of potential support for the Tamil insurgency.

In the *Northern* districts, the dominant elites are the Vellalar caste. The Northern Vellalars derive their considerable economic, political, and social power from their near-total caste dominance, which enjoys widespread legitimacy due to a vast array of supporting cultural patterns and religious rituals. In particular, Vellalars benefit from their social and economic domination of lower caste (untouchable) elements which comprise at least one-fourth of the population in Jaffna.

The Sinhalese government has pressed for social reform in Jaffna since the 1950s. Legal attacks on the caste system have . . . aimed at discrediting and demobilizing elite Tamil leadership and fragmenting Tamil political continuity. Using Buddhist-egalitarian rhetoric to justify its anti-caste posture, the Sinhalese state has consistently supported its denial of federalist demands for regional autonomy by stating its commitment to ending caste inequality in the North.

In addition to state-sponsored anti-caste activity, private organizations of Sinhalese leftists have supported lower caste challenges to the Hindu religious practice of maintaining temples closed to certain castes. Further, Buddhist missionary groups have extended offers of Sinhala-language education to underprivileged lower caste Tamils in Jaffna. Moreover, the establishment of Buddhism as the national religion in the 1972 constitution, also raised the spectre of state-sponsored religious conversions of 'untouchables' and more concerted, well-organized Sinhalese efforts at social reform in the North.

The aggressive social reform movement generated by the Sinhalese placed the Federal Party in a difficult position. In their attempts to build political coalitions, the liberal federalist leadership had advocated social reform in order to win lower caste and East Coast support. Thus, Tamil politicians were unable—and perhaps unwilling—to challenge the Sinhalese incursions.

TOWARD ELECTORAL SEPARATISM

By the early 1970s, Tamil political leaders were confronting formidable centrifugal forces within the Tamil community. First, the plight of young, educated Tamils seeking positions in

TABLE 1   Tamil Employment in Government Service (approximate %)*

Branch	1956	1965	1970
Ceylon (Sri Lanka) Administrative Service	30	20	5
Clerical Services (including postal, railway, hospitals, and customs)	50	30	5
Professions (engineers, doctors, lecturers)	60	30	10
Armed Forces	40	20	1
Labour Forces	40	20	5

*Source: Memo from Ceylon Institute of National and Tamil Affairs (CINTA) to International Commission of Jurists. Figures were calculated by Arasanga Eluthu Vinaya Sangam, a trade union of Tamil

the state sector was increasingly grim. This situation, combined with the ineffectiveness of conventional Tamil political parties, prompted Tamil university students and graduates to form the first Tamil guerilla organization, the Liberation Tigers (Kearney, 1978:530). The advent of a violent separatist struggle prodded the conventional liberal Tamil leadership to endorse an electoral separatist campaign in order to maintain influence over increasingly disaffected diploma-holders. Indeed, the formation of the pro-separatist Tamil United Liberation Front (TULF) in 1976 allowed for an influential, militant section of elite youth.

Second, many middle- and upper-class elders also demonstrated disapproval of the liberal, reformist bent of federalist politics. Specifically, they rejected the Federal Party's failure to condemn sufficiently the Sinhalese attacks on the caste system and the traditional preserves of Vellalar cultural practice.

Third, Tamil political eliters were confronted with the general breakdown of political alliances built during the 1950s. In addition to the fragmentation of Tamil political unity underscored by the resurgence of the Tamil Congress, elections of 1965 and 1970 saw declining interethnic support for the federalist agenda. The diminished salience of the language issue removed the chief incentive for Muslims to support Tamil parties.

In sum, elite youths, ideological conservatives, and others in the North were animated to support (a) the creation of an alternative system of social stratification free of Sinhalese interventions and (b) the construction of a new state apparatus, to be a source of employment and cultural support. Further, like its predecessors, the Tamil Congress and the Federal Party, the TULF and its leadership have been firmly rooted in the North.

The TULF has called for "the restoration and reconstitution of the Free, Sovereign, Secular, Socialist State of TAMIL EELAM" in the North and East (Kearney, 1978:532). The "restoration" and "reconstitution" refer pointedly to the often-romanticized Tamil kingdoms of the precolonial period. The rhetoric of cultural unity may have served effectively as a political instrument of Vel-

lalar elites to subordinate castes and to Tamil groups outside the Northern region. . . .

Indeed, during the 1977 legislative elections, the rhetoric of ethnic separatism emanating from the TULF may have drawn support from voters in Eastern districts who had previously forsaken the Federal Party. The escalation of ethnic militancy (separatism) and the rhetoric of cultural unity represented by the TULF attracted a notable degree of support in the 1977 legislative elections. . . .

CONCLUSION

. . . A study of the Tamil movement raises several important points regarding the structural bases and transformation of ethnoregionalism. The theoretical approaches to ethnic mobilization adopted by social scientists have focused primarily on relations among ethnic collectivities, all but ignoring the salience of intraethnic stratification patterns for ethnic politics. In particular, the focus on notions of "niche overlap" and "boundary selection" by proponents of ecologically-derived theories may divert attention from asymmetrical power relations *within* a collectivity. Selection in favor of certain boundaries of identification may benefit a particular segment of the collectivity disproportionately. Thus, it may serve the interests of those privileged elements to encourage certain types of "selection mechanisms" as bases of mobilization while discouraging others.

. . . This study has presented evidence suggesting the importance of various elite interests in the emergence of an electoral separatist agenda in the early 1970s. This paper also suggests the centrality of status and power, manifested as *caste* cleavages, within the national Tamil community. In advancing the dubious claim that all Tamils share a single cultural heritage and political legacy, it appears Northern elites have employed "ethnic historicism" to minimize sociopolitical challenges from subordinate castes and to maximize their leverage vis-a-vis ascendant Sinhalese strata. . . .

REFERENCES

DeSilva, C. R. (1978). "The Impact of Nationalism on Education: The Schools Takeover (1961) and the University Admissions Crisis (1970–1975)," in M. Roberts (ed.), Collective Identities, Nationalisms, and Protests. Colombo: Marga Institute.

Kearney, R. N. (1973). The Politics of Ceylon (Sri Lanka). Ithaca, N.Y.: Cornell University Press.

—(1978). "Language and the Rise of Tamil Separatism in Sri Lanka," Asian Survey 18:521–534.

Oberst, R. (1986). "Policies of Ethnic Preference in Sri Lanka." In N. Nevitte and C. H. Kennedy (eds.), Ethnic Preference and Public Policy in Developing States. Boulder, CO: Lynne Rienner Publishers.

Ponnambalam, S. (1983). Sri Lanka: The National Question and the Tamil Liberation Struggle. London: Zed Press.

Ragin, C. C. (1986). "The Impact of Celtic Nationalism on Class Politics in Scotland and Wales," in J. Nagel and S. Olzak (eds.), Competitive Ethnic Relations. New York: Academic Press.

Schwarz, W. (1975). "The Tamils of Sri Lanka," report no. 25, Minority Rights Group, London.

Tambiah, S. J. (1986). Sri Lanka: Ethnic Fratricide and the Dismantling of Democracy. Chicago: University of Chicago Press.

NOTES

1. The principal ethnic antagonists are the Sinhalese majority and the Tamil minority. The Sinhalese—roughly 70 percent of the population—practice mainly Theravada Buddhism and speak the Sinhala language. They dominate most areas of the island except for the Northern region and a narrow belt along the Eastern coast. The North is home to approximately two-thirds of the Sri Lankan Tamils. A smaller population of Moors (Muslims) reside primarily in East Coast districts. In addition, a sizeable population of Indian Tamils was brought to the island as plantation labor by the British during the nineteenth century. During 1949–1986, this group was disenfranchised by the Sinhalese-dominated state.

5.6 Ethnic and Class Mobilization in Kenya

Barbara P. Thomas-Slayter

We have seen, in various excerpts in this book, that societies are often divided in terms of ethnic group, regional, and class loyalties. The following excerpt begins by showing that contemporary Kenya is no exception to this pattern. The author also indicates that, as with many other societies, the ethnic and regional loyalties are stronger than the class loyalties.

The author then shows that the ethnic and regional divisions are both useful for, and an obstacle to, the operation of the power elite of Kenya. They are useful because the masses cannot readily come together to oppose the powerful. They are an obstacle, however, for any attempts by the elite to mobilize the masses to do as it wishes.

One way that some mobilization has taken place is around local self-help activities called "harambee." In a modest way, these activities, which are often locally-initiated, empower ethnic and regional groups and the poor. These activities are also being promoted wherever possible by the elite, when they serve their interest.

The author suggests that more widespread mobilization of people around common class interests which cut across ethnic groups and regions will be difficult to achieve because of the stronger ethnic and regional loyalties.

The Kenyan state is trapped by near overwhelming economic pressures arising from its position within the global economy. Moreover, its political situation is tenuous vis-a-vis a growing public dissatisfaction that some Kenyans have been in a position to take advantage of largesse arising through global economic linkages, and vis-a-vis its international allies who, in the declining days of the Cold War, may not be predisposed to meet the costs of maintaining strong friendships with Third World countries. On one hand, the Kenyan state desperately needs to mobilize both the political support and the economic resources of its rural people. On the other hand, it is prevented from fully utilizing these forces by its own fragility and its fears of losing control. Ethnicity remains the most compelling basis for community mobilization, as well as the energizing force which the state fears the most, given its own dependence on problematic, multi-ethnic coalitions while trying to build a strong, multi-ethnic nation. . . .

ETHNICITY AS A CATALYST FOR COMMUNITY MOBILIZATION

Throughout Africa, ethnicity is an important phenomenon and remains, today, the single most important variable around which individuals, households, and communities aggregate for common action. Ethnicity can be defined as a perception of common origins, as well as

Thomas-Slayter, Barbara P. (1991). "Class, ethnicity, and the Kenyan state: Community mobilization in the context of global politics." *International Journal of Politics, Culture, and Society* 4(3), 301–321. © 1991 Human Sciences Press, Inc.

shared history, norms, language, dreams and other ties and attributes which link a person to a given set of people. An ethnic group may be spatially defined as well. The consciousness of special identity permits and encourages people to organize to advance their common interests.

Ethnicity is often a political as well as a cultural phenomenon. Analysts of contemporary Africa emphasize that ethnic awareness, vis-a-vis other groups, is a consequence of the colonial period in which governance was often achieved through promotion of ethnic rivalries. In the post-independence period, ethnic groups, like other groups, place claims upon the state. They compete among themselves and with other groups for state controlled resources. In the political systems operative in many African nations today, ethnic loyalties and organizations play a significant role in advancing the material and other interests of their members. They usually do so through patron-client relationships which are a common phenomenon in the politics of many African states.

Ethnically-based communal solidarity, as found at varying levels of political and social organization, is a potent and often feared force in Kenyan institutional and organizational development. In a formal way, the Government of Kenya avoids overt policies or actions which encourage ethnic rivalries. In this regard, the most widely debated policy of the country has been its refusal to consider a multi-party system. Both former President Kenyatta and President Moi have viewed multiple parties as ethnically divisive and politically destructive, leading to competition based on ethnic loyalties. At top national levels, the Kenyan leadership makes considerable effort to incorporate a broad cross-section of ethnic representation in ministerial positions.

National policy de-emphasizes ethnic loyalties. Political ethnic associations are forbidden, and ethnic loyalties in other organizations are discouraged. Public documents
refer to provinces or regions rather than to
ethnic groups although they may be virtually
synonymous. Despite governmental policy,
ethnic loyalties are strong, no doubt in part
because of the regional or geographic identification which most ethnic groups retain.

An important undercurrent in Kenyan
politics today is a shift in the ethnic basis of
political power in the inner circle surrounding the Kenyan president. Under Kenyatta,
the Kikuyus were highly influential. President Moi comes from a small tribe within the
Kalenjen grouping. Those influential in the
president's office reflect a shift away from
perceived Kikuyu hegemony to Kenyans of a
different ethnic origin.

The convergence of ethnic, regional, and/or
district lines has important implications for politics and for community mobilization. For example, the ability of Kikuyus located throughout
the country to mobilize on behalf of local development (Harambee) projects within their home
communities in Central Province is a reminder
of the power of these ethnic ties. The Government, with its District Focus program of small
grants to individual projects through District
Development Committees, does not provide a
counter-weight to the informal and largely ethnic channels such as the Murang'a Harambee
Development Fund, a fund organized by and
for Kikuyus from Murang'a District. Given that
approximately four-fifths of Kenya's population
is rural; that rural communities have distinct
ethnic identities; and that ethnic ties are among
the most effective means to raise development
funds, the question of ethnicity in politics and
community mobilization promises to be paramount for some time to come.

CLASS AS A CATALYST
FOR COMMUNITY MOBILIZATION

While ethnicity continues as a dominant
influence, a new and potentially profound
force—social class—is a growing factor in the
Kenyan political economy. Perhaps the class
in Kenya most easily identified is that of
affluent, urban elites. Based in Nairobi and
often solidly tied to strong positions in the
government bureaucracy, these individuals
continue to have deep roots in a village community where they are widely regarded as
benefactors and "local success stories."

Of great importance is the connection
between Kenya's class structure and land
ownership. The well-entrenched elite families control not only much agricultural land
but also the bureaucracy which shapes the
policies affecting it. Large farms are likely to
be in the hands of Members of Parliament,
senior government administrators and other
civil servants, senior police chiefs, KANU
officials, current and former chiefs, members
of the diplomatic corps, and executives of
parastatals (Hunt, 1984:288). The Kenyan
elite is specifically and directly tied to large
scale and export agriculture, "maintaining relatively high export crop prices through their
direct and indirect affiliation with the government" (Bradshaw, 1990:17). Their ways of
assuring benefits are numerous, and they link
the traditional source of wealth, land, with
new forms of wealth based upon ties to foreign capital and emerging commerce and
industry. A member of Parliament may own a
large coffee plantation in his rural constituency, have access to bank loans at favorable rates, and serve on government regula-
tory boards. He is also likely to have multiple
investments in private businesses such as tex-
tiles, auto assembly, or pharmaceuticals,
based on indigenous or foreign capital. He is
not required to make public disclosures of his
finances. This illustration suggests an intri-
cate network of class-based elites with both
rural and urban interests, drawing on domestic and foreign capital, and utilizing both the
government's bureaucracy and patron-client
linkages.

Along with these privileged economic and
political positions go certain assumptions in
terms of educational opportunity. There is an
extremely narrow educational structure in
Kenya with access to university education
only for a small percentage of those who qual-

ify. While the system is based on examinations impartially administered, the capacity to compete is developed from the early years of primary school. Access to excellent education—a prerogative of affluence—is an important aspect of class structure in Kenya today.

In spite of the increasing evidence of privilege and wealth, a basic question remains. Can subordinate, impoverished rural people mobilize around issues which would be defined as class issues. By far the majority of the poor, not only in Kenya but in all of Africa, are rural folk who tend to be unorganized and, at best, tied into political organization and mobilization through patron-client networks. Poor rural Kenyans activate whatever purchase they are able to gain on the more influential and prosperous members of their own community. Mobilization that has occurred so far, through the Harambee mechanism, has focused primarily on development needs and questions of access and social mobility, not on redressing injustices or seeking equity. The objective for most has been to gain a toehold in the system. The approach rural Kenyans perceive as most likely to be effective is improved education. Most rural communities have focused their efforts on increasing educational opportunity, primarily through building secondary schools. Thus, transforming the system has not been an objective; rather, most have cherished a hope of gaining access to the system. Since independence, educational opportunity, as a way to gain access, has been the single most important issue around which rural Kenyans have readily mobilized for change.

CLASS AND ETHNICITY: CONFLICT AND CONVERGENCE

The elite Kenyan in recent years has embodied the convergence of class and ethnicity. Dominant in both spheres, he or she can work through both sets of linkages to maintain a position of strength within Kenyan society. For example, Members of Parliament are usually key patrons as well as members of the dominant ethnic group in the communities they represent. They are also likely to be well connected in the urban setting of Nairobi where they spend most of their time. Connections there may be both within and outside their own ethnic group.

The well-placed, affluent urban "patron" uses his social position well and provides a ladder to members of his own ethnic community, aiding them in a variety of ways from new jobs to permits, to contacts, while also maintaining strong ties with many of those in his own class who may or may not be of his ethnic group. There is, however, intra-ethnic rivalry as well as inter-ethnic rivalry. Clans, factions, schisms within ethnic groups do occur constantly. The levels of cohesion and fluidity vary according to the personalities, the issue and the situation.

The Kikuyus are Kenya's most numerous and most dominant ethnic group. Predominant during the Kenyatta years at high levels of government and economy, they were in a position to take advantage of government policies which strengthened the center. As the ethnic group best organized and most able to take advantage of the informal opportunities for development through Harambee, they have benefitted considerably. Kenyatta's death in 1978 led to a fundamental change in the regional, ethnic and economic basis of the Kenyan power structure. President Moi, whose support comes from a number of smaller ethnic groups to the West of the Rift Valley, has pursued a conscious policy of ethnic diversification. He has reduced Kikuyu influence in the high ranks of government, while at the same time solidifying his own sources of political support. Kikuyus continue to play a significant role in Kenya's economic and political structures, yet simultaneously, they feel they are being cut off from the critical sources of power, namely those surrounding the President.

Central Province, home to the Kikuyu, is the most affluent in Kenya, and, as a group, the Kikuyus are the most prosperous. Harambee contributions provide an indicator. Central Province raised its share of Harambee contributions from 30% of the total value contributed throughout Kenya in the mid-

1970s to nearly half the value in the early 1980s (Thomas, 1985:207). Central Province's small farmers are major producers of two of Kenya's primary earners of foreign exchange, tea and coffee, and have been more fully integrated into the cash economy, reaping some of the benefits when prices are high. Thus, there is a basis for the fears some have expressed concerning the potential for Kikuyu hegemony. These fears exist despite the fact that within Central Province there are many smallholders and increasing numbers of people dependent upon wage labor.

Moreover, the Kikuyus have forged ahead with secondary education and have the highest rates of Form IV completion for both males and females in the country. There is a dearth of employment opportunities appealing to those who have completed this level of education. Frustrations are quickly generated when the hopes of parents are dashed and the efforts of young adults to enter the system prove futile. In such situations, alienation and disaffection can readily arise.

Overall, evidence suggests that there is a sharply increasing awareness of class differences in Kenya. In the context of a rapidly growing population and galloping unemployment, economic and social inequities may become Kenya's paramount issue. It is likely, however, that these perceptions would be accompanied by a complex overlay of ethnic loyalties. As noted, there is a close fit between region, administrative unit, and ethnic dominance. Large numbers of rural poor depend to some extent on the largesse of their wealthier kinsmen. Most probably, class issues, based on the need for opportunity, justice and equity for Kenya's poor, would be played out within a power structure shaped significantly by ethnicity.

HARAMBEE: COMMUNITY MOBILIZATION, URBAN ELITES, AND THE GLOBAL ECONOMY

Harambee is the Swahili term for "Let's pull together." Harambee self-help started as a means for community members to work collec-

tively on small-scale projects such as schools, clinics, or cattle dips. Groups contributed cash, labor and materials, as well as management skills, to building and operating such facilities.

An outgrowth of traditional family and clan responsibilities, Harambee encourages a transfer of individual resources from the prosperous to the poor and from urbanites to rural residents. It provides a mechanism whereby some highly visible private wealth is put to public use in ways which are considered socially and ethically appropriate. Wealthy persons are supposed to distribute largesse, and Harambee provides a way to allow more than a few to benefit from the contributor's bounty while at the same time bringing a variety of returns to the donor. This obligation is intensified by ethnic and regional competition and loyalties, for one who prospers is expected to render some assistance, not only to family members, but to those of his own background who are less fortunate.

After independence, Harambee rapidly became an integral part of Kenya's electoral processes. Political candidates vied to assist with these projects; candidates based their campaigns on pledges to support Harambee schools and other facilities; and communities quickly learned how to manipulate this competition to their own advantage. Since 1978 when Daniel Arap Moi became President of Kenya, the term "Harambee" has been used more broadly to identify not only small-scale, local or district-level projects, but also efforts orchestrated by the center to support nationwide development objectives, such as a national scholarship fund or a technical university.

Thus, as a form of community mobilization, Harambee has roots not only in family and clan responsibilities, but also in the independence struggle occurring in Kenya from the 1920s onward. Yet, it has evolved in new wave over the past thirty years, reflecting the political system in which it is situated, the urban and elite sources of support on which it is partially dependent, and the characteristics of the international economy in which it is embedded. For political, economic, and social reasons, Harambee has been an important part of Kenya's development strategy. It is predicated on a philosophy of incremental change initiated by and shaped for grassroots communities. It is also based on principles of wealth-sharing and redistribution. . . .

In recent years, the Government has moved to capture control over Harambee. This is no small task for there are vested interests in the Harambee system. In one way or another Harambee serves the interests of Government, local elites, national elites and poor rural households. The Government has sought control in several ways. First, through the decentralization of the planning and implementation process, the "District Focus", the Government has attempted to incorporate Harambee resource mobilization into the planning process. Its chief purpose has been to regulate the mix of capital costs and recurrent expenditures, to control the sources of funds for each of these categories and to specify the relative contribution of state and local community. In part, this effort has been a response to Kenya's fiscal crisis and to policies of the IMF and World Bank which have put new pressures on the Government to regulate Harambee and to limit recurrent costs related to social services.

As a form of community mobilization and as a political phenomenon, Harambee has been characterized by the dispersal of power. Overall, it has constituted a minimal threat to those at the center of governance. In this context, self-help in Kenya must be viewed as politicized but powerless. At the local level it can provide effective grassroots development; at the national level, it does not jeopardize the status quo. However, even its local role may be diminishing as comparisons of Kenya's two most recent Development Plans suggest.

The Plan for 1984-88 specifies that cooperative effort through self-help will be encouraged and should be expanded during the Plan period (Government of Kenya, 1984:45). In a speech in 1985 President Moi stated, "Harambee is a basic Kenyan institution . . . and the cornerstone for local resources mobilization . . ." (Moi, 1985:1). This theme was echoed by the Minister for Finance and Planning who, in his Budget message, emphasized the theme of "mobilization of domestic resources for renewed growth" (*Weekly Review*, June 21, 1985:2).

The theme for the 1989-93 Plan is "Participation for Progress." The Plan mentions that the Harambee self-help movement is noted for its contribution to capital formation in the rural areas and notes that Harambee is "one of the concrete ways in which the theme of the Plan 'Participation for Progress' will be translated to positive action" (Government of Kenya, 1989:32) Harambee is lauded in terms of past accomplishments and in terms of its ideological significance. However, the Plan attaches no specifics to the Harambee contribution. One may infer that, at the present time, Harambee's development role is outweighed by its political significance. Harambee has always been important politically, but in the context of a more authoritarian state and increasing state-society tensions, the politics of Harambee take on new meaning. . . .

Clientelist politics, imperfect and inequitable though the system may be, offer some checks and balances and some flexibility for processes of access to and distribution of resources. With the increasing power of KANU this flexibility has diminished; politics is a "top down" process with the players kept in line by the authority emanating from the high levels of the party. Clientelist politics, accompanied by the Harambee approach to development, distract the attention of rural citizens from fundamental changes which would benefit Kenyans more broadly—changes in tax laws, land ownership policies, pricing on agricultural commodities, or regulation of behavior of members of statutory boards.

Harambee broadens political participation and some forms of community mobilization, but it does so primarily within the context of inequitable relationships, reciprocity between unequals, and benefits and services to be rendered to individuals or to specific communities. Rural communities have welcomed the opportunity to "tap" the resources of the center in ways provided by Harambee efforts, and in many cases they have learned to do so with skill and acumen. Nevertheless, this system of mutuality between national leaders and local communities, while enhancing some forms of participation and aiding some communities, does not alter fundamental power relationships within the political and economic systems. . . .

CONCLUDING OBSERVATIONS

To date in Kenya, locally-generated self-help through a clientelist political framework has been the primary method communities have employed to try to alter the distribution of goods, services, and opportunities and to try to diminish the inequities which characterize the nation. As an instrument for promoting development, Harambee has fostered an ad hoc approach directed toward "the squeakiest wheel." That is, those self-help groups and those communities which collect the most money and have the most articulate and well-connected leadership can command the most attention from outside donors, including the Central Government. Those who are best able to organize themselves can draw on the loyalties of their members who have prospered beyond the immediate locale.

Among other consequences, this process has sharpened the inter-elite conflicts and intra-elite linkages, as politicians and other leaders at all levels strive to shape coalitions which will benefit themselves and their communities. These elite linkages usually take the form of patron-client relationships with ethnic and regional foundations. In the rural areas ethnicity and geography overlap significantly. Reliance on community or ethnic connections for local development tends to strengthen these loyalties building vertical connections and obscuring identification with others in a similar socio-economic stratum. This approach also tends to exacerbate differences between rich and poor localities, regions, and ethnic groups. . . .

If economic conditions continue to deteriorate, as appears to be the case for many nations in Africa in mid-1990, and if hopes for increased prosperity dwindle, the paradigm for community mobilization is likely to change. Incremental change through Harambee is unlikely to appeal to growing numbers of frustrated rural and urban Form IV leavers who perceive little opportunity for themselves and observe great wealth at the top of a narrow pyramid within their social structure.

In the context of a deteriorating economy, the Government will probably foster Harambee self-help as a politically defusing mechanism, hoping to avoid political confrontations between dissatisfied rural communities and the Government. However, the options here seem to be declining. Elites, who have been contributing large sums to Harambee, face diminishing sources of largesse. For the urban middle class, employment pressures, inflation, shortage of goods and services, and the impact of various structural adjustment policies are certain to diminish their willingness to contribute to local development projects and to clarify their sense of grave injustice in a system in which a few are acquiring great wealth. Already pinched by numerous demands for their limited salaries, this group of middle management bureaucrats, secretaries, drivers, and office messengers is likely to find self-help contributions a heavy and unwelcome burden.

Most important, however, voices of courage, as well as anger and despair, descry the widening gap between rich and poor. As the Government closes off avenues for encompassing diversity, for constructive participation in the polity, and for assuring its own accountability, frustration is likely to grow and give voice to this despair. In this regard, linkages with the global political economy are complex. On the one hand, those linkages are oppressive in a variety of ways as noted above. On the other hand, through the international media, through the church with its international structure, and through organizations such as Amnesty International, they support the "staying power" of those who are trying to lead the way toward a more democratic, just, and egalitarian Kenya. In fact, we may be seeing in Kenya the emergence of a clearly articulated ideological stance which will mobilize Kenyans across most social categories. The visibility and support given to this effort from beyond Kenya's boundaries is not unimportant.

Given severe and growing class differences, class is increasingly a catalyst for mobilization. An urban-based, loosely-defined coalition of clerics and politicians is giving voice to these concerns. Ultimately, however, power derives from a rural population, constituting the vast majority of the people, which is divided along converging ethnic and regional lines. Thus, for the foreseeable future, community mobilization will be intricately linked to ethnic loyalties. In the Kenyan context, class remains in complex coexistence and inter-action with the alternative paradigm for mobilization, clientelist politics based on ethnic loyalties. For Kenya, and for many other African countries as well, this condition is likely to exist for some time to come.

BIBLIOGRAPHY

Ake, Claude. "The Future of the State in Africa." *International Political Science Review* 6, 1, 1985.

Barker, Jonathan S. "Political Space and Political Change" Concepts for Research and Theory November, 1989, unpublished paper.

Bienen, Henry. "The State and Ethnicity: Integrative Formulas in Africa," in Donald Rothchild and Victor A. Olorunsola (eds) *State Versus Ethnic Claims*, Boulder: Westview Press, 1983.

Bradshaw, York W. "Perpetuating Underdevelopment in Kenya: The Link between Agriculture, Class and State," *African Studies Review*, Vol. 33, No. 1, April, 1990, pp. 1–28.

Browne, Robert S. "Evaluating the World Bank's Major Reports: A Review Essay," in *Issue*. Journal of the African Studies Association. vol. XVI/2, 1988.

Callaghy, Thomas M. "Debt and Structural Adjustment in Africa; Realities and Possibilities," *Issue*, Journal of the African Studies Association. Vol. XVI/2, 1988.

Chabal, Patrick (ed). *Political Domination in Africa*. Cambridge: Cambridge University Press, 1986.

Chazan, Naomi, Robert Mortimer, John Ravenhill, and Donald Rothchild. *Politics and Society in Contemporary Africa* Boulder: Lynne Rienner, 1988.

Decalo, Samuell. *Psychoses of Power—African Personal Dictatorships*. Boulder: Westview Press, 19;89.

Durning, Alan B. "Ending Poverty," in Lester Brown et al., *State of the World*. New York: W. W. Norton and Company, 1990.

Evans, Peter B, Dietrich Rueschmeyer, and Theda Skocpol (eds.) *Bringing the State Back In*. Cambridge: Cambridge University Press, 1985.

Ford, Richard B. and Janet Welsh Brown. "Land, Resources, and People in Kenya," in Janet Welsh Brown (ed.) *In the U.S. Interest, Resources, Growth, and Security in the Developing World*. Boulder, Colorado: Westview Press, 1990.

Forest, Joshua B. "The Quest for State 'Hardness' in Africa." *Comparative Politics* 20, 4 July, 1988:423–442.

Ghai, Dharam. "Participatory Development: Some Perspectives from Grass-roots Experiences," *Journal of Development Planning* No. 19, 1989.

Government of Kenya, *Development Plan, 1989–1993*. Nairobi: Government Printer, 1989.

Government of Kenya, *Development Plan, 1984–1988*. Nairobi: Government Printer, 1984.

Government of Kenya, *Economic Survey*, Nairobi Government Printer 1990.

Holmquist, Frank. "Self-Help: The State and Peasant Leverage in Kenya." *Africa* 54(3), 1984.

Hunt, Diana. *The Impending Crisis in Kenya*, Brookfield, Vermont: Gauer, 1984.

Hyden, Goran. "Governance: A New Approach to Comparative Politics," a paper presented at the African Studies Association meeting, Chicago, 1988.

Industrial Review. No. 22. Nairobi: Stellagraphics Ltd., June, 1990.

Kasfir, Nelson (ed.) *State and Class in Africa*. London: Frank Cass, 1984.

Kasfir, Nelson. "Relating Class to State in Africa," *Journal of Commonwealth and Comparative Politics* 21, 3 November, 1983.

Lofchie, Michael. "Kenya: still an Economic Miracle?" *Current History*, Vol. 89, No. 547, May, 1990.

Nafziger, E. Wayne, *Inequality in Africa: Political Elites, Peasants, and the Poor*. Cambridge: Cambridge University Press, 1988.

Nation, The Daily and Sunday. Various issues between January, 1990 and July, 1990. Nairobi: Nation Newspapers, Ltd. 1990.

Nye, Joseph. "The Changing Nature of World Power," *Political Science Quarterly*, Vol. 105, Number 2, Summer, 1990.

Rothchild, Donald and Chazan, Naomi, (eds.) *The Precarious Balance: State and Society in Africa*. Boulder, Colorado: Westview Press, 1988.

Rothchild, Donald. "Complex Bargaining Coalitions: State and Societal Groups in Africa." Paper presented at the African Studies Association. 1988.

Samoff, Joel. "Popular Initiatives and Local Government in Tanzania," *The Journal of Developing Areas* 24, October, 1989.

Samuelson, Robert J. "End of the Third World," *The Washington Post*, July 18, 1990, p. 23.

Sklar, Richard L. "Democracy in Africa," in *The African Studies Review* Vol. 26, No. 3/4, 1983.

Sklar, Richard. "Beyond Capitalism and Socialism in Africa," *The Journal of Modern African Studies*, 26, 1, 1988, pp. 1-21.

Thomas, Barbara P. *Politics, Participation. and Poverty, Development Through Self-Help in Kenya*, Boulder, Colorado: Westview Press, 1985.

Weekly Review, The. Issues between January, 1990 and July, 1990. Nairobi: The Weekly Review, Ltd., 1990.

Wilson Ernest J. III. ""Privatization in Africa: Domestic Origins, Current Status and Future Scenarios." in *Issues.* Vol. XVI/2, 1988.

World Bank (a), *Social Indicators of World Development 1989*, Washington, D.C. IBRD, 1989.

World Bank (b), *Sub-Saharan Africa: From Crisis to Sustainable Growth*, Washington, D.C. IBRD, 1989.

World Bank (c), *World Development Report, 1989*, New York: Oxford University Press, 1989.

Wunsch James and Olowu, Dele (eds.) *The Failure of the African State*. Boulder, Colorado: Westview, 1989.

Zaki, Ergas (ed.) *The African State in Transition*. Houndsmills and London: Macmillan, 1987.

Section Review

Discussion Questions

1. Give four instances of laws in this country that favor men over women. Can you find some that favor women over men?
2. Ellison shows how language can be used for political purposes. Discuss other examples of this.
3. Moghadam sees "modernization" more than "exploitation" as the source of ethnic tension in Yugoslavia. There are similar arguments in Labaki's analysis in the previous section. Compare the two studies to find points of similarity and difference.
4. Suppose that Ellison and Flere compare their analyses of ethnic conflict. What common elements would they see in the two societies they have studied?
5. Siim argues that some changes in the Scandinavian states have strengthened male domination. Do you see any similar processes occurring in your own country?
6. Consider the question of whether ethnicity or class is the strongest vehicle for mobilization of people in your country, as Thomas-Slayter did for Kenya.

Data Collection Exercises

1. Gather some data on the gender and race of law makers (politicians and judges) in your country. How far from representative are the patterns?
2. Gather some data on the effects of British rule upon social inequality in one former British colony, and compare your findings with the results reported above for Sri Lanka.
3. Flere presents some data on modernization in Yugoslavia and links these data to ethnic antagonisms. Do the same type of analysis for another country currently undergoing civil strife (the former USSR, Canada, South Africa, Northern Ireland, or another country: You choose which one!).
4. Gather some information on laws that reinforce inequalities of class in your country.

Writing Exercises

1. Write a brief (500-word) essay considering the pros and cons of a nation, made up of two very different cultural or ethnic groups, breaking into two countries.
2. Write a brief (500-word) speculative piece on how laws might be different if women had been largely in control of making them instead of men.
3. Race, religion, and class are all related to power in Ellison's analysis of Sri Lanka. Keep a diary for a month on how these factors come up in your life, and the implications for power inequality.
4. Write a brief (500-word) report on which type(s) of authority—rational-legal, traditional, or charismatic—is/are most prevalent in the school you are attending now. (Refresh your thinking about these types of authority by reviewing the introduction to this section.)

SECTION 6
Responses to Power Inequality

6.1   Everyday Resistance in a Philippine Village

Benedict Kerkvliet

The next excerpt is about a response to power inequality: everyday resistance by the powerless. There are many ways that have-nots respond to their lack of power, and they range from acquiescence to resistance and protest. The words *resistance* and *protest* themselves conjure up images of organized groups of people fighting some perceived injustice. However, resistance is not always organized. It is not always public and visible. These points are demonstrated in the following excerpt.

The author, Benedict Kerkvliet, believes that unorganized, individual acts of protest can also be an effective form of resistance. He bases this view on observations made in the Philippine village of San Ricardo. The village consists of a few wealthy employers and a majority of very poor peasants. Here, the author finds individual protest to be common and effective.

What is **everyday resistance?** According to Kerkvliet, it is anything people do to express anger or opposition to what they regard as unfair treatment by people who exert some kind of power over their lives.

This definition allows for a wide variety of acts. These range from singing derogatory songs about one's boss while the latter is absent, to "foot-dragging" on the job, to sabotaging the farm machinery of an ungenerous employer. The common component in acts of everyday resistance is that they are not organized efforts. Thus the author differentiates between an individual sabotaging machinery and a band of guerrillas doing so.

The individual acts differ, however, along three dimensions: the likelihood the target is aware of the act, the amount of harm done to the target, and the risk to the actor. An employer is less likely to discover that a harvester is leaving husks of wheat ungleaned so that his family may come at night to take them, than he is to notice that a tractor has been deliberately damaged. In the latter case, the worker puts himself at greater personal risk, and the employer will probably go to great lengths to find and punish the culprit.

You may be thinking: Aren't these just deviant acts? What has this got to do with protest? And in truth, it is often difficult to distinguish between deviance and protest. The powerful in society determine what constitutes a deviant act. Most movements for social change by have-nots involve violations of laws and other norms they think are in need of change.

In the rural Philippines, people want better living conditions. However, poor people are uncertain about how to make claims to a better livelihood and more dignity. It is unclear who is "responsible" for the lot of the poor. Is it *the state, the employer, both, or neither? This uncertainty makes organized protest difficult. Who does one organize against? In this atmosphere of uncertainty, everyday resistance is perhaps the only means by which the poor can lay claim to a fairer share of things.*

. . . While studying in a Philippine village [named San Ricardo¹] for eleven months in 1978–79, I tried to be aware of various ways people might indicate discontent with their conditions. . . . I tried to discover the bases upon which people justify to themselves and possibly to others the hostile, angry, or indignant reactions they have to what other people or institutions do to them.

DEFINITION

Everyday resistance refers to what people do short of organised confrontation that reveals disgust, anger, indignation, or opposition to what they regard as unjust or unfair actions by others more wealthy or powerful than they. Through such resistance people struggle to affirm what they regard as just or fair—or less unjust, less unfair—treatment and conditions. They are expressions of people who perceive injustice but for various reasons are unable or unwilling to push for improvements in an organised, direct manner.

This definition only includes acts against or at the expense of individuals, groups, or institutions of or symbolic of better off or more powerful classes than those who are resisting. . . .

By definition, everyday resistance is done by individuals and small groups with little

Excerpted from Kerkvliet, Benedict (1986), "Everyday resistance to injustice in a Philippine village," *Journal of Peasant Studies*, 13(2), January, 107–123. Reprinted by permission from the second issue volume thirteen of the *Journal of Development Studies* published by Frank Cass & Company Limited, 11 Gainsborough Road, London E11, England. Copyright Frank Cass & Co. Ltd.

leadership. Resistance that involves co-ordination among large numbers of people and a set of leaders is not 'everyday'.

What is resisted are often specific individuals or institutions such as a certain moneylender, landowner, government official, or governmental agency, but it can also be a general condition. To the extent the target is rather specific, those who resist imagine their actions would not be condoned by the target.

Two contending values for which there is evidence from several parts of the Philippines are that people are entitled to be treated with dignity and entitled to livelihood. I shall refer to these as entitlement norms. . . .

These entitlement norms are ambiguous. What exactly constitutes livelihood, dignity, and, bringing them together, livelihood with dignity? The better-off should help the poor but what constitutes help? There is considerable room for interpretation. In political terms, this means probing, testing, and struggle among those with alternative, often conflicting sets of values and interpretations about how values should be practiced. Here we can find everyday resistance. . . .

BACKGROUND FOR EVERYDAY RESISTANCE

In order to appreciate the context in which everyday resistance occurs, I shall highlight six points. First, society in San Ricardo has become much more complex than it was one or two generations ago. . . . Economic diversity, competition for scarce work, and frequent moving in and out of the village has made such community customs as mutual aid and exchange labour difficult to sustain.

Second, paternalistic relationships that once characterised relations between large landowners (landlords) and share tenants are nearly gone. Share tenancy is now the exception rather than the rule. Most tenant farmers in San Ricardo and vicinity are leasehold (*namumuwisan*). Rather than giving the landowner a certain percentage of the harvest as share tenants did, leasehold tenants pay a fixed amount (in cash or *palay*). This means landlords can make no claims on tenants (other than the rent), but it also means that, unlike before, tenants can make no claims on them.

Third, within the last decade, new hybrid varieties of rice have almost completely displaced previous seeds. The new varieties require enormous amounts of cash (especially for chemical fertilisers and insecticides). But capital is scarce, and interest rates from moneylenders are high.

Fourth, poverty is widespread. About 30 per cent of San Ricardo's households live virtually hand-to-mouth. Another 60 per cent usually have enough rice and vegetables to avoid hunger and frequently have cash to meet small necessities. For big expenditures or emergencies, they need to borrow. Only about ten per cent of the households have ample food, well-constructed homes, and otherwise enjoy some comforts of life. A few here are very wealthy even by urban standards.

Fifth, San Ricardo was in the thick of unrest that grew in the 1930s as peasants protested against landlords who changed the terms of tenancy and against the government for supporting the landlords. This evolved into the Huk rebellion, which dominated politics in the region between the mid-1940s and mid 1950s (*Kerkvliet*, 1977).

Sixth, although no soldiers or police are in San Ricardo and its vicinity, people know that the central government can swiftly react to visible, organised signs of discontent. And, villages generally hold, the government is run by and for the benefit of well-to-do sectors of society.

The significance of these points is that even though the need for better living conditions is great, it is not clear to people where and how claims to livelihood with dignity can be made. Many previous customs helping to assure at least subsistence have disappeared with the demise of paternalistic relations with landowners and the increased complexity of society. Moreover, because cash and capital have become necessities, sheer subsistence is often inadequate for one's livelihood. The Huk legacy remains an inspiration to many villagers, as a period when 'little people' organised against oppression, but it was easier then to identify the oppressors—unscrupulous landlords, vicious soldiers, the police. Now it is often unclear who or what is to blame for impoverishment and degradation. Besides, during the rebellion many died and suffered tremendous hardship. The price for standing up was high and would undoubtedly be so again were villagers to organise today.

ENTITLEMENT NORMS

. . . Generally, it is to one's advantage to have a favourable reputation among people with less means. Otherwise, in the words of one middle-aged tenant farmer, 'that stingy fellow [who has means] is likely to be picked on, stolen from, even hurt by the poor people'.

For instance, two Tinio families, large landowners who evicted numerous tenant families in the 1950s–60s in order to mechanise farming operations and whom many in San Ricardo regard as the epitomy of selfishness and insensitivity, no longer live in the village but maintain large houses where family members stay while visiting their hacienda. But they will not remain in the area after dusk because, as some villagers said, 'they wouldn't dare', or as one Tinio member told me, 'it's too dangerous'. This man also said that unless the family hires guards (usually not from the area) during harvests, San Ricardo people 'rob us blind', sneaking into the vast fields at night to harvest. Confirming this to me, several villagers explained that they are not stealing; they are 'just taking' a little rice because 'we have none ourselves' and because the landowning family 'is so mean'.

Loans of money or rice with interest rates that are 'too high' are, as one elderly tenant said wryly, the kind that 'don't deserve to be paid back'. One local moneylender went broke because, in her words, 'ungrateful borrowers' never repaid several thousand pesos she had loaned. She received little sympathy from others who tended to say that she deserves her fate because the interest rate she charged was extremely high.

Another example of what a reputation can mean for better off people involves the quality of *miryenda* (snacks). When a landholder arranges through a *kabisilya* (labour recruiter and foreman) for planters, miryenda is not part of the agreement. But it is customary for the landholder to provide it at mid-morning and mid-afternoon. What the landholder serves is her choice. If the miryenda is cheap, planters may grumble, especially if they believe the landholder can afford to 'be a little generous.' In 1979 complaining planters in a couple fields went so far as to refuse to resume planting the fields of stingy landholders and marched to the fields of owners who were giving tasty miryenda.

There are, of course, limits. Transplanters who drag their feet when working for a landholder serving lousy miryendas might be replaced next time with others more desperate for work. And if no planters in the vicinity are to a landholder's liking, others might be imported from distant villages. The same goes for harvesters and other landless workers. Landholders, though, who ignore landless villagers can expect to hear about unflattering names that they are called or even to discover one morning that part of their field was harvested during the night.

Struggle involving entitlement norms is also reflected in other problems between transplanters and landholders. Landholder sometimes become careless about how they speak to transplanters, calling them lazy, stupid, or worse (for example, devils, animals). Or they might harshly criticise some workmanship. Transplanters often respond to such rudeness by purposefully planting sloppily or slowing down. There are also instances of planters abruptly leaving and

refusing to return until the landholder apologises. The same thing can occur in other work setting such as distant construction sites where San Ricardo residents are sometimes hired.

Entitlement norms are also expressed in controversies regarding land use. The two haciendas from which many tenants were evicted in the 1950s–60s have lately gone unplanted or only partially planted with sugar cane rather than *palay*.[2] The strong sentiment in San Ricardo is that 'it's not right' for land to sit idle while 'so many here are landless,' reduced, as many say, 'to living like chickens' scratching about for kernels. Twice in recent years fires have occurred in the sugar cane field. Arsonists did it, claim the Tinios. Some residents indicate arson is a possibility because people are angry at the inconsiderate and greedy (*matakaw*) Tinios.[3]

By custom, pasturing one's goats and carabao, foraging for edible wild plants and shellfish, and gleaning after harvest are permissible in any unplanted field, no matter who owns it. Sometimes landowners try to interfere and say that people are 'trespassing' or are 'destroying the dikes'. Frequently people will leave but later, when the owner is not around, return to forage or pasture their animals. 'It is not right to keep me out', complained one lady who had defiantly returned to a field she had previously been told to leave. 'My family needs something to eat.'

Entitlement is also expressed in justifications poor people have for taking from the better off. This 'taking' can be a way for people both to assert their right to a livelihood and to blame better off people for their impoverishment. Landlords and former tenants alike tell about how tenants used to take grain surreptitiously from fields prior to the actual harvest. Tenants justify this on grounds that their shares were too small or the landlord was too strict and lacked consideration. They also defend their deed by saying the landholder 'can afford' to lose a little grain. . . .

Another expression of the entitlement norm are reasons people sometimes have for not paying certain debts, rents, and fees. An illustration concerns several *Masagana-99* borrowers. Started in the mid-1970s, Masagana-99 is a government programme to extend loans to peasants who cannot otherwise qualify for bank loans because they lack collateral. In the first year or two of the programme, about 30 landholders from San Ricardo had Masagana-99 loans. By 1979, however, only eight continued to qualify. The others no longer did because they had not fully repaid previous loans. Their reasons were that due to poor crops or extraordinary family expenses (usually large medical bills), they had considerably less income to meet family needs and to pay all claimants.

Expecting that many households throughout the province would be unable to pay, villagers surmised—correctly—that the banking and governmental offices lacked adequate staffs to track down most delinquents. Possibly Masagana-99 itself would collapse, as so many governmental programmes have. Some borrowers also thought the government might or *should* give them consideration and not demand repayment. Especially important to many is their low regard for the Rural Bank through which they had received their loans. Besides having to wait weeks and make numerous trips to the bank before actually receiving the loan, they had to purchase the required fertiliser and other chemicals from a store owned by the bank's managing family, an illegal arrangement about which people felt powerless to do anything directly. Not repaying loans, so long as no repercussions came down on them, was a way to get back at the bank and the fertiliser store.

Significantly, people did not cut their family expenditures to bare bones subsistence in an attempt to meet all claims on their income. Some probably could have reduced expenses without going hungry had they wanted to pay their Masagana-99 loans. But they did not reduce drastically. They seem to be saying they are entitled to what they have and maybe even a little more. They will not forego that in order to pay everything that was claimed of them.

The view that a family is entitled to more than subsistence and that claims should be somewhat flexible . . . is a view of justice. It asserts that people have a right to live like human beings, not animals, and this means having enough resources in order to live with dignity.

CONCLUSION

. . . In San Ricardo there is a friction due to entitlement norms rubbing abrasively against values that encourage individuals and families to scramble to accumulate material goods and wealth. Most villagers experience conflicting values within themselves and may attempt to act according to both. It would be incorrect to say that the better off hold the acquisitive values while only the poorer ones have entitlement norms. The everyday resistance discussed in this article, however, reflects poorer residents' efforts, based on entitlement norms, to qualify and shape their relations with those who are better off.

Practicing entitlement ideas has been more difficult in recent years. A generation ago share tenants had a right to help from their landlords. That system of land tenure is gone, however, and no longer do share tenants compose the bulk of society. Earlier, socio-economic divisions within the village and surrounding area were sharper, mainly between the numerous poor share tenants and the few prosperous landlords. Now distinctions are more gradual and complex. Hence, struggles involving entitlement norms frequently occur in unfamiliar contexts and among people whose socio-economic differences are less pronounced. . . .

. . . Entitlement norms come from the past. But then so do rival ideas reinforcing self-enrichment and success. The meaning of entitlement has not remained constant. Its content and how and where it should be practiced are changing with new influences. Villagers have been attempting not only to maintain a standard of subsistence that was appropriate for an earlier period but to reach beyond it to some of what other sectors of society take for granted. The idea that education, sturdy housing, sanitation, and regular income are necessities—something the dominant classes have long enjoyed—has worked its way into San Ricardo people's thinking and is beginning to be expressed in entitlement terms when villagers associate these with human dignity and decent livelihood. . . .

Everyday resistance often brings important gains to the poor. The miserably paid workers' acts of defiance often help them to assert their humanity and put rice on the table. Second, the cumulative effects of everyday resistance can thwart the plans of those with more power and status. A small example from San Ricardo is that individuals' persistent day-by-day opposition to landowners who try to keep them from pasturing, gleaning, and foraging in fallow land has sustained these practices. . . . Finally, everyday resistance may help to nurture ideas of justice that can be the basis for far-reaching visions and protest movements in another time under different conditions. . . .

NOTES

1. Names of people are fictitious. San Ricardo is located in Nueva Ecija province, about 150 kilometres north of Manila.
2. The two families have other businesses and investments that are more lucrative, engaging, and, as they say, 'less headache' than their haciendas. In addition, siblings in one family are quarrelling about whether to farm or sell the 200-hectare hacienda and how to divide either the land's harvests or the land itself.
3. Signs of discontent became serious enough in 1978–79 to prompt village officials to petition the Ministry of Agrarian Reform to subject the haciendas to land reform. Some in San Ricardo are hopeful this will succeed. More, however, doubt it will ever happen.

REFERENCES

Kerkvliet, Benedict J., 1977, *The Huk Rebellion*, Berkeley: University of California Press.

6.2 People's Kitchens and Radical Organizing in Peru

Carol Andreas

The next excerpt is about another response to power inequality: radical organizing at the neighborhood level. The **People's Kitchens** of Lima (Peru), described in this excerpt by Andreas, are a lifestyle outcome of the experience of extreme poverty and a collective response by the urban poor to the hunger caused by Peru's severe and unpredictable economic situation.

The kitchens are operated and supplied by the pooled resources of some 20 to 25 households. Families contribute labor and money and receive meals from the kitchen. The cooperatives also provide meals to other community members in particular need of assistance.

The success and popularity of the People's Kitchens is evidenced by their increase in numbers: There are more than 1,500 in Lima alone. The realization that working together can make a difference has given people who manage the organizations, of which most are women, more self-esteem and a new sense of power. Another positive effect of the Kitchens has been their use by feminists as a springboard for women's agendas.

Women who work in the cooperatives can leave their houses without their husbands asking where they are going. This represents a significant step forward for Peruvian women. The success of the People's Kitchens also legitimizes women's critique of public policies relating to reproductive rights, marital issues, and violence against women.

Emerging as they have from poor neighborhoods, the People's Kitchens represent a significant departure from the factory as the primary locus of working class protest. They also suggest that traditional obstacles to working class community organizations can be overcome. They show a measure of success by the disadvantaged in combating each of the four basic obstacles to equality—scarcity, decoupling, disability, and exclusion.

There seems to be a breaking point in semi-colonial situations where unemployed or underemployed poor outnumber the employed so much that new conditions for class struggle come into existence. Distribution of goods and services becomes such an acute problem that issues of exploitation *per se* take second place to issues of survival or reproduction. The crisis in the family and community reaches a point of no return. Those who are excluded from regular wage work play an increasingly important role in defining political agendas, paving the way for the revolutionary transformation of daily life, not only in the production of goods and services, but also in the relations among women, men, and children in their communities.

Issues such as sanitation, public health, transportation, childcare, education, food, and housing are essentially reproductive concerns that are particularly acute in cities where massive migration generated out of these concerns prepare the poor to take collective responsibility for their lives.

A decade of economic crisis in Peru has spawned many such structures. The most notable of these are the People's Kitchens established by the urban poor. At least 1500

existed in Lima alone by the end of 1988. In each of these some twenty to twenty-five families pool resources and work cooperatively to help maintain family members and others who may be temporarily or permanently without a stable source of income.

Because most of those involved in the administration of People's Kitchens are women, the growing importance of these organizations has given women a new source of political power, a new sense of self-esteem, and the experience of radical praxis in political struggle against the state. . . .

BACKGROUND AND DEVELOPMENT

The People's Kitchens in Lima have their roots in the *olla común* (common pot), prepared during fiestas and community work projects in native communities in the countryside. The *olla común* is also traditionally prepared in support of striking workers in mines and factories, especially when families accompany workers on *marchas de sacificio*, in which workers walk for days or weeks to confront government officials with their demands. . . .

Another antecedent of the People's Kitchens can be found in the Mothers' Clubs established by the government and the Catholic Church (using surplus commodities from the United States). Some of these date from the 1950s and the 1960s. The Clubs were established to gain the political support of women and to establish a relationship of what Peruvians call *asistencialismo*— welfare clientelism. These programs "corraled" women with the enticement of individual allotments of basic food supplies such as cooking oil and flour, as well as certain sought-after items such as nylon hose, plastic kitchenware, and sewing supplies. In the 1970s, some Mother's Clubs escaped the bounds of *asistencialismo* and became centers for grassroots organizing efforts aided by progressive nuns influenced by the Popular Church movement and feminism.

The first People's Kitchens in the *barriada* of Comas (Lima) were organized in 1979. Some women were able to utilize food allotments provided by Caritas, a Catholic relief service, even though collective utilization of Caritas assistance was prohibited in other places by conservative church officials. Since the husbands of many women were hostile to the idea at first, and mothers were reluctant to be away from their homes for extended periods, the program operated out of individual homes. Families donated big cooking pots and other supplies, and women prepared meals for each neighborhood entirely on the basis of rotating labor. Those who were *socios*, or members of the program, came by to receive prepared food and carry it to their own homes.

Weekly meetings of those responsible for the planning, shopping, and cooking for People's Kitchens, and less frequent meetings of the entire membership, determined how much labor and/or money participants owed and on what basis free food and other assistance could be provided to the elderly, orphans, or others who couldn't contribute to the program for whatever reason. As the program expanded and became more centralized at the district level, and eventually at the city-wide level, those who planned menus were required to attend seminars in nutrition given by local health professionals. Savings were also effected, where possible, by organizing *almacenes* or food warehouses so that extra costs due to price speculation by individual businesses or market vendors could be avoided.

People's Kitchens are often organized in buildings or rooms that previously served

some other purpose, such as a clinic or school. Several women serve as "permanent staff" for a period of time and receive four or five portions of free meals for their families each day in return for their efforts. Others pay either by the meal or in advance. In some cases, outsiders such as workers from nearby factories come to eat at the People's Kitchen regularly and pay a higher price than *socios*. On weekends the locale is used by individuals or groups to serve meals to the general public as a way of earning money for neighborhood causes or personal needs. Young people support the People's Kitchens through volunteer labor and through helping connect the organization with other neighborhood programs such as literacy classes and political education.

While in most cases leaders of the People's Kitchens bring to these organizations years of neighborhood organizing experience and a certain amount of political sophistication, many *socios* are. . . shy at first about speaking at meetings or taking initiative or responsibility. Over the years, such women have been transformed by their participation in the People's Kitchens. Not only have they come to be outspoken and self-confident, they are critical of those who used the Kitchens for personal profit and those who attempted to manipulate the community's neediness to promote outside interests.

Fernando Belaúnde, who preceded Alán García as president of Peru, received U.S. government support in setting up official versions of the People's Kitchens, where inexpensive meals would be provided under government auspices. There was much fanfare over the establishment of several government-sponsored *comedores* (eating places). However, this was a token effort and did not undermine the People's Kitchen movement but instead encouraged the women to demand government support of their own efforts.

The existence of People's Kitchens that were not subservient to the central government was important in the success of another *barriada* program, initiated by the Left Unity mayor of Lima in 1984. Alfonso Barrantes secured foreign assistance (but not from the United States) in order to provide a glass of milk daily for children and nursing mothers in the *barriadas*. Local women's committees were set up to administer the program, which was centralized in an overall Emergency Plan. This caused chaos in the *barriadas*, as many party men resisted turning local power over to the women's committees, which were thought to be insufficiently loyal to the left Unity. In many cases, committee membership overlapped with that of the *comedores populares* of People's Kitchens. When Barrantes was no longer mayor, the Glass of Milk Committees struggled to retain autonomy from the ruling APRA party and still receive powdered milk allotments.

More often than not, food assistance from the Church and/or the government has been cut off whenever People's Kitchens begin to show solidarity with other causes by sheltering political refugees or organizing marches to make demands on the government. It is this process, more than anything else, that radicalized many members. In the end, most Kitchens have been forced to "go it alone." In Villa El Salvador, 156 such *comedores* became the core of the Popular Women's Federation of the *barriada*. Nearly half the *socios* were the sole support of their families (that is, single mothers). The People's Kitchens helped free these women to work outside their homes.

In 1985, when the female-based organizations of Villa El Salvador and other *barriadas* of Lima attempted to get official recognition from the city-wide Federation of New Towns (*barriadas*), organized primarily by the Left Unity electoral coalition, they were told to go home.[1] The women persisted, however, and female political party members eventually found it necessary to work within the People's Kitchens in order to legitimize themselves as political leaders. The myriad of political parties of the left attempting to win support among the *socios* of the People's Kitchens gave rise to political debates about the function of these Kitchens beyond the provision of low-cost food for the families who benefited from them. Thus, the process of centralization further radicalized some of the women who were involved in organizing People's Kitchens, even as it gave rise to internal conflicts.

By 1987, the People's Kitchens were experiencing a leadership crisis. Centralization of the movement was resulting in disputes over who were the legitimate representatives of the coordinating bodies. Some were accused of being "terrorists" (in this case, Shining Path guerrillas). Others were accused of being conciliatory with APRA. Women sympathetic to Shining Path had been slow to involve themselves in the People's Kitchen movement. However, as Church and government participation became marginal or nonexistent within the movement, women who had been influenced by Shining Path began to take part in the organizations and to work to redirect away from any remaining forms of *asistencialismo*.

Feminists were active in seeing the People's Kitchen movement through its initial political crises. Their involvement has been most effective when feminists are *pobladores* themselves, which is not as unusual in Peru today as it would have been even six or eight years ago. Feminists began to see the People's Kitchen movement as a potential springboard for women's agendas, ranging from a critique of public policies relating to reproductive rights, marital issues, and issues of violence toward women, to the legitimizing of collective domestic work.

In August of 1988, the Peruvian government reinitiated a temporary work program that had been forced to close down earlier because of scandalous misappropriation of funds. Critics had also charged that workers were used to break unions and to engage in activities specifically in support of APRA. The recreated temporary work program is modeled after OFASA, a work-relief program for *barriada* women administered by the Seventh-Day Adventist Church (as in the case of Caritas, this program enjoys the support of the U.S. government). According to grassroots leaders in the *barriadas*, these programs are aimed primarily at disrupting nongovernmental programs such as the People's Kitchen movement. Over 80 percent of those employed by the government work programs are female. Because these women work mainly cleaning up garbage dumps in the *bar-*

riadas, they are unusually susceptible to bacterial infections. *Socios* of the Kitchens complain that by the time women have finished working in government programs they are so sick they can't help with the work in the *comedores populares,* yet are in need of the services these provide.

During the past two years the coordinating bodies of the People's Kitchens, Glass of Milk Committees, and Mothers' Clubs in Lima have waged periodic campaigns to demand that their programs be financed, at least in part, directly from government coffers. The demands were at first met with defiance and repression on the part of the government. However, a new National Program for Food Assistance has been implemented. It is based in part on the issuance of food stamps for the "truly needy." Thousands of other women have also been attracted to newly-established *comedores* sponsored directly by APRA, and *apristas* have taken over many *comedores* which used to be considered autonomous.

Electoral politics in 1989 has turned many People's Kitchens into centers for the organization of conservative forces. Welfare clientilism is rampant. But other forces are also at work.

As the food crisis continues in the cities, some urban migrants are returning to rural areas. Noncommercial avenues of food distribution and the "requisitioning" of trucks carrying food products to urban markets are reportedly increasing. . . .

Organizations born in the *barriadas* are more than a reflection of workplace struggles. I think it is more useful to view them as direct expressions of popular discontent over issues of reproduction rather than production. These expressions bring into the political arena new social forces, predominantly female rather than male, and a new kind of revolutionary vision, not necessarily less radical than that of the urban work force.

It has been assumed that the primary locus for revolutionary change is at the point of production, among those who work for wages in strategic industries. Political economists have also tended to take as given an ever-increasing demand for labor in an expanding economy. The inexorable expansion of industry provides the main basis for working-class political power, even as periodic recessions are necessary for economic readjustment in capitalist societies. But conditions in debt-ridden "developing" countries are quite different. While workers on strike are a constant threat to stability, both government repression and efforts at "pacification" are often centered in working-class neighborhoods rather than at the workplace. In the neighborhoods, popular organization is facilitated by geographic concentration of the poor. Students, housewives, and unemployed workers are more active politically on a regular basis than are those employed in urban industries. The interests of these groups are also identified more closely with the interests of the rural poor. This is especially true in countries like Peru, where recent arrivals to the city are discriminated against as Indians. All these factors are important in assessing the significance of People's Kitchens in Peru and elsewhere.

It should be emphasized that the development of People's Kitchens in Peru has not been "spontaneous." Obstacles encountered by the women involved—from husbands, from political parties of both the left and the right, and even from within their own ranks as charges of opportunism and betrayal threatened to destroy their movement—have been at times overwhelming. However, many leaders have been able to resist cooptation and repression. Where women have succumbed to external or internal pressures, or retired from active involvement, often others have emerged to replace them.

In Peru, as People's Kitchens have assumed an ever more visible role in maintaining the physical well-being and promoting the collective strength of *pobladores,* the recognition of women's importance as political actors has been immeasurably advanced. And the possibility of a democratically-based revolution encompassing the larger concerns of families in their homes and communities as well as workers in the wage economy has also come into clearer focus.

NOTES

1. Cecelia Blondet, *Muchas Vidas Construyendo una Identidad: Mujeres Pobladoras de un Barrio*

Limeño, Documento de Trabajo No. 9 (Lima: Instituto de Estudios Peruanos (IEP), January, 1986), p. 61.

6.3 Empowering the Homeless in America

Michael Fabricant

The next excerpt in this section is about a third response to power inequality: empowerment through institutional restructuring. This time it is the empowerment of the homeless poor of New York City. Here the administrators of selected public agencies have initiated the activity.

The author reports on how selected agencies serving the poor try to do their work in such a way that the clients come to see their problems differently. The problems are defined as not their own failings, but problems of the system. The homeless are taught strategies for responding to their problems. The goal is not to "directly" help homeless people as much as it is to teach them to help themselves. In other words, the agencies try to combat the disabling beliefs that the homeless, and most other poor people, accept.

The agencies also try to remove unnecessary bureaucratic obstacles for the homeless. They welcome homeless people and involve them in the activities of the service. In other words, social exclusion and decoupling are recognized as problems and something is done about them.

Admittedly the activities the author describes are rather isolated. There are small local examples, hardly covering a vast majority of the nation's poor. However, if the techniques work here, with the most powerless and downtrodden in America, they should work among others under less extreme circumstances. These strategies are no substitute for better state welfare and training policies, that would even more greatly improve the economic lot of the poor, but they can be used successfully in conjunction with such policy changes.

. . . It has been estimated that during the 1980s millions of citizens experienced homelessness. The National Coalition for the Homeless and the Community for Creative Non-Violence have suggested

Excerpted from Fabricant, Michael (1988), "Empowering the homeless," *Social Policy*, 18(4), Spring, 49–55.

between 3 and 5 million citizens are presently homeless. . . .

This rapid upturn in homelessness has had substantial consequences for social service agencies. Municipal shelters, public welfare centers, and nonprofit agencies have been unprepared to meet the needs of the homeless. In general, these agencies reinforce a cycle that saps homeless people of their esteem and any sense of control or power over their lives. For instance, large municipal shelters frequently fail to protect the physical safety or property of the homeless. . . .

Nonresidential social service agencies are also not prepared to meet the immediate or long-term needs of the homeless. Consequently, the alienation and despair that often characterize life on the streets are reinforced by formal agency policy.

Most social service agencies are organized to meet the needs of their clientele through the delimited provision of services. However, the provision of services to homeless individuals and families requires flexibility. Clients may be unwilling or unable to visit the agency because of experiences associated with living on the streets.

Additionally, categoric definitions of assistance often will not meet the needs of homeless citizens who combine physical, emotional, and desperate material problems. Finally, the circumstance of living on the streets or the threat of being in such a situation requires a sense of urgency and rapid mobilization not often associated with large public welfare agencies.

The structure and content of social work expertise also fail to meet some basic needs of homeless people. Many agency-based models of practice encourage an objectivity, rationality, and distancing from client that is inappropriate for a group desperately isolated and in need of intimate forms of human connection that offer hope.

Finally, social service agencies simply do not have the material resources to meet all the needs of all the homeless.

This context offers homeless people little hope of recreating their lives. New service forms must be created that address the economic, social, and emotional needs of the homeless.

AN EMPOWERING FRAMEWORK

An alternative approach in working with the very poor has been to develop a service structure that promotes empowerment. . . .

. . .The critical question for social workers and agencies is how to create processes that enable the poor to believe they can change themselves and the world.

It has been suggested in the literature that a prerequisite for the development of empowering processes is the development of new types of relationships between client, worker, and agency. Barriers that separate the client from agency and social worker must be broken. These barriers include professional distance, hierarchy, cumbersome intake procedures, and agency messages that fail to validate the circumstances of the client. Alternatively, social workers must develop a process that enables clients to "articulate these views about matters of personal concern and over time to relate their personal interests first to similar concerns of others and ultimately to the broader problems of all powerless people.[1] For this to occur, a complex relationship must be developed between the client and worker and indirectly the agency. Relationships must be restructured to emphasize equity, reciprocity, hospitality, celebration, and, most critically, the validation of the dynamic interplay between the personal and political in defining the life circumstances of the poor.

Clearly, this formulation has pertinence to the homeless. In general, the homeless are isolated and personally powerless. Equally important, they are frequently blamed for individual deficits.

A number of small to mid-sized nonprofit agencies working exclusively with the homeless are struggling to implement empowering models of practice. The following will explore how some agencies have structured their encounters with the homeless to facilitate empowerment.

ADVOCACY WITH THE HOMELESS

A sample of six administrators who have been intimately associated with the development of empowerment services in the New York City metropolitan area was drawn for this inquiry. The administrators were identified by the National Coalition for the Homeless and the New York City Coalition for the Homeless as innovators who have successfully struggled to implement empowerment models. An openended interview schedule was developed, to elicit information regarding the services intended to empower homeless people. The qualitative data culled from these interviews have been organized thematically. . . .

An environment of hospitality is characteristic of the innovative organizations working with the homeless.

[W]hen a woman walks in the front door, we stop everything and make our best effort to mobilize resources to meet her need. You just have to be able to truly meet and encounter people as they enter the program. Otherwise you've lost half the battle before you've begun.[2]

When someone walks in the door, they can't be treated with disrespect. . . .You almost have to visualize their being somewhere, living somewhere, and having quality in their lives. You have to immediately struggle to see it so they can see it and also begin to connect to you. . . .[I]f they see that you're looking at them as a stinking lump of flesh then that's they way they'll feel and respond.[3]

Homeless people are isolated and in need of human encounters. The technical, rational models of social service delivery tend to emphasize relationships that encourage objectivity, expert distancing, and hierarchy. However, the alienation, distrust, and isolation characteristic of life on the streets must be penetrated. It is critical to seek out connections to the client's thoughts and feelings.[4]

Just as important, the homeless person's fundamental equality and worth must be incorporated into the practice relationship.

Homeless people have a real sense of hierarchy; they've been defined by everybody and everyone reinforces that they're at the bottom. That distance between them and everybody else has isolated them. I firmly believe that strengths don't emerge and change can't occur when people are isolated. It's therefore so important that the distance and sense of hierarchy with homeless people be bridged.[5] . . .

A variety of approaches that have been developed by alternative social service agencies to narrow distance, build on client strengths, and empower homeless people. The unifying theme is that each of these agencies has surrendered some turf to the homeless. This democratic restructuring may be as modest as offering greater equality in

practice relationships or as substantial as the development of new governance bodies that involve homeless people.

This sharing of power is an expression of respect that assigns value to homeless persons' experiences, opinions, and voice. The process is intended to offer homeless people choices and some control over their lives.

For instance, at Community Access we trained many clients on how to live in an apartment. This training was initially done by staff. Over time, however, more and more of this training was done by clients. You could almost see the jump in their sense of esteem. In effect we took some of their strengths, gave them an opportunity to put them to work, and not only did they do a marvelous job, they built on these strengths.[6]

At Women-in-Need we have a self-governance structure. The women have an opportunity to change everything from the content of the meals to the services. They truly have a voice in every facet of agency life. At times we as staff may have to identify when we are pressed against our limits and really can't make changes immediately that we define as needed. But at least we go through the process and together attempt to find an answer to the problem. It is through processes like this that many women learn that what they have to say is important and that they can make a difference.[7]

As homeless people begin to feel they are an essential part of the life of the agency and workers are recruited to not only sustain this involvement but to build upon it, the agency is transformed into a community. A number of critical elements of a first stage of transition to a community have already been identified: a welcoming, narrowing of distance, a sense of control, and choices within the agency environment.

However, the transition from living within an agency of mutual respect and concern to a community involves an array of factors that focus on the depth of interpersonal bonding. It is only through communal support that staff and the homeless feel sufficiently supported to create new ways of transforming their experience and pushing against their present limitations.

Staff needs to be supported in their development of ideas. They have to be willing to take the risk of expression crazy creative ideas and not feel that their ideas will be stolen or that they will have their legs shot out from underneath them. They must be able to present ideas and leave with a continued sense of possibilities.[8]

Clients shouldn't be forced to do things they don't want to do. But if this place feels safe enough, slowly but surely these homeless women will begin risking parts of themselves by applying for entitlements, going through legal systems, or sharing parts of themselves that have remained hidden for years. The women have to be pushed for this to happen, but for them to respond they also have to feel safe with us.[9]

In order for staff or the homeless to experience safety, however, they must feel they are integral members of a community who can individually or collectively make a difference. Each of these members must feel sufficiently invested, on the basis of shared values and concerns, to want to make a difference. Communal bonds will also evolve from personal feelings and commitments. These more personal responses can in part be traced to celebrations that are structured into the experience of this type of community. . . .

In our program we celebrate the women's birthdays or special events. These. . . enable us to begin to bridge our differences and offer a form of caring and often intimacy that simply can't be created any other way. It is only in this way that you can build a community that binds staff with residents, residents to residents, and staff to staff.

CREATING NEW CHOICES

Empowerment services require that programs attempt to meet neglected yet primary needs of their clientele. This can be accomplished, for instance, by helping to locate or create low-income housing for the homeless.

Service agencies have struggled to develop new responses to these needs. If, however, homeless persons' choices are persistently meager or nonexistent, then this vision of services and communal integrity demands that new choices be created. On this basis, many empowerment service agencies have progressed from shelter provision to transitional and permanent housing creation.

In effect, the scarcity of low-income housing has forced agencies to enter a new arena to address the most vital issue confronting homeless citizens.

One of the things we quickly discovered at the Elizabeth Coalition is that homeless people have more than sheltering needs. They have critical health problems, are often illiterate, and frequently families do not have the necessary child care to do an effective housing search. Consequently, we created a literacy training program with volunteers, a health program in conjunction with St. Elizabeth's Hospital, and are in the midst of attempting to develop a child-care center. These new programs and others that will follow were not created out of thin air. They represent an attempt by this agency to meet needs as they are articulated by homeless people.[11]

Look, it's all a big lie if we don't get into the business of creating transitional and permanent housing. How can we speak about choices or pretend we are engaged in a process of empowering people if we shelter people for x number of months and tell them to locate housing when we know full well such housing simply doesn't exist for everyone?[12]

These agencies are working with banks and state government to stitch together the finances for modest housing programs. Clearly, the federal government's disengagement from housing creation has provided part of the impetus for providers to enter this process.

Legislative lobbying, rallies, and militant action have consistently involved homeless people in key roles as speakers, organizers, and so forth. These activities underscore for many homeless the relationship between individual circumstance and public policy choices. A critical activity of empowerment is to highlight the connection between homelessness and the decisions of real-estate developers and legislators.

Mutual support groups enable homeless people to identify the shared nature of their experience. By talking with each other about how they became homeless, present struggles, or plans for the future, members not only strengthen their individual problem-solving skills, but begin to understand how their fate is intertwined with others. The individual begins to identify with a group of homeless people: This insight enables the homeless to believe they can alter their situation by acting to recreate parts of the social environment. In effect, the group becomes a bridge between the individual personal struggles of the homeless and collective action.

Often the women may try to support each other by providing tips on child care or an apartment they may hear about. More recently, however, groups have begun to focus on the fact that there just isn't enough housing to go around. Now what they're looking to do is find a way to do something about it.[13] . . .

. . . [I]n the course of our sessions the women came to see how the lack of housing was profoundly affecting all their lives. So they decided to do something about it. They are identifying housing abandoned by the city that is salvageable. Once they've completed developing their list, they intend to go to the city council with other groups, to press the city to rehabilitate housing for the homeless. They realize the process is going to be slow and difficult but they're excited to be in it.[14]

CONCLUSION

A range of tensions will continue to plague empowerment service agencies. The content of these services are dependent upon low staff/client ratios. However, given fiscal realities and the swelling homeless population, the agencies' control over these ratios may be increasingly marginalized. Increasingly, these agencies will be forced to walk the tightrope of providing empowerment services and meeting the daily demands of the state and those homeless citizens who remain in crisis.

Another tension is that the initial vision, energy, and sense of mission of leadership and line staff may be eroded over time. Their momentum and sense of direction can be drained away by the combination of new demands and less time. This array of factors undermined similar community-based programs in the 1960s and 1970s.

Additionally, these programs' growth may pose a threat. These organizations' capacity to function as an alternative to bureaucratic service may no longer be viable if they require similar centralizing organizational structures to manage their new tasks. This was the fate of similar programs two decades ago.

Clearly, if the integrity of empowerment service programs is to be retained, these agencies and their leadership must learn a number of vital lessons from their predecessors. Most critically, a balance must be struck between the growth of the agency and the need to maintain the communal facets of its structure as well as the missionary drive of its leadership. The absence of such a balance will result in many losses, the most important of which may be the creative or innovative impulse. . . .

NOTES

1. Michael Reisch, Stanley Wenocur, and Wendy Shermans, "Empowerment, Concientization and Animation as Core Social Work Skills," *Social Development Issues* (Summer/Fall 1981).
2. Interview with Tilly Schuster, president of the board of Women-in-Need, Sept. 1986.
3. Interview with Peggy Schorr, former clinical director of Community Access, Nov. 1986.
4. Donald Shoen, *The Reflective Practitioner* (New York: Basic Books, 1982).
5. Interview with Colleen McDonald, director of Olivieri Center, Sept. 1986.
6. Ibid.
7. Interview with Rita Zimmer, executive director of Women-in-Need, April 1986.
8. Tilly Schuster.
9. Colleen McDonald.
10. Colleen McDonald.
11. Interview with Joan Driscoll, director of the Elizabeth Coalition to House the Homeless, Sept. 1986.
12. Colleen McDonald.
13 Rita Zimmer.
14. Joan Driscoll.

6.4   Confronting Powerlessness in India

Sundari Ravindran

The next excerpt in this section is about a fourth response to power inequality: **empowerment** by building self-esteem. When disadvantaged groups like women unite, they often improve their situation. But before they can unite, they have to realize they share a common problem. This may be difficult for women, since they do not share a distinct ancestry (like an ethnic group) or work together in large organizations (like a working class). Special efforts must be made to bring women together.

This excerpt describes one such attempt among poor rural women in southern India. This organizing effort provided women with better knowledge of health and their own bodies. By better understanding how their bodies function, they gained more control over their lives. They also began to challenge the societal norms that keep women in a subordinate position.

For instance, many of the women only had a vague understanding of the connection between sex and children. Many felt life was a series of events beyond their control: They had children; they suffered miscarriages; their children lived or died; and so on. By getting together to discuss these events and their problems, they came to understand that it was possible to change and control somewhat the course of their lives.

INTRODUCTION

. . . Attempts are being made by women from the most exploited sections of society in many parts of the world, to define their priorities and to change their conditions of existence. This article describes one such attempt by a group of rural women belonging to the untouchable 'Paraiya' caste in S. India to build an organisation of their own and to help women in their communities organise themselves to challenge their oppression.

ORIGINS OF THE ORGANIZATION

Rural Women's Social Education Centre (RUWSEC) in Chingleput, S. India was initi-

Excerpted from Ravindran, Sundari (1985), "Confronting gender, poverty and powerlessness: An orientation programme for and by rural change agents," *Community Development Journal*, 20(3), 213–221. By permission of Oxford University Press.

ated in 1981 by ten women who belonged to the villages of Chingleput, and the author. The main focus of RUWSEC's work has been activities and issues related to women and health. Then women 'animators' began carrying out health-care, health education and working towards building a women's organisation in those villages. . . .These activities helped in the consolidation of women's groups in all the villages during the course of two years and women's *sanghams* or associations were formed. These *sanghams* have become well known for their involvement in village problems and health issues. As a result, there were requests from several villages in the neighborhood for the setting up of women's centres, and the animators decided to extend their work to five more villages.

They visited the five villages, explained their work and requested the community nominate their own animators. The animators thus nominated were young women between the age of nineteen and twenty-five. They were introduced to RUWSEC through a six-day orientation programme organised by the senior animators.

THE ORIENTATION WORKSHOP

Building Confidence Through Sharing Experiences

. . . The training programme began with a brief introduction by two animators about the organisation and its work. The first animators described their role as animators and shared some of their experiences and the difficulties they had faced. As women who were daring to venture into new vistas, they had come under criticism from the traditional male leaders in the community. One speaker asked the trainees not to feel inadequate or afraid. She assured them saying that if she could learn to be the assertive and confident person she was today, she did not see why the same was not possible for them. After this introduction, the objectives and programme plan were explained.

Participatory Training Techniques

The group was paired off in twos and after ten minutes spent in getting to know each other, each participant introduced her partner to the larger group.

This was followed by another game designed to stimulate discussion on the problems encountered by groups when trying to function democratically and as a collective. The participants, in groups of five, had to stimulate decision-making in an emergency situation of a rising tide which would sweep away their hut in ten minutes. They had to decide which household articles to take along. At the end of five minutes the group had to announce their decisions, and describe how they arrived at them. . . .

From working together in a group participants went on to the next activity, public speaking for two minutes on a given topic. Not only had none of the trainees ever done public speaking before, they had been brought up to be quiet and withdrawn, never assertive and never to have an opinion of their own let alone to state it in public. The women were very nervous. They were sure they could never do it. When they did do it, it was for them a great leap forward.

By the end of the first day all the trainees seemed to have broken out of their shells. The first basic theme of the programme—reflecting on the status of women in society—was introduced at this juncture.

Reflecting on Women's Position in Society

. . . Popular proverbs about women in vogue in their villages were discussed:

"Father of five daughters, even if he is a king, will be reduced to a pauper." (This refers to the custom of giving dowries and presents at and after marriage throughout the daughter's life.)

"Does the day dawn with a hen crowing?" (Do women do anything of importance?)

"If you trust a woman, you will be stranded on the streets."

"It is woman who caused the fall of Indra (King of Gods) and of Chandra (the moon God)."

"A girl who has attained puberty should be given away in marriage, be it to a *chakkiliya*." (*Chakkiliya* is a caste that works with leather and is considered lowest of the low).

The participants said such proverbs were constantly hurled at them. They expressed anger at the way women were degraded in the proverbs. This initiated a spontaneous exchange by the women of how voiceless they were in their own households. The exchange was charged with emotion, and at the same time an awakening as to how similar their plights were. One woman had to put an end to her fascination for books after her marriage since only a lazy woman whiled away her time reading, according to popular conception. Another, who had been married at thirteen and had borne seven children before she was twenty-five, told of how she seemed to have forgotten who she was. She as a person with desires and aspirations did not exist in the eyes of her husband and in-laws. Many animators already working in RUWSEC described having to contend with rumours of their being women of loose morals since they moved around several villages all by themselves.

The discussions, which ensued late into the night, were evidence they were totally absorbed in it.

The next morning began with small group discussions around two stories.

In the first story, Sita, the main character, finds herself treated as nothing but an additional hand to work for the family into which she has entered as daughter-in-law. Strict codes of conduct are laid down for her by her mother-in-law, and she does not even have the possibility to talk to her husband freely. In the second story, Golden Flower, a newly married young woman in pre-revolutionary rural China is in an identical situation.

The first story posed questions as to how a woman could react in a similar situation, and all the women eagerly participated in suggesting solutions. The woman could persuade her husband to set up house separately—or alternatively, she could live alone, but for that she would need regular employment. In the latter case, she would need a lot of support from other women, which was considered difficult to come by because a woman who supports another who had dared to break the rules of society is herself in danger of being labeled immoral. But should we not, it was suggested, try to break away from this vicious circle? The participants agreed, and the session ended on a hopeful note of trying to change rather than comply.

In the next session, participants worked in three groups, each group analysing respectively, the image of women in popular fiction, films and in film songs.

Creating New Attitudes of Self-Value

The third day of the workshop was designed to help the women to focus on traditional attitudes held by themselves and by society regarding women's social and sexual roles. It began with the presentation of a case-study of a rural woman's life by narration combined with drama.

The story was about Meenu, the daughter of poor peasant *harijan* parents. She went to school for two years, and at age eight stayed back to help with household tasks and to take care of her younger brother and sister while her mother worked in the fields. At thirteen she attained puberty. The occasion was celebrated with the customary rituals, beginning with her physical isolation for five days since she was "unclean". She was shocked and confused. In the days that followed more restrictions were imposed on her. She could not leave home after dark, she could not talk to boys or even come out of the house if men other than her family members were present. She was filled with fear and contempt for her new state, but got no advice from anyone about the facts of life.

At sixteen, Meenu was married to a young man from a neighbouring village. Her life followed in a drab rhythm thereafter—work, more work, pregnancies, childbirths, miscarriages, deaths of children—everything happening without her will or consent, without her being able to control or change anything.

The case study struck a familiar chord in all the trainees. Even those who were married and had children had had no idea of conceptions except that it was related in some way to copulation.

The rest of the day was spent going through the Tamil version of 'Child-Birth Picture Book'[1] which RUWSEC had produced. This dealt in detail with the reproductive system, puberty, conception, normal pregnancy and childbirth. The poverty of women which prevented adequate care following pregnancy was also discussed, through a narration of personal experiences by participants. The trainees said this was one of the most meaningful sessions.

Identifying Oppressive Attitudes and Structures in Society

The fourth day aimed at presenting the exploitation of women in the context of an unjust society mainly through games and stories.

The first was a game called "The Unequal Race." Participants divided into two groups, the rich and the poor. Each person was the head of a family and received 6 cards; one was an asset card detailing any assets the person had. The other cards denoted important events in a family's life cycle. Beginning with given assets they had to go through important events in the family's life cycle—like the birth of a child, education of children, finding them employment, arranging for their marriage, etc. which entailed spending money. At the end, the assets that remained with each person were calculated. The point was to stimulate discussion regarding popular misconceptions as to why some people are poor.

Following this there were two fables enacted. One was about a lone goose who dared to challenge the authority of a fox in a society where foxes occupied all important positions. She fell prey to the foxes. The second was the story of the wolf and the lamb. This time however, the lamb gathered together all the sheep and lambs, and together they succeeded in ejecting the wolf from the forest.

Next was a board game similar to Monopoly but it had true-to-life rules. Two players were landlords and the others were wage labourers. The landlords began with ten times more cash than the labourers, and already owned 25% of the property on the board when the game began. The last activity of the day was a skit by the senior animators, about a poor *harijan* woman called Valli.

Valli was a *harijan* woman who eked out a living doing agriculture wage labour. Her husband was also a wage labourer. Valli was tricked by the landlord for whom she worked into meeting him when he was alone and was raped by him. When she got back to the fields, she heard that her husband had been caught drinking water from the well of the upper caste people. The important landlords had assembled, and Valli's husband was awaiting their verdict for the 'crime' he had committed—'polluting' the well. The landlord who raped Valli was among them. Beside herself in rage, Valli rushed in front of the man and shouted whether he did not get polluted by raping a *harijan* woman? The 'untouchable' bitch and her husband were punished by a boycott by the landowners against hiring them for work.

Reflections of the participant on the day's activities summed up the concerns of poor *harijan* women. They had seen that society was divided into the rich and the poor, the powerful and the powerless, the exploiters and the exploited. Exploitation of women could not be seen in isolation.

The Socio-economic and Political Causes of Disease

In the fifth and the sixth days, trainees analyzed the inter-relationship of poverty, powerlessness and disease.

The theme was introduced with the story of Murugan, a village boy who died of tetanus. Participants had to identify the reasons that led to his death. For example, "Murugan's foot was pricked by a thorn when he was grazing cattle. Why? Because he wore no shoes, he was too poor. Why was he too poor? Further, he had not been vaccinated against tetanus. Why? Because the team from the health centre could not get to his village, there were no roads. Why didn't they make the effort, and why were there no roads?" and so on.[2]

The participants made a poster depicting the medical, social, economic and political causes of Murugan's death.

Later the trainees volunteered to enact a role play about how the poor were often treated by the health care system. The message was that villagers were apprehensive of going to hospitals because they were treated as stupid people with no minds of their own, and with no rationale behind their decisions.

Following the role-play and discussion, a paper entitled 'A post-mortem of our health-care system' was read and discussed. It dealt with the lop-sided priorities of the health-care system and how women—especially poor women—suffered most because of this. Women need medical attention not only when they are ill, but also during pregnancy and childbirth. The consumer-oriented health-care delivery system deprives them of care when they need it most, since it serves only *those who approach it*. The poor women are often preoccupied in their battle for survival and have neither the time nor the money to go to health centres.

EXAMINING THE ROLE OF ANIMATORS

The next task was to discuss the animators' role.

The animators saw their role as comprising curative health (for which they were to undergo further training), health education which aimed at identifying all the causes of disease, not only the medical ones, and organisation to eradicate all these causes.

They drew up a list of ways in which their work would be different from that of the existing health personnel. They would visit people at their homes at the latter's convenience, talk to them about preventive measures, mobilise action against diseases, treat patients as people with an ability to understand their own diseases and participate in their own healing. They would respect the wisdom and experience of the people, treat rich and poor alike, use local home remedies as far as possible, and take risks to strike at the root causes of disease.

Their main focus would be Women and Children's Health problems, and they would involve women in learning about symptoms and treatment of diseases while discussing the causes. Malnutrition for instance, may not be possible to eliminate without organising for higher wages for the work they do. They would also have to deal with the status of women, since their double oppression as women and as poor was causing most of their diseases.

The trainees had been introduced during the evenings to some of the ways ideas could be communicated and discussion stimulated. Street theatre based on rural women's life stories, role plays and problem dramas that portrayed women's problems and provoked discussion on how to change the situation, songs that told of their lives and struggles, and simulation games were all ways to involve women in reflecting about their lives and questioning what they had often taken for granted. The senior animators explained how this usually led on the formation of *sanghams*. However, the point was not to push for *sanghams* before the women felt the need for them.

The programme ended with an evaluation by the trainees and the animators. The trainees then returned home to begin their work . . .

NOTES

1. The 'Child-Birth Picture Book', ed. Frank P. Hosken is available from WIN News, 187 Grant Street, Lexington, Mass. 01273, U.S.A.
2. This exercise was taken from *Helping Health Workers Learn*, D. Werner and B. Bower, Hesperian Foundation, PO Box 1692, Palo Alto, California 94302, USA. 1982.

6.5 Guinean Women and The Promise of Liberation

Claire M. Renzetti and Daniel J. Curran

We have seen that political will is often not enough to effect meaningful change in a society. For example, achieving true gender equality means abandoning traditional family values and redefining gender and work. But too often, leaders and followers have been unwilling to do these things.

The next excerpt is about the high political and economic costs of equality. It uses an example of this from the behavior of the elite in the African republic of Guinea. This former French colony achieved its independence in 1958. The socialist government of former president Ahmed Sékou Touré came to power with, among other things, the promise of advancing the status of women.

Touré was one of the few African leaders to recognize the political advantages of appealing to women for support. He enacted many laws increasing the rights of women. He genuinely encouraged the advancement of women in the economic and political spheres. However, at the same time, his government called for a preservation of traditional family values.

Policies aimed at improving women's status have failed largely because of traditional attitudes to women that cannot be changed by legal reform. So, for instance, girls are still taught economically peripheral skills such as sewing and craftwork. Men are taught the technical jobs that are replacing old ones, further retarding women's progress.

Few women achieve higher education, due to the expectation that they will mainly fulfill the traditional female role in the home. Marriage and child-bearing are still considered the primary vocations of Guinean women.

A problem throughout much of the Third World as elsewhere is how to enforce legislative guarantees of gender equality so that they become more than just paper rights.

The present research examines this disparity between the written law and the law in action more closely. Specifically, this is a study of the progress toward gender equality in one Third World country, the Republic of Guinea, under the leadership of its former president, Ahmed Sékou Touré [and his socialist ruling party, the Parti Démocratique de Guinee (PDG)]. Guinea [a former colony of France] is situated in Western Africa on the Atlantic Coast. . . .

. . . The data were collected primarily by field observations and interviews in Guinea during the summers of 1982 and 1984. Additional data were gathered from content analyses of government documents, the written works and recorded speeches of Touré and issues of the *Hoyora* (the official state news magazine). Supplemental statistics were secured from . . . other international agencies. . . .

Excerpted from Renzetti, Claire M. and Daniel J. Curran (1986), "Structural constraints on legislative reform: Guinean women and the promise of liberation," *Contemporary Crises*, 10(2), 137–155. Reprinted by permission of Kluwer Academic Publishers.

[GUINEA'S PROSPECTS AT INDEPENDENCE]

Education

. . .After independence the Guinean government embarked upon one of the most extensive educational campaigns in all of West Africa. But given its limited financial resources, . . the program was only partially successful. . . . Eighty percent of the Guinean people remained illiterate in 1980.

Particularly disappointing was the sex differential in educational attainment. While. . . the percentage of girls attending primary school increased substantially after 1958—an 11.5 percent gain overall—the enrollment of girls still lagged far behind that of boys at all levels of the educational system. Among children 7 to 12 years old, only 24 percent of the girls were enrolled in primary school in 1980 compared with 45 percent of the boys. . . . And it was at the primary level, where females were admitted in the greatest numbers, that the curriculum for girls was designed to train them in basic 'women's vocational skills' such as sewing, food preparation, child care, and laundry practices. . . . Such courses . . . can seldom be utilized in the wage-labor market. . . . As one moves up the educational hierarchy . . . the disparity between male and female enrollments increases. . . .At the university level . . . the ratio of males to females exceeded seven to one in 1980. . . .

There are largely two reasons for these . . . differences in. . . educational attainment despite Touré's campaign in favor of schooling for both sexes. First is the extensive use of children, particularly girls, for . . . household chores and agricultural work. . . .Thus, even among girls enrolled in school, absenteeism was bound to be high. The right to obtain an education became meaningless for most females since household responsibilities made attending school impractical. . . .

Closely related to this [were] widespread. . . prejudices about a woman's 'proper place.' A commonly-held belief in Guinea was that the education of females is wasteful because their primary duties are to marry, maintain a household, and bear children. . . .

. . . The Revolutionary People's Republic of Guinea was . . . established in October 2, 1958 by its new president, Sékou Touré. . . .Both before independence and after, a number of serious obstacles had to be reckoned with. Not the least of these was the severe economic underdevelopment of the country. . . .

. . . Touré also faced the problem of tribal and regional differences among the Guinean people. . . .Despite repeated attempts to unite all ethnic groups under the banner of the PDG, confrontations erupted which threatened the . . . party. . . . Touré's primary means of resolving the dilemma was. . . [to] direct his efforts to the group he perceived as having the most to gain from change. . . . He appealed to the women of Guinea, whose interests he saw as cutting across ethnic and regional lines, to provide the foundations for the PDG. Prior to independence, he delivered speeches praising women as the 'future of the country,' the 'indispensable elements of life,' and even urging them to refuse sexual intercourse to their husbands until the latter joined the party.[1] After independence, Touré rewarded them for their support by instituting reforms which encouraged women to participate in the wage-labor force and in politics,

and to obtain an education. In addition, marriage and family laws were . . . revised to discourage polygamy and . . . allow women to obtain divorces. . . .

GUINEAN WOMEN UNDER SOCIALISM

. . . At the time of our first . . . visit, . . . few Guineans were . . . wage-earners: only six percent of the . . . working-age population. And of those only a tiny fraction were women, . . . concentrated in occupations which their employers—mostly Western bauxite mining firms—considered suitable female employment. The vast majority were secretaries and office clerks. . . . These women were not only subjected to the cultural biases of their own society, they were also confronted by outside prejudices. . . .

. . . Child-care facilities were nonexistent, and while many women . . . had the help of a female relative or neighbour, the working woman was still chiefly responsible for the care of her home and family. It is not surprising, therefore, that women sometimes missed work because of their domestic duties . . . This . . . gave employers an additional excuse for not hiring women.

Regardless of employment rates in the paid public sector, Guinea is clearly an agricultural society; 82 percent of the population was engaged in agricultural production in 1981.[2]. . . . Throughout West Africa, women traditionally have played a central part in the production and distribution of food, and Guinea was never an exception. The most important women in this respect have . . . been the 'market women.' Market women cultivate small plots of land in conjunction with their relatives, transport the produce to a . . . marketplace, and sell it for a profit. . . . Each woman has her own. . . . section of the market from which she sells her wares and for which she pays a rental fee to the state . . . .Virtually every housewife is a subsistence farmer. In addition, during Touré's presidency, each was expected to devote . . . time . . . to the cultivation of a local community garden which the government required them to maintain. In exchange, . . . they were given limited rights to sell the produce at the official state price. With the exception of the initial . . . clearing the land, the gardens were solely the women's responsibility. During our first visit to Guinea, we . . . found . . . it was in their household and community farming activities that . . . Guinean women most desperately needed assistance. . . . Planting was still done using a digging stick, and . . . weeding and harvesting were done manually, making the labor . . . arduous. Yet women were excluded from the government's program to reorganize . . . agricultural production. This was especially evident at the district level where the state established large, mechanized collective farms. There men were employed almost exclusively with the result that technological innovations, extension and improved seeds and fertilizers were made available only to them. Thus, although smallholder's (women) were responsible for practically all of Guinea's food production, they were bypassed by governmental programs which . . . could have lightened their . . . workload.

. . . This was happening . . . due to two competing . . . plans for the economic development of the country. On the other hand . . . were the programs of the . . . development agencies representing . . . countries of the West. . . .Their emphasis was on the introduction of machinery and advanced farm technology to . . . modernize production. . . . But underlying these programs was the Western notion of the sexual division of labor which associates machines and large scale production with . . . men. . . .

The role of women in economic production was blatantly ignored by Western development programs which either excluded women altogether or were designed to address areas irrelevant to their needs.

On the other hand, President Touré. . . was committed to traditional communal living as the basis for his socialist society. In Guinea . . . the center of the communal

lifestyle is the family in which the man is the head with undisputed authority. . . .

. . . The consequences of such norms are . . . illustrated by the case of one woman . . . we interviewed in 1982. She . . . had finally convinced her husband to help with the housework and child care only to have it abruptly ended by the other members of her village. One day, when several neighbors saw her husband cooking dinner, they began to ridicule him by calling him 'an old lady.' After that, she too was looked down upon as a bad wife. . . .

Marriage and the Family

. . . The president's commitment to a communal lifestyle served to reinforce women's subordination. . . . In 1982 we found . . . most men continued to take more than one wife, preferring to follow Islamic . . . doctrine rather than . . . state law. The law restricting polygamy was rarely enforced. Wives were . . . sometimes given . . . as gifts. And most women continued to be married by age 14 . . . At the same time, birth control was frowned upon. . . .Less than one percent of the female, childbearing population used contraceptives, and the average Guinean woman bore six children. . . .

A divorce, too, remained . . . difficult for a woman to obtain . . . . Typically one would be granted only if the woman could show . . . her husband had contributed *nothing* to her support or the support of their children, or that he beat her too severely. This latter point . . . illustrates another commonly-held belief that we encountered: . . . that a husband has the right to beat his wife if he has just cause—that is, for instance, if she showed him disrespect or flirted with other men. Should a woman . . . leave her husband for the home of her parents, she and her children would be promptly returned—few households could afford more mouths to feed. As a result, some women were forced to stay in unhappy . . . marriages. . . .

But perhaps in nothing was the endurance of custom more evident than in the practice of female circumcision.[3] In Guinea, the most common form of circumcision is excision, and virtually every girl between ages 7 and 14 is excised. However, recent awareness of the ritual in the West has generated controversy. Western feminists have labeled it a barbaric crime . . . and demanded that it be outlawed. African nationals, . . . men and women alike, have responded by accusing Western critics of 'cultural chauvinism' and imperialist interference. To them, female circumcision represents a 'link in cultural unity.'[4] This was . . . the prevalent attitude in Guinea where excision has . . . been considered one of the most significant events in a girl's life. . . .

. . . Following the excision, the girl would be sequestered . . . for about three weeks, after which she was reunited with her friends and relatives to celebrate her transition to adulthood. Wearing new clothes, she was presented to the village as older women sang and danced. . . . There would be feasting and the presentation of gifts. . . . The focus . . . was on the girl's new adult status because it signaled her eligibility for marriage. . . . An uncircumcised woman was not only considered 'dirty' by her peers, she also risked being ostracized by her community. In effect, she was rendered unmarriageable. . . .

Female circumcision . . . continues to be a means by which Guinean women exercise power and achieve recognition. . . . It is a fundamental part of the traditional culture which the Touré government was intent on restoring. . . .

. . . The debate surrounding female circumcision also illuminates how economic factors can restrict possible courses of action. Given women's exclusion from development programs, as well as their continued subjection to male domination, it may be expected . . . they would cling to one of the few avenues of power and status that remained open to them. What's more, it is perhaps unrealistic to expect people for whom mere survival is a daily struggle to recognize female circumcision as a major problem; the harmfulness of this . . . custom becomes dwarfed in comparison with other issues. . . .

The Polity

. . . During the Touré regime, all women belonged to the Union Revolutionnaire des Femmes de Guinée (URFG), the women's branch of the PDG. The organization of the URFG paralleled the . . . structure of the state party, running hierarchically from the grassroots village units (Pouvoir Revolutionnaire Local or PRL) to the National Directorate. It was at the local level that women participated most actively in political affairs. . . . Each PRL . . . served as a . . . self-help group. The cultivation of the . . . community gardens was coordinated by the PRLs and the proceeds from the sale of their vegetables were used for some mutually agreed-upon activity. . . . In addition, the PRLs organized adult literacy classes, although limited school supplies caused classes to be held only intermittently in many villages. Finally, [it] . . . was the PRL's charge to mobilize their constituents and ensure . . . women socialized their children in line with party ideology. . . .

Apart from their PRL activities, however, women's participation in . . . decision-making was low during Touré's presidency. . . . Women were poorly represented in the highest echelons of . . . government. Touré appointed no women deputy ministers or secretaries of state, and his one female cabinet member was in charge of a traditionally feminine area, social affairs.

The Minister of Social Affairs, . . . Mme. Cisse, described her job as first and foremost promoting the welfare of mothers and children. . . . She helped establish the Centres de Promotion Feminine (CPFs) in 1972 . . . to increase women's participation in the socioeconomic development of Guinea by teaching them profit-generating skills such as dying, pottery, and basket weaving. Typically, they attracted young women . . . who had never been to school or who had dropped out. The turnover rate was high—most women attended for less than six months—but they did generate income, especially in Conakry. . . . At the time of our first field visit, there were 37 CPFs, but because of financial and administrative difficulties, their focus was . . . confined to . . . the urban sector. They were largely unable to meet the acute needs of rural women who comprised a majority of the female population. . . .

CONCLUSION

. . . Several factors . . . rendered the . . . government's legal proclamations in women's interests insufficient . . . to guarantee change. One of these was . . . a widespread male supremacist belief system—a hybrid form of patriarchy blending customary prejudices with colonial biases. Under Touré it was perpetuated by the president's commitment to preserving traditional communal living patterns, by Islamic religious customs, and by Western influences in the commercial arena as well as in assistance programs which either ignored women . . . or enforced sexist divisions of labor.

Undoubtedly, however, the major problem was economic. . . . With a population of 5.8 million people in 1983, Guinea had a GNP per capita of US$300. Only 18 countries of the 126 from which the World Bank collects statistics had lower per capita GNPs in 1983. Life expectancy was 37 years, the lowest in the world in 1983, while the infant mortality rate ranked among the highest. Calorie intake is only about 84 percent of daily nutritional requirements and 88 percent of the population has no access to safe water.[5] . . . Faced with underdevelopment and poverty of this magnitude, the Touré government simply did not have the capital necessary to implement programs, such as the socialization of child care and domestic labor, which could have made women's realization of their legal rights more probable . . .

NOTES

1. Little, Kenneth (1973). *African Women in Towns: An Aspect of African Social Revolution* Cambridge: Cambridge University Press; Riviére, Claude (1968), op.cit.
2. Ibid.
3. Female circumcision—the partial or complete removal of the external female genitalia—is practiced in about 40 countries, mostly in East and West Africa. It can take three forms. Pharaonic circumcision, the most radical, involves the removal of the clitoris, labia minora, and at least two-thirds of the labia majora. The vagina is then stitched closed save for a tiny opening to allow for the passage of urine and menstrual blood. The two other forms are 'Sunna' and excision. Sunna circumcision is the mildest form and involves the cutting of the prepuce or hood of the clitoris analogous to male circumcision. But excision, the most common form of the operation, involves the removal of the clitoris as well as all or part of the labia minora.
4. The operation is usually performed by an elder woman of the village or a traditional birth attendant without an anaesthetic using a razor, a saw-toothed knife, or a piece of glass. Once completed, dirt, ashes, or herbs are rubbed into the wound in the belief that they will stop the bleeding and aid in healing. Medical complications are severe and frequent.
5. World Bank (1985). (see note 24)

6.6 Judicial Racism in Australia

David Thorpe

In the ideal egalitarian society, groups that make up a society will be represented in crime, the courts, and prison in roughly the same proportions as they appear in the society as a whole. But this condition does not exist in any society today. Certain dominant groups are over-represented outside of prison; other groups, often minorities, are over-represented inside prison.

Why do these disparities exist? The next excerpt, by David Thorpe, studies the situation of the Aborigines, the indigenous peoples of Australia. They are over-represented in the criminal justice system of that country. In the state of Western Australia, for instance, Aborigines make up a third of all prison inmates but only 2.5 percent of the population. In other words, they are over-represented in prison by more than a factor of ten. According to Thorpe, what is at work is a clash of values, where one culture (white European) imposes its code of acceptable behavior on another (the aboriginal) with complete disregard for legitimate differences.

Many of the crimes Aborigines are accused and convicted of fall into the category of "offenses against good order." It is easy to imagine how one culture's notion of this can differ drastically from another's. Nudity, for instance, is tolerated to differing degrees in different cultures. In Australia, Aborigines violate a white concept of order, by being nude, not one of their own. They frequently violate probation and parole, because these practices make assumptions about their lives that are invalid. Aborigines traditionally move around a lot and often do not live at a permanent address—a requirement of parole.

Often, arrests for offenses against good order occur in the absence of any public complaint or victim. In other words, the offense is police-defined. Police "racism" in Australia—including arbitrary arrests and harassment—is very similar to what blacks report facing in the United States and Britain.

Efforts to reduce the over-representation of Aborigines in the courts and prisons show promise of improving the situation. Free legal aid for Aborigines, for example, has had a positive effect. But such measures are not enough to achieve equality.

ABORIGINALS AND CRIMINAL JUSTICE: THE PROBLEM

. . . In 1984, the author was invited to visit Western Australia by the Department of Community Welfare which had recently begun a series of reforms in its work with juvenile offenders. The author was given the impression, while visiting two high-security youth institutions in Perth, that the majority of youngsters in those facilities were black[1] and the departmental officer who had organised the visit estimated 'over 60%' of the inmates were Aboriginal. She added that Aboriginals formed 'less than three per cent of the State's population'. The disparity is so striking that it is easy to leap to wrong conclusions— . . . that Aboriginals are either

Excerpted from Thorpe, David (1987), "Structures of judicial racism in Australia," Howard Journal, 26(4), November, 259–271. With permission of Blackwell Publishers.

deeply committed to crime or that Australian criminal justice system officials deal with Aboriginals in an exceptionally harsh fashion. Neither position is true.

As part of a review of Western Australia's Child Welfare Act, Professor Eric Edwards (1982) stated in his report that:

Calculated from the 1976 Census statistics the total of all children in the 10-11 year-old age groups in Western Australia is 210,584. The total of the Aboriginals in the same group is 6,701 (3.18%). The total number of offenses shown in the Children's Court statistics for 1980—81 is 14,532; of these, 4,721 (32.49%) are heard against Aboriginals. (Part 3, p. 37)

This calculation demonstrates Aboriginal youths were over-represented in Western Australia's juvenile criminal statistics by a factor of ten. In the adult system, a similar situation obtains. A study by Martin and Newby (1984) states:

The fact of excessive Aboriginal involvement in criminal law in Australia is well known; in W.A. the issue is particularly acute, with approximately a third of prison inmates and a fifth of court charges in any one year being drawn from an Aboriginal minority of 2.5% of the state population. (p. 295)

Some clue . . . to the reasons for this over-representation is offered by Martin and Newby's cross-tabulation of offense type and race on data taken from adult courts in seven towns in Western Australia.

They found that more than two-thirds of Aborigines were convicted of offenses against 'good order,' an offense usually arising from and defined by police presence and action. This issue will be taken up later in the paper.

The ethnic bias of Western Australia's criminal statistics is reflected in every other Australian state. In the 'welfare' sector, Aboriginal children are grossly over-represented in the care statistics. Stewart Murray (1984) shows that in 1974, 323 of Victoria's 3,107 Aboriginal children under age 18 were state wards. Murray calculates that effectively 9.6% of Aboriginal children in the state were in care, a rate . . . 16–20 times higher than that of non-Aboriginal children' (p. 81).

The . . . relationship of Aboriginal Australians and the Australian State offers a partial explanation of these statistics. In 1978, the Aboriginal population of Australia was estimated at 240,000 of which 7.4% lived in urban settings, 16% were settled on farms, 13.5 lived in 'outstations' (agricultural settlements) and the majority, 63.1%, lived in Aboriginal communities in remote parts of the state. These figures produced by the House of Representatives Standing Committee on Aboriginal Affairs show Aboriginal 'crime' is predominantly rural. It is likely very remote communities which rarely see white people or police officers will produce less 'crime'.

. . . [When] Australia was *founded* as a penal colony in New South Wales in 1788, *all* land was declared British territory. The British deployed the legal doctrine of *terra nullis* (empty earth) and the natives were

seen as savages to be exterminated. MacIlvanie (1984) points out that:

The Aborigines were simply relegated to the status of 'non-residents'. With their right to land ignored, and all land deemed to be vested in the Crown, a well concentrated—and British orchestrated—process of dispossession continued as 'settlement' extended. Massacres by soldiers, settlers and police are well recorded and while Aborigines fought a strong war of resistance, by 1860 the ongoing process and pattern of dispossession had been virtually completed. The establishment of the mounted police in 1825 marked a new era in Aboriginal/police relations. Assembled as a protecting force against escaped convicts, they were soon to become involved in violent confrontation with the Aboriginal population while performing tasks undertaken by the army in other frontier situations. The dual—yet entirely contradictory—roles of the police became those of 'protection' and 'prosecution'. Under the rule of law and in the guise of authority they became the force of dispossession, the dispensers of summary justice and, on many occasions, the instigators of massacre. (p. 118)

This 'dual role' has characterised police interactions with Aboriginals since that time. From the 1870s onwards, legislation was passed protecting Aboriginals from European predation. Ironically, protective legislation also increased police powers over Aboriginals. The 1909 Aborigines Protection act . empowered the police to decide where Aboriginals should live. As McIlvanie (1984) points out:

. . . They—and not the individual Aborigine—became the judge as to whether that person was, in fact, an Aboriginal person. According to the quantum of 'black' blood coursing through the veins of an Aborigine, he/she would be moved out of town and indeed out of the district. In addition, the police had the power to remove Aboriginal children from their parents if, in their opinion such children were seen to be in need of 'white' care and protection. (p. 119)

. . . The power to remove children in need of care and protection passed from the police to newly established social welfare agencies during the 1960s. These agencies also assumed many of the 'protection' functions of the old Aboriginal Protection Board of the 1920s and the Aboriginal Welfare Board in the post World War II period. . . .

History is nevertheless only one dimension of explanation. Another lies in the traditional Aboriginal modalities of social control which conflict with European-style criminal law and its administration.

TRADITIONAL SELF-REGULATION WITHIN ABORIGINAL COMMUNITIES

Until the British invasion . . . a number of mechanisms operated within Aboriginal communities which permitted self-regulation. Amongst more traditional tribal Aboriginals many of these regulations still exist although they have come under increasing strain since the 1960s. Self-regulation takes a number of forms. First, it operates as a result of the recognition of a *common* interest. Second, the regulations are transmitted by the socialisation of children, the use of myth, religious belief and tribal ritual. Third, the distribution of power and control within the tribe locates authority within particular kinship structures.

These prerequisites for self-regulation have been undermined by the impact of a European society and culture. In traditional Aboriginal societies, children were socialised by the women on food-gathering expeditions. These trips often took lengthy periods and the children were taught the rules through the medium of myth, magic and tribal lore. Under these circumstances, the imposition of a European type shop, or village or community store has the effect of eradicating the traditional system of socialisation. The imposition of European-model schools completes the destruction. Adults are left without a mechanism for socialisation. Children do not learn tribal lore. Adults then interpret delinquency not as a *failure* of socialisation and something for which they are responsible, but a result of children having 'no ears' (ears being at the centre of understanding), or 'no shame'. As Brady (1985) points out:

In this way, the Aboriginal conceptualisation of the degree of responsibility possessed by children for their actions *preludes* the possibility of influencing or diverting their actions. A child cannot be responsible if he or she has no understanding. Parents would shrug and say 'he can't listen.'

. . . Unsurprisingly, in the eyes of European police officers and welfare officials, Aboriginal parents appear inadequate and their children out of control.

Law enforcement in traditional Aboriginal societies occurred through kinship and tribal structures. People's interactions were determined by the status attendant on membership. The idea of judgment or punishment emanating beyond these boundaries was unthinkable.

Since traditional Aboriginal communities did not use money, live in houses or stay in the same place, the dispositions of bail, fines, incarceration and probation have no Aboriginal equivalent. Sanctions imposed within the kinship system, were swift and immediate. These might include physical punishment ranging from a single blow, through spearing to execution. More usually public denunciation was used.

Ironically, public denunciation as a sanction represents a way Australian criminal laws cut across traditional Aboriginal custom and create criminalisation. Writing of Aboriginals in the Kimberley Region of Western Australia, Syddall (1984) says Aboriginals still use the 'public harangue' frequently:

If a person feels aggrieved he will 'growl' his victim in the presence of other members of the community and cut him down to size. The pub, is the obvious place to do this especially when alcohol has raised memories of hurts—real or imaginary. Quarrelsome behavior is, of course, in European terms disorderly conduct and arrest and imprisonment often follow for doing what, in his eyes, is his right. (p. 135)

Syddall gives another example of how traditional Aboriginal behavior aimed at regulating social conduct is *criminalised* by European law with his reference to women undressing and standing naked between two men engaged in conflict. Since Aboriginal law requires males to avoid naked females, the fight inevitably ends. Such public nakedness is however an offense against 'good order.' Traditional Aboriginal penalties which involve striking one blow are also offenses against criminal laws. Even the procedures of European law courts violate Aboriginal tradition. Syddall comments:

Avoidance rules make courts difficult to run when a witness is not permitted to look at a defendant and, unless one is aware of this, a man's credit may be doubted. Again, the name of a deceased person can not be mentioned and a witness may refuse to look at a photograph of a deceased. Sometimes people will plead guilty rather than have a matter go to trial and run the risk of revealing tribal secrets or of repeating words which provoked an assault. (p. 137)

The impact of imprisonment on Aboriginals is more serious than for whites. Aboriginal life is tied up with tribe, with the land and with custom. At a stroke, prison deprives black Australians of virtually every experience which serves to maintain and reinforce their sense of self. Mention has already been made of the fundamental nature of kinship in traditional Aboriginal society. Similarly, avoidance (not looking at someone, not speaking to someone) is an important part of social interactions, which in part is defined by kinship. Unfortunately Aboriginals can be placed together in police or prison cells, or made to undertake tasks together when kinship rules dictate such proximity is not possible. Consequently they may fail to work or disobey orders.

Non-custodial sentences which involve elements of supervision are also problematic. Probation, parole and bail procedures usually involve conditions with regards to accommodation (living in a place with a specific address), employment and associations. In more remote Aboriginal communities these matters are impossible to supervise since Aboriginals are not likely to have an address in the conventional sense. Employment more often than not is out of the question and it is

difficult to have any control or . . . supervision over someone's associates. . . .

THE RESPONSE OF AUSTRALIAN CRIMINAL JUSTICE

A number of measures have been introduced into Australian criminal justice systems in an attempt to contain some of the effects of Eurocentric criminal justice practices at state and Federal levels.

The most prominent recent Federal initiative was the establishment of the Aboriginal Legal Service, which has had a marked impact on levels of legal representation. Eggleston (1976) claimed that in 1975, in South Australia, Aboriginals were two and a half times less likely to be legally represented than were whites. However, Sutton (1984) shows that by 1982, . . . more than 80 per cent of Aboriginal defendants facing charges requiring more than one hearing, and 34 per cent of those with a single appearance, had a lawyer. This compared with 77.5% and 26.3% for all others (p. 365).

Another important Federal development has been the enquiry into the recognition of Aboriginal customary law, by the Australian Law Reform Commission. This enquiry has produced a number of research and discussion papers. These papers begin with a recognition that the problem is a justice system which might be described as Eurocentric. The papers suggest a radical approach, which involves . . . looking at mechanisms whereby 'customary law defence' can be incorporated into the relevant criminal statutes.

However, it is clear from the conflicts between criminal justice agents and Aboriginals that many of the difficulties lie outside the realm of the 'fit' between the criminal law and tribal custom. Many conflicts centre on questions of 'good order'. These offenses involve a wide range of behaviors including drunkenness, brawling, using insulting words, vagrance and general 'misconduct'. They can be situations in which there may be no complaint from the public or even a victim in the conventional sense. They are very much 'police defined.' This suggests the problem is more one of criminal justice *practice* than of law. When a Department for Community Welfare official asked about police/Aboriginal relationships, the senior police officer in a Western Australian country town replied starkly 'they are the enemy.' It demonstrates endemic police racism is a factor which must be taken seriously.

In Western Australia, 'Aboriginal Aids' have been appointed as assistants to the police but police/Aboriginal relationships are such that the status enjoyed by aids within their own communities is not always high. It does however represent a step forward, since the police have been prepared to employ members of the minority group, in recognition of the conflicts. The Department for Community Welfare in that state has taken a range of steps in the areas of de-institutionalisation of juvenile offenders and community work. Since 1978, many Aboriginal youths committed to the care of the Department have been kept out of institutional care and have been sent to live with Aboriginal communities in remote areas. In addition, many Department officials have begun to work to minimise state control of Aboriginals. There is also a policy of employing Aboriginals as field and residential workers. The agency recognises that much of the child welfare legislation and child care practices of the past created wholesale institutionalisation and between 1983 and 1985 a significant number of youth correctional institutions were closed.

Despite these practices however, Aboriginals remain grossly over-represented in police arrest figures. A study by Gale (1985) in South Australia identifies race as a factor in determining police decisions in respect of arresting juvenile offenders, but she discovered that the single most important factor was unemployment:

In fact unemployment was found to have a predictive value ten times that of Aboriginality alone. Thus we concluded that a higher proportion of Aboriginal youth were being arrested, not just because they were Aboriginal but because a greater percentage of Aborigines were

unemployed. In reaching that conclusion, we are moving out of the arena of individual racism to an analysis of the societal structure or, as it is often expressed, a process of structural racism. (p. 8)

. . . Gale suggests the *welfare* orientation of South Australian juvenile justice discriminates against unemployed youth.

While the problems Australian Aborigines encounter with criminal justice systems may constitute one extreme example of the over-representation of ethnic minorities in prisons and institutions, Australian legal reformers, welfare workers and researchers are going to considerable lengths to come to grips with the issues. Their efforts may [offer] important lessons for those concerned with the way all criminal justice systems discriminate against such minorities. . . .

REFERENCES

Brady, M. (1985) 'Aboriginal youth and the juvenile justice system', in: A. Borowski and J. Murray (Eds.), *Juvenile Delinquency in Australia*, Sydney Methuen.

Edwards, E. (1982) *The Treatment of Juvenile Offenders* (A Study of the treatment of juvenile offenders in Western Australia as part of an overall review of the Child Welfare Act), Perth: Department of Community Welfare.

Eggleston, E. (1976) *Fear, Favour or Affection: Aborigines and the Criminal Law in Victoria, South Australia and Western Australia*, Canberra: A.N.U. Press.

Gale, F. (1985) *Aboriginal Youth and the Law: Problems of Equity and Justice for Black Minorities*, London: Australian Studies Centre, University of London.

McIlvanie, C. (1984) 'The struggle for law: Aboriginal-police relations and the role of the magistrates' court, North West New South Wales', in: B. Swanton (Ed.), *Aborigines and Criminal Justice*, Canberra: Australian Institute of Criminology.

Martin, M. and Newby, L. (1984) 'Aborigines in summary courts in Western Australia, a regional study: preliminary report on selected findings', in: B. Swanton (Ed.), *Aborigines and Criminal Justice*, Canberra: Australian Institute of Criminology.

Murray, S. (1984) 'Aboriginal children and youth in care', in: B. Swanton (Ed.), *Aborigines and Criminal Justice*, Canberra: Australian Institute of Criminology.

Sutton, A. (1984) 'Crime statistics relating to Aboriginal people in South Australia', in: B. Swanton (Ed.), *Aborigines and Criminal Justice*, Canberra: Australian Institute of Criminology.

Syddall, T. (1984) 'Aborigines and the courts', in: B. Swanton (Ed.), *Aborigines and Criminal Justice*, Canberra: Australian Institute of Criminology.

NOTES

1. Australians do not necessarily use the word 'black' as opposed to 'Aboriginal'.

Section Review

Discussion Questions

1. The "people's kitchens" described by Andreas are not at all common in North America. Speculate on why this is the case?
2. The "animators" who worked in villages described by Ravindran came from similar social backgrounds to people actually living in the villages. Discuss the pros and cons of this approach.
3. Why isn't there more affordable housing available to the very poor in North America? Discuss, with a particular emphasis on power distributions.
4. Is there a difference between "everyday resistance" and "deviance"? Indicate why you agree or disagree with Kerkvliet's analysis.
5. The excerpt by Renzetti and Curran suggests that gender equality calls for more than political will and fair laws. Discuss this observation.
6. There are higher crime rates among Native Americans, compared with whites, just as there are among aboriginal peoples compared with the majority group in Australia. Would you explain the North American pattern the same way as Thorpe has explained the Australian pattern? Why, or why not?

Data Collection Exercises

1. Kerkvliet does not produce much data to support his view that unorganized, individual acts of protest can be effective forms of "resistance." Indicate how we could go about testing this view.
2. Interview the administrators of any agency serving the poor in your community or region, as Fabricant did. Identify what aspects of empowerment of the poor are involved in this agency's activities.

3. The women in Ravindran's study often had very poor information about sex, birth, and health. What about women in North America? Consult some data to find out whether North American women have accurate information on these topics. How is information on sex and health distributed and controlled here?
4. Collect some information on homelessness in your country. Is it increasing or decreasing, and why?

Writing Exercises

1. Comparisons can be drawn between the untouchables of India and the homeless of North America, but the two categories of people are also very different. Write a brief (500-word) essay on the differences, and on the reasons why comparisons should be made with great caution.
2. Ravindran's article reminds us that information about health may be one of the most important scarce and unequally distributed resources among women in society. Discuss the issue in a brief (500-word) paper.
3. Women are taught economically peripheral skills in this country, as in Guinea (see Renzetti and Curran's excerpt), although not to the same extent. Write a brief (500-word) essay on why there is this difference.
4. In a short (500-word) essay, speculate on whether much of the deviance described by Thorpe is "individual resistance" as described by Kerkvliet. Say why it is, or is not.

PART III

INTRODUCTION
TO STATUS INEQUALITY

Status Inequality and Its Sources

The introduction to Part II argued that domination and submission are symbolized in a variety of ways. The symbols range from the tangible to the intangible, and the material to the behavioral. These **symbols of domination** are part of the apparatus of legitimation that keeps power relations just the way they are from year to year, decade to decade, even century to century. People who "have" set themselves off from "have-nots" through actions that create exclusion, decoupling, disability, and scarcity. They do this to protect their interests, and to "demonstrate" their advantage.

For example, many social roles require us to wear particular clothing (uniforms) and act in a particular way. The military is an obvious example; here, the uniform indicates each individual's rank and the deference (obedience and respect) he/she is owed. Another example is the hospital, in which the outfits worn by doctors, nurses, orderlies, and patients are all clearly different and instantly recognizable. Even where people do not wear uniforms, they are likely to use other symbols to show their status. The corner office, Rolex watch, expensive German car, in-ground swimming pool; these are all accepted and widely understood symbols of high status and success in our society.

We all understand these symbols of status and power and consciously try to use them to our advantage. This is why people go out and buy Rolex watches and expensive business suits. But often we are not aware of what we are accepting when we "buy into" these symbols of domination and submission, for there is an underlying message that is evident when we analyze the *kind* of symbols we use, and the ways we use them.

Then it becomes clear that our North American culture has come to embrace a particular notion of success: namely, success is macho, sexy, tough, and not necessarily moral. Our culture dresses up domination to make it seem fun and sexy. There can be no doubt that, in our society, dominance is equated with success, and with masculine qualities such as toughness. In our society, domination is not regarded as a moral issue: It is viewed like success in a contest—even a sport.

Efforts to create equality will mean changing these kinds of views: questioning, for example, whether domination equals success, and whether "success" really demands a masculine approach and imagery. It will also mean challenging people's beliefs and prejudices—especially their readiness to disrespect and hold negative, hostile attitudes toward members of other groups.

People belonging to different **social statuses** in a society not only receive different amounts of respect and deference: they also live in different ways. The first sociologist to get interested in lifestyle and its social meaning was Max Weber. Weber showed that the ways people spend money and time together are a basis for both social integration *and* social exclusion (Weber, 1986).

A second group of sociologists interested in lifestyle focus on the social and emotional content of "community life." This stream of thinking begins with the German sociologists Ferdinand Tönnies (1957) and Georg Simmel (1950), and is picked up later by the Chicago school of sociology (including Louis Wirth and his disciples).

Both groups depart from the thinking of Karl Marx, who had argued that economic and class relations determine all other social relations. For his part, Weber believed that social organization rests on a triad of principles: economic (or class), political (or party), and status group. People have economic and political allegiances, to be sure, but they also belong to *status groups* that influence their view of life and their behavior. These status groups do not always organize people vertically—the way we now think of "social status"; they organize people horizontally, too, in well-defined groups.

A person's status group might be organized around ethnic, religious, or racial differences from the rest of society, or around other symbolic and noneconomic principles. What is important—what defines a status group—is its degree of **commensalism:** literally, the degree to which its members eat together, or more generally share daily activities and a common world view. A status group in Weber's terminology would today be called a **subculture** or **lifestyle.** When we study the common behaviors of that group, we are studying a common lifestyle.

When people share a subculture, or lifestyle, they form a community. Community ties anchor people emotionally. Without them, people often suffer from isolation and "anomie," such as Durkheim (1951) discussed in his famous work on suicide. So even trivial things like where you eat and who you eat with, where you live (what neighborhood), who you do leisure activities with, and so on, can have an important symbolic, social, and emotional value in modern society. These are things that tie people together in social groups.

However, lifestyles not only tie people together but also push people apart. Thorstein Veblen's *Theory of the Leisure Class* (1934) shows how lifestyles can come to define exclusive group boundaries. The very rich invent ways of consuming their wealth that are "conspicuously wasteful" in order to clearly define who is part of the group and who is not.

By their nature, lifestyles of the rich and famous are limited to a very few; no one else can afford them. Moreover, people with the most wealth continue to invent ever newer forms of **conspicuous consumption** to delimit the boundaries of the **leisure class..** To be a member, you must have enough time and money to keep up with an endless, changing stream of fashions in conspicuous waste; you must also want to try.

Not all status groups test their candidates this rigorously to determine who is part of the group and who is not. But in practice, lifestyle behaviors, including consumption patterns, *always* distinguish insiders from outsiders. This is the reason sociologists have long claimed that you can tell a person's social position from his or her living room. Living-room furnishings display both the "taste" (hence, status group background) and pretensions (or desired status group affiliation) of the householder. (For a humorous update of living-room assessment, see Fussell, 1983.)

And since they have a hand in creating the boundaries, members of a subculture can read the status signals a person gives off. This fact is demonstrated in community studies conducted by Chicago sociologist Lloyd Warner and his students (see, for example, Davis, Gardner, & Gardner, 1941; Warner, Meeker & Eells, 1960). In one community after another, researchers found community members could easily sort local townspeople into status groups based on reputation.

When people do this task, they regularly identify the same numbers of distinct status groups and sort people into groups in similar ways. Moreover, they tell researchers similar things about the characteristics of each grouping: for example, how "upper-upper-class" people differ from "lower-upper-class" people. Thus, status groups, their membership, and behaviors appropriate to members, are all well known to people who live in small, stable communities.

In large, new, and transient communities the boundaries of status groups are harder to specify. As well, their membership, large and constantly turning over, is harder to agree on (Jaher, 1982). That is why, in large fluid communities, people rely more on visible behaviors to communicate their actual or intended status. Their behaviors not only signal who they think they are or want to be taken for, but also what kinds of people they want to interact with, and in what ways.

This is the reason why people—especially young city people—wear clothing with the designer labels prominently displayed: for example, Polo, Roots, Club Monaco, and so on. Or they wear clothing and hairstyles that convey a point of view: for example, punk versus "preppy." Increasingly, people spend their time and money to communicate who they are and who they want to be. In this way, they make themselves into a visible community within a larger society.

Consequences of Status Inequality: Stereotyping, Distance, and Discrimination

Groups with low status in our society—people who receive less than average respect and deference, and live in a way that people view as "lower class"—tend to suffer from discrimination, and they are often stereotyped by the popular culture. In fact, stereotyping, social distance, and discrimination are three ways in which people maintain status inequalities between men and women, whites and nonwhites, poor people and rich people.

Stereotypes are fixed, unchanging mental images of what is believed to characterize all members of a given group. When we stereotype people, we categorize them without regard to their actual characteristics. So, for example, if we equate success with dominance, and dominance with masculinity and toughness, we are stereotyping women as losers: They do not have what you need to succeed in life. Making this prejudgment is likely to lead men to exclude women from important roles in society, and to treat women with disrespect, even contempt. To the extent that women "buy" this evaluation, it is disabling.

Likewise, perceiving some ethnic or racial groups as possessing less valuable qualities leads to less respect and more discrimination. Consider the study by Berry et al (1977), which gave respondents in a national survey a list of Canadian ethnic groups and asked them to judge how "hardworking," "important," "Canadian," "likable," "clean," and "interesting" each ethnic group is. The respondents readily (with very few "don't knows") evaluated ethnic groups on these dimensions.

The results showed Canada's earliest settlers—the Anglo-Saxons and French—topped the list with the most desirable qualities: most likable, cleanest, most hardworking, and so on. Next came the Northern Europeans (Dutch, Scandinavian, Belgian), then Eastern Europeans (Hungarian, Polish, Jewish, Czechoslovakian, Russian, Yugoslavian, Ukrainian), then Southern Europeans (Italian, Portuguese, Spanish, Greek). *Least* clean, likable, hardworking and so on were the visible minorities—Canadian Indians, blacks, and East Indians—at least according to these respondents.

Some people think that racial and ethnic stereotyping has declined in the past 50 years in North America. More likely, stereotyping and prejudice still go on, but prejudiced people are more embarrassed to admit to their beliefs today. This is what some of the following excerpts suggest.

Another consequence of stereotyping and prejudice is the creation of "social distance" between groups that hold different amounts of respect for one another. **Social distance** is a measure of the amount of interaction between people who belong to groups that have unequal status.

A lot is known about patterns of social distance as a result of research based on a procedure developed by E. S. Bogardus. This measure asks people how close they would be willing to have members of a particular ethnic or racial group be—for example, Armenians. It asks respondents to answer questions like this: "Would you admit an Armenian . . .

1. to close kinship by marriage?
2. to your club as a personal friend?
3. to your street as a neighbor?
4. to employment in your occupation?
5. to citizenship in your country?
6. as a visitor only to your country?
7. or would you exclude him or her from your country?

The smallest social distance is marriage into your family: "How would you feel if your sister married an Armenian?" for example. People of widely different backgrounds—different income, regional, educational, occupational, and even ethnic groups—typically answer these questions in the same ways: That is, they value people like themselves more highly than others do, but they value the descendants of the oldest immigrant groups most highly.

So, for example, a Canadian study (Mackie, 1974) found respondents put white native-born Canadians and Anglo-Saxons at the least social distance, followed closely by Northern Europeans and French Canadians, then Eastern Europeans, and finally visible minorities—in descending order, Chinese, Japanese, West Indians, Eskimos, East Indians, Native Indians, and finally Metis (descendants of native/French Canadian marriages). The average respondent wanted twice as much social distance from a visible minority person as he/she wanted from a white Anglo-Saxon.

As noted, there is some variation in the results depending on who is doing the rating. Typically, people rate their own ethnic group higher on the list—indicating less social distance—than someone outside the group would do. For example, black respondents are more willing to have blacks up close than whites respondents are. Except for that, people rate ethnic groups in very similar ways. For example, Portuguese-Canadians want as much distance from Chinese- or Pakistani-Canadians as English- or French-Canadians do.

So majority opinion has a great influence, and people's *own* experiences of stereotyping and exclusion teach them nothing about other people's qualities and needs for acceptance.

Prejudice and social distance are naturally linked to **discrimination**. All of us discriminate in favor of some things and against others. As human beings, we all have people we like and people we dislike; people for whom we feel empathy and others for whom we feel antipathy. The danger occurs when we put these feelings of preference into action; for example, when a teacher gives a student he doesn't like an unfairly lower grade. That is discrimination.

Discrimination can take a variety of forms: job segregation, unequal pay for equal work, or a denial of promotion, for example. Often, acts of discrimination are very subtle and hard to see. However, there is plenty of evidence that the members of some ethnic and racial groups take advantage of others.

A study by Henry and Ginzberg (1985) showed the extent of racial discrimination in employment by conducting field experiments in a large North American city. In one set of experiments, the researchers sent two job applicants to apply for the same job. They were identical with respect to age, sex, education, experience, style of dress, and personality and differed in only one respect: one was white and the other, black. In all, teams of applicants sought a total of 201 jobs in this way. With the data they collected, Henry and Ginzberg conclude that "The overall Index of Discrimination is therefore 3 to 1. Whites have three job prospects to every one that Blacks have."

No less serious than such intentional discrimination is what is called **systemic or institutional discrimination**. This is largely unintended discrimination that is so deeply embedded in a society's institutions and customs that it is hard to recognize. Consider, for example, the height requirement for police officers and firefighters. Because northern racial and ethnic groups tend to be taller, this rule will discriminate against southern applicants. The taken-for grantedness of this height requirement is a main cause of the problem. Once people realize that such a rule is unnecessary—that shorter people can do just as good a job—the racial discrimination often disappears.

Different kinds of discrimination produce different kinds of "isms" **racism, sexism, age-ism**. So far, there is no "ism" term to describe prejudice and discrimination that is leveled against people simply because they are poor. Such prejudice flows from the stereotypes examined in the Texas study—the ideas that poor people lack drive, have loose morals, drink too much, squander their money, and are lazy.

What we call *racism* is racial discrimination carried to an extreme; it flows from the belief that one's own racial group is the measure of human perfection, and all other groups fall short. But racism is not simply ignorance: It also keeps the powerful in power. All stereotyping, social distance, and discrimination tends to serve the interests of the powerful by maintaining the status quo. Where racism is concerned, Li (1991:270) notes that "there is a close relationship between labor exploitation and the division of people into races (giving superficial physical traits social meanings). Over time, the cultural and physical characteristics of a subordinate group become inseparable from its work role and its subservient position."

So racism has the effect of seeming to justify one group's exploitation of another group. Members of the dominant, exploiting group blame the misfortunes of the subordinate group on such supposed racial characteristics as laziness, stupidity, aggressiveness, or bad cultural values.

However, the **split labor market model** of ethnic conflict claims that the source of antagonism is not race and ethnicity, but differences in the price of labor between two groups that are often divided along racial and ethnic lines. . . .

The emergence of a split labor market is related to two conditions, both of which arose from the development of capitalism in Western Europe. The first was the rise in labor cost of white workers, and the second was the availability of non-white labor from Third World countries as imperialism accelerated their underdevelopment (Li, op. cit,).

By this reasoning, a competition for scarce jobs, income, and housing is the true cause of most racism, so racist attitudes are most acute during times of economic hardship. That's when minority groups are likely to be seen as competitors, taking away jobs from white Anglo-Saxon males. At times like that—in fact, at times like today—the competition for available jobs often surfaces as interethnic (or racial or gender) conflict.

People with the most intense racist feelings are often people who stand to lose the most if the targets of their racism achieve equal status. Low-status members of the dominant cultural group—"poor whites"—are the people who are threatened most by economic competition from blacks and Asians (and women). But racism not only harms the minority group. It also destroys the unity of working people by drawing their attention away from economic exploitation, and focusing their attention on ethnic differences. So, one of the effects of racism is to strengthen the position of employers.

Racism may develop out of a need to justify the exploitation of another group, but it does not simply disappear after the conditions that gave rise to it disappear. Racist attitudes and beliefs pass from generation to generation, through the process of socialization. These ideas are learned at a very young age, so they seem "natural" to the people who hold them. People learn to look for evidence that confirms their attitudes and ignore evidence that does not—a practice psychologists call the **confirmation bias**.

In the end, the exploitation that caused inequality in the first place is legitimated by "evidence" of the senses. Creating equality will mean breaking down these tendencies to derogate and isolate certain groups of people for reasons of their race, gender, or class at birth.

It will be clear from the above discussion that we have returned to the four supporting mechanisms of social inequality. The process of stereotyping and its consequences in discriminatory behavior and practices of social distance are examples of the *mechanisms* of social inequality with which we began in the introduction.

Whenever race, gender, or social class groupings develop status consciousness—come to see themselves and their interests as different from those of others—they are on their way to producing, as consequences, the mechanism of inequality. There generally follows some form of social exclusion and decoupling of the less advantaged outgroup, disabling of the outgroup, and attempts to control scarce economic and power resources. The excerpts in Part III will show that these processes occur in a wide variety of societies for racial and ethnic groups, social classes, and genders.

References

Berry, J. W., R. Kalin, and D. W. Taylor (1977). *Multiculturalism and Ethnic Attitudes in Canada*. Ottawa: Ministry of Supply and Services Canada.

Bogardus, E. S. (1959). *Social Distance*. Yellow Springs, Ohio: Antioch College Press.

Davis, A., B. Gardner, and M. Gardner (1941). *Deep South: A Social Anthropological Study of Caste and Class*. Chicago: University of Chicago Press.

Durkheim, E. (1951). *Suicide: A Study of Sociology*. J. Spaulding and G. Simpson (Trans.) New York: Free Press (original work published, 1897).

Fussell, P. (1983). *Class*. New York: Ballantine Books.

Henry, F. and E. Ginzberg (1985). *Who Gets the Work?* Toronto: Urban Alliance on Race Relations and the Social Planning Council.

Jaher, G. C. (1982). *The Urban Establishment: Upper Strata in Boston, New York, Charleston, Chicago, and Los Angeles*. Urbana: University of Illinois.

Li, P. (1991). "Race and ethnic relations," Pp. 257–286 in L. Tepperman and R. J. Richardson (eds.) *The Social World: An Introduction to Sociology*. Toronto: McGraw–Hill Ryerson.

Mackie, M. (1974) "Ethnic stereotypes and prejudice: Alberta Indians, Hutterites, and Ukrainians" *Canadian Ethnic Studies* 10, 118-129.

Simmel, G. (1950). *The Sociology of Georg Simmel* (Trans. Kurt Wolff). New York: Free Press.

Tonnies, F. (1957). *Community and Society*. East Lansing: Michigan State University Press.

Veblen, T. (1934). *Theory of the Leisure Class*. New York: Modern Library.

Warner, L. W., M. Meeker, and K. Eells (1960). *Social Class in America*. New York: Modern Library.

Weber, M. (1968). *Economy and Society*. New York: Bedminster Press.

Suggested Readings for Part III

Anderson, Margaret C. and Patricia Hall Collins (1992). *Race, Class and Gender: An Anthology*. Belmont, CA: Wadsworth. *A rich array of feminist scholarship, focused around, but not limited to, U.S. examples of race, class, and gender phenomena.*

Badinter, Elizabeth (1981). *Mother Love: Myth and Reality*. New York: Macmillan. *This book challenges the belief that mothers have some sort of instinct that better equips them to be caretakers of infants, a role they perform in most societies. It argues that "maternal love" is a historically and culturally conditioned concept.*

Lane, David (1982). *The End of Social Inequality? Class, Status and Power Under State Socialism*. London: Allen and Unwin. *A detailed analysis of the three forms of inequality in socialist countries.*

Sennett, Richard and J. Cobb (1973). *The Hidden Injuries of Class*. New York: Vintage. *An interview study, with provocative interpretation, on how people come to grips with the fact that they are at the bottom of the community's status and class structures.*

Steinberg, Stephen (1981). *The Ethnic Myth*. Boston: Beacon Press. *The author provides a careful historical analysis of the evaluation of blacks, and of institutional racism, in the United States.*

Van den Berghe, Pierre L. (1981). *The Ethnic Phenomenon*. New York: Elsevier. *This volume contains a wealth of comparative data, from several societies, on racial and ethnic stratification.*

Vanneman, Reeve and Lynn Nebber Cannon (1987). *The American Perception of Class*. Philadelphia: Temple University Press. *A summary of evidence on awareness of class and status dimensions. It argues that many people are conscious of inequality and discontented with it, and they reject the ideology that there is open opportunity.*

Veblen, Thorstein (1934). *The Theory of the Leisure Class*. New York: Modern Library. *The author develops a theory of how and why people of advantaged status "display" their status.*

Vorst, Jesse et al., eds. (1991). *Race, Class, Gender: Bonds and Barriers*. Toronto: Garamond Press. *Eleven authors try to clarify the relationship between race, class, and gender, with an emphasis on the possibilities for breaking down the barriers of inequality.*

Wolf, Eric (1982). *Europe and the People Without History*. Berkeley: University of California Press. *A sweeping worldwide perspective on how expanding European capitalism, and colonialism, affected precapitalist societies, including their structures of status, class, and power.*

SECTION SEVEN
Patterns of Status Inequality

7.1 Class and Status Hierarchies in Japan

Hiroshi Ishida

Among other things, lower-class people are typically granted low status—little prestige or deference—in the community. For example, the following excerpt by Ishida examines the connection between social class and social status in Japan and the United States (see also, e.g., the following excerpt by Sawinski and Domanski). Ishida finds that in the middle class there is less connection between income and status, but at the ends of the continuum—among the rich and poor—there is a strong connection.

Among the middle classes in modern societies, status distinctions get blurred. Many middle-class people can afford to own a nice home or complete a college education. Their lives are not dramatically different from those of people who earn half as much or twice as much money as they do.

But the wealthiest people are very different from the poorest. People with a lot of money tend to live very well indeed and receive a lot of status and deference, while people with very little money are held in low regard. This is, of course, part of the process of social exclusion of the poor and lower classes.

INTRODUCTION

This paper addresses the issue of the relationship between class structure and status hierarchies in contemporary Japan. . . . This paper will empirically examine four hypotheses related to the relationship between class structure and various dimensions of status hierarchies (such as hierarchy in occupational status, or education, or income). These hypotheses are called the status homogeneity hypothesis, the bipolarity hypothesis, the status inconsistency hypothesis, and the dual structure hypothesis.

The homogeneity hypothesis derives from the work of Murakami (1977; 1984), a theoretical economist, who argued for the emer-

Excerpted from Ishida, Hiroshi (1989), "Class structure and status hierarchies in contemporary Japan," *European Sociological Review*, 5(1), May, 65–80. With permission of Oxford University Press.

gence of 'the new middle mass'. . . . The hypothesis is that the status composition of different classes will be highly homogeneous.

. . . According to the bipolarity hypothesis, the distribution of status characteristics is polarised along the lines of the ownership of the means of production, forming two extremes of capitalists and workers. Therefore, this hypothesis predicts that with respect to their status attributes classes are divided into two basic groups. . . . The status inconsistency hypothesis predicts that status characteristics of classes are inconsistent so that classes cannot be characterised by consistently high or low status attributes.

Finally, the dual structure hypothesis emphasises the importance of firm size in the labour market stratification of employees (cf. Koike, 1988). . . . According to the dual structure hypothesis, employees in large firms will tend to show more favourable status attributes than those in small and medium-sized firms, even though they belong to the same class.

In order to examine these hypotheses empirically, this paper will analyse the distribution of various status characteristics—occupational prestige, education, income, home ownership, and stock investment—among classes. A similar analysis will be performed on an American data set to provide a comparative reference.

DATA AND VARIABLES

The Japanese data set used in this study comes from the 1975 Social Stratification and Mobility National Survey (hereafter called SSM). The 1975 SSM is based on a sample consisting of men between the ages of 20 and 69 residing in Japan in 1975. The data were collected in personal interviews and follow-ups, and the usable sample size was 2724.

The American data set comes from the 1980 Class Structure, Class Biography, and Class Consciousness Survey (hereafter called (CSCC). The data were collected in a national telephone survey conducted by the Survey Research Centre at the University of Michigan, and the usable sample size was 1761 (Wright, 1982; Wright et al., 1982). This study is restricted to the employed male labour force between the ages of 20 and 65. Since the 1975 SSM includes only male respondents, female respondents are excluded from the CSCC. Students, unemployed persons, retirees, and house husbands are also excluded from the analysis reported.[1]

Five different dimensions of status are considered in this study: education, occupational prestige, income, home ownership, and stock investment. Education is measured by years of schooling which range from 0 to 16 or more years. Occupational prestige is represented by the International Occupational Prestige Scores (hereafter IPS) assigned to the respondents' current occupation (Treiman, 1977).[2] Income is the respondents' estimated total annual income in US dollars before tax.[3] Home ownership and stock investment are determined by whether the respondents own their home and have invested in stocks and bonds.[4]

Three additional indicators of status attributes are available in the Japanese survey: land holdings, sports club memberships (for golf, tennis etc.) and air-conditioned homes.

Classes are defined by position in the social relations of production and by marketable skills. . . .

The six classes distinguished—the employer class (which includes owners and members of a board of governors), the petty bourgeoisie, the professional-managerial class, the non-manual working class, the skilled working class, and the non-skilled working class—are constructed using survey items on employment status, managerial status, and occupation.[5]

Finally, the size of the firm in which respondents were employed was distinguished. Respondents employed in a firm with 500 or more employees are classified as employees in a 'large firm'. Public sector employees are also included in the 'large firm' category. Respondents employed in a firm with less than 500 employees are classified as employees in a 'small and medium-sized firm'.[6]

STATUS CHARACTERISTICS OF CLASSES

. . . The composition of classes is examined along the five dimensions of status stratification—education, occupational prestige, income, home ownership, and stock investment. These variables are measured by average years of schooling, average occupational prestige score, average total individual income in dollars, the proportion of individuals owning homes, and the proportion investing in stocks and bonds.

The employer class occupies the most advantageous position in the distribution of resources and rewards in both societies. Its members' incomes and non-pecuniary rewards (home ownership and stock holdings) give them a distinct advantage over other classes. In both societies, the employer class has the highest average income, the highest proportion of stock ownership, and a high proportion of home ownership. In both societies about 80 per cent or more of persons in this class have their own homes and over 40 per cent of them hold stocks. The only exception to their dominant position is in their educational attainment. The employer class in both societies has a lower educational standard than the professional-managerial class and the non-manual class.

The petty bourgeoisie is far less privileged than the employer class in both Japan and the United States. Its members fare better in home ownership (especially in Japan), but their other status characteristics are consistently lower than those of the employer class and are often lower too than those of the professional-managerial class and the non-manual class. Furthermore, the Japanese petty bourgeoisie reveals the lowest level of educational attainment. The low level of average education (9.4 years) and the high rate of home ownership (87 per cent), the two distinctive characteristics of the Japanese petty bourgeoisie, can be in part explained by the fact that this class includes a much larger proportion (50 per cent) of independent farmers than does the American petty bourgeoisie class (16 per cent). When we exclude farmers, the status composition of the Japanese petty bourgeoisie becomes closer to that of its American equivalent.

The professional-managerial class is characterised by high educational achievement and occupational prestige, and to some extent by high income. The American professional-managerial class tends to enjoy these status advantages to a greater degree, since their average education (13.6 years) and prestige score (51) are higher than in the case of their Japanese counterparts (12.1 years and 49, respectively).

The non-manual working class appears to occupy a mid-way position between the professional-managerial class and other working classes in both societies. However, the non-manual class is much closer to the professional-managerial class in level of education. In the United States the non-manual class appears to occupy a more advantageous position than the professional-managerial class in terms of home ownership and investment: 82 per cent of the non-manual class own their homes and 29 per cent hold stocks while the corresponding figures for the professional-

managerial class are 67 per cent and 25 per cent. The Japanese non-manual class, however, is located below the professional-managerial class in all dimensions of status stratification.

The lower status characteristics of the professional-managerial class in the United States is probably due to its age composition. The proportion of the young people in the professional-managerial class is greater than in the non-manual class: the average age of the professional-managerial class is 37 years and the average age of the non-manual class is 42 years.

Finally, the skilled working class and the non-skilled working class constitute the bottom of the status hierarchy in both societies. In particular, these classes are disadvantaged as regards share-holding; only 15 per cent of both skilled and non-skilled workers in Japan owned stocks, as did only 11 per cent of skilled workers and 9 per cent of non-skilled workers in the United States.

Overall, the status composition of classes shows a remarkable resemblance between Japan and the United States. Three important cross-national differences are, however, worth mentioning. First, the American non-skilled working class is particularly disadvantaged in resources and rewards in the labour market: its members' average education, occupational prestige, and income are all far below the averages for the skilled working class. In contrast, in Japan, status differentiation within the manual working classes appears to be minimal.

Secondly, the status advantages of the American employer class are more pronounced than those of the Japanese employer class. . . .

Thirdly, the American non-manual class appears to fare better than its Japanese equivalent. . . .

Table 1 shows the further differentiation among classes in Japan with respect to land holdings, sports club memberships, and air-conditioned homes. . . .

The composition of classes with respect to these three items in Japan resembles the pattern found above. The employer class shows the highest average proportions of sports club memberships and air-conditioned homes and a high proportion of land holding. The petty bourgeoisie is characterised by its high level of land holding while it scores low on the other two items. In contrast, the professional-managerial class and the non-manual class score higher on sports club memberships and air-conditioned homes but lower on land holdings than the petty bourgeoisie. The skilled and non-skilled working classes occupy the most disadvantaged position.

The results do not provide support for the hypothesis of the homogeneity of status characteristics in Japan. . . . Furthermore, there is no evidence that the Japanese classes are more status homogeneous than the American classes. While status differentiation within the manual working classes (skilled and non-skilled) appears to be much smaller in Japan than in the United States, the overall patterns of status composition show a remarkable resemblance.

The bipolarity hypothesis does not receive much support from the findings either. While in both societies the employer class occupies the most advantageous position and the two manual working classes constitute the bottom of status hierarchy, the remaining classes do not show any tendency towards polarization.

CLASS AND STATUS INCONSISTENCY

The issue of status consistency and inconsistency among classes [can be] summarised in five points.

(i) The two manual working classes in both societies score consistently low on all status characteristics.

(ii) The most status inconsistent class is the professional-managerial class. Both in Japan and in the United States, the professional-managerial class scores high on education and occupational prestige while low on home ownership. The fact that a relatively high proportion of the American professional-managerial class do not own a house may reflect the demographic composition of the class. In fact,

Table 1   Distribution (average proportions) of land holding, sports club memberships and air-conditioned homes among classes in Japan [a]

Class	Land holdings	Sports club membership	Air-conditioned homes
Employer	0.714 (0.452)	0.246 (0.432)	0.495 (0.501)
Petty bourgeoisie	0.794 (0.405)	0.026 (0.159)	0.153 (0.360)
Professional and managerial	0.603 (0.490)	0.090 (0.287)	0.240 (0.428)
Non-manual	0.562 (0.497)	0.080 (0.272)	0.195 (0.397)
Skilled	0.462 (0.499)	0.027 (0.161)	0.118 (0.324)
Semi- and non-skilled	0.545 (0.499)	0.023 (0.150)	0.133 (0.340)
Grand mean	0.633 (0.482)	0.077 (0.267)	0.217 (0.412)
ANOVA F-value	27.49	38.95	43.00
p-value	$p < 0.001$	$p < 0.001$	$p < 0.001$
Petty bourgeoisie excluding farmers	0.627 (0.485)	0.038 (0.191)	0.267 (0.443)

Note: [a] Standard deviations are in parentheses.

the proportion of home ownership among the American professional-managerial class jumps from 66.6 to 86.6 per cent when the sample is restricted to men aged 35 and over. This increase is far more dramatic than the increase in, for example, the non-manual class (from 81.5 to 89.9 per cent).

(iii) In both Japan and the United States, the employer class generally occupies the upper end of the status hierarchies.

(iv) A striking cross-national difference can be found in the status composition of the petty bourgeoisie. The Japanese petty bourgeoisie shows a strong tendency towards status inconsistency, while its American counterpart shows a strong tendency towards status consistency. The Japanese petty bourgeoisie occupies the lowest position in the educational hierarchy but shows the highest proportion of home ownership and land holdings. In contrast, the American petty bourgeoisie occupies an average position on all dimensions of status stratification. The exclusion of farmers from the Japanese petty bourgeoisie reduces the tendency of status inconsistency, but the Japanese non-farm proprietors remain more status inconsistent than the American petty bourgeoisie.

(v) The non-manual class also shows cross-national variation, although on a smaller scale. The Japanese non-manual class occupies a slightly below-average position on all dimensions of status, except for educational attainment where it is located at the top of the distribution. In contrast, the American non-manual class fluctuates around the mean status score. Its levels of education, home ownership, and stock holdings are well above the mean, but occupational prestige and income fall below the mean. The status composition of the American non-manual class is thus much more inconsistent than that of its Japanese counterpart.

Table 2 summarises tendencies towards status consistency or inconsistency among the different classes in Japan and the United States. . . .

Overall, our results do not support the statement that the Japanese classes are more status inconsistent than the American classes. This would apply only to the petty bourgeoisie.

At the two extremes of the class structure, that is, among the employers and among the manual working classes status characteristics are either consistently high or consistently low in Japan and the United States alike.

Status inconsistency seems to prevail among the professional-managerial class and to some extent among the non-manual class. . . .

STATUS DIFFERENTIATION BY FIRM SIZE AMONG EMPLOYEES

The dual structure hypothesis predicts that in Japan, workers in large firms will tend to have more advantageous status characteristics than those in small and medium-sized firms even though they occupy the same class positions. Two findings emerge from this study. First, in Japan workers in large firms have higher levels of education, occupational prestige, and income than those in small and medium-sized firms within each class of employee. In addition, among the professional-managerial class and the skilled working class, workers in large firms are more likely to hold stocks than their counterparts in small and medium-sized firms. Firm size appears to be a powerful factor in differentiating employees within classes.

Second, in the United States the differentiation by firm size appears only among the professional-managerial class. Professional and managerial workers who are employed in a large firm have higher levels of education, occupational prestige, income, and home ownership than those who work in a small or medium-sized firm. However, among non-manual, skilled, and non-skilled workers, firm size does not seem to affect the distribution of status characteristics. The only exception is that non-skilled workers who are employed in large firms have a higher average income than those employed in small and medium-sized firms.

There is, therefore, a striking cross-national variation in the role of firm size in explaining differentiation among employees.

Table 2 *Tendencies towards status consistency and inconsistency among different classes in Japan and the United States*

Class	Japan	US
Employer	Consistent	Consistent
Petty bourgeoisie	Strongly inconsistent	Strongly consistent
Professional and managerial	Inconsistent	Strongly inconsistent
Non-manual	Weakly consistent	Inconsistent
Skilled working	Strongly consistent	Consistent
Semi- and non-skilled working	Consistent	Strongly consistent

SUMMARY AND CONCLUSION

This paper has examined the relationship between class structure and status hierarchies in contemporary Japan. The analysis was aimed at testing four hypotheses about the status composition of classes.

The dual structure hypothesis, which focuses upon the internal stratification of employees, has been supported by our analyses. Employees in large firms tend to have more favourable status characteristics than those in small and medium-sized firms even though they occupy the same class positions. The size of the firm where workers are employed appears to be a crucial factor in explaining differentiation among Japanese employees.

The bipolarity and the status inconsistency hypotheses also received partial support from our analysis. Bipolarity in status attributes is evident at the extremes of the Japanese class structure; the employer class occupies the most advantageous positions in the distribution of most status attributes, while the manual working classes are at the bottom of all the status hierarchies.

However, classes which occupy partially dominant and contradictory locations in the social relations of production (Wright, 1979; 1985) tend to show status inconsistency. The professional-managerial class is the most status inconsistent class; it scores very high on education and occupational prestige but low on home ownership. The Japanese petty bourgeoisie also shows a tendency towards status inconsistency.

It can be said, then, that the Japanese class structure is characterised by a combination of polarisation and inconsistency of status characteristics, with a further differentiation among employees by firm size. The American class structure can be characterised by the same combination found in Japan with the notable exception of the differentiation among employees associated with firm size. . . .

The same proportion 47 per cent of the male labour force can be called members of status inconsistent classes in each of the two societies.[7] These results support neither Imada or Hara's (1979) claim that status inconsistency is a generalised feature of Japanese society, nor . . . Okamoto's prediction (1982) that status inconsistency is more pronounced in Japan than in any other society. . . .

REFERENCES

Imada T, Hara J. (1979): 'Shakaiteki Chii no Ikkansei to Hiikkansei' (Consistency and Inconsistency in Social Status), in Tominaga K, (ed), Nihon no Kaiso Kozo, Tokyo: Todai Shuppan Kai.

Ishida H. (1986): 'Educational Credentials, Class, and the Labour Market: A Comparative Study of Social Mobility in Japan and the United States', unpublished Ph.D dissertation, Harvard University.

Koike K. (1988): *Understanding Industrial Relations in Modern Japan*, London: Macmillan.

Murakami Y. (1977): 'Shinchukan Kaiso no Genjit-susei' (The Reality of the New Middle Class), *Asahi Shinbun*, evening edition, 20 May.

—— (1984): *Shin Chukan Taishu no Jidai* (The Age of New Middle Mass), Tokyo: Chuo Koronsha.

Naoi A. (1979): 'Shokugyoteki Chiishakudo no Kosei' (The Construction of the Occupational Status Scale), in Tominaga K, (ed), *Nihon no Kaiso Kozo*, Tokyo: Todai Shuppan Kai.

Okamoto H. (1982): 'Seikatsu no Kiban toshiteno Seisan to Rodo' (Production and Labor as the Basis of Life), in Matsubara H, Yamamoto E, (eds), *Ningen Seikatsu no Shakaigaku*, Tokyo: Kakiuchi Shuppan.

Okamoto H, Hara J. (1979): 'Shokugyo no Miryoku Hyoka no Bunseki' (The Analysis of Prestige Evaluation of Occupations), in Tominaga K, (ed), *Nihon no Kaiso Kozo*, Tokyo: Todai Shuppan Kai.

Siegel P M. (1971): 'Prestige in the American Occupational Structure', unpublished Ph.D Dissertation, University of Chicago.

SSM National Survey Committee. (1976): *1975 SSM Survey Code Book*, Tokyo: SSM National Survey Committee.

Treiman D. (1977): *Occupational Prestige in Comparative Perspective*, New York: Academic Press.

Wright E O. (1979): Class Structure and Income Determination, New York: Academic Press.

—— (1982): 'The Questionnaire on Class Structure, Class Biography and Class Consciousness', Comparative Project on Class Structure and Class Consciousness Working Paper Series Number 2, Department of Sociology, University of Wisconsin–Madison.

—— (1985): *Classes*, London: Verso.

Wright E O, Hachen D, Costello C, Sprague J. (1982): 'The American Class Structure', American Sociological Review, 47: 709–726.

NOTES

1. After incorporating all restrictions, the sample size was 2633 for SSM and 739 for CSCC.

2. The International Occupational Prestige Scores (IPS) are highly correlated with the occupational prestige scores developed independently in Japan (Okamoto and Hara, 1979; Naoi, 1979) and the United States (Siegel, 1971): High correlations suggest a great deal of similarity in the hierarchy of occupations perceived by people in Japan and the United States. The IPS are used because the scores allow us to measure occupational status on the same scale in Japan and the United States.

3. Yen were converted into dollars by applying the average exchange rate of 300 yen = 1 U.S. dollar in 1975, and income for the American respondents was deflated by the Consumer Price Index to account for the inflation in 1970s.

4. CSCC asked the respondents whether they received 'any income from investments other than real estate or savings, such as from stocks, bonds, profits from business, and so on', rather than whether they invested in stocks and bonds.

5. For details of the construction of class categories, see Ishida (1986). This distribution of respondents by class categories in Japan and the United States is as follows: the employer class, 13 per cent in Japan and nine per cent in the United States; the petty bourgeoisie class, 23 per cent and eight per cent; professional-managerial class, 22 per cent and 38 per cent; non manual class, 14 per cent and nine per cent; skilled working class, 11 per cent and 13 per cent; and non-skilled working class, 16 per cent and 24 per cent.

6. I also used 1000 employees as the dividing line and obtained basically the same conclusions.

7. The identical proportion of people being status inconsistent does not imply that they belong to the same class categories in the two societies.

7.2 Prestige Hierarchies and Social Change in Poland

Zbigniew Sawinski and Henryk Domanski

The next excerpt is about the difference between what we might call "condition" and "deep-rooted" **occupational prestige.**

In every society there is some degree of consensus on rankings of occupational statuses. What are these rankings based on? Ishida's study suggested that income is important. What else is involved? Also, do the rankings change much over time? These are the questions addressed in the next excerpt. The research is based on responses from sample surveys in Poland, carried out over recent decades.

It is clear that, despite marked social change in Poland over the study period, occupational status rankings have remained quite stable. Stability in rankings is the strongest impression one draws from the results. The authors attribute this to a consensus in people's views on the value of various jobs for Polish society, and to the income, power, and educational levels of different occupations.

However, some interesting "anomalies" appear in the data. In particular, occupations of the "intelligentsia" receive higher prestige than would be suggested by their comparative low income level in Poland. This suggests that education levels of occupation incumbents, at least in this instance, carry greater weight in status evaluations than income. Also, part of the explanation may be that people perceive the intelligentsia as having greater power, despite their lower incomes.

There is also some evidence that changes in the economy of Poland—to a more prominent role for technical, industrial occupations and to greater importance of mining exports—are reflected in changes in the evaluations of occupations. It is fair to say that this change has created many interethnic conflicts where none existed previously.

...The analysis in this paper extends previous research on temporal stability in [occupational] prestige ratings in Poland beyond 1975, that is from the last survey onward.

We did not expect substantial changes in the hierarchy of occupational positions, because of its cross-time invariance in other countries across decades. Nonetheless, some change might be expected because, over the last few years, Polish society underwent great changes.

Excerpted from Sawinski, Zbigniew and Domanski, Henryk (1991), "Stability of prestige hierarchies in the face of social changes: Poland, 1958–1987," *International Sociology*, 6(2), 227–241. With permission of Sage Publications.

After rapid economic growth in the first half of the seventies, Poland faced a sharp economic crisis with a marked decline in the standard of living. In 1980, a political crisis brought about the establishment of 'Solidarity' and the imposition of martial law. These phenomena caused changes in people's values as shown in recent survey data. For example, from the early 1980's, when asked about the most important things to achieve in their life, people put greater stress on material needs (housing, consumption) and money. Similarly, people are now less likely to value higher education attainments and occupational advancement . . . . They are also more reluctant now to enter supervisory and managerial jobs (Nasalska and Sawinski 1989).

All these changes could prompt people to reassess prestige. In particular, high incomes are more valid in the eighties, so occupations offering high incomes should rise in prestige. By contrast, educational attainments and managerial or supervisory positions have been downgraded, so their prestige should decrease. The same should be true of jobs endowed with prerogatives of authority and supervision. . . .

DATA AND METHOD

We compare hierarchies of occupational prestige established in preceding years with data obtained in a survey conducted in May 1987 by the Institute of Philosophy and Sociology of the Polish Academy of Sciences on a national, random sample of 1,894 working men and women. Questions on occupational prestige were replicated from the 1975 questionnaire. Respondents were asked to rate 29 occupational titles according to the prestige they have in the raters' personal judgment. A five-point scale was applied with scores ranging from (1) very high prestige, to (5) very low prestige. We repeated the exact wording of the 29 occupational titles employed in the 1975 survey as well as the same ordering on the list presented to respondents.

To extend the comparison, the occupational rankings from 1975 and 1987 will be set against hierarchies obtained using the same analytical schema (Pohoski et al. 1976), based on surveys conducted in Warsaw and in rural areas. In Warsaw data were collected using quota sampling in 1958 and 1975 within the population aged above 18. Respondents were given the same 29 occupational titles, 24 of them identical with our list from 1987. Research among the rural population in 1960 was based, in turn, on a random sample. These data were rendered comparable with a sub-sample of the 1975 national survey selected to cover rural areas. Respondents rated 21 occupations.

The prestige score for each occupation was computed as the arithmetic mean of ratings made by respondents on the five-point scale. We transformed average scores for all hierarchies into a standard metric from 0 to 100. The absolute scoring was established with the maximum possible rating ('very high prestige') coded 100 and subsequent ones coded 75, 50, 25, and 0 respectively ('very low prestige'). Scores calculated this way locate occupations on the absolute scale. The relative scoring was determined with the occupation having the highest average absolute score coded 100, and the occupation with the lowest score coded zero for each survey. The scores on this metric identify relative place of occupations on the prestige ladder.

DYNAMICS OF PRESTIGE RATINGS

A comparison of scores for 1987 and 1975 offers insight into whether changes in occupational prestige occurred (see Table 1). The first two columns give average scores on the absolute scale. The correlation between them stands at 0.94, indicating high correspondence in the ranking, so there is substantial continuity.

In 1987 respondents were more likely to avoid extreme, especially negative, ratings. For example, the lowest absolute mean rating for an occupation was 32 in 1975 and 44 in 1987. This produced an increase in scores at the bottom of the scale. . . .

As discussed above, our relative scores range from 0 (for the occupation with the lowest prestige) to 100 (the highest average rating). This procedure shows the prestige ratings occupations would have if the distance between the top and the bottom were the same in both surveys. We present relative average ratings for 1975 and 1987 and their average annual increment in the last three columns of Table 1.

We begin with the intelligentsia represented by 'university professor', 'physician', 'lawyer', 'journalist', 'teacher', 'industrial engineer', 'agricultural engineer', 'and 'priest'. There is no unidirectional change. One can see a decline in the relative position of some occupations as well as an increase in the rank of others. The magnitude of changes is small except for the 'industrial

Table 1   Absolute and relative occupation scores for national samples in 1975 and 1987

Occupational Title[1]	Absolute			Relative		
	1975	1987	Δ[2]	1975	1987	δ[3]
University professor	90	87	− 0.3	100	100	+ 0.0
Miner—skilled worker	72	83	+ 0.9	68	90	+ 1.8
Physician	86	82	− 0.3	93	89	− 0.3
Factory manager	76	79	+ 0.2	76	81	+ 0.4
Teacher	77	79	+ 0.1	78	81	+ 0.2
Government minister	85	78	− 0.6	91	80	− 0.9
Journalist	71	71	+ 0.0	67	63	− 0.3
Nurse	62	70	+ 0.7	52	61	+ 0.8
Solicitor	64	69	+ 0.4	56	60	+ 0.3
Industrial engineer	72	69	− 0.2	68	59	− 0.8
Priest	69	69	− 0.0	64	58	− 0.5
Agricultural engineer	69	69	− 0.0	64	58	− 0.5
Farmer	51	66	+ 1.3	33	52	+ 1.6
Army captain	65	65	+ 0.0	57	51	− 0.5
Manager of state farm	61	65	+ 0.3	51	49	− 0.1
Locksmith—own business	50	64	+ 1.1	32	48	+ 1.3
Turner—skilled worker	56	64	+ 0.6	41	47	+ 0.4
Electrician	55	63	+ 0.6	40	45	+ 0.4
Office manager	61	63	+ 0.2	49	44	− 0.4
Tailor—own business	49	62	+ 1.1	30	43	+ 1.1
Truck driver	49	61	+ 1.0	29	40	+ 1.0
Factory foreman	58	60	+ 0.1	45	38	− 0.6
Sales assistant	45	56	+ 0.9	23	28	+ 0.5
Shopkeeper	45	55	+ 0.8	23	26	+ 0.2
Office clerk	42	46	+ 0.4	17	6	− 0.9
Unskilled construction worker	38	44	+ 0.6	10	3	− 0.6
Secretary	41	44	+ 0.3	15	2	− 1.1
Cleaner	32	44	+ 1.0	0	1	+ 0.1
Unskilled agricultural labourer	34	43	+ 0.8	3	0	− 0.3
Maximum rating	90	87		100	100	
Minimum rating	32	43		0	0	
Difference	58	44		100	100	

Note: In order to obtain absolute scores the highest possible ratings ('very high prestige') have been coded as 100.0 and the lowest one as 0.0 ('very low prestige'). Relative scores were obtained by assigning 100.0 and 0.0 to the highest and to the lowest mean of absolute prestige ratings respectively.
1. In the questionnaire schedule occupational titles were arranged in a different way from Table 1 but identically in the 1975 and 1987 surveys.
2. Average yearly increment of prestige scores measured by units of absolute scale.
3. Average yearly increment of prestige scores measured by units of relative scale.

engineer' whose prestige diminished by 9 points (i.e. by 0.8 a year).

We distinguish between intelligentsia occupations connected with authority and supervision, such as, government minister', 'factory manager', 'army captain', 'manager of state farm', and 'office manager'. Accord-ing to our hypothesis presented above, prestige given to authority should have decreased. Our results confirm that most of these occupations received lower prestige in 1987 than 12 years earlier.

The remaining non-manual occupations include 'electrician', 'nurse', 'office clerk', and 'secretary'. The dynamics in this category are inconsistent. Some increment in relative scores for electrician and nurse was accompanied by the opposite tendency for clerical jobs. The latter decline in prestige was the highest of all downgrading trends. Adherents of the thesis on the proletarianisation of the middle class would say our results point out the growing gap between routinised clerical jobs and the rest of the non-manual categories (Abercrombie and Urry 1983).

Turning to manual categories, all skilled occupations improved their position (miner, turner, truck driver), while unskilled labourers fell to the bottom of the scale (construction worker, cleaner, agricultural labourer). This suggests the differential between higher and lower segments of the working class has grown. An apparent departure from this is some drop in the relative position of the factory foreman. Nonetheless, factory foremen may be perceived as representatives of 'authority.' That would lower their prestige in popular imagery.

In relative terms, the greatest upgrading is enjoyed by the miner. Its second position in 1987, just after university professor, is astounding, even in the Polish context, where consecutive surveys have proved the higher prestige of skilled workers compared to capitalist societies. Most critical for the advancement of the miner's status might be the growing recognition of the crucial role of mining for the recovery of the Polish economy.

Finally, farmers and small business people (locksmith, tailor, shopkeeper) received higher prestige in 1987.

Having identified the main trends in prestige ratings, we now attempt to interpret our findings. First, some growth in disapproval of positions connected with authority corresponds to a fall in the prestige of managerial and supervisory jobs. This confirms our expectations based on research into the dynamics of value systems in Polish society (Wisniewski 1989).

The opposite is true in the case of the hypotheses claiming, first, a decline in prestige of occupations with higher education credentials, and, second, an increase in the prestige of highly rewarded jobs. A devaluation of the highest educational level in Polish society has been uncovered in several surveys (Koralewicz 1984). Contrary to expectations, however, there are no signs of decline in the prestige of occupations, in the intelligentsia, which command the highest educational credentials. In the case of occupations offering substantial monetary benefits, changes in their relative position neither support nor falsify the prediction advanced above. On the one hand, the prestige of the occupational roles securing considerable incomes increased (e.g. non-agricultural business people). But, under-rewarded jobs (nurse, teacher) remained practically on the same, relatively high, level.

Occupational prestige and values declared in social surveys come to be discrepant. To explain this discrepancy one may hypothesise that norms which people apply to rate occupational roles are more persistent in comparison to values and life preferences revealed in the research we referred to (Nasalska and Sawinski 1989).

Prestige ratings may be determined by perceptions of the social utility of occupational roles for society and the social system in a given political and economic context. Occupational prestige ratings express normative views as regards the proper organization of the social system. According to this interpretation, transformations in the Polish political system and economy at the turn of the seventies and eighties led to a reassessment of occupational roles. With rising prosperity in the first half of the 1970s, the institutional arrangements of the political and economic system gained legitimacy and widespread approval. However, in the period that ensued the system proved ineffective which promoted a challenge to the status quo by the majority of the Polish people.

A reorientation of this kind could explain many changes in occupational prestige disclosed in our data. In comparison to 1975 there was an overall decline in the prestige of positions constituting an integral part of the system dominant in the 1970s, that of managerial and supervisory staff and minister representing governmental power. In contrast, non-agricultural owners, representing free market forces, gained prestige. Similar attitudes could give way to a relative increase in the position of farmer. One may hypothesise that an additional source of the relatively high prestige enjoyed by a farmer in 1987 was the growing belief that state agriculture offers weak prospects for an improvement in the food supply.

There are other signs of the increasing role of attributes of effectiveness and rationality in the rating of occupations. The most conspicuous appears to be some growth in positive judgements of occupations that require high professional qualifications and hard work. At the same time, jobs with low skills, unspecified, and simple tasks, lose respect. These regularities are detectable in the rise of prestige of the nurse, manager and skilled workers, and in the decline of esteem for clerical jobs.

To provide additional support for our interpretation, we re-analyse changes in occupational prestige before 1975. Note that the data refer only to inhabitants of Warsaw and rural population.

Correlations between hierarchies in the three populations under analysis reveal high stability in prestige ratings that conforms to earlier findings. Interestingly, among Warsaw inhabitants and in the rural areas one finds higher correlations between 1987, 1958 and 1960 than between 1987 and 1975. Changes of occupational prestige in Warsaw did not correspond to changes in rural areas and sometimes ran in the opposite direction (for example, in the case of non-agricultural business people). However, some regularities conformed to each other. There was an increase—up to the mid-seventies—in the prestige of occupations carrying prerogatives of authority, alongside a decline in the relative positions of manual workers and farmers. Both tendencies are consistent with the interpretation advanced above. The placement at the top of occupational roles marked with authority and power might have resulted from the widespread approval of the strategy for economic growth realised by government in the first half of the 1970s. At the

time, the mass media fostered an unfavorable image of private agriculture. The parallel growth in prosperity gave rise to an ideology of consumption that reduced the high evaluation of manual work promoted by the official ideology in the early stage of socialism.

THE POLISH IDIOSYNCRASY

While in Poland earnings correlate with prestige at .24 (Domanski 1991), in most capitalist countries it stands well above .40.

The decomposition of earnings and prestige in Polish society must be seen against the background of the normative character of prestige ratings. Prestige expresses opinions on the fair distribution of rewards. When hierarchies of occupational prestige and occupational earnings declared as 'fair' have been compared, the correlation between them has not fallen below .9.

The explanation of why occupations differ in prestige is they have different requirements for recruitment (educational level), a different position in authority hierarchies, and differ in relative rewards (income). The level of earnings in this model plays a critical role as a direct source of prestige, along with education and other attributes of social status. The cross-country analyses by Treiman (1977) offered empirical support for this explanation. The correlations between hierarchies of occupations according to education, income, and prestige for about 15 countries proved moderately high.

In apparent contradiction to most countries, the Polish case exhibits peculiarities. While there is a strong connection between occupational hierarchies of prestige and educational levels ($r = .73$), the earnings of some occupational strata significantly deviate from their rank on the prestige scale. We refer chiefly to the intelligentsia and semi-professionals (teacher, nurse) who are granted high prestige but are undervalued in financial rewards. When our data were collected —the intelligentsia in non-technical jobs (physicians, lawyers, scientists, etc.) had average earnings below skilled workers. Semi-professionals earned about the same as unskilled labourers working in manufacturing. The marked disparity of occupational prestige and financial reward did not reveal significant change between 1982 and 1987 (Domanski 1990). . . .

The unchanging top prestige of the Polish intelligentsia indicates its relatively lower earnings have not been legitimised on the normative base. People have not accepted its decline into the lower levels of the income order and have contested the overall disparity between earnings and occupational skills, training and education. Surveys carried out over the 1980s showed that in wide sections of Polish society the existing patterns of financial reward were regarded as unjust. It was meritocratic rules of distribution that respondents commonly pointed out as fair (Zaborowski 1983; Koralewicz 1984). Thus, the prominent prestige of the intelligentsia may be seen as indicative of the widespread claim that top qualifications, high educational levels and specialised knowledge should be granted the highest financial returns.

If Communist rule had lasted longer than 45 years, a basic reorientation might have taken place in the criteria for occupational assessment by adjusting prestige ratings to the shape of the economic order. At present—with the growing marketisation of Polish society—the opposite may be true, that the distorted economic reality will be changed to the persistent prestige norms.

CONCLUSIONS

In our treatment of occupational prestige hierarchies in Poland we compared the results of a national survey from 1987 with surveys in 1958, 1960 and 1975. The comparison supports previous findings that show continuity of prestige ratings over time. No dramatic shifts in the occupational ladder were detectable, although changes in the relative position of some occupational roles occurred. From 1975 to 1987 the most significant change was the decline in the prestige of occupations connected with supervision, authority and power. In contrast, we found some increase in the prestige of small business people, skilled workers and technical staff who in the popular image are presumably identified with social utility. It may be that the trends displayed in our findings reflect changes in people's values or a reassessment of criteria of social utility and effectiveness by people in the evaluation of jobs.

REFERENCES

Abercrombie, N. and Urry, J. 1983. *Capital, Labour and the Middle Class.* London: Allen and Unwin.

Domanski, H. 1990. 'Dynamics of Labor Market Segmentation in Poland 1982–1987'. *Social Forces* 69.

Domanski, H. 1991. 'Effect of Education and Earnings in Australia and Poland'. *The Australian and New Zealand Journal of Sociology* (forthcoming).

Koralewicz, J. 1984. 'The Perception of Inequality in Poland, 1956–1980'. *Sociology* 18.

Nasalska, E. and Sawinski, Z. 1989. 'Przemiany celow i dazen spoleczenstwa polskiego w latach 1977–1986 w swietle wynikow badan ankietowych' (Changes in life goals and aspirations of Polish scoiety 1977–1986: empirical findings) Kultura i Spoleczenstwo XXXIII.

Pohoski, M., Slomczynski, K.M. and Wesolowski, W. 1976. 'Occupational Prestige in Poland 1958–1975'. *Polish Sociological Bulletin* 4.

Treiman, D.J. 1977. *Occupational Prestige in the Comparative Perspective.* New York: Academic Press.

Wisniewski, W. 1989. 'Education in the System of Values of Polish Society'. *Sisyphus, Sociological Studies* 6.

Zaborowski, W. 1983. 'Economic Inequalities and Distributive Justice: Opinions of Inhabitants of Warsaw'. *Polish Sociological Bulletin* 1–4.

7.3 The Status of Moslem Women in Turkey and Saudi Arabia

Yakin Erturk

The next excerpt is about secularization and the relationship between religion and the status of women. Women, like racial minorities, suffer from low status and prejudice. For example, Islam has given female sexual purity and family honor a legal and sacred status. According to this excerpt by Erturk, the status of women in Moslem countries in universally low. Yet, the Islamic religion may not be the cause of women's subordination in Moslem countries so much as its justification.

This is suggested by the fact that the status of women varies a lot between Moslem countries —between Turkey and Saudi Arabia, for example. These two countries give women very different amounts of status. Turkish women gained the right to vote in 1930. In contrast, Saudi women have no vote and are even forbidden to drive cars. The fundamental difference is that Turkey separates religious thought from politics and the law, and Saudi Arabia does not.

. . . This paper will explore points of divergence and convergence in two Islamic societies representing different models of national transformation and compare the impact of these experiences on the status of women. While the cultural and structural variability is illustrated, by focusing on such seemingly contradictory examples it will also be argued that it is not Islam per se (i.e. the implementation of the *Sharia*) that accounts for the subordination of women but rather that it is the religious, political and social tradition which is so profoundly embedded in the intimate levels of consciousness and identity of gender roles. Therefore, it is necessary to approach the problem at two levels:

1. The *structural* level, where Islam as a way of life is interpreted and institutionalised within a concrete socio-political entity within which the status of women is determined. Analysis at the structural level will require us to examine the formal aspects of gender relations and ask 'Is the public domain accessible

Excerpted from Erturk, Yakin (1991), "Convergence and divergence in the status of Moslem women: The cases of Turkey and Saudi Arabia," *International Sociology*, 6(3), September, 307–320.

to women?' The emphasis will necessarily be the quantitative representation of women in the public sphere of life and the socio-political orientation of the state which organises this realm.

2. The *conscious* level, where Islam as an ideology is internalised into identities and personal structures of both men and women. As a result, gender inequalities become perceived as natural rather than social. At this level of analysis the concern is on the qualitative aspects of identity and gender relations. Therefore, here the question shifts to whether sex-role stereotyping is eliminated at all levels of social relations and consciousness, while at the same time creating alternative gender roles.

THE CASES OF TURKEY AND SAUDI ARABIA

A. *Turkey.* Turkey represents a secular approach in terms of the relationship between state and religion. Turkish secularism implies the subordination of the latter of the former rather than a complete divorce between the two. In the process of national transformation, modernising elites of Turkey chose to separate the two institutions and introduce reforms aimed at emancipating women from centuries of seclusion. It must be emphasised, however, that the actual seclusion of women under Ottoman rule was more of an urban upper-class phenomenon, just as the main impact of the secular emancipatory reforms that followed was on that group of women. The Civil Code of 1926 outlawed polygamy and gave women the right to divorce and child custody. Civil marriages replaced religious marriages. In 1930 women were granted their right to vote and to be elected to office. While Turkish modernisers took measures to integrate women into the public domain, crucial aspects of gender relations (sexuality, domestic division of labour, and so on) and the sex bias of the public/private domains remained untouched.

After the 62 years since the reforms were initiated, in practice the situation is far from what might be expected. Women in the rural areas have faced more of a paradox than emancipation in the face of some of these changes.[1] The laws granting them rights are quite irrelevant to the objective conditions of their daily lives. Many, especially in the Eastern provinces, are still married by religious ceremony and some are still subject to polygamy. In both cases under the new secular/modern system the conventional legitimacy of their marital status, and the protective mechanisms it provided for women, no longer hold. As a result these women are confronted with real hardship in cases where the husband abandons them or dies. Furthermore, they are unable to make any legal claim over their children or inheritance from their husbands. Since they lack the know-how and means by which to function within the modern external institutions (such as courts), they are left to the mercy of their men and the effectiveness of the traditional mechanisms by which rights and obligations were customarily arranged.

As for urban women, the situation varies significantly by social class. For the majority of lower- and middle-class women the burden of having to contribute to the family budget has been added to the existing burden of domestic responsibilities. At the same time, the working woman had to assume a somewhat 'Victorian modesty' to prove her worthiness of being admitted to the 'club.' They 'voluntarily' accepted the ideology of the public domain for the sake of not only being accepted by it, but also for the greater cause of the new role granted to them in the modern nation-state. The first generation of Republican women in particular promoted emancipation as part and parcel of nationalism and the road to modernity. One positive outcome of the state-initiated reformist approach was that the indiscriminate recruitment of women during nation-building into many jobs avoided the emergence of sex stereotyping, especially in the professions.

In the light of recent developments, however, it is questionable whether this trend still holds. As the social transformation becomes more settled and the need for mobilising female labour becomes less urgent, women are being discretely discouraged from the more prestigious positions within the occupational hierarchy. The most obvious areas for such closure are the high administrative positions in state and private enterprises (Gülmez 1972) and in the medical profession, where women are particularly discouraged from becoming surgeons. Often the ideological justification offered is that some positions are neither compatible with female psychology and a woman's innate qualities nor with their primary duties as mothers and wives. Despite these drawbacks, perhaps the most significant and irreversible outcome of women's entry into the occupational structure is the fact it provided new role models for the younger generations (Öncü 1981). At the same time, however, the growing fundamentalist movement cannot be overlooked as a competing trend. There appears to be an increasing appeal of the Islamic ideology to young university students even in major urban centres. This has undermined the significance of the urban/rural-modern/traditional dichotomy which was believed to have characterised the women of the Republic of

Turkey. Instead, a secular/Islamist differentiation among the educated urban women is
gaining precedence.

Kemalist reforms paved the way for the
emancipation of women, while at the same
time undermining their motivation to struggle for change. In other words, the reforms
had a co-opting effect. The average middle-
class woman saw little need to struggle for
her liberation since she faced no obvious formal barrier. However, this co-optation has
not been free of contradictions for urban
middle-class women. Pressures arising from
the conflict within and between the traditional demands of the private domain and the
public domain are forcing women to search
for alternative ways of organising their lives
and exerting their power to produce new gender roles at home and at work. In addition,
the intensity of labour migration within the
past two decades had an impact on traditional relations as this process left women
with the responsibility of managing their
household affairs. In some cases, women
joined the labour force as the primary
providers for their families. This change, in
turn, has required new legislation to accommodate the emerging needs. For example,
since 1981 women are allowed to pass citizenship rights to their offspring (a right previously obtained only through the father). Parallel to these changes is the emergence of a
more radical women's 'consciousness' along
feminist and Islamist lines. The latter sees
the ultimate liberation of women in a total
submission to the will of Allah; the former
regards all forms of submission as an obstacle
to women's liberation.

B. Saudi Arabia. Saudi Arabia came into
being as a result of the hegemony of one tribe
over others. The power of the Al-Saud hegemony relied on: 1) the Wahhabi[2] connection,
which provided the ideological legitimacy of
the Saudi regime; and 2) strategic marriages,
which allowed them to form alliances with
other powerful tribes (Salameh 1980). This
process was supported by oil wealth which
reinforced the political-religious alliances of
the Al-Saud and Al-Shaikh families.[3] Thus,

the material and ideological preconditions for
the preservation of traditional institutions
were secured. It became feasible for Saudi
Arabia to 'modernise' without having to
restructure their society. Women could participate in the public domain only within pri-
vate/segregated female institutions. Especially after 1960, the Saudi government
extensively supported the education of
women and created new employment opportunities in health, commerce and social services among others.[4] The import of sophisticated technology along with foreign domestic
labour has freed women from household
chores. Private drivers and special women's
sections in public buses have given women
some physical mobility and independence.
These practices allow women to acquire a
more diversified image of themselves and
their abilities.

How much opportunity will be made available to Saudi women, however, is a contested
issue. The contradictions confronting the
regime manifest themselves in the constant
loosening and tightening of 'Islamic principles'. It is therefore not possible that under
the existing political order the public integration of Saudi women will improve.

Saudi society is literally divided into black
and white, private and public, with little
chance to deviate from the norm except in
secrecy. This sex-divided society is most readily observable in the dress code, i.e. black
abaya for women and white deshdasha
(robe) for men. It is also reflected in the
organisation of the urban physical environment. Even modest houses or apartments
are designed with internal divisions to allow
for the observance of the public/private
domains.

Overemphasis on morality and strict control of public behaviour has created widespread hypocrisy in Saudi society. Taboos are
broken behind the walls. The private domain,
which is reserved for the observance of hon-
our, purity and morality, in some cases serves
also for 'immorality'. The by-products of the
oil boom—supermarkets, videos, cars, tele-
phones, foreign domestic help and so on,
have, on the one hand, increased the concern

for morality, and, on the other, undermined control over individual behaviour. And the veil, in fact provides a disguise for those women who indulge in the 'forbidden.'

While the contradictions produced by the concern to preserve segregation, on the one hand, and the need to educate Saudi women, on the other, is mounting, the system is responding with new ideologies of consumerism and 'Saudi superiority.' The former acts to keep women preoccupied with the consumer market; the latter emphasises the need to distinguish oneself as a Saudi in the face of an influx of expatriates. The veil and the abaya symbolically serve such distinctness. Even the more critical Saudi women carefully arrange their veil in the 'proper' style so as not to be mistaken for a foreigner. The ideology of 'Saudi superiority' works in two ways to preserve the status quo: 1) it assures the conformity of Saudi men and women and 2) it makes self-appointed managers out of them as they keep an eye on the expatriates they work with. In other words, the Saudis in both state and private institutions act as managers of the managers. The native/foreign distinction is also supported by a higher pay scale for Saudis.

Beneath the black and white outer appearance, there is a quiet but persistent revolution. The risk involved in being rebellious bears a heavy price. Even those who are less challenging must put in much effort to gain very little. For example, in 1980 a group of Saudi women from King Saud University decided to attend a conference at the male campus. They observed the veil carefully so that their intentions would not be misinterpreted. The authorities were taken by surprise. They did not lose much time, however, in controlling the situation by confining the women to a separate room where they were allowed to listen to the speaker and submit their questions in writing. Subsequently the issue was never again brought up—as if it never happened.

In November 1990 about 50 women, completely veiled, were reported to have driven their cars in the streets of Riyadh to protest against the Saudi tradition which prevents women from driving. The protestors used the Gulf Crisis as a pretext. They claimed that in the event of war men would be away fighting and they would be left immobilised. This time, however, the response of the authorities was direct. Six protesters who were professors at King Saud University were suspended from their jobs. The reaction of other women in Saudi Arabia has been mixed. The fundamentalists charged the protesters with being infidels. Others from the professional community expressed concern that the act would have adverse consequences for women in the long run. Aside from such incidents there are a number of women writers who write regularly in local magazines and newspapers on women and oppression. Life for these women is not easy. They are constantly harassed by the authorities, their right to publish is periodically or permanently withdrawn, and pressure is brought to bear on their male guardians who are ultimately responsible for their conduct. Most of these women do not attribute the restrictions imposed on them to Islam, rather they see Islam as a political weapon used by the regime. The following quotation from a Saudi woman in the *Wall Street Journal* reflects a commonly held viewpoint. 'The royal family is using religion like a lash on our backs to stay in power. They know it's all hypocrisy. The Koran doesn't require veils. We should be a model Islamic society and not accept the word of fanatics.' (House 1981).

Declining oil prices and a multitude of problems arising from the presence of a large foreign workforce is increasing the pressure on Saudi rulers to replace the expatriates with an indigenous workforce. This is a potential challenge to the existing balance which is allowing them to maintain the sex-segregated institutions of education, law, banking, and so on. The Saudisation of the labour force, which must rely on every skilled and experienced Saudi, will require the recruitment of those women who have already acquired these skills in the all-women institutions.[5] A drastic restructuring of society will follow. Within this process, Saudi women, as double victims of oppression, are strategically placed to become a potential force in giving direction to change, more so than their male counterparts.

CONCLUDING REMARKS

When taken at face value, the above discussion obviously begs the question: How can so seemingly different cases of women's status be compared? Turkey is a secular Republic where indulgence in women's rights issues outdate its existence. Saudi Arabia, on the other hand, underwent a swift change from what was largely a tribal/nomadic society to a unified Kingdom only at the beginning of this century.

In both societies the patriarchal-Islamic culture continues to impose standards by which the moral and structural positions of women are defined. Women's natural drives, individuality and independent participation in the public realm, are seen as destructive of the institution of the family, and hence society. Therefore, the protection of the family and social order justifies the subordination of women to patriarchal institutions. These linkages are, no doubt, manifest in Saudi society where male and female distinctiveness is emphasised in segregated but sometimes parallel spheres of activity. The situation is somewhat discrete in Turkey. The Saudi case further illustrates that women are the central targets of regimes which appeal to political-religious alliances for their legitimacy. Similar trends are making their way into the Turkish political life.

The Turkish experience shows that the problem of women in Moslem societies is not merely one of gaining entry rights to the public domain. As important as this is, it can only lead to piecemeal reforms and a few token women in high positions. This is only a precondition. Beyond this it requires alternative models of gender roles at all levels of social relations. This can only be achieved by a conscious effort for change—individually and collectively. In this respect, women in Moslem societies are in a more advantageous position vis-à-vis men. They have access,

even under the veil, to the male world. They can observe and become acquainted with male gender roles. In contrast, men's familiarity with women is, in most cases, limited to the more subordinate and traditional female roles. As a result they are not equipped when confronted with women in an unfamiliar context. At the societal level this gap provides women with the opportunity to challenge conventional expectations and to impose an alternative image and self. Of course, the hard reality of political regimes, rising Islamic fundamentalism, and the brutal force men exercise over their wives and daughters cannot be dismissed. Hence, efforts for change must be directed towards both the external and internal obstacles embedded in identity as well as institutional structures.

REFERENCES

Gülmez, M. 1972. 'Kamu Yönetiminde Feminizasyon Olayi' (Feminisation in Public Administration). *TODAIE Dergisi* 5(3): 51–71.

House, K.E. 1981. 'Modern Arabia: Saudi Women Get More Education, but Few Get Jobs'. *The Wall Street Journal*, June 4.

Kingdom of Saudi Arabia, Ministry of Finance and National Economy, Central Department of Statistics. *Labour Force Statistics in Saudi Arabia, 1397 A.H.–1977 A.D.* Riyad: Central Department of Statistics.

Öncu, A. 1981. 'Turkish Women in the Professionals: Why so Many?', In Abadan-Unat, N. (ed.), *Women in Turkish Society*, Leiden: E.J. Brill. pp. 81–193.

Salameh, G. 1980. 'Political Power and the Saudi State'. *Merip Reports* October: 5–22.

NOTES

1. While legal changes concerning the status of women and the family were being introduced, Turkey was also experiencing processes such as national integration, rural transformation and the internal contradictions created by Turkey's position within the world system. These latter processes have probably had a more profound impact on the role and status of rural women. Most studies reveal the changes have preserved

traditional formations while modifying their form.

2. Wahhabism, a movement started in the eighteenth century by Abdul Wahhab, called for a return to the fundamentals of Islam as preached by the Prophet Mohammed. The association of Abdul Wahhab and the Al-Saud family formed the basis of Al-Saud's victory over other tribes and the unification of Arabia.

3. The members of the Al-Shaik family who hold religious power today are descendants of Abdul Wahhab.

4. Teaching, social work and medicine were the first areas to open up for Saudi women. Positions in the service sector followed. With the exception of medicine, all jobs are carried out in segregated institutions. In the past ten years women have also been appearing on television as news readers or programme directors.

5. According to the Central Department of Statistics, the employment status of the Saudi population over 12 years of age shows that, while 59.3 per cent of the men are in the labour force, this is true for only 4.8 per cent of the women. Over 90 per cent of the Saudi women in the workforce are secondary school and university graduates. It would not be wrong to assume that women in the labour force are employed in professional and administrative positions. These figures do not include the traditional informal sector. (Although the above data were published in 1977, women's participation in the labour force could not have increased significantly.)

7.4 Concepts of Women in Urban China

Margaret R. Weeks

The next excerpt is about the burden of women's role models. In China, as in Islamic societies, prejudice against women remains strong, and even official efforts to improve the status of women founder on the rocks of tradition.

According to this excerpt by Weeks, Chinese attitudes toward women have been shaped by a long history of male dominance. And, if anything, they have been strengthened by the official Communist party views of gender and women's issues. Classical Marxist theory puts gender issues in second place to economic and class issues. Because gender issues are considered secondary, they remain under the control of the traditional male-dominated family structure.

In the party-supported scheme of thinking, a woman is supposed to strive to be a "virtuous wife and good mother"—the traditional Confucian ideal of women. This conjures up images of the dutiful wife who is selfless in her devotion and considers only the well-being of her family. To be a good woman is to uphold the harmony of the family. As well, women are encouraged to be productive members of the workforce and maintain domestic duties at the same time. Communism or not, these Chinese views are similar to what one finds in India and the Arab world, where they also end up maintaining sex segregation and limiting opportunities for women.

Excerpted from Weeks, Margaret R. (1989), "Virtuous wives and kind mothers: Concepts of women in urban China, "Women's Studies International Forum, 12(5), 505–518. With permission of Pergamon Press Ltd. Oxford, England.

The 1980s have been a time of dramatic change for urban China. Yet forty years of socialist development have done little to dislodge attitudes of male privilege and concepts that give form to gender relations of male dominance. . . .

. . . The following discussion analyzes some popular traditional gender concepts as they relate to contemporary gender relations. . . .

In comparing the concepts I make use of the comments and experiences of my urban Beijing informants.[1] The more than seventy people I interviewed at length from 1982 to 1984 fell into three occupational categories. Officials, male and female, such as representatives of the National and Beijing Women's Federations and factory managers, generally provided the Party line on gender issues. Factory and nonprofessional service workers, both men and women, were the second category. These people, who I will refer to as the working class, constitute the majority of the urban labor force. The third category, college-educated intellectuals and non-administrative professionals, constituted the largest portion of my interviews.[2] . . .

MODELS FOR THE NEW CHINESE WOMAN

The traditional model for women is summarized in the still popular phrase "*xian qi liang mu*," which can be translated "virtuous wife and good mother." This phrase epitomizes the Confucian ideal of women. It suggests a woman's efforts should all go to serving her husband, family, and children.

Stories of "model" women publicized by the Women's Federation and in national and local media praise married women—most with paid jobs of their own—who take on the entire burden of domestic responsibilities so their husbands may put full effort into success at work. At the 12th National Party Congress in September 1982, Hu Yaobang, then General Secretary of the Communist Party's Central Committee, said that in addition to their economic contribution, women "have a particularly significant role to play in building

socialist spiritual civilization" ("A new year's message," 1983).[3]

The concept of women as having responsibility for upholding and teaching morality in the family and in society, is an integral part of the present leadership's call for women to build "socialist spiritual civilization." This varies strikingly from traditional ideas of the polluting power of women and the need to keep them under tight control (Ahern, 1975). But this recently bestowed responsibility opens them up to blame and criticism if domestic tranquility is not maintained.

Women's role in creating "socialist spiritual civilization" is outlined in a transcription of a Shaanxi Province radio broadcast:

Within the household, the main role of the female head of the family is to insure the stability of family relationships such as harmonious relations between husband and wife, support of the aged, education of the young, proper arrangement of the children's weddings [that is, no lavish ceremonies—author], and organization of the family's regular activities. The state of women's thinking and the height of their moral values are related to the level of civilization in the family. Likewise, every family's level of civilization directly affects society. Therefore, giving full play to women's enthusiasm in building spiritual civilization is a question of utmost importance. (*Jiating wenti*, 1982. pp. 1–2)

Significantly, this passage makes no reference to women's nondomestic jobs, either to encourage their participation there or to acknowledge that most women do hold jobs outside the home. As unemployment continues to rise with China's economic reforms, this omission may open the door to increasingly discriminatory hiring practices by employers.

The idea of the "virtuous wife and good mother" is officially counterposed by a second model of the ideal working woman. This model relies heavily on an image of the well-known scientist Marie Curie. The Chinese praise dedication such as hers to the development of science for the greater social good while still playing a supportive role in her family. Many Women's Federation leaders feel Marie Curie should be an inspiration for Chinese women to do the same in working for China's Four Modernizations economic program. But this leads to ambiguity about where women should focus their energy.

Women's Federation representatives agreed that the modern Chinese woman must try to be both a "virtuous wife and good mother" and a Marie Curie and concede this is not easy.

Official views of women's roles modify the traditional ideal of women to fit the modern context. My working class women informants indicated they accept the tradition more than they do these official modifications. Popular notions of "xian qi liang mu" emphasize the personal sacrifice women must make for men and the family. The comments of a woman who works in a Beijing sweater factory reflect a widely accepted definition of the "virtuous wife and good mother":

The traditional idea of what a woman should be is that she should do a lot of domestic work and her husband should not do anything. She must take very good care of him so the man will feel the warmth of the woman. . . . The "traditional" woman thinks that her husband is her soul. She takes good care of him so he's free from worries at home. She doesn't worry about her own job—just does it OK. The "best" woman is the one who never thinks of herself. In the countryside today, women are like this. They eat last and the least, and they work the hardest. They give everything to others and enjoy very little themselves.

In cities, husbands and wives discuss and compromise in domestic decision-making more than traditional practices allowed. But a modern-day "virtuous wife" is still expected to subordinate her own needs and goals.

Many working class women felt it is virtually impossible to achieve the Women's Federation's ideal balance between the traditional and modern roles. These women said they will do their best in domestic and nondomestic responsibilities. Yet for many, the "virtuous wife and good mother" is the role on which they prefer to concentrate. A young female store clerk summed up these ideas:

After marriage a woman forgets about everything except home and children. There's no need to put much energy into her job. . . .

Many women, whether cadre, intellectual, or working class, felt strongly that full time paid employment is absolutely necessary in terms of the money it brings in and the effect that being an independent wage earner has on women's status in the home. But a high proportion of the urban working class also maintain. . . . a woman's first job is to manage and care for her family.

More highly educated and professional women were less concerned with being "virtuous wives and good mothers," though they did not reject the goal altogether. Many college-educated women would like to achieve the goal of balancing the "virtuous wife and good mother" and the Marie Curie models. They feel husband and wife should work together, and each should have his or her own interests, ideas, and voice in decision-making. But they also see that an educated professional woman who wants to be successful in her work and a good wife and mother will have numerous difficulties trying to accomplish these goals.

Educated and professional women have an additional problem associated with a pervasive traditional belief illustrated in the old saying "talent [or education] is no virtue for a woman." A number of Chinese cities report an increase in the 1980s in unmarried educated women over thirty. Many urban college-educated women, especially with graduate degrees, are almost 30 before they begin seriously looking for a husband. Postponing marriage is necessary for women to insure they have adequate time and energy to complete their degrees and establish their careers before taking on the responsibilities of marriage and family.

Their difficulty in finding husbands comes from the widely held belief that a man should be better than his wife in every way, including education, status, and intelligence (Zhang, 1984). The few "eligible bachelors" for professional women are mostly unwilling to marry a woman who they think will put a lot of time into work at the expense of her domestic duties.

FURTHER OBSTACLES TO WOMEN'S EQUALITY

Major concepts affecting gender roles and feminist consciousness in China today include attitudes about the relatively greater importance of men than women. These ideas are summed up in the phrase *"zhong nan qing nü* ("exalting males and demeaning females"), which the Chinese also translate as "concepts of male superiority." . . .

. . . The prevalence of "exalting males and demeaning females" is evident in the popular preference for sons over daughters. . . .The preference for sons has resulted in husbands and parents-in-law verbally and physically abusing women who produce only female off-spring. A related consequence is female infanticide. . . .

The phrase "exalting males and demeaning females" also refers to continuing discriminatory practices that deny women equal opportunities. Such practices translate into material power for men, thereby substantiating the preference for sons. For example, employers give preference to males in hiring, especially in factories.

Men are also given preferred admittance into colleges and universities, and even some high schools (Tan, 1982, p. 25). Popular perceptions of women's innate characteristics affect ideas of their capacity for learning. Women's Federation officials and many educated women criticized the idea women are less intelligent than men. But many working class people (women as well as men) and officials outside the Federation, and even a few intellectuals, feel women cannot learn as well as men in higher education. A woman working in a Beijing automobile parts factory summarized the position:

When girls are small, they study better than boys. Boys are too naughty. But in higher levels of education, women do badly. Some do as well as men, but many do not. This is a natural phenomenon. It is what women have discovered about themselves in practice. Their brains can't handle it.

Chinese critics of this view say the belief itself leads to a "female inferiority complex" (Hao & Zhou, 1985, p. 3). This causes the decrease in the percentage of women who pass college entrance exams because these women have lost confidence in their ability to do so. . . .

Furthermore, there is a strong notion that women are not well suited to scientific and technological fields despite increasing publicity of women's contributions in these areas. With the Four Modernizations program initiated in 1979, scientific and technological fields have become highly desired areas of study. In addition, recent Party policies have begun to favor those trained in technical fields for administrative positions. But women continue to be channeled into arts and languages while men predominate in the hard sciences. In Qinghua University, China's top school for science and engineering, only 16.5% of the students enrolled in 1982 were women (Tan, 1982).

In promoting people into Party and government leadership positions, the same attitude is at work as in factory hiring practices.[4] Those making the decisions see women's domestic duties and activities as limiting their ability to be good administrators. . . .

IDEAS OF WOMEN'S EQUALITY

The three groups of women I interviewed expressed quite different views of the degree to which women have achieved equal status with men in China.

Women's Federation representatives said women and men are equal in China today. They referred to China's socialist economic relations and to the laws they say unequivocally state women's equal status and rights. But they recognize problems that adversely affect women, especially by hindering full implementation or protection of women's legal rights. This seeming contradiction in their perspective is a result of their assumption that continuing "feudal ideas," such as the concept of male superiority, are only an *ideological* problem, not an *economic* one.

With this explanation, they feel that a sufficient solution to inequality is to counteract traditional concepts with ideas reflecting China's new economic conditions and to publicize the laws protecting women.

Yet, the Federation's efforts thus far in "educational" and persuasive techniques to change gender relations have had limited results. Their educational programs deal with problems as individual cases, rather than as resulting from the social structure and requiring broader political means of elimination.

In addition to "feudal ideas," the Federation acknowledges women's general level of skill and education as a major obstacle to eliminating discrimination against them. Federation leaders believe that only long-term efforts to improve women's access to education will solve this. Housework also presents a major obstacle, one that Chinese officials believe the developing economy will overcome by mechanizing or socializing domestic tasks. Additionally, some Federation leaders noted that the reticence of certain factory managers to hire women is not necessarily discriminatory, but a reasonable response to women's generally lower skills and education, and their greater responsibility for domestic tasks. . . .

Urban working class women and men both commonly felt males and females are already equal in China. They believe there is no need for a separate and active grassroots women's movement. For my urban working class informants, legal equality is important, but "practical equality" is more so. This has two aspects, both of which they feel have been satisfactorily achieved.

The first aspect is "economic equality," specifically, both men and women having jobs and getting equal pay for the same job. Many said a man and a woman standing next to each other on the assembly line earn the same wage. They were content with this and overlooked differential placement of a greater number of men in industries that pay higher wages and offer better benefits. These informants, too, disagree with use of the term "discrimination" against women with reference to differential hiring and job placement. They see it, rather, as the need to place women in jobs suitable to their "natural" qualities. Like the Women's Federation, they accept these practices as the factory managers' logical response to problems created by women's greater domestic role and lesser education and skills. But unlike the Federa-

tion, they also explain it as resulting from women's generally "weaker" physical condition.

The second aspect of practical equality is "equality in the family," that is, sharing domestic tasks and decision-making. Virtually every working class individual to whom I spoke said men and women now share housework. In the families of many of my informants. this division of domestic labor places a substantially heavier burden on the woman, especially in terms of labor hours required. Because many working class women accept the traditional model of the "virtuous wife and good mother," they feel if men do *any* housework it indicates women's status in the home has improved greatly. This, coupled with the relative economic independence that holding a job brings, causes these women to feel they have equal say in the family. . . .

. . . The overall changes since the revolution lead working class women to feel satisfied with the gains already made in improving their social status. . . .

Intellectual and professional urban women tend to be critical of Chinese women's status. Many see a need for feminist political activity, though they avoid approaching the Women's Federation as a means to change. Also, they seldom use the word "feminist" to describe their interest in increasing women's opportunities because of the Party's interpretation of the term as implying a separation of the woman question from class analysis. . . .

The college-educated women were less consistent than working class women in their definitions of women's innate capabilities. Many reject the idea women do not work or study as well as men. They resent the burden housework creates for their educational and professional goals. Several stressed that policies to make housework more convenient for women do not necessarily aid in improving their status. Some, however, voiced the feeling that the husband should always have greater opportunity to advance in his career.

My college-educated informants were often critical of the popular working class acceptance of the current situation. . . .

. . . Education broadens these women's experiences and perspectives and leads them to have higher expectations of themselves and of society for opportunities. . . .

CONCLUSION

. . . Few women in China seem to desire to further women's social power or status unless their personal goals have been hampered by traditional expectations and behaviors resulting from male chauvinist attitudes. This more often happens for urban professionals than for working class women. . . .

. . . What amounts to a feminist critique, then, is being made primarily by an educated elite of women who see the need to further feminist demands beyond asserted equal pay and limited participation of men in domestic duties. Educated and professional women often have more conflicts and contradictory perspectives on women, women's roles, and women's status. Many feel the need to incorporate traditional definitions of women into their behavior while trying to break away from these definitions. They find it difficult to resolve the conflict between their newly expanded aspirations and the social pressures and demands placed on them to conform to older values.

In the end, many professional women must comply with social pressure to accept traditional gender roles and lessened opportunities to participate in their career activities. A very few who do not wish to do this choose to give up marriage and a family altogether. But the many pressures to get married cause virtually all women to avoid this option. Others try to find a husband who is willing to take on a sizeable portion of the domestic burden. But even if they can find such a man, the "superwoman" faces more difficulties than her cooperative husband.

Even with the consistent efforts of the Chinese government to eliminate concepts of women's inferiority, such beliefs persist, as do discriminatory and even criminal behaviors against women consequent to accepting such ideas. This indicates the causes of gender inequality and of concepts of gender inequality have not been adequately addressed.

REFERENCES

Ahern, Emily M. (1975). The power and pollution of Chinese women. In M. Wolf & R. Witke (Eds.), *Women in Chinese society* (pp. 193–214). Stanford, CA: Stanford University Press.

Hao, Keming, & Zhou, Yu. (1985, April). Growth of women's education. *Women of China*, pp. 2–3.

Jiating wenti ershi jiang [Twenty issues about the family]. (1982). Shaanxi Province: Shaanxi People's Publishing House.

A new year's message. (1983, January). *Women of China*, p.1.

Tan, Manni. (1982, March). Equal opportunities for women: Many gains, some problems. *China Reconstructs*, pp. 22–25.

Zhang, Yonglin (1984, April 14). Clash of machismo and strong women. *China Daily*.

NOTES

1. I conducted open-ended interviews lasting from three to four hours with over 50 women and some 20 men, and had numerous briefer discussions with others in the city on topics related to my research.
2. In my sample, officials comprised approximately 30% of my informants, all but two of whom were women. Working class informants made up around 23% of my interviews, and about 46% were with college-educated intellectuals. All those interviews, except for some officials, fell between the ages of 20 and about 45.
3. "Socialist spiritual civilization" refers to appropriate culture, morals, and ethics for the modernized Chinese socialist society (Su, 1983).
4. A report published in 1984 indicates that on Bureau, Ministry, and higher levels of the Party Central Committee and the central government, only 5.2% were women, among Provincial government heads and their deputies, 4.6% were women; and in regional offices above the county level, 4.7% were women cadres at that time ("Zhide zhuyi," 1984).

7.5 Untouchables and Brahmins in an Indian Village

S. S. Sharma

The next excerpt is about the ways religious beliefs support status hierarchies. As we shall see, in India different racial or caste groups lead different lives.

Status differences between these groups are age-old. The most extreme form, **untouchability,** is a prohibition against contact with the caste-less harijan for fear of pollution and loss of karma. Untouchables perform the most lowly and menial work. They are India's street sweepers and toilet cleaners. Though India depends on their labor, untouchables are people without any status in Indian society. They do not even have proper names.

An excerpt by Sharma shows that, today, the practice of untouchability persists even though it is illegal. While higher-caste Hindus have largely accepted contact with harijan ("untouchables") in public places, they continue to avoid private interaction. Public interaction allows them to claim to have stopped practicing untouchability. For example, in the markets and temples, untouchables roam freely. Yet they continue to practice untouchability in their private lives.

In many parts of India, untouchability is a sensitive topic that is difficult to study. Harijans want more interaction with, and less social distance from, high-caste Brahmins—a sentiment that is not reciprocated. Most of all, the harijan want private acceptance.

An attempt is made in this paper to identify the pattern of interaction between the upper caste and the 'untouchables' or the scheduled castes. The specific questions are: What is the pattern of interaction between the Brahmins and the Harijans as perceived by each of the communities? What is the extent of initiation for mutual interaction in both castes? Which of the social situations in public and private are preferred for acceptance by each caste? What social factors account for untouchability as perceived by each caste? . . .

The present study proposes to use an interactional approach for exploring the

Excerpted from Sharma, S. S. (1986), "Untouchability, a myth or a reality: A study of interaction between scheduled castes and Brahmins in a Western U.P. Village," *Sociological Bulletin*, 35(1), March, 68–79.

existing relations. The assumption is that so long as the upper castes feel polluted by a bodily contact of the scheduled caste, the scheduled castes are in effect 'untouchables'.

Since it is an exploratory study, 30 heads of households of each of the castes, Brahmin and scheduled castes, were interviewed. The respondents were selected on the basis of their preparedness to grant interviews. This became necessary, because it is too sensitive an area of enquiry in the village. Of the respondents, however, 4 scheduled castes and 3 Brahmins refused to answer one question; 2 scheduled castes declined at another stage and three Brahmins and two scheduled castes dropped out at the last stage of the survey. The Brahmin caste was selected on the basis of the researcher's own experience as a rural Brahmin. A schedule of 10 questions was prepared. The questions were explained to the respondents, so that reliable information might be obtained. The systematic information was supplemented by asking the respondents to narrate the most remarkable events of untouchability which they experienced in their life. The field work, done during June, July and August 1984, was conducted in Machhra Village.

VILLAGE

Machhra is about 20 Km. from Meerut on the Meerut-Lucknow Road. It is a multi-caste village with a population of about 2587 voters. The Tyagi caste is numerically at the top, being 22.24%. The others are Brahmins 20.1%, the scheduled castes 19.13%, Muslims 9.8%, Balmiki 4.1%, Nai 3.1%, Gujars 2.94%, Saini 2.82%, Potter 2.5%, Badhai 2.4%, Khatik 2%, Sikkigar 1.58%, Bania 1.28%, Jogi 1.2%, Sunar 0.92%, Dhinwar 0.93%, Chhipi 0.66%. The Tyagis, the Brahmins and the Gujars are land-owners and cultivators. This village has provided an M.L.A. from among the Brahmins to the preceding U.P. Legislative Assembly. The village is irrigated and electrified.

ECONOMY

The whole life of the village depends on land. The main feature of landed property in the rural setting is that it is unequally distributed. Landownership has been the privilege of higher castes, barring a few exceptions of Harijans. This village is not typical in this sense. The Survey of 30 families of Brahmin caste revealed that on average a Brahmin household holds 30 bighas of land and its range varies from 10–80 bighas. On the other hand, scheduled caste households own eight bighas of land on average and the range varies between five and 14 bighas. Every one of the scheduled castes is either an agricultural labourer or an unskilled mason, or a rope-maker or a cot-weaver. His earnings are insufficient by any criterion. He lives in unhygienic conditions with inadequate accommodation.

This village has educational facilities from elementary to graduate level. Among the scheduled caste respondents, about half (13) are illiterate, almost the same (12) have primary education and only one-tenth have gone up to Junior High School. Of the 28 Brahmin respondents about one-fifth (6) are illiterate, 12 are primary, five are Junior High School, three are High School, one is B.A. and one is M.A. The age range of both caste groups remaining the same, the disparities in their educational attainments are significant.

The educational achievements of the two castes may be compared at other levels too. In all 27 scheduled castes boys have been reported as engaged in their studies. Of them, 20 are in Primary, Junior High School, or High School classes and only one has studied beyond and he . . . is in the Intermediate class. In the case of the Brahmin caste, 28 boys are studying at different levels. The range also is wider as 20 of them are up to High School classes, two are in Intermediate, four are in Graduate and two in Post Graduate classes.

The Brahmins and scheduled castes differ in respect to employment of educated boys, also. The former have 21 such cases. It is significant that one-third could get jobs after completing High School, nine after Intermediate, two after B. Sc. and three after Post Graduation. In case of the latter, the situation is by and large the same. In all, 5 could get a job and among them 3 after Intermediate, one after Graduation and one post-Graduation. In the families under study, 17 educated Brahmin boys have settled in agriculture. Such families have sufficient land to absorb the younger generation in agriculture. Only three have been reported as educated unemployed. One has qualified for the Intermediate, another has failed at the Graduate level and the third possesses a professional degree in teaching. The situation is worse in the case of the educated scheduled caste boys. There are 12 cases who have left education. Of them, two have finished at Primary, five at Junior High School, five at High School and one at Intermediate level. They are selling their physical labour in the village and report themselves as unemployed. In general, scheduled caste boys finish their education at High School level or below and only a few continue beyond. . . .

UNTOUCHABILITY

Information was obtained from the respondents along two lines: One by studying a few cases according to case study method; second, by posing specific questions related to the context in which the respondents feel untouchability is observed viz. social, political and economic.

Case I:

A scheduled case Sub-Inspector of Police while on duty had to stay for a night with the Pradhan in a village in U. P. The Pradhan sent one of his sons to the local scheduled caste family to bring utensils to be used at dinner for the Sub-Inspector, who somehow came to know of it and instantly refused to take dinner at the Pradhan's house and insisted on having it at the scheduled caste's house from which the utensils were brought.

Comments: Vertical occupational mobility is not a ladder for vertical social mobility.

Case II:

The same scheduled caste Sub-Inspector of Police happened to be deputed as Security Officer in an Industrial Organization in Rajasthan. He along with his colleagues was served tea by a tea-stall boy. When one of them came to know that the tea-stall boy was a scheduled caste, all of them were annoyed and asked the owner of the shop not to keep the boy at his shop. The Sub-Inspector introduced himself as Chaudhry and thus could get acceptance in the High Caste group.

Comments: The urban setting is not quite different from the rural one with respect to observing untouchability.

Case III:

The same scheduled caste Sub-Inspector of Police got admitted to a Sanitorium at Bhowali in District Nainital. One of the Muslim employees there somehow came to know his caste. The Muslim employee advised him to conceal the caste, otherwise he would be deprived of facilities and services of the staff. He pretended to be a Jat and thus could adjust to the situation.

Comments: It is not true that untouchability has been removed from public places.

Case IV:

At the instance of one Tyagi leader from among the most respected and influential traditional elite caste, a scheduled caste in the village happened to invite a few Brahmins and Tyagis to a feast. The Tyagi who was an enthusiastic social reformer advised the scheduled caste host to serve dishes to the Brahmin and Tyagi guests. The Brahmins as well as the Tyagis, but for the Tyagi social reformer, left the feast untouched.

Comments: Untouchability is a reality. Food is considered to become polluted the moment it is touched by the hand of a scheduled caste.

Case V:

In October a cultural activity called 'Rama Lila' is celebrated in the form of a drama depicting the fight between Rama the symbol of God and Ravana the Demon King. It is strictly prohibited on the grounds of purity to allocate the role of Rama to a scheduled caste boy. However one educated scheduled caste boy was accepted as a member of the organizing committee of the Drama Club.

Comments: God is considered to become polluted even when he is impersonated by the scheduled caste.

DEPRIVATIONS

An attempt was made to identify the nature of deprivation felt by the scheduled castes in this village. To make the observations precise and specific, a few items indicating social, economic and political deprivations were projected in the interview. . . .

With regard to public places, it was reported by the scheduled castes that they do not dare enter the temple. It was observed that the Brahmins too are not regular in visiting the temple, nor do they perform many rituals. Many do not even wear the sacred thread. The scheduled castes feel their entry into the temple is not by itself a sufficient indicator of their being accepted by the Brahmins.

With regard to private places, the general impression of the Brahmins of this village is that their women folk are more conservative than the men. The women work as a constraining counter force on males in bringing about any social change with regard to untouchability in private life and after much conflict and altercation between the men fold and the women folk, the women prevail.

With regard to political affairs which fall under public dealings, [neither] caste observed any untouchability. Politics, it was reported, encouraged a closer contact between the two castes and members of both castes were satisfied with this state of affairs.

To explore the intensity of social interaction on the part of each caste, a question was raised 'Are you interested in having social interaction with each other? The four alternative responses were mentioned as 'most', 'more', 'less', 'least'. The responses 'most' or 'more' have been taken as an indicator of active and 'less' and 'least' of passive extent. The results are shown in Table 1.

The difference between the responses of scheduled castes and Brahmins is so great that the hypothesis of equal intensity of interaction is rejected. Scheduled castes are actively interested in interaction with Brahmins, whereas Brahmins are passive in this regard.

There is sufficient qualitative evidence to indicate there is acceptance of scheduled castes more in public than in private places. Brahmins and scheduled castes were asked: 'In which situation do the scheduled castes and Brahmins insist on acceptance?' The former in our study is denoted by refusal to scheduled castes to enter into temples and the latter is denoted by denying scheduled castes permission to enter the inner part of the house and to take meals on a common table. The responses are given in Table 2.

The difference between the responses of scheduled castes and Brahmins is very high. Brahmins insist on accepting scheduled castes in public places whereas the scheduled castes insist on being accepted in private places.

A closed question was put to identify the reasons for non-acceptance of the scheduled castes as viewed by the Brahmins and scheduled castes themselves. The earlier studies have suggested ideological and material reasons. . . . The indicators of ideological reasons were, for the purpose of this study, the theory of Karma and nature of food, and of material reasons were poverty and lack of possessions. A choice between ideological and material and undecided reasons was given in the responses. The responses are presented in Table 3.

The discrepancy between the responses is highly significant. Brahmins consider ideological reasons for non-acceptance of scheduled castes, whereas the scheduled castes consider material conditions responsible for non-acceptance of themselves by the Brahmins.

TABLE 1. Extent of intensity of interaction among Brahmins and scheduled castes.

Caste	Active	Passive	Total
Scheduled Castes	15	11	26
Brahmins	10	17	27

TABLE 2. Acceptance of scheduled castes by Brahmins and vice-versa in public and private places

Caste	Public	Accepted in Private	Both	Total
Brahmins	22	1	7	30
Scheduled Castes	7	16	5	28
Total	29	17	12	58

Table 3. Reason for non-acceptance of scheduled castes according to the Brahmins and scheduled castes

Castes	Ideological	Material	Undecided	Total
Brahmins	19	5	3	27
Scheduled castes	9	18	1	28
Total	28	23	4	55

CONCLUSIONS:

In this study, an attempt was made to enquire into the pattern of interaction between scheduled castes and Brahmins in Machhra village. The study confirmed that untouchability is observed by Brahmins in social life, whereas it is not in political aspects. Perhaps the social is the core and the political is the periphery for both castes. Contrary to the widely held belief that occupational mobility may lead to upward social mobility the study indicates that an educated scheduled caste with an achieved status of police official was not considered as touchable by the higher castes when in a public place like a hospital. Ascrip- tion takes precedence over achievement. The scheduled castes insist on being socially accepted in private places. The Brahmins prohibit them from doing so but concede their free entry into public places. The reasons are obvious in that the Brahmins do not make their daily prayers in the temple of the village and those who do so have started to have mini temples in their residences. Thus it should not be interpreted as a substantial change. Lastly, the Brahmins and scheduled castes are diametrically opposed to each other with respect to reasons for untouchability. Ideology is the basis of untouchability according to Brahmins and material conditions are vital according to the scheduled castes.

7.6 Ethnic Social Distance in the Netherlands

Joseph Hraba, Louk Hagendoorn, and Roeland Hagendoorn

Some sociologists have favored a "colonial model" to account for the development of boundaries between different racial and ethnic groups. The argument is that exploitation of workers is easier when it is justified by ideological beliefs about the lower competence of groups of workers. People who have been colonized and oppressed are easier to label in this way, it is said, justifying their exclusion from status, power, and economic equality.

We often find a clear and consistent status hierarchy of ethnic or racial groups in the views of white majorities in industrial countries. Researchers measure this using a social distance scale. As we have seen, this scale measures how close particular social groups would like others to be to them. Questionnaires ask respondents how they would feel about having a neighbor of a certain ethnic origin, or about having their child marry such a person. The level of acceptable intimacy thus emerges.

When we examine the results from the scale we find most people view the society they live in as a collection of groups with differing levels of prestige. As well, most people agree on the order of the hierarchy. Usually, they put whites at the top and blacks at the bottom. The latter are least wanted as neighbors, friends, or kin.

However the next excerpt, on social distance in Holland, shows an exception to this rule. In this study, the respondents put Europeans at the top and former colonials next down (as the colonial model would have predicted), but Turkish immigrants were at the bottom. This hierarchy does *not* run from darkest-to-lightest-skinned people, a deviation that leads us to ask, Why are the Turkish immigrants rated so low?

The answer would seem to lie in the way the economics of current European societies operate. The Dutch no longer rule colonies in the Third World. However, like the Germans, Swiss, and other prosperous Europeans, they benefit from the economic control of migrants from many Mediterranean countries, including Turkey. In effect, the Turks are the blacks of Europe. Their low social status reflects their low position in the European economy.

Note, however, the distinction that these authors draw between discrimination *among* and discrimination *against* different groups.

Common-sense theories about social reality are called social representations. Social representations contain beliefs, imagery and implicit evaluations. . . .

. . . Our intention was to apply social representation theory to Dutch students' social distance towards Holland's minorities, testing whether the static or dynamic interpretation of social representations is more suitable.

There are two types of social distance distinguished in this research. One is the amount of social distance towards an ethnic group, a discrimination *against* the out-group. The second is discrimination *among* out-groups in social distance (Hagendoorn & Hraba, 1987). Some out-groups are kept at a greater distance than others. This pattern can be evidence for a hierarchical conception of ethnic groups in a multi-ethnic society.

Hypothesis 1: More respondents would discriminate among ethnic groups than would discriminate against ethnic groups in social distance.

Excerpted from Hraba, Joseph, Louk Hagendoorn and Roeland Hagendoorn, (1989), "The ethnic hierarchy in the Netherlands: Social distance and social representation," *British Journal of Social Psychology*, 28, 57–69.

Is an ethnic hierarchy a social representation, and is its form and content static or dynamic across populations and contexts of use? These are questions addressed by this research.

Consensus over the content of an ethnic hierarchy is tested by scalogram analysis (Pettigrew, 1960).

If a scalogram of ethnic groups in social distance evolves across all respondents, then the cognitive representation of the stimulus (Holland's minorities) is shared. If no stable hierarchy emerges across all respondents, consensus within subcategories of respondents can be tested in the same manner.

Hypothesis 2: Respondents would share the content of the ethnic hierarchy.

The form of an ethnic hierarchy can be dynamic. Respondents can unfold or collapse a hierarchy across a stable sequence of outgroups. Some might use a dichotomous or three-fold hierarchy while others use a fuller hierarchy. Furthermore, the unfolding and collapsing might vary by subgroup or individual characteristics of respondents.

Hypothesis 3: Respondents would vary in how they unfold and collapse the form of the ethnic hierarchy.

Respondents can also unfold and collapse an ethnic hierarchy across contexts of use. Domains of contact from marriage to temporary encounters, are one context of use. Another is the gender of the ethnic group member with whom the respondent has contact.

Hypothesis 4: Respondents would unfold and collapse the form of the ethnic hierarchy across domains of contact and gender of ethnic group member.

METHOD

Subjects

In the first survey, the respondents were 224 first-, second- and third-year students of psychology at the University of Nijmegen, The Netherlands, and 67 pupils in a social problems course in a high school near Nijmegen. The age range for the university students was 18–21 years, and for the high school students, 16–18 years. The respondents were contacted in April 1984. Sixty-two per cent of the respondents were female. All were ethnic Dutch and more than 90 per cent were middle class.

In the second survey conducted in May 1986, the respondents were 145 first-year students of psychology at the University of Nijmegen, 28 and 47 pupils from a Nijmegen high school and a secondary school, respectively, and 55 and 29 pupils of vocational schools in Leiden and Amstelveen. The age range for the university students was 18–46 years, and 16–18 years for the high school and vocational school pupils. Ninety per cent of the respondents were between 16 and 24 years. Seventy-seven percent were female. About 30 per cent of the respondents had a working-class background; the others were middle class. Four per cent were not ethnic Dutch and were excluded from the analysis.

Procedure

In the first survey there were eight statements about social distance towards outgroups in different domains of interpersonal contact. They were:

1. I would be annoyed if my neighbours were . . .
2. I would be annoyed if my work colleagues were . . .
3. I would be annoyed if my children's school had a lot of . . .
4. I would be annoyed if my physician was a . . .
5. I would be annoyed if my superior at work was a . . .
6. It would not occur to me to marry or to have a relationship with a . . .
7. I would be annoyed if my children married or had a relationship with a . . .
8. It would not occur to me to become friends with a . . .

Under each statement was a list of ethnic groups, including English, Jews, Moroccans, Spaniards, South Moluccans, Surinamers and Turks. The five response categories followed a Likert-type format ranging from agree to disagree.

In the second survey, five statements about social distance from the first survey were repeated. These concerned marriage, neighbours, work colleagues, schoolmates and friends. In the list of groups under each statement 'the Dutch' were added. The subjects were randomly assigned to four treatment groups in which the list of ethnic groups under each statement was specified for (*a*) a general ethnic label, e.g. Turks; (*b*) female representatives of the ethnic groups, e.g. Turkish women; (*c*) male representatives of these groups, e.g. Turkish men; of (*d*) both a general, female and male ethnic label. The purpose was to test for variation in the ethnic hierarchy across specific ethnic representatives as well as domains of contact.

In the second study, the respondents indicated their school type (vocational school, high school or university), their first preference for a political party (out of the 13 parties represented in Dutch Parliament), father's occupation later coded into six and

recoded into two categories (Van Westerlaak, Kropman & Collaris, 1975), religious
denomination (Roman Catholic, Protestant
or none), gender and previous contact with
each out-group, which was then transformed into a contact sum score across
groups. . . .

Analysis

First, social distance towards ethnic groups
across domains of contact and the percentage
of subjects sharing a hierarchical conception
of Dutch multi-ethnic society were determined and the effect of respondent characteristics on the use of this hierarchical conception was tested.

The next step was to determine consensus
over the content of the ethnic hierarchy by
scalogram analysis. This was done across
domains of contact and for each domain of
contact and ethnic label separately.

The following stage was to determine
consensus over the form of the ethnic hierarchy by testing the effects of respondent
characteristics on the number of discriminations among ethnic groups. Likewise, variations in the number of discriminations
among ethnic groups due to domains of contact and ethnic representatives were determined.

RESULTS

Discrimination Against
and Among Ethnic Out-groups

The amount of social distance respondents
expressed towards ethnic minorities in different domains of contact is a measure of discrimination *against* these out-groups. In the
first study, the average social distance of all
respondents towards all out-groups across
domains was 1.95 on a scale from 1 (no distance) to 5 (maximum distance). Only 4 per
cent of respondents rejected (scores 3.5–5)
ethnic minorities in average social distance
across domains and groups. Twenty-four per
cent showed a neutral score (2.5–3.5) in social
distance.

In the second study, the average social distance towards all groups across all domains
was 2.35, i.e. greater as compared with the
first study. Again 4 per cent of the subjects
rejected out-groups, but 40 per cent showed a
neutral score in average social distance across
domains, out-groups and labels.

In the first study, 76 per cent of the respondents discriminated *among* ethnic groups in
social distance. This percentage was lower in
separate domains. In the second study, 80 per
cent of the respondents discriminated among
groups in social distance. These results pertain
to the label 'people.' A greater percentage of
subjects discriminated among ethnic groups
represented by women and a smaller percentage
in the case of men. More respondents discriminated among ethnic groups than against them.

In total 69–80 per cent of the respondents
had a hierarchical conception of multi-ethnic
Dutch society. By contrast, only 4 per cent
discriminated *against* ethnic groups. As predicted in hypothesis 1, more subjects discriminated *among* ethnic groups in social distance
than discriminated *against* them.

Catholicism and a Christian-Democra-
tic/Conservative political preference contributed to the use of a hierarchical conception of Holland's ethnic groups. Eighty-eight
per cent of the respondents with a preference
for right-wing parties discriminated among
ethnic groups in social distance, whereas 71
per cent with lift-wing preferences did so.
Eighty-two per cent of the Roman Catholic
respondents discriminated among groups,
but 73 per cent of the non-denominational
and 59 per cent of the Protestant respondents did the same. While the hierarchical
conception was shared by a majority, it varied
across some subcategories of respondents.

Content of the Ethnic Hierarchy

Scalogram analysis was used as a test of the
shared nature of the ethnic hierarchy. In the
first study, the dichotomized social distance
towards out-groups emerged cumulatively in
the following sequence towards (1) Turks, (2)
Moroccans, (3) Surinamers, (4) South Moluccans, (5) Spaniards, (6) Jews, (7) English. The

TABLE 1. Ethnic hierarchy scalograms by representatives of ethnic groups and domains of contact

Representatives of ethnic groups	n	Domains	Sequence	CS[a]	Rho[b]
People	139	All	EN JE SP SU MO TU SM	0.85	0.95
Men	93	All	EN JE SP SU SM MO TU	0.93	0.97
Women	85	All	EN JE SP SU SM MO TU	0.94	0.97
People	140	Marriage	EN JE SP SU SM MO TU	0.82	0.94
People	141	Neighbours	EN JE SU SP TU MO SM	0.82	0.95
People	142	Colleagues	EN JE SP SU TU MO SM	0.90	0.97
People	139	School mates	EN JE SU SP SM TU MO	0.95	0.98
People	140	Friends	EN JE SU SP SM MO TU	0.91	0.97

Key. MO = Moroccan; TU = Turks; SM = South Moluccans; SU = Surinamers; SP = Spaniards; JE = Jews; EN = English.
[a]CS = scalability coefficient.
[b]Rho = reliability coefficient of the scale (Mokken, 1970).

most social distance was towards Turks and the least towards English.

In the second study, social distance emerged cumulatively through South Moluccans, Turks, Moroccans, Surinamers, Spaniards, Jews and English.

This hierarchy deviates from the one in the first study in only one aspect: Moluccans are placed lower. Comparable coefficients were obtained when the number of domains in which a group is not accepted was used as a measure of social distance.

Social distance responses towards ethnic groups represented as men and women formed comparable Guttman scales (see Table 1). In both scales the South Moluccans are placed higher in the ethnic hierarchy than for the label 'people'.

The sequence of the groups changed with domain, however. These were largely shifts in adjacent positions, for example, between the Spanish and Surinamers. The one exception is that South Moluccans were placed at the bottom of the ethnic hierarchies for neighbours and colleagues (Table 1).

The results from both studies are in line with the second hypothesis. The respondents have the same group sequence in mind on the ethnic hierarchy. Across domains of contact and ethnic representatives, however, there is some variation in the content of the ethnic hierarchy.

Form of the Ethnic Hierarchy

Not all respondents with a hierarchical conception discriminated among ethnic groups to the same degree. In the first study, 18 per cent of the respondents discriminated among two groups, 19 per cent did so among three, 16 per cent did so among four, 12 per cent did so among five, 7 per cent did so among six groups, and 4 per cent discriminated among all groups on the ethnic hierarchy. The number of discriminations was computed on social distance scores for ethnic groups averaged across domains. Results from the second study are comparable to those from the first.

These results suggest the form of the hierarchy is not shared across respondents. Respondents are predisposed to unfold and collapse the . . . hierarchy from one domain to another. Likewise, different ethnic representatives affect the number of discriminations used. This means respondents have some larger hierarchy in mind that they unfold and collapse across domains and ethnic representatives.

Two other factors can affect respondents' discriminations among ethnic groups. First, it is impossible to discriminate among ethnic groups without expressing increasing amounts of social distance. The amount of social distance can restrict or enhance the number of discriminations. Secondly, respondents' beliefs and social characteristics can affect the number of discriminations they make. Only this second factor is truly relevant to consensus on the form of the ethnic hierarchy.

. . . There is an association between the number of discriminations among ethnic groups and the amount of social distance, but it is not strong. With higher amounts of social distance in the second study, the association is slightly curvilinear.

Secondly, the effect of respondents' beliefs and social characteristics on the number of discriminations among groups was tested by a repeated measures MANOVA. The effects of eight factors were concurrently tested in the second study. Respondents who did not discriminate among ethnic groups or had missing scores on any of the eight variables were excluded from the analysis. 86 respondents remained in the test.

There were no significant effects on number of discriminations by gender, father's occupational status, political party preference, and prior contact with ethnic groups. However, type of school and denomination had significant effects on number of discriminations. High school students used more discriminations than did vocational school and university students. Protestant respondents used more discriminations than did Catholic respondents, and both used more discriminations than did non-denominational respondents. There is no consensus across all respondents on the form of the ethnic hierarchy as proposed in hypothesis 3.

The Use of the Ethnic Hierarchy

In the MANOVA above, contact domains had a significant effect on the number of discriminations. The form of the ethnic hierarchy unfolded when interacting with neighbours and in regard to marriage, and it collapsed when interacting with work colleagues, schoolmates and friends. Respondents' gender interacted with domains on the number of discriminations. Females discriminated more with respect to marriage, whereas males discriminated in regard to neighbours, colleagues and schoolmates.

The type of ethnic representative also had a significant effect. Respondents made more discriminations with respect to people than men and women representatives, and this was especially true for male respondents. The personalization of ethnic out-groups by male and female representatives, results in fewer discriminations.

As stated in hypothesis 4, the form of the ethnic hierarchy varies across domains of contact and gender of the ethnic group member.

DISCUSSION

Discriminating among ethnic groups in social distance is the more pervasive form of discrimination in Dutch society. Up to 80 per cent of the respondents discriminated in this way. This type of discrimination can indicate a hierarchical conception of ethnic groups by societal members.

The majority of respondents shared a hierarchical conception as well as the content of the resulting ethnic hierarchy. It is a hierarchy of European, former colonial and then Islamic groups. Hence, the ethnic hierarchy is a shared cognitive representation of ethnic groups in Holland. We can call it a social representation as conceived by Moscovici (1981, 1984).

The refinement of the ethnic classification underlying this social representation, however, was not shared to the same degree by all respondents. Consensus on the number of ethnic distinctions was affected by religion and school type, i.e. the ideological and social characteristics of the respondents.

Moreover, this social representation is not static. Respondents collapsed the hierarchy with the personalization of the ethnic representatives and unfolded it into fuller rankings with more impersonal representatives. This was stronger for male than female respondents, indicating an interaction effect with respondent characteristics. Of course, a collapsed form also means collapsed content of the ethnic hierarchy.

The respondents also unfolded and collapsed the ethnic hierarchy across domains of contact. Female respondents unfolded the hierarchy especially when interacting with potential marital partners, and males did so when interacting with neighbours, colleagues and schoolmates. Males unfolded the ethnic hierarchy in domains connected to class standing, while females did so in the domain of marriage.

This social representation serves pragmatic purposes. According to the situation, the representation is able to bring out the number of ethnic distinctions that are relevant more when ethnicity is particularly salient, consequences of contact are lasting and significantly affect life-chances, and when norms do not necessarily inhibit ethnic preferences. Discriminations are not so refined where consequences of contact are not great and norms run counter to the display of ethnic preferences.

REFERENCES

Hagendoorn, L. & Hraba J. (1987). Social distance toward Holland's minorities: Discrimination against and among outgroups. *Ethnic and Racial Studies*, 10(3), 317–333.

Mokken, R. J. (1970). *A Theory and Procedure of Scale Analysis*. The Hague: Mouton.

Moscovici, S. (1981). On social representations. In J. P. Forgas (Ed.), *Social Cognition: Perspectives on Everyday Understanding*. London: Academic Press.

Moscovici, S. (1984). The phenomenon of social representations. In R. M. Farr & S. Moscovici (Eds), *Social Representations*. Cambridge: Cambridge University Press.

Pettigrew, T. F. (1960). Social distance attitudes of South African students. *Social Forces*, 38, 246–253.

Van Westerlaak, J., Kropman, J. & Collaris, J. (1975). *Beroepen Klapper (occupation categorization)*. Unpublished manual, ITS, Nijmegen, The Netherlands.

Section Review

Discussion Questions

1. Drawing on Ishida's discussion of Japan and the United States, distinguish between class and status. How do they differ. What do they have in common?
2. Kato's earlier excerpt on women and power suggests much more marked differences between the United States and Japan than does Ishida's study of male workers. What does this suggest about the need for guidelines for comparative research on power and status inequalities?
3. Research in North America also shows a pattern Weeks reports for China, namely, the lower the social class, the more the support for traditional views of women. How can we account for this pattern?

4. Do you think the proportion of women in an occupation affects the status ranking of that position? If it does, what explanation would you offer?
5. "There is generally less status consciousness among women than there is among minority ethnic groups." Do you agree with this statement, or not? Discuss.
6. Sharma's study touches on the religious legitimization of inequality in India. Are there any religious underpinnings to inequality in your own country?

Data Collection Exercises

1. For two days when you are "out in public" a lot, record in a diary the symbols of status others confront you with, and the symbols of status you employ with others. Identify the meanings of these symbols.
2. Design a brief questionnaire that will show that people differentially evaluate the statuses of women and men; then carry out the study. Give the questionnaire to a few fellow students or family members. Check for differences in the evaluation made by females and males.
3. How would we best conduct a study to show, in a compelling way, that there is racial discrimination in employment?
4. How can we adapt the methods of Hraba et al. to measure the social distance between men and women in our own society? Would evidence of a sexual double standard be relevant in measuring social status?

Writing Exercises

1. Like everyone else, you have a gender status, a class position, and a racial status. Write a brief (500-word) essay on which of these three has the most influence upon your behavior and life chances, and why.
2. Weeks suggests that economic power and gender status are inextricably tied together. Write a brief essay supporting or rejecting this view, in relation to any country you wish. Muster the best evidence you can for your arguments.
3. Write a brief essay on the implications for social status of contemporary power struggles around affirmative action policies in your own country.
4. "Groups with more money usually have more status, and they take actions to ensure they get more of both." Comment on this statement in a brief essay that takes into account the findings of Hraba et al.

SECTION EIGHT
Explanations of Status Inequality

8.1 Brown Racism and a World System of Racial Stratification

Robert E. Washington

Is there an internationally prevalent pattern of racial status rankings whereby whites are consistently seen as better than "brown" people and black people? And, if so, what accounts for it? The next excerpt by Washington argues that there *is* an internationally recognized ranking system, and that the rankings run from white to brown to black people.

In effect, western culture is a source of worldwide racism. The author explains the pattern in terms of the European dominance of other countries during the colonial period, and the views of colonials of the time. Whites were seen by the Europeans to be supreme, and blacks as unworthy. Racial mixes came to be seen as somewhere in between.

Many decades later, the author argues, similar views continue to influence those in other nations because of continued Western economic and cultural penetration of these other societies. People in other countries aspire to Western cultural behavior, and, in the process, "unconsciously" accept Western ideas about race. The influence of Western culture upon other cultures extends to the transmission of the idea that evaluations of people should be based on skin color. There is brown racism, according to the author.

Note, too, that the author presents various social psychological explanations of why brown people, under the influence of Western culture, might want to devalue blacks and set themselves apart from blacks.

Probably no problem of race relations in the contemporary world has been more free from critical scrutiny than brown racism. I use "brown" here . . . in the figurative sense, as a reference to the neither white nor black but colored peoples of the third world (the Chinese, East Indians, Filipinos, Mestizos, etc.).

Excerpted from Washington, Robert E. (1990), "Brown racism and the formation of a world system of racial stratification," *International Journal of Politics, Culture, and Society*, 4(2), 209–227.

These peoples occupy an intermediate position along the black-white spectrum of color classification. By brown racism, I refer to the prevalence of prejudice among these fair complexioned colored groups and societies toward blacks, especially those of African ancestry.

. . . Brown racism is commonplace throughout the third world. . . .

. . . In what follows I shall contend . . . that the current form of brown racism, and the global system of racial stratification through which it is manifested, are post-colonial adaptations of white Western imperialism and are effected through the latter's cultural hegemony in third world societies. . . .

THE FORMATIVE PHASE: COLONIAL SYSTEMS OF RACIAL STRATIFICATION AND THE EMERGENCE OF BROWN RACISM

It has been widely recognized that European colonial expansion into Asia, Africa, and the Americas was legitimated by beliefs in white racial superiority. As one author has noted:

The dilemma of the imperialist democracy was much more happily solved if 'the native' was permanently and genetically inferior. . . . It seemed manifest that evolution had culminated in the people of North-Western Europe and North America, who dominated the world and, in their own eyes, surpassed all others in skill, intelligence, beauty and moral standards. (Mason, 1970a: 31–33)

Often European colonial conquests were viewed as religiously mandated obligations to spread Western civilization and assume control over the backward people of color throughout the world. For instance.

A. T. Beveridge . . . in 1900, lectured his colleagues in the United States Senate: 'God has not been preparing the English speaking and Teutonic peoples for a thousand years for nothing but vain and idle self-contemplation and self-admiration. No! He has made us the master organizers of the world to establish system where chaos reigns. . . . He has made us adept in government that [we] may administer government among savage and servile peoples. (Banton, 1967: 49)

The effect of early European colonial conquests was the emergence of localized dual layered systems of racial stratification comprised of white Europeans at the top and "natives" at the bottom. "In European colonies all natives were treated alike, regardless of the numerous distinctions they made among themselves" (Shibutani, 1969, 1969: 201). These localized dual layered systems of

racial stratification, however, were seldom of long duration. Either because of a shortage of European women or the importation of non-white laborers from other regions or both, they evolved into multi-layered stratification systems which were maintained by direct European colonial domination (Ballhatchet, 1980; Mason, 1970a; Schermerhorn, 1970).

In one type of situation, where sexual relations between European men and native females resulted in offspring, a status distinction was established between those of mixed race and those born of the native population. The dominant European groups drew boundaries of the color line, placing the mixed race group into a separate and intermediate racial category. . . .

The appearance of these mixed race European-native groups in colonies and their identification with the Europeans resulted in the first pattern of brown racism: the antipathy of mixed race groups toward the native groups.[1] The antipathy of these mixed race groups resulted from their having internalized the color valuations of the European colonials and from the superior status privileges granted them—such as separate schools, better employment opportunities, and in some cases, the right to emigrate to the mother country. These privileges were denied to the darker skinned native groups. . . .

Early manifestations of brown racism were also evidenced in situations where there was importation of groups from one colonial region to another for the purpose of providing labor. Such policies often resulted in the co-presence of brown skinned and black African groups.

What is significant about the above patterns is the formation of localized multi-layered stratification systems comprised of white Europeans at the top, mixed race and/or brown groups in the middle, and Africans at the bottom. (Morner, 1970). Interestingly, the status distinction between browns and blacks originated by European colonials became so ingrained that the moral objections to the abuse of browns were seldom extended to blacks (Mason, 1970a; Rout, 1976). As one British student of racial relations notes in reference to Brazil,

It is pertinent to recall that many of the liberal Portuguese who . . . championed the cause of the South American Indians at this time, did not regard the enslavement of Negroes as wrongful or protest so strongly about their ill treatment. (Banton, 1967: 259)

It is also noteworthy that Mahatma Gandhi, who began his resistance movement against the racial policies of British colonialism in South Africa, restricted his protest to the treatments of Indians. He ignored the plight of the much larger and more severely oppressed African group. The pariah status imposed on Africans was deliberately contrived to prevent integration of brown and black communities and thereby fragment opposition to white European colonial domination. This status distinction between blacks and browns can also be seen in the colonial policies of Queen Isabella of Spain which exempted Amerindians, but not Africans, from slavery (Rout, 1976: 22). The consequences of that status distinction have been described by a historian of race relations in Latin America.

Under the Spanish system, no black or mulatto could have an Indian servant, but Indians could and did have Africans as slaves. Moreover, Indians had cooperated with Spaniards and hunted down rebellious blacks in Hispaniola in 1522. . . . Furthermore, once the native came to understand that the Spaniards regarded Africans as an inferior being, they were often prone to adopt the same attitude (Route, 1976: 121). . . .

During the colonial era, to briefly recapitulate, brown racism arose out of European administrative and military domination and the status gradations the latter created through elaborating a racially based ideology. . . .

THE TRANSITIONAL ANTI-COLONIAL PHASE AND THE ILLUSION OF UNITY

Throughout much of the third world, the post World War Two era was characterized by national independence movements oriented to both anti-colonial and anti-racist ideology. Among third world intellectuals and political elites of color a feeling of unity evolved based on the view that racism was the prejudice of white Easterners toward nonwhites.

The high point in this movement of solidarity among third world leaders of color was the conference in Bandung, Indonesia in 1955. In the words of a *Newsweek* magazine article:

The Columbo Powers (India, Pakistan, Ceylon, Burma, and Indonesia) convoked an unprecedented conference of officials from 30 Asian and African nations, representing more than half of the world's people. . . . The sponsoring powers seemed to be aiming vaguely at a sort of Monroe Doctrine against colonialism. Their basic philosophy was that Asian and African nations have some common destiny, freeing them from the power politics of the white race and setting them aside from the Atlantic and Soviet blocs. (*Newsweek*, 1955: 32)

The effects of a number of world shaking events led up to this movement of third world unity. First, there were Marxist influences. As one author has noted, "Lenin's dicta . . . that 'colonialism is the worst and the most extreme form of capitalism, but also its last' could not fail to impress anti-imperialists from Asia and Africa" (Kimble, 1973:3).

Second, there was the feeling of a bond among non-white peoples influenced by the shared experiences of racial oppression. In fact, as early as the beginning of the century, we can see an assertion of this view of a simple white/nonwhite division of the world in the declaration of W. E. B. DuBois, the black American pan-Africanist leader, that "the problem of the twentieth century is the problem of the color line" (Tuttle, 1973: 65). This sentiment was echoed by Richard Wright, the exiled black American writer, who attended the Bandung Conference and characterized that gathering as a meeting of "the despised, the insulted, the hurt, the dispossessed—in short—the underdogs of the human race" (Wright, 1956: 12). . . .

The spirit of Bandung fueled the anti-colonial movement and gave it a new impetus. . . .

Significantly, however, no one mentioned the color prejudice of brown groups toward Africans. Apparently that prejudice was deemed insignificant in the face of the overwhelming force of European colonial domination and the deep-rootedness of white racism. . . . No doubt some were motivated not to mention the brown racism issue because of its potentially disruptive effect on the solidarity of the anti-colonial struggle.

THE NEO-COLONIAL ERA AND
THE EMERGENCE OF THE WORLD
SYSTEM OF RACIAL STRATIFICATION

Western imperialism during the post World War Two era shifted from a colonial to a neo-colonial form of domination. White Western capitalism forged ties of economic dependency between itself and the former colonies as well as those third world regions that had escaped colonialism.

While much has been written about the economics of neo-colonialism, too little attention has been paid to its cultural process. What had been previously achieved through direct administrative and military control was achieved during the post war era through cultural hegemony—the propagation of Western values through which third world peoples are conditioned to acceptance of a world view that facilitates Western economic domination. Two crucial preconditions lay behind this development: the political displacement of direct European colonial control and the transformation of the technology of cultural communication. Under the control of white Western nations, this new technology of cultural communication facilitated the diffusion of Western popular culture—via films, radio, television, etc.— throughout the third world. . . .

Among the values diffused by Western culture are color valuations based on ideological assumptions of white superiority. This is evidenced in the consistency of race/color rankings throughout the contemporary world.

The valuations underlying this global stratification system are perceived not as racial but modern because white Western films, magazines, television and news publications project such values in a subliminal form. Thus, the images of white superiority propagated by these cultural products largely escape the notice of the recipient societies. Indeed, the same cultural influences that create attractions to hamburgers, Western music, Western clothing fashions and Western style home furnishings also create attractions to Western categories of color valuation. Third world societies, subjected to this cultural hegemony, soon began to evidence clear tendencies toward brown racism—manifested in positive valuation of whiteness and negative valuations of blackness.

Whereas the colonial form of brown racism was the result of contacts between browns and blacks, the neo-colonial form often exists independent of such contact. Thus, when we find these negative valuations of blackness in an ideological form (that is, expressed in terms of beliefs about the biological inferiority of blacks) in societies that have had no contact with blacks except that derived from white Western cultural media, we must conclude these are products of white Western culture.

THE MANIFESTATIONS
OF BROWN RACISM

What is most striking is the extent of antipathy toward blacks among brown groups throughout the world. This antipathy, based on beliefs about the innate inferiority of Africans—beliefs which typically precede contacts with the latter, is the result of the assimilation of white Western culture in the post colonial era. An illustration of how these negative race/color categories are formed is provided by the experience of black American soldiers when first stationed in Oahu, Hawaii, during World War Two.

The presence of a large number of white soldiers from the mainland had much to do with the importation of stereotyped conceptions. At first, many Hawaiian girls treated the Negroes like all other soldiers, but they soon found themselves under pressure to make distinctions. Girls who danced with Negroes at the U.S.O. were ostracized; in time most hostesses refused to dance with Negroes, even though they had initially assumed that they were to entertain all servicemen. (Shibutani, 1969: 205) . . .

Parallel problems are encountered by blacks in China. In . . . May, 1986 at Tianjin University, a skirmish between African and Chinese students occurred. It was a five hour long rock and bottle throwing brawl between 300–500 Chinese students and approximately 18 foreign (mostly African) students (Scott, 23 June 1986: 51). Shortly afterwards, in June 1986, as a result of the incident, there was a mass demonstration of 200 African student in Beijing to highlight racism in China. Complained one African student from Togo, "The Chinese do not consider us human" (Scott, 19, June 1986: 20).

According to the African Student Union (which monitors cases of racism against African students) "most cases of trouble with university or government authorities involve Africans who dated Chinese women" (Scott, 23 June 1986: 51).

Brazil—another society that evidences a pervasive brown racism— is often mistakenly thought to be free of racial prejudice because the few blacks who attain upper class status are socially defined as whites. However, this token exemption in no way obviates the negative categorization of blackness. As one scholar has pointed out:

The Brazilian outlook assumes that everyone would like to be white and that the whiter a person is the higher he is likely to be in the social status scale. . . . The psychological effects upon dark skinned people of a wholesale desire for whitening are also unfavorable. They entail acceptance by dark people of the belief that whites are justified in discriminating against them (Banton, 1967: 280).

This pattern is hardly restricted to societies where blacks constitute a minority. We see a similar hierarchy of race/color in the West Indies where the majority populations are black. Referring to Jamaica, Henriques notes: "The important point is that all the different groups, from the black to the white, accept that the European is the ideal and the Negro inferior" (Henriques, 1964: 128). . . .

Hundreds of illustrations of brown racism could be cited.[2] Its prevalence in such countries as Mexico, Saudi Arabia, Sudan, Dominican Republic, Thailand, Morocco, and Venezuela is documentable.

THE SOCIAL PSYCHOLOGICAL DYNAMICS BEHIND BROWN RACISM

Like any other racism, brown racism is based on a culturally embedded categorical system of classification. In this instance, the system is absorbed concomitant with Westernization. This process facilitates the largely unconscious assignment of negative valuations to blacks based solely on their physical appearance. However, it does not explain the social psychological functions of those valuations. To explain this, it is necessary to understand the psychological implications of the Western white oriented racial stratification system from which brown racism derives. That stratification system is distinguished by the following characteristics:

1. It is based on the ideal of white racial features.
2. It consists of a continuum of color valuation— that is, the further away one's group is from the ideal, the lower its status.
3. Because the system has a positive and a negative mode, it possesses only two unambiguously defined statuses: whiteness at the top and blackness at the bottom.

For individuals and groups who fit neither the positive or negative ideal, the consequences for their color/racial identity of acculturating the white Western world view (i.e., Westernization) are marginalization and psychological anxiety. Because they occupy an ambiguously defined position, browns fear being categorically identified with blacks. Their preoccupation with segregating themselves from blacks reflects their desire to avoid the stigma associated with blackness. This helps to explain why there is considerably more fraternization between whites and blacks and whites and browns than between browns and blacks. Whites, who possess the clearly defined superior status in the racial hierarchy, need not fear being subsumed under the same category as blacks. Whereas browns, lacking such a clearly defined superior status, are plagued by this fear. And for this reason, they . . . exert strenuous energy to segregate themselves from blacks.

It is not only brown groups' repulsion from blacks but also their attraction to whites—indeed in many cases their aspirations for whiteness—that are produced by marginalization and the attendant psychological anxiety. This helps us to understand another curious fact. Among brown/white, black/white and brown/black rates of intermarriage, the latter are always—and by a considerable degree—the lowest. And in those few instances where members of a brown group marry a black person, they will tend to be ostracized by their community.

It might be argued that these low intermarriage rates between browns and blacks are merely the effect of ethnic differences, i.e., of the desires of brown groups to retain their distinctive ethnic cultures. However, this thesis fails to account for the consistently higher rates of intermarriage of browns to whites and to members of other brown groups who have different ethnic backgrounds.

Insofar as brown groups internalize the Western world view, they will experience a psychological need to distance themselves from blacks in order to validate their claims to superior racial status within the hierarchy of Western white color valuations. Thus, their anxiety about their racial status has the paradoxical effect of causing them to inadvertently support the principle of white superiority and the hierarchy of color stratification. That is, it causes them to support the system which also defines them as inferior. . . .

REFERENCES

Ballhatchet, K. *Race, Sex and Class Under the Raj*, New York: St. Martin's Press, 1980.

Banton, M. *Race Relations*, New York: Basic Books, 1967.

Henriques, F. *Jamaica, New York*: London and Maxwell, 1964.

———*Children of Conflict*, New York E. P. Dutton, 1975.

Kimble, D. *The Afro-Asian Movement*, Jerusalem: Israel Universities Press, 1973.

Mason, P. *Patterns of Dominance*, Oxford, England: Oxford University Press, 1970a.

———*Race Relations*, Oxford, England: Oxford University Press, 1970b.

Morner, M. *Mixture in the History of Latin America*, New York: Little Brown, 1967. *Race and Class in Latin America*, New York: Columbia University Press, 1970.

Newsweek, "Asia—A Place in the Sun," 17 January, 1955.

Rout, L. B. *The African Experience in Spanish America*, London: Cambridge University Press, 1976.

Schermerhorn, R. A. *Comparative Ethnic Relations*, New York: Random House, Schiller, H. I. *Communication and Cultural Domination*, White Plains, N.Y.: International Arts and Sciences Press, 1976.

Scott, M. "Blacks and Red Faces," *Far Eastern Economic Review*, vol. 132, 19 June, 1986.

———"Black Students and the Tide of Prejudice," *Far Eastern Economic Review*, vol. 132, 23 June, 1986.

Shibutani, T. and Kwan, K. *Ethnic Stratification*, New York: McMillan, 1969.

Tuttle, W. M. (ed.) *W. E. B. DuBois*, Englewood Cliffs, N.J.: Prentice Hall, 1973.

Urdy, J. R., Bauman, K. E., Chase, C. "Skin Color, Status, and Mate Selection," *American Journal of Sociology*, v. 76 (Jan. 1971).

Wright, R. *The Color Curtain*, Cleveland and New York: The World Publishing Co., 1956.

NOTES

1. This incipient pattern of brown racism differs from the modal pattern in that it was not characterized by Afrophobia. Nevertheless, it shared the basic characteristics of the modal pattern—identification with whites and antipathy toward the darker skinned native population.
2. Actually, symptoms of brown racism can be found among groups with African ancestry.

For instance, until relatively recently, fair complexioned African Americans (e.g., often those of mixed racial backgrounds) tended to express prejudice against darker skinned African Americans. (see: Urdy *et al.*, 1971: 722–733).

8.2 Educational Failure and Positive Discrimination

Jonathan Potter and Margaret Wetherell

The next excerpt in this section is about one of many ideological causes of status inequality: "common sense" explanations of failure and success. Here, in a look at the subtleties of racism, Potter and Wetherell examine the ways white New Zealanders discuss "positive discrimination."

This is a set of policies that aims to improve the access of the native Maori people to higher education. Criticizing positive discrimination is a delicate matter in liberal-minded New Zealand. An outright rejection of the policy would be seen as racist. But certain ways of speaking allow people to express anti-egalitarian sentiments that would be socially unacceptable if voiced in other ways.

The researchers find two polite ways of objecting to positive discrimination in common use. First, many respondents claim that positive discrimination increases the division between whites and Maoris by causing resentment. Second, many argue that universities and colleges should admit only the most qualified students, regardless of race or ethnicity, since doing otherwise means lowering the standards.

Potter and Wetherell provide an explanation, and example, of how majority group members resist change to greater racial equality. The "new" authority or legitimacy (positive discrimination) is being resisted by invoking apparently some contradictory legitimacies—the idea that success should occur only according to merit and the idea that we should seek relative harmony between races.

This paper is derived from a broader project concerned with racism and specifically with the discourses of white majority group members in New Zealand as they make sense of 'race relations' in that country. One aim of this project was to examine how situations of exploitation, discrimination and unequal power are legitimated. As Thompson has argued, 'to study ideology is to study the ways in which meaning (signification) serves to sustain relations of domination' (1984: 131). . . .

Excerpted from Potter, Jonathan, and Margaret Wetherell (1989), "Fragmented ideologies: Accounts of educational failures and positive discrimination," *Text*, 9(2), 175–190. With permission of Mouton de Gruyter, a division of Walter de Gruyter & Co. Publishers, Berlin and New York.

The analysis that follows is concerned chiefly with two closely related topics. First, we will examine one of the ways white New Zealanders accounted for putative educational inequalities between Pakehas (whites) and Maoris in schools; second, we will examine the ways in which 'positive discrimination,' programs of affirmative action to provide educational support for Maoris and other minority groups, were criticized. The focus will be on the interpretative procedures and resources that participants bring to bear when arguing against 'positive discrimination'. . . .

BACKGROUND TO THE STUDY
AND SELECTION OF EXTRACTS

The study was conducted in New Zealand in 1984 focusing on Pakeha (white) majority group members. Sixty five open ended interviews were conducted across a sample with a range of ages and political affiliations, including both sexes. The adults were mainly in professional occupations; two small groups of final year school students and some individual students were also interviewed.

For this study we searched the interview transcripts for references to 'educational inequalities' and 'positive discrimination' and equivalent notions. Although 'educational inequality' was addressed in fifty-four interviews, only twenty eight of these also included discussion of 'positive discrimination'. Of these, ten expressed predominantly approving views of 'positive discrimination', five were both approving and disapproving, while thirteen expressed predominantly disapproving views. Our focus for the rest of this paper will be solely on the latter two groups.

ANALYSIS

We will start with a complete passage—chosen because it was brief and broadly typical—which illustrates the way different themes can be meshed together. These themes will be elaborated using passages from other interviews. The respondent, Pratt, is a female

high school student aged seventeen whose father worked as a computer engineer.

Extract One: Pratt

Interviewer. Yeah. Why, there's quite, there's such a big gap between, er, Maori and Pakeha educational attainment, although it is decreasing, so you find very few Maoris at university or technical colleges and so on. Why?

Pratt. They can't afford to go most of the time. Ha, ha.

Interviewer. Or say in the seventh form even, at school; why do you think, what's that about, causing that?

Pratt. Um well, they's trying to fit into something that they don't (.) belong to. We find it far easier because it's in us, because our people are the ones who are setting the exams to their standards in the first place, but the Maori people, their old Maori elders aren't the ones setting the exams for them, and so I suppose everything, they think about things differently and it comes out. And of course they have more trouble expressing English (yeah) so I suppose that must be a big disadvantage.

Interviewer. Yeah. What do you think about positive discrimination, in the sense of say keeping aside places at university for Maori students, er, or if a Pakeha and a Maori are both eligible, giving a preference to the Maori student? Do you think those sorts of moves are reasonable ones?

Pratt. I don't, no. Because, while it might sound all very nice, it's just going to cause more um (.) disharmony. I mean, that means that the Pakeha people are going to get upset because, I mean, that person who's missing out is going to be pretty mad. And I don't know, I don't think so. I think just whoever comes in the top should get in. . . .

THE ACCOUNT
OF EDUCATION INEQUALITY

The respondent answers the question about the cause of educational inequality by specifying factors which are different between Pakeha and Maoris—styles of thinking, ease in expressing English—and observing that exams are set by Pakehas. For Pratt these things seem to be *intrinsic* to the social groups Maori and Pakeha, for she talks about them being 'in us' and uses the powerfully charged notion of 'belonging'—the problem for Maoris is they don't belong. Thus she offers a lay psychological and socio-psychological account which explains differential attainment by way of underlying differences in ways of thinking and the differences in examinations which follow from them.

The second feature to note is Pratt does not formulate the described situation as unfair. The situation could be glossed as 'unfair', where standards are biased toward the skills of one group, or even by proto-sociological ideas such as 'cultural domination'. It seems, however, that the situation is being offered by Pratt as one where the disadvantage is a consequence of *natural* differences between social groups where who belongs and who does not is pre-defined.

THE RESPONSE
TO 'POSITIVE DISCRIMINATION'

Undermining togetherness

The respondent's negative answer to the question about 'positive discrimination' is immediate and unhedged; and her rejection of 'positive discrimination' is quickly followed up by a warrant. The warrant has an interesting dual structure using what has been dubbed a reality/appearance (R/A) device (Potter, 1987; Eglin, 1979). As its name implies, the R/A device posits an apparent, superficial or surface version of some event, phenomenon or objective and then contrasts this with the real, or true version. In this case, 'positive discrimination' is said to:

'sound all very nice'

(the appearance) but:

'it's just going to cause more um (.) disharmony'

(the reality).

The metaphors of harmony and disharmony are recurrent features of the 'togetherness' repertoire. In the logic of this repertoire, togetherness is a harmonious state which can be destabilized by interventions which stress conflict or difference. The 'togetherness' repertoire thus provides a resource for criticising 'positive discrimination.' Disharmony is depicted as caused by the 'positive discrimination' and 'positive discrimination' is constituted as the kind of thing that would cause disharmony.

Another feature of this segment of talk provides more evidence of the care with which the respondent orientates to issues of blame and criticism. There is delay indicating some care or possibly lack of certainty in the selection of an appropriate descriptor for the effect of 'positive discrimination':

'it's just going to cause more um (.) disharmony'

and the term chosen is not only a central term in the 'togetherness' repertoire, it is also ideal for withholding or limiting attribution of blame and causality (Kress and Hodge, 1979; Potter and Reicher, 1987). Just as 'police shoot strikers' may be transformed to 'sad loss of life' in a right-wing newspaper account to obscure problematic causal processes (c.f. Trew, 1979) so 'Pakehas resent/threaten Maoris' may be transformed into the less blaming formulation: 'disharmony'.

The respondent goes on to specify how this disharmony will present itself in the Pakeha people getting upset and this in turn is immediately accounted for:

'because, I mean, that person who's missing out is going to be pretty mad.'

So although the disharmony is re-formulated as unrest in a particular group, the blameworthiness of the unrest is undermined by giving it a reason (Scott and Lyman, 1968): they are 'missing out'.

One final detail of the passage is worth noting. When the respondent was accounting for putative educational inequality she used pronouns in an inclusive manner—'they' for Maoris; 'we', 'us', 'our people' for Pakeha. However, in the response on 'positive discrimination' she uses more distanced constructions: 'the Pakeha people', 'the person who's missing out'. She seems to be orientating to the potential culpability of Pakeha 'upset' and separating herself from it.

Overall in this passage, then, we see this respondent designing her talk in a way that provides a criticism of 'positive discrimination' constructed out of the 'togetherness' repertoire. The fact that the 'togetherness' repertoire has the status in this community of a taken-for-granted common-place makes it a powerful rhetorical resource.

While the respondent in Extract One stressed the disharmony facet of the 'togetherness' repertoire other respondents stressed positive discrimination was bad because it was discrimination. For example:

Extract Two:

Border. The very heart of that is discrimination. I mean discrimination itself has very negative terms. I mean there's also the point if you point positive and a negative together, you get a negative. (ha) I mean I think the very fact that it's discrimination cancels out the fact that it's er perhaps an advantage. [ ] . . . I think the key word is discrimination really. It's a negative word.

The notion of discrimination can itself be seen to have the status of a common-place whose badness is taken for granted. As such, the very terminology for describing this policy carries the resources for its own criticism; these sorts of difficulties are no doubt one reason why policies of this kind are now often dubbed programs of *affirmative action.* Other ways of deploying the 'togetherness' repertoire to construct criticisms of 'positive discrimination' involved redescriptions of the policy which formulated it in terms of the creation of division. For example:

Extract Four:

St. Pauls, Pupil Z. It's apartheid.

Although it was common for criticisms of 'positive discrimination' to be warranted by reference to its role in undermining togetherness, constructions of this kind were typically

minor elements in participants' responses. An alternative form of account was more common and, can be formulated as a criticism of 'positive discrimination' for undermining meritocratic ideals.

THE RESPONSE TO 'POSITIVE DISCRIMINATION'

Undermining meritocracy

In their criticisms of 'positive discrimination' respondents recurrently used formulations involving a meritocratic repertoire organized around three central assumptions:

1. New Zealand society has social mobility allowing everyone to have equal opportunity;
2. people have natural levels of ability which the education system is able to assess by, for example, examinations;
3. the people who have the most ability should get the places in advanced courses and the most demanding and best paid jobs. . . .

This form of discourse could be used to criticise New Zealand society for failing to live up to this normative ideal.

Coming back to Extract One, the respondent ends her criticism of 'positive discrimination' in the following way:

'I think just whoever comes in the top should get in'.

We can see how this criticism is constructed by implying 'positive discrimination' undermines meritocratic ideals, specifically the ideal that students with the best marks should receive places in higher education.

Two features of this criticism are notable. First, it is taken to be an appropriate argument in itself. Indeed, this taken-for-granted quality is characteristic of meritocratic discourse across the sample.

The second point is the potential tension between this criticism and the respondent's earlier account of educational inequality. Within the limited domain of meritocratic discourse 'coming top', in exams say, is a straightforward index of ability. That is, the appropriateness of those 'coming top' being offered positions is predicated on the objectivity of the measures used to rank students. Furthermore, the meritocratic model presupposes that people are sorted only by merit and motivation rather than by essential group attributes. However, in the respondent's account of educational inequality she had questioned the basis of examinations as culturally impartial arbiters of ability and laid heavy emphasis on basic (racial) differences between Pakeha and Maori ways of thinking. Indeed, we could take the 'joke' that the participant offers ('They can't afford to go most of the time') as embodying serious information (Drew, 1987; Mulkay, 1988); namely, that inequalities in resources restrict Maori educational success. This too fits uneasily with the meritocratic account offered later.

It is possible to make sense of this variability in discourse by thinking about the different kinds of interpretative tasks the respondent was engaged in. The idea that Maoris do not do well at school because their ways of thinking are not suited to Pakeha exam standards is a possible way of making sense of educational inequity. However, it is not a form of reasoning suited to criticising 'positive discrimination'. On the contrary, members of our sample on occasion argued *for* 'positive discrimination' on the grounds that it increases equality by overcoming systematic cultural biases of the kind described by Pratt.

The meritocratic ideal is much more suitable for criticising 'positive discrimination' because of its assumption of the neutrality of qualifications and freedom of social advancement. It embodies an implicit social model in which 'positive discrimination' can be depicted as unfair and discriminatory.

In line with other studies of natural discourse, then, we see Pratt varying her claims and explanations according to the details of the interpretative context.

The following, edited, extracts illustrate some further facets to meritocratic discourse:

Extract Six: Ackland, Border, Irvine, Munman, Williamson

Ackland. You know it could have a tendency to lower the standard if you (Mm.) took it in on the numbers basis rather than an ability basis.

Border. Uh, I would probably get upset if I was passed over in that position. But by the same token, a Maori would too. But, um, I, I agree that if the standards are the same it's all right, but I don't, the standards got—I mean, if the Maori's going to be in European society, he's got to live up to European standards, I mean there's no way you can lower the standards and expect him to stay in the society.

Irvine. Well, the medical profession is probably our, is one of our, it's a terribly important profession, you know. (Ha ha.) Heaven's above! [ ] You can't, you can't have a person who gets thirty percent who, you know, becomes a doctor, you know, it just [end of tape].

Munman. Well, I don't think that they should have quotas, I think that they should get in on merit.

Williamson. They're talking about dragging the educational system down now to the standard of the Maori.

All these passages formulate the consequences of 'positive discrimination' policies, namely that it will 'lower standards'. Again, the notion of standards is neither made accountable nor decomposed; standards are treated as unproblematic.

However, standards are on occasion tied to the social categories Maori and Pakeha. This is true, for example, of the Border and Williamson passages quoted in Extract Six. And such accounts are redolent of traditional racist notions of a natural hierarchy of the races. There is a subtle irony to such accounts; for the critical force of meritocratic thinking seems to be principally derived from the idea that ability or merit should decide furtherance rather than category membership. Yet here the standard for assessing ability seems *itself* to be tied to category membership. Border identifies 'European standards' with the appropriate standards for a modern society.

CONCLUSION

In this paper we have looked at the organization of one respondent's discourse concerning educational inequality and 'positive discrimination' and at the way some of the themes in this discourse are reiterated and developed in the discourse of other respondents. In particular we examined the deployment of the 'togetherness' repertoire and the use of meritocratic discourse.

The 'togetherness' and meritocratic repertoires are taken-for-granted normative ideals which 'positive discrimination' is taken to conflict with. Togetherness would be disrupted by the erection of barriers between groups and the discrimination involved in 'positive discrimination' would undermine the meritocratic organization of education by working from quotas rather than merit.

The effectiveness of these approaches (at least measured by their wide deployment amongst the critics of 'positive discrimination') is partly a consequence of their meshing of practical and principled elements. Thus the meritocratic model could be supported as efficient (the best people do the most demanding work) and just (colour blind). Likewise, togetherness could be taken as something both good in the abstract and, in practice, making for a well run, harmonious society.

We are not suggesting these themes are mechanically reproduced as fixed models. Indeed, the concept of interpretative repertoire emphasises both the process of selection from the various facets of the repertoire to fit the occasion at hand and the work that goes into using those facets in context sensitive ways. It is notable that respondents used the 'togetherness' and meritocratic repertoires to manufacture criticisms of 'positive discrimination [and] on other occasions used these same repertoires to construct warrants for it.

We have tried to indicate the way these respondents fashion their activities (accountings, criticisms) out of a patchwork of pre-existing resources. What we have found striking is the fragmentation of these resources; the way disparate interpretative systems are drawn on by the same respondent.

REFERENCES

Drew, P. (1987) 'Po-faced receipts of teases,' *Linguistics*, 25: 219–53.

Eglin, P. (1979) 'Resolving reality disjunctures on Telegraph Avenue: A study of practical reasoning', *Canadian Journal of Sociology*, 4: 359–77.

Kress, G. and Hodge, B. (1979) *Language as Ideology*. London: Routledge and Kegan Paul.

Mulkay, M. (1988) *On Humour: Its nature and its place in modern society*. Cambridge: Polity.

Potter, J. (1987) 'Reading repertoires: A preliminary study of some techniques that scientists use to construct readings', *Science and Technology Studies*, 5: 112–21.

Potter, J. and Reicher, S. (1987) 'Discourses of community and conflict: The organization of social categories in accounts of a 'riot', *British Journal of Social Psychology*, 26, 25–40.

Scott, M.B. and Lyman, S.M. (1968) 'Accounts', *American Sociological Review*, 33: 46–62.

Thompson, J.B. (1984) *Studies in the Theory of Ideology*. Cambridge: Polity.

——(1988) 'Mass communication and modern culture: Contribution to a critical theory of ideology', *Sociology*, 22: 359–84.

Trew, T. (1979) 'Theory and Ideology at Work', in R. Fowler, B. Hodge, G. Kress, and T. Trew (Eds.) *Language and Control*. London: Routledge and Kegan Paul.

8.3 Merit and Power

Brian Martin

We often think of bureaucracies as workplaces that operate very "rationally"—
as places where merit (in the sense of people's skills and abilities and performances) is carefully assessed. These assessments are then used to place people
at different occupational status levels, it is believed.

The next excerpt is about another ideological cause of status inequality: the
belief in stratification by merit. In this excerpt the author explains that our
beliefs provide essential support for, or legitimation of, inequality in the work
world. Indeed, so compelling is **the merit principle** that it is used by both
supporters and opponents of affirmative action in the workplace. We just saw
(above) another example of opponents' uses of the merit principle in Potter
and Wetherell's study.

The author shows how the belief that merit can be the basic determinant of
job placement and advancement is quite erroneous. Problems in measuring
merit, the arbitrary use of power by employers, seniority systems, and pools of
available talent that are bigger than the number of good jobs all work against
there being a close correspondence between merit and advancement.
Because of this, the author sees no reason to accept the critiques of affirmative
action using the merit principle.

Note that the author suggests that the merit of *workplaces* could, and
should, be assessed. We should ask how well they maximize the uses of their
human resources and the opportunities provided for personal growth of workers. Some policies for moving in these directions are put forward.

. . . Paradoxically, the concept of merit has
become a catchphrase of both supporters and
opponents of legislated equal employment
opportunity. Advocates of women's and
minority rights have supported application of
the merit principle, underpinned by affirmative action to remove unfair starting handi-
caps, to provide real equal employment
opportunity. On the other hand, traditional
bureaucratic elites have invoked the merit
principle to oppose what they allege is
reverse discrimination against white middle-
class males. Merit is being used by both sides

as a tool. To understand how this comes
about, it is necessary to examine the power
structures of organisations.

The merit principle is most commonly
applied in bureaucratic or semibureaucratic
organisations. These organisations are constructed on hierarchy and a division of
labour. The classical picture sees bureaucracy as an instrument for rational administration, operating on the basis of universalistic principles (Weber 1964). Merit, an
assessment of a person's ability, experience
and motivation relevant to performing a job,
would seem a suitable principle for measuring and rewarding performance in an ideal
bureaucracy.

What is merit in the conventional theory
of bureaucracy? "Ability plus effort" is a typi-

Excerpted from Martin, Brian (1987), "Merit and
power," *Australian Journal of Social Issues*, 22(2),
May, 436–451. With permission of the Australian
Council of Social Service.

cal formula. There are three standard ways of assessing merit: examinations, credentials and work experience and performance. . . .

In practice examinations, credentials and performance are mixed together in the assessment of merit. . . . The question which needs to be faced by supporters of equal opportunity is whether merit can be applied in a relatively unbiased manner. If this cannot be done, it may not be wise to rely too heavily on merit in overcoming discrimination in employment. To approach this issue, I will look critically at the way power is exercised in large organisations. . . .

THE POLITICAL PERSPECTIVE ON ORGANISATIONS

The traditional Weberian picture of bureaucracy as a rational system has strongly influenced organizational theory. Nevertheless, it is widely recognised that actual bureaucracies do not behave precisely according to Weber's ideal-typical picture. There is a constant struggle for power within bureaucracies, a process which includes power relations embodied in interpersonal discourse, competition between internal factions, conflicts between bureaucrats and clients, and struggles between bureaucracies.

Rejecting the Weberian assumptions is the political perspective on organizations presented by Deena Weinstein (1977, 1979), according to which bureaucracies are best understood as political systems. Individuals and groups within bureaucracies exercise power using the social and material resources available, including control over labour power, positions, clients, funding, and knowledge. Overt political activity by workers is inhibited by fear of reprisals and by habits of acquiescence, often based on beliefs or fear.

The key role of power is obvious when oppositions form within bureaucracies. What usually happens is not a rational assessment of the claims of the dissidents, but suppression of the dissidents: corporation executives who speak out critically about their employer's behaviour typically will be sacked;

soldiers who rebel will be courtmartialed; rank-and-file revolts by trade unionists may be smashed by expulsions (Weinstein 1977, 1979; see also Anderson et al. 1980; Perrucci et al. 1980; Zald & Berger 1978).

Weinstein likens bureaucracies to authoritarian states in that control is exercised from the top with few opportunities for popular participation. Democratic structures are token or non-existent, and the elites control the main political and economic resources. The main difference between bureaucracies and authoritarian states is that normally bureaucratic elites cannot use violence to enforce their control. One consequence of this power struggle is that the goal of the bureaucracy may be displaced from outer service to inner control (Hummel 1977).

A similar analysis of professions developed in recent years sees occupational groups using knowledge and skills as resources to increase their power, wealth and status. Doctors for example use credentialing and licensing systems to deep down numbers in the medical profession and then use their control over the resulting scarce resource of "legitimate" expertise to push for higher salaries and control over medical decision-making (Freidson 1970; Johnson 1972; Larson 1977; Parkin 1979; Willis 1983). Opposition movements also arise in professions. The medical profession has routinely taken action to deny status and resources to challengers such as practitioners of "fringe therapies", for example by lobbying to deny their inclusion under medical benefits schedules.

The political picture of bureaucracy and professions provides a useful way to begin to analyse their interactions with systems based on class, gender and ethnicity. For example, there are various ways male domination is maintained in bureaucracies and professions. Overt discrimination against women is made possible by control of the top decision-making positions by men. Secondly, external support systems for employees are biased against women. Since women continue to carry most of the burden of housework and child care, most women employees are doing 'double duty' compared to men who have the support of wives for these tasks. Thirdly, organizational styles usually favour those with personal characteristics which are typically masculine, such as aggressiveness and competitiveness. Finally, the gender division of labour excludes most women from opportunities to rise in organizational or professional hierarchies. Similar mechanisms are used to limit the advancement of members of ethnic minorities, those who maintain links with working class culture, and those who take threatening political stands.

This example of the meshing of bureaucracy and patriarchy is silent about the precise mechanisms of domination and group cohesion within bureaucratic and patriarchal systems. One possible analysis could be based on the material interests of most men in patriarchal systems and of most bureaucratic elites in their positions. These elites, for example, mobilise the support of other men, lower in the job hierarchy, by supporting them against the challenge to jobs or status by women. This can explain management's acceptance of a constantly renegotiated gender division of labour (Game & Pringle 1983) which keeps women in the inferior jobs at the cost of overall efficiency.

How can the conventional application of the merit principle be compatible with the sort of bias consequent on the routine exercise of power to serve group interests? Let me look in turn at examinations, credentials and job performance.

The strengths of examinations in assessing merit include uniformity and anonymity (of those taking an examination to those marking it). But this does not remove the possibility of cultural bias. Examinations usually select out those schooled in the 'cultural mainstream' and those skilled in taking examinations, which is again an indication of success in the dominant culture within the schooling system.

Studies have shown the class bias in IQ tests (Kamin 1974). A few decades ago, only a . . . small fraction of children completed high school and therefore those who competed for professional and managerial jobs were a select group, mostly from better-off families. As progress through high school became more universal, it seemed everyone would be able to share in the 'common culture' sufficiently to obtain equal opportunity through examinations. But as schooling has become universalised, its focus has changed from preparation for elite careers to inculcating middle-class culture (Collins 1979)—something which works better for those with the appropriate class background and family support. Working class boys, for example, typically resist this process (Willis 1977). In any case, the outcome is culturally biased: those with the appropriate cultural background will learn most readily and be able to show their skill on ostensibly neutral examinations.

Another problem with examinations is that most of them have limited relevance to the job.

Even if these problems with examinations could be overcome, there is the problem of their limited use. Typically, examinations are used in recruitment, but once inside a bureaucracy, tenure is reasonably secure. A true merit system would have regular open competitions, in which any person could vie for any post. In only a few occupations, such as competitive sports and performing arts, is there a continuous and public examination of talent and performance which affects a person's standing and career. Significantly, these occupations are notable for their absence of formal examinations, and for the relative ease with which individuals can establish themselves without credentials.

Credentials, like examinations, commonly have little relevance to the job. Most of the skills for professional and managerial positions are learned on the job (Collins 1979). The role of formal education in reproducing and legitimating the social class structure has been widely documented (Bowles & Gintis 1976). Credentials are the symbols and currency of competence, but numerous studies have shown there is little connection between educational performance and job performance. . . .

What about job performance? The first point is that it is hard to separate out the performance of an individual worker within a bureaucracy (Collins 1979; Emery & Emery 1974). Work requires cooperation with other people and resources provided by other groups. Above all, performance depends on working as part of an overall system, on making the whole operation go smoothly. Who is to say what was a particular individual's contribution?

This question is key. People in the top positions evaluate performance. This gives them the opportunity to judge on the basis of conformity to the cultural norms of the organization. The concept of "political labour" is a valuable one here (Collins 1979). Much of the activity in bureaucracies and professions, especially in the higher echelons, consists of interacting with others through conversations, committee meetings, lunches and so forth. What is happening is a continual process of "social negotiation" over preferences, policies and alignments. The status of any individual is at stake in this process. Those who play the game poorly, or opt out, are liable to lose out in some reshuffle or power play. Others are able to forge alliances and mobilise resources to promote the interests of themselves and those similar to them (Kanter 1977). The problem here is that political labour depends on possessing the right cultural attributes and resources. Verbal skill, personal attributes and social compatibility are important.

The importance of political labour means it is difficult for cultural outsiders to get ahead.

A further problem is that most assessments of merit are confounded with simultaneous assessments of "loyalty" and "fitting in": whether a person gets along with workmates and superiors, is unlikely to rock the boat, associates with the right people, etc. This conformity is especially prized by organizational elites, since an uncommitted employee is a potential leader of or trigger for wider opposition. . . .

As long as the organizational resources are available to be used in power struggles, they will be used to maintain and extend the power of those who are best able to deploy them.

Within bureaucracies, the Weberian model of rational administration is itself a powerful rhetorical and ideological resource for maintaining commitment to the organisation. The belief in bureaucracy as administration is promoted especially by those who are successful in the system, since it attributes that success to individual performance rather than to being on the winning side of a power struggle.

In summary, individual productivity has a relatively low impact on career performance in large-scale organisations. Advancement depends greatly on jockeying for position, for example by forming alliances, obtaining personal credit for collective work and increasing the evaluation of particular types of contributions. In this struggle for position, resources provided by culture—namely the dominant white middle-class male culture—are vital.

While the struggle for advancement is part of a wider power struggle, it is no longer acceptable to admit the importance of system biases in an era in which egalitarian sentiments are strong. Hence it is convenient to justify decisions on the basis of merit because this legitimates inequality. This is the basis of the defence of "merit by traditionalists who oppose changes in the gender and ethnic composition of hierarchies. The supporters of legislated equal opportunity on the other hand recognise the biases built into normal selection processes and therefore push for "true" adherence to the merit principle, in other words merit stripped of its links to gender stereotypes, middle-class culture and so forth. This is the explanation of the paradox of merit: that both opponents and proponents of equal opportunity make appeals to it. . . .

THE DIVISION OF LABOUR

. . . The idea of merit in many circumstances is of great value to disadvantaged groups: the most blatant forms of discrimination are harder to sustain. But merit is not a perfect tool for creating equal opportunity: it has a fundamental flaw.

The most massive barrier to application of the merit principle in bureaucracies is the division of labour. It is virtually impossible for a cleaner or a steno-secretary to move into top management—or even to move from her position—no matter how well she does her job. In any situation where there are large differences between jobs, the problem arises that people can't be judged as unsuitable until they have been given a chance in the other job.

In some bureaucracies a limited degree of job rotation is practiced. This has the advantage of allowing individuals to show their ability in a variety of positions. But usually job rotation is only carried out with tasks on a similar level. Managing directors are not rotated to be gardeners, nor vice versa.

The main way this is justified is through appeal to the merit principle! For example, typists are refused opportunities to undertake research positions because they have neither the right credentials nor appropriate experience.

The problem is credentials usually have little relevance to the job, and previous experience says little about a person's ability to handle a different type of job.

This brings me to what I believe is a fundamental flaw in the usual conception of the merit principle. The application of 'merit' assumes the existing occupational slots are suitable for the allocation of meritorious workers to them. In other words, the merit principle assumes the slots are fixed while people are chosen for them—not vice versa.

The difficulties in this can be illustrated by a not-so-hypothetical example. Assume there are 10 people working in a section. They are all literate and have an average potential for learning. In a bureaucratic system, the 10 people are ranked 1 to 10: one person administers from the top while those at the bottom do routine work requiring little or no initiative. The person at the top develops a broad view of the operations, hobnobs with corresponding figures in other sections, obtains inside information about the organization and gains increasing confidence and self-assurance through the exercise of power and

from the deference of subordinates. The point is that the initial distribution of workers into slots could almost have been done at random, and the result would have been the same. The power system creates the very differences in information, confidence and performance which are used to justify it.

In practice, the workers are *not* allocated at random to different slots. White middle-class men hold most of the positions of power, and they use that power to maintain themselves and those like them in the top positions. The merit principle helps to sustain this system by justifying it: the merit principle may be the best justification yet for a highly stratified society (Young 1958).

But to be fair, it is not the merit principle which lies behind stratification. The most important support for system bias is the hierarchy itself. Resources are given to small groups which they use to maintain their privilege. It is inevitable that groups with more cultural resources will use those resources to gain organizational power, and use organizational power to promote group interests. While insisting on the application of a 'true' merit principle has the potential to make inroads into this system, a more far-reaching approach is to restructure the job hierarchy and division of labour. . . .

Under the project of socio-technical design (Herbst 1974), merit is just as usefully attached to the organization of work as to individuals. The most 'meritorious work organization' is the one which maximizes the performance, satisfaction and personal growth of all individuals, within the constraints of current knowledge and resources.

For example, socio-technical design typically implies elimination or automation of jobs which are satisfying to no one, rather than automation of the basis of profits and material productivity. . . .

. . . . It is important to realise that using merit as a lever for the advancement of individuals does nothing for the bulk of workers relegated to dead-end jobs and it may help to legitimate the whole system of inequality and privilege. Instead of applying the merit principle only to individuals, it should also be applied to work structures. Instead of workers being judged according to how they fulfill fixed job specifications, work structures should be evaluated according to how they allow the greatest use and development of each person's potential contribution.

REFERENCES

Anderson, R.M., Perrucci, R., Schendel, D.E. and Trachtman, L.E. (1980), *Divided Loyalties: Whistle-blowing at BART*, West Lafayette, Indiana: Purdue University.

Bowles, S. and Gintis, H. (1976), *Schooling in Capitalist America*, New York: Basic Books.

Collins, R. (1979), *The Credential Society*, New York: Academic Press.

Emery, F.E. and Emery, M. (1974), *Participative Design*, Canberra: Centre for Continuing Education, Australian National University.

Freidson, E. (1970), *Professional Dominance: The Social Structure of Medical Care*, New York: Atherton.

Game, A. and Pringle, R. (1983), *Gender at Work*, Sydney: Allen and Unwin.

Herbst, P.G. (1974), *Socio-technical Design*, London: Tavistock.

Hummel, R.P. (1977), *The Bureaucratic Experience*, New York: St Martin's Press.

Johnson, T.J. (1972), *Professions and Power*, London: Macmillan.

Kamin, L.J. (1974), *The Science and Politics of IQ*, Potomac, Maryland: Lawrence Erlbaum.

Kanter, R.M. (1977), *Men and Women of the Corporation*, New York: Basic Books.

Larson, M.S. (1977), *The Rise of Professionalism: A Sociological Analysis*, Berkeley: University of California Press.

Parkin, F. (1979), *Marxism and Class Theory: A Bourgeois Critique*, London: Tavistock.

Perrucci, R., Anderson, R.M., Schendel, D.E. and Trachtman, L.E. (1980), 'Whistle-blowing: Professionals' Resistance or Organizational Authority', *Social Problems*, 28, 149–164.

Weber, M. (1964), *The Theory of Social and Economic Organization*, New York: Free Press.

Weinstein, D. (1977), 'Bureaucratic Opposition: the Challenge to Authoritarian Abuses at the Workplace, *Canadian Journal of Political and Social Theory*, 1, 31–46.

Weinstein, D. (1979), *Bureaucratic Opposition: Challenging Abuses at the Workplace*, New York: Pergamon Press.

Willis, E. (1983), *Medical Dominance: The Division of Labour in Australian Health Care*, Sydney: Allen and Unwin.

Willis, P. (1977), *Learning to Labour*, Westmead: Saxon House.

Young, M. (1958), *The Rise of the Meritocracy 1870–2033: An Essay on Education and Equality*, London: Thames and Hudson.

Zald, M.N. and Berger, M.A. (1978), 'Social Movements in Organizations: Coup d'etat, Insurgency, and Mass Movements', *American Journal of Sociology*, 83, 823–861.

8.4 Models of Conflict and Ethnocentrism

Daniel Bar-Tal

In the introduction to this part we emphasized that stereotyping and discrimination are commonplace in interactions between status groups. In the next excerpt, Daniel Bar-Tal drives home this point by presenting a sweeping array of international examples of *extreme* stereotyping and discrimination. Its effect: the delegitimization of outsiders.

The author's basic purpose is to show that a process of **delegitimization** is involved in all instances of stereotyping and discrimination. Typically, the ingroup comes to see the outgroup as less than fully human, and deserving of both social exclusion and aggressive attacks. Drawing on theories of conflict and ethnocentrism, the author shows that perceptions of *threat* to the ingroup from the outgroup are always involved in cases of delegitimization. This is both a cause and consequence of the process of delegitimization.

Bar-Tal features examples from racial and ethnic conflict, and conflict between nations, but it is easy to see how the same processes may occur in class relations and gender relations.

... The concept, delegitimization, describes *categorization of a group or groups into extremely negative social categories that are excluded from the realm of acceptable norms and/or values* (Bar-Tal, 1988, 1989a). Delegitimization permits moral exclusion. The most common means of delegitimization, which are not mutually exclusive, are :

1 *Dehumanization:* labeling a group as inhuman by characterizing members as different from the human race—using either categories of sub-human creatures, such as "inferior races" and animals, or categories of negatively valued superhuman creatures, such as demons, monsters, and satans.
2 *Trait characterization:* describing a group as possessing extremely negative traits such as aggressors, idiots, or parasites.
3. *Outcasting:* categorizing members of a group as transgressors of such pivotal social norms that they should be excluded from society and/or institutionalized—e.g., murderers, thieves, psychopaths, or maniacs.
4. *Use of political labels:* describing a group as a political entity that threatens the basic values of the given society,—e.g., Nazis, fascists, communists, or imperialists.
5. *Group comparison:* labeling with the name of a group that is negatively perceived, such as "Vandals" or "Huns."

Delegitimization: (a) utilizes extremely negative, salient, and atypical bases for categorization; (b) denies the humanity of the delegitimized group; (c) is accompanied by intense, negative emotions of rejection; (d) implies the delegitimized group has the

Excerpted from Bar-Tal, Daniel (1990), "Causes and consequences of delegitimization: Models of conflict and ethnocentrism," *Journal of Social Issues*, 46(1), 65–81.

potential to endanger one's own group; and (e) implies the delegitimized group does not deserve human treatment and therefore harming it is justified.

The present paper explores the phenomenon of delegitimization by analyzing its causes and consequences. Two models are described—the conflict model and the ethnocentric model. . . .

CONFLICT MODEL

Every intergroup conflict begins with the perception that one group's goals are incompatible with the goals of another group (Bar-Tal, Kruglanski, & Klar, 1989; Pruitt & Rubin, 1986). The perception that a conflict exists means a group finds itself blocked because the attainment of its goal or goals is precluded by another group.

Two conditions in a conflict most frequently incite delegitimization: perception of the outgroup's goals as contradictory, far-reaching, and sinister; and the occurrence of extreme violence.

Threat and Delegitimization: Explanation and Derivation

An ingroup experiences threat when it perceives it cannot easily achieve its goals because of outgroup opposition (see Fig.1). The crucial questions in explaining the appearance of delegitimization in the early phase of conflict are: (a) How are the goals of the opponent perceived? (b) What is the nature of one's own goals that are perceived as blocked?

The first proposition is that *when a group perceives that the negating goal(s) of an outgroup is (are) far-reaching, especially unjusti-*

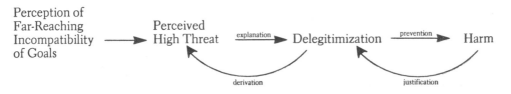

FIGURE 1   Conflict model: far-reaching incompatibility of goals.

fied, and threatening to the basic goals of the ingroup, then the ingroup uses delegitimization to explain the conflict. These aspects are linked; when the goals of the outgroup are perceived as outrageous, farfetched, irrational, and malevolent, they are also seen as negating fundamental ingroup goals and therefore as threatening.

Usually this is a zero-sum type of conflict. The perception that the outgroup will achieve its goals poses a danger to the very existence of the ingroup. The danger can be economic, political, or military.

Threat perception in general is accompanied by stress, uncertainty, vulnerability, and fear. These feelings arouse the need to understand and structure the situation quickly, thus allowing explanation and prediction (Y. Bar-Tal, 1989). Delegitimization fulfills this function. It explains why the other group threatens and predicts what the other group will do in the future (see Fig. 1).

Figure 1 illustrates this situation where the ingroup uses delegitimization to explain the outgroup's enraging aspirations and demands. As examples, delegitimizing labels provide an explanation to Poles about why German Nazis decided to occupy their country, or to Americans about why the Soviet Union strives to dominate the world. Who else would do such things other than a group that is imperialistic, satanic, or fascistic?

Once employed, delegitimization leads to inferences of threat from the delegitimizing category (see Fig. 1). Thus, the labels "aggressive," "ruthless," "devious," or "oppressive" indicate the outgroup is capable of destruction, violence, or brutality, and this further disrupts the ingroup's sense of security. In this way, the perception of severe threat and delegitimization feed each other....

Delegitimization and Harm: Prevention and Justification

In most serious conflicts, delegitimization leads to harm. Once the ingroup delegitimizes the outgroup with labels that imply threat and evil— "imperialists," "fascists," "terrorists"—acts for preventing danger usually follow. Because the outgroup is delegitimized, preventive measures can be severe, for delegitimized groups are perceived as not deserving human treatment.

Deportations, destruction, and mass killings of civil populations are not unusual in these cases. An example of this phenomenon was provided in an insightful statement by an American soldier in the Vietnam War:

When you go into basic training you are taught that the Vietnamese are not people. You are taught they are gooks, and all you hear is "gook, gook, gook, gook. . . ." The Asian serviceman in Vietnam is the brunt of the same racism because the GIs over there do not distinguish one Asian from another.... You are trained "gook, gook, gook" and once the military has got the idea implanted in your mind that these people are not humans, they are subhuman, it makes it a little bit easier to kill 'em. (Boyle, 1972, p. 141)

Exceptionally violent and harmful actions by the ingroup augment the delegitimization because they seem to justify further actions that exceed normative behavior (see Fig. 1). The more violent the behavior, the more delegitimization occurs because more justification is needed to explain the harm done. In addition, violent acts of the delegitimized group during confrontation reinforce delegitimization because they explain the deviant and extreme behavior of the delegitimizing group. Thus, the second proposition states that *a violent conflict leads to delegitimization to justify and explain it.*

A current example of delegitimization based on far-reaching incompatibility of goals exists in the Middle East. Israeli Jews and Palestinians persistently delegitimize each other to explain the threat that each group poses to the other and to justify the harm they inflict on each other (Bar-Tal, 1988, in press a). Both groups have struggled for the same land over the present century, and today, despite attempts to bridge the irreconcilable goals, the conflict continues. . . .

The protracted conflict intensified the perception of threat and caused mutual attempts to exclude the other group from the community of nations through delegitimization. The continuing mutual harm and violence has strengthened the delegitimization process. The Palestinians label Israeli Jews as "colonialists," "racists," "aggressors," "Nazis," "imperialists," "fascists," and "oppressors." They call them "Zionists," and consider Zionism a "colonialist movement in its inception, aggressive and expansionist in its goals, racist and segregationist in its configurations, and fascist in its means and aims" (Article 19 in the National Covenant of the Palestine Liberation Organization [PLO]—Harkabi, 1979).

The Israeli Jews, from the beginning of their encounters with Palestinians, viewed them as primitive, bandits, cruel mobs, and failed to recognize their national identity. Later, with the eruption of violence, they delegitimized Palestinians with labels such as "robbers," "criminals," "gangs," "anti-Semites," "terrorists," and "neo-Nazis." In the last decades, special efforts have been made to delegitimize members and sympathizers of the PLO, which represents the national aspirations of the Palestinians. On September 1,

1977, the Knesset of Israel adopted a resolution by a vote of 92–4 saying

The organization called the PLO aspires, as stated in its Covenant, to destroy and exterminate the State of Israel. The murder of women and children, and terror, are part of this organization's ideology, which it is implementing in practice.

. . . Not all conflicts begin with far-reaching incompatibility between the goals of the parties involved. Conflicts may also begin with less incompatibility that does not involve a high level of threat. Although such a situation can continue as a stalemate for a long time, this can also escalate into violent confrontation.

As Fig. 2 shows, delegitimization emerges from violence because an ingroup needs to justify and explain harm perpetrated by its members, as well as explain similar acts performed by the members of the outgroup. . . .

ETHNOCENTRIC MODEL

Delegitimization does not occur only in conflict. A group may also attribute delegitimizing labels to another group as a result of ethnocentrism. Ethnocentrism, a term introduced by Sumner (1906), denotes a tendency to accept the ingroup and reject outgroups. Delegitimization can serve this tendency. Using delegitimization, ingroup members see themselves as virtuous and superior, and the outgroup as contemptible and inferior (LeVine & Campbell, 1972).

Figure 3 illustrates how the ethnocentric tendency can foster delegitimization. Nevertheless, a necessary mediating condition for delegitimization is fear and/or contempt toward the outgroup. Subsequently, delegit-

FIGURE 2   Conflict model: deterioration

FIGURE 3   Ethnocentric model

imization can engender harm when the ingroup attempts to prevent the danger implied by the delegitimizing label, or to treat the outgroup inhumanely, "as deserved."

Delegitimization is used in extreme cases of ethnocentrism because it maximizes intergroup differences and totally excludes the delegitimized group from commonly accepted groups, implying a total superiority of the ingroup. It denies the humanity of the outgroup.

A mere perception of difference and devaluation does not lead necessarily to exclusion, for arousal of fear and/or contempt for the outgroup is also necessary (see Fig. 3). The third proposition states, *delegitimization is used when a group perceives another group as different and devalued, and feels fear of it and/or contempt for it.*

The more the two groups differ, the easier it is to delegitimize.

The most salient differences are based on physical appearance because they enable a clear distinction and an easy identification. Thus, skin color, physiognomic features, hair color, body structure, or even dress permit unmistakable differentiation between groups. Throughout history, these differences were most often the bases for differentiation and delegitimization. People also differentiate and delegitimize on the basis of religion or ideology. In these cases, however, external identification may be impossible.

In addition to intergroup differences, devaluation is necessary for delegitimization to occur. Devaluation results from the ethnocentric tendency (Brewer & Campbell, 1976) for ingroup members to feel positive about their own group and attribute favorable characteristics to it, while feeling antipathy

toward outgroups and attributing unfavorable characteristics to them (see Adorno, Frenkel-Brunswik, Levinson, & Sanford, 1950).

The final necessary condition, which not only evokes delegitimization but causes it, is fear and/or contempt. Fear is elicited when the different and devalued group presents a threat or a mysterious aspect. In this case, the ingroup uses delegitimization to explain their fear (see Fig. 3). Feelings of contempt emerge when the outgroup is perceived as absolutely inferior, based on perceived cultural, economic, military, scientific, and/or political achievements.

There are two main reasons for ethnocentric delegitimization: first, the desire to completely differentiate the outgroup from the ingroup in order to exclude it from humanity; second, the desire to exploit the outgroup. These two reasons do not necessarily appear together. . . .

. . . A prime example of delegitimization used to rationalize exploitation is the enslavement of Black people by White people. Delegitimization was, perhaps, the most important justification for slavery. Otherwise, how could the moral, deeply religious, and gallant Southerners have treated these people so inhumanly? Black people differed from Whites in physical appearance, folkways and mores, religion, language, and culture, and these characteristics were also greatly devalued, so that Black people were a perfect target for exploitation.

Stampp (1956) pointed to three beliefs that undergirded slavery: (a) the "all wise Creator" had designed Black people for labor in the South; (b) being inferior in intellect and having a particular temperament, Blacks were the natural slaves of White people; and (c)

Black people were barbarians who needed rigid discipline and control. These perceptions legitimized slavery in the Southern states.

Delegitimization and Harm: Intention and Justification

Once invoked, delegitimization can open the way to harm. Delegitimizing labels may indicate either that the delegitimized group is inhuman and therefore harming it is allowed, or that it is threatening and therefore, to prevent the danger, harm should be carried out. In addition, delegitimization may lead to intergroup conflicts. The goals of the ingroup and the outgroup may clash because of the superior and imperialistic feelings of the ingroup. Then, when harms are committed, delegitimization serves to justify inhumane treatment of the outgroup (see Fig. 3).

The delegitimization of the American Indians facilitated cruel behavior toward them. Once they were labeled "savages," "inferior," or "animals," it was but a short distance to harm. Because "inferior" and "savage" men do not deserve human treatment, Europeans did not hesitate to destroy, to enslave, to drive them away, or to kill them.

The strengthening of delegitimization after harming others is illustrated in the development of defenses by White people to justify their enslavement of Black people. Doctors, scientists, and phrenologists in the South searched for physiological differences to substantiate the assumed temperamental and intellectual differences:

Dr. Samuel W. Cartwright of Louisiana argued that the visible difference in skin pigmentation is also extended to "the membranes, the muscles, the tendons, and . . . [to] all fluids and secretions. Even the Negro's brain and nerves, the chyle and all the humors, are tinctured with a shade of the pervading darkness" and Dr. Josiah C. Nott of Mobile proposed that Negro and Whites do not belong in the same species. (Stampp, 1956, p. 8)

One striking case of ethnocentric delegitimization that led to tragic consequences is the treatment of Jews in Germany between 1933–1945. . . .

Between 1933 and 1945, Jews in Europe were subjected to exclusion, deportation, expropriation, expulsion, pogroms, mass killings, and ultimately genocide. During 1939–1945, about 6 million Jews perished as a consequence of starvation, deadly epidemics, mass executions, and systematic gassing. There is little doubt that as these actions were carried out, Germans justified them with delegitimizing beliefs, which first encouraged the atrocities and later supported and reinforced them.

CONCLUSION

Delegitimization, the exclusion of an outgroup and denial of its humanity, is a phenomenon with cognitive, affective, and behavioral aspects. On the cognitive level, delegitimization organizes "reality" by providing an explanation for the perceived characteristics and behaviors of the outgroup and a prediction of potential future events. On the emotional level, delegitimization is a reaction to feelings of fear, threat, or contempt stimulated by another group. Its occurrence not only strengthens these feelings, but also may provoke new negative emotions. On the behavioral level, delegitimization leads to an array of behaviors including malevolent treatment and preventive steps to avert potential danger to the ingroup. Delegitimization is also a consequence of brutal and cruel behavior because it serves as a justification mechanism.

Delegitimization, as an extreme case of stereotyping and prejudice, is a widespread phenomenon. Two related models of the process have focused on situations that elicit delegitimization: conflict and ethnocentrism. Delegitimization occurs in conflicts that involve a perception of far-reaching, outrageous, and incompatible goals between groups and/or a high level of brutal violence. Delegitimization occurs in ethnocentrism when an outgroup is perceived as very different and is devalued.

REFERENCES

Adorno, W., Frenkel-Brunswik, E., Levinson, D.J., & Sanford, R. N. (1950). *The authoritarian personality.* New York: Harper & Row.

Bar-Tal, D. (1988). Delegitimizing relations between Israeli Jews and Palestinians: A social psychological analysis. In J. Hofman (Ed.), *Arab-Jewish relations in Israel: A quest in human understanding* (pp. 217–248). Bristol, IN: Wyndham Hall.

Bar-Tal, D. (1989). Delegitimization: The extreme case of stereotyping and prejudice. In D. Bar-Tal, C. Graumann, A. W. Kruglanski, & W. Stroebe (Eds.), *Stereotyping and prejudice: Changing conceptions* (pp. 169–188). New York: Springer-Verlag.

Bar-Tal, D. (in press). Israeli-Palestinian conflict: A cognitive analysis. *International Journal of Intercultural Relations.*

Bar-Tal, D., Kruglanski, A. W., & Klar, Y. (1989).

Conflict termination: An epistemological analysis of international cases. *Political Psychology, 10,* 233–255.

Bar-Tal, Y. (1989, January). *Coping with uncertainty.* Paper presented at the International Conference on Psychological Stress and Adjustment in Time of War and Peace, Tel-Aviv, Israel.

Boyle, R. (1972). *The flower of the dragon: The breakdown of the U.S. Army in Vietnam.* San Francisco: Ramparts.

Brewer, M. B., & Campbell, D. T. (1976). *Ethnocentrism and intergroup attitudes: East African evidence.* New York: Halsted.

Harkabi, Y. (1979). The Palestinian Convenant and its meaning. London: Valentine, Mitchell.

Pruitt, D. G., & Rubin, J. Z. (1986). *Social conflict.* New York: Random House.

Stampp, K. M. (1956). *The peculiar institution: Slavery in the ante-bellum South.* New York: Vintage.

Sumner, W. G. (1906). *Folkways.* New York: Ginn.

8.5 Social Class and Child-Rearing Practices in Taiwan

Li-Chen Ma and Kevin Smith

Where do different social classes get their ways of thinking—their class subcultures? To answer this question, we need to know something about the ways children are socialized to believe the same things as other members of their social class. North American research on childrearing has repeatedly found evidence that middle- and working-class people differ fundamentally in their approach to parenting. In general, parents tend to stress conformity while middle-class parents encourage independence in their children.

But the following excerpt by Ma and Smith finds no clear difference in parental values in Taiwan across classes. In fact, on matters such as the value attached to conformity, the two classes are remarkably similar. Both value conformity in their children—the opposite of what American research finds.

The authors suggest two possible explanations for this finding. First, only nontraditional parents encourage self-direction in their children and there are few such parents in Taiwan today. Second, rapid modernization has brought prosperity to much of Taiwanese society and, in this way, has reduced the differences in values between classes.

The results of this study should give us pause in making quick generalizations about class differences across cultures. This is not to say that family socialization processes are not important in what class members learn and the values they acquire, but the content of what is taught and learned varies across cultures.

INTRODUCTION AND LITERATURE

Kohn (1969), using a 1964 National Opinion Research Center (NORC) survey of fathers of 3- to 15-year-old children, presented evidence that the tendency to value self-direction increases with social class. More specifically, middle-class parents emphasize internal control of behavior, whereas working-class parents emphasize external control. Kohn explained these differences by tying them to the occupational experiences of the two classes of parents. Working-class parents, accustomed to jobs that are routine, repetitive, and closely supervised, are likely to value conformity to external authority and practice it in child rearing. On the other hand, middle-class parents whose jobs require initiative, independent judgment, and the ability to work with people and abstract ideas are more likely to value autonomy and self-motivation and stress these qualities in child-rearing practices. . . .

This research attempts to examine Kohn's thesis using data from a recent national survey in Taiwan. Two points of Kohn's thesis are addressed. The first pertains to "self-direction versus external conformity." Is it true that today's middle- and working-class parents in Taiwan stress different values in socialization? If so, do the differences match those found in Kohn's research? Second, do middle- and working-class parents discipline their children in similar or different ways? Bronferbrenner (1958) concluded that "in matters of discipline, working-class parents are consistently more likely to employ physical punishment, while middle-class families rely more on reasoning, isolation, appeals to guilt, and other methods involving the threat of loss of love." Echoing this observation, Kohn (1976) reasoned that working-class parents are more likely to emphasize the consequences of the child's actions, whereas mid-dle-class parents are more likely to emphasize the child's intentions. Our research attempts to answer these questions and examine these issues using data from Taiwan.

DATA, SAMPLING, AND MEASUREMENT

Data for this research were collected as part of the Basic Survey of Social Changes in Taiwan Region (hereafter called Basic Survey) in 1984 to 1985. Two questionnaires were used in the survey; each version was used for interviews with approximately 4,500 household members. A stratified random sample was used. First, the island of Taiwan was divided into three subuniverses: Taipei, Kaohsinng, and Taiwan. Then all of the Li's (an administrative unit) and villages in the island were stratified as cities, townships, and villages according to "industrial types" determined by several specific criteria (Institute of Ethnology, 1987). Three hundred Li's and villages were randomly selected from the three subuniverses. Based on household listings for each of the chosen Li's and villages, 30 households were systematically drawn. Of these, the 15 drawn with odd numbers were interviewed with Questionnaire 1, and the rest with Questionnaire 2. All of the interviewed were between 20 and 70 years of age.

Twelve questions pertaining to parental values and child-rearing practices were included in Questionnaire 2 and were used in this research. The analysis sample was selected from the 4,199 household members who completed Questionnaire 2, were employed, were married with a spouse present, and had at least one child 3 years or older at the time of the interview. The actual sample size was 1,210 parents (1,002 fathers and 208 mothers).

Social class, the major independent variable, was measured for both fathers and mothers by Taiwanese Census occupational levels instead of Hollingshead's two-factor "index of social position," which was used in Kohn's initial study. . . . Parents were defined as middle class if they were: (1) professional, technical, or kindred workers, (2) administrative or management workers, or

Excerpted from Ma, Li-Chen and Kevin Smith (1990), "Social class, parental values, and child-rearing practices in Taiwan," *Sociological Spectrum*, 10(4), October-December, 577–589. Reproduced with permission of Taylor and Francis, Inc., Washington, D.C.

(3) supervisory or sales workers. They were defined as working class if they were: (1) service workers, (2) production, transportation, operational workers, or (3) physical laborers. Agricultural, forestry, fishery, hunting, military, and police workers were excluded.

The 12 child-rearing items were factor analyzed and reliability tested in an attempt to formulate self-direction and conformity scales. However, scaling problems were encountered, and the 12 items were analyzed individually.

Child-rearing practices were measured in terms of the action taken by parents: (1) to punish their children for misbehavior, (2) to correct their children's misbehavior, (3) to discipline their children for fighting with other children, and (4) to reward their children for their good conduct.

FINDINGS

Social Class and Parental Values

Of the 12 value items, only 2 had mean scores that were significantly different for the middle- and working-class fathers. Middle-class fathers were more likely than working-class fathers to emphasize filial duty as an important trait for youngsters. The same pattern of difference was observed for the samples of mothers and parents (combined samples). Obedience was another item marked by significant class differences. Working-class fathers stressed obedience slightly more than middle-class fathers.

Despite the exceptions just mentioned, scores for the "conformity" items were remarkably similar for working-class and middle-class parents. Two explanations could account for the lack of significant differences. First, perhaps elements of traditional Confucian ethics overshadowed class differences. The other explanation is that rapid modernization in Taiwan, and mass educational achievement, have reduced the value variations across all social classes.

SOCIAL CLASS AND CHILD-REARING PRACTICES

To test Kohn's hypothesis that working-class parents are more likely to respond in terms of the immediate consequences of the child's action whereas middle-class parents are more likely to respond in terms of their interpretation of the child's intent, this study examined the actions taken by parents to: (1) punish, correct, and discipline their children for misbehavior and (2) reward their children for good conduct.

Table 1 shows the kinds of punishment reported by middle- and working-class parents

TABLE 1. Percentage of Middle- and Working-Class Parents Who Reported Action Taken to Punish Children When They Misbehave

Action applied by parents	Fathers, Middle-Class (N = 480)	Fathers, Working-Class N = 517	x^2	Mothers, Middle-Class (N = 91)	Mothers, Working-Class (N = 116)	x^2
Physical	36.4	44.9	7.30**	49.5	48.3	0.00
No allowance	9.6	6.2	3.5	9.9	6.9	0.27
Stand and kneel	55.2	61.9	4.32*	51.6	51.7	0.00
To do household chores	19.6	21.3	0.34	22.0	23.3	0.00
Grounding	31.7	30.2	0.19	25.3	34.5	1.63
No food	2.1	3.3	0.95	1.1	5.2	1.49
No TV watching	35.6	42.0	3.95*	30.8	33.6	0.08
To do school work	24.2	21.9	0.62	8.8	20.7	4.65*
Social isolation	11.5	7.5	4.02*	13.2	10.3	0.17

*$p < .05$.   **$p < .01$

for children's misbehavior. Bronfenbrenner's assertion that working-class parents are more likely to use physical punishment whereas middle-class parents are more likely to use reason, isolation, and appeals to guilt is partially supported by the analysis. Working-class fathers spanked their children and made them "stand and kneel" more frequently than did middle-class fathers. Middle-class fathers, on the other hand, were more likely to use isolation to punish their children. Also, middle-class fathers used other nonphysical punishments (such as withholding allowance, grounding, and work) more frequently, although the differences were fairly small and nonsignificant. No clear patterns were found for mothers.

Table 2 shows the data on corrective actions reported by middle- and working-class parents when their children misbehave. Working-class fathers and mothers scolded their children significantly more frequently than did their middle-class counterparts. In addition, they were more likely to use methods such as mild admonishment, verbal threats, and punishment than did their middle-class counterparts. On the other hand, the middle-class fathers' disciplinary strategy was more situationally based than was that of working-class fathers. Middle-class mothers also relied more on the situation in deciding the proper corrective action, although the difference was not statistically significant. Overall, the findings offered some support for Bronfenbrenner's hypothesis that middle-class parents tended to use rea-

son and psychological techniques more frequently in correcting children's behavior.

When children fight with other children, over 70% of the middle-class fathers said they would first determine the reasons for the fight and then decide what to do. This compares with less than 65% of the working-class fathers. Over 20% of the middle-class fathers reported they scold their children, whereas more than 33% of working-class fathers said they did. Overall, class differences in fathers' disciplinary action were highly significant. The same patterns were also observed among mothers, but the differences were nonsignificant.

When children behave well, middle-class fathers are more likely than working-class fathers to praise them or take them to a movie or picnic, and are less likely not to respond. Similar patterns were also observed among mothers, although again to a lesser degree. On the other hand, working-class parents reacted to children's good conduct more frequently with materialistic rewards such as giving them gifts or extra money and increasing their allowance. This evidence supports Kohn's (1976) contention that working-class parents are more likely than middle-class parents to use external control.

CONCLUSION AND DISCUSSION

Of the 12 parental value items examined in our study, only the one pertaining to "obedi-

TABLE 2. Percentage of Middle- and Working-Class Parents Who Reported Action Taken to Correct Their Children's Behavior When Committing Faults

Action taken by parents	Fathers, Middle-Class (N = 482)	Fathers, Working-Class N = 520	x^2	Mothers, Middle-Class (N = 91)	Mothers, Working-Class (N = 117)	x^2
Admonish mildly	70.3	71.0	0.02	61.5	73.5	2.85
Scold	42.1	51.5	8.54**	46.2	60.7	4.35*
Verbal threat	67.2	72.5	3.07	49.5	51.3	0.01
Punish	74.3	76.3	0.47	63.7	68.4	0.31
Depends on situation	67.2	56.3	12.04***	51.6	47.9	0.16
Don't know what to do	0.4	0.8	0.10	1.1	0.0	0.02

$*p < .05$ $**p < .01$ $***p < .001$

ence" was statistically significant and in the expected direction. Although differences on filial duty were significant, they were not in the hypothesized direction. The comparisons of 10 other items were all nonsignificant. Data from this research thus suggest the class-value relationship in Kohn's theory is not generalizable to Taiwan.

Why Kohn's theory encounters difficulties in Taiwanese society is difficult to answer. First, it may have to do with the cultural conceptualization of social class and the difficulties of cross-cultural measurement. In American society, social class is more of a socioeconomic than an occupational concept; in Chinese society, the reverse is true.

Second, Taiwan is still a society in which Confucian ethics and values are taught to children of all social classes. Confucianism is basically oriented to system stability and maintenance, stressing conformity and adaptation values and norms (Weber 1964). Li, the social element, is used as the concrete and immediate guide of human behavior. Thus, throughout Confucian teachings, Chinese educational systems, and family socialization process, Li has been stressed as a core value. The higher the social class, the more access to the teachings of Li, and thus the more exposure to conformity and adaptation norms and values. As a result, middle-class positions promote conformity and adaptation values and norms in Taiwanese society. In fact, in many respects, there is close affinity between Eastern Confucian values and the Western work ethic.

Third, the similarities between middle- and working-class parental values in Taiwan may result from rapid social changes. As a society undergoes dramatic socioeconomic and political change there tends to be a leveling-off effect on its value system. Bronfenbrenner (1958, p. 425) pointed out that class differences in parental values and child-rearing techniques were narrowing. Alwin (1984) made a similar observation on value convergence when he examined data on parental

socialization. Furthermore, he noted that education was a significant and consistent factor in the diminution of value variation between white- and blue-collar workers. The educational improvement of all classes, particularly the working class, amid rapid modernization and social changes in Taiwan in recent years, has undoubtedly equalized access to Confucianism and its conformity and adaptability values, thereby contributing to the leveling off of class-value differences.

This analysis found some support for the hypothesis of social class differences in child-rearing practices. The support was more prevalent among fathers than mothers. The weak relationship observed among mothers may also be related to Confucianism. Under Confucianism the disciplinarian role in the family falls largely on husbands. Thus, in punishing, correcting, and disciplining children, mothers would not act as decisively and firmly as would fathers.

In conclusion, this cross-cultural examination of Kohn's theory indicates the theory may not be applicable in Eastern societies where Confucianism is a major influence and where rapid social change and modernization have occurred.

REFERENCES

Alwin, Duane F. 1984. "Trends in Parental Socialization Values: Detroit, 1958-1983." *American Journal of Sociology* 90:382.
Bronfenbrenner, U. 1958. "Socialization and Social Class Through Time and Space." Pp. 400–425 in *Readings in Social Psychology*, edited by E. Macoby, T. Newcomb and E. Hartley. New York: Holt, Rinehart & Winston.
Kohn, Melvin L. 1969. *Class and Conformity: A Study in Values*. Homewood, IL: Dorsey.
——— 1976. "Social Class and the Exercise of Parental Authority." *American Sociological Review* 41:538-545.
Weber, Max. 1964. *The Religion of China: Confucianism and Taoism*. New York: Macmillan.

8.6 Why Europe's Business Class Opposed Social Security

Abram de Swaan

Between 1880 and 1930 governments in Europe and North America introduced the first social insurance programs. These programs were aimed at protecting the working classes from possible income loss due to illness or unemployment. In effect, they aimed at reducing economic inequality.

Members of the petty bourgeoisie, or small business class, strongly opposed these programs. Some required employers to contribute to insurance funds for the benefit of their employees. We can understand their opposition to these plans. However, the same group also opposed plans where small businesses did not have to contribute. How do we explain this resistance when the employers stood to lose nothing material from the gains of the working class?

According to the author the resistance was an example of **"downward jealousy."** As defined in this excerpt, such jealousy differs from envy. Envy is the desire to have what those above you have, or to be what they are. Jealousy is the fear that others will take what you have, as with the jealous lover who fears losing his/her beloved to another.

In jealous group relations, an advantaged group resents the mere idea of a lower-status group gaining the privileges it has acquired. Thus, the petite bourgeoisie saw any gain by the working class as a loss for them. This is not to say that the loss was imaginary. They *did* stand to lose something, but it was not something tangible.

Saving money for the future was, and to many still is, an oppressive feature of middle-class life. Social insurance programs aimed to relieve the poor of this burden. According to the author, the petite bourgeoisie opposed the programs because they could not stand to see the working class handed the same degree of security they had struggled so hard to achieve.

This kind of jealousy may be an inevitable part of all group relations. People often resent the gains of others when it lessens inequality, the gap between groups. For example, the working poor often voice the strongest opposition to improved benefits for the unemployed. Governments may not be able to prevent such sentiments.

If the kind of downward jealousy described in this excerpt is inevitable, it does not lend hope for greater equality in the world, whether for status, economic well-being, or power. It suggests that people in an advantaged position will always oppose, and perhaps sabotage, the steps that governments take to reduce inequality. This is both a cause and consequence of economic inequality.

Excerpted from Swaan, Abram de (1989), "Jealousy as a class phenomenon: The petite bourgeoisies and social security," *International Sociology*, 4(3), 259–271.

JEALOUS GROUP RELATIONS

... When jealousy emerges as a group feeling, relations between groups tend to acquire a conflict-ridden quality. The advantages, which one side believes to accrue to the other, it perceives as losses to itself, regardless of whether it had to give up or forego anything as a result. Bitterness at the sight of other people's good fortune appears. Such jealous group relations may occur in both directions, upward among the less well off who envy their luckier counterparts, and downward among the better off who cannot bear others to increase their well-being even if it is at no cost to themselves.

A social psychological interpretation of group relations purely in terms of "jealous relations" risks reducing a real conflict of interests to a mere psychological misperception. Such psychologisation is dangerous since it reduces real interests and justifiable claims to infantile emotions. But this caveat does not rule out an analysis of the role of jealousy in group relations.

Envy and jealousy, in game theoretical terms, transform "variable-sum" situations into "zero-sum" games. In other words, these emotions increase the conflict potential of the situation, because the partners concerned perceive their interests as completely opposed, where an outsider might see mutually satisfying solutions if only jealousy had not changed the parties' evaluations. ...

These negative comparisons are of the essence when social differentials themselves are at stake. The satisfaction of money need not be in having more of it than others, it may reside in having enough of it for oneself. But the satisfaction that goes with social prestige is by its very nature bound up with being higher than others are, since it involves comparisons. Prestige distribution are always competitive and conflict-ridden.

RELATIONS BETWEEN
THE PETITE BOURGEOISIE
AND THE WORKING CLASS

At this point the argument may be applied to the analysis of a historical episode: the emergence of compulsory social insurance for wage workers and the petite bourgeois opposition against such schemes.

Between 1880 and 1930, compulsory and collective nationwide insurance against income loss from the vicissitudes of industrial working life was introduced in Europe and North America. Elsewhere I have argued that these arrangements were brought about by an activist political regime in coalition with large employers or organised workers, or both (cf. de Swaan 1988, especially Ch. 6).

In general, the opposition against these innovations came most of all from the petite bourgeoisie: from those people who saw themselves positioned "between capital and labour," and who indeed both employed their capital and applied their own labour as independent entrepreneurs.[1] Of course, they often also employed foreign capital and many among them did hire workers, but they themselves worked along with their employees and privately owned the means of production. This definition covers groups as diverse as small and medium farmers, shopkeepers, artisans, traders, manufacturers, and independently established professionals, such as lawyers and doctors. These categories shade into other social strata, when the enterprise grows so large that the owner no longer works alongside his employees, or when it becomes so small that it hardly involves any capital at all and comes to resemble casual or "hired-out" labour. ...

Because the *petite bourgeoisie* was such a motley category and rarely united behind exclusive political organisations of its own, party positions on issues of social legislation cannot be identified unambiguously with the opinions of small entrepreneurs on the issues. More generally, in the present approach, a class need not be treated as a unitary agent, unanimous in its animosity. ... But by and large small independent entrepreneurs opposed workers' insurance, and often quite vehemently at that.

Why they did so is by no means obvious. In so far as they were employers, they feared having to pay insurance contributions and some schemes indeed imposed fees, many economically marginal enterprises could hardly afford.[2]

But some plans excluded enterprises with a small number of employees and all excluded those in which only family members worked. Such proposals were opposed nevertheless.[3] If the insurances were financed from the general tax fund, small entrepreneurs might still resist it for increasing the overall tax burden and their share in it. But those plans that entailed no contribution from general taxes still met with objections from small entrepreneurs. Moreover, had they perceived the issue strictly in terms of financial costs and benefits, the small employers might have appreciated the savings on the disbursements they made privately or through commercial insurance to their incapacitated and aged workers. Support of needy or elderly employees was not usually a legal obligation, but a moral one of widely varying stringency. Yet, by and large, employers did object to the replacement of moral commitment by legal compulsion. It is difficult to understand what privilege was lost thereby, other than the freedom not to fulfill one's moral obligations. Voluntariness allows benefactors and employers to adjust their handouts to the changing proceeds of risky enterprise.

Employers did resent bureaucratic interference with their entrepreneurial autonomy. Especially the small masters, unaccustomed to any administration, hated the *"paperasserie"*. The small, independent middle class sensed that social insurance was another major addition to big government, which it feared and hated as much as it did big business, department and chain stores, or consumer cooperatives.

The autonomy of the small entrepreneur was an essential myth. Wage earners were dependent on the whim of their employers, tenants on the caprice of their landlords, but the *petits bourgeois* were boss in their own shop and their own house. That made them superior to working people, both in their own eyes and in those of the workers. In so far as they were indeed independent, their autonomy rested solely on the ownership of the means of production they worked with (and on the ownership of the major durable means of consumption, such as their own

house, partly workshop, partly family dwelling).

The basis of relative autonomy was private property. Property served the twofold function of working capital and insurance against adversity. This property was accumulated by individual saving. Social insurance represented an alternative to private property in its providential functions. It entailed the collective and compulsory accumulation of transfer capital to be disbursed in times of need. It thus relieved wage workers from the continuous compulsion to save for the future which was so essential and oppressive a feature of middle-class life. With social insurance, workers too, would be sure in times of disease and disablement, during old age and often even during periods of unemployment. This caused jealousy among the petite bourgeoisie and made them oppose the insurance plans.

In the second half of the nineteenth century, the small independent entrepreneurs increasingly lost the field to large enterprise. At the same time, workers gained more income and security, while their social prestige also rose. A salaried position increasingly became an alternative for members of the petite bourgeoisie. In other words, workers and *petits bourgeois* increasingly became involved in a competition for status, which was intensified because they often lived close together in the same *quartiers*, shared a common urban neighbourhood culture and met as shopkeepers and customers, or worked together as craftsmen on the shop-floor. Workers who had succeeded in putting away some savings often established themselves in independent business, and businessmen frequently had to hire themselves out as employees or saw their children accept salaried employment.

As class boundaries were vague, changing and precarious, it seemed all the more pressing to maintain the small differences in status between the independent entrepreneur and the wage-dependent worker: "It is likely that fears of proletarianisation led many craftsmen and shopkeepers to exaggerate the remaining "small differences"—home-owning, the absence of unemployment (although not under-employment), or outward badges of respectability" (Blackbourn 1984 : 48). The regularly employed workers were equally eager to distance themselves from casual workers, vagrants and paupers whom they considered their social inferiors (cf. de Regt 1984). The *embourgeoisement*, which characterises so much of working-class culture in the unions, housing societies and friendly societies since the late nineteenth century, served to demarcate a boundary between these decent and steadily employed workers and the others, the dregs of society. The same emulation of middle-class forms of life acted as pressure upon the independent middle class, which in turn sought to maintain its lower boundary by adhering even more strictly to the ways of the propertied classes (cf. Elias 1982).

During the first half of the nineteenth century, factory labour was generally considered an anomaly which would disappear as increasing numbers of workers would succeed in putting aside a small working capital to establish themselves in independent business. And many workers shared those illusions. They had been craftsmen or peasants before, in rural areas they often still kept a few animals and worked a small plot of land on the side. In the cities, factory work alternated with casual jobs and "cottage industry" at home, while wives or children often also worked in the factory and operated a tiny shop of their own. The ideal for working people was to own a small business or a piece of land, and a house of one's own to live in: private property remained the ideal, to be realised through individual savings. Property was considered as venture capital in the first place, for the owner to work by him or herself; even a privately owned house was first of all a shop or a farm to work in and next, a dwelling space for the family. The second function of private property was to provide financial security. This may seem less obvious now, after traumatic episodes of hyperinflation, and when small enterprise is associated with risk-taking. But at the time, wage dependency was considered even riskier.

A fundamental equation of nineteenth-century society runs: individual savings = private property = economic independence = financial security. In this light the question was why workers did not save to acquire the blessings of propertied existence. The simplest answer is also the best: they did not earn enough to save. But even when they could afford to put aside a small sum, they often spent it anyway. In a social environment of dire poverty, whoever has unused resources at his or her disposal is under constant and intense pressures from less fortunate kin, neighbours and fellow workers to lend or give them money. Refusing such requests means either refusing help to those who once did help one, or destroying long-standing solidarities which might be a vital necessity on some future day and thus a source of security in themselves. In other words, poor people do not save because their peers demand they spend their surplus on them and there is more security in heeding that request than in keeping one's surplus to oneself (and this—with the fear of the taxman — also explains the traditional secretiveness of hoarding peasants in rural societies) (cf. Popkin 1979).

In other words, the formula—savings = property = independence = security—did not apply to the working class. For the small middle class, however, it became a moral precept. Private accumulation was also considered proof of moral and social rectitude and earned one the esteem of one's fellow citizens. On the other hand, the poor who did not save were thought of as improvident spendthrifts who had gambled away their claims to sympathy. This comfortable view of social inequality was not just hypocrisy. Small middle-class families must have made great sacrifices and foregone many pleasures for the sake of private accumulation. And, as the century proceeded, in many cases this self-denial produced ever more niggardly results. Economic independence often did not lead to a secure existence, but on the contrary to ever increasing dependency on banks, large suppliers and big industrial customers. Craftsmen found themselves driven out of business by factory production and shopkeepers by department stores and cooperatives. Small enterprises often proved the most vulnerable to the risks of economic conjuncture, while inflation ate away fastest at small savings which could not easily be invested elsewhere.

The middle-class ideal was still to leave one's sons a 'nice business' and marry one's daughters to a propertied suitor. As these goals proved increasingly difficult to realise, small entrepreneurs began to invest in education for their children, ensuring them of a position in the cadre of a corporation or a government bureaucracy (cf. Crossick 1984 : 21). "In this manner the second generation did not so much climb or step down on the social ladder, it rather made a step aside, crab-wise", into the hierarchy of the new salariat (Blackbourn 1984 : 44).

In the last quarter of the nineteenth century, the conditions of the industrial proletariat began to improve. Urban sanitation spread. A beginning was made with working-class housing. The worst abuses of industrial labour were contained by factory legislation. And industrial workers increasingly were being considered as the backbone of the nation, factory production as the true source of national wealth. New ways were being sought to make the existence of wage workers more secure. And if individual workers did not manage to save enough to provide against adversity, then they might succeed collectively in accumulating funds: the recipe of the friendly savings associations. These mutual funds were an important transitional institution on the road to compulsory collective insurance on a national scale. . . .

. . . Wage earners, protected by social legislation and national insurance, were no longer a prey to emiseration at the first stroke of adversity. And this eliminated an important difference between the petite bourgeoisie and the working class, one which was at the core of the status distinction. And so it was experienced by small entrepreneurs, for example by Frank Bulen, as his *Confessions of a Tradesman* of 1908 testify (quoted by Crossick 1984 : 263):

The doctrines I heard preached by the socialists in the open air simply filled me with dismay. For it was nothing else but the unfit and incurably idle, the morally degenerate, at the expense of the fit, the hard-working, and the striving classes.

And:

It makes me positively ill to hear the blatant cant that is talked about the working man, meaning journeymen and labourers only. The small London shopkeeper toils far harder than any of them, is preyed upon by them to an extent which must be incredible to those who don't know . . .

. . . Behind middle-class protests there may have been "a vigilance in maintaining and guarding something": jealousy of a working class that stood to gain the security which once had been the sole privilege of the propertied classes. It is not easy to document this group feeling adequately. It was often hidden behind more elaborate ideological stances, if it was expressed at all. And it may only be uncovered by studying private sources, such as personal correspondence, diaries, and letters to the local press.

The assumption may also serve in interpreting more recent group feelings. For example, in countries such as the Netherlands, where minimum wage incomes are not much above maximum benefits, a downward jealousy can be sensed: what workers earn by hard work, others receive without effort or merit (cf. Verhey and van Westerloo 1984). Here too, the small financial difference masks a crucial status distinction. And again, these jealous relations are ambivalent, since employed workers are aware they may be next to go on the dole. . . .

REFERENCES

Blackbourn, D. 1984. 'Between Resignation and Volatility: The German Petite Bourgeoisie in the Nineteenth Century', in Crossick, G. and Haupt, H.-G. (eds.), *Shopkeepers and Master Artisans in Nineteenth-Century Europe*. London: Methuen.

Crossick, G. and Haupt, H.-G. 1984. *Shopkeepers and Master Artisans in Nineteenth Century Europe*. London: Methuen.

De Regt, A. 1984. *Arbeidersgezinnen en Beschavingsarbeid*. Amsterdam: Arbeiderspers.

De Swaan, A. 1988. *In Care of the State: State Formation and Collectivization of Health Care, Education and Welfare in Europe and America* in the Modern Era. New York/Cambridge: Oxford University Press/Polity Press.

Elias, N. 1982. *The Civilizing Process: Power and Civility*, Vol. 2. Oxford/New York: Blackwell/Pantheon.

Popkin, S.H. 1979. *The Rational Peasant: The Political Economy of Rural Society in Vietnam.* Berkeley: University of California Press.

Verhey, E. and Van Westerloo, G. 1984. 'De Pont Van Kwart over Zeven', in *Ons Soort Mensen.* Amsterdam: Raamgracht.

NOTES

1. Cf. Crossick (1984 : 9): "We find the unique feature of the petite bourgeoisie in the fact that its livelihood is derived both from its capital and its own labour . . . it is the former that sets it apart from the proletariat, the latter from the bourgeoisie . . . any labour it hires is on a very limited scale".

2. Payroll taxes were sometimes paid by workers, sometimes by employers, most often by both; sometimes the state added its part. In practice, the formal division of shares between employers and workers did not make much difference, since each party would try to make the other pay for it by adjusting wages, and since the parties together would try to compensate for insurance fees by increasing prices.

3. For example, the English unemployment insurance of 1911 initially covered only heavy industry and the building trades; the French *"insurance sociale"* of 1930 excluded agrarian workers; the Dutch Workmen's Compensation Act of 1901 excluded agrarian workers (cf. de Swaan 1988 : Ch. 6).

SECTION REVIEW

Discussion Questions

1. "Language influences thought." Discuss this observation in relation to the excerpts you have read in this section.

2. Washington argues in his study that views and policies originating many years ago still influence patterns of racial group evaluation. Discuss some similar long-standing influences upon relations between social classes, or between genders.

3. Do you agree or disagree with Martin about the difficulties involved in assessing merit (say, for measures of skills and abilities)? Why?

4. Bar-Tal discusses ways in which ethnic and racial groups are "delegitimized." Discuss ways that women are delegitimized in your own society.

5. Extrapolating from Bar-Tal's analysis where appropriate, discuss ways in which the poor and the lower classes, in a society of your choice, are also delegitimized.

6. Swaan describes a middle-class backlash against welfare rights for the poor. Are the "sexual politics" of virginity another kind of backlash against women, aimed at limiting their economic value and economic power?

Data Collection Exercises

1. Ask Potter and Wetherell's questions—about affirmative action in the workplace—of some 10 to 12 people. What are the characteristics of the socially acceptable replies you receive?

2. Consult some available studies of race relations in your home country and ask whether *threat* plays the sort of role suggested by Bar-Tal's article.
3. Try to recall when you first learned about race and its evaluation. What did you think then? How have your views changed?
4. Do the same exercise as in number 3 above, but for your first impressions of social classes.

Writing Exercises

1. "The same cultural influences that create attractions to Western music, fashions and home furnishings also create attractions to Western categories of color valuation." Write a brief (500-word) essay showing why you agree or disagree.
2. Ask a couple of friends who are not in your sociology class to discuss their views on use of the merit principle in schools. Write a brief essay on ways the responses are consistent with the analyses by Potter and Wetherell and Martin.
3. In a brief essay draw on your own experiences with your family to describe the values related to social inequality that were taught there.
4. Write a brief review of a popular movie, book, or television program, revealing how it puts forward ideas on status distinctions and the legitimitizing ideas provided for these distinctions.

SECTION 9
Responses to Status Inequality

9.1 Perceptions of Women's Opportunity in Five Industrialized Nations

---

Jesper B. Sorenson

This section looks at various consequences of being placed in different status groups. We begin with an excerpt by Jesper Sorenson, which compares data from the United States, Great Britain, Australia, Italy, and the former West Germany. It is about self-limiting beliefs about one's opportunities.

Respondents in each country were asked to report their views on women's and men's chances of going to university or college. They were also asked to rate the job opportunities of equally qualified men and women.

Sorenson finds that men's and women's perceptions differ quite a bit, and that they differ more in countries where a larger proportion of women work for pay. Here, especially, women see more discrimination than men do. This suggests that differing perceptions, and gender conflict, may increase in the very countries where inequality is actually declining.

... This paper attempts to clarify the nature of beliefs about women's opportunity. Using a unique cross-national data set, two issues are explored: (1) the conditions under which people are likely to perceive gender discrimination in higher education and the occupational structure; and (2) whether the determinants of beliefs about women's opportunity are the same in different societies.

...The five nations studied in this paper—the Federal Republic of Germany, Italy, Great Britain, the United States and Australia—differ in the extent to which women attend universities and work. They also differ in their perceptions of women's opportunity and support for affirmative action. This allows us to explore whether there exists a

Excerpted from Sorenson, Jesper B. (1990), "Perceptions of women's opportunity in five industrialized nations," *European Sociological Review*, 6(2), September, 151–164. With permission of Oxford University Press.

systematic relationship between the social position of women and the nature of beliefs about women's opportunity.

The survey employed in this paper was conducted by the International Social Survey Program in 1985 and 1986. Two questions measuring perceptions of women's opportunity are used. The first asks whether, compared to men, women have an equal chance of going to university or college. The second asks whether the job opportunities of equally qualified men and women are the same (Zentralarchiv, 1987). ...

STRUCTURAL CONDITIONS AND BELIEFS ABOUT WOMEN'S OPPORTUNITY

... The survey questions ask the respondent to evaluate whether the stratification system systematically denies opportunities to women.

We can expect the position of women with respect to the stratification system (i.e. the extent to which they are involved in direct competition for status) to be an important variable in shaping perceptions of women's opportunity.

In Western, industrialized nations, as women have increasingly become more committed to work, status attainment has gained new relevance for them. This change influences the way in which experience may shape perceptions of women's opportunity.

Imagine two societies, A and B, which are alike in every aspect except one. In Society A, women work primarily to supplement family income but not for status attainment; in Society B, women devote their energies to careers precisely because they are interested in status attainment. Women in Society B compete for status directly with men, while women in Society A do not. The social status which can be derived from work is more important to woman in Society A.

In Society A, women are less likely to compete fully, so both men and women will be less likely to perceive the stratification system as unfair towards women. On the other hand, since men and women in Society B are equal competitors, there is a greater likelihood that these mechanisms will be perceived as unjust by women in Society B.

The situation is different for men. If men in Society B accept women as equal competitors, they may adopt the view that men succeed more often, because their qualifications were objectively seen as better in a fair competition. On the other hand, if men in Society B do not view women as equal competitors, there is no real difference between men in Society A and Society B. Thus men will not be more likely to perceive discriminations in Society B. It follows, then, that the differences in perception between the sexes will be greater in Society B than in Society A.

The effects of structural position, such as occupational status, in the two societies may differ in a fashion similar to the effects of gender. Since women in Society A are less likely to compete than in Society B, respondents in occupations are less likely to perceive discrimination than similar respondents in Society B, even when controlling for gender differences in perceptions.

... In short, it appears a person's experience in the stratification system will have a greater effect on his or her perceptions of women's opportunity in situations where women compete for status directly with men than in situations where women are more tangential to the stratification system.

CROSS-NATIONAL DIFFERENCES IN THE SOCIAL POSITION OF WOMEN

In order to test the theory, we must characterize the nations considered in terms of the relationship of women to the major arenas of status attainment process. ...

... Arguably, the increasing importance of the service sector influences the relationship between men and women in the stratification system, since the system rewards technical skill to a higher degree, 'with education as the necessary route of access to skill' (Bell, 1976: 361). Through education, women can independently accumulate the resources necessary to compete directly with men for status.

Figure 1 presents the sectoral distribution of the labor force in the five nations studied here.

FIGURE 1   *Civilian Labour Force by Major Sectors, 1986.* Source: OECD, *Labour Force Statistics, 1966–1986.*

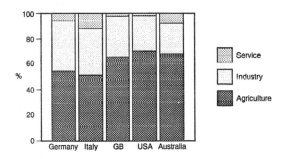

A natural way of looking at Figure 1 is to draw a vertical line between Italy and Great Britain. To the left of the line are nations (Germany and Italy) where approximately 55 per cent of the labor force can be found in the service sector. On the right side of the line—in Great Britain, the United States and Australia—the service sector employs approximately 65 per cent of the labor force. For the remainder of this paper, the countries to the left of this line will be termed 'Type II' nations.

Given the suggested link between the size of the service sector and women's economic activity, we would expect that women in the Type II nations (Great Britain, the United States and Australia) participate to a greater extent in the stratification system than women in Type I nations (Germany and Italy). Table 1 presents the female labor force participation rates for each nation.

In neither of the Type I nations are more than 52 per cent of women aged 15 to 64 economically active. . . .

The difference between the two types of nations goes beyond the relative size of the service sectors. Women are less likely, in Type II nations, to stand outside of one of the major arenas—the occupational structure—in which individual status is determined; they are hence also less likely to be completely dependent on their husbands for social status. Women in the Type II nations are therefore also more likely to compete for status directly with men.

TABLE 1   *Female labor force participation rates, 1966–1986*

	1966	1976	1986
Type I:			
West Germany	48.5	49.5	51.1
Italy	33.4	30.6	42.0
Type II:			
Britain	49.9	60.2	63.2
United States	45.4	56.1	66.5
Australia	42.6	49.8	56.4

Source: OECD, *Labour Force Statistics*, 1966–1986.

. . . Women are still under-represented in higher education (OECD, 1986b). This is true of all of the nations studied here, where women constituted approximately 40 per cent of university enrollments in 1980, with the exception of the United States, where women constitute half of university enrollments (OECD, 1986a).

In the Type II nations, approximately 80 per cent of the female labor force is employed in the service sector; the corresponding figure for the Type I nations is 60 per cent (OECD, 1985b).

It is possible to construct two general hypotheses to guide the analysis of the survey data. First we might expect the level of perception of sex discrimination to be consistently higher in the Type II nations, where more women are directly involved in the stratification system. Secondly, we would expect greater differences in beliefs between men and women and between respondents in different structural positions in Type II nations. . . .

DATA AND METHODS

. . . The surveys took the form of self-administered questionnaires and were fielded between 1985 and 1986 (Zentralarchiv, 1987).

Dependent Variables

Two questions concerning the opportunity of women relative to men were asked in the ISSP survey. In the first, each respondent was asked to compare the relative opportunities for university education of women and men. In the second, respondents were asked to compare the relative job opportunities of men and women with similar education and experience. Respondents were allowed to choose between answers on a five point scale ranging from 'Much better for women' to 'Much worse for women'. . . .

Independent Variables

The variables fall into three categories: ascriptive characteristics, structural position variables, and general beliefs. There are two ascriptive variables, sex and age, with respondents grouped into ages: under 35, 35–54 and 55 and over.

Six independent variables measuring social position are used, the most important being educational attainment and employment status. Respondents are assigned to three categories of educational attainment: compulsory schooling or less, upper secondary schooling (high school in the United States) and college or university education. Respondents are categorized as employed on the one hand or unemployed or not in the labor force on the other. In addition a current occupational status variable is included to see whether beliefs about women's opportunity vary with the respondent's position in the occupational hierarchy. Respondent earnings are also included. The final structural variable divides the respondents into not married, married but spouse not working, and married with spouse working.

Finally, only one variable measuring general beliefs is included, namely party affiliation. Respondents are grouped according to whether they align themselves with the left, the center (or no preference), or the right.

The determinants of beliefs about women's opportunity will be explored through weighted logistic regression. . . .

LEVELS OF PERCEPTION

It was argued earlier that Type II nations should consistently have a higher proportion of respondents stating opportunity for women is worse than for men. This hypothesis is not supported by the data. Regarding educational opportunity for women, the Germans and British are significantly more likely to perceive discrimination than respondents in other nations; Australians and Americans are significantly more likely to perceive discrimination than Italians. The two Type I nations are at opposite ends of the spectrum, with Germans being the most likely to perceive discrimination. What is most striking is the small percentage of respondents who believe educational opportunity is worse for women (between 10 per cent and 21 per cent).

Substantially larger proportions of each nation believe occupational opportunity is worse for women, ranging from 87 per cent in Germany to 45 per cent in Italy. Again, our hypothesis is not supported. Germany and Italy are at opposite ends.

DETERMINANTS OF PERCEPTIONS OF WOMEN'S OPPORTUNITY

The second question is whether sub-group variations in the perception of discrimination differ between countries. We are interested in whether, as the hypotheses predict, gender, educational attainment and occupational status are significant determinants of perceptions in Type II, but not Type I nations. Starting with educational opportunities, we find a strong age effect in Germany: the two older cohorts are significantly less likely to perceive worse opportunity in education for women than are the respondents under age 35. It may be that the young, who have better educational opportunities than previous generations, also have higher expectations.

The perception of discrimination does not vary significantly with educational attainment in Germany, but does vary with employment status. Thus, in Germany the perception of discrimination is not directly dependent on a respondent's personal experience of the educational system, a finding consistent with our hypothesis. Men and women do not differ significantly in their perceptions, despite the fact they have different levels of educational opportunity. It may be that Germans form their opinion of the extent of gender discrimination in higher education according to a general conception of the educational system, and not through their own experience.

The lack of any significant coefficients in Italy may be due to the fact that some of the independent variables are not available for Italy. It may also be due to problems in the translation of the question or the low percentage of people who believed educational opportunity was worse for women (9 per cent).

In the Type II countries, one finds significant effects of gender and educational attainment on perceptions of women's educational opportunity. This supports the hypothesis that in the Type II societies, the respondent's experience of the structure of opportunity plays a direct role in the formation of beliefs.

The difference between Type I and Type II nations is perhaps best illustrated if one compares Germany with Australia and Great Britain. Consider first the effect of education. In Germany, the respondent's educational attainment did not affect his or her perceptions, despite the fact that women are under-represented in higher education. In Australia, however, where women are also under-represented in higher education (OECD, 1985a), the perception of discrimination increases as one moves up the educational ladder. . . .

In Great Britain, educational attainment also has an effect on opinions. British men in the two upper educational categories do not differ significantly from men with only a compulsory education; neither do women with compulsory or upper secondary schooling differ significantly from this group of men. Women with a university education, however, are significantly more likely to perceive discrimination. In both Australia and Great Britain, then, the respondent's own experience (although only for women in Great Britain) in relation to the structure of opportunity in education plays a role it does not play in Germany.

In both the United States and Australia women are significantly more likely to perceive discrimination in higher education than men, controlling for other factors. This is revealing in light of the fact that gender effects were not found in Germany. . . .

Turning to the determinants of perceptions of women's occupational opportunity, the same patterns are found. Among Type I nations, neither the respondent's sex nor variables relating directly to the labor market status of either the respondent or the respon-

dent's spouse play a significant role in determining perceptions of women's job opportunities. In Germany, the perception of women's job opportunity only varies by age, with the older cohorts being less likely to perceive discrimination than respondents under age 35. Age also plays a significant role in Italy, but it is Italians aged 35 to 54 that are most likely to perceive discrimination.

In Italy, educational attainment is also a significant predictor of beliefs: respondents who have gone to upper secondary school are more likely to perceive discrimination than respondents who have completed no more than compulsory schooling; the odds of perceiving discrimination increase even more if an individual has a university education.

In the Type II nations, as in Italy, educational attainment is positively related to the perception of sexual discrimination in the job market. But other factors, which were not significant in Italy or Germany, are influential in these nations. For example, sex has an independent effect in both the United States and Great Britain, where women are significantly more likely than men to believe job opportunity is worse for women than for men, independently of any other characteristics. In Australia, a difference between men and women is found among respondents who are currently employed.

In addition the relation of the respondent to the labor market helps determine perceptions in these three nations. In Australia and the United States, beliefs about women's job opportunity vary with the occupational status of the respondent. While there are differences between the two nations, the two highest white collar categories are the groups most likely to perceive discrimination.

Finally, two structural variables in addition to education and employment status are significant predictors of opportunity beliefs in Great Britain. The odds of a respondent perceiving discrimination increases with the income of the respondent; the well-off are therefore more likely to perceive discrimination than are the poor. Finally, British respondents whose spouses work are significantly more likely to perceive worse job opportunities for women than respondents who are not married or whose spouse does not work.

The findings with respect to party affiliation are ambiguous. Where party effects are found, they consistently reveal that respondents who align themselves with the right are the group least likely to perceive inequality of opportunity for women. However, the effects of general beliefs do not vary with the type of nation considered.

DISCUSSION

Several findings stand out. First, there is no strong correspondence between type of nation and the aggregate level of perception of discrimination. It suggests other factors— such as general stratification beliefs, the salience of issues of women's opportunity and the extent of affirmative action programs for women—need to be taken into account when explaining aggregate levels of perceptions of women's opportunity.

Secondly, men and women do not necessarily differ in their perceptions of women's opportunity. Indeed, sex differences only arise in those nations where women constitute a greater presence in the labor force as a whole (Type II). This confirms the hypothesis that sex differences arise out of the nature of women's position in the stratification system and not simply out of increases in the participation of women. . . .

The last major finding also supports the notion that differences in the social position of women in the two types of nations have important consequences for the ways in which perceptions are formed. In Type I nations, the perception of women's opportunity does not vary with the respondent's success in the opportunity structure, while such variations do exist in Type II nations. In the United States and Australia, for example, the odds that a respondent will perceive occupational discrimination increase as one moves up the occupational ladder. This effect is not found in Germany.

The extent to which women have entered into the once predominantly male spheres of competition has a substantial effect on beliefs about women's opportunity. As men and women begin to compete with each other for status, differences in perceptions begin to run at a deeper level. Perceptions of women's opportunity are less ideologically determined, but instead fundamentally reflect an individual's experience in the stratification system. . . .

REFERENCES

Bell D. (1976): The Coming of Post-Industrial Society: A Venture in Social Forecasting, 1973, New York: Basic Books.

Organisation for Economic Co-Operation and Development (OECD). (1988): *Labour Force Statistics, 1966–1986*, Paris: OECD.

———(1986a): *Girls and Women in Education*, Paris: OECD.

———(1986b): *Living Conditions in OECD Countries*, Paris: OECD.

———(1985a): *The Integration of Women into the Economy*, Paris: OECD.

———(1985b): *Labour Force Statistics, 1963–1983*, Paris: OECD.

Zentralarchiv für empirische Sozialforschung. (1987): *The International Social Survey Program Role of Government Module 1985*. Codebook. Cologne, FRG: Zentralarchiv für empirische Sozialforschung.

9.2 Shadow Education and Allocation in Formal Schooling in Japan

David Lee Stevenson and David P. Baker

"Shadow education" is a type of educational activity that occurs outside the formal school system. This activity is designed to give the student an advantage over other students not using the activity (or to make the student competitive with other students using the activity) in the pursuit of marks and advancement in the formal education system.

The excerpt shows how very widespread this activity is in Japan. The authors report results from a study of students who were interviewed near the end of high school and again later.

The study shows that families of different socio-economic backgrounds vary in how effectively they use shadow education. As is often the case, higher status families are better able to take advantage; they use shadow education more than other families. The authors show that shadow education does pay off for students, giving them better success in getting into the highly competitive university system in Japan.

The capacity of formal schooling to differentiate students is central to allocation theories of education (Bourdieu and Passeron 1977; Bowles and Gintis 1976). Allocation processes, however, vary across educational systems in terms of the criteria by which allocation decisions are made, in the timing of such decisions, and in the factors that influence those decisions (Eckstein and Noah 1989). Allocation processes also can have institutional effects on schooling itself (Meyer 1977).

An example of such an institutional effect is the way allocation processes encourage the development of shadow education, a set of educational activities outside formal schooling that are designed to improve a student's chances of successfully moving through the allocation process.

Certain characteristics of the educational allocation process foster the development of shadow education. First, and most important, is the use of formal examinations—particularly centrally administered examinations. Second, shadow education flourishes if schooling uses "contest rules" instead of "sponsorship rules" (Turner 1960). And third, shadow education is prevalent when there are tight linkages between the outcomes of educational allocation in elementary and secondary schooling and future educational opportunities, occupations, or general social status.

When these qualities occur together, extensive shadow education can be observed. For example, in Taiwan, graduates of elite universities have significant advantages in the labor market, and there is extensive shadow education to prepare students for university entrance examinations (Lin 1983). In Hong Kong, graduates' hiring and pay

Stevenson, David Lee and David P. Baker (1992). "Shadow education and allocation in formal schooling in Japan," American Journal of Sociology; 97(6), May, 1639–1657. ©1992 by the University of Chicago.

rates are partly dependent on their performance on secondary-school-certificate examinations, and shadow education takes the form of tutoring and after-school classes to prepare students for the examinations (Mitchell 1968; Sweeting 1983). In Greece, because admission to an elite secondary school is considered critical for acceptance at a prestigious university, students use tutors and attend special after-school classes to prepare for the national entrance examination for secondary school (Katsillis and Rubinson 1990).

The timing, use, and forms of shadow education are shaped by allocation rules. We use the term "shadow" to denote the strong connection between allocation rules and nonformal schooling; we do not imply that these activities are hidden. Indeed, in systems such as Japan's, these activities make up a large, open enterprise.

SHADOW EDUCATION
AND CONTESTED SPONSORSHIP
IN JAPAN

Educational allocation in Japan is organized around the institutional qualities that foster the development of shadow education. First and foremost is the use of formal examinations in the educational allocation process, particularly since the examinations are central to the allocation process, the weight of nonexamination criteria in the selection process is minimal, and there are few critical school-to-career transition points (U.S. Department of Education 1987; Amano 1990). Second is the clear and immutable connections between the outcomes of the educational allocation process and future occupational positions or general social status (Brinton 1988; Rosenbaum and Kariya 1989). The Japanese combination of meritocratic examinations and rich educational rewards shapes an allocation process that can be described as "contested sponsorship." Contested sponsorship arises from the organization of Japanese education that shifts from more compulsory and nonselective schooling in the lower grades to increasing levels of selectivity by the end of high school. . . .

Increasingly larger numbers of students attempt to enter college, in part because the potential prize is entrance to one of the most prestigious universities, which leads to recruitment into a sponsored elite. As elsewhere, universities in Japan have social charters: the ability "to define people as graduates and as therefore possessing distinctive rights and capacities in society" (Meyer 1970, p. 59). But the clear hierarchy of Japanese universities has produced a set of "narrow" charters so that *which* university one attends affects one's occupational career and general social status (Amano 1986; U.S. Department of Education 1987).

University graduates are recruited by firms directly from university and many spend their entire work career with their first employer (Brinton 1988). Recruitment by employers begins in November and, within a five-day period, almost 80% of the spring graduates have selected an employer (Ushiogi 1986). Major companies and elite departments of the civil service only recruit graduates of certain departments in the most prestigious universities. Graduates employed by major companies have life long advantages over graduates employed by small firms in terms of salaries, promotion opportunities, benefits, job stability, and yearly bonuses (Ushiogi 1986).

The tight linkages between education and work and the narrow charters of Japanese universities produce intense competition for admission to the most prestigious universities. In 1980, for example, 13,000 applicants competed for 3,077 places at Tokyo University (Rohlen 1983). For admission to the prestigious departments of law, economics, and medicine, the ratio of applicants to places may reach 7 : 1.

It is clear, then, why Japanese students with college aspirations arduously prepare for the entrance examinations. The importance of this transition point is heavily emphasized in the name "examination hell" (*juken jigoku*). The intensity of the competition is captured in the popular phrase, "four pass, five fail," which admonishes students that those who sleep four hours pass their entrance examinations but those who sleep five hours fail.

The contested sponsorship process in Japan is ripe for the development of shadow education. The dominance of examinations, the social and financial rewards for success, and the concentration of allocation at one time point intensify the growth of shadow education.

There are two sets of Japanese shadow-education activities: one used primarily during secondary school and the other used immediately after high school. During the secondary school years, students participate in after-school and weekend preparation activities such as private cram schools, correspondence courses, and practice examinations. If high school graduates do not earn admission to the university of their choice, they may spend one or more additional years preparing. Such students are known as *ronin*, a word that was used to describe lordless samurai. Ronin do not legitimately belong to either the world of formal schooling or the world of work. They spend their time engaged in preparation for the university entrance examinations, often in intensive preparation schools (*yobiko*).[1]

Shadow education encompasses a large set of varied educational activities that are firmly rooted within the private sector. Students and their families pay tuition for private schools to prepare them for examinations, purchase workbooks with questions from previous examinations, and pay for practice tests that are administered and graded by private companies. Since there are millions of students competing for university entrance examinations, shadow education is a vast market representing an industry worth 870 billion yen (in U.S. currency, approximately $7 billion) in 1986 (Katsuki 1988). . . .

---

1. Practice examinations (*mogi shiken*), provided and graded by private firms, assess a student's chances of being admitted to university. Students receive a report comparing their performance with national norms, are notified of subject areas that require greater study, and are given an estimate of their chances of being admitted to a particular university.

2. Correspondence courses (*tsuchin tensaku*), purchased from mail-order companies, provide exercises for entrance examinations that are mailed back and then returned graded.
3. Private tutors (*katei kyoshi*) are primarily used for staying abreast of regular schoolwork and used less for examination preparation.
4. Private after-school classes (*juku*) come in two types: *gakushu juku*, which are remedial classes, and *shingaku juku*, for preparation for the university entrance examinations. *Juku* vary in the size of the classes from small classes that may meet in the home of the tutor to large classes in a school. Students in primary school may participate in *juku* to develop academic abilities in coordination with the curriculum of the formal school, while secondary students in *juku* prepare for university entrance examinations. There is a great deal of variation in the atmosphere and demands of *jukes* but there is a general opinion that participation in a *juku* is an important part of a student's school career (Cummings 1980; White 1987).
5. Full-time preparation following high school (ronin) is a strategy used by students who do not gain admission to any university or by those who do not gain admission to the university they wish to attend. Ronin take a year or more to prepare solely for university entrance examinations and often attend *yobiko*, a private examination preparation school (Tsukada 1988).

PREVALENCE OF SHADOW EDUCATION

Because shadow education is both a large industry and is publicly defined as useful for educational advancement in Japan, we would expect to find high proportions of students using these educational practices, particularly among those students who definitely plan to attend a university. Table I presents the percentage of students who participate in shadow education activities during high school and the percentage who are willing to become ronin after high school. The first column shows the participation of all base-year students and the second column shows the participation of only those base-year students

TABLE 1 Participation in Shadow Education by Japanese Students during High School (Base-Year Sample)

Shadow-Education Activity	Total Sample of Students (%)	Students with College Plans* (%)	School Period when Student Began to Plan for College				x^2
			Early Elementary School (%)	Late Elementary School (%)	Junior High School (%)	1st-2nd Year, High School (%)	
Practice examination (mogi shiken)	54	68	72	69	68	60	40.0†
Correspondence course (tsushin tensaku)	30	43	45	41	35	26	99.2†
Private tutor (katei kyoshi)	8	11	15	12	8	7	66.9†
After-school class (juku)	35	46	52	43	38	29	144.4†
Plans to be a ronin after high school	29	32	41	33	26	19	123.0†
N	7,240	5,352	1,740	826	1,924	862	

Note.—Fifty-four percent of all students took a practice examination; 46% did not.
*Students with college plans represent 74% of base-year sample.
†P < .00001, df = 3.

who have college plans (about 74% of the base-year sample).

Japanese students are voracious consumers of shadow-education activities. Eighty-eight percent of those students with college plans participated in at least one activity during high school and 60% participated in two or more of these activities. Almost a third of the seniors were willing to become ronin after graduating if they needed additional preparation for the university examinations.

We have argued that the use of shadow education is related to its perceived educational benefit. If that is so, we should find that students' participation varies with their plans for postsecondary education. The last four columns in Table 1 show that participation is related to the age at which students stated they planned to attend a university. Students who had college plans early in elementary school were most likely to use shadow education, while the rates of participation declined among late planners.

DETERMINANTS OF PARTICIPATION IN SHADOW EDUCATION

Although shadow education is pervasive, participation may not be equally spread across all students. The transition to university offers significant benefits, and many students engage in extraordinary preparation activities, but, because these educational activities are expensive and time-consuming, we expect children from families with more resources to participate more in shadow education than children from poorer families. Differential investments in shadow education also can occur within families. For example, because of the better job prospects for Japanese males and perceptions about gender and social opportunity (Brinton 1988, 1989), families may tend to invest their resources in the education of sons rather than daughters. Or families may invest in shadow education for only their most promising child or do so only when they live in areas, such as cities, in which these activities are most available.

To examine this we estimated logistic regression equations in which the dependent variable is whether or not the student ever participated in a particular shadow-education activity. We find that investment in shadow education for students is associated with three measures of family's SES, even after student and school characteristics are controlled for. Students from wealthier families and families in which the parents have higher levels of education are more likely to purchase shadow education. These effects are moderate, generally adding only 4%–5% to the likelihood of participating in a form of shadow education, but taken together they increase the probability of undertaking shadow education by 12%–15%. For the majority of activities, all three indicators of family SES increase the likelihood of shadow participation.

There are moderate to large gender differences in participation for every activity except after-school classes. Compared with females, males participate more in practice examinations, correspondence courses, and are more willing (54% more) to become ronin after high school. Almost one-half of the male seniors had plans to become ronin if not admitted to university, while only one-tenth of the female students had similar plans.

Scholastic characteristics also influence participation; students with better grades (academic standing) and students in academic curriculum tracks purchase shadow education. The latter effect is large as students in the academic track are 22%–68% more likely than other students to use shadow education, while the largest effect of grades increases participation by only 7%. The curriculum-track effect indicates the strength of the connection between shadow education and educational allocation.

High school reputation has a mixed effect; students from high schools that are successful in university placement use shadow education, except for *juku* (after-school classes). Among these students *juku* is not used because in many prestigious high schools examination preparation activities are now incorporated into an extracurricular schedule, by creating within-school, after-school classes. This shows how pervasive systems of shadow education can in turn influence the instruction and organization of formal schooling.

Finally, living in an urban area moderately increases the use of shadow education, except for the purchase of correspondence courses, the only form of participation not restricted by proximity.

We examine one final issue of participation in shadow education. Some students, who are either not admitted to any university or are admitted but decide to continue to prepare for the examination of a more prestigious university the following year, undertake perhaps the most extensive form of shadow education—the ronin year. Since no limit exists as to the number of times a student can participate in the annual examinations, up to 25% of examination takers in any one year are ronin. While ronin activities can keep the student preparing and competing for the prestigious positions, the financial, social, and emotional costs can be quite high. The average tuition for *yobiko* (private cram school for ronin) ranges from the equivalent of $2,000 to $2,800 per year, but can go as high as $20,000 for *yobiko* designed for entrance to special programs, such as medicine. For some there are additional room and board costs. Other costs for ronin come in the form of emotional stress from constant pressure to prepare, damaged social and peer affiliations, and anxiety about uncertain futures (Tsukada 1988).

To assess which students become ronin, we analyzed those students in the follow-up who, as seniors, had had college plans (69% of the follow-up sample) since this is the pool from which ronin will come. Of this group 27% became ronin the year immediately after high school.

We find that, as is true of participation in shadow education during the high school years, family resources have a modest influence on becoming a ronin after high school. Students whose families have more money and whose parents have more education are more likely to continue in the most extensive

forms of shadow education. These effects are small however, adding only about 5%–6% to the likelihood that a student undertakes the ronin year. Family expenditure and student sacrifice for the ronin year is far more motivated by the gender of the student. Males dominate the ranks of ronin, and we find that, even after we control for a number of other factors, when we compare males with females, the former are 49% more likely to become ronin if this is necessary for continuance in the allocation process. Naturally students who failed examinations during the first year are more likely to become ronin and students from rural areas less likely to, because of the higher costs of sending a student to live in the city to attend a *yobiko*. Finally, students from prestigious high schools tend to become ronin, most likely because they are taking the most competitive entrance examinations.

CONSEQUENCES OF SHADOW EDUCATION

We examine the consequences of participation in shadow education for university attendance at two points in time: (1) the first year out of high school and (2) the second year out of high school. The first point includes all base-year students with university plans and the second point includes only those follow-up-year students with university plans who did not attend university after high school.

Because we have no measure of the quality of the shadow-education experience, our analysis provides a limited assessment of the effect of participation in shadow-education activities on university attendance. We can, nevertheless, determine whether participation in shadow education increases the student's chances of attending university, in addition to including various control variables, such as student, family, and school characteristics, in order to assess the relative contribution of shadow education to allocation outcomes in Japan.

We find that among students two years out of high school with college plans, high school shadow education had a diminishing effect on attending university, but the effect of being a ronin is dramatic because it increases university attendance by 80%. There is a strong association between the ronin year and continued competition in the race for university; among this part of the follow-up sample 86% became ronin and of these 72% entered college compared with only 6% of the non-ronin from this group. This is particularly true among the males, who are much more likely than females to become ronin. A further 19% of the original ronin continued for a second year to prepare for another round of university examinations. Even though the dominant effect in this model is that of the ronin, shadow education as a group of activities still adds significantly to the background model.

DISCUSSION

As we have seen, many Japanese high school students participate in preparation activities that are not offered in formal schooling, and many high school graduates continue such preparation activities during the two years after high school.

Although rates of participation in various forms of shadow education are uniformly high, there are different patterns of participation. The likelihood of participation increases if the student is male, or has good grades in high school, or is from a higher SES family. These patterns of participation in shadow education reflect broader patterns of stratification by gender, secondary schooling, and SES. Such evidence suggests that participation in shadow education is not a remedial strategy used primarily by students who have difficulty meeting the academic standards of a formal school setting, but is instead a proactive strategy used primarily by students who have already accumulated significant advantages in the formal educational system. Shadow education provides an avenue for parents to enhance their children's chances in the educational allocation contest.

Consequences of participation are modest for some forms of shadow education and large for others. Becoming a ronin is an institutionalized way for one-time losers to stay in the educational allocation contest, and staying in the contest seems to have its pay-offs. Forms of shadow education are designed to help students increase their knowledge in order to improve their performances on the entrance examinations. Gaining admission to a Japanese university is, however, not merely a transfer of family background through investment in shadow education. The meritocratic contest of university admission in Japan emphasizes the academic ability of the student and measures of previous academic performance have large, direct effects on university attendance.

Shadow education is designed to enhance the school careers of students. Its content and existence is tightly coupled to the organization of transitions both within schooling and from school to the workplace. For some societies, the study of shadow education will enhance our understanding of the process by which students are allocated within formal schooling and how social advantages are transferred across generations.

REFERENCES

Amano, I. 1986. "Educational Crisis in Japan." pp. 23–43 in *Educational Policies in Crisis*, edited by W. K. Cummings, E. R. Beauchamp, S. Ichikawa, V. N. Kobayashi, and M. Ushiogi. New York: Praeger.

———. 1990. *Education and Examination in Modern Japan*. Tokyo: University of Tokyo Press.

Bowles, S., and H. Gintis. 1976. *Schooling in Capitalist America*. New York: Basic.

Bourdieu, P., and J. Passeron. 1977. *Reproduction in Education, Society, and Culture*. Beverly Hills, Calif.: Sage.

Brinton, M. 1988. "The Social-Institutional Bases of Gender Stratification: Japan as an Illustrative Case." *American Journal of Sociology* 94:300–334.

———. 1989. "Gender Stratification in Contemporary Urban Japan." *American Sociological Review* 54:549–64.

Cummings, W. 1980. *Education and Equality in Japan*. Princeton, N.J.: Princeton University Press.

Eckstein, M., and H. Noah. 1989. "Forms and Functions of Secondary-School-Leaving Examinations." *Comparative Education Review* 33:295–316.

Katsillis, J., and R. Rubinson. 1990. "Cultural Capital, Student Achievement, and Educational Reproduction in Greece." *American Sociological Review* 55:270–79.

Katsuki, N. 1988. "The Learning Business." *Tokyo Business Today* (January), pp. 34–36.

Lin, C. 1983. "The Republic of China (Taiwan)." Pp. 104–35 in *Schooling in East Asia: Forces of Change*, edited by R. M. Thomas and T. W. Postlethwaite. New York: Pergamon.

Meyer, J. 1970. "The Charter: Conditions of Diffuse Socialization in Schools." Pp. 564–78 in *Social Processes and Social Structures*, edited by W. R. Scott. New York: Holt, Rinehart & Winston.

———. 1977. "The Effects of Education as an Institution." *American Journal of Sociology* 83:55–77.

Mitchell, R. 1968. *Pupil, Parent and School: A Hong Kong Study*. Taipei: Orient Cultural Service.

Rohlen, T. 1983. *Japan's High Schools*. Berkeley and Los Angeles: University of California Press.

Rosenbaum, J., and T. Kariya. 1989. "From High School to Work: Market and Institutional Mechanisms in Japan." *American Journal of Sociology* 94:1334–65.

Sweeting, A. 1983. "Hong Kong." Pp. 272–97 in *Schooling in East Asia: Forces of Change*, edited by R. M. Thomas and T. W. Postlethwaite. New York: Pergamon.

———. 1988. "The *Yobiko*: The Institutionalized Supplementary Educational Institution in Japan: A Study of the Social Stratification Process." Ph.D. dissertation. University of Hawaii, Department of Sociology.

Turner, R. 1960 "Sponsored and Contest Mobility in the School System." *American Sociological Review* 25:855–67.

U.S. Department of Education. 1987. *Japanese Education Today*. Washington, D.C.: Government Printing Office.

Ushiogi, M. 1986. "Transition from School to Work: The Japanese Case." Pp. 197–209 in *Educational Policies in Crisis*, edited by W. K. Cummings, E. R. Beauchamp, S. Ichikawa, V. N. Kobayashi and M. Ushiogi. New York: Praeger.

White. M. 1987. *The Japanese Educational Challenge*. New York: Free Press.

NOTES

[1] There was a similar status of intensive preparation for aspiring feudal Chinese literati (*shen-shih*) whose existence was referred to as an "examination life" (Franke 1963).

9.3 Male and Female Conversational Styles in Sweden

Kerstin Nordenstam

The next excerpt is about specialized gender roles in social interaction. Specifically it is about how (and why) men and women make conversation differently.

The excerpt reports on results of studies of how women and men speak with each other and together. The studies used tape-recorded sessions of pairs of people in Sweden. The author provides a fine-grained analysis of amount of talking, topics and topic organization, topic shifts, interruptions, and simultaneous speaking—all across the genders.

What do you think are the male-female differences in these respects? Some of the differences follow from our knowledge that men dominate women. Other patterns of difference show that women and men have markedly different interests and experiences. See for yourself.

Note, also, that the author concludes that there are various forms of evidence for the proposition that "interaction is the work women do."

... To study language variation in as informal a situation as possible I used tape recordings made by the participants in their homes. The choice of topics of conversation was entirely free. To make possible gender differences apparent, I compared the language usage of single-gender dyads (conversations between two women or two men) with language usage in two-gender dyads (conversations between a woman and a man).

MATERIAL

My material consists of tape recordings of men and women, born in Sweden and living in Gothenburg. These individuals were chosen as a random sample from different age and social groups. A person, around either 25 or 50 years old, selected a conversational partner from among his or her friends or relatives and kept a conversation going for about half an hour. The recordings were made by the participants. The person selected for the task received a state raffle ticket as remuneration. It was made clear they were taking part in a language study.... The recordings were made in 1979.

I have chosen three groups of conversations: six dyads where a man talks to another man, called MEN, six dyads where a woman talks to another woman, called WOMEN,

Excerpted from Nordenstam, Kerstin (1992), "Male and female conversational style," *International Journal of Sociology of Language*, 94, 75–98. With permission of the Mouton de Gruyter, a division of Walter de Gruyter & Co. Publishers, Berlin and New York.

and six dyads where a man and a woman talk to each other, called MARRIAGES. ...

WORD DISTRIBUTION

As is shown in Table 1, the number of words in the corpus is approximately 86,000, distributed over 8,400 utterances. The average number of words per utterance is 10.3. MEN have the longest utterances, with an average of 12.3 words per utterance, and WOMEN the shortest, with an average of 8.2 words per utterance. The figure for the MARRIAGES is 11.3.

However, in the married couple's conversations the average male utterance consists of 8.7 words, the average female utterance of 13.9 words. This is the reverse of the proportion in the single-gender dyads.

The distribution of words in the dyads varies between an equal distribution of the two parties using 50 percent of the words each, to the most unequal distribution of 72 percent versus 28 percent. The most equal distribution occurs in the WOMEN's dyads. Here none of the talkers utters more than 58 percent of the words. In the MEN's dyads, in four of the six dyads, one person utters more than 60 percent of the words, while in the two-gender dyads the number of words uttered by one party exceeds 69 percent in three of six dyads.

Inequality of distribution is greatest in MARRIAGES. The three most talkative married people (with 69%, 71%, and 72% of the words) are also women (500, 507, 618). These three women are the ones selected for the recording and have chosen their husbands as conversational partners. The men who

TABLE 1 Differences between the three main groups

	Men (%)	Women (%)	Marriages (%)	m	f	Total (N)
Number of						
words	20,268	28,048	29,362			86,678
utterances	2,371	3,427	2,602			8,400
turns	2,223	3,089	2,437			7,785
Words/utterance	12.3	8.2	11.3	8.7	13.9	10.3
						(p < 0.001)
Simultaneous speech/	94	192	119	56	63	405
cooperative overlap	(4.2)	(6.2)	(4.8)			(p < 0.01)
Interruption of turns	74	73	149	82	67	296
	(3.3)	(2.3)	(6)			(p < 0.001)
Back-channeling signals	148	338	129	65	64	615
	(6.2)	(9.9)	(4.9)			(p < 0.001)

choose their wives to talk to do not act in the same way. Only one (635) talks more than his wife (61%).

I interpret these findings as the married women's fulfilling their task particularly thoroughly. There is a general tendency for the people who have been allotted the recording task to talk more than the others.

The three husbands chosen by their wives as conversational partners seem uninterested and uneasy and yawn on several occasions. No woman yawns in my recordings. Could yawning be a characteristic of male conversational style?

TOPIC AND TOPICAL ORGANIZATION

... We know from other studies and our own experiences that men talk to each other about manly things—cars, sports, jobs—and women talk to each other about womanly things—children and personal relations. This is also the case in my study. In my study, however, the women also talk about their jobs and courses. As regards the married couples, the tendency is the same, but here the wife tends to talk about one thing and the husband about another (see 635, where he talks about tape recorders and other equipment, and she talks about black currants and neighbors).

I tried to estimate my informants' interest in people by counting the number of people they mentioned by name. WOMEN talking to each other mention almost twice as many names as MEN do talking to each other (48 and 26 respectively). As for the MARRIAGES, the wives mention almost four times as many people as the husbands (30 versus 8).

Furthermore, as in other findings men talk about other men, while women talk about both women and men in my corpus.

TOPIC SHIFT

The number of main topics is 236 divided: MEN 77, WOMEN 91, and MARRIAGES 68. Thus WOMEN change topics most frequently, followed by MEN. The person selected for the recording initiates a larger number of topics than his or her counterpart in the single-gender dyads. 59 out of 77 new topics in MEN were initiated by the people selected. The corresponding figure for WOMEN is 56 of 91. For the MARRIAGES, however, there is no difference: 34 of 68 main topics are introduced by the person allotted the recording task. Here, sex seems a stronger variable: 42 out of 68 initiatives are taken by women. Thus, Zimmerman and West's (1975) hypothesis that *men decide the topic of conversation* in mixed groups does not apply to my corpus.

Topic changes can be managed in different ways. The sudden change of topic, I call *abrupt*. The person who takes the turn presents a topic not previously discussed. No boundary markers are used. Second, topic change may be *smooth*, characterized by the occurrence of a formal boundary marker (such as 'by the way,' 'this is changing the subject but'), meta comments, fillers, and the like, usually combined with clues as to content like *preclosings* or former topic endings.

Since Tannen sees abrupt topic shifting as a sign of *high-involvement style* (1984: 30), I sorted out the instances of topic shifts that could be considered abrupt.

For WOMEN, around 30 percent of the 91 main topics discussed in this group are introduced abruptly. For MEN, the figure is 23 percent, and for MARRIAGES 19 percent. Out of the 13 abrupt topic shifts in the latter group, nine are made by women. So there is a tendency for women to begin new topics in a more direct way than men do.

The MEN's dyads, on the other hand, make extensive use of phrases like 'this is changing the subject but,' 'talking about this,' 'while I remember,' etc., which often give a formal impression. WOMEN do not normally use expressions like 'by the way' for renewal of a topic, though it is common in the other groups.

Abrupt topic shifts may be the consequence of a quick talking pace and a great deal of personal involvement between the conversational partners. The partners in my corpus generally help each other carry on a conversation.

TOPIC SHIFT AFTER PAUSE

Another way of measuring the pace and involvement in a conversation is to check which topic shifts are preceded by an inter-turn pause. . . .

In MARRIAGES, 37 percent of the topic shifts are preceded by a pause, in MEN 22 percent, and in WOMEN only 3 percent.

I believe the pause before topic shifts is usually a sign of these talkers' uneasiness. They have difficulties finding a "natural" topic of conversation. Some MEN mention this difficulty directly. . . .

None of the female dyads seem inhibited: they neither turn off the tape recorder, nor talk about difficulties in the situation, nor pause when introducing a new topic.

In dyads where men are present, one party is often in focus. A in (620), explicitly expresses the idea that he, not his partner, is the object of study. Men's conversations are often more like interviews than dialogues. . . .

. . . In sum, when women talk to each other and to their husbands, their language usage is characterized by several of the features Tannen (1984) finds typical of *high-involvement style*. Women

–prefer personal topics.
–shift topics abruptly,
–introduce topics without hesitation.

I now want to report on other traits which Tannen (1984: 30) includes under pacing: *cooperative overlap* and *participatory listener-ship*, to see if they too are typical of women's conversational style.

INTERRUPTION
AND SIMULTANEOUS SPEECH

To discuss *cooperative overlap*, we must first sort out the difference between interruption and simultaneous speech. . . .

I define interruption as a turn taking which violates the current speaker's turn. The speaker is not allowed to finish his turn. This could occur with or without simultaneous speech. . . .

I use the term *simultaneous speech* for overlapping speech which does not violate the speaker's turn. This includes three types.

1. *Overlap.* Speaker shift takes place at a transition point, when the first speaker has more or less finished his turn but makes a short addition. It is to be seen as bad timing on the part of the second speaker and is common in rapid spontaneous speech. . . .

2. *Butting-in interruptions.* The listener tries to take over the turn but is not successful. . . .

3. *Cospeech.* The listener is talking at the same time as the speaker in short sequences of parallel speech. He fills in comments and phrases, usually of a supportive nature. I distinguish these from back-channeling signals by virtue of their length and sentence structure. Thus I classify 'of course' as a back-channeling signal, and 'yes do that' (555: 240) as simultaneous speech. . . .

Cospeech is a sign of the listener's involvement in the speaker's talk. The floor is, as it were, equally shared.

I regard *overlaps, butting-in interruptions* and *cospeech,* as generally cooperative strategies.

DISTRIBUTION OF INTERRUPTIONS

MEN have 74, WOMEN 73, and MARRIAGES 149 interruptions. Figured as a percentage of the number of turns in each group, 6 percent of the turns are interrupted here, compared to the all-MEN's group where 3.3 percent and the WOMEN's group where 2.3 percent of the turns are interrupted. In the single-sex groups, interruptions are also significantly unequally distributed (5% level), and men use interruptions more often than women do. Previous researchers have proposed interruption is a male strategy of dominance. My results support this idea.

In MARRIAGES husbands interrupt their wives more than vice versa, but the difference is not significant. The wives keep up with their husbands fairly well. One reason for this could be the speech setting. The home is the women's domain.

My most striking finding, however, is that the marriage situation gives rise to so many more interruptions than talk between friends. . . .

DISTRIBUTION
OF SIMULTANEOUS SPEECH

There are 305 cases of simultaneous speech, MEN have 94 cases, WOMEN 192, and MARRIAGES 119. (Significant at the 1%

level) There are also more women talking simultaneously with their partners in the mixed groups, 63 against 56, but here the difference is not significant. . . .

Women's talk during the other speaker's turn is a normal part of relaxed informal conversation between equals. Women also address the talker, frequently interpolate remarks, and offer enthusiastic comments during the other speaker's turn. In all-women interaction, such behavior is seen as evidence of active listening. Men's interruptions, on the other hand, seem to have as their goal the seizing of a turn. This is why men's use of interruptions in mixed conversations can result in women's silence (Coates 1986: 153).

This could explain why, in my study, simultaneous talk is not as common in MARRIAGES or in the MEN's dyads as in the WOMEN's dyads. The speech situation is not as relaxed in the first two groups, and the participants are not equals to the same extent as in the same-sex women's dyads. However, interruptions are comparatively common in MARRIAGES, where the "manly" norm prevails.

Thus, WOMEN, when talking to each other, use cooperative overlap to a much greater extent than MEN do. I define cooperative overlap as synonymous with simultaneous speech.

BACK-CHANNELING SIGNALS

Back-channeling signals are uttered during the other speaker's turn, usually at a transition point. Their function is (a) for a listener to show she or he has heard and/or understood and/or agrees with the speaker, and (b) to support the speaker's continuing her/his turn (Linell and Gustavsson 1986: 54). Different types of back-channeling signals are found in my material; 'yes' with various elaborations is the most frequently used, while exclamations are few (Nordenstam 1987: 47).

Back-channeling signals, are most frequently found in the all-WOMEN's group. Out of 615, 338 are found there. In the all-MEN's group there are 148, and in MAR-

RIAGES 129 (significance 0.1 level). The hypothesis that *women back each other up more than men do* when in single-sex groups is supported (see Table 1).

In MARRIAGES the 129 back-channeling signals are equally distributed between women and men. The comparatively high number among men is probably a consequence of women's talking in the longest turns, which is bound to evoke a certain number of back-channeling signals from their husbands.

All the exclamations or exclamatory questions of surprise, the emotionally loaded exclamations or questions, are uttered by women: 'oy,' 'oh,' 'ugh yes,' 'ugh no,' 'you don't say.'

Men, on the other hand, only burst out in a balanced way: 'eh,' 'ok,' 'yes ok,' 'that's it,' 'yes right.'

The tendency is the same if we look at variants of 'yes' (Nordenstam 1987: 49). WOMEN have the greatest number of types. And in MARRIAGES it is the same impatient husband who utters all four variants (618). Clearly enthusiasm is lowest among the married couples.

Thus, not only the quantity of the back-channeling signals but also the quality of those used by the women reinforces the idea that women are better listeners than men. Their involvement is certainly higher. . . .

DIFFERENCES AND STYLE IN THE THREE MAIN GROUPS

MEN dyads

The male dyads often organize themselves hierarchically. They have difficulty finding topics of conversation and are obsessed with the tape recorder. They talk in significantly longer turns than the WOMEN's dyads. They use more formal topic shifters and tend to introduce a new topic after an interturn pause. They interrupt each other significantly more often than WOMEN. Only men yawn.

WOMEN dyads

Female dyads discuss their own personal relations or those of their friends. As mentioned above, MEN talk more about jobs, sports, etc. WOMEN talk about both men and women, whereas MEN mainly mention other men. WOMEN talk about a greater number of topics. New topics are introduced without hesitation. (There are hardly any interturn pauses.) WOMEN use abrupt topic shifts more often than MEN and do not have difficulty finding topics of conversations. They do not seem bothered by the tape recorder. WOMEN support each other while talking: they use significantly more cooperative overlaps when talking simultaneously than men. They also use significantly more back-channeling signals. Thus they are better listeners than MEN. Their back-channeling signals are of a higher intensity and thus qualitatively different from MEN's . WOMEN in single gender dyads use a high-involvement style.

MARRIAGE dyads

In the conversation of the married couples, some of the characteristics of the single-sex dyads remain, others are lost. Thus with respect to topic choice there are certain similarities: women show a greater interest in human relations and talk about both sexes, while men mainly mention other men. Husbands more often introduce new topics after interturn pauses that signify hesitation than wives do, but the difference is smaller here than in the single-gender dyads. Wives use more abrupt topic shifts (but the figures are too small to be significant), and they initiate more topics. They also talk in longer turns than their husbands do.

My study supports Fishman's (1978) proposal that *interaction is the work women do.* This work seems to be particularly well handled by the wives in my study in that they also do their recording task so conscientiously. I interpret their greater talkativeness and their initiative with respect to finding conversational topics as greater eagerness to be useful in contributing to the study.

The married couples' conversation shows signs of competitiveness. There are comparatively many interruptions and few instances of cooperative overlap and back channeling signals, compared with the conditions of the WOMEN's group in particular. The enthusiasm is low in the married couples' conversations. It seems the high-involvement style women use when talking to each other is not used when they talk to their spouses. The husbands seem indifferent to the idea of recording half an hour's marital conversation in their homes.

Is it, then, presumptuous to conclude by suggesting we might twist another of Tannen's concepts (1984: 58 and 66) and regard men as *enthusiasm constraints* on women in casual conversation?

REFERENCES

Coates, J. (1986). *Women, Men and Language*. London and New York: Longman.
Fishman, P. (1978) Interaction: the work women do. *Social Problems* 25, 397–406.
Linell, P.; and Gustavsson, L. (1987). *Initiativ och respons. Om dialogens dynamik, dominans och koherens*. SIC 15. University of Linköping, Department of Communication Studies.
Nordenstam, K. (1987). *Kvinnlig och manlig samtalsstil*. Göteborg: Institutionen för nordiska sprak.
Tannen, D. (1984). *Conversational Style: Analyzing Talk Among Friends*. Norwood, NJ: Ablex.

9.4 Armenian Survivors and Their Children

Donald E. Miller and Lorna Touryan Miller

Family socialization is one of the major ways in which we learn about our ethnic and social statuses, including our family backgrounds and the histories of our ethnic/racial groups. Parents and grandparents are key transmitters of ethnic/racial group traditions, and ethnic identities and culture.

Exceptional problems occur for the intergenerational transmission of ethnic identity and culture when there are traumatic events in the history of the group. This is vividly demonstrated in the next excerpt about personal identification with the grief of a historical group. This excerpt studies Armenian survivors of the **genocide** that was perpetrated by the Turks at the beginning of this century. Sad to say, social inequality often has extended to the practice of genocide upon one group by another.

Using interview data, the authors show that there have been all manner of responses, by parents and children, to knowledge of the genocide. These responses range from commitment to a life of terrorism against the Turks to ignoring or denying the event occurred.

The study shows that parents and children have some control over how they define (and redefine) their ethnic identities and ethnic traditions. If this is true for those who have experienced the trauma of genocide against their ethnic group, it is very likely to be true of people without this as part of their history.

Note, finally, that the author generalizes from the Armenian example to put forward elements of a theory of identity of descent.

Excerpted from Miller, Donald E. and Lorna Touryan Miller (1991), "Memory and identity across the generations: A case study of Armenian survivors and their progeny," *Qualitative Sociology*, 14(1), 13–38.

From 1915–23, approximately 1.5 million Armenians died in Ottoman Turkey in what has been called the first genocide of the twentieth century. . . .

This article examines the ways in which the trauma of this genocide has affected the identity of survivors, their children and grandchildren. To approach the topic we have borrowed a methodological principle from one of America's most eminent philosophers and psychologists, William James.

In *Varieties of Religious Experience*, James (1961:pp. 24–25) asserts he will map the terrain of the religious life by studying those for whom religion has been a passion: the saints, mystics and, as he calls them, the "geniuses" of religion. From these extreme cases, James believes one can better understand persons for whom religion may be a much blander commitment.

We have adopted a similar methodological principle. In this article we will elaborate the case histories of several Armenian terrorists for whom the Armenian cause, and the genocide in particular, has been a commitment for which they were willing to die. Although their commitment may be extreme, they embody many issues and conflicts present more generally in the Armenian population.

THE ARMENIAN TERRORIST MOVEMENT

Between 1973 and 1985 the terrorist movement claimed the lives of 30 Turkish diplomats or members of their immediate families; in addition, 34 non-Turks were killed and over 300 persons were wounded (Gunter, 1986, p. 1). These assassinations occurred in the Middle East, Western Europe, and North America. Their objective was to focus world attention on Armenian claims, and to counter the continuing denial of the genocide by the Turkish government.

Two groups masterminded the attacks. The Justice Commandos of the Armenian Genocide (JCAG) were relatively discrete in their tactics, killing only political representatives of the Turkish government. The Armenian Secret Army for the Liberation of

Armenia (ASALA), on the other hand, claimed credit for attacks that involved the deaths of non-Turks as well as Turkish civilians and diplomats.

METHODOLOGY

There are three sources of data for this study. First, between 1974 and 1986 we interviewed more than one hundred survivors of the 1915 genocide. These interviews lasted a minimum of two hours. Survivors were at least seventy years old when interviewed, and averaged between 11 and 12 years of age at the time of the genocide.

Second, in 1990 we interviewed four Armenians who were arrested in 1982 for terrorist activities against Turkish targets, and are currently serving prison sentences or else are on parole. At the time of their arrests, they ranged in age from their late teens to middle twenties. All are grandsons of survivors, and all indicated the Armenian genocide played an important role in motivating them to pursue the political actions which resulted in their arrests and convictions. . . .

A third source of data is the personal experience of the authors. Lorna Touryan Miller is the daughter of two survivors. Seven of her father's nine family members died in the genocide. Half of her mother's family lost their lives.

SUMMARY OF OUR INTERVIEWS

Grandparents and Grandsons

Because of the extended family network among Armenians, the bond between grandparents and grandchildren has been extremely strong. In the case of the terrorist Levon, his primary education regarding the genocide came from his grandparents.

This was not exceptional. For example, Shaunt (not his real name), another terrorist, was born in Lebanon. In Beirut he lived in an extended family setting in which his uncle's house—where his maternal grandfather also lived—adjoined his own. Shaunt described his relationship with his grandfather:

He loved us tremendously, both of us [referring to his older brother]. I remember him kissing my forehead every morning. . . . I think my personality was developed when my grandfather was carrying me around . . . talking to his survivor friends about the horrible times. I think my responsibility started to be conveyed to me even that early . . . as he walked through parks . . . he holding my hand and talking to me. . . . These conversations about the genocide were ubiquitous.

. . . When Shaunt was 12, the family moved to the United States. This move was preceded, however, by the deaths of his grandfather and uncle. These losses saddened him greatly, and when reflecting on his commitment to the Armenian cause, he commented his involvement was in direct response to a felt obligation to the vision of his uncle and grandfather.

I was so immersed and committed to this belief of making my grandparents proud, my uncle proud, and giving them the message, "See, I did what you expected me to do. I died for the cause."

This statement by Shaunt parallels Levon's comment that his involvement in a terrorist plot was a way of fulfilling his grandfather's desires.

Vahe (not his real name), said he did not know much about his grandparents. At the time, we took this at face value. However, several weeks after he wrote to us saying he had talked to his mother about his grandparents, and she had said that as a child he had been obsessed with their stories. He reported he was surprised at how he had "filtered out the 'tragic' and converted the 'memory' of suffering into political phenomena." His mother told him his paternal grandfather had been killed in the deportations, along with his brother. Also, his great grandfather, on his mother's father had escaped death by being sent to hide among friendly Kurds. At some level these stories, or the anger surrounding them, had been communicated to Vahe, and had contributed greatly to his political consciousness.

Turning from terrorists to our sample of survivors (i.e., grandparents), the pattern becomes more complex. Survivors varied remarkably in their response to the tragedy of their childhood. A substantial number said they never spoke with their children about the genocide. Often they would say something like "My story is too sad; I didn't want to burden my children with it." A majority, however, had told their children at least pieces of their story; and many said their grandchildren frequently asked them about their experiences.

A small, but significant, group of survivors appeared reconciled to their past. They seemingly have forgiven the perpetrators of the violence against them, sometimes drawing on religious imagery, and even religious conversion experiences, to explain their attitude. Other survivors seemed resigned about the past; indeed, many might be labeled clinically depressed. Other survivors were vocal about the injustices of the past, with some limiting their rage to verbal expression, while others suggested specific political goals related to reclaiming their homeland in Turkey. The latter group tended to affirm assassinations of Turkish diplomats as legitimate political expression. . . .

Some survivors, who objected to political violence, instead put the responsibility on God, saying God would avenge the Turks. And other survivors struggled with what they felt should be their *Christian* response to the genocide, as opposed to what they said their *human* feelings were.

On the other hand, survivors who have been vocal with their children and grandchildren about the genocide sometimes expressed ambivalence about the effect of these conversations, as is expressed in this statement:

We don't want to fill our children with revenge. Also, we don't want to trouble or hurt their hearts. But we feel that our children should know what kind of people their ancestors were and that obviously includes how they were killed.

Another survivor said she used to tell her husband not to tell their children about his experiences in the genocide: "But nothing would stop him. Now my sons are filled with revenge. Even my grandchild comes and asks him questions."

... Nearly universal among the one hundred survivors we interviewed was the desire for their grandchildren to maintain their Armenian identity. For many, Armenian identity is tied to the Armenian language. They also commented on the importance of knowing the history of the Armenians and maintaining a commitment to the Armenian church.

Parents and Children

Some Armenian parents isolate their children from non-Armenians because assimilation is a threat to any ethnic minority. ...The terrorists we interviewed all came from homes where assimilation was very low. We attribute the depth of their feelings not only to the influence of grandparents, but to the significant role played by parents.

Raffi (not his real name) told us that when he was growing up his grandmother used to tell stories of her childhood to his older sisters. He would overhear these stories and wonder at his grandmother who wept as she talked. Raffi's father would say to the grandmother, "It's no use to talk about the past." But Raffi said he noticed his father's own eyes would water as he listened to his mother's stories.

His father's communication about the genocide was always indirect. To offer a further example, he repeatedly told Raffi to "be good"—meaning, not to be influenced by revolutionary rhetoric—but then he would teach his son the revolutionary songs from the 19th century which *his* father had taught him. Raffi said there was one song his father could never complete:

Every time my father sang [this song] he would never finish because he would cry. He always cried as he sang that song and choked. And whenever I sing that song today, I also cannot finish it. (paraphrase)

When he was arrested, Raffi said his father never asked "Why did you do it?" Deep

inside, said Raffi, he must have felt that what his son had done was right.

Indirect communication between fathers and sons may be one of the most powerful forms of communication. ...

The Role of Socializing Institutions

... In Levon and Shaunt's experience, school functioned to reinforce as well as to universalize the stories they had heard at home. At school they came to realize all Armenians had been touched by this tragedy.

Vahe believes his primary political education came from Armenian political organizations: the Scouts which he joined at age 7 or 8, and the Junior Organization of the ARF, which he joined at 13.

In Lebanon, as a member of the Junior Organization, Vahe received informal military training to serve as an armed guard at the gates of his own school. The Armenian community made heroes of these young men who were willing to defend Armenian institutions.

When he came to the United States with his family at age 16, he was upset at leaving the Armenian community that had been so affirming of him.

Psychosocial Development

... Shaunt believes his radical commitment to "the cause" was a way of filling a deep personal void occasioned by the death of his grandfather and uncle, as well as a profound sense of rootlessness that he felt upon coming to the United States at 12 years of age. In high school he felt abused because of his foreignness and accent. This pushed him further into the Armenian subculture and he started to read voraciously in Armenian literature. In college, his accent actually got worse; in his view, this was symbolic of his rejection of American culture and his attempt to root himself in Armenian history and culture.

In reflecting on the terrorist activity in which he was involved, he said "as the opportunity developed to do something that would make me feel more anchored as an Armenian, I think I grabbed it." As quoted earlier, his commitment to "the cause" was also a symbolic way of telling his grandfather and uncle that he had lived up to their expectations. . . .

Two individuals raised another issue that we believe has developmental implications. Both Vahe and Raffi said that as children what bothered them greatly was the image of large groups of Armenians being deported by a handful of gendarmes. How could the Armenians have been so weak, they wondered. This feeling was compounded by a perception Armenians are always on the losing side.

Vahe said that when he first heard of the assassinations, he could not believe it for two reasons: First, Armenians don't kill; and secondly *Armenians are not capable* of killing. Vahe said he became fascinated with Armenian terrorism, and at first he did not include in his analysis the fact that people were losing their lives. It was the *capacity* to kill, the counter to Armenian impotence, that interested him.

In a somewhat different interpretation, Levon said the assassinations were something the Armenian community "needed" in the 1970's and early '80s to counter the *powerlessness* they were feeling.

Moral Commitment and Identity

Those who engage in terrorist acts usually understand their own actions in moral terms (Jacoby, 1983). Levon, for example, spoke of himself as being "half a person" so long as the genocide went unacknowledged. Likewise, Vahe understood his political actions within a moral framework.

Vahe's prelude to involvement in the terrorist movement was extensive reading in literature dealing with equality and justice. He was not a Marxist, but read extensively in Marxist criticism. Furthermore, he became fascinated with the socialist roots of the ARF, and read voraciously in Armenian liberation literature of the late 19th century.

When we asked Vahe whether imprisonment and the political struggle to which he was committed is worth it, he answered with a secularized version of Jesus' statement "Man cannot live by bread alone." His expression was "man cannot live with objective things alone." Life is not worth living, he said, unless it is a life committed to justice. In his words, "If you are not willing to die for something, then your life does not have meaning.". . .

THEORETICAL EXTRAPOLATIONS

Can one generalize from the Armenian experience of memory transmission among generations to a more expansive theory of identity of descent? We offer the following points for consideration.

First, traumatic events such as genocides potentially serve as the axial point for group and generational self-understanding. Conversations that link generations radiate around these events. These traumatic events become the template through which generations relate to each other and through which group self-understanding evolves. These events define the parameters of communal conversations, thus providing the components from which collective identity is built.

Secondly, grandparents are primary carriers and transmitters of collective group memories. Grandparents symbolize the past to grandchildren, and embody the collective memory of the family or group. For all of their protests, grandchildren hunger for roots that define from whence they have come.

Third, when our stories of origin include moral contradictions, we may reject them because they paralyze and threaten us, or we may seek to correct our past in an effort to achieve personal wholeness and healing. What may appear to be fanatical behavior may be based in battles with demons rooted in the injustices (and failures) which surround the stories of our predecessors.

Fourth, parents establish the context for mediation between grandparents and grandchildren. Parents communicate in direct and indirect ways whether the stories told by grandparents are to be valued.

Fifth, parents and grandparents together bear primary responsibility for creating and maintaining the institutions that preserve cultural and group values.

Sixth, there is nothing mechanical about the transmission of memory from one generation to another. Children exercise considerable control in what they accept and reject, which is another way of saying individuals exercise considerable freedom in constructing their personal sense of meaning.

REFERENCES

Gunter, M. (1986). *"Pursuing the Just Cause of Their People,"* A Study of Contemporary Armenian Terrorism. New York: Greenwood Press.
James, W. (1961). *The Varieties of Religious Experience.* New York: Collier.
Jacoby, S. (1983). *Wild Justice: The Evolution of Revenge.* New York: Harper and Row.

9.5 Residential Segregation by Skin Color in Brazil

Edward E. Telles

The next excerpt is about racism within a color continuum. We know that in North America there is much **residential segregation** of whites and blacks. The two racial groups tend to live in different areas. This is one of the ways in which social exclusion around race manifests itself. Also, the higher the income levels of whites the greater the residential segregation, showing that differential access to economic resources by race, and the high prices for homes in certain areas, are among reasons why residential segregation occurs.

But what about patterns in other countries? We would expect similar processes wherever there is racism and differential access to economic resources by race. The next excerpt tests for patterns of residential segregation in Brazil. This is an interesting country in which to pursue the question because it has been shown that this country has high levels of interracial interaction, at least among the poor (in intermarriages and friendships). Also, the "official" ideology of the government says that there is little or no racism in this country.

The author shows that residential segregation does exist in Brazil. However, it is not as extreme as we find in North America. As in North America, segregation in Brazil is more prevalent for higher-income whites who can better afford to practice it. There is also a suggestion of a "color continuum" in the results; whites are more segregated from blacks than from mulattos.

This study also shows there is very little residential segregation by race among the poor. This may be because the poor cannot afford to practice segregation. Nonetheless, the result apparently is that there is very little racial conflict among the poor. Again, perhaps the poor cannot "afford" such conflict. Just getting by economically is a difficult enough task without compounding problems. Or perhaps people of different races with a common economic circumstance—poverty—see themselves more in terms of class than race.

... Virtually nothing is known about racial residential segregation outside of the United States. Brazil's African-origin population is the second largest in the world only after Nigeria's. Unlike the United States, Brazil has had no race-based laws that encourage residential segregation since Abolition in 1888, yet segregation by skin color is prevalent. I examine overall levels of white-black, white-brown and brown-black residential segregation as well as segregation patterns among color groups within income groups. I then analyze factors that may contribute to variation among Brazilian metropolitan areas in residential segregation.

METHODS AND DATA

I focus on *evenness*, i.e., the extent to which minority and majority group members are evenly distributed across an urban area (Massey and Denton 1988). Evenness is measured with the index of dissimilarity, D, defined as the proportion of one group that would have to change census tracts to achieve the same spatial distribution as the other group (Duncan and Duncan 1955).

The value of D varies from O, when two groups are evenly distributed, to 1, when there is complete segregation.

$$D = .5 \times \Sigma |(x_i/X) - (y_i/Y)|, \qquad (1)$$

where X and Y are the metropolitan area populations of the groups being compared and x_i and y_i are their respective populations in census tract i.

Residential dissimilarity indices among whites, browns and blacks in 35 metropolitan areas were computed for the total population and within family income groups. The 1980 Population Census of Brazil, produced by the *Instituto Brasileiro de Geografia e Estatistica* (IBGE) is the source for computing segregation indexes based on census tract data from the 25 percent sample of households that

answered the long form census questionnaire. The independent variables in the regression analysis were also calculated from this sample.

Metropolitan areas are defined as contiguous urbanized areas in one or more municipalities and were defined in a previous IBGE publication (Vetter 1988). I chose 35 of the 40 metropolitan areas with populations over 200,000 in 1980. The five excluded areas are in the North and Central-West regions (the Brazilian frontier) where a higher concentration of Indians and their descendants among persons identifying as whites, browns, and blacks suggests a system of race relations distinct from most of Brazil in which there is a continuum from European to African. The 35 metropolitan areas include 36.1 percent of Brazil's total population in 1980 and 53.5 percent of its urban population.

The study of residential segregation in Brazil has been impeded by the lack of data available at the neighborhood level. However, an agreement by the IBGE to compute segregation indexes using census tract level data overcame this problem.

In Brazil, census tracts in urban areas contain about 250 to 300 households. ... The average census tract population in Brazilian urban areas is about 1150.

The 1980 census asked respondents to identify themselves as to their color. Possible responses were white (*branco*), brown (*pardo*),

TABLE 1. Regional Distribution of Total Population by Region for Color Groups: Brazil, 1980

| Region | Color | | | |
	White	Brown	Black	Total
Northeast	14.5	49.6	33.2	29.3
Central-East	24.0	16.8	33.6	22.5
São Paulo	29.0	11.5	17.9	21.1
South	24.8	5.0	8.5	16.0
North	1.8	9.7	2.2	4.9
Central-West	5.7	7.6	4.5	6.3
Total	99.8	100.2	99.9	100.1

Source: Instituto Brasileiro de Geografia e Estatistica 1983, Table 1.11.

Excerpted from Telles, Edward E. (1992), "Residential segregation by skin color in Brazil," *American Sociological Review*, 57, April, 186–197.

black (*preto*), yellow (*amarello*), and other. Fully 99 percent of the responses were in the first three categories. *Brown* refers to both Indians and mixed race persons, i.e., those whose skin color is between black and white.

Although the native Indian population is categorized as brown in this census, a survey showed that persons who would identify themselves as "Indian" comprise a very small proportion of the national population although they are a significant proportion of the population in the Amazon (North) region and in the Central-West (Oliveira Filho 1987). . . .

. . . The concentration of Indians and their descendants in the two regions of the Brazilian frontier along with current struggles for indigenous land rights (Oliveira Filho 1987) contributed to a system of race relations in those areas that differs from the eastern half of the country where about 90 percent of Brazilians reside. Thus, the problems of including large numbers of Indians with the mulatto population and of classifying persons with Indian admixture as "white" are attenuated by eliminated North and Central-West metropolitan areas from the analysis.

RESULTS

Regions

In Brazil, nonwhites are a numerical minority in the more developed areas of the country while a majority in the less developed Northeast, which was the center of the slave based economy prior to 1888. Table 1 shows the distribution of color groups by region. The majority (53.8 percent) of whites live in the industrialized, highly populated and relatively wealthy state of São Paulo and the South, a region comprising three slightly less developed states. Conversely, about one-half of browns and one-third of blacks live in the poor and underdeveloped Northeast. Indexes of dissimilarity reveal browns and whites are more regionally segregated from each other ($D = .447$) than are blacks from whites ($D = .286$) or blacks from browns ($D = .268$).

Metropolitan Areas

The racial composition of individual metropolitan areas varies widely. Whites are a minority in all 13 urban areas of the less developed Northeast but make up more than 80 percent of the population in 10 of the 14 areas in São Paulo and the South. Brazil's two giant cities, São Paulo and Rio de Janeiro, both have white majorities (71.5 and 60.0 percent) but have African origin populations surpassing three million.

By U.S. standards, values of D between .3 and .6 are considered moderate (Massey and Denton 1987). Thus residential segregation by color in Brazil is moderate—all but one of the dissimilarity indexes are below .6. One factor that may depress these indexes is the tendency for domestic workers and building guards and their families, who are predominately nonwhite, to live in the same household or building as their employers. On the other hand, the smaller average population size of Brazilian census tracts (1,150 compared to 4,000 in the United States) may inflate Brazilian segregation indexes.

The mean segregation of blacks versus whites (.450) for these 35 urban areas is only slightly greater than that for browns versus whites (.397), a pattern typified in 29 of the 35 urban areas. In the remaining six urban areas, four of which are in the Central-East region, the black-white segregation index was lower than the brown-white index. White-black dissimilarity was highest in all 13 metropolitan areas of the Northeast.

Interestingly, the mean index of brown-black segregation (.407) was higher than that for white-brown segregation (.397). However, white-brown and white-black segregation indexes may be misleadingly low because of the tendency for many nonwhite domestic workers to reside with their white middle-class employers. Nevertheless, the moderate level of segregation between browns and blacks, who are of similar socioeconomic status, demonstrates the importance of the color continuum.

Average residential dissimilarity by region is highest in the Northeast and South, followed by São Paulo and finally, the Central-East.

Socioeconomic Segregation

To examine the extent to which color segregation is independent of social class, I computed residential dissimilarity indexes among the three color groups within household income brackets.

Dissimilarity indexes within income levels were calculated using households as the unit of analysis and defining color as the color of the family head. Results are presented in Table 2. Indexes were not calculated if either of the two color groups in an income bracket averaged less than three households per tract. This was done to avoid random departures from evenness that might otherwise occur by using very small populations in the calculation of D. This criterion meant indexes could not be calculated for many income groups in many of the urban areas, which reflects the concentration of nonwhites in low income categories. Thus, *residential isolation of whites is virtually assured by the absence of a significant nonwhite middle class.*

Household income is measured as the number of "minimum salaries," a common procedure in Brazil where high inflation makes actual dollar or *cruzeiro* values less meaningful. In September 1980 when the census was taken, one minimum salary was worth about 75 U.S. dollars per month. Indexes were not presented for the "less than one minimum salary" category because results were inconsistent with those for the other income categories, suggesting substantial misreporting at the low end of the income spectrum.

The seven metropolitan areas presented in Table 2 are those for which the greatest number of indexes could be calculated. Table 2 shows that in metropolitan areas in which blacks and mulattoes *are* represented in the various income groups, moderate segregation persists independent of income. In fact, segregation indexes tend to *increase* with income. This pattern is unmistakable for white-black dissimilarity and the general pat-

TABLE 2   Indexes of Dissimilarity Among Whites, Browns, and Blacks by Family Income Group: Seven Metropolitan Areas in Brazil, 1980

Metropolitan Area and Income Group (Numbers of Minimum Salaries)	White vs. Black	White vs. Brown	Brown vs. Black
Salvador			
1.01 to 2	.519	.499	.391
2.01 to 3	.547	.519	.411
3.01 to 5	.547	.511	.418
5.01 to 10	.618	.497	.483
10.01 to 20	—	.509	—
20.01 and over	—	.507	—
Feira de Santana			
1.01 to 2	.514	.468	.348
2.01 to 3	.572	.464	.439
3.01 to 5	.585	.481	.445
5.01 to 10	.615	.465	.549
10.01 to 20	—	.518	—
Rio de Janeiro			
1.01 to 2	.419	.382	.399
2.01 to 3	.456	.389	.424
3.01 to 5	.452	.387	.409
5.01 to 10	.543	.421	.479
10.01 to 20	—	.546	—
Belo Horizonte			
1.01 to 2	.435	.412	.405
2.01 to 3	.450	.419	.437
3.01 to 5	.462	.416	.450
5.01 to 10	.568	.454	.518
10.01 to 20	—	.554	—
Barra Mansa-Volta Redonda			
1.01 to 2	.355	.387	.423
2.01 to 3	.360	.358	.406
3.01 to 5	.377	.362	.422
5.01 to 10	.421	.361	.439
10.01 to 20	—	.549	—
Juiz de Fora			
1.01 to 2	.318	.337	.337
2.01 to 3	.380	.415	.408
3.01 to 5	.410	.436	.449
5.01 to 10	.568	.465	.556
Campos			
1.01 to 2	.377	.335	.376
2.01 to 3	.411	.374	.451
3.01 to 5	.448	.384	.461
5.01 to 10	.618	.450	.604

tern also holds for brown-black and white-brown segregation. In addition, the increase in white-black segregation over the income groups is greater in all seven areas than that for white-brown segregation while brown-black segregation increases are intermediate. . . . These cases demonstrate the importance of the color continuum in which black is perceived as lower status than brown and brown-black distinctions are made even by nonwhites. The pattern becomes clearer as income increases—segregation is greater among high income households where housing options are greater. . . .

The fact that residential segregation by color is lowest among the very poor may help explain why race relations among the poor have been comparatively amicable—historically there has been little race-related violence (Skidmore 1974). The low levels of segregation among the poor may also reflect the precarious living conditions of the poorest sectors of the Brazilian population. Residential choices are limited and must often be made on the basis of survival chances. For the poor, the decision about where to live is likely to be based on criteria like walking distance to work or where friends live who can assist in tasks such as child care or housing construction. This often means living illegally in makeshift housing. Extreme poverty coupled with an absence of overwhelming social pressures to segregate by color make concerns about color a low priority. At income levels where housing options are greater, color can become a criterion in neighborhood selection.

Salvador is significant in that it has a significant mulatto middle class (Azevedo 1953). Salvador has high white-brown and white-black segregation but relatively low brown-black segregation. The relatively high segregation between whites and nonwhites may promote social solidarity, as manifested spatially, between browns and blacks in Salvador. Also important in Salvador is the strong presence of African-origin culture and institutions which further differentiates the social lives of Afro-Salvadorans from Salvadorans of European origin.

Explaining Inter-Urban Patterns

The causes of differential segregation are tested using an OLS regression model that considers segregation indexes as a function of social context, socioeconomic status, and housing market variables. Dissimilarity indexes are transformed into logits because of their limited range. Social context variables include industrialization, immigrant influence, and heterogeneity. Industrialization is the percent of the total labor force in manufacturing. Immigrant influence is estimated by the percent Italian- and German-born individuals among the white population aged 60 and over in 1980 because such immigration continued only until the 1930s (Merrick and Graham 1979). In the absence of ethnicity data, this approximates the relative immigrant influence. Heterogeneity is calculated using the formula:

$$H = 1 - (w^2 + m^2 + b^2), \qquad (2)$$

where w is the percent white, m is the percent brown and b is the percent black (Gibbs and Martin 1962).

Socioeconomic status is measured using two variables: (1) male occupational dissimilarity indexes between paired color groups in each metropolitan area and (2) mean household income for the entire population of each area. Color inequality is commonly postulated as the sole source of residential segregation in Brazil where housing markets merely reflect a social division of labor; income provides the economic resources that permit residential mobility.

Any analysis of residential segregation must consider the local housing market. I control for three housing related factors: residential turnover, homeownership, and density. High housing turnover in an area indicates a high level of internal movement and migration. Turnover is measured as the percent of households living less than two years in their current dwelling. Persons in high turnover areas are freer to choose their residences than are those in tight markets. Movers are often channeled into relatively homogeneous neighborhoods through social networks. This may either increase segregation or contribute to expanding areas of transition, thus reducing segregation. Homeownership is the percent of the households that are owner-occupied. Homeowners see their homes as long-term investments so they are more likely than renters to be concerned about who their neighbors are. If neighborhood homogeneity is preferred, then segregation is likely to be higher where homeownership is high. Finally, a given level of segregation is entirely different in a dense urban area where persons live in close proximity to each other compared to areas that are more spread out. If whites want to avoid nonwhites, they would be physically closer to African-origin neighbors in a dense neighborhood, thus making segregation more likely in dense areas. Density is operationalized as the percent of households living in apartment buildings.

The results are fairly consistent across the three models although levels of significance vary. Overall, variables representing socioeconomic status and the housing market are better predictors of segregation than are the social context variables. None of the social context variables are significant. Areas with high industrialization, greater immigrant influence and lower racial heterogeneity tend to have higher segregation but these relationships are not significant.

As expected, occupational dissimilarity has a significant positive relationship with white-brown and white-black segregation, but its relationship is not significant for brown-black segregation. The lack of a relationship for brown-black segregation is not surprising given the small differences in status between browns and blacks. Mean household income has a significant negative relationship for white-black segregation and brown-black segregation—residential segregation between blacks and both whites and browns is especially high in low income urban areas.

Urban areas with high residential turnover have higher segregation as indicated by the significant positive coefficients in all three models. Urban areas with high levels of home-ownership are significantly associated

with greater white-brown and white-black segregation.

DISCUSSION AND CONCLUSION

By U.S. standards, residential segregation among color groups in Brazil is moderate.

Results show that residential segregation among color groups cannot be accounted for by socioeconomic status—moderate segregation along color lines occurs among members of the same income group. Furthermore, segregation levels increase with income in those metropolitan areas with substantial numbers of whites, blacks and mulattoes in the income categories. Thus, the Afro-Brazilian middle class is more spatially dissimilar from middle-class whites than poor Afro-Brazilians are from poor whites. In most metropolitan areas, though, the absence of a significant African origin middle class ensures middle-class neighborhoods remain predominately white. The low color segregation among the poor suggests limited housing options make color a low priority when choosing a place to live.

Despite the suggestion in the literature that industrialization and immigration in Brazil are crucial to understanding regional differences in Brazilian race relations, my analysis shows these factors have weak effects. On the other hand, an area's socioeconomic status and its housing market are significantly associated with patterns of segregation. Urban areas with relatively high occupational inequality tend to be more segregated and high income urban areas tend to be more segregated. Urban areas with high housing turnover or a high rate of homeownership also tend to have higher segregation.

The existence of a color continuum in Brazil is thus supported in the case of residential segregation. Whites are more segregated from blacks than from mulattoes, both overall and within income groups. There is also significant residential segregation between blacks and mulattoes, often higher than white-brown segregation (but lower than white-black segregation), suggesting mulattoes also disdain blacks. The fact that segregation increases faster with increasing income for both white-black and brown-black segregation than for white-brown segregation suggests black skin color is especially salient for higher income groups in the same area. Bivariate and multivariate findings indicate segregation of *blacks* from both whites and browns is clearly greater than white-brown segregation in poorer and less developed areas.

Moderate segregation has implications for other features of Brazilian race relations. These are: (1) a relatively low level of race consciousness and organization among the African origin population, and (2) relatively high levels of interracial interaction. Whereas extreme segregation in South Africa and the United States has led to a high degree of race consciousness and corporate organization, moderate segregation and the absence of clearly-defined racial categories have led to their relative absence in Brazil. Along with an ideology that denies racism, the fact that blacks, mulattoes, and whites live in similar neighborhoods may strengthen a general perception that race has little or no effect on life chances. In this sense, the pervasive racism and racial inequality of Brazilian society is less conspicuous. Also, the absence of extreme segregation in Brazil has precluded the formation of parallel institutions, a condition fundamental to the rise of black social movements in South Africa and the United States. Finally, Brazil's less extreme segregation has meant far greater prevalence of interracial friendship and intermarriage, at least among Brazil's large poor population.

REFERENCES

Azevedo, Thales de. 1953. *Les Elites do Couleur dans une Ville Brésillienne.* Paris: UNESCO.

Duncan, Otis D. and Beverly Duncan. 1955. "A Methodological Analysis of Segregation Indices." *American Sociological Review* 20:210–17.

Instituto Brasileiro de Estatistica e Geografia. 1983. *Censo Demografico: Dados Gerais-Migração-In-Strução-Fecundidade-Mortalidade.* Vol. 1, ser. 4, no. 1. Rio de Janeiro: Instituto Brasileiro de Estatistica e Geografia.

Massey, Douglas S. and Nancy A. Denton. 1987. "Trends in the Residential Segregation of Hispanics, Blacks and Asians: 1970-1980." *American Sociological Review* 52:802–24.

———. 1988. "The Dimensions of Residential Segregation." *Social Forces.* 67:281–315.

Merrick, Thomas W. and Douglas H. Graham. 1979. *Population and Economic Development in Brazil: 1800 to the Present.* Baltimore: Johns Hopkins University.

Oliveira Filho, Joao Pacheco. 1987. *Terras Indigenas no Brasil.* São Paulo: Centro Ecumênico de Documentação e Informação.

Skidmore,Thomas E.

———. 1974. *Black Into White: Race and Nationality in Brazilian Thought.* New York: Oxford University Press.

Vetter, David. 1988. *Indicadores Sociais: Regioes Metropolitanas, Aglomeracoes Urbanas e Municipios com mais de 100 Mil Habitantes.* Rio de Janeiro: Instituto Brasileiro de Estatistica e Geografia.

9.6 New Ways to Evaluate the Undervalued

Riane Eisler and David Loye

Research has shown a relationship between gender inequality and violence. Comparisons across societies show that cultures that have more gender inequality have more violence toward children and women, have more blood vengeances, and conduct more wars against other societies. The authors of the next excerpt review the relevant studies on these relationships.

The authors also remind us that new historical and anthropological studies, many by feminist researchers, show that there have been some cultures without gender inequality. This demonstrates, they argue, that such societies can be formed—if we put our minds to it.

Part of the required solution, the author emphasizes, is a "paradigm shift," a major transformation of culture to elevate to highly held values the principles of the "ideal" female character—nonviolence, cooperation, and compassion. These values must be made more important than the male values of many cultures—violence, competition, and dominance.

The authors emphasize that cultural change in these directions should lessen levels of violence and the threat of war, including catastrophic nuclear war. It also should lessen gender, ethnic/race, and class conflict. Whether it would eliminate them is another question.

As several of the other selections in this volume have suggested, the roots of inequalities of condition and opportunity are difficult to eliminate. Value change that meant that other people's interests were held high in our priorities—with "others" defined as the broad collectivity, irrespective of class, race, and gender—would certainly take a major step in the direction of equalizing opportunity and condition. Can it be done?

HUMAN IDEOLOGY
AND THE WORLD PROBLEMATIQUE

We have a mounting body of data from national and international agencies, as well as from the social sciences, indicating that, when viewed in systems terms, sexual inequality and equality are central to the better understanding and eventual solution of the world problematique.

At first glance this may seem absurd. But study after study documents the power of perceptual blindness induced by the prevailing social and ideological organization. Of such ideologically induced blindness, none has been as powerful as that relating to the social facts about sexual inequality, so taken for granted that they are invisible.

Émile Durkheim observed how social facts are like the air we breathe.[1] Just as we take air for granted until it is not there for us to breathe, so social facts only become visible as

Excerpted from Eisler, Riane and David Loye (1983), "The hidden future: A global view from another paradigm," World-Futures, 19(1–2), October, 123–136. Reproduced with permission from Gordon and Breach Science Publishers, Inc.

we become aware of their presence through social change. In the contemporary laboratory of social change, sexual inequality has become increasingly visible. But what is only gradually becoming visible is the all-pervasive effect of sexual inequality in the ideological sphere, where it acts as a kind of filter, distorting and obscuring perception, invisibilizing the obvious, and blocking appropriate actions.

Despite the urgent necessity for global population control, almost everywhere on our planet religious and secular ideologies defining women primarily in terms of reproduction-related functions prevent the formulation and implementation of the necessary policies. That this is not a function of lack of knowledge is evidenced not only by the masses of readily available reports on the necessity for policies vigorously promoting reproductive freedom of choice and other fundamental changes in the status of women.[2] It is also explicit in statements by people like Robert F. McNamara, President of the World Bank, on how "greater economic opportunity for women and the greater educational opportunity that undergirds it would substantially reduce fertility," and how, in cost effective dollars and cents terms, this would be "a very good buy."[3]

To further illustrate how the problem is ideology, let us move on to two additional aspects of the world problematique. The first is the growing problem of global poverty and hunger, with all its ramifications for global economic development and global security, where once again we encounter the deleterious policy effects of the prevailing world view which trivializes and/or invisibilizes "women's issues." Were it not for these ideological dynamics, policy makers could not speak of economic development and the elimination of poverty and hunger while ignoring the mounting data indicating that the female half of humanity and the children primarily dependent on their mothers for sustenance are the poorest of the world's poor and the hungriest of the world's hungry. . . .

Reports are explicitly documenting, how there is little likelihood that economic development and foreign aid programs will ever achieve their aims as long as the people who need this aid the most—women—are systematically excluded from financial aid, from land grants, from loans, from training, from education for modernization.[4] Nevertheless, these programs continue to be based on the premise that the economic development of men will automatically result in economic development for women and children. And instead of paying particular attention to women and children, these programs continue to be almost exclusively geared to men.[5]

But perhaps nowhere is our ideologically induced blindness as potentially lethal as in relation to the danger of nuclear war. For if we look at war, as some social scientists do, as basically a function of demographic factors—of population pressures which create conflicts over scarce resources—we again come back to the issue of population control: the need for policies where women are not only given free access to birth control technologies but are also no longer barred from nonbreeding life and work roles. And if we look at war, as other social scientists do, as a direct derivative of the socialization of men to be tough and warlike, we once again come face to face with a so-called women's issue—stereotypical sexual socialization.

NEW FINDINGS FROM SOCIAL SCIENCE

This link between sexual inequality and warfare is being increasingly examined and the result has been a growing body of studies indicating significant statistical correlations. For example, in a 1976 study, anthropologists Divale and Harris found a significant correlation between the extent to which a tribe or society engaged in warfare and measures of its sexual inequality.[6] A 1978 study by Arkin and Dobrofsky focused on how the he-man, conquest-oriented male stereotype and male-dominance over women is central to the way the military teaches soldiers to kill.[7]

Even more significantly, these kinds of correlations have been found to extend to social violence in general. For example, using a randomly selected sample of primitive cultures, McConahay and McConahay in 1977 observed a statistically significant relationship between violence and rigid male-female stereotypes; societies with more pronounced sexual inequality had a higher degree of social violence, ranging from punitive violence in child-rearing to rape, wife-beating, and blood vengeance within the group and a higher incidence of violence against other groups in the form of raids and wars.[8]

Anthropologist Geoffry Gorer has suggested a key element in societies characterized by low social violence is a lack of concern for having males learn adult sex-role definitions idealizing aggressiveness, as well as a general indifference about which sex fills the important roles in the society.[9] Summarizing the statistically significant behavioral characteristics associated with primitive societies which rigidly restrict women's freedom of reproductive choice by severely punishing abortions, anthropologist R.B. Textor found that such societies tended also to practice slavery and polygyny; to kill, torture, and mutilate enemies captured in war; to be generally sexually repressive; and to be patrilineal rather than matrilineal. In primitive societies which did not have such restrictions, there was a statistically significant converse relationship.[10]

There is also a growing number of studies indicating that societies where there is marked male-dominance tend to be authoritarian and that a central component of what psychologists call the authoritarian personality type is a rigid internalization of stereotypical sex roles. One of the studies in this area is *The Authoritarian Personality,* in which a group of scientists, alarmed by the threat of fascism, conducted extensive research into the kind of personality that would tend to support and comfortably function in such a system.[11] The co-principal investigator, Else Frenkel-Brunswik, found that individuals high in prejudice, and with such potentially violent and explosive personality traits as a high degree of repressed anger and hostility and inordinate difficulties in forming satisfactory love relationships, characteristically saw women and men in terms of rigidly stereotypical masculine-feminine roles.[12]

NEW FINDINGS FROM HISTORY AND PREHISTORY

... Such data present startling implications. And yet, if we think about it, it is not so strange that societies which see women and men primarily in terms of ranking rather than linkage should also see humanity in general in such terms. And so, it is not so strange that, as historians are beginning to look at social configurations from the perspective of what happens when there is movement toward sexual equality, they are finding there is movement away from authoritarianism and social violence.

Some of the most interesting data are from studies of the early Christian movement. Scholars are now able to reconstruct a picture of the group dynamics of some of the early Christian communities, where women and men lived in sexual equality. Here, Christians not only preached Jesus' teachings of equality—that we must work for a moral order where there shall be no master and no slave, no male or female—but actually lived

that way, with women taking leading roles as teachers, and the Deity was seen as both Mother and Father. They also lived and preached nonviolence, until they themselves fell victim to the authoritarian Church structure that later evolved, which hunted them down as heretics and burned and expunged their writings from the Holy Scriptures— writings like the 52 Gnostic Gospels recently discovered after being buried for over 1,600 years in Egypt.[13]

One final area which is, perhaps to some, providing the greatest shock of all, is the new data from prehistory.

We now know civilization was not, as we have been taught, born in Sumer about 5,000 years ago, but that there were a number of cradles of civilization, all of them thousands of years older.[14] For example, in Europe there is now evidence of stable Neolithic societies where the arts flourished, where people peacefully tilled the soil, traded, and engaged in crafts, and where there seems to have been a written script predating Sumerian writing by 2,000 years.[15]

In these societies, the social organization was basically egalitarian. Differences in status and in wealth were not marked. Moreover, women priestesses, women craftspeople, and the supreme deity conceptualized as female are all indications that these were *not* male dominated societies. Likewise, these societies do not seem to have had wars. Throughout the digs revealing this ancient culture from Europe into Asia, there is a general absence of fortifications, as well as an absence in their extensive art of the glorification of warriors and wars.

These findings are meeting with a great deal of resistance, both by lay people and academicians, because they are truly heretical. In short, it is information that is being met much the way the information that the world is round was once met, because that, too, went against Holy Scripture and against everything people knew to be the truth.

There is, of course, always resistance to anything new and unfamiliar—although this actually is *not* unfamiliar information. We are familiar with it, from many ancient stories, about a more innocent time when humanity lived in a garden (as these people did because they were the first farmers), a time before woman was (as the Biblical story has it) condemned by a male god to henceforth be forever subservient to man. We have all, in fact, heard of these prehistoric societies through our most ancient texts: not only the Bible, but Chinese texts, Sumerian texts, and Greek texts. They are referred to in the works of the Greek poet Hesiod, who wrote just before Homer, and who told of an earlier and nobler golden race who also lived in a garden and did not make war,[16] and in legends of Atlantis, now believed to be a garbled memory of Minoan Crete, where this type of social organization prevailed.[17]

PERTINENT QUESTIONS
AND EFFECTIVE SOLUTIONS

The importance of the increasing number of studies that are focusing on the hitherto invisible women's issues lies in what they tell us about sexual equality and inequality in systems terms.

Viewed in this context, the data surveyed here can serve to stimulate thinking so that we may begin to ask whether and how, at this juncture in global history, sexual equality might be a key to the creation of a more peaceful, more egalitarian world.

One such question might be whether it is merely coincidental that those who are trying to push women back into so-called traditional male-dominated roles in the home are at the same time ideologically committed to a social order run by a small male elite, with little respect for the civil and economic rights of the mass of not only women but men.

We might further ask whether it can be coincidental that the great modern surge toward sexual equality should come at a time when our world desperately needs a new way of running human affairs.

And we might conclude all this is *not* just coincidental, and that what we are seeing today in the struggle over sexual equality is the struggle of two very different ways of living.

One, the way based on sexual inequality, is the idea of ranking as the primary organiza-

tional principle in human affairs. This way has led not only to the subordination of women, but also to the conquest of one nation by another, and to man's so-called conquest of nature, a conquest against which nature herself is now rebelling in countless ways. It is the way of strong-man rule that has led to authoritarianism, totalitarianism, racism and colonialism.[18]

The other way seems to have been the original path for our species, from which we have undergone a 5,000 year detour. It is a way based on linkage rather than ranking in human relations, and it is the way that is beginning to reassert itself, not only in the partnership as equals between women and men, but also in the general movement toward egalitarianism and democracy and in our growing understanding of the necessity of finding a more peaceful way of living on this Earth.

Which of these two ways will be the way of the future still hangs in the balance. What is here suggested is that at its most fundamental level, the much discussed shift in paradigm generally recognized as a pre-requisite to a better future is a shift in our paradigm (or world view) about the relationship between the individuals associated with femininity and masculinity. . . .

NOTES

1. E. Durkheim, *The Rules of Sociological Method* (Free Press, New York, 1964).
2. See e.g. *Draper World Population Fund Report, no. 9: Improving the Status of Women,* October 1980.
3. R. McNamara, *Accelerating Population Stabilization through Social and Economic Progress,* (Development Paper 24, Overseas Development Council, Washington D.C., 1977).
4. P. Huston, *Third World Women Speak Out* (Praeger, New York, 1979); H. Loutfi, *Rural Women: Unequal Partners in Development* (International Labour Organization, Geneva, 1980); M. Rihani, *Development As If Women Mattered* (Occasional Paper no. 10, Overseas Development Council, Washington D.C., 1978).
5. See e.g. E. Boserup, *Woman's Role in Economic Development* (Allen and Unwin, Lon-

don, 1970); B. Rogers, *The Domestication of Women* (St. Martin's Press, New York, 1980).

6. W.F. Divale and M. Harris, "Population, Warfare, and the Male Supremacist Complex," *Am. Anthropologist* 78, 521–538 (1976).

7. W. Arkin and L. Dobrofsky, "Military Socialization and Masculinity," *Journal of Social Issues* 34, 1, 151–168 (1978).

8. S. McConahay and J. McConahay, "Sexual Permissiveness, Sex-Role Rigidity and Violence Across Cultures," *J. of Social Issues* 33,2, 143–143 (1977).

9. G. Gorer, "Man Has No Killer Instinct," in A. Montagu, *Man and Aggression*, first edition (Oxford University Press, New York, 1968).

10. R.B. Textor, *A Cross Cultural Summary* (HRAF Press, New Haven, Conn., 1967).

11. T.W. Adorno et al., *The Authoritarian Personality* (Harper and Row, New York, 1950).

12. *Ibid*, Part II.

13. See e.g., E. Pagels, *The Gnostic Gospels* (Random House, New York, 1979).

14. See e.g. J. Mellaart, *The Neolithic of the Near East* (Scribner, New York, 1975).

15. See e.g. M. Gimbutas, *Goddesses and Gods of Old Europe* (University of California Press, Los Angeles, 1982).

16. Hesiod, *Works and Days*, in J.M. Robinson, *An Introduction to Early Greek Philosophy* (Houghton-Mifflin, Boston, 1968), pp. 12–17.

17. See e.g. J.V. Luce, *The End of Atlantis* (Thames and Hudson, London, 1969).

18. R. Eisler, *The Blade and The Chalice*, work in progress.

SECTION REVIEW

Discussion Questions

1. Discuss the way "shadow education," or some equivalent to it, was practised by your peers in secondary school. Was the practice as widespread as we saw in the study from Japan above? Why, or why not?
2. "Parents and grandparents together bear primary responsibility for creating and maintaining . . . group values." Discuss.
3. Residential segregation by race tends to occur wherever people have the economic resources to segregate themselves (and others). Discuss.
4. Discuss studies of the ways women are less violent than men. What are the best explanations for the differences, and why do you think so?
5. Discuss how some of the sex differences in conversational style described in Nordenstam's study are likely caused by social inequality. Do you think the differences in conversational styles help reinforce inequality? Discuss.
6. Thinking about the neighborhoods you have lived in, was there evidence of residential segregation by race? Describe the evidence.

Data Collection Exercise

1. Conduct some informal observations of men and women talking in pairs. Are the patterns you observe consistent with Nordenstam's results? Offer interpretations of any differences you find.

2. Reflect upon Miller and Miller's research approach, that is, learning about ethnicity by studying people who have passion for ethnicity. Assess the strengths and weaknesses of this approach in a brief essay.
3. This section has discussed various beliefs and behaviors associated with status differences; but they are simply selected differences and we have ignored many others. Gather some data from published sources on three *other* ways in which the beliefs or behaviors of social classes differ.
4. Do the same exercise for ways in which the genders (or race/ethnic groups) differ in their beliefs and behaviors.

Writing Exercises

1. Write a brief essay on the various forms of shadow-education that may be practised in your country. Try also to estimate how effective they are in attainment of university education and higher status occupations.
2. Write a brief essay speculating on what types of cultural values would be required to decrease social inequality as much as possible, and why.
3. Write an essay on what stands in the way of the kind of "paradigm shift" called for by Eisler and Loye. Estimate whether the shift will occur in your country in your lifetime. Indicate what relevant changes are *likely* to occur in that period.
4. Write an essay on the pros and cons of residential segregation by ethnicity or race. For example, indicate how segregation affects social conflict, and prejudice and discrimination.

Glossary

achieved status   A social status based on characteristics over which the individual exerts some control, such as educational attainment, marital status, or type of employment.

affirmative action   A type of legislation (particularly related to recruitment, hiring, and promotion practices) aimed at ensuring that certain types of people (whether women, racial minorities, or otherwise) who have previously been excluded will enjoy a slight advantage over all competitors in the future.

age-ism   A prejudiced attitude and/or willingness to discriminate against people of a particular age, especially elderly people.

ascribed status   A social status based on the position into which an individual is born or on characteristics (like gender) over which he or she exerts no control (Contrast with *achieved status* above.)

authority   The ability of an individual or group to issue commands and have them obeyed because their control is perceived as legitimate.

bourgeoisie   In Marxist terminology, the group of people who own the means of production, i.e., capitalists. Sometimes also used to refer to the middle class in a capitalist society. The bourgeoisie employ the *proletariat,* who own none of the means of production and sell their own labor power.

brown racism   Refers to prejudice among "brown" groups towards blacks; "brown" is used in the figurative sense to refer to neither whites nor blacks but other people of the third world.

caste system   A hierarchy of groups separated from each other by rules of ritual purity and by prevention from intermarrying or changing castes through mobility or holding jobs.

charismatic authority   A type of authority that gains its legitimacy from *charisma,* an exceptional capacity to inspire devotion and enthusiasm among followers.

class system   A hierarchy of groups with different market conditions, work situations, and life chances. In Marxist theory, classes stand in different relations to the means of production.

commensalism (or commensality)   The act of eating together or (literally) sharing the same table. Often this both symbolizes and reinforces the boundaries of a status group.

confirmation bias   The process whereby people tend to look for evidence that confirms their attitudes and ignore evidence that does not.

conflict approach   A theoretical perspective that emphasizes conflict and change as the regular and permanent features of society because society is made up of various groups who wield varying amounts of power.

conspicuous consumption   Consumption (of material goods) that is for show alone, in order to establish the boundaries of a status group (especially, a wealthy "leisure class") and exclude others.

decoupling   The disconnection of certain groups from key institutions and rewards. The lack of connection leads to a lack of information about available opportunities and ways of taking advantage of them.

delegitimization   The process whereby powerful "ingroups" come to define some "outgroup" as less than fully human and, therefore, deserving of social exclusion or even aggressive attacks.

de-skilling   The tendency of new technology to take the skill and challenge out of jobs.

differentiation   The process whereby various sets of activities are divided up and performed by a number of separate institutions. A complementary process is *integration,* whereby various elements of a society are combined to form a unified whole.

disability   The reduction of a person's life chances, often because the person has been convinced that he or she cannot succeed in a particular type of activity.

discrimination   The denial of access to opportunities that would be available to equally qualified members of the dominant group.

domination   The exercise of control over an individual or group who must submit to that person's power. (See also *submission.*)

downward jealousy   Where one group, or class, resents the gains of others less advantaged than themselves.

elite   A small group that has power or influence over others and that is regarded as being superior in some way. (See also *power elite* below.)

empowerment   Any act or process that gives a disadvantaged group or individual more control over their life chances.

ethnocentrism   A tendency to view social life from the point of view of one's own culture, which enters into both common thought and also social research.

everyday resistance   What people do, as individuals, to express anger or opposition to unfair treatment by those who exert power over their lives; not organized resistance; individual resistance.

feminization of poverty   The growing tendency of the poor to be comprised predominantly by women, due to lone parenthood or impoverished old age.

functional theory of stratification (also, structural functionalism)   A theoretical perspective that emphasizes the way each part of a society functions to fulfill the needs of society as a whole. In relation to inequality, it argues that unequal rewards are needed to ensure society is supplied with highly trained, highly motivated workers.

gender   The socially (or culturally) constructed idea of what attributes and behaviors are appropriate to a given sex.

genocide   The state-planned and systematic murder of people who belong to a particular ethnic, racial, or religious group.

inequality of condition   An inequality in the distribution of social goods (food, housing, health, wealth, respect, authority, power, and so on) in society.

inequality of opportunity   An inequality in the chances that individuals or groups have to increase their social goods relative to other individuals or groups. (See, also, *inequality of condition.*)

legitimacy   A willing acceptance of existing social arrangements (especially, inequalities of condition or opportunity, or existing authority relations).

leisure   Any time or activity that is controlled by the person or people who are participating in the activity.

leisure class   The class of people who have inherited wealth and use their time in nonwork (often, frivolous and wasteful) activities.

merit principle (meritocracy)   A view that society is, or should be, organized in a way that rewards most highly the most "meritorious" (that is, the most socially useful and valuable).

modernization theory (also, industrialization and socio-economic development)   Theories about the process by which a society becomes industrialized, urbanized, and Westernized.

occupational prestige   The prestige or respect that members of a society commonly attach to a particular occupation or occupational group (e.g., doctors, assembly-line workers).

peoples' kitchens   Cooperative kitchens operated and supplied by the pooled resources of several poor households; the participating families contribute labor and money and receive meals from the kitchens.

power   The capacity to exercise one's will despite resistance. In Marxist theory, power is the capacity of one class to realize its interests in opposition to other classes.

power elite   The ruling group in a society, which rules by controlling the dominant organizations in society.

prestige   Social honor and treatment with respect, a dimension of stratification that is separate from income, authority, or class position.

racism   The belief that one's own race is superior to all others.

radical feminism   The view that the oppression of women by men is the longest-lasting, most pervasive, most harmful, and most basic form of all social inequality

rational-legal authority   A type of authority that gains its legitimacy through appeals to reason, legal contract, and concerns with efficiency.

residential segregation   The geographic setting apart of two or more different groups (especially, racial or ethnic groups, or social classes) within a single city, state or country.

sexism   A prejudiced attitude and/or willingness to discriminate against people of a particular gender, especially women.

social distance   Reserve in social interaction between people who belong to groups ranked as superior and inferior in status.

social mobility   The movement of individuals among different levels of the social hierarchy, defined occupationally. Movement may be vertical or horizontal, inter-generational or intragenerational.

social status   People's "standing" in the community, as measured by the amount of respect, deference, or prestige they are granted.

socially constructed (reality)   Behaviors or interactions that result from a shared perception or belief (for example, belief in the inferiority of women or of non-white people).

socioeconomic status (SES)   A method of social ranking that combines measures of wealth, authority (or power), and prestige.

split labor market model   A theoretical approach to the study of work that argues that only people with certain characteristics are eligible for certain kinds of opportunities and benefits. The result is a two-tiered job system, in which one tier lacks high rewards, job security, good working conditions, and respect.

status group   A group that shares certain key social characteristics (e.g., ethnic or class origins), forms an identity based on these characteristics, and promotes interaction mainly among group members.

stereotype   A fixed mental image embracing all that is believed to be typical of members of a given group.

stratification system   A system of inequality that integrates class, status, and domination with other forms of differentiation, such as gender, race and ethnicity.

subculture of life style   A group in society that shares some of the cultural traits of the larger society but also has its own distinctive values, beliefs, norms, style of dress, and behavior.

submission   Subjection to control by another group or individual whose power is based on a higher class position or higher status position.

symbol (of domination)   A sign—for example, a gesture, artifact or word— that can meaningfully represent the superiority (or control) of one individual over another.

systemic (or institutional) discrimination   The unintended denial of opportunities to members of particular groups because of certain physical or cultural characteristics.

traditional authority   A type of authority that gains its legitimacy through appeals to custom and time-honored tradition.

untouchability   A traditional distinction between certain Indian castes that forbids any kind of social contact.